Systems of Psychotherapy

Systems of

A Comparative

John Wiley and Sons, Inc.

New York · London · Sydney

Psychotherapy

Study

Donald H. Ford and Hugh B. Urban

The Division of Counseling

The Pennsylvania State University

Preface

We think the writing of any book is presumptuous. It implies that the authors believe they have something to say which is new and may be interesting and useful to others. Anyone so bold should offer an explanation. We offer two reasons.

First, ten years of daily experience with psychotherapy in both hospital and outpatient settings, extensive involvement in research on psychotherapy, teaching, and attempts to keep up with theory and research in psychology have left us with a discomforting sense of the incompleteness of current theories about human behavior. "Personality" or "psychotherapy theories" have seemed more human, "psychological behavior theories" more rigorous. During this period we have tried to work within the boundaries of first one and then another existing theory, but have found each to be unsatisfactory. This led to the conclusion that further improvement in our own work required rethinking what we were trying to accomplish and formulating a more complete way of thought and a more effective way of procedure. Since personal satisfactions have led us to emphasize our roles as professional psychologists rather than as teachers or researchers, and since the most influential theories about human behavior have, in our judgment, been formulated by psychotherapists, we decided to begin our task with a careful and systematic examination of the ideas of psychotherapists. We have spent five years at the task and now wish to share the results with those who are interested.

Second, both of us have spent a good bit of time training young clinical psychologists, both in formal classrooms and informal seminars in the professional setting where we work. We have been impressed with their difficulty in understanding various psychotherapy theories and in making comparative judgments about them. The idiosyncratic language of many of the theorists seemed to us to be a prime culprit in producing this difficulty. Repeatedly, discussions in graduate seminars and case conferences became confusing because different concepts were used to refer to similar events, and the same concept to refer to different events. We thought it might be helpful to graduate students if some effective way of comparing concepts were available. We decided that this could be developed only by returning to the "data level," just as some therapists have concluded that patients can cure themselves only by returning to the "data level" of their basic sensations and perceptions.

A few comments about the way we have proceeded may be helpful to the reader before he reads this book. We have tried to establish some of the characteristics of a complete therapy system, and in doing this have recognized that we are talking about an ideal. We all expect to fall short of ideals; that is no less true of our attempts to study these theories than of the theories themselves. But the very purpose of ideals is to provide objectives toward which to work, criteria by which to guide one's efforts to improve. We hope no reader will be offended if we say that his pet theory falls short of an ideal, just as we shall not be insulted when it is observed that we have fallen short of our own goals in this book.

In the chapters which follow we have tried to avoid continually modifying, qualifying, and hedging what we say. We have tried to write in a straightforward manner, because we think that ideas asserted clearly can be more easily comprehended and submitted to test. Naturally, we think the ideas are sound, but we also expect that in the future we shall develop more effective ways of thinking. If not, we shall be disappointed in our own growth.

This is a book about theory. As such we recognize that it is not "easy" reading. One early reviewer suggested that we include more clinical anecdotes to make the material "come alive." How often and how to exemplify a point is a difficult choice. Extensive use of clinical material would have restricted seriously the number of theories we would have had space to examine. We agree that clinical material is helpful in thinking about theory, and we have found our own daily practice invaluable in this regard. There is no substitute for being immersed in the data a theory is intended to explain. However, we have chosen to try to write this book with an attitude of sober reflection, rather than to suffuse it with the excitement and poignancy of human hope and misery. The student should realize that comprehension of theory requires diligent study, and no theory can be understood thoroughly without several readings, interspersed with periods of reflection and thought.

We have tried to approach each system with the attitude that it contains valuable and important ideas. To this end, the body of each chapter presents the theorist's ideas without criticism or evaluation. First, we try to lay bare the essential ideas. Then, at the end of each chapter, we present some comments that occurred to us as a consequence of the analysis. This gives each reader the opportunity to form evaluations of his own before reading ours. The ten systems were selected to represent the great variety of theories extant in the field of psychotherapy. Some of them were selected also on the basis of their prominence (e.g., Freud), or their current popularity (e.g., Existentialism), and others because of their special influence (e.g., Rank in relation to social workers), or the distinctiveness of their approach to treatment (e.g., Wolpe).

Two reactions have occurred so frequently to portions of this manuscript that we wish to alert the reader to them. The first has to do with our definition of behavior. Apparently, in American psychology there are strong feelings attached to the distinction between "behavior" such as obvious overt acts, and what one reader referred to as "pre-behavioral organization," such as attitudes, thoughts, and frames of reference. We take a monistic position, defining both as instances of behavior, a view which has an established history in psychology. One of our experimental colleagues has advised us to expect to be criticized for utilizing a definition different from that which is current: that behavior is a function of the operation of muscles and glands. Some clinical readers have been downright upset that we called such events as thoughts or affect "behavior." They argue that if you change "behavior," you only change symptoms, and that every good therapist deals with those more important events which lie behind "behavior"—"pre-behavioral organizations" of various kinds. Clearly, our monistic definition violates established habits and may challenge distinctions which some clinicians have felt with pride distinguished their work from that of others. We agree that psychotherapists long have recognized certain human characteristics as important, and that academic psychology has underemphasized many of them. Let us not leave it that way. As we see it, there are different kinds of human responses, all part of the same package, and we need to study each to see how it functions, rather than arbitrarily to limit ourselves by definition.

Second, some who have read this manuscript have criticized us for "implying" that psychotherapists are a kind of stupid lot and researchers are much better thinkers. We have not meant to imply that. Others felt we were not sufficiently critical of "fuzzy-brained" theorizing. Frankly, we do not think anyone has a monopoly on either good or rigorous ideas. We think that, in general, psychotherapeutic theory tends to have more provocative ideas about human behavior, and experimentalists tend to exercise more rigor in their evaluation of ideas. Which is more important? Neither is much good without the other. Why argue about it when we can pool our talents?

We shall be pleased if this volume helps other psychotherapists to examine and more clearly formulate their own ideas about therapy. We hope some who have devoted their lives to research will be stimulated to investigate some of the alternative hypotheses revealed by our analysis. We shall be even more gratified if students find it helps them to become effective professionals. For the informed layman who enjoys thinking about why humans are what they are, we hope what we have done stirs his thoughtful brew a bit more.

We have found that this book can be used several different ways as a text. It can be studied chapter by chapter to develop a full understanding of each point of view. Since all chapters are organized in essentially the same form, the book may be studied across chapters, section by section, as a means of accentuating the similarities and differences in the separate aspects of the various systems. For example, students might be asked to read each section on behavior disorder to gain a more immediate appreciation of the different views. Finally, students have profitably used this same method of analysis to examine still other systems of psychotherapy not included in this volume.

Our undertaking has been a collaborative effort in the fullest sense. The ideas were formulated through extensive discussion, and the writing was accomplished jointly. Although we have quite different writing styles, we have tried to maintain a unified style for the readers' benefit. We found that each idea proposed by either of us was always inadequate in its initial form, but by treating each other's ideas with respect and attempting to polish each proposal before discarding it, we have emerged with something that is truly the product of two minds. For all of these reasons, there is truly no senior author. Neither of us could have written this book without the other. Which author should be listed first? Urban is to be credited with the initial idea for a comparative study of therapy systems. However, because Ford prepared the first draft of seven of the ten system chapters, he has been listed first. We would prefer to be thought of as a single author.

We think it is impossible to specify and therefore credit the sources of one's ideas. However, we would like to note that our colleagues in the Division of Counseling and the Department of Psychology at The Pennsylvania State University, and many of the graduate students we have taught and worked with, have indirectly contributed much to the development of our thinking and of this project. We extend our thanks to Rollo May for his critical reading and commentary of an early draft of the chapter on the Existential point of view.

Carol Ford and Myrtle Ely share our gratitude for taking care of many of the clerical details involved in preparing a manuscript. John Fry was very helpful in doing library work and checking references for us. And to the secretarial staff at the Division of Counseling go our heartfelt thanks.

DONALD H. FORD
HUGH B. URBAN

University Park, Pennsylvania
September 1963

Contents

Section I

A Method for Comparing
Systems of Psychotherapy

Chapter 1

Individual Verbal

Psychotherapy

The primary purpose of this book is to provide a comparative study of several major systems of individual verbal psychotherapy by analyzing each one in relation to a common set of issues, in order to reveal major areas of agreement and disagreement about these issues. The book is built on three major ideas.

BEHAVIOR CHANGE

First, the authors believe that psychotherapy must be developed around the concept of behavioral change. At first glance this statement may evoke surprise. The reader may wonder about it since psychotherapy is described so often as a procedure for producing change not in "behavior," but in "pre-behavioral" organization; therapists

3

sometimes assert that the changes to be produced are changes in personality organization, underlying attitudes, perceptions, and the like. Such an objection is based on a distinction between overt behavior and something else. This something else includes the covert world of thoughts, feelings, attitudes, and similar events, none of which is considered to be a behavior.[1] Behavior from this vantage point is a "symptom," and symptomatic treatment is to be avoided.

And yet the statement that psychotherapeutic procedures should be related to the notion of behavioral change takes on meaning when we note that the definition of behavior employed in this volume is far more inclusive than ones typically employed. For by behavior the authors mean not only the overt actions and movements a person makes with his hands, or the speech sounds he produces, but also what he thinks, how he sees, and what his emotional reactions are like. Moreover, the term includes the more complex patterns of response, such as the attitude of one person to another. The reader will discover, as we discuss these issues in greater detail in subsequent chapters, that the authors espouse a monistic view of human behavior. For the moment he should understand that the term behavior as presently used encompasses the antecedents to overt behavior, that is, "personality organization," as well as the motor and glandular events which most people label behavior.

Man has always been faced with the problem of changing behavior, as that term is used in the larger sense. People in most, if not all, ages and cultures have suffered to some degree from the types of problems brought to the psychotherapist in our culture. In every age, the kinds of behavior problems that developed, the ways they were treated, and the explanations given have varied with the dominant cultural motifs of the period. Points of view have frequently been contradictory. For example, the Stoics taught the suppression of "natural impulses" in the interest of reason and virtue, and the Epicureans proposed that free expression of "natural impulses" was basic to a satisfactory life. Despite contradictory ideas, however, every society developed ways of attempting to alter undesirable behaviors and to encourage the desirable ones long before psychotherapy came into existence. For example exhortation, punishment, the use of incentives, and praise are ancient but still widely used techniques. Brain washing, faith healing, and Dianetics have all demonstrated some success in changing

[1] It will be recognized also that such a position is a form of *dualism,* analogous to the mind-body dualism in the history of psychology.

behavior. Even in societies where pathological behavior was believed to have no natural causes, changes in aberrant behavior were attempted through appeals and sacrifices to gods and spirits. Moreover, societies charge people and institutions with the responsibility for arranging the modifications in the way its members think and act. Teachers, parents, and prison wardens are all in the "business"; thus behavior change is not the exclusive domain of the psychotherapist.

Some behavior patterns, however, have consistently defied change attempted through the application of ordinary techniques. With the advent of individual verbal psychotherapy a set of procedures for producing change in these as well as in other patterns became available, and it is now one of the most widely used approaches in attempting changes in some kinds of behavior. The language used by various writers—psychotherapy attempts to make possible self-actualization or maturity; to reduce fears and restore higher mental processes; to bring the patient back to reality; to reduce anxiety and improve interpersonal communication—tends to obscure the fact that each is concerned with changing behavior in some fashion. *Since psychotherapy's avowed purpose is to change behavior selectively, it would seem that the development of sounder systems of psychotherapy requires a study of the conditions under which specified behaviors will change in specified directions.*

PSYCHOTHERAPY AND THE SCIENTIFIC METHOD

A second theme in this book is that increased understanding and effectiveness of psychotherapy lies in systematic and rigorous application of scientific methods to its study. Most existing systems have developed out of the richness of clinical observation. Careful observations followed by serious attempts to make sound generalizations from them have provided the wealth of ideas with which the field is now faced.

It is clear that many types of therapies can legitimately claim to be effective in some ways. Even so, therapists will acknowledge that many procedures surrounding psychotherapy are unverified and reflect a kind of folklore. Moreover, contradictory proposals by equally reputable therapists as to what is an effective procedure are characteristic of the current field. Such controversies can be resolved only by methods that permit the making of observations that are repeatable and verifiable by others.

Naturalistic observation has had a long and respectable history in medicine, exemplified by the case study method employed by physicians from Hippocrates to the present. The emphasis on case study was an important antidote to ancient medical superstition and folklore, much of which persisted into the seventeenth, eighteenth, and nineteenth centuries. Many examples of important discoveries growing out of careful observation of individual cases could be cited.

The limitations of the case study method became readily apparent, however, as more rigorous approaches, such as experimentation, came into use. The conquest of yellow fever by Walter Reed and his associates is a dramatic example of the use of more controlled methods of observing disease processes. More recently, Jonas Salk's careful experiments with a polio vaccine established the effectiveness of a preventive treatment which no amount of bedside observation could have accomplished.

It is the contention of this book that psychotherapy, like medicine, will make much more rapid strides if it can find ways of utilizing the methods of science in the study of the specific behavioral changes with which it is concerned. These include systematic and controlled observation, on the one hand, and experimentation, on the other.

In a sense, practicing psychotherapists *are* "experimenting" daily, since they try out different hypotheses and procedures with each patient. In this sense, therapy is a natural experimental setting. Faced with the problem of changing selected behaviors, therapists explicitly or implicitly formulate hypotheses about the origin and nature of the troublesome behavior patterns and then institute procedures to produce the desired change. After observing the effects of these procedures, the therapist alters his hypotheses and tries again.

The difficulty with this type of "experimenting" is that it is unsystematic and uncontrolled. It involves none of the procedures that have been developed to reduce the unintentional distortions of the subjective observer. Personal psychotherapy for the therapist may help, but it certainly is not sufficient. From the early work on reaction time, triggered by Bessel's interest in differences among astronomers' observations at the Greenwich observatory in 1795, up to the more recent research on the effects of social factors and unconscious processes on perception, the evidence has consistently demonstrated the necessity for controlling experiments for observer bias. Therapists *must* acknowledge that their observations are as prone to bias and distortion as are those of anyone else, perhaps more so because of their emotional involvement in the process, and therefore they must seek supplementary procedures for verifying their theories.

The same considerations apply to therapy techniques. Unless a standard set of procedures is used in a systematic and controlled fashion upon selected groups of subjects, it becomes exceedingly difficult to generalize about the results from one patient to another. Further elaboration of the weaknesses of this kind of "experimenting" is probably unnecessary. It may produce rich and provocative hypotheses, but it is demonstrably unproductive of verified principles upon which psychotherapeutic practice can be built.

Under ordinary conditions, however, the practicing therapist cannot conduct experiments in the strict sense of the word, since his commitment to the patient places severe restrictions on what he sets out to do—objectives—and the methods he chooses to employ—techniques. He and his patient both are embedded in social groups, and this fact requires him to take the values of the group into account in planning treatment for any individual. These value judgments affect who is considered in need of treatment and what changes will be regarded as improvement. His task of "healing" patients restricts the observations he can make on their behaviors, limits the collection of data, and circumscribes the variety of treatment conditions he is permitted to employ. Finally, faced with the demands of service to human beings, the therapist usually has little time for the extensive thought, the precision of logic, and the systematic and controlled investigation of the therapeutic process required by the research scientist.

Thus, a therapeutic system or theory, which is based primarily upon the observations, records, and confirmations of the therapist, will rest upon a rich and impressive mass of data that has serious shortcomings when considered as evidence on which to base a scientific theory. Not only would the requirements of scientific proof be lacking, but also they typically would have to take second place to the practitioner's treatment obligations.

This does not mean that the practitioner is unable to study the problems of behavior change in a systematic and controlled fashion when he works in some *other* setting. But his clinical observations and construction of theory cannot proceed independent of the more basic disciplines of science and their use of the experimental method under controlled laboratory conditions.

It should be clearly acknowledged that scientific methods become of value only *after* one has generated some interesting hypothesis or hunch which is worth attempting to verify. Thus, careful and accurate observation and thought, in both the clinic and the laboratory, are essential to the use of scientific methods.

PSYCHOTHERAPY AND BEHAVIOR THEORY [2]

The third idea is that psychotherapy must be firmly rooted in the more general sciences of behavior. Most prominent among these are psychology and human biology. An examination of recent issues of the *Psychological Abstracts* quickly reveals that psychologists are devoting extensive work to fundamental aspects of human behavior, such as motivation, emotion, perception, sensation, thinking, learning, and the developmental process. The psychotherapist deals with the same kinds of behavior in his daily practice.

A medical analogy may clarify this point. William and John Hunter, two eighteenth century Scottish physicians, demonstrated that surgery could be greatly improved if it were based on a knowledge of the more fundamental fields of anatomy and pathology. In 1858, Theodor Schwann published his highly important theory that the human body is composed of cells which reproduce themselves. His theory profoundly modified existing conceptions of pathology. Similarly, without disciplines such as chemistry and bacteriology, the power of antibiotics would never have become available to medical practitioners. By building on such basic disciplines, the effectiveness of medical practice has been tremendously improved.

The same bright future would seem to be possible for psychotherapy if it builds on its more basic disciplines. Psychotherapy, like industrial, engineering and educational psychology, is a field where the application of knowledge about human behavior occurs; it is not a unique discipline. In discussing their cases, therapists consider problems of learning ("How can I help my patient alter his trouble-producing hostile behaviors?"), motivation ("Why does my patient avoid women?"), perception ("Why does my patient seem to watch for behaviors he can interpret as unfriendly, and not notice friendly gestures?"), and other typical psychological problems. From this point of view, the theories and experiments in learning, personality, motivation and emotion, perception, and other branches of psychology can be expected to contribute to psychotherapy theory and practice. Psy-

[2] Note that *behavior theory* as herein used is synonymous with other writers' use of the phrase *psychological theory,* encompassing both traditional behaviorism and personality theory. Behavior theory as used here is not the same as "behaviorism."

chotherapy would be expected to profit from the findings of the more basic branches of psychology, just as medicine has prospered by cultivating its more basic disciplines. Similarly, just as medical practitioners have suggested problems and ideas to their colleagues, psychotherapists daily confront difficult problems and formulate provocative hypotheses which psychologists in other branches of the discipline would be wise to take account of. The idea that psychotherapy should be firmly rooted in the broader discipline of psychology is not new. It has been a recurrent theme in the conferences sponsored by the American Psychological Association on graduate training (1950, 1959).

Psychotherapy Is an Application of Behavior Theory

It is quite clear that the practice of psychotherapy is an applied field. A therapist's primary purpose is not to establish principles of behavior, but rather to apply established principles to achieve behavioral change. His primary purpose is to "cure" patients rather than to build theory. Thus, it may be unreasonable to expect a practicing therapist to develop elaborate and carefully organized theories. On the other hand, these same therapists require some principles by which to proceed. Theoretical statements are needed to account for the manner in which unwanted behaviors arise and for the procedures whereby they can become changed. Without a systematic point of view, therapists are likely to be quite inefficient and on occasion perhaps even haphazard in seeking behavioral change in their patients. A detailed discussion in later chapters will emphasize that the data available in the clinical interview represents an extremely limited source of information on which to build a therapy theory. Only limited propositions can arise from observations within such a narrow situation. Since therapists require an adequate set of propositions on which to base their efforts for change, and since many of the behaviors they seek to change are not directly accessible to their observation during the therapy interview, the propositions of the therapist necessarily must rest on theories developed from study of much wider ranges of behavior.

This point of view runs counter to those who argue that psychotherapy represents a special condition, sufficiently different from other behavioral situations that it requires a psychology of its own. In some instances, the effort to arrive at separate formulations particular to therapy is explicit. In other writings, this idea is more in the form

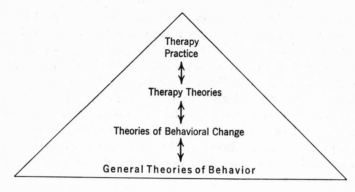

Figure 1. Schematic representation of relationships among theories.

of an implicit assumption. The thoughts lying behind this position are often summed up in the phrase: psychotherapy is a unique relationship. Psychotherapy may differ along certain dimensions from behavior at large, but it is evident that if therapy were strictly a unique circumstance, no observation about behavior outside this unique event could have any relevance whatsoever to behavior within it, and thus cross-generalization would be impossible.

Our argument implies that a hierarchy of theory exists which might be represented in a diagram such as that shown in Figure 1. Several points are represented here. First, the practice of therapy must ultimately depend on general theories of behavior, typified by the field of psychology, for example, personality theory, perception, motivation and emotion, learning. More specifically, it must depend on theories of behavioral change, for example, learning, of which therapy theories are a special case. The diagram illustrates an increasing degree of specificity as one proceeds toward the level of application. Arrows point in both directions to indicate the interdependence of these various levels of conceptualization and to imply that the practice of therapy can be rendered more effective if built on more general theories, yet that these same general theories will require further refinement as their relative strengths and weaknesses are encountered in the practice of psychotherapy.

It is true that the psychotherapist may legitimately question the relevance of many of the theories available in the more basic disciplines of psychology and physiology. Many of them rest on highly restricted and far less complex behavior than the therapist encounters. Some have been developed on subhuman organisms and have not been demonstrated to be relevant to human behavior. It is hard for a psychotherapist to see how procedures effective in conditioning salivation or eyeblinks can be applied to a depressed and retarded human in whom behavior has virtually come to a halt. Similarly, his experimental or research colleague may question the extent to which psychotherapists have tried to understand basic theories and to imagine how they might apply to the therapy situation. The experimentalist may feel that he is so ignorant of the actual therapy situation that he does not know how to make his theories relevant to it. If only the two could get together, how productive the union might be. The psychotherapist has a wealth of clinical observations and ideas. His experimental colleague has the time, training, and procedures to sharpen those ideas and put them to experimental test. Both have demonstrated that they are highly ingenious in developing ways of thinking about and dealing with very complex and difficult problems. It is the writers' belief that the precision and applicability of general behavior theory as well as the effectiveness and efficiency of psychotherapy would grow much more rapidly if collaboration between therapists and research psychologists became a matter of course.

WAYS OF CHANGING BEHAVIOR. Upon what more basic theories of behavioral change can psychotherapy be built? There appear to be three generalized ways in which behavior can be changed. First, the responding mechanism can be altered. An individual who loses both eyes no longer can see. A patient wrapped in a camisole cannot strike his neighbor. The severing of the vagus nerve reduces in some measure the autonomic reactivity of a person. Second, the situational events that operate to elicit particular behaviors in the organism likewise can be altered. An angry child can often be distracted by interesting alternatives. Autistic thought sequences in a schizophrenic can often be replaced by interpersonal behaviors if he is confronted by interested and congenial people. Third, the individual's response repertoire itself may be changed through learning. An American visitor to Japan must alter his driving patterns in order to conform to traffic regulations which differ from those to which he has been accustomed. A patient may come to love rather than fear his father, or the "attitudes" he holds toward himself may be changed.

In general the nature of the psychotherapeutic interview is such that changes in behavior are sought through effecting changes in the patient's response repertoire. It is clear that this depends partly on a knowledge of the physiological substrate of behavior; that is, the physiological determinants and the physiological limits of behavior change must be known. This involves the question of what behaviors can and cannot be altered, and to what degree, as determined by the limitations of the organism. If anger is an innate response, it ill behooves a therapist to try to "remove" it.

Likewise, it is evident that the conditions that elicit behavior must be taken into account when attempting to change the response repertoire. Not all behaviors are the result of within-therapy events. Determinants other than those occurring in the therapeutic hour continuously operate throughout the therapy sequence, and an adequate account of the behaviors concomitant with therapy requires knowledge of these conditions and their operation. Social psychology, sociology, and anthropology are disciplines which study such events in detail. Even so, the predominant focus of the psychotherapist's efforts to produce change lies in the realm of altering the patient's responses themselves. Psychotherapy must utilize the general field of psychology as a fundamental base upon which to develop improved psychotherapeutic rationales and techniques. It must rely upon general psychological theory.

THEORY IS FUNCTIONAL. The necessity for a theoretical substructure is not peculiar to the field of psychotherapy. It occurs in other applied disciplines as well. A good example is found in the realm of economics. The appearance of Keynesian economic theory has had tremendous impact upon the ways in which economic trends are managed in the United States. After the First World War, efforts to deal with inflation and recession were erratic and pragmatic with little or no rationale. In the latter days of the Hoover administration and the early stages of the Great Depression of the 1930's, a variety of remedies were proposed and put to trial. Most were simply guesses, and some were contradictory. Legislators had no set of economic propositions to guide their efforts. In contrast, during the recession of 1957–1958, there was almost unanimous agreement among legislators in both political parties at state and national levels concerning the steps necessary to change the economic picture. Argument centered not around what should be done, but around the scope and timing of the actions to be taken. In the 25-year interim legislators had acquired a theory by which to guide their behavior. Whether the theory is right or wrong, it brought about organized and systematic efforts to change the economic behaviors of the country.

The foregoing discussion may seem to imply that the therapist's choice is one of theory versus no theory, system versus no system. That is rarely if ever true, of course. As soon as a therapist begins to act, he does so on the grounds of some expectation, in terms of some frame of reference. Implied in what he does is a system of some sort. Therapists do not differ with regard to the presence or absence of a theoretical point of view, but rather in terms of the degree to which their system has become elaborated and made explicit. They vary in the degree to which they are aware of and can communicate to others the system they employ. It is probable that every therapist has a system of a sort. What is needed is to encourage each therapist to evolve a system that is explicitly formulated, regularly evaluated, and subject to modification.

These three major ideas, that psychotherapy should build on the notion of behavior change, that psychotherapy should seek refinement through application of scientific procedures to the study of its theories, and that psychotherapy should employ more basic behavior theory, will recur and become elaborated throughout the book. Out of these major assumptions and their implications, a framework for the analysis of therapy systems has been developed. Alternate assumptions are possible, but it should be clearly recognized that the analyses in later chapters are strongly influenced by the three major ideas. Different assumptions would undoubtedly lead to different analyses. This book is not simply an attempt to summarize several therapeutic positions retaining the idiosyncratic language of the various theorists. Rather, the authors have attempted the more difficult task of translating each point of view into a common framework. If the reader examines this book from a different point of reference, he is likely to be dissatisfied with this view of therapy systems.

CURRENT STATUS OF PSYCHOTHERAPY

Historical Perspective

To give some perspective on its current status, some comments about the development of psychotherapy as a treatment procedure may be helpful.

The Renaissance gave back to learning independence from the supremacy of the religious dogma of the Middle Ages. With this independence, new ideas and new methods of learning developed and were concentrated on understanding and controlling physical nature. Similarly, new ideas and methods for understanding and controlling human nature began to develop. The development of a humanistic and naturalistic point of view about man made it unnecessary to look upon man's widely deviant behavior patterns as the result of magic, evil spirits, or punishment, or as special dispensations from the gods. Rather, deviant behaviors could be viewed as susceptible to being changed by the efforts of man. Once it became possible to believe that neurotic and psychotic behavior patterns could be changed, interest was renewed in aberrant behaviors and more understanding consideration of them developed. This new perspective led to the development of a variety of procedures for attempting to cure the "insane."

Charcot applied hypnosis to the "treatment" of hysteria. Breuer hit upon a procedure in which the patient was encouraged to talk himself out freely and uninhibitedly to the physician. Freud, strongly influenced by both Breuer and Charcot, carefully and extensively explored the use of hypnosis and the "talking cure." Little by little, through long experience, careful observation, and brilliant theorizing, Freud formulated the first extensive system for treating serious behavior disorders.

The theories and techniques for changing behavior evolved by Freud and his associates were not universally successful. One patient would change markedly as a result of the approach, but another would change little, if at all. Some patients changed significantly but rapidly regressed to the earlier state. Because it was only a partially effective tool, others began proposing alternate theories or techniques. Adler, Jung, Rank, Horney, Rogers, Dollard and Miller—these names symbolize a continually expanding variety of theories and techniques.

For example, in terms of theory, some have emphasized the hereditary base of behavior disorders, and others, environmental influences. In terms of techniques, some emphasized the impersonal, analytical activities of the therapist, and others emphasized the personal, accepting, and clarifying activities of the therapist. Some theorists argue for highly active and continual intervention by the therapist in the patient's behavior patterns. Others argue for a more passive role. Freud saw interpretation as the primary technique. Rogers proposed that reflection and clarification of feeling were the therapist's basic response forms. Some therapists are confident that a verbal re-enactment of an *original* situation is the necessary vehicle for change to be effected in the behavior of patients. Others are equally confident that the verbalization of *current* feelings toward the therapist is required.

Recommendations differ in regard to length of interview series, frequency of contacts, roles to be played by therapist and patient, the manner in which the relationship is defined, and virtually every other facet of psychotherapy.

Thus, starting with a new way of looking at man, building on careful and extended observations of actual patients, and inductively developing some theories about human behavior, an extensive, elaborate, and frequently confusing mass of ideas and beliefs about psychotherapy has developed. The validity attributed to each of the various points of view has been achieved primarily by the test of clinical experience and observation. As pointed out earlier, such unsystematic and uncontrolled validation has many weaknesses. As a result, considerations of the relative merits of various theories and techniques have been primarily theoretical, philosophical, or personal-emotional, simply because no agreed upon body of observations has developed which all can use in deciding among the contending ideas and beliefs. The clinical study of cases has been remarkably fruitful in the development of stimulating ideas about human dynamics and therapeutic procedures. As might have been expected, it has been remarkably unfruitful in determining which ideas, hypotheses, theories, and techniques are the more sound.

This multiplicity of theory and technique, untested and sometimes untestable by systematic, controlled, and repeatable procedures, has led some zealots to give the status of fact to what originally were offered frankly as hypotheses. They have tended to convert into dogma what was originally offered as theory intended to be tested and revised. Polemics rather than controlled and systematic observation sometimes have been the avenues chosen to settle theoretical disputes. Enthusiastic proponents of various points of view sometimes have seemed to imply that one set of procedures is appropriate for all problems and to ignore the possibility that their set of procedures may be severely limited in applicability.

Definition of Individual Verbal Psychotherapy

Although much of the foregoing discussion has emphasized the diversity in the field, there appears to be an underlying consensus as to what is generally meant by the term individual psychotherapy. In the seventy-odd years since Freud and Breuer first reported on "the talking cure," most therapists, theorists, and practitioners have agreed on its general characteristics even while they have disagreed on its particulars.

Individual verbal psychotherapy appears to have four major elements. First, it involves two people in interaction. The interaction is highly confidential. The patient is required to discuss himself in an intimate fashion seldom if ever required in other types of human relationships. To facilitate this self-revelation, the interaction is usually highly private and unobserved by others. It is typically a very personal kind of interaction. A patient cannot reveal his most carefully hidden ideas, his craziest notions, his deepest fears to a relative stranger unless he develops trust and respect for that stranger—the therapist. Similarly, no matter how hard he tries, the therapist finds it difficult to avoid becoming somewhat involved in the achievements and disappointments of each patient. Because the interaction is so personal, the patient and therapist react to one another not only as "doctor" and "patient," but also as emotion-arousing and satisfying human beings.

Second, the mode of interaction is usually limited to the verbal realm. The participants talk with one another. The patient talks about himself, his thoughts, feelings, and actions, describing the events in his life and the way he responds to those events. The therapist in turn listens, occasionally responding in some fashion to what the patient says to provoke further responses. It is through this very limited type of exchange that the major effects of therapy must occur. Many other types of responses are generally prohibited in the traditional relationship. For example, they do not go to movies together; they do not live together; they do not caress one another. They think, talk, and share their ideas. In so doing, they are likely to arouse emotional reactions in each other, but the mode through which this is accomplished is primarily verbal.

Third, the interaction is relatively prolonged. A friendly conversation with a bartender or a confidant has something in common with a psychotherapy interview, but is not likely to produce marked, permanent behavioral changes of the same order. A single conversation may temporarily relieve anxieties, make one feel less lonely, or give one a feeling of well-being. However, fairly extensive and permanent behavioral change ordinarily takes time.

Fourth, this relationship has as its definite and agreed purpose changes in the behavior of one of the participants. Although the therapist may obtain some personal gratification from the relationship, that is not its primary objective. The focus on only one of the two participants is one of the important ways in which the psychotherapy relationship differs from most other close relationships. In contrast to relationships with friends, parents, or siblings, the patient need not be concerned about the personal happiness or preferences of his therapist. The patient must agree, however, to devote most of his energies to attempting to change himself.

We emerge with a characterization of individual verbal psychotherapy as a procedure wherein two persons engage in a prolonged series of emotion-arousing interactions, mediated primarily by verbal exchanges, the purpose of which is to produce changes in the behaviors of one of the pair.

It seems legitimate to characterize psychotherapy as, in part, a "healing art," rather than primarily a "healing science." It is an art in the sense that the consequences of psychotherapy vary extensively from therapist to therapist, from patient to patient, and for the same therapist in frequently unexplained fashion; there are few scientifically verified principles which govern its practice; major portions of the treatment procedures depend on the character of the therapist and must be learned largely by practicing therapy under the guidance of more experienced practitioners; procedures effective in the hands of one therapist are frequently ineffective in the hands of another; and the therapist is often unable to specify the treatment procedures that produced observed changes.

Selection of Psychotherapy Theories and Techniques

The present unsatisfactory state of affairs has disturbed many serious students of psychotherapy. The practicing therapist faces a difficult dilemma. He is confronted with a multiplicity of behavioral changes he wishes to produce in his patients and with a variety of theories and techniques from which to choose his treatment approach. On what basis can a therapist decide which set of theories and procedures will produce the desired changes for a given patient?

Currently, the selection of treatment procedures is based on several criteria. The first is personal experience, or what seems reasonable to the therapist. This is a very idiosyncratic criterion. A therapist works with a variety of patients. As he does so, he finds certain procedures useful in achieving whatever goal he had in mind. Sometimes his reasoning takes the form, "It worked with X, so perhaps it will work with Y." At other times, it takes the more elaborate form, "It worked with X; Y is like X in certain ways; therefore, it will work with Y." In the current state of knowledge, in relying on his personal experience to a considerable extent, each therapist encounters many hazards. At best, an individual's observations are distorted by the limited number and restricted variety of patients with whom he deals. Also his own reactions will undoubtedly distort his judgments about the effectiveness of his activities. At worst, this procedure leads a therapist to provide therapy solely on the basis of "intuitive" feelings.

A second criterion used is consensus among experts. This really represents the pooling of personal experience, and it suffers from the same weaknesses as individual personal experience. In a sense, it is somewhat more adequate because it provides a wider variety of experiences from which to make judgments, and the effects of systematic personal biases may be somewhat reduced. To be impressed with the inadequacy of expert judgment, however, one need only remember that the finest physicians once agreed that the letting of blood was an excellent treatment for a variety of ills. A serious danger involved in this criterion is that the pooled judgments of experts can exert a strong pressure for conformity and restrict experimentation with new treatment procedures. The cautions of experience must be heeded, but not overemphasized.

A third criterion is prestige. Younger practitioners tend to defer to the judgment of their more experienced elders or to the opinions of professional men they admire and trust. Disciples are not restricted to religions. Established treatment procedures are more likely to be used than those less well-established. A publicly acknowledged and valued system, developed and supported by accepted authorities, will usually take precedence over "Johnny-come-lately" ideas. Prestige also tends to operate as a pressure toward conformity and as a brake on innovation.

A fourth criterion is a theory supported by a public and verified body of knowledge. Psychotherapy has many theories. Unfortunately, no really coherent body of evidence is as yet available. There are many empirical and some experimental data available; but these are fragmentary, and are prone to overgeneralization.

The growing body of empirical and experimental research, however, is encouraging. Carl Rogers has had a remarkable and significant effect in promoting systematic attempts to evaluate therapy. The recent growth of extended research programs in psychotherapy is a promising development (Rubenstein and Parloff, 1959). Certainly the growing public acceptance of and desire for psychotherapeutic services demands refinement of present theories and procedures. One need not prove that therapy is "effective." To ask whether therapy is effective is a misleading question. A more useful question to ask is: what kinds of treatment procedures will produce what kinds of behavioral changes in what kinds of individuals? From this point of view, effectiveness in producing specified behavioral changes in specified types of patients becomes the point of emphasis. It is the contention of this book that all those concerned with therapy—theorists, researchers, and practitioners alike—must strive to develop a public and verified body of knowledge about psychotherapy. Initially, this requires explicit formulation and careful scrutiny of the great variety of propositions under which therapists operate. The comparative study of psychotherapeutic systems in this volume is offered as a step toward that goal. This should be followed by an examination of the basic literature of psychology for evidence pertinent to these propositions. The third step requires rigorous empirical and experimental examination of the various hypotheses to determine which are the most fruitful. Until such an approach is undertaken, the conduct of psychotherapy and the training of new psychotherapists is likely to remain primarily an art rather than a science.

Psychotherapy must be refined as a treatment procedure. Presently, it is too expensive and too time-consuming to meet more than a small portion of the current need for therapeutic treatment. There is the strong suspicion that quicker methods can be developed for identifying the nature of people's problems and helping them to solve them. The need is too great for patients to stand in line at the psychotherapist's office for one to three years awaiting treatment. We believe psychotherapists should take the initiative in encouraging all possible research into the principles and techniques by which human behavior may change. By so doing, therapists should eventually be able to increase their own professional accomplishments while rendering greater service to society.

SYSTEM AND PSYCHOTHERAPY

The title of this book is *Systems of Psychotherapy*. The book grew out of the belief that systematization was essential for the growth and development of effective psychotherapy. We believe that knowledge, no matter how big or how small a piece of the total realm of knowledge it may represent, must be systematic if it is to be communicable and verifiable. Since the emphasis throughout the book is on the necessity for being systematic, the significance of systematization should be examined. What does it mean to be systematic? What good does it do? What are the consequences of being unsystematic?

What It Means to Be Systematic

The term *system* has three principal meanings, all of which apply to our problem. First, a system is a method of classification or codification, a taxonomy, a classificatory scheme. To be systematic, we must define a set of classes into which the phenomena or events of concern may be placed and thereby differentiated from one another. Second, a system is a regular method or order. To be systematic is to be methodical, orderly, and consistent in following a set of procedures. Third, a system is a collection of objects, facts, ideas, or principles related in some fashion to form a coherent whole. In this sense, to be systematic is to operate within a coherently related framework; in this latter sense, the terms system and theory may be synonymous. Let us examine each of these three meanings in turn to show that a systematic approach is crucial to the conduct of therapy as well as in the scientific study of behavior.

SYSTEM AS CLASSIFICATION. Classification is the first step toward full systematization. It is also the first step toward generalization. Classification involves the grouping of phenomena in terms of some identifying characteristics. For example, humans may be classed as men or women according to their possessing specifiable attributes. They may also be classed as blonde, brunette, or redhead according to the color of their hair. The second set of classes cuts across the first, that is, either men or women may have the various colors of hair. The classes chosen depend in part on our purposes or the kind of phenomena with which we are concerned. If we wish to develop a championship football team, we may classify men in terms of their size, strength, and agility. On the other hand, if we wish to develop a male chorus, we may classify men in terms of the tone, volume, and control of their voices. Size, strength, and agility would have little relevance in developing a good chorus.

Why be concerned about ways of classifying behavior? Classification is a way of imposing order on heterogeneous events by grouping them together on the basis of their similarities or differences, that is, on the basis of characteristics they hold or do not hold in common. Thus, a classification scheme defines the attributes of events to which we should attend and becomes a vehicle for sorting relevant from irrelevant data. It is impossible to attend to all events at once in a therapy interview, and thus some way of determining what is relevant for the therapist's purposes becomes very useful. For example, if a therapist's theory leads him to look for responses in "feelings," he need not attend so closely to motor activity, the content of thought and speech, or the physiological responses, except insofar as they have some relation to feeling responses.

Perhaps even more important is the value of classification in facilitating generalization. An event placed within a class on the basis of some attributes may be found to share other attributes of that class as well. We may be tempted to predict that such is the case. It works in the opposite direction as well. If a new characteristic of an event is discovered, it suggests the possibility that all other events within the same class also may share the new attribute. If one discovers that iron will conduct electricity, one might immediately wonder if all other metals also conduct electricity since iron belongs to the class, metals. In psychotherapy, if one finds that a patient has a persistent fear toward his mother, one might suspect that the patient may have similar responses to all women since mother belongs to that general class. Thus, classification is an efficient step toward generalization about the behavior of one or more individuals. Generalization leads to prediction. Prediction is implied whenever psychotherapy is used as a procedure for changing behavior.

Since a variety of classifications is possible, one must have a way of determining which classification scheme is best. Whether or not a classification scheme is "right" or "wrong" depends to a considerable extent on its utility for a specific purpose. This was illustrated in our attempt to select males for a football team and a chorus. Similarly, classification of behavior patterns as schizophrenic, paranoid, or hysteric is of very little value to the psychotherapist if he is going to use the same psychotherapeutic procedures to change the behavior, regardless of class.

It is pointless to question whether or not classification is good or bad, helpful or not helpful. It is an absolute necessity! Therapists are concerned with human behavior and the events that influence it. However, they cannot deal with all events at once. They must choose what is relevant and irrelevant, what is important and unimportant, or what is useful and what is not. When a patient relates what he thinks of his family (his mother, father, sister, brother, grandparents), what emotional reactions he has toward them, the way they treat him, the way he would like them to behave, and also describes their social, economic, and personal qualities, the therapist cannot respond to everything at once. He may respond to the statements about the father and ignore the rest. Or he may respond to the significance of the patient's statements for the family in general, but then he is choosing to ignore the individual members of the family. He may choose to respond to the emotion the patient is expressing rather than the words. He may respond to the general theme but not to the specific content. There are many choices he can make, *but he must choose.* He cannot deal with a patient's behavior all at once, but must deal with aspects of it at a given moment. As soon as he does that, the therapist is breaking behavior into classes. Thus, it is apparent that every therapist uses some classification scheme, although it is likely that many are not explicit or consistent about the classes they use.

Human behavior has been classified in multiple ways both by laymen and psychotherapists, and literally thousands of words referring to behavior exist, often with overlapping and obscure meanings. Analogies and allegories, the emotional impact of certain words, their harsh or musical sounds, and their implication are all important to the author or poet. Such flexibility of language represents a serious barrier to the psychotherapist or scientist who must have precise, distinct, and stable classes if he is to develop generalizations which are both valid and useful. Not only is there a large number of words that refer to classes of human characteristics, but they also overlap greatly and frequently are unreliable. They overlap in the sense that many words seem to refer to approximately the same events. For example, what are the differences in behavioral characteristics to which the following concepts (classes) refer: defensiveness, cautiousness, guardedness, inhibition, constriction, evasiveness, repression, hypercontrol, blocking, and coarctation? Or empathy, insight, and warmth? Or abreaction and ventilation? Or double approach-avoidance conflict and a double bind? Lack of systematization in the sense of a clearly defined, consistently used classification scheme leads to fuzzy and confused thinking, poor communication, if communication is possible at all, useless controversy, and most important of all, wasted effort and gross errors in generalization.

SYSTEM AS ORDERLY, CONSISTENT PROCEDURE. It is not enough to be able to classify events. A set of procedures which may be used to observe relationships of events within and among classes is also needed. For example, it does not suffice for a therapist to classify anxiety as a negative emotion. He wants to know the events that precede or accompany the anxious response and the events that follow. In other words, he wants to generalize about the relationships among events and classes of events. Without such generalizations, the therapist cannot proceed to cure his patient. If he can establish that angry behavior by the father always precedes anxiety attacks in the patient, and if he has some generalizations about how to break the connection between angry behavior by the father and anxiety responses in the patient, he may then proceed to operate on the relationship to effect a change.

Generalization requires that the same event or events be observed on a variety of occasions by one observer, the typical therapy situation; or that the same events be observed on the same occasion by a variety of observers. Note that a single observer, observing a single event on one occasion, cannot make a generalization. Since an observation must be repeated on more than one event, or on more than one occasion, or by more than one observer, clear specification of the *procedures* for arranging the events, observing them, recording them, and interpreting them is essential. Otherwise, generalizations may be in error because the methods of observation differed rather than because the events themselves varied. Moreover, the fact that the procedures used have the same label does not necessarily mean that the procedures were the same. Two therapists may argue, with one insisting that anger toward the therapist is routinely observed and the other objecting that it is an infrequent occurrence. It is likely that the source of this difference lies in the therapeutic technique, with one set of procedures making anger likely and another rendering it improbable.

We have been focusing on systematic procedures of observation, but the same requirement holds for other procedures as well, such as procedures for modifying behaviors. Orderly and consistent procedures should be formulated explicitly, and the more this is done the more successfully the same therapist can replicate them for a particular purpose; the more successfully some other person—therapist or researcher—can replicate them; and the more successfully the effects of specific procedures can be studied. Specification and explicit description make the method potentially reliable and communicable, and observations that follow from it can be checked. Thus, systematic procedures are an essential condition for the verification of observations. Without verification, no body of knowledge can be firmly established.

SYSTEM AS THEORY. Having a classification scheme into which the events of concern can be ordered and a set of consistent procedures by which to manipulate and observe events makes it possible to establish generalizations about the relationships among classes of events and characteristics of events. The work of Carl Rogers (1942) offers a simple example. He specified a class of events labeled emotional responses. He specified a procedure for the therapists—*clarification of feeling.* Through consistent application of this procedure to patients' statements involving emotion or feelings, he was able to demonstrate an increase in the frequency with which patients made such statements. System as classification and system as procedure are essential to the development, testing, and verification of system as theory. Each meaning of the term system has significance in relation to the others, and together they represent a kind of hierarchy of systematization.

A set of hypotheses, propositions, or principles about human behavior which are rationally and logically interdependent are crucial for the practicing psychotherapist. He cannot preselect his problems through his ability to conceptualize and measure the phenomena, or through his interest in a particular aspect of behavior, as does the experimentalist. Patients confront him with a complicated and varied set of behavior patterns which are of concern to them but with which the therapist may have little experience or about which little may be known. *Psychotherapists are frequently asked to proceed beyond the boundaries of verified knowledge about human behavior.* The therapist may choose not to try, but if he does try, he may have to make the attempt on some basis other than established knowledge. The most desirable basis other than verified knowledge to guide his attempts to deal with the new psychotherapeutic problem is a logically interrelated set of hypotheses about behavior—that is, a theory—which can be used *as if* they were verified. Therapists have an ethical obligation to proceed carefully and systematically, since their efforts can make patients worse as well as better. Errors in treatment occur, but a systematic approach helps to limit them and reduce their recurrence.

Some theorists, such as phenomenologists, are concerned about imposing an inappropriate conceptual scheme on an individual's behavior. This is a legitimate concern, but the solution is not the alternative of simply adopting the individual's own conceptual scheme which may be loaded with many inadequacies, as in disordered individuals, although some extremists in the phenomenological movement propose its adoption.

Consequences of Being Systematic

Why should the therapist be systematic and orderly in his conceptualization of behavior? There are respected therapists who believe therapy is such a sensitive, delicate, individualistic process that the therapist must "fly by the seat of his pants." "Intuitions," "gut feelings," the "third ear," the hypotheses which spring into being without prior specification of the observations upon which they are based, are given considerable importance by such therapists. The authors would be the first to agree that orderly conceptual systems and observational procedures are not the only source, and perhaps not even the best source, of important ideas. The history of knowledge suggests that truly important ideas can occur under almost any circumstances—even while shaving! It is likely that the sensitive psychotherapist, through some combination of observation and intuition, is an excellent source of provocative new ideas about human behavior, and the experimentalist or laboratory scientist is likely to find a gold mine of hypotheses in clinical lore. This is not to say that systematic approaches will not produce important new ideas. It simply points out that the need for system cannot be demonstrated on the basis that it alone can produce them.

The special advantages of being systematic lie in effectively elaborating, evaluating, and verifying new ideas and relating them to one another. This is what the sensitive, intuitive, unsystematic observer or psychotherapist cannot do. He may formulate many new hypotheses, but his procedures for recording observations upon which they are based and for checking them later are grossly inadequate. It is our conviction that those therapists or clinicians who insist on being unsystematic will not help create the verified body of ideas that effective clinical practice requires. They will only add to the mountains of hypotheses already produced.

How may a systematic way of conceptualizing behavior help in "effectively evaluating, elaborating, and verifying ideas" about behavior? First, it keeps one's attention focused on the concrete behavioral events with which therapy practitioner, theorist, and researcher are all concerned. Within the multitude of events occurring simultaneously and continuously, it can help determine the events to which one should say "these events are classed as behavior; those are not." Further it should specify that one set of behaviors differs from another with regard to certain characteristics—for example, fear has different consequents than love. Thus, for any particular purpose one may be guided in choosing the particular set of events to be examined under the more general class of events labeled behavior.

As a consequence of influencing the choice of events to be observed, a systematic conceptualization also influences which observations one chooses to record, which observations one decides to analyze and think about, and what one eventually does as a result of those observations. For example, suppose a patient complains of gastric distress on going home from work each evening. Such a complaint represents a report of a small bit of human behavior. If one assumes that such behavior occurs as a result of some physical disorder, the observations made and analyzed probably would involve barium X-rays of the intestinal tract, an examination of the individual's report of his digestive history, and analyses of blood samples, leading to physical medication. On the other hand, if one assumes that the behavior reported is specific to a particular set of situational events rather than primarily the result of some physical disorder, the observations would probably include an investigation of what going home from work means for the individual. Such things as his relationship with his wife, his children's responses to him, or the tasks he has to perform on going home might be studied to identify the factors that produce anticipatory fear, or anger, and thereby generate the gastric symptoms. As a consequence of such observations, the treatment chosen might be psychotherapy rather than physical medication or some combination of both.

To take a second example, suppose a researcher wished to determine the causes of schizophrenia. If one assumed that the behaviors subsumed under the label of schizophrenia were caused by some physical malfunction of the human body, one would probably study differences in blood characteristics, endocrine secretions, etc., between schizophrenics and normals. On the other hand, if one assumed that the symptoms resulted from behavior learned to control excessive fear, one would probably study the events which produced the fear, the behavior which controlled it, and ways of reversing the learned behavior.

A systematic approach helps one to observe in an orderly fashion. The data obtained will be more orderly as a consequence. Analyses of more orderly data tend to be more orderly themselves. Without a systematic framework, a therapist would be likely to observe a patient's concern over sexual matters for a while, then jump to observations of the patient's intellectual functioning, and later change to the patient's fears of being hurt, without any particular reason except that each seemed interesting and important at the moment. Relating observations about intellectual functioning to fears or the observations concerning fears to those concerning sexual matters would be awkward unless one were to assume that everything always is related somehow to everything else. If one assumed that fear was the focal event, however, it would then be possible systematically to explore all other classes of behavior, such as thoughts and sexual responses, in terms of their relationship to fear or to the events which produce fear.

A systematic approach facilitates a comparison of different observations, which is essential for accurate generalizations about one individual's behavior or about behavior in general. However, comparison requires that the observations are comparable, that they were made under standard conditions. There is no point in making such comparisons unless the observer has noted the same phenomena under the same conditions and can do so consistently on each occasion. It may be worth noting at this point that the fact that two observers use the same label for their observations—for example, oedipal complex—is no guarantee they are talking about the same behavioral events. Unfortunately, psychotherapists and others tend to use labels loosely.

CONSEQUENCES OF BEING UNSYSTEMATIC. If one does not have a systematic scheme, a series of problems follow. One does not know to which of a myriad of events one should attend. Without system there are no explicit criteria by which to determine what is relevant and what is irrelevant for one's purposes. The observations recorded will be related or unrelated in some unknown fashion. As a consequence, what one does is likely to be as unsystematic as the observations on which the action is based. Accurate generalization from occasion to occasion is highly unlikely, since there is no known order in the events from which the generalization is to be made.

The authors do not mean to imply that most psychotherapists are unsystematic. Psychotherapists work with extremely complex patterns of behavior, and at the present stage of knowledge it is unreasonable to expect rigorous system in everything they do. Most therapists are systematic to some degree. They have relatively consistent ways of observing and are somewhat consistent in the phenomena they seek to observe. Many therapists, however, have not made explicit for themselves the consistencies and system of their approach. They have developed some systematization gradually without being fully aware of it. As a consequence, such therapists are usually "inconsistently systematic." Since the assumptions on which they operate are not explicit, they cannot verify or communicate clearly either their assumptions or procedures. At the very least, every therapist should be as explicit as possible to himself about the nature and degree of system in his approach. Only in this way can he intentionally improve his skill as a psychotherapist.

One cannot help but view the future of psychotherapy with optimism. Psychotherapists are learning to turn to their psychological colleagues, seeking answers to the puzzling questions of perception, motivation, and learning, since these are part and parcel of the problems that patients bring to them. The realization is developing that one need not feel defensive if one is at a loss for answers when there is no scientific base of knowledge from which they can be obtained. Along with this goes the recognition that research findings assume significance when they are applied to the solution of important human problems by practitioners like themselves. For it is in the area of application that deficiencies in theory become apparent, and significant hypotheses are generated and become the focus of future research.

THE PROBLEM

The purpose of this book is a comparative study of varying therapy approaches. A comparative study requires some stable reference point, some standard to which the various points of view can be referred. Several courses are possible. A single system such as that of Freud or Rogers could be selected and all others could be studied as they relate to it. A second course would be to take a theoretical model from psychology which has been fairly extensively developed, such as Hullian learning theory, and consider the different therapy systems in terms of that model. We have rejected both possibilities as too restrictive. Theories of therapy deal not only with problems of learning, but also with questions of physiology, emotion, motivation, perception, ideational processes, and interpersonal relationships, as well as others. These are classes of behavior that are extremely inclusive, and the selection of a theoretical model from a single branch of psychology or psychotherapy as a reference point would impose severe restrictions on the issues represented in the psychotherapy theories to be examined.

For this particular study we propose to examine each therapy system in terms of a common set of issues, thus making it possible to refer any one system to any other. It has seemed most appropriate to select the series of questions that we believe any therapy system should seek to answer.

The reader should be aware at the outset of several limitations to our procedure. First, any statement of the issues by which therapy systems may be compared can be only tentative and will certainly need major revision as increasing knowledge accrues with the development of the field. Second, it is unlikely that any one system of therapy so far devised will be adequate in all respects. Therapy writers characteristically have focused their interests on certain aspects of therapy and correspondingly have tended to neglect or ignore others. Further, not all theorists agree as to the type of statements a therapy system ought to make. Perhaps most important of all, any theory or system can be safely predicted to be incomplete to some degree, for there is still much to be learned about the therapy process.

The reader is encouraged to proceed through this book in the same spirit in which it has been compiled, namely, as an attempt to specify and then to compare each psychotherapy system on various issues, seeking to draw the best and most from each system. If the reader is an adherent of one of the systems to be considered, we hope he will be stimulated to an objective appraisal of that system and of the several others, and thereby become directed toward a more adequate formulation of his own system. The therapy systems to be examined should be considered as working models, hypothetical formulations, or possible ways of conceptualizing whose workability has yet to undergo adequate empirical and experimental testing.

The task in the next three chapters is the development of the issues to be used in the comparative study. This development of issues can be facilitated by exemplifying the kinds of questions a practicing therapist must face in a concrete clinical setting. Let us take the case of Mr. X, who applied to an outpatient clinic for assistance and was treated by one of the writers. He is a patient who would ordinarily be classed as a schizophrenic.

THE CASE OF MR. X

Mr. X was found to be personable, quite confiding, and considerably more youthful in appearance than his 20 years would seem to warrant. He was evidently disturbed and, as it developed, anxious to achieve the cessation of a wide range of distressing events. The types of difficulties which he recounted in the course of an hour's time were multiple; only a few of the more prominent are related here.

He began by reporting that he was being repeatedly disturbed by fearsome dreams, which contained themata that he felt to be inescapable indications of homosexuality and of aggressive-sadistic impulses toward his mother. The dreams had come to be nightly disturbances from which he would awaken in the midst of a severe panic, remaining unsure whether the dream events actually had occurred.

His waking hours were also punctuated by alarming experiences. He complained of a recurrent feeling that people were inserting penises into his rectum. He told of his attempts to resist the sensation, to deny its existence, but it remained so persistent that he was forced to admit he felt it. That admission led him to conclude that something was radically wrong, and that he needed help. He noted that the problem had progressed to the point where if he were accidentally to brush up against other people, he was in instant fear that either he would inject his penis into their rectum or theirs would intrude into his. He was unable to say which consequence was more likely.

His affinity toward children troubled him; he found himself becoming enraged when he observed one crying, but paradoxically he became equally infuriated when he saw them laugh and appear to be happy. Wishes to rape a ten-year-old girl of his acquaintance were unsettling and troublesome to control.

He complained of uncertain control over intense emotional states, citing occasions of extreme rage toward members of his family, particularly his mother. His contacts with people were fraught with fear and, he was certain, distorted and unreal. His fear of others was often concretized in such things as experiencing alarm lest cars in the street back up and run over him. Etiologically speaking, he pointed to chronically disturbed relations with his family as being importantly causative. His relations with his mother had been particularly difficult. He felt it was his uncertainty as to whether she wanted him to be a boy or a girl that was a principal contributor to his present difficulties. By present difficulties he seemed to refer primarily to his disturbed rectal sensations, his sexual appetites toward children, and his increasing affiliation with homosexuals. On the latter point he related that he had maintained strong feelings of guilt over several early adolescent experiences in which the passive homosexual role had afforded him great pleasure. His subsequent history on this score was one of attraction to and association with confirmed homosexuals, with himself growing increasingly close to overt homosexual behavior. Episodically he would realize the nature of the development, become panicked, and withdraw, only to discover himself being drawn later to another circle of homosexuals. Here the cycle of ambivalence would continue, with his finding himself pleased when he could attract them with "feminine" and alluring gestures, until the threat of overt involvement became too evident. He had sought to maintain to himself that he had no homosexual strivings, but he confessed that it was becoming virtually impossible to continue to assert this.

As one would expect, further sessions served to elicit more and more accounts of difficulty. It was soon apparent that most facets of his behavior were in considerable disarray. We have provided sufficient report of this case for our present purposes; however, we shall refer to this case repeatedly through the next three chapters, in order to exemplify the issues being formulated for use in our later analysis of therapy systems.

Chapter 2

System as Classification and a Method for Comparing Concepts

PROBLEMS OF CONCEPTUALIZATION

Mr. X described hundreds of events, including such diverse things as fear, dreams, mother, panic, alarm, sensations, judgment that something is wrong, rage, wish to rape, control, homosexuality, femininity, cars, feelings of unreality, and the like. Even though his actual verbal description has been abstracted by the writers, one recognizes the impressive array of happenings he reported. This plethora of experiences is bewildering to him, and one of the reasons he is consulting a therapist is his hope that someone more sophisticated can make some sense out of what appears to him to be senseless and disorganized. Were he

32

to take the same description to a layman he would be apt to encounter a reaction much like his own. The ordinary person would probably listen with feelings of disbelief and despair over being unable to understand the contradictory, confusing, and strange occurrences.

It is precisely because psychotherapists purport to be able to understand such happenings that patients seek them out. What is entailed in making sense out of all this? Obviously, some generalizations or abstractions must be drawn from so many discrete events, whether the therapist's method will entail helping the patient to build his own useful understanding of what is happening, or whether it involves the therapist developing one and transmitting that to the patient.

Some Conceptual Alternatives

For example, Mr. X says that he gets afraid. What is meant here? Is that *an* event? Should that he called a *fear* response? Or is it a pattern of events, a combination of happenings including such things as sensations and feelings, physiological activity, and overt movements visible to another person? Even if it is a pattern, can it be treated as a unit, such that one can talk about an event leading to fear, and fear, in turn, leading to something else? If it is treated as a unit response, is it distinct from other response units? Is it the same as *anxiety*, so that when Mr. X says he is anxious, or apprehensive, or has a feeling of dread, these represent just different ways of saying he is afraid? Or are fear and anxiety different kinds of things?

How about the "homosexual" happenings? Are they all aspects of a larger pattern? In one instance Mr. X talks about making alluring *gestures,* in another he says he has rectal *sensations,* and then again he talks about *thinking* and *dreaming.* Should these be treated as separate kinds of things, or is it better to think in terms of a homosexual *role* of some kind? Is it possible that Mr. X is mistaken, that it is inappropriate to label these as homosexual? Perhaps it is better to think of these as different ways of relating to people, which have more significance as *interpersonal patterns* than they do as sexual ones.

This approach leads to a larger possibility. Perhaps Mr. X is not attending to the significant things at all. Perhaps the events presented in the first interview were reported because they were less disturbing to him, and therefore easier to discuss, than other, more important things. Or perhaps his concentration on specific difficulties is missing the essential nature of the problem, and rather than taking his conceptualization of events at face value, maybe a better way of thinking about them can be found. Perhaps it is because of the way he is thinking about them that they do not make sense to him. Maybe he should be looking for *feelings of inferiority* which are implicit in what he is thinking and doing, and until they are made explicit none of the rest will make any sense.

The therapist is aware of the fact that the various therapy theorists have provided many different ways of viewing such happenings. He knows, for example, that "homosexual" events can be considered instinctual sex urges which have become "attached to" inappropriate objects, or that they can be regarded as compensatory strivings to overcome intense feelings of inferiority, as patterns of defense in relation to underlying anxiety, as misguided patterns of moving toward people, or as part of a larger self-concept which values love and affection between men as opposed to conflict and competition.

The fear alluded to by Mr. X can be represented by many different theorists in as many different ways. One may conceive of it as an innate emotional response which becomes attached to various events through learning. Another may consider it as one of several manifestations of "basic anxiety." A third may interpret it as a form of tension resulting from conflicting and contradictory responses, and a fourth may class fear among "safeguarding tendencies" and consider it similar to actions such as deprecating other people, finding excuses to avoid situations, and the like.

Considerations in Choosing a Conceptual Framework

The therapist is faced with a number of choices. One of the things he might do is use the patient's way of analyzing and construing what is happening. The patient's analysis of events, his "view," becomes the set of concepts that the therapist employs. On the other hand, the therapist can adopt a set of concepts advocated by some theorists, analyzing the events according to some system, for example, Freudian or Sullivanian. Finally, he can be "eclectic" and employ some of the concepts of the patient, some of his own, and those of a variety of systems whenever they seem to be appropriate or of some real utility. He knows that he must exercise care, however, because the concepts he uses will determine what he listens to, what he considers to be important, and how he relates all the different kinds of events to one another. And he runs risks in each of these choices. If he adopts a systematic framework of analysis such as the Freudian, there is the danger that he might force the patient's behavior into a mold it does not fit. If he adopts the view of the patient, he may be using a set of concepts that will not serve him any better than they have served the patient in understanding what is going on. If he fails to be systematic and merely uses whatever concepts and ideas occur to him at the moment, he runs the risk of confusing himself and his patient as well. In a word, if he employs the *wrong* sets of concepts, the behavior will not become intelligible, and he and his patient will fail in the enterprise.

It is the purpose of this chapter to develop a way of examining the similarities and differences existing among the numerous concepts that the many therapy theorists have proposed as useful. During the remainder of this chapter we shall concern ourselves with explicating a method by which the various concepts of the systems may be represented and subsequently compared.

Criteria for Selecting a Method for Comparison

Several criteria were used in choosing a method. First, the method must be sufficiently general to encompass the great variety of concepts represented in therapy theories. Second, it must encompass notions in the general field of psychology and personality theory as well as psychotherapy, following from the basic idea that these various levels of theory should eventually interrelate with one another. Hopefully, this should implement and speed the interrelationships which undoubtedly exist. Third, the scheme chosen should be appropriate and useful for both the practitioner and researcher. That is, the same way of thinking about behavior should serve the purpose of experimental and empirical as well as clinical analyses of behavior, so as to facilitate generalization from the clinic to the laboratory and vice versa. Fourth, it should be applicable to and convenient for the analysis of behavior change. It should help clarify considerations of therapeutic technique. The reader will recognize that these criteria represent an application of the three basic assumptions presented in Chapter 1.

LIMITATIONS OF THE METHOD. Any proposal for analyzing behavior must be presented with some diffidence, particularly if it must be designed to accommodate remarkably different approaches to the study of human responses. The method that follows is undoubtedly incomplete in many ways. First, the basic problems that plague psychology and psychotherapy are also problems here. Second, by trying to devise a procedure to encompass so great a variety of concepts and propositions without being excessively complex itself, we have necessarily had to use grosser points of reference than would have been necessary had we been analyzing or building only one type of system. Despite its limitations, however, the method that follows represents the most workable one the authors could evolve after prolonged struggle with the problem over a period of five years.

A METHOD FOR COMPARING THERAPY CONCEPTS

The Nature of Concepts

The central concerns of the psychotherapist are behavior and the kinds of events that influence it. Characteristically he is faced with complex behaviors following one another in rapid succession. Unable to deal with all events simultaneously, the therapy theorist decides to pay attention to some events now and to others later. As he observes and studies the behavioral stream, he notices that certain kinds of behavior appear to have things in common with one another. For example, criticizing a friend, or striking him, or taking away one of his belongings might all be seen as destructive acts or might carry the implication of anger toward the person. One might employ the label "aggression" to refer to all such acts. In doing this, one is developing an abstraction about a collection of events. In the example cited, the term aggression or aggressive behavior, is a concept that refers to a group of behavioral events which are judged to hold certain characteristics in common with one another. Thus, concepts are abstractions: they represent particular classes of events. Concepts and their labels are shorthand, convenient methods for thinking about, analyzing, and generally dealing with many discrete occurrences and the generalities among them. Concepts are built and employed by the man in the street in essentially the same way. Of course, the scientist's concepts must be a good deal more precise, since they are designed to accomplish more exact goals than those to which the layman typically aspires.

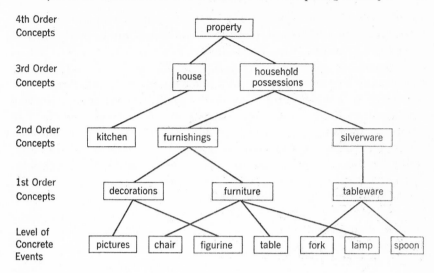

Figure 2. Concepts and their relationships within a hierarchical arrangement.

LEVELS OF CONCEPTUAL ABSTRACTION. Scientists and laymen also agree in arranging their concepts in a hierarchy of abstractions, ranging progressively from lower- to higher-order groupings. The scientist's groupings are likely to be more tightly related. An example of a commonplace hierarchy of concepts would proceed from table—a particular limited kind of observable event—to furniture—a class encompassing not only tables, but also chairs and beds—to household belongings—including linens, silver, and other items as well as furniture. Thus, arrangements of concepts can be represented meaningfully in the form of a pyramid, where first order concepts represent groupings of relatively discrete events, second order concepts represent groupings of concepts of the first order, and so on. There may be many levels in the pyramid, but the apex represents the highest level of abstraction, the most inclusive concept—the universe.[1] Figure 2 represents such a pyramid.

Many of the concepts (event-classes) that are characteristically employed in personality and therapy theories fall at the higher levels of abstraction and thus stand for, represent, or "point to" large num-

[1] The whole question of concept formation is an important and complicated issue which we cannot discuss in detail here but can only note certain salient features. How concepts come to be formed and used is probably one of the most important theoretical and research areas in psychology.

bers of more specific events. Personality theorists have tended to feel handicapped in the use of small concept units when they have attempted to account for complex interpersonal behaviors.

Of course, not all concepts in therapy theory are *molar,* or inclusive, though they do seem to predominate. Allport (1937) proposes that units of all sizes are theoretically legitimate and highly useful for the conduct of research. In such an instance, the choice of unit size will depend on one's purposes. Allport suggests a group of units that can be arranged in increasing order of complexity, including the conditioned response, habit, attitude, trait, and self, with personality being the largest unit of all. Cameron (1947) employs a comparable listing: response, attitude, pattern, role, and personality.

Higher-order concepts have the virtue of being more inclusive. It is more convenient and efficient to think about complicated behaviors occurring over months and years in inclusive fashion. To cite an absurd case, one would hardly set out to represent the course of a person's episode of 18 months of depression by an analysis of the intricate sequences of muscular movements which occurred in that period. Typically the more behavior to which the theorist points, the more useful inclusive concepts will be.

HAZARDS RELATED TO LEVELS OF ABSTRACTION. Real hazards, however, follow upon conceptualizing at these higher levels of abstraction. These hazards result from the fact that the more removed from relatively discrete observable events one becomes, the muddier and more confused may be the interrelationships between the concepts at the upper reaches of the pyramid and the behavioral and situational events at the bottom. Rotter (1954) has illustrated a number of unwanted consequents which are likely if these interrelationships are not kept explicit and in order. Without going into detail, some of these difficulties will be mentioned.

If a theorist does not make explicit the events to which his lower-order concepts refer, and if he similarly fails to make clear how higher-order concepts are related to those of a lower order, confusion will result. Different workers will not be able to employ the concepts in reliable fashion. The same term will mean different things to different people; the same concept will be used by the same person to refer to different events at different times. Communication will be poor, and reliable observations will be unlikely. Rotter has illustrated the frequency of such concepts in the field of personality and therapy theory.

Moreover, unclear formulations result in a profusion of concepts, with considerable overlap. Many writers have remarked upon the bewildering array of concepts in personality and therapy theory. But without clear formulations of what the concepts refer to, it becomes quite impossible to determine where the overlap is occurring and which concepts are duplicative. It is also likely that gaps exist, that some events are not represented adequately by corresponding concepts, but such gaps are difficult to identify if it is unclear as to how much of certain kinds of behavior or situational events is included in the concepts.

Another danger is the tendency to categorize individuals into dichotomies or into one of a limited number of classes or types. As Rotter has shown, this is a particular case of the error of overgeneralization. It occurs when a theorist observes a restricted group of responses and then conceptualizes the group *as if* it characterized all of behavior—that is, treats it as if it were a concept near the apex of the pyramid. For example, a patient who refuses to answer a single question may be labeled hostile or resistive.

Then again, there is the logical error of reification, where the theorist tends to forget that his concepts are abstractions and begins to think of them as being entities. If a therapist is not careful he will find himself slipping into such statements as "He has schizophrenia," "His ego has been poorly formed," or "His idealized self is . . ."

The emphasis placed on operational definitions by some theorists offset the hazards of precipitous concept building at the higher levels of abstraction. The theoretician, however, does not have to remain at the operational level if he builds a progression of concepts that are explicitly related to one another and to the event base.

CONSIDERATIONS IN CONCEPT-SELECTION. One might complain about this procedure, arguing that the analysis of behavior into kinds and classes is arbitrary. It *is* arbitrary, but only in the sense that it is an act of theoretical choice. Clearly a variety of choices is possible, but the choice of units should not be arbitrary in the sense of being whimsical.

The selection of units for analysis is really a very important step in system construction, and it is determined by several considerations. First of all, it depends on the purpose of the theorist. If he is setting out to account for the operation of the eyeblink reflex, units as large as "personality," "life style," and "self dynamism" are inappropriate. Correspondingly, the analysis of a one-year span of an individual's life cannot proceed in terms of units as restrictive as the eyeblink reflex.

For one purpose, one level of analysis is appropriate, for a second purpose, a different level is to be desired. However, there always remains the stricture that analysis at the more molar level should not violate or contradict established facts at the more molecular level, even though the concepts used need not be the same.

A second important consideration is pragmatic. Will one set of concepts work more effectively than another for the accomplishment of given purposes? Thus, the theorist's choice of units is always open to some empirical evaluation. His proposal will be displaced by others if his concepts are poorly defined, are too general to be manageable, or are irrelevant to the task for which they were designed; in short, if they do not work.

TWO WAYS IN WHICH CONCEPTS VARY. We should anticipate that as different therapy theorists observed their patients they may have been impressed by somewhat different aspects of the behavioral stream and therefore may have developed different concepts. It is also possible for them to have been impressed by the same responses but to have labeled them differently. In this case, concepts of two theorists might only *seem* to be different.

A second way in which theoretical concepts seem to differ is in the various ways in which the separate events come to be *combined*. Some concepts, such as aggression, may include only behavioral events. Other concepts link both behavioral and situational events under a single rubric; for example, claustrophobia refers both to the behavioral event of fear and to a type of situational event under which it occurs, namely, small enclosed spaces. Diverse concepts point to different combinations of behavior over varying periods of time. Concepts range in size from those that refer to small bits of behavior occurring over a limited period of time—*wish*—through *reaction formation*, which refers to a greater variety of behavior over a more extended period of time, all the way to *life style*, which encompasses huge amounts of behavior over many years' time.

It is convenient to think about these combinations of events in two ways; first, in terms of one following or leading to another, that is, as *sequences of events*, and second, as occurring at relatively the same point in time, that is, as *patterns of events*.

Actually, if a person conceives of behavior as a continuous stream of events which he attempts to study and analyze, then he can hardly avoid analysis in terms of sequence and patterns if he attempts to represent behavior in its original complexity. Behavior occurs in a never-ending series throughout life, through the conditions of sleep and coma as well as the waking state, and the only way it terminates is for the individual to die. And yet, not even death is a discrete event, since even after the heart stops beating, other chemical and cellular changes (responses) continue for some time. It is even possible under some conditions to re-arouse the heart into activity, when "death" had been presumed to have occurred.

Similarly, several kinds of responses are always occurring at approximately the same point in time. Consider the driver who speaks to his companion as he pilots his car through traffic, or the high school student who miraculously finishes his homework while attending to the television.[2] These are instances in which it is most difficult to think of a person as behaving in a holistic fashion, and the superiority of thinking in terms of parallel and interrelated chains of simultaneously occurring events becomes apparent. Thus, adequate representation of behavioral complexity requires one to deal not only with sequences of behavioral and situational events as they occur in time, but also with the concomitancies of such events as they occur at relatively the same point in time.

Complexity and the Choice of Conceptual Units

Clearly, the theorist has many options about the kinds of conceptual units he will devise and use. First, the concepts may differ in terms of the kinds of events to which they refer. Second, they may differ in terms of the amount of behavior encompassed. And finally, concepts may differ in terms of the way the kinds of events within the concept are related to one another. Figure 3 represents the manner in which concepts may be considered in terms of these three attributes of complexity.

An arrangement such as Figure 3 helps to clarify the ways in which theorists may have divided the behavioral stream into chunks of different types and sizes, that is, have developed concepts representing different levels of behavioral complexity. Unit 1 represents concepts involving a limited variety of events over a brief period of time, such as the concept of fear—*kind of events*. Unit 2 represents concepts in-

[2] The reader will have noted the number of times we have employed examples drawn from everyday life and have wondered at their appearance in a discussion of therapy. The writers have done this deliberately as another way to emphasize their conviction that "behavior is behavior," in therapy and out, and that the data of psychotherapy are also the data of general psychology.

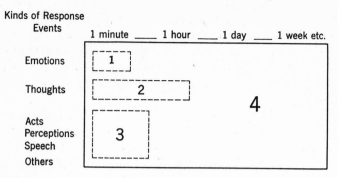

Figure 3. Behavioral concepts compared according to the kinds of events, amount of events, and relationships of events.

volving a limited variety of events over an extended period of time, such as the concept of delusion, which signifies a sequence of thoughts extending over time—*sequences of events*. Unit 3 represents a greater variety of events occurring over a brief period of time, such as the concept of assault, where the patient seizes upon another person and curses and strikes him—*patterns of events*. Unit 4 represents a great variety of events occurring over an extended period of time, such as the complicated and elaborate pattern of behavior occurring over the course of a week, as is encompassed within the concept "the honeymoon," that is, concepts representing *pattern-sequences of events*. Some concepts represent the periodic repetition of pattern-sequences; these are *recurrent pattern-sequences*.

Concepts and Their Comparison

Any method for comparing concepts, then, must be prepared to allow for differences in level of abstraction, in the kinds and variety of behavior encompassed, in the amount of behavior, and in the way the kinds of behavior are related through time.

THE CONTENT OF CONCEPTS

The psychotherapist is concerned with two kinds of events, the patient's behavior and the conditions that affect that behavior. The therapist needs to know not only that the patient is fearful, but also what is feared and what events will modify or eliminate the fear. To begin with, we may divide the events that concern the therapist into two groups: the behavior of the person being studied or treated and the events surrounding that behavior. We shall call the latter *situational events*. First we shall discuss the classification of behavior and then proceed to problems involved in the classification of situational events.

Behavior and Its Classification

The need for a way of representing or classifying behavior seems self-evident. The phenomena of behavior are the data of psychotherapy. All other considerations are relevant only insofar as they are related to or affect human behavior, how it develops, and how it changes. It is impossible for a therapist to work with behavior in its entirety. He must deal with only portions at a time. He cannot consider a patient's whole life at once, but he must be concerned with the particular fears, doubts, thoughts, and actions which are troubling the patient that month, that day, that hour. The pieces the therapist chooses to deal with, then, are of crucial importance.

Although the terms behavior and behavior change have been used with great frequency, we have employed them up to now in a rather glib and unsystematic fashion. We must now proceed to identify or define this class of events.

A DEFINITION OF BEHAVIOR. We can begin by defining human behavior as any change in any attribute of a person. The words *event* or *response* will be used to characterize such changes. Of course, in one sense, everything is continually changing. For the purposes of the behavior theorist, however, attributes of the physiological structure usually change so slowly that they are treated as if they were stable. Thus a finger is not ordinarily considered to be behavior, but the movement of a finger is. Similarly, a stomach is not thought to be behavior, but the chemical changes and muscular movements that accompany digestion are.[3] The structural properties of a person's body

---

[3] We observe that something that has changed requires a specification of the point of observation to which the observation of change is referred. This notion will be discussed in more detail later, but note here that the recognition of change refers to a relation between two observations.

are very important, of course, because they define and limit the kinds of changes that can and do occur. For our purposes, however, we do not anticipate that this distinction will introduce any crucial difficulties.

This is self-consciously a very inclusive definition in contrast to some which restrict the concept of behavior to efferent functions (motoric and glandular). It encompasses what are often referred to as physiological events, as well as walking, speaking, dancing, and "acts" that are more familiarly given the label behavior. It also includes events such as perceptions, images, ideas, and attitudes, which have sometimes been considered to be of a different order than overt and instrumental actions. This point is worth some emphasis, since the reader's habits of thought may involve using the term behavior in a much more restricted sense.[4] If this is true, he should remind himself periodically that the authors include in the class, behavior, events that occur within as well as without the skin; visceral as well as motor responses; thoughts as well as movements; subjective feelings as well as overt indices of those feelings; "personality" as well as "behavior."

Characterizing behavior in this fashion follows the course of general psychology, which has found it both difficult and fruitless to attempt to make distinctions between physiology on the one hand and psychology on the other. The mind-body problem was an expression of such an attempt. Similarly, psychology has ceased to try to maintain the layman's distinction between actions on the one hand and "thoughts" on the other, with the restriction of the term behavior to actions alone. The man in the street has been accustomed to speak of thoughts, feelings, and memories as belonging to a different domain from behavior, and he has shared the implication that different rules and principles apply to each. Although the latter may be so, it seems more parsimonious and a matter of superior theoretic strategy at this time to follow the definition of behavior we have proposed rather than to think of instrumental acts as "behavior" and all other behavioral events as "something else," while acknowledging that different principles may govern different kinds of behavior.

The definition proposed helps to clarify the distinction between psychologists and other scientists. They can be distinguished by the

---

[4] For example, one early reviewer, who strongly rejected the idea that the purpose of psychotherapy is behavior change, reported that several other therapists he talked with agreed that they did not attempt to change "behavior" (symptoms), but changed "personality." We have avoided this implicit dualism, choosing a monistic definition which we consider more in accord with the facts.

kinds of behavioral changes they elect to study. Biological scientists and medical specialists are concerned primarily with the physiological structure and changes closely related to that structure, while the psychologist is concerned primarily with the behaviors that are possible within the limits set by the structure. The definition also makes clear why there is some overlap among such disciplines.

The term *behavior* will be used to refer to the general class of events just defined and illustrated. The term *response* will be used to refer to particular events within the more general class; responses are subclasses of behavior.

THE CHOICE OF BEHAVIOR CLASSES. There are innumerable ways in which behavior can be subclassified. Familiar classes which have been used include dominant and submissive, adient and avoidant, and respondent and operant responses. Responses might be classified in terms of some physiological attribute; for example, whether they occur as a function of striped or smooth muscle activity. They might be classed in terms of the sensory modality involved, such as auditory, visual, olfactory, and kinesthetic responses. They might be classified in terms of functions, such as eating, sleeping, and talking. The behavioral stream has a variety of attributes, and it is possible to sort behavior into classes according to any identifiable attribute.

How can one choose from among the variety of classification schemes possible? We have chosen the following scheme in terms of the purposes to which it will be applied. One of our purposes is to make it possible to relate the theoretical and experimental work in general psychology to that in psychotherapy. An inspection of the topical organization of *Psychological Abstracts,* of volumes of the *Annual Review of Psychology,* and of various introductory psychology textbooks suggests some traditional classes, for example, sensation, emotion, motor behavior.

A second purpose is to facilitate the comparison of the variety of concepts present in the literature on psychotherapy. We have decided this can be done best by using as a common base the more specific responses to which various concepts refer—the particular responses that confront the psychotherapist in his office. Starting from this "data base," we hope to be able to compare intricate concepts such as ego and self-concept by asking "How are they alike and how do they differ in the behavioral events they encompass?" To accomplish this we have chosen a system based upon (*a*) the observational vantage point from which the behavior is viewed and (*b*) differences in the nature of the behavior itself, that is, response content.

The First Set of Subclasses:
I. The Observational Vantage Point

All observations must be anchored to some reference point or points. By so doing, we relate one observation to another and the observations take on certain significance relative to one another. Thus, we can speak of the movement of planets relative to the position of the earth and describe their movements precisely enough to be able to hit them with a rocket fired from earth. Movement itself cannot be observed unless there are other objects or events to which the moving object can be related. What is observed may differ according to the vantage point one chooses from which to make the observations. Many everyday examples illustrate this fact. When one looks down on a city from an airplane, one sees far different things than if one stands on the ground in the middle of the city. The old story about three blind men illustrates the same point. Each observed an elephant by feeling its body, and came to different conclusions about what it was because one felt a leg, another felt the trunk, and the third touched its tail.

Human behavior has been viewed from more than one vantage point also, and, as in the story of the three blind men, disagreements have arisen as a consequence. For example, the nature of human behavior and how it functions looks very different to the objective behaviorist and the phenomenologist. The objective behaviorist views behavior from the vantage point of an outsider watching it occur. The phenomenologist views behavior from the vantage point of the behaving individual who reports how his behavior looks to him. We should expect their observations and concepts to differ since they have chosen quite different points from which to view behavior. One need not argue that one is right and the other wrong. They are different because their vantage point causes them to observe different events and therefore to arrive at somewhat different conclusions.

We expect to find both observational vantage points used by therapy theorists. Indeed, there are important advantages if the therapist uses both, something that we shall later discuss. At this point, however, we wish to note that a person's behavior can be characterized as falling into two broad and general categories. Some behaviors are public, open to the observation of other people and therefore subject to objective appraisal. Other behaviors occur "privately" and are much less open to objective inspection. Unverbalized thoughts, images, feelings, attitudes, fantasy sequences, and the like occur with great frequency in humans. The fact that they are difficult to observe in no way denies their occurrence, or their central importance in understanding the operation of the individual's behavior.

THE SUBJECT AS AN OBSERVER. It is not so much, however, that events occur which an outside observer can and cannot see, but rather that in any particular situation in which one person is observing another there are, in effect, two observers in operation. *The person whose behavior is being observed is an additional observer.*

It is a property of humans that they can perceive and symbolically comment on many of the behaviors they emit. To some extent, they can respond observationally to their own behavior as they do to the world of objects and people around them. Not only can a person watch his form as he plays tennis, but he can also evaluate his thoughts, correct his logic, and judge thoughts of a hostile rejoinder to be a social error and proceed not to verbalize them. In almost any situation in which his behavior is being subjected to study and analysis, it is almost certain that the subject continually observes his own behavior, privately responding to what he is thinking, feeling, and doing. The persistence of these behaviors makes him an experimental nuisance on many occasions, since his private observations often interfere with the responses an experimenter wishes to study. Interpolated activity between experimental trials, for example, is a method by which the experimenter seeks to prevent the subject from "reflecting upon" the conditions to which he was exposed and the ways in which the experimental setup caused him to feel and think. Typically it is very difficult to arrange conditions to prevent such behaviors from occurring in experimental arrangements where they are unwanted.

If one considers the behaving person as an additional observer, the question of accessibility becomes: to which observer or observers are the behaviors accessible? And, if they are accessible to only one, by what means do they, or can they, become accessible to the others as well?

THREE BEHAVIOR CLASSES.[5] With two sets of observers, the behaving person on the one hand, and objective observers on the other, re-

[5] The reader should be cautioned in two ways at this point. First, the distinctions between the three classes of behavior here are *not* the same as the more traditional differentiation between "overt" and "covert" behavior, since both of the latter stem from the vantage point of the objective observer. Secondly, the use of symbols (such as S, R, and r) should *not* mislead the reader into thinking that we are presenting a typical "behavioristic" view. Such symbols are the property of psychology as a whole and do not denote an "S-R position" as such.

sponses will fall into one of three main classes, depending upon their differential accessibility: behavior which is accessible to both, to one but not the other, and to neither observer at all.

Objectively observable responses (*R*). In the first class will fall the behaviors that are accessible to the observation of both observers. The subject may strike a match; both he and the observer can identify and react to this event. Similarly, the subject can assert that he is angry, and again both he and the external observer can hear the statement as it is being made. It is helpful to represent classes in terms of symbols, and the use of *R* to represent behavior which is accessible to both observers follows convention. Accessible means either actually observed *or* potentially so with the means at hand.

Thus, the symbol *R* is being used to refer to potentially observable responses made by the subject, even though at any particular point in time one of the therapy observers may not identify its occurrence. The subject's eyes can water without his being "aware" of it, even though it might be quite evident to anyone watching him. Similarly if the subject's attention is focused upon something other than his behavior, a therapist can note a host of events of which the subject is quite ignorant, for instance, changes in facial expressions or changes in posture. Moreover, the patient can make verbal statements and be unaware that he has made them; sometimes this occurs simply because his attention was on something else, for example, when his "thoughts race ahead of his speech." Correspondingly, the subject can observe his responses at times when they are not accessible to the observation of the therapist, as he does, for example, when he makes a gesture of disgust around the corner of the desk hidden from the therapist's view.

It should be noted that the classes proposed provide for within-skin events which are accessible to the outside observer and thus are potentially accessible to the behaver as well. Observation by means of instruments often makes this possible, for example in the use of the stethoscope to listen to the sounds of heart and chest. Thus, any response that can be observed directly by another person as the response occurs, with or without the use of instruments, even though the response may go on within the skin, is an *R* event. Advances in instrumentation often make new responses available to objective observation and thus create the opportunity for additional advances in knowledge.

In a therapy setting, the fact that there are two individuals who can observe responses is of major significance. If there were just one observer, the therapist, watching the subject's behavior as it sequentially unfolded, the possibility of error would be tremendous. Since there are two observers, however, the possibility of validating the observations of one of the pair exists. It is critical that both therapist and patient have a second observer with whom either can check the accuracy of what he heard or what he saw. Without at least this degree of "consensual validation" therapy could not proceed at all.

Subjectively observable responses (r). Although objectively observable responses (R) lend themselves more readily to observation and study, they still represent only a part of the human response repertoire. Humans engage in numerous intervening or mediating responses, and in the adult these have become extremely rich and extensive. Again, following convention, the symbol r will be used to refer to all such mediating or subjective events, such as the myriad thoughts, wishes, beliefs, attitudes, memories, sensations, and feelings which apparently occur continuously. As opposed to the plant of the botanist and the rat of the physiologist, in whom analogous intervening events might be presumed to occur, the human subject can and does act as an observer and reporter, and he can relate to some extent his observations of these "inner" processes. He can produce a verbal representation of them to another individual; he can also represent them in gestures, postures, and graphic drawings. It is common to suppose that communication of thoughts and feelings is likewise possible through the media of music, sculpture, and creative art. These responses are not *directly* available to the examination of another person, though some of them might eventually become so. Although legitimate events, they are so difficult to study that with some the term "subjective" behavior has taken on a derogatory connotation.

Therapists have emphasized these mediating events, and this emphasis has represented both a boon and a serious handicap. Psychologists who are concerned with maximal objectivity have questioned why the personality theorist and the therapist become embroiled in the problems associated with studying these intervening responses. It can be a relatively easy matter to illustrate how the subject's observations are unreliable and influenced by a number of unwanted and uncontrolled events. Moreover, most agree that therapy subjects are in therapy precisely because they ignore, deny, distort, repress, and pay no attention to many of the significant events of their subjective experience. Exclusive reliance upon verbal reports of a subject at one point in time often has led more than one investigator to inaccurate and embarrassing conclusions, for example, Freud's trauma theory.

The personality theorist has persisted in his attempts to deal with such responses, however, for a variety of reasons. First of all, they represent a large proportion of the behavior of any matured individual. His thoughts are characteristically extensive, and the difficulties inherent in their study in no way deny their operation or importance. Actually, in some individuals, such as those who become highly reflective and "thought-laden," such responses assume preponderance over the more obvious and active things that they do.

It is not only that they may simply outnumber the objectively observable responses in any particular individual, but also that they are thought to be very important. Many therapy theorists have concluded that the way a person sees, thinks, and feels are the crucial antecedents to his other responses.

Parenthetically, it seems to the writers to be difficult to overemphasize the importance of this group of responses—the logical, careful, orderly ideas used in studying a mathematical problem, or the succession of designs that pass before the architect's "eye." Society has typically rewarded the "creative" individual who was able to accomplish an intellectual or an artistic product after prolonged thought and reflection. It took thoughts, feelings, and harmonic sensations to produce the music of Beethoven. Intricate and complex sequences of subjective responses (r) resulted in the accomplishments of the da Vincis, the Newtons, the Platos, and the Jeffersons who filled our world with art, helped man to develop control over the world around him, established great and influential ideas, and molded the politico-economic contexts in which we live. Man's capacity to employ symbols in mediational fashion permits him to communicate better and to learn to solve more intricate problems than any other living organism.

American behaviorism, in following the example set by J. B. Watson, has developed a rigorous methodology and an ingenious instrumentation. But it seems ironic that for some behaviorists the very mediational responses which they use to solve the problems of behavior and to develop the science of psychology are responses which are deemed inaccessible or even inadmissible to scientific analysis. The concern which some experimental psychologists have for this problem was illustrated by an address of the president of the American Psychological Association a few years ago (Hebb, 1960).

Psychologists know of two general ways by which objective observers can learn about subjective events. The first possibility, the one most frequently employed, is to ask the subject to report his observations. He can report just what he felt or saw; the content of his thoughts;

the way he went about solving a particular problem; the sensations arising from his stomach; or what he remembers of previous occasions and experiences. The verbal report of mediational responses can be treated as an objectively observable response (R). However, the degree of correspondence between the subjective response and the individual's verbal representation of it remains a knotty problem. They may be congruent, but of course they are not the same. The congruence is reduced if the patient reports falsely, either inadvertently or on purpose. Patients are sometimes reluctant to speak of some of their private thoughts and feelings. As a matter of fact, much of our interpersonal relations are based on an implicit assumption about the degree of correspondence, or lack of it, between what friends, associates, loved ones, and politicians say and what they "really" feel and believe. *Subjectively observable responses cannot be observed by an outsider; they remain a matter of inference for the objective observer.*

The key to sound judgments about the correspondence between verbal report and subjective responses is twofold. First, repeated observation—the typical condition in sequential psychotherapy interviews—enables one to compare consistencies in behavior over time and thereby obtain evidence as to the degree of correspondence. Second, by examination of the relationships among various kinds of responses, contradictions may become obvious. The patient who reports he is neither tense nor anxious, but who is flushed, sweating profusely, moving restlessly about in his chair, and stammering as he speaks, seems to be manifesting other responses that contradict his verbal report. Simply because the mediational responses and the verbal report of them are not completely isomorphic is no reason to dismiss them as useless. The conditions under which they correspond and the interrelationships which do exist are topics of concern to psychotherapy theory as they should be to the general field of psychology.

A second avenue of access to mediational responses is difficult in a different way. It requires the intricacies of instrumentation, such as the X-ray or the fluoroscope. However, instrumentation for objective observation of responses such as thoughts is not in sight in the foreseeable future. Thus, the burden for studying and attempting to change such responses must continue to fall primarily on the subject's verbal report, although helpful inferences based on other responses, such as blushing, trembling, or smiling, are also possible.

Unobservable responses (r_i). Finally, one must presume that behavioral events are operative which are inaccessible to the direct observation of anyone. An obvious example is the constant chemical changes occurring in the cells of the body. Similarly, the chemical reactions leading to the sensation of taste are not directly observable, but the sensations themselves can be observed and reported upon by the subject. The notation r_i represents this class of events, the subscript carrying the implication that such events are *in*accessible and *in*ferential, and are presumed to be intervening between some set of observable events.

The Second Set of Subclasses: II. Response Content

In the preceding section we developed three major subclasses of behavior: objectively observable behavior (R), subjectively observable behavior (r), and unobservable behavior (r_i). Our task now is to subdivide them further according to *kinds* of responses, or what is frequently referred to as *content classification* or *content analysis*. The content is the "what" of a response, in contrast to other characteristics such as its amplitude, its frequency, or its function, any of which could also be used as a basis for classification.

THE IMPORTANCE OF RESPONSE CONTENT IN PERSONALITY AND PSYCHO-THERAPY THEORY. Emphasis on the "what" in personality theory is readily apparent in the language used by personality theorists—needs, anxiety, guilt, perception, and self-concept. The question of the "what" in personality analysis has typically been the basis for the development of personality inventories, projective techniques, and many other psychometric instruments. For example, the Thematic Apperception Test is primarily a content instrument with which one attempts to determine which responses in what sequences are prominent in a patient's habits of thought. Of course, "structural" or "stylistic" factors are also facets of response sequences which can be studied. For example, attention is paid to both content and structure in the typical Rorschach analysis. Recent work on stylistic factors in personality inventories (Jackson and Messick, 1958) indicates the complementary fashion in which analyses, in terms of content and style, can proceed.

Diagnostic categories represent another content distinction. Psychotherapists sometimes argue against the use of diagnostic classificatory systems because they are poorly constructed, they do not permit adequate differentiation, they are phenotypic in nature, or they fail to be pragmatic, since frequently differential treatment procedures do not derive from the diagnostic effort. Less often do such critics realize that they merely proceed to "diagnose" using a different classificatory procedure, when they seek to differentiate between patients in terms of their "underlying dynamics" or the nature of their problems. Their evaluative reports merely approach the problem of response content in different conceptual terms.

In the realm of the individual psychotherapy interview, the "what" of behavior is equally critical. It matters very much whether the individual is fearful or aggressive, depressed or elated, whether he feels he may be persecuted or is certain that he is.

The use of content classes of behavior may demonstrate that only certain kinds of responses are characteristically attended to in each of the therapy systems, others quite literally ignored, and still others deemed impossible to change. For example, it is generally believed that psychotherapy constitutes an effective procedure for changing unwanted reactions of fear, inappropriate self-reactions, and the like. However, for changes in behaviors such as car driving, dancing, writing, esthetic judgments, social prejudices, or political attitudes, other training procedures are usually proposed. One can be equally dissatisfied with such behaviors, yet rarely is psychotherapy deemed the appropriate method for changing them. All of this is by way of emphasizing two points not always recognized. First, there are likely to be some behaviors which are totally ignored in certain therapy viewpoints. Second, there are some behaviors the changing of which may be more economically accomplished by procedures other than psychotherapy.

THE CONTENT SUBCLASSES. The system of content classification in terms of which the therapy systems will be analyzed and compared is represented in Table 1. The content subclasses have been categorized according to the observational vantage point, that is, the threefold classification R, r, and r_i. Each of the subclasses has been identified with an adjectival label intended to imply the general characteristic of the class. It should also be noted that for each objectively observable response class there is a parallel or related subjectively observable response class. For example, the objectively observable responses of looking at or touching a piece of sculpture (sensory orienting responses) are expected to be accompanied by sensations, perceptions, or sensory images. Thus the parallel classes suggest the most direct inferences, though certainly not the only ones, that might be made from the objectively observable responses.

The content subclasses listed in Table 1 are intended to encompass the major kinds of behavior with which psychotherapists have been

Table 1   Subclasses Based on Response Content

NEVER NEED TO BE INFERENTIAL	ALWAYS INFERRED BY OBJECTIVE OBSERVERS BUT NOT BY SUBJECTIVE OBSERVERS	ALWAYS INFERRED BY BOTH OBSERVERS
Objectively Observable Responses (R)	Subjectively Observable Responses (r)	Unobservable Responses (r_i)
1. Physiological responses	1. Interoceptive response—perceptions, sensations, or sensory images	
2. Motoric responses	2. Proprioceptive responses—perceptions, sensations, or sensory images	Presumed chemical changes, "biological energies," etc.
3. Attending (sensory orienting responses)	3A. Exteroceptive responses— perceptions, sensations, or sensory images	
	3B. Attention and awareness	
4. Emotional responses	4. Affective responses	
5. Communicative response (speech, writing, and "gestural language")	5. Thoughts	

concerned, while at the same time retaining considerable relevance to the traditional areas of inquiry within more academic psychology. At first glance, it may seem that such large inclusive classes might not advance an analysis of concepts particularly well. In addition, the distinctions made are likely to be awkward to maintain in some instances. Of course, the same type of awkwardness is present in the literature of psychology and psychotherapy. It appears necessary, however, to arrive at a compromise between no classificatory approach at all and a complete and detailed set of classes. The value of this proposal will be tested by its usefulness in drawing distinctions among the theories examined in later chapters.

Before discussing the kinds of responses included in each, some general differences among the classes should be noted. Under objectively observable responses (R), the physiological and motoric subclasses are relatively denotative. It is possible to point to particular behavioral events independent of other factors as being appropriate to those two classes. The remaining three subclasses in that group, however, are a good deal less denotative. Sensory orienting, emotive, or communicative acts will have motoric components, for example, but their significance lies in the implications or context of the act rather than in the fact that they are expressed through motoric responses. The simple fact is that we have been unable to manufacture a set of completely denotative classes to encompass psychotherapy concepts and relate to the basic field of psychology. This problem will become clear as the subclasses are discussed.

Under subjectively observable responses, the first three classes differ essentially in the source from which sensory data arise. The general field of psychology has found it awkward to maintain a distinction between sensation and perception, and thus no such distinction is made here even though it may be legitimate and ultimately possible. In addition, we have used the term perception in a limited sense. As Prentice (1958) has pointed out, the term perception has been used as a label for a great variety of phenomena. We have limited its use to the identification or awareness of events as represented in sensations. Other events to which the term perception has been applied, such as judgment, discrimination, and reasoning, we include in the subclass of thoughts. We believe such a distinction will prove useful for our purpose and is not wholly inconsistent with the general field.

Finally, the subclasses chosen make it clear that inferences may be based on several different kinds of objectively observable responses (R). For example, a patient may state that he is disturbed and depressed by his parent's death, leading to the inference that his thoughts are of regret at the loss and his affective responses include sorrow, fear, guilt, or depression. At the same time he may smile as he reports the death, leading to the inference that his feelings are those of relief. While he talks, he may show agitated activity (motoric) and sweating and tearfulness (physiologic). These observable responses would tend to support the first inference rather than the second. This kind of validation of his inferences is extremely important to the psychotherapist, and any way of classifying the behavioral events with which he deals must make it possible.

Physiological and interoceptive responses. These include manifestations of autonomic, smooth-muscle, and glandular activities. Such would include the respiratory, cardiac, gastrointestinal, genitourinary, and dermatological functions. One particularly important characteristic of responses in these two subclasses is that they are generally considered to reflect changes in emotion and in the state of arousal of a person and to be less subject to voluntary control than many others. *Physiological responses* include such objectively observable responses as perspiring, deep and rapid breathing, blushing or a sudden paleness of the skin, "goose flesh," skin rashes, and dilation of the pupils. With instruments to aid observation, other responses such as changes in blood pressure and the galvanic skin response may be observed. *Interoceptive responses* include such subjectively observable events as one's heart beat and palpitations, gastrointestinal sensations such as cramps, nausea, and hunger pangs, a dry mouth and throat, bladder discomfort, uterine pains, and the warm feeling of a blush.

The responses in these two classes are frequently among the symptoms which have distressed the patient enough to cause him to seek therapy. Disturbances in these responses are the defining characteristics in the psychophysiologic or psychosomatic disorders and can be involved in the hysterias and schizophrenias. In milder conditions, when heart palpitations, chronic nausea, or similar events occur without understandable reasons, people generally become frightened. The patient may assume they arise from some physical disorder, or he may recognize them as symptoms of emotional distress. Psychotherapists may view them either as mere by-products of the basic difficulty or as important elements in the disorder itself. The disappearance of, or reduction in intensity of, such responses in therapy is frequently one occurrence which impresses patients and encourages them to continue to try to make progress. The general field of psychology has shown its concern with these responses in such areas as psychopharmacology, somesthetic sensation, pain, and the like.

Motoric and proprioceptive responses. These include functions of the striate muscles in combination with the skeletal framework. *Motoric responses* that might be observed during a therapy interview would include tense posture, restlessness, facial gestures, chewing, nail biting, walking, hand and other body movements. The motor behavior which may be observed in the interview is ordinarily quite restricted since the patient is usually seated or reclining. The patient's description of his behavior outside the therapy condition, however, may be filled with reports of complicated motoric acts of all kinds. *Proprioceptive responses* include those sensations arising from the muscles, tendons, and joints of the body, sometimes called kinesthetic sensations. Such events provide the information by which a person judges and guides his body movement, position, and balance. Thus, patients may report they feel tense, that it hurts to move their leg, that they cannot move, that they feel no sensation from their arm, or that they cannot co-ordinate their movements. Into these categories fall the many instances of autonomy and inactivation in the hysteric groups—tics, paralyses, and seizures—as well as the ritualistic compulsions of the obsessive-compulsive and the bizarre motor activity of the catatonic schizo-phrenic.

It is difficult to overemphasize the importance of these responses. In many respects the manipulatory and locomotive patterns are among the most impressive in the human repertoire, because they represent the instrumentality by which man controls his environment. Man's capacity for building structures, for manipulating intricate and delicate instruments, and his arrangements for moving through space are indeed significant accomplishments. The general field of psychology has shown its interest in this area through research in motor learning, motor skills, body awareness, and phases of engineering psychology.

Sensory orienting and exteroceptive responses. These include events related to the external senses of vision, hearing, touch, taste, and smell, representing the means by which an individual obtains information about his environment. *Sensory orienting responses* include all those objectively observable responses which relate some sense organ to an object or phenomena that may stimulate it. Examples include cocking one's head toward a sound, turning up the volume on the radio, look-ing at a book or a picture, placing food in one's mouth, sniffing a bottle of perfume, and exploring the outlines of an object with one's hands. On the other hand, responses in this group may also remove a sense organ from the influence of events as demonstrated in avoidance be-havior. Covering one's ears, closing one's eyes, spitting out distasteful food, and walking away from a situation are all typical examples. It is important to note that sensory orienting responses are also motoric responses. They are treated as a separate subclass, however, because of their crucial function in orienting a person toward or away from external events, and because there are important subjective responses related to the external sense organs. *Exteroceptive responses* include all those subjectively observable responses arising from the senses of vision, hearing, touch, taste, and smell. Thus sounds, colors, shapes, movements, textures, flavors, and odors all fall in this subclass. These are frequently the primary events to which the term "experiencing" is applied. For our purpose, the recall of sensory images will be included in this subclass along with the original responses, although thoughts about such sensory images are not included here.

These responses have received considerable attention from psychotherapists. For example, in psychoses, distortions, illusions, or hallucinations are frequent. In hysteria, disorders may range all the way from the disruption of restricted response patterns, for instance, anosmia, to gross and inclusive dissociative phenomena. Psychology has shown its interest in these subclasses through research in vision, audition, the chemical senses, orienting acts, perceptual learning, and perception. In fact, most of the research on perception has been based on these senses, probably because they are more convenient to work with than some of the others.

Attention and awareness. We are giving these phenomena the status of a special kind of response, although they may turn out to be response attributes instead. They are placed here because sensory orienting responses (R) are often the base for inference about attention. We expect therapy theorists to emphasize this response class. Academic psychology has tended to ignore it since the advent of Behaviorism, even though it has reappeared in the guise of concepts such as vigilance, set, perception, and the like.

Emotional and affective responses. These two subclasses include the expressive acts typically considered emotional and the subjective phenomena that accompany them. *Emotional responses* include objectively observable acts which have the connotation of emotional expression. As was true of the previous two subclasses, this one manifests motoric and physiologic responses. Whether an act is considered emotional depends on the sequence of observable behaviors that precede and follow it and on the related situational events. The characterization of emotional responses has been difficult for both psychology and psychotherapy, although their extreme forms have not been too difficult to identify—for example, the rage of the catatonic schizophrenic or the profound melancholy of the depressive. The differentiation of less intense responses has been far more difficult. Nevertheless, when a patient shouts while criticizing his parents, smiles, shakes his fist at the therapist, laughs, or cries, therapists typically consider the emotional expression more important and the motoric or verbal act subsidiary. Thus, while this class may tend to merge into others, we expect it to prove useful in the analysis of the different systems. *Affective responses* include the subjective experiences of fear, joy, relief, resentment, hate, shame, disgust, guilt, love, and others which are likely to be significant in therapy literature.

Communication and thought responses. These final subclasses are intended to include both the overt aspects of communication and the intervening symbolic responses. *Communication responses* are all those objectively observable responses by which information is communicated. They include all speech and written communication. Occasionally, a few other responses appear such as "sign language," that is, gestural communicating, but most responses in this subclass are verbal-symbolic. *Thought responses* include all those subjectively observable responses, both imagistic and verbal, characterized as thinking, reasoning, analyzing, imagining, memories, remembering, and the like.

Words and thoughts are the basic tools in verbal psychotherapy, despite their drawbacks. Consider the unreliability of verbal report. The degree of correspondence between thoughts and the statements purporting to represent them is sometimes virtually zero. Patients are notorious for the ways in which they misreport, mislabel, and thus mislead the therapist with or without intention. One of the first tasks of psychotherapy is to bring about a high degree of correspondence between what a patient thinks and what he reports. Consider also the intricate interrelationships that can and do develop among thoughts, verbalizations, and responses in other subclasses. All or nearly all human behavior can influence or be influenced by symbolic activity.

The value of utilizing verbal behavior, however, seems to outweigh its liabilities. The power of words resides in their function as symbols that can represent objects and events in their absence and be used to foreshorten time and space, bringing events from near and far and from present and future immediately into the therapy room. Consider the tremendous limitations which would occur if responses were contingent *only* on the events in the original learning situation. For example, to change a patient's reactions to his father, he would have to be brought back into the treatment setting. Creating the original conditions could be quite awkward—if the father were dead, or if one wished to extinguish a fear response pattern developed during a series of bombing raids in Shanghai, China.

Apparently, it is through the interrelationships of verbal-thought responses with other types of responses such as emotions that therapeutic behavior change is effected in verbal psychotherapy. Therefore, these two subclasses of responses are crucial for psychotherapy.

There is a particularly important set of thoughts which we will call *self-evaluative thoughts*. For example, feelings of inferiority, inadequacy, and worthlessness frequently appear in disordered people and reflect a common self-critical and self-derogatory evaluation, the word *self* connoting the reflexive nature of such responses. They can also be positive, as in the congratulatory responses in manic disorders.

Psychology has given language responses considerable emphases— for instance, the extensive research upon cognitive functions, thinking and problem solving, concept formation, the higher mental processes, verbal learning, and psycholinguistics.

Situational Events and Their Classification

Behavior does not occur in a vacuum. People do not merely respond, they respond in terms of the conditions surrounding them. Thus, behavior is, in part, a function of events that are not a property of the behaving person himself. Whether one drives to work is determined by the presence of an automobile in workable condition. One can hardly eat steak if only drinking water is available. Sounds affect responses. The behavior of other people affects one's behavior. It appears that almost any aspect of one's environment can come to affect one's behavior.

And these become very critical in the conduct of psychotherapy. Therapists have long been aware that the place where the interview is conducted, or whether another person is present, may have a profound effect on the way the patient responds in an interview. Similarly, a question phrased in one way will elicit a denial whereas the same question differently phrased will prompt the patient to become quite confiding. It is commonplace to note that an unkempt appearance, a harsh manner, and a derogatory tone of voice are all conditions that will repel a patient and adversely affect the therapy process.

SITUATIONAL EVENTS IN PERSONALITY AND BEHAVIOR THERAPY. Personality theorists have been somewhat divided on the question of the importance of situational events in determining or influencing behavior. There are several positions in personality theory which decidedly de-emphasized the stimulus. For some theorists the proper study of personality involves the generality of behavior—the analysis of relatively stable and enduring response patterns which characterize the individual across different situations. This interest in cross-situation behavior uniformities is sometimes reflected in trait theory, where the person is conceived as having relatively enduring patterns of behavior which can be expected to occur under a wide range of situations. This led to attempts to measure traits such as anxiousness, dependency, dominance, or aggressiveness. The degree to which behavior can be conceptualized as generalized and situationally independent on the one hand, and particular and situation-specific on the other, is still open. It is undoubtedly both, and this fact encourages disagreement for lack of a simple answer.

There is another source of disagreement as to the role of situational events, and it is best illustrated by the phenomenological point of view. This group of theorists has been particularly impressed by the interindividual differences in reacting to and perceiving what appears to be the same situation. Recognizing that a person's behavior is often determined by what he thinks a situation to be, they have tended to emphasize the response aspects of the person-environment exchange. To this group, it is less the situation itself than it is the *situation as perceived*, that is, a response, that became the focus of analysis.

On the other hand, the modern behaviorists have placed a strong emphasis upon the situational variables. Dollard and Miller (1950) and others share the proposition that behavior is a function of the conditions under which it occurs, that is, the Gallilean point of view (Lewin, 1936). Therefore, responses come to be studied insofar as they relate to, or are contingent on, environmental events. From this standpoint, the analysis of situational events is crucial for the effective analysis of the way behavior works. We are likely to find that most, if not all, theorists give some attention to both kinds of events but with differing degrees of emphasis. Thus, provision must be made for both responses and situational events.

DEFINITION OF SITUATIONAL EVENTS. Before proceeding further, we should designate more precisely the kinds of events to which we are referring. *By situational events we mean all those events occurring around an individual which are not a property of the individual himself.* This is an "outside the skin" definition, referring to events external to the individual whose behavior is under study. Note that this definition is tied to an observational vantage point. The behavior of one individual may be a situational event for another. We will use the symbol S to designate situational events.

We have chosen to use the term "situation," rather than "environment," because we believe it connotes a more particular, specific set of events. We mean the term situation to refer to only the portion of the environment that is available to influence behavior at a given point in time and space. In this sense, it is more like Murray's use of the term "press" (1938).

This definition is different from the usual meaning of the term "stimulus" in several important respects. The latter is typically defined as any event that leads to a response, and thus stimuli may be external or internal, and responses can be stimuli. The term stimulus therefore refers to the *relationship* between events and is not identifiable in terms of what *kind* of event it denotes. Since we have sought a class definable in terms of kind of event, we have avoided the use of this term.

RESPONSES AS "STIMULI." In the search for antecedents of behavior, it has often appeared that streams of responses are triggered by specific events, and research in psychology has demonstrated some of the particulars of how this occurs. For example, the child may cringe from a hot stove, or the husband may start at his wife's criticism. Such responses follow upon specific external or situational events. There are many responses, however, which appear to have no observable antecedents. An individual, seated in his home, may suddenly announce that he is hungry, or get up and go to the bathroom, or abruptly cry out in pain. If we assume the existence of a "cause" that is not objectively observable, then it may be proposed that the responses were initiated by something going on within the person (r or r_i events). Needs, drives, impulses, instincts, or motives are often proposed as ways of conceptualizing these response initiators.

Actually, any response can be thought of as having "stimulus properties." For example, when a child learns to count from one to ten, his recitation of the successive numbers can be thought of as a series of responses, each functioning both as a response and as a stimulus to later responses.

This type of conception can become awkward and confusing as well as cumbersome. The concept of motivation, for example, appears to be in difficulty partly because it has been conceived in this way (Cofer, 1959). With behavior occurring in a continuous stream, one has the phenomenon of responses occurring after each other in a never-ending fashion, and these sequences are more simply conceived as *response-producing responses*. This alternative will be followed in the present volume. When a system speaks of drives, motives, or needs, our framework of analysis will represent these as behavioral occurrences—that is, responses—which lead to other responses in a particular way that is defined by the system's propositions. As the reader will see in the later sections on propositions, this will permit the ready differentiation between S-R laws and R-R laws as statements which relate situational events to responses on the one hand and response events to responses on the other.

This manner of thinking has been dictated partly by the purposes of the volume. It is devised to encompass systems as divergent as stimulus-response positions, phenomenological theories, and psychoanalytic and dynamic points of view. The fact that the symbols S, R, r, and r_i are used, or that reference is made to S-R laws, should not mislead the reader to thinking that the framework of analysis is thereby "behavioristic," or a stimulus-response position in the usual sense. He should keep clearly in mind that the S in this approach is completely different from the typical notions of stimulus for which it is often used, and that the definition of response is a great deal more inclusive.

SITUATIONAL EVENTS ARE CONTINUOUS. Situational events, like behavior, are often thought of as discrete events. A honking horn, a friend's smile, a mountain view, a pretty girl's wink, the heat of a fire, a parent's angry voice—all are instances of situational events. However, we must remind ourselves that, like behavior, situational events are constantly occurring in a continuous stream, and any division into discrete or separate events becomes an act of analysis. For example, a family argument lasting over a period of two hours can be thought of as an event, or it can be subdivided into who said and did certain things in what order. Similarly, what preceded and followed the argument might be considered. The stream is always changing and yet is always there.

The recognition of the continuity of situations carries with it the realization that the stream cannot be dealt with in its entirety but must be broken down conceptually into component parts. The parts so chosen become situational event classes.

But how should the stream be subdivided, or which situational classes are to be chosen? Hypothetically, the possibilities are as many and varied as are the observable attributes of the situations themselves, although presumably certain classes are best for certain purposes. The problems here are identical with those involved in the analysis of behavior itself.

Ordinarily, for the development of stimulus classes, psychology has tended to select dimensions of external events which have some direct relationship to behavior. For example, one might classify plants in terms of size or shape, attributes which would carry little connotation of the relationship between the plant and human behavior. On the other hand, plants classified as poisonous or nonpoisonous to humans are subdivided according to the responses they are likely to produce. Thus, psychology has classes identified in terms of the sensory apparatus with which they interrelate, for example, visual or auditory. Examples of other classes are *relevant* and *irrelevant stimuli* and *structured* and *ambiguous stimuli.*

It is clear, then, that psychologists do employ various situational event classes in their study of behavior. We expect to find that therapy theorists have also done this, although perhaps not always explicitly. For example, when a therapist speaks of his patient as being afraid, he is omitting the situational reference, but as soon as he designates it as fear of his mother, he is identifying both the response and the situational events to which it is related.

THE SUBCLASSES OF SITUATIONAL EVENTS. We believe it will be useful for our purposes to subdivide situational events into at least two very general subclasses. One will involve the behavior of other people and the second will include all nonhuman phenomena.

The behavior of other humans. The behavior of other people, parents, friends, wife or husband, children, and boss, are usually the most significant situational events in a person's life. The responses of one person are situational events for a second person if it is the second person's behavior that is under consideration, and vice versa. This reciprocal relationship, in which the behavior of each individual serves to determine the behavior of the other, is important in the development of both normal and disordered behavior.

People, psychologists and laymen alike, have recognized that training methods greatly influence the types of behavior a growing child acquires—the questions parents ask, the demands they make, the way they treat one another, and the rewards and punishments they administer. Neurotic conflicts are rarely generated with respect to chairs and tables, or trees and rocks, but rather in relation to people. It is often suspected that the variability of human events as opposed to that of physical matter, and the inconsistency with which people behave toward an individual, prompt the individual to develop ambivalent and inconsistent responses to people.

It is also important to note that individual verbal psychotherapy involves the use of the behavior of one person—the therapist—to make up a set of situational conditions to modify the behavior of a second person—the patient. Thus, when we deal with the problem of technique, we shall be considering the kinds of situational events the therapist can control and manipulate in an attempt to modify the patient's behavior. Most prominent among these conditions will be the behavior of the therapist himself.

Since the therapy systems to be studied have probably not considered the issue of situational events in great detail, we shall not develop further subclasses of human behavior for our purposes. Of course, the classification of objectively observable responses might be used as situational classes when one person's behavior is viewed as situational events for another.

Nonhuman events. For our purposes, this subclass probably need not be further subdivided, although any completely adequate system would consider them in detail. Animals, enclosed space, water, textures, odors, music, storms, day, and night are all examples of nonhuman events which have been tied up in different behavior disorders. The experienced therapist can undoubtedly think of many more examples. In terms of therapeutic technique, occupational therapy, art therapy, music therapy, shock therapy, drugs, and even custodial treatment represent, at least in part, the manipulation or use of nonhuman situational events in an attempt to bring about behavioral change in a patient.

HIGHER-ORDER CONCEPTS

Kinds of Events as the Base

Through the preceding section the discussion was centered about the kinds of events with which therapists have to deal. We expect to find, however, that therapy systems have been concerned with complicated patterns of behavior and have developed more abstract and inclusive concepts to accomplish their purposes.

For purposes of this study, we are proposing that observable events are the starting point of any system of concepts. They are the building blocks which are then combined, grouped, and ordered into various combinations for the purpose of thinking and conceptualizing about them and for drawing generalizations about their occurrence. Observables are the raw materials out of which systems are built, and all therapists and theorists start with them. The subject winks, avoids his therapist's gaze, has a feeling of rage, or recalls an image of his mother. These are events, but, of course, they do not determine the way in which a theorist thinks about the events—which ones he attends to, how he will group them, or how he will relate one set of events to others.

The preferred procedure would be to compare concepts by starting with the kinds of events to which they refer. If this is possible, the reviewer will be able to tell whether two concepts lie at the same or different levels of conceptualization, whether one includes another, whether two concepts with different labels are being used to apply to the same bits of behavior, and so on. Of course, there are limits to the clarity with which this might be done, particularly if a theorist has been careless in denoting the events to which his concepts refer, or in what ways his higher-order concepts are related to concepts lower in the conceptual hierarchy.

Characteristics

A theorist could choose to remain close to the level of observable events and employ concepts denoting a limited variety of events, each of which extends over very brief periods of time, such as the motion of a hand, the wink of an eyelid, a lover's caress. However, we expect to find that therapy theorists have characteristically employed concepts of a much higher order of abstraction in their attempts to deal with complex human behavior. We also expect them to differ among themselves as to which level of abstraction is most appropriate. It will be helpful to consider some choices available to the therapy theorist, as a way of clarifying the kinds of differences we are likely to meet.

Let us suppose that each theorist has available to him the same bit of data concerning a youth in therapy, namely, that whenever he sees his mother in close physical contact with his father he becomes distressed and characteristically gets up, leaves the room, and begins another solitary period at the piano. A theorist can analyze such phenomena into units of many different kinds. One of the things he can do is to remain at the level of observables and represent this set of events as a *sequence* of responses occurring through time: sees mother and father → distress → arises → leaves → plays piano. He can employ a larger concept instead, encompassing more events under a single rubric. He might use the term *threat* to refer to two sets of responses occurring at virtually the same point in time: becomes distressed as he sees parents interacting. A *pattern* of events is referred to here with a single concept label. Or the entire package of events might be described with the label *isolation:* whenever threatened he withdraws to some sanctuary. Such a concept refers to a *pattern-sequence;* that is, to both the variety of responses occurring together and their relationship through time. Finally, this might be thought of as a part of a larger organization of behavior which might be called *oedipal complex.* Such a concept would refer to a constellation of response patterns, occurring singly and in sequence, which are recurrent over a period of weeks, months, and years. Thus, some concepts represent *recurrent pattern sequences.*

These possibilities cover some choices available to the theorist when he considers the response aspects of his behavioral analysis alone. But situational events occur in sequences also, and the nature of those sequences has important consequences for one's behavior. The theorist has many options with respect to these events as well. He may choose to ignore them in the sense that he concentrates on the person's immediate response to the situational conditions rather than being concerned with the situational events themselves. He may characterize some as important (the interpersonal ones) and choose not to analyze others. He may accord them equal significance with the response events themselves, and thus analyze the events in terms of situation-response relationships; such a theorist might object to the concept of fear, and might insist that the situation to which it refers always be specified— fear of mother, fear of animals, or fear of water. Finally, a theorist might choose to develop units of analysis that encompass situational conditions and responses in a single concept. Some of these alternatives are exemplified in the concept of *hydrophobia.* In this instance, a single term is used to refer to a sequence of situational and response events—water(S) → fear(r) → avoidance(R). We can anticipate that the therapy theorists have employed many different courses in their treatment of situational events and their relationship to behavior.

SUMMARY. When we come to the analysis of the various systems, then, we shall be interested in a variety of questions. We shall ask, for example, to what kinds of events do the concepts of this system typically refer? This will provide some notion of the ones judged to be significant. It will reveal whether the system has emphasized some events—

for example, thoughts—and deemphasized others—for example, motoric or situational ones. It will help to identify those systems built on the assumption of response events which remain unobserved (r_i) either by the therapist or the person in whom the events are occurring. Looking at systems in this fashion, we should have a better appreciation of the relationship of one set of concepts to another.

We can move on now to consider the level of abstraction at which the system's concepts typically lie and their relationship to observable events. The extent to which a system has been careful to explicate how the higher order concepts relate to those lower in the hierarchy, and how each of these, in turn, build on the base of observable events, should become apparent from such an analysis.

Chapter 3

System as Theory and a Method

for Comparing Propositions

Concepts are the building blocks of a systematic analysis of behavior. The "mortar" of a theoretic system is composed of the statements by which such blocks are tied together. Since few statements in psychotherapy can be made in the form of scientific laws, we refer to these as propositional.

The varieties of such propositional statements that a theory might develop are multiple. Of course, several sets of restrictions apply to theories in general, and to therapy theories in particular. All theories must include statements relevant to their concepts. If a theory employs anger as a central event, the system should include a series of statements about how anger interrelates with other events, the conditions under which it occurs, what it characteristically leads to, and the like. To exemplify the variety of propositional statements that therapy systems might include, we refer once more to Mr. X and his opening interview.

The reader will recall that Mr. X sought relief from disturbing thoughts, frightening emotional reactions, conflicting interpersonal patterns of responding, and other upsetting behaviors. It is clear that all his requests may be summed under a single rubric: a request for help in modifying his reaction patterns, a *change* in his present response repertoire. It is easy to understand his distress over his responses and the consequences for his life situation, particularly since he is relatively lucid in his account and is able to specify with more precision than can many patients the particular responses that are causing him difficulty.

The request for help in achieving a behavioral change is considerably less explicit in many situations therapists may encounter. Consider the statement: "My wife and I don't get along, and we agreed we ought to see someone like you about it." Such a person differs from Mr. X in two important respects: (1) he does not state explicitly that he wishes to achieve changes in his characteristic ways of thinking, feeling, and acting; and (2) he does not specify particular responses in his thoughts, emotions, or overt behavior with which he is dissatisfied. The first of these, however, is likely to be implicit in his appearance at the office of the therapist. Later interviews may be sufficient to establish the specific responses he would like to see altered, even though his list may prove to be more extensive in the case of his wife's behavior than in the case of his own.

Not infrequently a therapist will also encounter an interviewee who comes to see him following the machinations of some other person. A wife's ultimatum may have proved sufficient to lead a patient to a therapist; the parents of a rebellious adolescent may require his attendance; an in-patient in a mental hospital may be assigned to therapy as a part of his treatment program, or he may be induced to undergo therapy as a condition of discharge. In instances like these it is less at the insistence of the patient than of someone else that a request for behavioral change materializes. Implicit or explicit in such referrals, however, is the assertion that the patient holds within his repertoire response characteristics which are unwanted by "someone," an assertion which the patient may or may not endorse. The consideration of therapy for any particular individual, therefore, hinges on the necessity, desirability, or feasibility of attempting to accomplish behavioral change. The decision by a therapist to undertake therapy signifies that he believes that the conditions of psychotherapy to be utilized may be effective in producing the changes in behavior being sought. Thus, *psychotherapy is a set of procedures for changing behavior.*

PROBLEMS OF THEORY

When someone comes in and states that something is wrong with someone's behavior, in this case his own, and that something should be done about it, a host of questions arises. There is first of all the question of whether the person is correct: is there something wrong with the behavior that is going on? If there is, what is it? Which of all the myriad things which the patient is reporting represents the difficulty?

What Behavior Should Be Changed

One can imagine the variety of questions that are apt to flood the therapist's mind as he listens to Mr. X report on his difficulties. "What's wrong here? Obviously he is in great distress, since he reports on many things about his behavior that he finds unsatisfactory. Some of what he doesn't like is quite obvious. Clearly the strange sexual sensations he has require change. His panic reaction must obviously be brought under control. His homosexual impulses appear to be something he both likes and dislikes. His hostile and fearful relationships with people must certainly place him in an almost constant dilemma. I wonder how these things are related."

These kinds of thoughts and questions reveal the therapist's first concern. He must be able to specify which behavior patterns require changing. Experience has taught him that it is a rare patient who can put his finger on the events that are producing the difficulty and thereby guide the therapist directly to them. Much of the therapist's training has led him to expect that responses of which his patient is unaware are influential; that frequently patients fail to report their behavior as others more objective than they would be apt to do; and that often patients will seek help in changing responses which, in turn, are contingent upon the successful change of a whole series of quite different response groups.

MOST KINDS OF RESPONSE MAY BECOME DISORDERED. Patients request changes in tremendously varied sets of behavior. No class of behavior apparently has yet proved to be immune to the inroads of disruption and disorder. Perceptual responses, acts of intellect or of judgment, unwanted feelings and emotional states, and excessively intense drives, wishes, or motive states exemplify the range of disruption therapists deal with. Psychotherapists have elected to try to change an impressive array of behavior sequences and have claimed success with problems as varied as ulcers, homosexuality, psychopathy, tics, compulsions, delusions, hallucinations, and sexual responses. It would appear that psychotherapists have been optimistic about the effectiveness of their techniques.

Clearly a therapist cannot help a patient to resolve difficulties, to change his problematic behaviors, unless he can form some idea of what is wrong. He needs a guide by which to tell disordered behavior from behavior that is not disordered. Not only must he recognize disordered behavior when it occurs, but he must also know how it works. In the case of Mr. X, he must know not only whether dreams such as Mr. X has been having are indicative of disorder but also where they come from, what they signify, and to what other behaviors they are related. Whence comes his fear of cars, to what does it lead, upon which other responses does it depend?

KNOWLEDGE OF DISORDERED BEHAVIOR. The therapist needs a set of propositions about disordered behavior, how it develops, and how it works. If the therapist concludes, for example, that he wishes to help Mr. X change his homosexual pattern, and if he believes that this homosexual pattern results from a biochemical imbalance, he might proceed to change the behavior by attempting to remedy the biochemical imbalance. On the other hand, if he believes that Mr. X's homosexual behavior results from faulty self-perceptions, he may try to establish a set of conditions under which those faulty self-perceptions could be corrected through learning.

A theory is required to account for the manner in which disordered responses are acquired and for their persistence in spite of the fact they are unwanted, ineffective, and inappropriate. This information is essential in deciding whether psychotherapeutic procedures will be effective in changing the responses. Not only does the therapist need some ideas concerning the process whereby disorder develops, but he also needs some hypotheses about the resultants of the process—for example, whether certain behavioral sequences once developed are irreversible, or whether highly varied symptoms may result from the same process.

We propose, then, that a therapy system must rest on a theory of behavior disorder. Any attempt to correct a problem must stem from an analysis of what is wrong. Certainly no therapist ever intends to change every aspect of the patient's behavior, and as soon as he begins to limit the extent of change to be attempted, a theory of psychopathology becomes essential. The decision, whether implicit or explicit, to attempt to modify certain behaviors while avoiding modification in others, requires some assumptions about how disordered behavior works. As soon as the therapist begins "doing something" he is using some theory of psychopathology because it implies that he has decided what is wrong and what may be modified by his procedures. All therapists use some theory of psychopathology. They differ in the degree to which they acknowledge and make explicit their theory.

CHANGE TO WHAT? Changing one set of behavior leads to the implication that other behaviors will take their place. If one decides that some behaviors need to be changed, then one is deciding implicitly that the person will develop others as alternatives. But the question is: which shall they be, and how shall they be determined? In a very general sense we refer to what many therapists speak of as the *goals of therapy*.

Let's follow the therapist's thoughts concerning Mr. X again: "Well, there appear to be a number of behaviors he wants changed, but what will take their place? Shall I wait and assume appropriate ones will naturally occur once he starts to change? That's what Professor Y always used to say: 'Let your patient lead you.' But some of this is pretty obvious. He doesn't like his anger feelings or his panicky feelings, and they seem to interfere with other responses. If they are reduced we shall have achieved one goal. He also says he wants to get along better with his mother. That's pretty vague so I probably need to determine more what that means. I'm not sure whether he wants to get rid of his homosexual impulses or whether he simply wants to stop being uncomfortable about them. I wonder if he's concerned about being able to hold a job and other practical things like that? He doesn't mention these, but I wonder if they aren't just as important."

THE VALUE OF SPECIFIC OUTCOME STATEMENTS. Here the therapist is faced with a second category of problem which follows logically from the first. Not only does he need to decide what behaviors need to be changed, but he requires some hypotheses about the direction in which changes should occur, what to facilitate the changes toward, changing which behavior to what. The question of how he reaches his decision will be considered shortly. Here we are emphasizing that if he is to work effectively he must know specifically what outcomes he expects of his labors.

It is evident that a very general formulation of the goals of therapy is always possible, so general, in fact, that few indeed would take issue with them. The therapist could state, for example: "Mr. X is unhappy and should be capable of enjoying life," or "Mr. X can't seem to get along with his mother, and he should have a mature and satisfactory relationship with his parents." There is probably an inverse relationship between the generality of such statements about outcome and their utility.[1] The utility of an outcome statement can be judged in part by the specific therapeutic procedures that derive directly from it. *Specific and precise therapeutic operations are more likely to arise from specific and precise outcome statements.* Therapy is similar to other problem-solving tasks. A knowledge of the objective helps to define the ways it can be accomplished.

For the sake of utility, a therapist should assert as precisely as possible the behaviors he seeks to produce as alternatives to the behaviors judged to be disordered. If the therapist proposes to eliminate Mr. X's response of fear, "which characteristically occurs in the presence of dominating, coercive females," he will have made an outcome statement of greater therapeutic utility than one expressed in general terms, such as "to enable him to get along with women better."

WHO SHOULD SELECT THE GOALS. Without a specification of desired outcomes, the therapist is faced with two alternatives. If he fails to specify the outcomes to which his techniques are directed, he permits changes to occur without foresight and planning and reconciles himself to whatever changes emerge, or he permits the decision of desired change to be made by someone else, such as the patient, the patient's family, or community opinion. Under these conditions the therapist proceeds to the alteration of behavior at the request of another person. However, the changes which the therapist might seek to produce may not coincide with those that others might choose. Mr. X might wish to retain his homosexual pattern of behavior, although the community disapproves of this same pattern. The therapist cannot satisfy both influences. Unplanned change is likely to be inefficient and erratic.

[1] The failure of psychotherapy "outcome" research to demonstrate the effectiveness of psychotherapy is probably a function of inadequate specification on this point.

A patient, a therapist, or *someone* implicitly or explicitly chooses a direction of change, and the direction chosen has an important influence on the nature of the therapeutic interview. We propose that explicit objectives are to be preferred to implicit ones, and that whether the therapist selects them or whether he chooses to implement the objectives of someone else, he should be explicitly aware of what they are.

It is important to note that the question of the nature of the change to be sought, or the behavior patterns to be developed, is related logically to the question of which behavior patterns are disordered and should be changed. It also implies the identification of response patterns that either cannot be subjected to modification or do not require it.

THE PROBLEM OF VALUES. It should be clear that theoretical propositions describing how behavior operates, and how it becomes disordered, are not sufficient in themselves to define the goals of therapy. The practitioner, working within a particular cultural setting, must also consider those behaviors that by group demand must be changed, or are deemed advisable to be changed. The question of "ought" and "must" are value questions, and therefore the practicing therapist is inextricably involved in them. He cannot avoid repeated implicit or explicit value judgments throughout the course of his therapeutic work.

KNOWLEDGE OF NORMAL BEHAVIOR DEVELOPMENT. How can one decide what would represent appropriate forms of behavior without some notion of what appropriate behavior looks like and how it works? If Mr. X is experiencing inappropriate feelings toward little girls, what should be his feelings instead? Someone might respond by saying that affectionate nonsexual feelings should be operating when he interacts with them, that he ought to feel kindly and loving toward them. If that is the case, where does one get kindly loving feelings, where do they come from? Are they biological givens, such that a rearrangement of conditions is required to elicit them? Does one learn to love and feel affectionate? Again, how about the homosexual patterns of which Mr. X complains? Where do they come from? Are they part of normal development? Are they biologically determined and thus not susceptible to change? Are they the product of learning, but of such a status that they are unlikely to be changed; or, on the other hand, are they an aspect of behavioral development into which changes are readily introduced?

All such questions make it clear that the therapist must have some hypotheses concerning the way in which normal behavior develops, hypotheses which specify which behaviors are determined biologically and therefore are less amenable to change, as well as which behaviors develop as a result of experience or learning, and are therefore alterable by the same process, that is, *re*learning. And since he knows that a change in one behavior may entail changes in others, he must have some notions as to how interrelationships among behavior patterns become formed and continue to operate.

We are proposing that a therapy system must rest on a theory of normal behavior development as well as a theory concerning the acquisition of disordered behavior. The reader will recognize that the two complement one another and may have concluded that both are necessarily reciprocal, since it is difficult to determine whether some form of disordered development has occurred unless one knows how the normal course of development proceeds.

A METHOD FOR COMPARING PROPOSITIONS

Propositions represent the second major step in the formal or logical aspects of system building. Their development follows the selection and definition of concepts. After having chosen the pieces of behavior with which he is to be concerned, the therapy theorist is faced with the question of how and in what ways these events relate to one another. Theoretical propositions are statements about functional interrelationships. "Obsessive thoughts represent outgrowths of earlier phobic response patterns," and "anxiety leads to a narrowing of the span of attention" are examples of propositional statements. These particular statements are cast in sequential form: one set of events is antecedent to and leads to another. Propositions can also express other forms of relationships.

TYPES OF PROPOSITIONS. Although we shall not attempt here to present a detailed classification of types of propositions, it may prove useful to distinguish between a few major kinds which have frequently characterized system building. Propositional statements could be developed to represent the relationships between one set of observable events and another. Often these are referred to as *empirical propositions*. At higher orders of abstraction, however, where concepts relate to concepts, the propositional statements are often referred to as *formal*—that is, hypothetical or theoretical—*propositions*. We can expect to encounter propositions of both sorts in the various systems.

A second major distinction may also prove useful in thinking about the variety of propositions included in therapy theories. This difference will be found to vary with the degree to which the theorists concern themselves with situational events and their role in the analysis of behavior. Some propositions relate situational to response events and have come to be called *S-R or S-r laws*. Others relate response to response, and may be called *R-R, R-r, or r-r laws*.

It will probably prove helpful to bear these major kinds of propositions in mind when the actual analysis of the therapy system is undertaken. The reader is referred to several considerations of this distinction between propositions—the considerations of their relative merits and the consequences which follow upon their respective use (McClelland, 1951; Marx, 1951; and Spence, 1956).

Another distinction between types of propositions has frequently been made and has become the focus of considerable controversy in the field of personality and therapy theory. Since the time when Adler introduced the notion of studying individuals as individuals (1927) up to the point at which Allport (1937) brought it to a clear and explicit formulation, there had been a group of theorists who entertained considerable doubt as to the possibilities of accounting for behavior in a specific individual if one were to have available only principles that were appropriate to the general case, that is, people in general. It has been argued that laws governing the occurrence of a general class of events (*nomothetic propositions*) would be insufficient for understanding an individual's behavior, and laws particular to his own behavior would have to be developed. Such *idiographic propositions* assume that each individual behaves lawfully, but according to "his own laws." Discussions of this controversy and the problems associated with the attempt to maintain the idiographic position have recurred in the literature (Phillips, 1956, and McClelland, 1951).

ASSUMPTIONS IMPLICIT IN THE DEVELOPMENT OF PROPOSITIONS. Of course, embedded in this theoretic approach to the study of behavior lie the assumptions that *the behavioral stream occurs in a lawful fashion, and that not only are the events which go to make it up orderly, but also that this order is potentially identifiable through careful and systematic analysis*. Without such assumptions, the development of principles of behavior could not proceed. The presumption is that an adequate and complete representation of the behavioral stream is possible, if given the appropriate units by which to analyze the continuing events and the capacity for identifying the ways in which they relate to one another.

A corollary should also be noted. If behavior is lawful, and if it occurs in a continuous stream within the context of the situational flow of events, *every behavioral event must be presumed to be related to some antecedent, concurrent, or consequent events in some way*. Such an assumption does not imply that *every* antecedent event is related to *every* subsequent event; only that every event must be related to *some* other event or events. Such events and their relationships are presumed to be identifiable.

The Relationships between Concepts and Propositions

A primary problem for the personality and therapy theorist who perforce must deal with many different kinds of events is the question of whether differences in the classes of responses—concepts—carry with them differences in the manner in which these responses operate. Or, stated another way, if responses can be distinguished from one another, that is, placed into different classes, does this necessarily imply that different propositions govern their functioning? For example, because love and anger feelings are discernibly different, does this mean that they function differently?

No, the selection of differing classes of events and their arrangement into behavioral concepts does not necessarily entail propositions specific to each. Two other general possibilities arise, and both are likely to be represented in the therapy systems we shall consider.

The first of these has been espoused most often by modern behaviorists and finds its strongest proponents among those who have been strongly influenced by the learning theorists of experimental psychology. It argues that the simplest and most parsimonious hypothesis on which to base early research is to assume that the same principles govern all behavior regardless of kind. It acknowledges that individuals differ markedly in the content of their behavior and that this primarily accounts for the impressive individual differences which are readily apparent. It also proposes, however, that people do not differ with regard to how these various response patterns operate. To put it more succinctly: people differ in what they learn, not in how their behavior is acquired and maintained.

Other groups of theorists, unwilling to proceed on such assumptions, have proposed that behavioral principles are somewhat more specific. They deem it more likely that explanatory principles will be found to vary with the kind of behavior involved; for example, emotional responses develop and operate differently than verbal responses. Thus, differential theories develop: a theory of perception, a cognitive theory, a theory of motor behavior, a set of principles by which to account for motivation.

A good illustration of this controversy in recent research is represented in the critical exchange between the New Look perceptionists and those who argued for a more traditional approach to the study of perception. Murphy and Proshansky (1942), Lazarus (1951), and Erickson (1951), among others, set out to verify the proposition that perceptual responses are subject to the same laws as pertain to the acquisition and maintenance of other responses that are superficially quite different, to wit, motor habits, intellective problem-solving, or the learning of nonsense syllables. Thus they sought to demonstrate the effects of reward and punishment upon perceptual habits and to verify the hypothesis that acts of seeing, judging, and interpreting are acquired in the same fashion as motor skills.

The opposite position is demonstrated in an article by Pratt (1950). Believing that the weight of evidence points toward perceptual behavior as relatively immune to learning, Pratt argues that the determinants of perceptions reside within the physiological structure of the perceiving organism and the basic organizing factors within the stimulus-organism interaction. He suggests that wherever the effects of learning appear to have played a part in determining the nature of a perception, it is likely that some artifact of observation has misled the investigator. Thus Pratt, as far as this exchange was concerned, argues for special laws governing perceptual behavior.

Variety of Propositions in Therapy Theory

Up to this point we have considered the nature of propositions in general, some of the forms which propositional statements may take, and the major assumptions underlying the development of propositions. However, another large source of variance lies in the content of the propositions themselves.

A considerable range of content can be expected in the propositions of the systems. We cannot do more at this juncture than to call the reader's attention to their heterogeneity and perhaps to indicate a few of the common issues to which the propositions are frequently directed.

The majority of human response patterns are congruent and integrated. In other words, concurrent responses are related appropriately to one another and do not lead to mutually contradictory consequences. A cardinal feature of theories of disordered behavior and of the therapy procedures devised to correct them has been to emphasize the role played by incongruent or inappropriately related response patterns.

One group of these conceptions involves the notion of simultaneously but inappropriately related response patterns and sequences, that is, those which are *discrepant* but not necessarily conflicting. One such idea which has gained almost universal adoption is the distinction between covert and overt responses, permitting what Cameron has referred to as "behavioral duplicity" (1947). For example, a mediating emotional response of anger may lead to both an angry thought and a friendly verbal statement. These latter responses are discrepant but not mutually conflicting, since they can and do occur together. Much of our training is devoted to the suppression of some responses in favor of more effective and less damaging alternative responses.

A second group of conceptions involves simultaneous response patterns or sequences, which are not only discrepant but also lead to mutually contradictory consequences. Propositions about *conflicting* behaviors would be included here. Characteristically, conflict is conceptualized as the occurrence of two or more response sequences which are directly incompatible, mutually contradictory, and thus cannot be completed simultaneously. The running-off of one sequence simply precludes the completion of another.

Perhaps the most common kinds of propositions for a therapy theory are those that are concerned with the relationships between verbal-symbolic responses and response patterns of other types. Most of the therapist's techniques for eliciting behavior in therapy, and for subsequently effecting changes in that behavior, involve verbal procedures on his part and entail verbal response sequences on the part of the subject. Working with the media of communicative responses, the therapist must be concerned repeatedly with how these words and statements of the subject are related to what the patient feels or does inside and outside the therapy hour; he must have some notions about how talking to a person makes the patient think differently, feel differently, and act differently on other occasions. The interrelationships of verbal and symbolic events with other events is therefore a particularly important set of propositions for a therapy theory. The puzzle of exactly why talking to a person *about* his behavior can produce change in the behavior itself remains one of the great enigmas of individual verbal psychotherapy. These examples are illustrative of the heterogeneity of propositions we are likely to encounter.

THE QUESTION OF LEVELS OF BEHAVIOR. The reader may have noticed the absence of any terms denoting *depth* in the foregoing material; he may have recognized that behavior has been represented in terms of two dimensions, concomitance and sequence, and that a third dimension could be added to the scheme. Angyall (1941) has done as much, and referred to variables of depth as the vertical dimension. Were such a dimension to be employed, it would follow those theorists who have tended to characterize behavior as : (1) composed of differing levels; (2) characterized by differing degrees of accessibility, that is, the unconscious; or (3) organized in terms of an hierarchical structure. Each of these three ideas of level is basically a question of the *relationships among response sequences.*

When depth is described in terms of *levels of behavior,* it is typically given a developmental definition. At the "deeper" levels lie response sequences that develop early in the individual's life and "on top" of which has accumulated a superstructure of increasingly mature forms of behavior. It is implied that responses learned earlier are more difficult to change.

When depth refers to *hierarchical structure,* it appears to mean that a response may be a part of more than one response sequence at the same time. Such a multiple role makes it possible for a response, or a group of responses, to interrelate a number of response sequences functionally. It serves as a kind of "bridge" from one pattern sequence to another. It is not necessarily a response acquired early in the developmental sequence.

When a theorist refers to "depth" in terms of *degrees of accessibility,* this would be represented by responses that either (1) are more remote from the sets of observable events or (2) retain few direct interrelationships with responses that would make them accessible to awareness. It is also possible for conflicting or contradictory responses to be operative, preventing the quick elicitation of the "deeper" events—inhibiting responses, repression, projection, and the like. However, one must be careful not to slip into the conceptual error of thinking that the longer it takes to elicit a response, then the "deeper" it must be.

If a response is to determine behavior, it must be currently opera-tive, albeit unlabeled, unrecognized, or perhaps "defended against." This same point applies to the question of layers of behavior. To think of some responses either as implicitly operative, as relatively inaccessible to identification or verbal representation, or as playing a central role in a configuration of response sequences would seem to be a more appropriate way in which to think of such behavior, rather than in terms of the "stacking" of one set of response patterns on top of another. Thus, a third dimension seems unnecessary. We believe we can more parsimoniously represent the same phenomena to which these notions of verticality refer through the use of concomitant or sequential patterns of response. This is the manner in which we shall attempt to represent propositions of "depth" in the different therapy systems.

SUMMARY. At this point we can review some of the questions which we shall entertain as we consider each of the systems in turn. We want to inspect the degree to which each theorist has been systematic in defining the functional relationships among his classes of behavioral and situational events. We wish to know the extent to which proposi-tions have been developed to tie the concepts together into a logical and orderly system and what the nature of those propositions are. We shall be interested in whether they tend to refer to situation-response $(S-R)$ or response-response relationships $(R-R, r-r)$ or both $(S-r-R)$. It should become apparent whether a system is committed to formal propositions to the exclusion of empirical ones. It will also be important to discover whether different kinds of functional rela-tionships are proposed for different kinds of behavioral events, or whether a single set of principles is thought to suffice for all.

We shall be interested in the content of the propositions in several respects. In particular we wish to know what the system's propositions are with respect to the development of "normal" behavior and the facets of that development that can be attributed to heredity, matura-tion, and learning. We shall ask what the system's position is on the development of disordered behavior—how it is that the normal course of development goes awry, the conditions under which it occurs, the course it typically follows, and the outcomes that characteristically appear. As part of this propositional network, we shall examine each system to determine whether statements have been developed to ac-count for the persistence of disordered or inappropriate behavior in spite of the fact that it may be unwanted, inefficient, self-defeating, and the like.

Chapter 4

System as Procedure and

a Method of Comparison

This chapter falls into two major subdivisions. Initially we must consider the therapist's concerns as to how to change behavior during the therapy itself and how to provide for the transfer of these effects to other situations in the individual's life. It will encompass that aspect of systematization involving consistent procedures for altering behavior in specified ways. Then we shall deal with a second aspect of procedure, the therapist's concerns as to how to verify the fact that behavior change has occurred, and how to establish the validity of the theory and procedures he used to accomplish that change. These represent two of the operational aspects of a system.

CONDITIONS FOR BEHAVIOR CHANGE

A first task is to develop ways of analyzing a theorist's ideas about how to change disordered behavior in desired directions. One point in common among all the theorists can be assumed at the outset. All apparently agree that something more than the patient's behavior is required to produce a change. Some kind of intervention from events "outside" the patient is necessary. If this were not true, there would be no need for psychotherapists. Thus, the situational events defined earlier are crucial in considering therapy technique.

How to Change Behavior

Let us return to Mr. X's therapist and see where his thoughts are leading. "Mr. X is very distressed at the moment, but once this flood of problems subsides, he will undoubtedly find it much more difficult to talk with me. What kind of relationship should I establish with him? It's likely he hates adults, so perhaps I should avoid too dominant a role or I will obtain those hostile reactions toward myself. But, if I remain passive, he may find it difficult to initiate talk about thoughts and feelings that obviously disturb him. Since I've decided I must elicit his anger toward his mother, how do I encourage that? Should I ask him to tell me about it, or should I simply respond to it every time it appears? How frequently should I see him? Perhaps I should see him more than once a week, since he seems quite panicky."

The Therapist Arranges Conditions

The moment the therapist asks what shall I do, what shall I say, what behavior do I want to encourage in the patient, how frequently should I see him, and so on, he is considering the problem of technique. He is aware that he must know *how* he can go about facilitating the changes. Assuming that he has decided to seek particular changes in behavior in specified directions, the therapist recognizes that he must know something about the conditions under which behavior change will occur, and that several courses are possible.

The traditional psychotherapeutic interview places severe limitations on the treatment procedures therapists might try. In typical psychotherapy the basic instrument of change is talk. The therapist may consider what he can talk about, what to encourage the patient to talk about, when to talk about it, to what extent, and in what tone of voice. Some nonverbal behaviors such as hand gestures, smiles, and nodding of the head may also be used to help control the patient's feelings toward the therapist. Situational variables such as the physical surroundings of the therapy room, the length of interview, the frequency of interviews, and the cost of services may be varied. The "relationship" which the therapist attempts to establish, the interpretive and reassuring things he says, the accepting and nonevaluative attitudes he evidences are all behaviors and represent the instrumentality through which changes in the patient's behavior are sought. The crucial notion, however, underlying all these potential actions is that *the techniques of therapy, or perhaps more accurately the behaviors of the therapist, constitute a set of conditions that can be varied by the therapist.* The conditions he can vary include aspects of the situation and how he himself behaves. When one arranges conditions, one is performing operations, and in doing so the therapist is "operating on" the behaviors of his patient. We have found that many therapists are uncomfortable with the statement that they "operate" on their patients' behavior. We think that this reaction stems from some implicit ethical position they may hold, to the effect that it is "bad" to manipulate the behavior of another person. The fact is that all therapists manipulate conditions in the expectation that their patients will thereby be helped. If this were not so, there would be no reason for therapists. The question is not whether he does or does not manipulate events; he does. Rather, the question is what kinds of manipulations does he perform, and to what effect. There are both the technique question of *how* changes can be accomplished and the value question of *what* changes should be sought.

The question of therapeutic procedure presupposes a prior set of ideas about the manner in which behavior change occurs. General propositions, principles, or laws stating how behavior, particularly disordered behavior, may be altered are necessary before one can proceed to a description of the therapeutic procedures or operations. A specification of the conditions which the therapist can manipulate to produce change is required. It is likely that each theorist will have taken some position about technique, although for certain of them the position may be that detailed specification of technique is not possible. Again, we have chosen the following framework in order to facilitate a relationship between the field of psychotherapy and that of general psychology.

PROPOSITIONS ABOUT THERAPEUTIC TECHNIQUE

Given a definition of the behaviors to be changed and the directions in which they should be changed, the therapist needs to know *if* they can be changed and *how*. He needs some principles of learning. In addition, he needs to specify the kinds of behavior to which the principles apply, if he proposes that different responses obey different laws.

BEHAVIORS THAT MAY BE MODIFIED BY LEARNING. Humans are born with a living, changing body. The typical American baby is 16 to 20 inches long. The typical American man is 66 to 69 inches tall. No amount of learning will change the fact that the man will be considerably taller than the baby. One's muscles, bones, sense organs, and other parts of the body gradually develop and deteriorate during one's lifetime. As a consequence, the behaviors one may perform or emit are determined by the degree of bodily development. An infant cannot walk until the organs and integrating structures have developed to the point where a variety of sensations or perceptions can result in co-ordinated muscular movements. An aged person cannot run and jump as can a teenager. Thus some behavior change occurs as an inevitable consequence of the maturation of body processes and the physiological properties of the body in which responses occur.

On the other hand, it has been clearly shown that great varieties of human behavior can be modified or developed through training. Billions of dollars are spent each year supporting the nation's schools on the expectation that verbal behavior in thought, speech, and writing develops through training. Football coaches are hired on the assumption that they can train special patterns of behavior. Budding artists study with renowned men on the assumption that their artistic behaviors will be modified as a consequence. Obviously, modification of behavior occurs as a consequence of both maturation and learning. Any complete statement of a psychotherapy technique must indicate which behaviors it considers to be modifiable by learning, and more specifically, the particular kinds of behaviors to which its techniques apply.

There are two primary aspects of behavior alteration—the shedding of unsatisfactory responses and the acquisition of new and effective ones.

BEHAVIOR ACQUISITION. The learning of new, more comfortable, "healthier" behaviors is, of course, one of the major results that patients seek as a consequence of a psychotherapist's help. They wish to make more friends, to be happier with themselves, and to lead constructive lives. If an ordinary citizen is asked how he came to do something, he will usually give one of three kinds of reasons. "The situation seemed right so I did it." "I did it to get relief." "I did it because it looked like it would be fun." These represent the layman's counterpart for three major kinds of principles about how behavior operates. The first reason involves simple contiguity of events, and the second and third involve contiguity of particular kinds of events in particular relationship to one another.

First, *principles of simple contiguity* seem a necessity. Situational events and the person whose behavior they are expected to modify must come together in time and space in order to be likely to have influence on one another. It may be possible that some phenomena exist, like extrasensory perception, for which spatial and temporal contiguity are not necessary, but until more convincing evidence appears, it seems more accurate to assume otherwise. In its most general form, this principle asserts that when a combination of situational events occurs contiguous in time and space with a set of response events, those same responses are likely to recur on future presentations of the same situation. A principle of this type appears in formal learning theories (Guthrie, 1935; Skinner, 1938). In its pure form it may appear at points in various psychotherapy systems.

Second, *principles in which contiguity results in response termination* can be expected to be found—for example, eating to reduce hunger. Such a principle assumes that a response sequence takes place and leads to instrumental behavior. This in turn terminates the response sequence if certain results occur. On future occasions when the initial response sequence occurs, the probability becomes greater that it will be followed by instrumental behaviors that lead to the events that had previously terminated it. The phrase response termination rather than behavior termination is used to suggest that a specification of the kinds of events involved is important. The principle of drive reduction or drive-stimulus reduction in some learning theories (Hull, 1943; Spence, 1956) is essentially this notion, as well as the idea of stimulus avoidance or escape behavior (Olds, 1955; Skinner, 1938; Miller, 1957).

Third, *principles in which contiguity has as a consequence response arousal* will undoubtedly be encountered. These parallel the layman's notion that he does things because they are fun, or because they are stimulating. They assume that instrumental behaviors, when associated with some other events, may be followed by the arousal of responses. When the events associated with response arousal recur, the instrumental behaviors that lead to response arousal are also likely to recur. As in the second class of principles, the *kinds* of behavior and situational events must be considered. This is similar to the idea of stimulus-seeking behavior, which has been demonstrated to be a factor in behavior modification (Olds, 1955; Harlow, 1954; Miller, 1958). Some theorists have proposed that the arousal of positive affect is the crucial event (Young, 1955, 1959; McClelland et al., 1953).

BEHAVIOR REMOVAL. Getting rid of painful, uncomfortable, unwanted behaviors is a second major concern of therapy patients. They want to be less afraid, to discontinue a failure pattern, or to stop alienating friends and family. It is precisely because they have behaviors that are making themselves and their associates unhappy that patients come to a psychotherapist in the first place. Therapy theorists may propose principles concerning the removal or extinction of such unwanted behaviors which are similar to those for behavior acquisition, or they may propose that the principles governing each are quite different. In general psychological theory, counter-conditioning and reactive inhibition are examples of procedures having to do with response removal.

Modified behavior in nontherapy situations is the ultimate goal of all patients. Being able to change behavior while with the therapist may be of some temporary satisfaction, but the patient does not spend the major portion of his life with the therapist. He wants to become less afraid of his mother and all other women. He wants to be able to talk freely with his boss, his wife, and his friends. He wants to be able to think clearly and constructively at school, at work, and in social conversation. He wants to feel comfortable and happy all the time, not just when he is in the therapy situation. Principles by which behavior applies to new situations are needed. The concepts of stimulus generalization and response generalization in learning theories (Hull, 1943; Skinner, 1938) exemplify this issue.

It is our expectation that most therapy theorists' principles about behavior change will be in terms of contiguity, contiguity with response termination, and contiguity with response arousal. If this is true, then it provides for another potential bridge between the fields of therapy and basic psychology, although we must also be prepared for the occurrence of principles particular to therapy, which have no counterpart in more academic psychology.

PSYCHOTHERAPY TECHNIQUES

Preconditions for Therapy

Before initiating psychotherapy, therapists must make decisions about whether the conditions are present under which their propositions about behavior change apply. Two kinds of considerations enter into such decisions. The first of these has to do with the behavior of the patient, and the second with the behavior of the therapist.

PATIENT FACTORS. These become important if psychotherapy is not an appropriate treatment for some types of behaviors that patients bring to therapists. For example, headaches, nausea, and dizziness might arise from protracted fear or from a malignant tumor. It is unlikely that psychotherapy would be effective in curing a tumor. A therapist needs to be able to specify the responses which must be present if his therapy procedures are to be effective. Mr. X entered his first interview explicitly acknowledging he was disturbed and requesting help. Is such an avowal or commitment on the part of the patient a necessary precondition for achieving change in psychotherapy? Must the patient have a certain level of intelligence? Must he be able to verbalize effectively, to report introspectively upon his intervening response events? Is it true that he must entertain some initial "motivation for change," or "capacity to tolerate anxiety," or express sufficient dissatisfaction with his behavior for procedures or techniques to operate effectively? Are techniques available by which recalcitrant patients can be led actively to seek change? The therapist's answers to such questions could well determine whether or not he accepts Mr. X for therapy.

THERAPIST FACTORS. These become important if it is assumed that special knowledge and skills are required for effective treatment procedures. Probably all theorists have subscribed to such an assumption, to some extent at least. If not, they would not have expounded their respective points of view. But must the therapist have a historically oriented analysis of the disordered behavior and its development? Does he require some understanding of the response patterns as they operate? Can he proceed to treatment without any knowledge of the nature of the patient's disordered behavior? Some therapists propose that the way to change a set of behaviors is independent of the way in which they were acquired. Others argue that a knowledge of the conditions under which the behavior originally developed is essential, since this will identify the conditions one needs to reproduce in order to change it. Still others argue that a single therapeutic procedure will suffice for all and therefore no knowledge of the antecedents is required.

Empirical data are not yet available to resolve these differences, but Mr. X's therapist must take some position on this issue or he cannot proceed. It will make a great deal of difference which one he selects. One therapist might proceed early in his contacts to elicit information about the events in Mr. X's life when the patient first noticed his symptoms, in order to discover the conditions under which they were initially acquired. On the other hand, if the therapist believes that such knowledge is irrelevant, he is more likely to try to discover the interrelationships among Mr. X's current response patterns as a guide to selecting his therapeutic technique.

How much must the therapist know about Mr. X's current situation before he can try to institute changes? Obvious questions in this regard include, "How is Mr. X feeling today? Will he be able to speak freely or will he be highly guarded?" For example, few therapists would press for admissions of sexual misconduct on a day when the patient was already profoundly depressed. Do certain response characteristics of therapists make it harder for them to work with some patient behaviors than with others?

Certainly, in their day-to-day practice, therapists make such judgments. For example, we have heard colleagues and trainees comment that they just cannot work with "masculine females," or "dependent, clinging people," or "silently resistant patients." Therapists occasionally comment, "If a patient isn't motivated for therapy, I can't do anything for him." Distinctions are made among diagnostic groups. Some therapists report they find it easy to effect changes in hysterics, find it harder to effect changes in obsessive-compulsives, and find it impossible to do anything with psychopaths. We expect at least some theorists to discuss such preconditions.

INTERVIEW PROCEDURES. The therapist must now face the two main issues of technique: (1) what the patient must do in order to produce behavioral change; and (2) what the therapist must do to facilitate or effect changes in the patient's behavior. In other words, (1) what are the behavioral events that must occur, and (2) what are the situational events that must be manipulated to arrange for them to happen. These are the two critical ingredients in the therapeutic setting. Of course, Mr. X must respond, for unless he "does" something, subjectively or overtly, in the interview situation, the therapist is helpless. Generally it is believed in psychology that a response must occur or be closely related to one which does occur, to be subject to modification. However, not all behavior on the part of the patient is useful or appropriate. He must make *certain kinds* of responses. Nor will his typical responses be sufficient, since patients have been attempting for some time to change their own behavior to no avail. It takes the intervention of the therapist's behavior in appropriate ways at appropriate times to facilitate the necessary changes.

Specification of the complex patterns of behavior in both patient and therapist and of the interaction of these patterns is an intricate and still uncompleted task. We suspect some therapists despair of the possibility of such precision. The complexity of therapeutic events is of such an order that thorough specification will undoubtedly be extremely slow in coming. It appears to be the *sine qua non* of the finished system, however, so that one can state it as a criterion toward which systems should aspire.

PATIENT BEHAVIORS. What should Mr. X talk about? Of what importance are his feelings and attitudes toward the therapist? Should Mr. X be encouraged to feel friendly toward the therapist, or will it be necessary for Mr. X to feel angry in the presence of the therapist as a necessary step toward recognizing hostile feelings toward his mother? Should Mr. X engage in associative chaining to permit the emergence of certain desired thoughts and feelings? Should he seek introspectively to reproduce the feelings and attitudes appropriate to earlier events? Does he have to abreact? Is intellectual "insight" required as an intermediate stage before certain changes can be expected?

THERAPIST BEHAVIORS. How about the therapist, whose behaviors constitute the therapeutic situational events for the patient? In what ways and at what times should he intervene to implement the principles he believes govern behavior change? Should Mr. X be instructed as to the kinds of responses he needs to produce? Should the therapist make statements by which he defines the relationship he and Mr. X should maintain? Should he interpret defense mechanisms as he sees them occur? Should he make explicit the love feelings Mr. X seems to have? Should he ask questions? Should he reinterpret statements Mr. X has been making? Or perhaps nonverbal procedures should be used, such as smiling or nodding at those times when Mr. X is behaving in a way that the therapist would like to see recur. Then, too, of what importance are the therapist's feelings and attitudes toward the patient? Can the therapist be effective if he feels disgust for Mr. X's homosexual activities? Can he systematically facilitate changes in Mr. X's behavior if he feels anger at the youth's desire to rape a small girl? Must the therapist always maintain kindly, accepting, and affectionate attitudes, or should he sometimes be genuinely angry as a way to modify Mr. X's approach to people?

For purposes of this comparative study, it may be helpful to think about therapeutic techniques *according to the kind of influence* they are intended to have on the patient's behavior. The therapist faces two general problems. First, he must make behavior occur in the therapy situation; he must elicit behavior. Second, once the behaviors have begun to occur, he must do something to modify them.

BEHAVIOR ELICITORS. If the patient does not perform responses in the therapy situation, behavior change will not occur as a consequence of the therapy. This does not necessarily mean that overtly observable responses (R) have to occur, but the changes achieved without them are likely to be severely limited. It is a maxim in psychology that a response has to occur before it can be subjected to change. Therapists who have had hostile teenagers referred to them for treatment by the courts or by school officials, or who have been faced with the problem of treating psychotic patients who are mute or catatonic, are well aware of both the difficulties and the importance of finding techniques that will get behavior started. Moreover, it is not just a question of getting any behavior in general started, but rather of getting particular sorts of behavior to occur. For example, unless the hostile teenager can be brought to confide in the therapist, treatment cannot proceed. Unless the mute psychotic can eventually be induced to talk, verbal psychotherapy can never be applied as an effective treatment procedure. Considerable attention has been given by therapists to the techniques that will get a patient to "reveal himself" honestly and frankly to the therapist. In psychotherapy, discussions of "structuring," of teaching the patient how to use psychotherapy, of tying the patient to the treatment, of establishing rapport, and of developing the relationship all refer, in part if not entirely, to arranging situational conditions that will get particular patterns of behavior to occur within therapy.

The importance of this class of technique can be understood by referring to the behavior classifications described earlier. The therapist has available to him only the patient's objectively observable behaviors (R). If his purpose is to elicit and then to modify the subject's feelings, thoughts, or attitudes—subjectively observable responses (r)—he can come to know about them through two avenues: (1) the subject's open report about them, and (2) the inferences the therapist can make from what he observes. For either of these, the responses of speech or writing are critical, since it is through them that a patient reveals *his* observations about his private behavior. If the therapist's inferences about the subjectively observable behaviors (r) are to be accurate, it is important that he be able to establish conditions under which the patient will talk accurately and freely (R) about his private events (r). If the patient distrusts or fears the therapist (r), the patient may lie (R) about what he is thinking and feeling (r). In this case, the therapist's inferences will be inaccurate unless some other types of behavior, such as blushing or averted eyes (R), reveal the lie. It is because other types of objectively observable behavior (R) such as blushing, sweating, and trembling are less easily falsified or denied than symbolic report that they are of considerable value to the therapist. Thus it is apparent that the therapist requires techniques by which he can reliably elicit both R and r behaviors in particular patterns so that they become accessible to modification. Techniques for doing this are frequently encompassed in the generalized phrase "building a relationship."

Moreover, the therapist needs techniques for verifying the fact that particular behaviors are occurring. Fortunately, as was discussed under the sections on behavior classes, the therapist may check his observations of the patient's responses with the patient's observations of the same events, and he can check his inferences about the patient's intervening responses with the patient's observation of those same behaviors. If the two concur, this constitutes a measure of validation. Of course, the therapist must still assess the validity of the subject's assent. A therapist might observe "Have you noticed that each time you talk about your father you flush, sweat, and grow restless?" The patient might reply, "You're right! What do you suppose causes that?" The two observers agree, and they can begin to look for the intervening behaviors related to this sequence. On the other hand, the patient might reply only hesitantly, "Well, maybe you're right." Observer agreement in this instance is quite dubious, and to begin to look for related thoughts and feelings may be ineffective until better observer agreement is established. It goes without saying that the therapist should be alert for error in his own observations as well as in the patient's. The patient may be restless because she has a very painful boil on her hip, and she may be blushing as a consequence of embarrassment at the thought of telling the therapist about it. The fact that such objectively observable events occurred in conjunction with her talking about her father may be purely coincidental.

Some elicitors are designed to *start* certain behaviors. For example, the suggestion "Just let your thoughts come out" often operates to start a general stream of talk. The suggestion "Tell me what you think of when you are afraid" is intended to start talk about specified events. Other elicitors are designed to start other behaviors by *stopping* the ones currently underway. For example, the suggestion "Why don't we turn our attention away from this, so that we can talk about . . ." is one designed to stop speech on one topic so as to direct it toward another. These two kinds of elicitors parallel the notions of behavior acquisition and behavior removal which were earlier discussed.

BEHAVIOR MODIFIERS. If the therapist does not know what to do with the behaviors once they occur in therapy, stable and permanent behavior modification is unlikely. For example, "classical psychoanalysts" concern themselves with the possibility that the transference might be mismanaged. By this they mean that neophyte therapists may obtain "transference" from their patients, but if they fail to recognize its occurrence or do not know how to deal with it once it appears, then therapeutic change is not likely to occur. The problem is one of manipulating situational events so as to modify patient behavior in particular ways. The desired modification has at least two characteristics. First, it is intended to be relatively permanent. The intent is not to change the patient merely for the balance of a particular therapy hour. Rather, it is to produce a change that will manifest itself in the therapy hours that follow. Second, and more important, the change must also appear in situational settings external to the therapy itself. Ideally, then, the therapist will have techniques for producing relatively stable behavior change in the therapy situation and techniques by which to ensure the transfer of the changed behavior into other situations as well. A therapist may be able effectively to reduce a patient's anger responses toward him, but fail to achieve the more general objective of reducing the patient's anger responses toward his father, toward others, or both. As was pointed out earlier, the two general classes of behavior change include modification by getting rid of undesired behaviors—behavior removal—or by acquiring new behaviors—behavior acquisition. For example, the likelihood that thoughts such as "I am a terrible person!" will occur may be reduced or the likelihood that thoughts such as "I am a good student but a poor athlete" may be increased. Most therapists probably use techniques to achieve both kinds of modification.

This distinction between events as elicitors and events as modifiers runs through learning theories in psychology. Hilgard (1948) noted, "Two main theoretical problems arise: the problem of the nature of the original adjustment ending in the correct act, and the problem as to how this adjustment is facilitated when the situation is repeated." The terms cue and reinforcer refer to this same distinction.

SEQUENCE OF BEHAVIORAL CHANGE. Systems of therapy concern themselves with the question of "process." The same issue is sometimes referred to by the term "stages of therapy." It is evident that the therapist cannot focus his attention and techniques on all behavior patterns simultaneously. He will have to deal with one and then another, but the question then becomes, *In what order* should these changes be sought?" A therapist is aware of the problem of sequence when he begins to consider such questions as the following: "What shall I encourage Mr. X to talk about first? He has many conflicting reactions to his mother: feelings of hate, fear, and love, as well as sexual impulses. Which of these should be talked about first? Perhaps the hostility, since he is less aware of his hate feelings than of the others. I must anticipate that making them explicit will bring fear and guilt along with it, so I must be prepared to deal with them next." Is the "transference neurosis" a necessary antecedent to the "abreaction" of infantile responses toward parental figures? Must "negative attitudes toward the self" be expressed before attitudes of "self-acceptance" can fully develop? Here we are trying to illustrate that in addition to setting long-range goals for the interview series, the therapist must, and at least implicitly does, work toward intermediate goals.

TRANSFER OF BEHAVIOR CHANGE. We have confronted the therapist with enough questions to tax the Delphic Oracle, and yet he must face still another aspect of therapeutic technique and the problems underlying it. This has to do with the procedures for insuring the generalization of the within-therapy changes to the real-life situation itself. If the therapist, whom we might suppose to be female, succeeds in reducing

Mr. X's fear of her as a woman, can she assume that he will be less afraid of other women also? Or will such a generalization require some additional steps by the patient or therapist? This is an aspect of therapy, a type of activity, that often goes unnoticed from a theoretical standpoint.

It is clearly an important issue. The successful change of behavior patterns in the patient's day-to-day experiences is the ultimate focus of all the involved and painful efforts of patient and therapist alike. Characteristically it is such things as crippling feelings of inferiority in social situations, or unfortunate relations with family and friends which both participants propose to change. Few patients would seriously consider persisting indefinitely in a therapy relationship, and even fewer therapists would look forward to the perpetuation of such a relationship with a patient.

Too often events within therapy are made the primary focus, and the main purpose of producing changes in behavior outside of therapy is only indirectly considered. Patients learn rather quickly to discuss topics in ways that the therapist wishes to hear them. This change in the way patients talk about themselves sometimes deceives therapists into believing fundamental changes have taken place. It is no longer unusual for a therapist to have patients in treatment who have previously worked with other therapists. When this occurs one may frequently find former Freudian patients discussing themselves in Freudian terms and former Rogerian patients discussing themselves in Rogerian terms. Unfortunately, changes in therapy behavior are not perfectly correlated with behavior outside of therapy. The therapist may help Mr. X to respond kindly and without fear toward him but still face the problem of getting Mr. X to generalize the new response pattern to other situations.

A focus on therapy events to the exclusion of extratherapy behavior may represent a faulty overemphasis, although it is understandable that such an imbalance of attention might occur. Therapy processes and techniques represent extremely complex and involved events in and of themselves. Relating within-therapy behaviors, some of which are difficult to observe, to extratherapy behaviors, which the therapist observes only indirectly, is indeed a puzzling task.

Such generalization will probably occur fortuitously if not by plan. Here again, order and system should replace haphazard events. If transfer or generalization must occur, it would follow that more carefully delineated statements about such generalization will produce greater efficiency in fostering and encouraging it. Thus, a therapy system should specify the kinds of responses the patient should perform in real life and whether one can anticipate their automatic occurrence following changes in therapy. If not, it should specify what the therapist should do to facilitate changes in the patient's extratherapy behavior.

ELICITORS AND MODIFIERS ARE SIMILAR. It is probably more accurate to refer to all types of techniques as modifiers. Situational events which elicit responses are really producing a temporary modification of behavior in a particular situation. For example, if a patient is describing a party he attended and the therapist asks, "Why did you go?" the patient will probably stop discussing the party and start discussing his reasons for going. Thus his behavior was modified by the question. That modification is not likely to carry over into other situations at other times, however, and it was probably not intended to do so. Elicitors can have more permanent effects, however, and one concern of the therapist is that the techniques he uses to elicit behavior from the patient do not restrict the occurrence of, or interfere with, other behaviors in the patient. A threat may induce a patient to talk, but it may keep him from talking about his distrust of the therapist. On the other hand, situational events as modifiers produce more permanent change and serve to get the change to appear in other situations as well. For example, if a therapist says, "Have you noticed that each time you get your headache it follows an argument with your husband?" to a patient who has been attributing the headaches to a brain tumor, the purpose is to produce a permanent change. That is, on any occasion when such headaches occur the patient is encouraged to consider them an aftermath of an argument with her husband. Thus, the difference is one of degree in terms of permanence and in terms of the kinds of situations in which the modified response will occur in the future. Although there are common factors in elicitors and modifiers, it would appear to be useful to maintain the distinction in the analysis of therapy systems.

Summary

In later chapters, then, we shall ask each theorist two major questions about his techniques. First, we shall ask what propositions he believes govern behavior change. We shall look for distinctions among the kinds of behaviors that he believes his techniques will modify.

We shall look for his principles governing the modification, including discussions of developing new behavior, removing unwanted behavior sequences, and getting changes to occur in situations external to the therapy hour. We shall also look for discussions of the preconditions that must be present to make therapy possible. Second, we shall ask what procedures the theorist selects to implement his propositions. We shall look for discussions of procedures for getting the kinds of behaviors that concern the therapist to occur, and procedures for producing relatively permanent behavior change once the behaviors of concern begin to appear. This question will also lead us to look for discussions of the sequences in which change must occur and procedures for making changes occur in extratherapy situations as well as in the therapy hour itself.

VALIDATING PROCEDURES

Our second task in this chapter is to develop a way to analyze the theorist's ideas about how to verify the fact that his procedures are producing the changes intended, and how to validate his general theory as well. Since most therapy theories have been developed by practitioners whose efforts have been to help patients and who have concentrated their attention on the clinical setting, we may find that many of the systems to be examined have little to say about the process of validation. Not only did some of the theorists have insufficient time available for extensive validational work, but also some had relatively little training and sophistication in the use of such procedures. The clinical setting was their primary domain. We do not expect to find detailed consideration of validational procedures among these theorists. This is an extremely complicated problem, partly because of the phenomena involved, and we can only touch on some of its aspects here.

VERIFYING CHANGE IN BEHAVIOR

As treatment proceeds, the therapist's thoughts turn to a final set of difficult problems. "How will I know when I'm right? Suppose I proceed to deal with the hostility first and then deal with Mr. X's fear second. How will I know when these emotions have been adequately modified in real life? How can I determine when Mr. X has completed therapy?"

The first sorts of validational procedures any system must include are those designed to establish whether behavior change has occurred in the patient. This judgment determines the course and length of therapy. When the therapist sets up the treatment sequence, planning for behavior x to be changed, followed by changes in behavior y and then behavior z, he has a situation in which he must be able to determine that x has changed before he proceeds further. Similarly, when the question of terminating therapy is reached, judgments have to be made about whether the desired behavior change has occurred, or if it is unlikely to occur even if therapy were to be continued. Hence, this kind of verification is of important practical consequence to the therapist.

This task of periodic assessment of the effectiveness of technique over the course of a therapy series often receives scant attention from practicing therapists. Hours are spent in diagnostic testing and interviewing; still more may be spent in staff discussions and the planning of treatment. Seldom is adequate time devoted to careful evaluation of the effects of the treatment plan. Obviously, such evaluation is difficult and time-consuming. Under the pressure of day-to-day treatment responsibilities in the typical clinic, therapists are forced to use treatment procedures without taking time to evaluate their effects carefully. However, minimal evaluation is always necessary. For example, the decision to terminate treatment must eventually occur. Such a decision implies evaluation no matter how gross and superficial it may be. Of course, the responsibility for evaluation may be abandoned by the therapist; the patient may be considered the authority. Since it is usually the "first case" with which the subject has worked, and yet is one about which he has more direct information than the therapist, it would seem that the best evaluation would require the participation of both.

This requires a specification of the behavioral events in the patient that are to be selected for evaluation, a definition of the persons or instruments by which the evaluation will be made, and the process by which it will be conducted. The therapy theories to be examined may have relied on naturalistic observation or on standardized evaluational procedures for this purpose.

Naturalistic Observation

Several varieties of naturalistic observation are possible. They differ in terms of the persons making the observations and in terms of the situations in which the patient is observed.

THE THERAPIST. He may observe the patient's objectively observable behavior (R) during the therapy hour, make judgments about the extent to which it has become changed, and make inferences as to the extent to which the subjectively observable behavior (r) has changed. This kind of verification is subject to at least two major kinds of error. First, the situation in which the behavior is observed, the therapy hour, is extremely limited, and the behavior exhibited in that situation may not be like the behavior exhibited in other important nontherapy situations. Thus, the therapist can only guess at the generality of behavior change across situations. Second, the kinds of behavior that can be observed are seriously limited. For example, the patient's interaction with his parents, spouse, boss, or friends is not directly observed. Even though limited, naturalistic observations in therapy are useful.

THE PATIENT. He may observe his own behavior (both R and r) in the therapy hour as well as in a variety of other situations and report his observations to the therapist. This has the advantage of assembling a variety of observations across a variety of situations. However, it, too, has serious limitations. One of the characteristics of persons who seek psychotherapy is that they do not observe their own or other people's behavior accurately. Their problems lead them to ignore some events, distort others, and screen what they will report to their therapist. They may report they have observed changes in themselves which actually have not occurred so as to please their therapist, or to terminate gracefully a therapy sequence that they wish to escape. Their reports sometimes will be at best only a crude or approximate representation of the events themselves. On the other hand, the patient remains the most convenient source of observations about changes in his subjectively observable behavior (r), and therefore his report of change is useful. It is a therapeutic task to develop the conditions that facilitate accurate reporting. Similarly, if the therapist has no way of observing the patient in other situations, the patient's report of those situations may be the therapist's only source of information, inadequate as it may be.

OTHER PEOPLE. Outside observers may report about patient behavior. Parents, spouses, nurses, and friends have an opportunity to observe a patient's behavior in situations different from that of the therapy hour. Their observations may be used as supplements by providing information about the patient's behavior in real-life situations. They suffer from many of the same limitations as those of the therapist's, but with one additional liability. Whereas the therapist may be a carefully trained observer, most other people are not. Because they may be personally involved with the patient, they too may overlook or distort some of the crucial events. In the absence of opportunities to observe the patient directly in such situations, however, reports of other people may be useful. In providing therapy to children, for example, observations about the child's behavior at home by the parents is absolutely necessary as a source of information about behavior change, since the child is inadequate to the task of reporting on the intricate events that occur.

OBSERVATIONS IN CONTROLLED SITUATIONS. The therapist, or other trained personnel, may observe the patient in situations other than the therapy hour. One of the advantages of placing a patient in a hospital, for example, is that extended observation of the patient by trained personnel is made possible. Similarly, artificial situations may be contrived in which the patient's behavior can be observed—for example, psychodrama, or confrontation of the hospital staff. The general limitations discussed earlier also apply here, but this source of observation may provide information about additional behavior in different situations which may help to verify or refute those initially made.

Standardized Evaluational Procedures

Psychological tests are probably the primary example of procedures in this group likely to have been used by therapy theorists. The purpose of such procedures is to control the conditions under which observations are made so that they may be reliably repeated on a variety of individuals on a variety of occasions by a variety of observers. Careful control of the circumstances of observation makes possible the comparison of observations, an essential step toward generalization. Since we do not expect to find many therapy theorists who have relied on such procedures, we shall not take space in this book to discuss many important related issues.

VALIDATION OF THEORY

Is it assumed that the therapist's hypotheses are logically compelling? Are his hypotheses consistent with clinical observations? Can his propositions be verified through empirical and experimental research? Without some systematic way of checking his propositions, concepts, and techniques, a therapist faces the danger of his hypotheses becoming dogma and his treatment procedures becoming habitual, perhaps even ritualized. Rigor mortis may well set in.

While the formulation of theory is primarily a creative effort, the careful, precise validation of the theory is primarily a scientific one. On the other hand, the most elaborate and refined scientific procedures have relatively little importance unless used in the service of theory development and validation; scientific procedures are no substitute for sound ideas about human behavior. There has been some concern recently that psychology may be training people who excel in the procedures of science, without training them adequately to perform the creative act of formulating meaningful theories about behavior. The procedural tail may be wagging the psychological dog. For our purposes, procedures for validating theories may be considered in three categories: clinical observation, descriptive research, and experimental research.

Clinical Observation

This term has generally been used to refer to observations made in the "clinic," that is, the treatment setting, while diagnosis and treatment are proceeding. Sometimes the term is used to refer to naturalistic observation in general. Of course, clinical observation is a particular kind of naturalistic observation. We expect to find that most of the naturalistic observations which have contributed to the theories will have been made in the therapy or treatment setting.

In this kind of observation, one attempts to observe things as they occur naturally, to find consistencies and variabilities among events that seem significant. This is what the therapist does constantly. He watches what the patient does and says. He looks for concomitancies, that is, for events that seem to occur together. For example, the therapist watches for topics of discussion which are accompanied by signs of emotion. He looks for consistencies or inconsistencies, such as whether or not patient statements containing angry or fearful verbal content are accompanied by the appropriate emotions. Similarly, the therapist looks for sequences—events consistently leading to or followed by other events. For example, he may note that if he initiates a discussion about father, responses of body tenseness, sweating, and voice quavering are likely to follow. He may note that whenever the discussion approaches the topic of sex, the patient changes the subject or in some other way avoids discussing sex. Such observational procedures are absolutely essential to the conduct of therapy. The therapist cannot stop and give the patient a psychological test or check his heart rate and his GSR before making each response to the patient. Skill in making accurate naturalistic observations is one of the first essential skills for a good psychotherapist.

It should be noted that measurement is usually not involved in clinical observation in the sense of quantification (S. S. Stevens, 1951). Classification is involved, however, in the sense of looking for relationships among *kinds* of events. The limitations of clinical observation for validating theories were discussed earlier.

Despite its limitations, one very important fact about naturalistic observation should be noted. *We should recognize that observations by humans is the base for all scientific procedures including the formal experiment.* Scientific procedures are simply tools for facilitating accurate and efficient observation of events and relationships among those events. They are not substitutes for careful observation but a means of making such observations more precise and repeatable. For example, assigning numbers to events according to some set of rules and analyzing those numbers with statistical or mathematical procedures—another set of rules—is done simply because the relationships among the events we are trying to observe are so complicated or so obscure that the use of measurement and mathematical analysis helps us sort out the relationships that interest us. If we could observe the events of concern accurately and consistently without resort to measurement and statistical analysis, the simpler procedure would be the most desirable. The scientific method is a set of rules and procedures by which observers can arrive at agreement about observations relevant to a specified set of events. In this sense, it is similar in principle to the psychotherapist's notion of "consensual validation," but of course aimed at much greater precision and control.

Descriptive Research

Sometimes referred to as empirical research, this type of investigation seeks to establish those relationships among events that typically occur. It differs from naturalistic observation in that it involves measurement and therefore the possibility of precise mathematical analysis of observations. It also makes possible more precise prediction of future events, with some known degree of error, than is possible with clinical observation. The most usual sort of descriptive research involves measuring two different variables and then examining the measures to ascertain the degree of relationship between them. For example, one might develop measures of the "traits" of dominance and of aggressiveness and then correlate them to see if they are related.

The major characteristics of such studies is that measurement, controlled observation, and mathematical analysis are used to try to determine existing interrelationships among specified events as they typically or naturally occur. This type of research is valuable when control and manipulation of the events to be studied is not possible. Typical kinds of statistical analyses presented in such studies include means, medians, standard deviations, various kinds of correlation, multiple correlation and prediction, and factor analysis.

Experimental Research

Experimental research builds on an observational base and is similar to descriptive or empirical research in that controlled observation, measurement, and mathematical analysis of observations is involved. There is a very crucial difference, however. W. S. Ray (1960) defined this difference simply and clearly. He pointed out that an experiment is an event planned and staged by a researcher to obtain information about a specified set of events. In it, the scientist actively "controls, manipulates, and observes." He is an "interventionist who deliberately and systematically introduces changes into natural processes" and observes the consequences. In nonexperimental research, the scientist is a "passive observer, interested in recording the behavior of objects or organisms in a relatively undisturbed natural setting."

There have been psychotherapists, particularly some psychoanalysts, who have said that experimentation is exactly what they do. In a very gross way it is. The psychotherapist develops some notion about some aspect of the patient's behavior and how to change it. He then uses certain therapeutic interventions at appropriate times to attempt to produce the desired changes. If the interventions have the expected consequences, his notion and therapeutic technique appear to have some validity. If the expected consequences do not follow, the therapist revises his approach and tries again. This kind of "experimenting" was discussed in Chapter 1. It differs from formal experimental research in two crucial ways. The first major difference lies in the concept of controls. The experimental researcher tries to devise situations in which all influences except the variables under study are eliminated from the analyses. Elaborate, complicated, and ingenious equipment and procedures are sometimes necessary. Such researchers usually prefer to use artificial laboratory settings to isolate and study selected variables; they may use nonsense syllables rather than formal language to study verbal learning so that they can get more control and precision into their observations. Of course, they later have to extend their findings to natural settings if the findings are to be of practical use. The second crucial difference lies in the use of measurement and mathematical analyses to facilitate systematic examination of the observations and to provide a consistent way of making inferences from the observations obtained.

Some people despair of ever being able to subject the complex phenomena of psychotherapy to study under the rigorous conditions of the formal experiment. Certainly, ethical considerations seriously limit the kind of experimenting that can be done with helpless, unhappy patients. However, the power of the formal experiment has served so well in so many disciplines that we expect at least that some of the theorists to be studied later will have subscribed to its use.

Summary

In later chapters, then, we shall ask each theorist about the validating procedures he proposes should be used. We shall ask how he verifies that behavioral change actually occurs in his patients. In addition, we shall ask how he proposes to validate his theories of behavior development and change and how the effectiveness of his therapeutic procedures can be established.

OUTLINE OF ISSUES

It may be helpful to close this section with an outline of issues that provide the basis for the analyses of systems that follow. Each system chapter will follow the same outline, thus facilitating comparisons. This is not the only outline possible, and the justification for its use lies in the preceding chapters. The degree of utility will unfold in the following chapters.

Introduction
    Biographical Information
    Central Themes
The Normal Course of Behavior Development
    Innate Characteristics
    Learned Characteristics
The Development of Behavior Disorder
    The Sequence of Development
    Characteristics of Disordered Behavior
The Goals of Therapy
    The Choice of Goals and Their Nature
Conditions for Producing Behavior Change
    Characteristics of Patients and Therapists
    Principles of Change
    Techniques for Change
    Sequence of Change
    Transfer of Change to other Situations
Evaluation of Behavior Change
    Appraisal of Behavior Change
    Verification of Therapy Theory
Comments

Section II

The Systems

Chapter 5

Sigmund Freud's Psychoanalysis

Sigmund Freud, as is known widely, developed the phenomenon of the "Talking Cure." The entire field of individual verbal psychotherapy has been built upon his initial work. Later systems have differed about theory and technique in certain respects, but all of them have been constructed around Freud's basic discovery that if one can arrange a special set of conditions and have the patient talk about his difficulties in certain ways, behavior changes of many kinds can be accomplished. More important, changes can be effected in behaviors which appear to be inaccessible to change by any other method. This great contribution was not so much the result of a strong desire to help suffering humanity as it was Freud's interest in psychoanalytic procedures as a group of investigatory techniques. Freud himself was aware of an intense interest in understanding the genesis, development, and functioning of human behavior, particularly of the "mind."

He felt that a study of psychopathological conditions might open the door to the secrets of the human mind and eventually to a psychology of human behavior. Although he was careful not to subordinate the welfare of his patients to his scientific interests, it seems clear that his major satisfactions lay in his contributions as a scientist and a scholar rather than as a practicing physician. The latter role began and continued out of financial necessity. Fortunately, Freud's practice as a neurologist and psychotherapist provided the raw observational data from which he went on to develop his theories, rather than prevented his theoretical development, which is the more frequent fate of practitioners.

Freud lived for 83 years, and more than 50 of these were spent in clinical practice and the development of his theories and techniques. It was his basic premise that one must "let the facts speak for themselves." As a consequence his theories underwent continual modification. He never saw them as complete, nor did he believe that he alone would succeed in completing them. He would stubbornly adhere to a theoretical position when he felt the facts supported it, despite rejection by colleagues, professional ridicule, and isolation. However, he had the courage to reject a position he had earlier defended with vigor, if he became convinced that the facts no longer supported it. This is touchingly illustrated in his painful acknowledgment that his sexual trauma theory of neurosis was incorrect. The continual modification and development of his theories has led inevitably to some confusion among those who have attempted to understand and follow Freud. This particular analysis of Freud's several theoretical positions leans heavily on the recent masterful biography of Freud by Ernest Jones (1953; 1955; 1957), in which he carefully traces the development of and the changes in Freud's theories.

BIOGRAPHICAL INFORMATION

Anyone interested in Freud as a person should treat himself to Jones' three-volume biography. The following facts were painstakingly developed by Jones from Freud's voluminous personal correspondence, his published works and public records, and from personal observations by Freud's family and friends.

Sigmund Freud was born in Moravia in May, 1856, and died in London in September, 1939, from cancer of the jaw. His father, Jakob, was a merchant who married twice. He had two sons by his first marriage; his second marriage was to a 20-year-old girl when he was 40 years of age. Freud was the first child born of this second union. In addition to Sigmund, Amalie, Jakob Freud's second wife, bore five girls and two other boys. Freud was thus the oldest child in a large family. As Jones represented it, Freud's childhood must have been a relatively happy one, although the father's business fortunes suffered somewhat, and the family had to move to Vienna when Freud was about three years old.

Jakob was a liberal-minded Jew of progressive views. He was apparently a loving father with a good sense of humor. However, he also required respect from his children and apparently represented authority and discipline to Sigmund. The mother is described as having a lively personality, and Freud remained fond of her until her death at 95 years of age. She was very proud of her first-born and gave him considerable affection and attention. Freud felt he acquired his sensitive temperament from his mother.

Freud is described as having been a well-behaved child. Intellectual interests seem to have characterized his boyhood. His room contained a desk, and he spent a great deal of time reading and studying. His reading was apparently quite precocious. For example, he started reading and enjoying Shakespeare at the age of eight. In his teens he would eat his evening meal in his room so as to lose no time from his reading and studies. He was an excellent student. His father allowed Freud to choose his own profession, and after considerable deliberation, he settled on medicine. The choice was apparently based as much on dislike of the other possibilities as anything else. There was no great and driving wish to become a physician.

He entered the University of Vienna in the fall of 1873 at the age of 17. After only two and a half years as a student, he began the first of his original researches. At the end of his third year he decided there were many departments of science in which he was not very capable, and settled on physiology as one area where he could anticipate success. Throughout his life he complained about not having been given a better brain. A significant set of influences entered his life at this point when he began to study in Brucke's Institute of Physiology. Brucke was a member of an outstanding group of men, including Helmholtz, who set out to destroy vitalism in physiology. It seems likely that Freud's deterministic position and his belief in scientific knowledge as the prime solution to the world's ills were shaped under Brucke, whom he greatly admired.

In 1876 Freud obtained an appointment as a sort of research scholar in the Institute under Brucke. It was here that his neurological studies first began, several of which represented important original findings. Interestingly these findings emerged as a consequence of empirical observations; on three occasions Freud in this period tried to utilize the experimental method in his researches, but with no success. He finally got up courage to take his examinations and was awarded his MD in March, 1881. Because of Freud's impoverished financial state, Brucke advised him to resign from his research position and enter medical practice where he could make some money, and this Freud did with some regret. He moved to Meynert's Psychiatric Clinic and became involved in brain anatomy. About this same time he fell deeply in love with his future wife. He spent three years as a resident in the hospital. In 1885 he was appointed a private docent at the University, an honorary appointment which provided the privilege of teaching but paid nothing.

About this same time he won a grant which permitted him to study with the famed Charcot in Paris from October, 1885 to February, 1886. It was Charcot's interest in hysteria that influenced Freud. By that time Freud was eager to be married, but he had little money. He returned to Vienna and set up private practice in April of 1886, and married in September of the same year at the age of 30. By this time he was a good neurologist and began to attract patients. He wrote an interesting book on aphasia in which he attacked current beliefs and proposed other hypotheses.

It was in this period that his development of psychoanalysis really began. He had met Joseph Breuer in the 1870's at the Institute, and they had been friends since that time. From 1880 to 1882 Breuer treated the famous Anna O case, in which the patient introduced the "talking cure." Freud learned of the case and was fascinated. In his private practice he began to explore both the procedure and what it revealed about the human mind. He began to speak of his new ideas in professional meetings and met with rejection by his colleagues. His growing emphasis on the sexual basis of neuroses brought ridicule and censure. He was considered a crackpot. His private practice rapidly declined, and by January, 1900 he reported he had had no new cases in the last 8 months and was deeply worried about his financial plight. The ten-year period from 1890 to 1900 was one of intellectual loneliness for him, according to his own report. He was working out his first theories and had no one with whom to discuss them. However, submission was not in Freud's nature. He believed very strongly in his ideas. At first he was surprised at the opposition he met but finally resigned himself to it as natural resistance to tabooed ideas.

Freud had suffered from some discomforting symptoms for quite some time. He apparently concluded they were neurotic in character and embarked on a painful and extensive self-analysis in 1897. At this same time he began writing one of his most important books, *The Interpretation of Dreams,* and also began formulating his theories of sexuality. There is little doubt that his own self-analysis contributed greatly to the formulation of his theories.

Finally, in the early 1900's his lonely work began to attract attention. He had continually been passed over for appointment to associate professor at Vienna University, largely because of his emphasis on sex. In 1902, however, a female patient went to great effort and finally got the appropriate minister to approve Freud's promotion in exchange for a painting the minister wanted very badly. In 1920 Freud was made a full professor but did relatively little teaching at the University and, strictly speaking, was never an academician.

In the fall of 1902 he initiated weekly discussions with a small group of men in his home at the suggestion of Stekel, and this grew into the Vienna Psychoanalytical Society. Even though there was still little recognition in Vienna, workers in a number of other countries followed his publications and became deeply interested. This led to the institutionalization of psychoanalysis in an attempt to control its growth, and the International Psycho-Analytical Association was formed. Freud continually held that he alone had the right to decide what should be called psychoanalysis since he had developed it. He did not mind others developing other points of view, but he vehemently objected to their using the name of psychoanalysis since he felt this would confuse the public and reduce the effectiveness of his movement. It was primarily for this reason that splits such as those with Jung and Adler occurred.

In 1909 Stanley Hall invited Freud to give a series of lectures at the twentieth anniversary of Clark University in the United States. Freud was excited about the trip, pleased to know his ideas were being seriously considered elsewhere, and touched when they conferred upon him an honorary doctorate. It was at this time that the dying William James told Freud he thought the future of psychology belonged to Freud's work.

From this point on, Freud's following grew and his private practice flourished. A look at his typical day is instructive. He saw his first patient each day at 8 a.m. and continued seeing patients until 1 p.m.

Each patient was allotted 55 minutes with a five-minute break between patients to enable Freud to prepare himself for the next one. At one o'clock he had lunch with his family and then took a walk. At three o'clock he began seeing patients again and continued his consultations until 9 or 10 p.m. At that time he had dinner and followed it with another walk with his wife or a member of his family. He then returned to his study, answered his voluminous correspondence, and worked on his manuscripts. He retired at one or two o'clock in the morning. Eleven or twelve psychoanalytic hours each day and he still had energy for scholarly work!

Although he deeply resented the treatment he had received from the professional groups in the city of Vienna and had occasionally toyed with the idea of leaving, he never did so. Ernest Jones had to persuade Freud to move to London when fear for his welfare under a Nazi regime developed. It was in London that Freud finally succumbed to cancer, continuing to work up to the end.

Freud's ideas grew from the narrow base of psychopathology. He read widely, but apparently his ideas developed largely from his own experience. He was heavily influenced by the attitudes of the natural sciences, particularly his mentors in physiology. Freud might be called opinionated in the sense that he believed very strongly in his own ideas and apparently felt betrayed when close associates rejected his ideas for theirs. For example, Jones reports Freud once commented that he continually sought friends who would not exploit and then betray him. Jones believes Freud disliked dependence and having his freedom of action restricted. He did not want to owe anything to anyone. This independence of thought made him willing to believe in the improbable and unexpected, however, and may have led to some of his major discoveries. He had a passion for getting at the truth, and Jones believes he had amazing intellectual courage characterized by absolute honesty and integrity. He was tediously patient and rationally factual. He had great self-discipline, as evidenced in his daily schedule. He was very self-critical and once commented that this was perhaps his best attribute, next to his courage. Perhaps most of all he was deeply considerate of and concerned about his fellow human beings although, with his usual candor, he acknowledged in a letter to Dr. Putnam in the United States that he knew not why it should be so (Jones, 1955, pp. 417–418).

THEORETICAL FORMULATIONS

Freud was a prodigious writer and even continued to write during the final stages of his very painful cancer which he endured without narcotics, preferring to tolerate the pain so as to keep his thoughts clear. In addition to his own writings, many followers have made significant contributions, some of which Freud accepted, others of which he rejected. The latter prompted him to reformulate his own theories to account better for phenomena that "deviants" such as Adler, Jung, and Rank discussed. In the face of the voluminous literature, it has been necessary to make some decisions about the material to be included in this chapter. We have based this presentation entirely on Freud's work for three reasons. First, his writings represent the major and original structure of psychoanalytic theory, a structure which has undergone some remodeling but the basic outlines of which still stand today. Second, a number of "neo-analytic" formulations will be examined in later chapters and will illustrate the variety of changes and modifications that have been proposed. Third, this restriction to Freud's own work avoids the problem of attempting to choose from among the great variety of other contributions those that Freud would have considered legitimate extensions of his theories.

The writings of Freud on which this chapter is based were chosen to represent his most significant publications. Two references (1915; 1932) represent Freud's attempt to present his ideas to a lay audience and are reasonably adequate summaries. His final book (1938), written during the last painful stages of his illness, is a good brief summary. Although many synopses have been published by others, there is no substitute for reading Freud in the original. He pursued the implications of an idea tenaciously and logically until he was satisfied the facts fit and there were no logical inconsistencies, or until his reasoning convinced him an alternate formulation was necessary. He was careful to distinguish between his empirical observations and the abstractions he developed to explain them. Sometimes he seems to have written as much to clarify his own thoughts as to communicate them to others (1925). He was usually dissatisfied with what he had written, even though he was a far more lucid writer than most who attempt to present complex ideas.

Freud made major modifications of his theories at several points during his lifetime. He stubbornly defended his ideas and struggled to explain within their framework all the phenomena he observed. When the empirical data derived from his observations could not be logically accounted for, however, he relinquished his ideas and formulated new ones. His distressing discovery that his patient's childhood memories of sexual seduction, upon which he had built his entire theory of neurosis, were more fantasy than fact is an excellent example. He was understandably very discouraged, because it appeared that the entire theoretical structure would fall when that foundation stone was removed. He could no longer deny the fact, however, and set out to account for it. This led to his discovery of the crucial role of fantasy itself. Such changes in his theory make it somewhat difficult to represent him and one must choose to present each change in turn or to choose from among them. We have selected the latter course. In each instance we shall give major emphasis to his later formulations, referring to his earlier ones where appropriate and helpful. This course enables us to present his most elaborate theoretical position, because his observations did not change but the higher-order abstractions he developed to account for them did, and because important threads of continuity run throughout his formulations.

THE NORMAL COURSE OF BEHAVIOR DEVELOPMENT

General Point of View

Freud was trained in the biological sciences and medicines; throughout his life, he considered psychic phenomena a manifestation of biological phenomena. He saw man as a biological creature and a part of the natural world, whose behavior was impelled by biological urges (instincts). He was explicitly irreligious. He did not attempt to trace the biological roots of the psychic phenomena he attempted to explain. Rather, he believed the biological knowledge of his day inadequate to the task, freely formulated his theories in terms of psychic phenomena, and left it to posterity to develop a biological science that could be used as a base for understanding human behavior. Although he admired Darwin, for some unexplained reason he consistently represented a Lamarckian point of view in his theorizing (Jones, 1957, Vol. III, pp. 312–313). For example, he proposed that the id contained residues of certain types of experience inherited from primitive ancestors.

He maintained a strictly deterministic point of view. The simplest everyday occurrences he believed could be traced to a complicated set of antecedents of which the person was typically unaware (1904). The individual is seldom, if ever, aware of all the antecedents to any of his behavior since the contents of the id are always unconscious, in Freud's judgment (1932, p. 43). Jones stated that psychoanalysts have found they are justified in treating the concepts of causality and intent as "extensively interchangeable" (Jones, 1957, Vol. III, p. 272). Freud considered the discovery of unconscious determinants of behavior, first presented in his work on dreams (1900), one of his most, if not *the* most, crucial contributions (1923, p. 9). His technique of free association was a direct application of this premise, and many of his major concepts, such as repression and resistance, are also outgrowths of this position.

A particularly important outcome of Freud's deterministic position was his construction of a developmental or "genetic" psychology. The kind of behavior that develops to reduce the biological tensions is the consequence of human experience. Present behavior is understandable in terms of the life history of the individual, and the crucial foundations for all future behavior are laid down in infancy and early childhood. The most significant antecedents or determinants of present behavior are the "residues" of past experiences—that is, learned responses—particularly those developed during the earliest years to reduce biological tensions.

His focus was primarily on response events. He obviously considered situational events important—for example, the "reality principle" and his emphasis on the crucial role of parents—but most of his theoretical efforts were directed toward the formulation of the response-response relationships, which he considered the primary governors of human behavior. He was primarily interested in the "economy," "dynamics," and "topography" of the "mind." A central thesis seems to pervade all his writing. As Jones puts it, Freud was a stubborn dualist, "seized with the conception of a profound conflict within the mind, and throughout his life he struggled to discover and define the nature and characteristics of the opposing forces" (1957, Vol. III, p. 266).

INNATE CHARACTERISTICS OF NORMAL DEVELOPMENT

Antecedents to Behavior

Freud conceived of behavior occurring as the consequence of two kinds of events: stimuli (situational events) and instinctual drives [1] (innate psychological energies). He gave far more emphasis to the latter, however, and most behavior was aimed at tension or drive reduction. Thus, situational events play their greatest role in his theories as events to be sought and utilized as a means of facilitating energy reduction. They also differ significantly in that the individual can escape physically from the stimulation of situational events but not from the sources of stimulation within the body which operate "as a constant force" (1932, p. 132).

INSTINCTUAL DRIVES. Freud (1932, p. 131) recognized the speculative nature of his theory of instincts, calling them "our mythology" and "superb in their indefiniteness," but he considered them absolutely essential for an adequate account of why and how human behavior occurs.

He proposed that these innate psychological energies (instincts) have several attributes. First, they are *quantities of energy* which may vary in intensity (pressure), and the more intense they are the more imperative it is that responses be made to reduce their intensity. Second, these psychological energies are *constantly occurring*, despite variations in intensity, and consequently must be regularly reduced (discharged) to avoid excessive accumulation. The individual *must* behave. Third, their *source* lies in the biological functioning of the organism, although the exact source may not be identifiable at our current state of knowledge. Fourth, their ultimate *aim* is to produce consequences that will reduce the intensity or quantity of the accumulated psychological energy, thus implying some selectivity in their functioning. Fifth, they seek *an object or event* through which the tension reduction can be accomplished. This may be a part of the individual or a situational event (1915). They also have the quality of combining with one another regardless of source, and thereafter may be reduced by achieving one set of consequences—that is,

[1] The German "trieb" has been translated both as instinct and as drive, and Freud's usage is similar to, although not identical with, American "drive" psychology.

aims or objects—even though the psychological energies combined may have come from different sources (1932, p. 133). In fact, Freud proposed that all psychological energies that can be studied are made up of fusions or alloys of energies arising from different biological sources (1925, p. 125; 1932, p. 143).

These various psychological energies (or *needs*, 1915, p. 119) require certain behavioral results to keep them at an optimum level. In his final formulation, Freud reasoned that this tendency to maintain an equilibrium of tension among the various sources of psychological energy is a general characteristic of human life; an "urge inherent in organic life" to restore "an earlier state of things" which had been disrupted by the intervention of situational events. This principle of equilibrium would tend to produce a stable—that is, "conservative"—behavior pattern rather than a changing one [2] (1919, p. 36).

What kinds of events are these? Freud began with the assumption that ultimately all events derive from the biological structures of the organism and the energies they produce. However, neurophysiological events in turn give rise to behavioral events, which Freud came to label *psychic energy*. As Rapaport (1960) has explained, Freud was clear in proposing that these events are not the consequence of events originating outside the organism; they are generated within the organism itself. But they are not the same as the psychological energies—somatic processes—themselves. Moreover, Freud wished to keep the relationship between these somatic events and the psychic energies they produced deliberately vague, lest "psychological concepts be prematurely equated with or tied to specific physiological processes" (Rapaport, 1960, p. 194). Freud was retaining a thorough psychological determinism; behavior must be studied without reference to molecular physiological processes. In the discussion to follow, we shall employ the term *psychological energies* to represent these instinctual drives, considering it to be a kind of response which is clearly inferential (r_i).

Thus, we have a situation in which psychological energies arising from different sources, varying in quantity or intensity, joining in different combinations, elicit responses to some objects or events through which the constantly accumulating energy can be discharged. Freud rejected the notion of a great many particular kinds of psychological

---

[2] This implies that behavior changes and develops only because of the stimulation of situational events, an implication he never extended systematically, except perhaps in the reality principle.

energy and at first proposed two groups which he called ego, or self-preservative, and sexual (1915, p. 124). Later, when the First World War and some of the resulting behavior disorders had thoroughly impressed Freud with aggressive and destructive human behavior, he changed his classification to include two other groups, Eros, which included both the previous two groups, and Thanatos, the death instinct (1925, p. 14).

EROS OR THE LIFE INSTINCTS. The aim of this group is constructive—"to establish ever greater unities," "to bind together," self-preservation and procreation (1938, p. 20). Initially, there are no built-in connections between the psychological energy associated with this group—energy that Freud called *libido*—and responses to situational events which would have the consequence of reducing, or discharging, the accumulating energy. It simply serves to maintain the optimum equilibrium of tension by serving as a balance to other kinds of psychological energy; it neutralizes them. Freud sometimes referred to Eros as "the love instinct" (1938, p. 21).

The *self-preservative* portion of this group includes physiological responses which elicit behavior to maintain life, such as thirst, hunger, the need for oxygen, and so forth. His theories paid little attention to these because they are seldom, if ever, antecedents to disorder. And for a very good reason! Their gratification *must* occur regularly and with relatively little delay or the person dies. Thus, there can be no accumulation of energy, a circumstance which has crucial consequences in the case of other instinctual drives (1932, p. 134). Freud remained somewhat vague about this aspect of the concept.

The *sexual energies* and their consequences are the group that Freud first emphasized. In his earliest statements, he seems to have meant sexual in the usual sense of erotic genital sensations and sexual intercourse, including thoughts and fantasies about sex and wishes for sexual relations (1900; 1905), that is, a drive for procreation. He soon broadened his definition, however, to include a great variety of sensations when he abandoned his first theory of childhood sexual trauma and developed his theories of infantile sexuality and narcissism (1905; 1914). He then emphasized that one should distinguish between the broad concept of sexual and the narrow concept of genital. In the latter theory he proposed that sexual energy was at first nothing more than relatively discrete, pleasurable sensations arising from the erogenous zones of the body. He proposed that any portion of the skin may give rise to such sensations but three, the mouth, anus, and genitals are especially sensitive zones (*organ pleasure*) (1905, p. 587). In addition, some unidentified "inner" responses, when they achieve a certain intensity, may also yield similar pleasurable sensations [3] (1905, p. 602). Under normal circumstances, these separate sensations come to function as a unit at puberty, that is, become *the* sexual instinct, and sexual life involves "obtaining pleasure from zones of the body" (*organ pleasure*, 1915, p. 135) which may lead to reproduction, but "the two functions often fail to coincide completely" (1938, p. 26).

This development automatically proceeds through several maturational stages, identified by the three most sensitive erogenous zones. During the first year of life, the mouth is the primary focus of pleasurable sensation, not only because it is the means of nourishment but also because sucking in itself appears pleasurable (*oral phase*). The incorporation of food appearing in this stage is considered the prototype of all later incorporations, such as *identification*.[4] In the latter part of this stage teeth begin to erupt, biting and mastication of food begins, and the first destructive or aggressive (*sadistic*) behaviors are said to appear. At the end of the first year the anus comes to be a primary source of pleasurable sensations (*sadistic-anal phase*). Satisfaction is sought in aggression and the retention or expulsion of feces. The "attitude" the infant takes toward mastery of this bodily function, whether active control or passive compliance, is said to represent a prototype for the development of other complicated behaviors. Thus, pleasure in collecting stamps may be considered an extension of this phase.[5] At about the age of three, the penis or clitoris is discovered as a source of pleasurable sensation (*phallic stage*). This leads to complications which will be discussed later. From the age of five until puberty (*latency phase*), sexual interests are in the background, only to appear again at puberty in the form of normal genital sexuality if

[3] It is interesting to note that this is a less frequent use of the term pleasure for Freud (the arousal of certain responses). His typical use of pleasure, for example, the pleasure principle, involves response termination, that is, the reduction of psychological tensions.
[4] This type of generalization by analogy from an actual physical act to a higher-order concept of complicated behavior, such as eating-incorporation-psychological identification or biting-destruction-aggression, is both typical of Freud and somewhat questionable.
[5] Some analysts discuss this phase of development (toilet training) in terms of its being one of the first complex interpersonal situations confronting the infant. Although this may have been Freud's intent, he did not make that clear but seemed to treat it as a maturational development.

all goes well. Thus, beginning with many sources of pleasurable sensations a predestined developmental path is traversed, culminating in the (integrated) sex pattern.

THANATOS OR THE DEATH OR DESTRUCTIVE INSTINCT. In his early formulations, Freud seemed to consider aggression as one of the innate self-preservation responses. In his final formulation, however, he set this apart as a most fundamental psychological energy which was in opposition to the life-maintaining energies (1932, p. 141). Its aim is destruction, "to undo connections," "to destroy things" (1938, p. 20). By pursuing the idea of destruction to its logical conclusion, he decided the ultimate aim of this drive must be to reduce living things to their previous inorganic state—thus, the "death instinct." He had no term for this psychological energy, in contrast to his use of the term libido to refer to the energies formed from the life instincts. However, it too could accumulate, become diverted, and combine with other psychological energies. It can only be observed when it is diverted outward in the form of destruction, such as aggressive and destructive acts toward oneself. In fact, one can only be aware of psychological energies through ideas, or affective responses which are their consequents (1915, p. 177).

Thus Freud conceived of a pool of psychological energy, derived from several biological sources and eliciting responses that served to reduce and balance the energy level. Which responses and situational events are utilized to effect and control such discharge is not innately determined and is therefore apparently a product of learning. Behavior will not occur by itself; it is all elicited (caused) by some psychological energy, typically of the constructive kind—libido. Thus, even thoughts were said to be a manifestation of the "sexual drive."

Kinds and Attributes of Responses

Freud did not directly formulate a statement of the innate response equipment of humans. In his extended discussions, however, several kinds of responses are clearly considered to be innate responses, and therefore we shall present them as such.

THE ATTRIBUTE OF AWARENESS. This Freud considered to be one of his most fundamental concepts. The division of mental life into responses that are conscious or unconscious is a "fundamental premise on which psychoanalysis is based" (1923, p. 9). There is a marked change in his usage of the concepts from his early to his later writings, however, and apparently some analysts feel he actually discarded this classification when he divided mental functioning into id, ego, and superego.

In his early usage of the terms he combined the *quality* of human awareness with the notion of the content of awareness. Thus, for example, he proposed that the unconscious was composed, in part, of thoughts that had been repressed, that is, certain *kinds* of responses. In his final formulation, however, he subclassified *kinds* of response events into the id, ego, and superego, which we shall discuss later (1923). From this point on he treated the idea of consciousness and unconsciousness purely as the "mental quality" of human awareness, and this quality could become an attribute of the various kinds of responses included under each of his new subclasses (1938, p. 33). This distinction between *kinds of responses* (id, ego, and superego) and one's *awareness of them* (conscious, preconscious, and unconscious) led to important changes in his way of speaking about behavior development and disorder, but it is important to realize that this was simply a different way of classifying the events of concern and not an entirely new set of phenomena. Thus, in his early discussions he spoke of conflicts between "the" conscious and "the" unconscious with "the" censor intervening between the two. In his later discussions he spoke of conflicts between "the" id, "the" ego, and "the" superego, and whether one was aware of certain kinds of responses in each of these three classes was considered a manifestation of this conflict. Thus, our discussion of consciousness will deal with it as a response attribute, in the same sense that intensity or frequency of occurrence are attributes, rather than as a kind of response. Let us first consider his conception of unconsciousness.

UNCONSCIOUSNESS. Freud used the term "mental" to encompass all responses that the present writers refer to as subjectively observable (r) and responses completely inferred (r_i). We shall use the term subjective responses (r and r_i) hereafter, since for many readers the term mental has either the connotation of a particular kind of response, for instance, thoughts, or the attribute of awareness. Each of these connotations is far too restrictive for Freud's usage. It was in his work on dreams that he first presented his views concerning the unconscious, and throughout his life he considered this one of his most important works (1900).

Freud assumed that *all* subjective responses occur without one being aware of them; that is, they are at first unconscious (1925, p. 31).

He meant all, too, because he included not only sensory responses of all kinds but also thoughts. In his earliest writings he argued that there were unconscious streams of thought in associative memory (1904, p. 49), and that highly complex patterns of subjective responses (mental operations) were possible without the co-operation of consciousness (1900, p. 529). He maintained this position in his last brief summary (1938, p. 38). He did assume that the subjective responses which occur outside awareness are probably "physical or somatic processes" of which phenomenalike thoughts may become the conscious manifestation (1938, p. 34). He made it clear that his concept of unconscious processes was an inference and compared it proudly to inferential concepts in the natural sciences, such as force, mass, and the like. His inference was based on the observation of unexplainable breaks and inconsistencies in the sequences of conscious responses, and on the occurrence of responses which the person did not "intend" but which were frequently embarrassing or downright harmful. However, by assuming that response sequences continually occur outside of awareness, only some of which the person can or does become aware of, he was able to fill in the gaps and account for the inconsistencies, better to understand, predict, and modify his patient's behavior (1938, p. 37). His books on dreams (1900) and everyday inconsistencies in behavior (1904) were his most extensive efforts to demonstrate this behavioral phenomenon and the usefulness and power of the inferential concept, *unconscious process.*

Freud also observed that some subjective responses were readily available to awareness, whereas becoming aware of others required a considerable amount of effort. Moreover, sometimes help from someone else such as a therapist was required if awareness of them were to occur at all (1932, pp. 101–102). Those responses readily available to awareness, or capable of becoming conscious, were termed *preconscious*—for example, memories—and those that required a considerable struggle to be introduced into awareness were called *unconscious.* This latter group plays an important role in behavior disorder and therefore requires some additional discussion.

He argued that responses are not unconscious simply because they are unnoticed. There seems to be a force—*resistance*—involved in keeping them from awareness, a process Freud called *repression.* This inference arose from his observations that: (1) a very great effort is required to concentrate enough attention on unconscious responses to bring them into awareness; (2) when one becomes aware of them they seem utterly alien and opposed to what one believes one's responses are, and one promptly disavows them; or (3) they elicit distressing negative affect, particularly anxiety (1923, p. 5). Where this force comes from and how it develops will be discussed in the section on learned development. Summing up, then, Freud proposed that all subjective responses occur outside awareness and that this is the "true essence of mental life" rather than consciousness, as is popularly believed. This is a clear expression of his biologically oriented determinism, namely, that behavior is directed by complicated responses, many of which occur outside awareness. To put it crudely, we may only think we know why we do things and for what we are striving.

CONSCIOUSNESS. Freud considered consciousness a fact "without parallel," defying "all explanation or description," a fact that "we know immediately and from our own most personal experience." He considered this a very important aspect of human behavior and strongly disagreed with "extreme lines of thought," like "the American doctrine of behaviorism," which try to develop a psychology that disregards the fundamental phenomena of human awareness (1938, p. 34). He characterized the qualities of human awareness and unawareness as "the single ray of light" penetrating "the obscurity of depth-psychology" (1923, p. 18). By this he seems to mean that without the capacity to observe our own responses (r and R), knowledge of how behavior works, that is, of "mental life," would be impossible. Only the subjective observer can shed light on the crucial human mediating responses.

We interpret Freud to mean that consciousness is itself a response, a behavioral event, which is not a product of learning. The response follows upon or entails the responses of attending—we are aware of what we attend to (1900, pp. 224, 529). Thus, sleep would involve the discontinuance of attending responses. Here and elsewhere (1915, p. 171; 1932, p. 106) he speaks of consciousness as a sense organ which receives impressions from the external world through exteroceptors, as well as receiving interoceptive and proprioceptive sensations from the body as well. This special function of attention, however, is not a passive receptor. It searches actively for sense impressions rather than waiting for their appearance (1911, p. 220). This helps to make it clear that *what* one is conscious of and the *act* of consciousness are different. The "contents" of consciousness are different than consciousness itself. In regard to the events of which one is aware, Freud emphasized their transitory nature. "[A]n idea that is conscious now is no longer so a moment later, although it can become so again under certain conditions that are easily brought about" (1923, p. 10). The events of which one is aware at any given point in time are limited and are constantly changing from moment to moment.

In summary, Freud's view seems to be that a variety of subjective responses are continuously occurring and influencing the behavior that follows. A special response of attending monitors some of the occurrences, and one is aware of those responses that are attended. What kinds of responses can be attended?

SENSORY AND MOTORIC RESPONSES. Freud acknowledged these but did almost nothing to fit them systematically into his theory. He stated that the typical sequence of behavior proceeded from the sensory to the motor. He spoke of the sense organs as being the individual's contact with situational events (reality), as being closely associated with consciousness, and as being closely related to the system of responses he called ego. He also spoke of auditory responses as the primary avenue through which the child learns language and vision as the primary source of images that provide the material for dream representation. He referred to motoric activity as a means of dealing with situational events (accommodating oneself to reality). Occasionally he discussed disordered motor functions as neurotic and psychotic symptoms. He spoke of voluntary movement as being controlled by the ego system of responses. Motor behavior reduces the accumulating psychological energy. These were only fragmentary discussions, however, and apparently he found it unnecessary to deal with them further in his theory.

THOUGHTS AND SPEECH. These responses are fundamental in Freud's system. Strictly speaking, thoughts and speech themselves are not innate, but the capacity to think and speak apparently is.[6] Freud specifies two kinds of symbols. The first of these, *images,* are particularly important in dreams. Imagistic representation is typical of infancy and early childhood, and later imagistic dreams have roots in such early habits. Logical thought is not possible through images. The second type of symbol, *words,* develops through contact with situational events. Words and their usage are learned through hearing and speaking them. Verbal thought may be logical and gives the individual powerful responses for controlling and manipulating psychological energies and situational events, and for making value judgments. Most thoughts

[6] Freud suggested the Lamarckian hypothesis that some thoughts, particularly sexual or Oedipal fantasies, might be inherited, but he did not extend this idea into his theories in any serious way.

are elicited by situational events through the sense organs. One group, however, called *fantasies*, are never "tested against reality" and resemble hallucinations (1911, p. 222). Both verbal and imagistic thoughts differ fundamentally from other responses in that they are the only ones that leave *memory traces* (1915, p. 178).

EMOTIONS, FEELINGS, AND AFFECTS. These responses were important in Freud's theories from the beginning. Positive affective responses mentioned by him include love and pleasure. Negative ones include anxiety, fear, guilt, shame, hate, and painful affect. Of these, anxiety was the only one to which he gave extensive treatment. Emotions, feelings, and affects are never unconscious (1915, p. 177).

Love seems to be Freud's term for awareness of the psychological energy (libido) which leads to positive constructive behavior. He never detailed quite what the term meant, although he used it often. Most frequently it related to actual sexual desire and relationships (1910). He also spoke of love objects. For example, he proposed that a person may love: (1) what he is, that is, himself, (2) what he was, (3) what he would like to be, (4) someone once a part of himself, *or* (5) the woman who feeds him, (6) the man who protects him, and (7) any of the substitutes who take their place throughout life (1914, p. 90). Here the connotation is less strictly sexual. He occasionally used the term tenderness to refer to affectionate relationships without a direct sexual connotation. *Pleasure*, too, is a term he used somewhat ambiguously. Occasionally he seemed to be referring to a positive affect such as pleasurable sensations, but more frequently pleasure referred to the reduction of psychological energy, without necessarily meaning awareness of pleasurable sensations from the reduction of tension.

Anxiety is a fundamental response which Freud discussed extensively. He discarded his initial concept of anxiety as a consequence of or transformation of accumulated psychological energy that could not be discharged because of repression (1900; 1915), and finally considered it an affective response which occurred automatically under certain circumstances (1925). What are these antecedent conditions? They are situations of danger (1925, p. 80). Any circumstance that produces a growing tension which the individual is helpless to terminate is dangerous (1925, p. 137). The antecedents may be situational events, psychological energies, or thoughts (1925, pp. 146–150). Stated another way, anxiety will occur if: (1) the individual is flooded with intense, uncontrollable stimulation, such as the sights and sounds of an intense battle at the time he is wounded; (2) uncontrollable events prevent reduction of innate psychological energy—for instance, an individual is prevented from breathing; or (3) responses produce painful consequences—for instance, a child assaults someone and gets severely beaten as a result. The antecedents will change during development, and Freud proposed that every developmental stage has its own particular conditions for anxiety (1932, pp. 122–123). One is not innately helpless in any situation, however, so whether a situation is "dangerous" depends upon learning. Initially, some events produce excessive tension which the individual is unable to relieve—a *traumatic situation*. He is thus helpless and experiences severe anxiety: *automatic anxiety* (1925, pp. 81, 166). The sequence is automatic and innate.

Situational events (S) or innate responses (r) → excessive tension (r) → helpless to terminate (ineffective R's) → intense anxiety (r)

Thus, some kind of painful events are always the original antecedents of anxiety, and it is only through learning that other responses, such as thoughts and memories, acquire this function.

Later, similar situations will be reacted to as dangerous; they will be "recognized, remembered, expected situations of helplessness." Thoughts of, memories about, or expectations of the occurrence of such danger situations elicit mild anxiety. This automatic sequence Freud called *signal anxiety* (1925, pp. 81, 166).

Situational events (S) → memories, thoughts, or expectations (r) → mild anxiety (signal anxiety) (r)

This development is considered crucial for self-preservation, because the signal anxiety is less intense, occurs before any actual traumatic situation develops, and makes possible preventive action.

What are the consequences of anxiety? The individual automatically tries to avoid the precipitating circumstances, whether the anxiety is traumatic or signal (1915, p. 373). *Anxiety leads to avoidance.* In the case of situational events, the person may avoid attending to or thinking about them. Or better yet, he may physically remove himself from their presence. With response events, motoric flight is not possible, so avoidance can only be accomplished by not attending to or thinking about them (*repression*) (1925, pp. 92–93). Thus, repression is the automatic consequence of anxiety and not the reverse as Freud originally had proposed. Physical avoidance, inattention (repression), or both probably occur when the degree of accumulated tension and consequent anxiety is intense (1925, p. 94). The avoidance of signal anxiety serves to prevent more intense anxiety.

What are the characteristics of anxiety? The most striking symptoms are breathlessness and heart palpitations, and since these also occur in acts of copulation, Freud at first considered anxiety a manifestation of sexual excitement (instinct). He later discarded this notion. Anxiety is a subjective response, a feeling. It has a marked character of unpleasure all its own, although it is not the only unpleasurable feeling. The clearest and most frequent physical manifestations which the individual notices involve respiration and the heart, thus providing evidence of motor discharge (1925, p. 132).

Hate is an affective response which seems to be the conscious manifestation of psychological energies that innately lead to aggression (death instinct). *Guilt* and *shame* appear to be derivatives of this same energy source resulting when aggression is turned against the self.

All negative affects connote discomfort and undesirable consequences which the individual innately tends to avoid. On the other hand, the positive affects seem to have a desirable quality about them and innately lead to constructive and approach behavior.

Innate Controlling Principles

Freud proposed three apparently inborn and automatic principles which control behavior. The first has been called lust-unlust, pleasure-unpleasure, pleasure-pain, or more frequently simply the *pleasure principle*. The second he called the *reality principle* and the third the compulsion to repeat or *repetition compulsion*. Historically the latter one was developed much later than the others, in conjunction with his death instinct.

THE PLEASURE PRINCIPLE. This principle is familiar to American psychologists in the form of drive reduction and is similar to Cannon's Principle of Homeostasis and Fechner's Principle of Constancy. The "mental apparatus" functions to keep excitations as low as possible, or at least to keep them constant (1919, p. 9). Freud proposed that as psychological energy accumulates, the increase in tension is felt as discomfort (unpleasure). This increase automatically impels action, the purpose of which is to reduce the quantity or intensity of the accumulated energy (1900, p. 533; 1919, p. 9). Freud referred to this consequence as pleasure, and thus a fundamental purpose in life is to achieve pleasure *in the sense of tension reduction*. This is *not* a response-arousal type of principle; it does not seek to arouse pleasurable sensations. A more descriptive name would be the tension or energy-reduction principle. In the infant, psychological energy elicits dreams and waking fantasies, which are ineffective tension reducers, and the motoric activity performed, if any, is undirected and also ineffective. This undirected effort at immediate gratification without effectively relating it to situational events, but with a memory image or "hallucination" of something desired rather than the real thing involved, is called the *primary process*. This image is sometimes called a *wish*. When imagining does not produce tension reduction, the infant must turn to the external world.

THE REALITY PRINCIPLE. The pleasure principle asserts that behavior is controlled by the requirement of tension reduction but does not determine which behaviors will be performed. The behavioral consequences that will produce tension reduction almost always require interaction with situational events (reality). Usually several possibilities exist, and one must select from among them. For example, one might seek sexual release with any available woman or obtain a wife of one's own. Circumstances may require a delay until situational events can be arranged or obtained to achieve the tension reduction; it may take some time, for example, for a man to obtain a wife. The reality principle simply refers to the tendency to seek and utilize situational events to achieve tension reduction without incurring other difficulties. It does not state how this is accomplished (1911, p. 219; 1919, p. 10). It involves foregoing a momentary pleasure with uncertain results to gain an assured pleasure at a later time (1911, p. 224). Thus, delayed and effective reduction of psychological energies (drives) along socially acceptable lines is implied in the functioning of this principle. It substitutes thoughtful, logically organized behavior for completely impulsive, unco-ordinated attempts at self-gratification, and this reliance on awareness, thought, memory, and judgment related to environmental factors is called the *secondary process*. What is represented in the "mind" is no longer what is "agreeable" but what is "real," even if it is "disagreeable" (1911, p. 219).

THE REPETITION COMPULSION. The first two principles function together, but the third one may override them. Freud observed that behavior was repetitious, or occurred over and over again—that is, much of behavior is habitual. What was puzzling was that it frequently did not serve to reduce tension. For example, he recognized that the increase of sexual tension was pleasurable and was exactly contradictory to the tension-reduction principle. In fact some of this repetitious behavior involved great discomfort and intense anxiety, and represented the re-enactment of very painful experiences. For example, recurrent self-injuring behavior which some people manifest—the tendency of some children and psychoanalytic patients to act out over and over again painful experiences of the past, or the patients with "war neuroses" in whom terrifying experiences recur in their dreams—were all cited as inexplicable by the tension-reduction or accommodation to reality principles (1919, pp. 18–35). Freud proposed that the purpose of this innate tendency to repeat was to "master" or "bind" a flood of sensations so that they could become subject to control and direction. It would follow that the more varied and intense the stimulation from both external and internal events the more repetition might be necessary to effect control. The implication is that if stimulation were excessive and uncontrolled, the behavior that followed would be chaotic and not in the service of the psychological energies of the organism. Thus, "mastering" or organizing stimulation—apparently this would mean sensory responses of all types—is a necessary prerequisite for the other processes to occur, to wit, tension reduction through the use of situational events (1919). Freud related this to his death instinct, since its ultimate logical extension would be for life to seek to repeat its earlier inorganic state. In a sense this seems to be another way of avoiding noxious, or excessive, stimulation.

SUMMARY. Thus, behavior is guided by a tendency to reduce psychological tensions, a tendency to accommodate behavior to situational events, and a tendency to repeat earlier behaviors in order to get stimulation under control. Biological processes produce psychological energy which must be discharged, most naturally through motoric acts. Sensory mechanisms bring evidence of the external and internal environment to the individual. Consciousness, through its attending function, examines the evidence of the senses and controls the motor discharge of the psychological energies. Thoughts or symbolic representations of past experience may be acquired—a form of notation in Freud's terms. Affective responses are subject to conscious control, though less so than motoric responses, and they may signify the accumulation or operation of some psychological energy, indicate that the individual has been overwhelmed or flooded with stimulation which he is helpless to control (trauma), or signalize the possibility of such a situation occurring.

LEARNED CHARACTERISTICS OF NORMAL DEVELOPMENT

Freud specified that behavior is learned for two purposes (Jones, 1957, Vol. III, p. 436). Behavior must be learned to reduce psychological energies (drives) effectively, in accordance with the possibilities permitted in the social circumstances in which one lives and to control such energies so that they do not elicit behaviors which might lead to immediate gratification but might also lead to other severe and undesirable consequences. Thus, behaviors instrumental in both achieving desired consequences and avoiding undesirable consequences must be learned.

One of Freud's major contributions to psychology was his emphasis on the influence of childhood learnings on adult behavior. He argued that what is learned in the first few years significantly influences behavior and development throughout the rest of life. He came to this conclusion largely because so many of his patients' significant memories were of childhood experiences and fantasies. Most of his ideas about normal development were interwoven with his discussions of the sexual developmental stages. Secondly, some of his ideas about development appear in his discussions of the ego and superego systems. And finally, his discussions of behavior mechanisms or dynamics furnish further ideas about behavior development. The present writers have taken these three types of material and, for convenience, have organized them around the stages of infancy, early childhood, late childhood, adolescence, and adulthood.[7]

Infancy

There are three characteristics of infant behavior. First, there are a group of functioning subjective responses. The most important are psychological energies, which automatically vary in quantity and intensity. In addition there are all the inherited response characteristics and automatic reflexes. Second, behavior is quite unorganized, and the subjective responses elicited are haphazard and fragmentary. All behavior is directed at immediate tension reduction (pleasure principle). Third, the infant is unaware or unconscious of all these events.

[7] Other analysts have written much about developmental patterns, not all of it in agreement with Freud's ideas, but the reader will recall we are concerned here only with Freud's ideas.

There are no values, no conception of time, no sense of contradiction or conflict among responses, no awareness of situational events, and no self-awareness. No behavior is consciously controlled or planned. This entire group of phenomena Freud named id (German *Es*, or *It*) to connote the completely impersonal nature of this state of affairs (1923; 1938, pp. 14, 208). In Freud's colorful terms, the id is a "cauldron of seething excitement," somewhere in contact with somatic processes. Quantitative energy dominates its processes. "Instinctual cathexes seeking discharge,—that in our view, is all that the id contains" (1932, p. 105).

It is inferred that the infant's first awareness is of a mass of confused sensations, fragmentary and unorganized. The infant is first aware of bodily sensations of all sorts, and does not distinguish sensations arising from its own body processes from those which are elicited by situational events (*primary narcissism*). Behavior is directed only toward its own body. At this point, the mouth or oral cavity is the infant's most prominent source of pleasurable sensations. To put it crudely, the infant is primarily a mouth. Through eating, it not only reduces a psychological tension but also derives pleasurable sensations. Sensations eventually become part of a mature sexual pattern, and Freud considered this the beginning of the child's sexuality. The desire to suck is partly the desire for the mother's breast, the first object of sexual desire, and begins a long sequence of attempts to gain sexual gratification (*oral phase*) (1905; 1915).

The mouth is also the first response mechanism to deal with the outside world. It is through sensations of the mouth that the infant first comes to know about situational events and begins to develop its first habits of responding to such events. Their main characteristic is incorporation or taking in, for example, eating. Habits of relating to other people also begin, of which the dependent, trusting, comfortable relationship with the mother during feeding represents the prototype. If the infant persists in developing this kind of relationship, if it becomes *fixated* at this stage, its adult behavior will be characterized by a dependent relationship to the world, expecting the world to mother and take care of it, and by an attitude of friendliness and generosity and an expectation that things will turn out all right without special effort on its part. Thus, a kind of passive, helpless, but affectionate and friendly adult behavior pattern may develop from this early start (*oral receptive character*).[8]

[8] This conception of basic character types, originally suggested by Freud, has been considerably elaborated by other analytic theorists.

During the first year, teeth begin to erupt, biting and chewing begin, and a new way of relating to the world becomes possible. Freud considered chewing and biting to be the first manifestation of an aggressive and destructive relationship to the world and the potential beginning of a whole, complicated pattern of behavior: fixation at the oral sadistic phase. The adult pattern that may emerge from this is characterized by aggressive and exploitative behavior toward others with subjective responses of envy, ambition, rivalry, and perhaps anger or hate—*oral sadistic character.*

During this same period, a kind of imagistic thought begins to develop. When increasing psychological energy must be reduced by some kind of response, the infant imagines sources of satisfaction; whatever was "thought of (wished for) was simply presented in a hallucinatory manner"—(wish) as a means of obtaining gratification (1911, p. 219). Since the infant does not realize that the image is not the same as the real source of gratification, it expects the image (hallucination) to terminate the tension. This may be considered the prototype of all later forms of *magical thinking.* Of course, since psychological energy cannot be reduced by hallucinations, the infant is forced to form "a conception of the real circumstances in the external world and to endeavor to make a real alteration in them" (reality principle) (1911, p. 219). This means the sense organs must bring sensations from situational events to the central nervous system, and the infant must attend to them, that is, become conscious or aware of them. Whereas the infant was originally aware of only the response qualities of pleasure and displeaseure, now it begins to attend to and discriminate other sensory qualities as well. It also begins relating differently to its environment by active exploration, utilizing the newly developed function of attention, to discover the resources available for terminating imperative psychological tensions. It begins to develop habits of seeking certain events for its satisfaction, that is, it forms *object relations.* At the same time, symbolic representations of experience (a system of notation) emerge, resulting in memories as a consequence of the periodic activity of consciousness; presumably Freud meant verbal symbols (1911, pp. 219–220). All of this represents the beginning of the group of responses Freud called the *ego.*

Near the end of the first year, the anus becomes a zone of considerable interest and an important source of pleasurable sensations—the *anal-sadistic phase.* Although reflective defecation, with accompanying pleasurable sensations, occurs from birth, now the parents begin trying to teach the infant to control its eliminative processes, and the infant begins to acquire its first control over an innate urge. Feces come to represent objects of considerable interest, and therefore, defecation represents another prototype situation for forming habits of relating to objects. If response control is achieved without difficulty, therein lie the beginnings of satisfaction in achievement and a belief that mastery of other objects is possible. On the other hand, if it does not go well, the infant may either defy the training efforts or comply anxiously. Adult patterns of behavior may develop from this base. Successful mastery may lead to an adult who is creative and productive. Mastery achieved through considerable difficulty may produce one who is hostile, obstinate, stingy and possessive, untidy or meticulous, self-centered, destructive, or fearful of throwing anything away: *anal-retentive character*. They are usually unproductive; they will not freely release their feces.[9]

In infancy, then, the child begins to make distinctions between its body and situational events, to experience its first sexual desires and gratifications, to have its first try at developing behavioral control, and to begin to develop and use symbolic responses. Behavior patterns begin which may lead to complicated adult patterns.

Early Childhood

Around the third or fourth year, the genitals become a major source of pleasurable sensations and the object of considerable exploration—*the phallic phase*. The penis and clitoris become both a source of pleasure and a matter of pride. Any threat to their existence or function is quite distressing—*castration fear*—and may be a prototype of situations in which threats to take things away from the child may elicit fear; that is, they are symbolic threats of castration. Sexual exploration in this period reveals to the boy that girls do not have penises, making the threat of castration concrete. Similarly, girls make the distressing discovery that boys have penises and they do not. They repudiate their love for their mother, whom they tend to blame, and may repress some of their sexual impulses; and may deprecate all women—*penis envy* (1932). The stage is now set for development of

---

[9] It is interesting to note that most of the character traits proposed as possible outcomes of "fixation" at this phase of development have a "bad" connotation. Throughout all the developmental phases, one sees the characteristic reasoning by analogy so clearly illustrated here.

the Oedipal complex, but first let us summarize other developments during this period.

THE DEVELOPMENT OF THOUGHT. Thoughts begin developing in infancy and assume an increasingly important developmental role. Through the active functioning of attention and awareness (the perceptual-conscious system), thoughts identifying situational events occur. These remain in awareness only briefly, since it is a characteristic of consciousness that its contents are transitory. However, all conscious thoughts leave residues in some portion of the nervous system, that is, *memory traces*. The earliest such thoughts (perceptions) are images of objects rather than words or other symbols; they are "optical memory-residues." Thus, imagistic thought, "thinking in pictures," is considered the earliest type. Imagistic thinking cannot be relational or logical, however, and is therefore severely limited: "the relations between the various elements of this subject-matter, which is what specially characterizes thought, cannot be given visual expression" (1923, p. 23). It is an important characteristic of these and all other memory residues that they can become conscious again. This "thinking in pictures" never completely disappears, even in adult life, since dreams and many waking fantasies are characteristically imagistic rather than verbal and since this phenomenon appears frequently in such behavior disorders as hallucinations.

Thinking in words is far more important in adult behavior, however, so we must ask how thoughts are learned. They are acquired primarily from "auditory perceptions," and the visual images of words acquired through reading are secondary. Sensorimotor images of words are important only in deaf mutes. "The essence of a word is after all the memory-trace of a word that has been heard" (1923, p. 22). All memory residues must at one time have been conscious thoughts, and, therefore, the only thoughts that can enter consciousness are those elicited by current events or memories of past perceptions.

But what about subjective response events? Can one observe or become aware of these? The answer is yes, but with certain qualifications. First, like perceptions of external events, several of which may occur simultaneously—for example, visual, auditory, olfactory, and kinesthetic perceptions—subjective sensations may come from several sources at once and have different or even opposite qualities. Freud stated that the only subjectively originated sensations about which we know very much are the pleasure-pain series. He used the term *feeling* to refer to these sensations, and at other times the term *affect* seemed to fall in the same class. Feelings have the characteristic of becoming directly conscious, in contrast to other unspecified subjective events of which one may be aware only by attaching a verbal symbol to them. Of course, feelings become connected with verbal images also, but that is not a necessary condition for one to be aware of them. Freud sometimes referred to feelings such as guilt, anger, and anxiety as unconscious but in a different sense than he usually used the term. In this instance, he meant the affect was misidentified—for example, pain rather than anger—or prevented from occurring entirely. If it occurs it will become conscious in some form (1919, pp. 177–178).

Freud proposed that thought processes could go on outside of awareness and are "worked out upon some sort of material which remains unrecognized." To enter awareness these unknown thought processes must somehow come into connection with memory residues of verbal images, once perceptions, which correspond to them. "It is like a demonstration of the theorem that all knowledge has its origin in external perception" (1923, p. 26). Thus, it appears that thought with verbal symbols can only take place in awareness. We are left in the dark as to the kinds of responses involved in "unconscious thought," although Freud was quite emphatic that it occurred and asserted that even solutions to complicated mathematical problems were so developed (1915; 1923).

THE FUNCTION OF THOUGHT. Through logical thought with verbal symbols, individuals achieve control over their behavior (reality principle). In contrast to the reflexively controlled infant (pleasure principle), the process of thinking secures a postponement of motor discharges and achieves control over motoric behavior. Similarly, thinking enables the individual to achieve control over his feelings, although the latter is much more difficult to maintain than motoric control. It is particularly important for therapy, however, that anxiety can be controlled with thoughts and words (1895, p. 389). By thoughtful control of the ways in which psychological tensions are reduced, the individual can avoid unfortunate consequences in the external world. In addition, by controlling his motor activity the person can manipulate situational events to achieve more effective consequences. Through the control of feelings the individual can avoid having his behavior disrupted by them. Control over affective and motor responses is the defining characteristic of normal development.

One special group of thoughts identifies the individual as an entity separate from situational events around him. All thoughts are ultimately derived from bodily sensations of one sort or another, chiefly those arising from the surface of the body, that is, exteroceptors. It is a special characteristic of the body that multiple sensations are occurring simultaneously; to the touch, the body yields sensations arising from touching any other object *and* a sensation arising from the body as a consequence of being touched. This dual type of sensation apparently provides the basis for discriminating oneself from other objects; and around it, over time, whole constellations of self-identifying thoughts are acquired. This illustrates another point Freud made. Certain ideas or thoughts are crucial or "directing ideas"; they acquire associations with other thoughts, which in turn may or may not be associated with one another (1900, p. 533). These "directing" thoughts play a much more influential role than others in the control of behavior.

With thoughts, the individual is able to "test reality." Not only does thinking function to postpone behavior and to enable the person to tolerate increased tension during the postponement, but it is also a kind of experimental acting in which the individual uses verbal symbols to try out various possibilities before selecting one which is used to discharge instinctual energy (1900; 1911; 1923).

One special group of thoughts, however, are not required to be in accord with reality, including *fantasying,* which begins "in children's play," and later *daydreaming.* Both "abandon dependence on real objects" (1923, p. 22). Although they are not unusual in children or adults, they have a special significance in behavior disorder.

Freud referred to all these phenomena with the term *ego.* One can easily see why he characterized these, whose central element is thinking and consciousness, as representing "reason and sanity" in contrast to Id phenomena "which contain the passions." He found it necessary to state that these ego phenomena were simply developments of portions of Id phenomena for two reasons. First, the response events, the sensory responses, upon which the thinking process must build are a part of the innate equipment of the individual. Second, since all responses have to be impelled by psychological energy, it was reasonable for him to suppose that thoughts could occur only if they were somehow connected with the energy source.

It should be noted here that Freud spoke of two fundamentally different kinds of thought processes, which he called primary and secondary process thought (1895; 1900; 1911). For analysts this is a crucial distinction, and Jones (1953, p. 397) termed the discovery of two different kinds of principles governing thought one of Freud's most important contributions. *Primary process thought* does not follow the rules of formal logic; it is unreflective; its temporal relationships and sequences are disorderly; it tends to be imagistic rather than verbal, though not entirely; contradictory ideas and images may exist together; separate images tend to fuse into one (condensation); and changes in relationships among images or verbal thoughts readily occur, such as the reversal of figure-ground relationships. Such thought is generally organized around experiences or aims related to psychological energies or responses (instinctual drives). Dreams exemplify such thought.

In contrast, *secondary process thought* is logically organized; uses verbal symbols; is reflective; is closely related to situational events, rather than being dominated by physiological events; and shows clear distinctions between past, present, and future events. Primary process thought develops first and characterizes infancy and early childhood, but it becomes overshadowed by logically organized, reality oriented (secondary process) thought in the adult. Since it is developmentally more fundamental, however, if logical thought processes are disrupted for some reason, the more primitive thought process will come to predominate again. To put it very simply, Freud seemed to be saying that first there was the biological organism with an innate, though unorganized, response repertoire (id), and then additional responses, the most crucial of which are thoughts, are acquired through learning (ego).

In summary, ego phenomena include attending and awareness; all memory residues, the most crucial of which are verbal; logical thought processes; the experience of affective responses; perception of situational and response events; self-identifying thoughts; and the functional control of psychological energies through controlling affective responses and motoric activities. It is striking that Freud grouped almost all learned responses under his concept of ego; thus, it might simply be translated, learned behavior. All such responses tend to become organized and function as a unit; "the ego has a tendency to synthesize its contents," and to "unify its mental processes" (1932, p. 107).

THE OEDIPUS COMPLEX. We must now return and pick up the theme of sexual development in early childhood. Associated with the child's sexual explorations and realization of the pleasurable sensations arising from penis or clitoris, a prelude to adult sexuality, comes a special relationship with the mother and father. The boy's tender feelings for his mother become transformed into a desire to possess her sexually, in the literal sense of intercourse, and he becomes jealous of his father whom he views as a hostile rival. He fears his father may remove his genital organs because of his incestuous wishes toward his mother—castration anxiety. At the same time he has hostile fantasies about killing his father or in some other way removing him so the son can have the mother all to himself. The girl child follows a somewhat similar pattern. It will be recalled that upon discovering she did not have a penis, the girl privately blamed her mother and developed hostile feelings toward her. At the same time her affectionate feelings toward her father increase and turn into a desire to have his penis, simultaneous with fear of her rival, the mother, and with fantasies of somehow removing the mother so she can take the mother's place in sexual intercourse. This whole process is a matter of private wish and fantasy, and the parents may be quite unaware of it. However, the child of four or five still confuses thought with deed and may be distressed equally by either.

Freud suggested this phenomenon was universal and proposed two possible antecedents. First, the child may actually have observed the parents during intercourse (children are notorious "peeping toms"), and there may be positive rivalry and jealousy between the child and the parent of the same sex. In addition, Freud speculated that some of these incestuous thoughts may have been inherited from primitive man, and pointed as evidence to the frequency of ancient myths and legends about rivalry between father and son for sexual possession of the mother.

Of course, the incestuous relationship is seldom possible, and the child seeks to resolve the situation. This is accomplished either by repressing the wishes and thoughts (this concept will be discussed later) or by completely destroying them, and by identifying with the same sex parent. By *identification,* Freud seemed to mean simply that the child tries to be like the parent, believe what he believes, like what he likes, and do what he does. He comes to view the parent as what he would like to be (1920, p. 106). The whole experience is likely to be somewhat less severe for the girl than for the boy.

SELF-EVALUATIVE THOUGHTS. During this same period of childhood, a special and very important group of thought responses is acquired. Being thoughts, they are a part of the learned constellation, the ego. However, because they play a very powerful role in behavior, Freud gave them the special title of *superego* (1923). The idea originated several years before its final formulation, when it was referred to as the *ego-ideal* (1914; 1920). The learning of these "self-regarding attitudes" depends on "love," and they are different in normal persons and neurotics (1914, p. 98).

Many of Freud's patients revealed excessive self-criticism and guilt, and Freud puzzled over the significance. He finally concluded that each person acquired two types of self-evaluative thoughts (1923, pp. 76–77), which served to monitor or criticize the rest of his behavior. The first type includes both what one "ought to be" (conscious ideals in a positive sense) and what one "would like to be" (ego-ideal). The second group represents "what one must not be," or one's "conscience." In very simple terms, there are thoughts that evaluate some behaviors as good and thoughts that evaluate other behaviors as bad (1923, p. 44).

How are they learned? From the parents primarily. At first Freud said the father, but later noted that it might be more accurate to say parents. By trying to become like the parents, by identifying with them, the child accepts their values. As Freud put it, the identification is more with the parents' "superego" than with their "ego," with their habits of evaluation rather than with what they do. Freud believed that these evaluative responses represented the higher moral and spiritual side of human nature and emphasized that they are learned. It is this identification with the parents that resolves the oedipal problem. By bringing the rival "inside" so to speak, and making it part of oneself, the obstacle in relationships with the parents is removed. However, the more intense the longings and fantasies associated with the ambivalent loving and hating responses toward the parents, the more severe will be the critical thoughts. The innate aggressive energy (instinct) will manifest itself in severe self-evaluations, if it is not adequately discharged through motoric behavior. Guilt and shame are the consequence of self-derogatory thoughts. Although the parents are the primary teachers of these evaluative thoughts, other authority figures may teach additional ones, but "the power of their injunctions and prohibitions remains invested in the ego-ideal" (1923, p. 49). The beginning of the development of self-evaluative thoughts (superego) brings to a close the early childhood period.

Late Childhood

About the age of six, Freud believed that the child had acquired habitual responses for controlling and reducing psychological energies and for relating with persons and objects in the environment. Although more complicated behaviors later developed, he believed they were extensions of this basic pattern, which remained relatively stable throughout the rest of life. This period is characterized by a lessening of sexual interest and energy, and for that reason was called the *latency period*. Freud had little to say about it.

Adolescence

With the onset of puberty, the intensity of the biological sex energy drastically increases again. With it comes a reactivation of the responses and thoughts about sexual stimulation acquired during the first six years. If the original sexual development proceeded smoothly through the earlier stages, and if the sexual desire for the opposite sex parent was adequately resolved, the adolescent acquired the rudiments of responses necessary for adult sexual relationships. During adolescence these response patterns are practiced and are more fully and adequately developed.

Adulthood

If all has gone well, by the time the individual reaches adulthood effective patterns of behavior have developed for alleviating psychological energies and for relating with persons and objects in the environment. In addition, a set of values, or more accurately a set of self-evaluative thoughts, will have been acquired, which serve to select the behaviors to be performed and those to be avoided. Responses, primarily thoughts, have been acquired to control and direct the psychological energies so as to gain adequate release without eliciting undesirable situational consequences, and in accord with the learned values. In Freud's terms, the ego serves three harsh masters and is continually "menaced by three serious dangers: from the external world, from the libido of the id, and from the severity of the superego" (1923, p. 82). He stated that a judgment of whether an adult was a normal, well-adjusted individual had to be based on the "practical result," that is, on how far the adult was capable of a sufficient degree of capacity for enjoyment and achievement in his life activities (1915, p. 398). One requirement to achieve this result is to free oneself from one's parents, psychologically not physically (1915, p. 295).

What kinds of response patterns does the individual develop to accomplish this difficult task? Freud had relatively little to say about effective habitual behaviors that developed without any difficulty. Most of the response mechanisms he discussed emerged as a means of blocking or diverting psychological energies from "natural" or reflex discharge, to avoid the occurrence of unhappy consequences in the environment and of self-criticism. For this reason they are frequently called defense mechanisms (1925). At times, one gets the impression from Freud's writings that no adult behavior is biologically "natural" and that it is all the defensive consequence of struggles with psychological energies. If this characterization is true, life must be considered one constant defensive battle, and the creative activities of man are simply by-products, like the trenches and empty cartridges after a real battle. Certainly, he considered defenses to be response mechanisms typical of normal people as well as neurotics and psychotics. In any event, several such mechanisms will be discussed to exemplify the idea.

REPRESSION AND RESISTANCE. This is one of Freud's earliest ideas and is closely related to his notion of unconscious process. The reader will recall Freud postulated unconscious processes after observing that his patients were frequently unable to recall certain ideas or memories without great effort in concentrating "enough attention" on them to bring them into awareness. He assumed there must be some energy or force keeping them from awareness; this he called resistance, and the whole sequence of psychological energy → unconscious thought → force preventing awareness, he called repression. How does this come about? At first Freud simply described it and was unable to explain how it happened. He noticed that painful affect was associated with the process but assumed it was a *consequence* of repression and represented transformed psychological energy. When he reformulated his theory of anxiety, he decided that anxiety was the *cause* of repression (1925). He argued that one of the ways in which people terminated their anxiety was to stay out of the situations that elicited it. However, when the event eliciting anxiety is another of one's own responses, namely, psychological energies and associated ideas, the mechanism of physical avoidance cannot be used. Even so, the mechanism of anxiety avoidance is considered reflexive in nature, and if motoric flight is not possible, some other kind of avoidance response must be used. But what kind? To our knowledge, Freud did not spell this out, but his statements that attention is the special response by which one becomes aware of events, and that one must concentrate "enough attention" to bring repressed events to awareness, clearly implies that inattention may be the indicated avoidance.

It seems reasonable to summarize the process of repression as follows: situational events and intense levels of psychological energy elicit intense anxiety—*trauma*. The tension-reduction principle (pleasure principle) leads the person to get away from the antecedent situational events and to disregard the thoughts and sensations which are also antecedents in order to terminate the anxiety. Repression separates the connection between thought and affect, and the latter will not recur until some associated perception or thought enters awareness. Thus, anxiety is the "force" (resistance) which opposes the psychological energy, and active inattention to the events antecedent to anxiety is the terminal avoidance response. The aim of repression is to suppress the development of affect (1915, p. 178).

The situation just mentioned represents the original learning of repression. Notice that it is not the psychological energies that are kept from awareness but the thoughts and sensations associated with them. The energies continue, and thus the repression must be maintained. This is accomplished through signal anxiety which was discussed earlier, and through anticipation of the anxiety-producing conditions. The learned repression sequence looks like this:

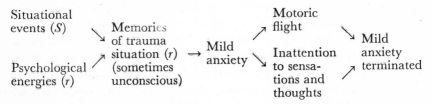

The thoughts and motoric responses have dropped out of the sequence. Thus, the individual has no opportunity to learn whether he can deal adequately later with the antecedents or whether he is still helpless before them, and new learning cannot take place. What is repressed remains unaltered with the passage of time (1932, p. 104).

DENIAL. Another set of responses which can be employed is to think and make statements to oneself to the effect that it never really happened in the first place. It is not clear how this is supposed to work, but it appears to be response substitution. The individual substitutes denying thoughts and statements for the memories and thoughts directly associated with the events leading up to anxiety.

In a grade school play, for example, a girl omitted some of her lines and made a speech that was supposed to occur somewhat later in the play. The other actors followed her cue, and a section of the play was omitted. Later, the teacher pointed out the omission, but the girl flatly and vehemently denied it even though all the other children agreed with the teacher. Apparently, thinking and making statements to the effect that she had made a mistake would have upset her, but by substituting their opposite, she avoided the occurrence of negative affect. She preferred the disapproval of her peers to the admission to herself of error. This kind of magical thinking is not unusual in early childhood; if you pretend it isn't there it will go away.

REACTION FORMATION. In this case, the responses substituted are exactly the opposite of those that are directly related to the precipitating tension and its associated affect. For example, a mother who did not wish to have another child may resent the child. However, since hating one's own child is tabooed, learned self-critical thoughts lead to guilt. To terminate the guilt, the mother performs loving acts and makes loving statements, thus preventing the occurrence of hateful thoughts and acts. In a sense, this too is a pretending it is not so. Substitute responses may be differentiated from genuine ones because they are excessive, extreme, and showy. For example, teenage girls and boys who are strongly attracted to a member of the opposite sex will often tell everybody they really hate the person.

PROJECTION. This is another form of denial and response substitution. Freud argued that it is much easier for an individual to deal with negative affect when it is elicited by situational events rather than by his own responses. Thus, by denying the existence of responses in himself and attributing them to situational events, the individual can control his own affective responses. He substitutes one set of thoughts for another. Instead of thinking "I have been bad and should punish myself," a person may think "Other people are trying to persecute me"; or instead of thinking "I hate him," he may think "he hates me." One avoids anxiety by "throwing the rascals out," so to speak.

RATIONALIZATION. Very simply, this type of response substitution involves making up thoughts and statements to explain one's actions. As a defense mechanism, it implies that the explanation is not accurate, but rather one that will not lead to negative affect. Of course, people frequently try to explain why they do things, but not always with the intent to avoid anxiety within themselves or to deceive others.

UNDOING. Freud frequently found this mechanism in compulsion neuroses. An individual may follow one response with another either to try to "blow away" the consequences of some event or to dismiss the event itself. Saying "I'm sorry" after performing an undesirable act is a common manifestation of this mechanism. In compulsive rituals, however, motor activities frequently have this as their purpose. Undoing has a magical quality about it, in the sense that one symbolic act is expected to cancel out another with opposite significance. It is as if to say, "That was not my intent."

ISOLATION. At times the individual somehow prevents a troublesome response, usually a thought, from developing associative connections with other responses, thereby keeping it from disrupting these other response sequences. For example, recurrent thoughts of murdering someone may occur but not be associated with self-derogation or the negative affect one would normally expect.

COMPROMISE. It will be recalled that the psychological energy eliciting the responses which are blocked is not itself destroyed but persists in producing responses aimed at tension reduction. Frequently, some other response occurs which provides for at least partial tension reduction, without eliciting anxiety. A compromise has been reached. The anxiety-producing responses do not occur, but the psychological tension achieves some reduction through another response. Freud proposed that hysterical symptoms such as motor paralysis were typically such compromise responses.

DISPLACEMENT AND SUBLIMATION. These are particular types of compromises. In *displacement,* the response is emitted toward some object other than the one toward which it would be most appropriately directed. An example would be the wife who, afraid to express her anger at her husband, "takes it out on the children." In *sublimation,* a psychological tension such as sex, which would most appropriately be reduced by sexual intercourse but which leads to anxiety when given a sexual expression, may be reduced partially through substitute responses such as intellectual or artistic activities which are constructive and socially approved. It was through this mechanism that Freud believed man to be able to build his complicated social structure and fill it with all kinds of magnificent creations at the expense of curbing and redirecting his sexual and aggressive "instincts."

FIXATION AND REGRESSION. At various stages of behavior development different response patterns occur. Thus, the infant's patterns of responding become a part of more involved childhood patterns, and so on. Sometimes behaviors prominent and effective at a particular developmental stage continue to predominate, rather than give way to progressively more elaborate and effective behaviors as one matures and learns. Freud called this *fixation*, and proposed that it occurred when excessive anxiety was associated with the transition from one developmental stage to another. The individual avoids the occurrence of anxiety by continuing the old familiar responses, even though they are no longer as effective in the new developmental stage, rather than by trying to learn new responses. A child may continue its dependent relationship with its parents into adulthood to avoid the anxiety that might result from forming new adult relationships. On the other hand, the child may develop normally, but at some later point in his life experience extensive anxiety. When this occurs, the individual may discontinue the behaviors appropriate to adult life and revert to those characteristic of an earlier stage. Freud called this *regression*. It appears to be another type of response substitution.

There appear to be several general attributes of defense mechanisms. They all develop to terminate or avoid anxiety. The simplest modification is to avoid or disregard the crucial antecedents to anxiety, such as repression and flight. Another way is to change the object toward which the anxiety-eliciting sequence is directed through projection and displacement. A third and most frequent way, apparently, is to substitute some other set of responses for those that lead to anxiety. The most typical substitution seems to be to replace one set of thoughts with another, such as denial or rationalization, sometimes in combination with the substitution of motoric and other responses as well— that is to say, reaction formation, compromise, and sublimation. A fourth way is to prevent the troublesome thoughts from becoming associated with other thoughts, affective responses, or motoric activity through isolation. And finally, there is the suggestion that when new response sequences are ineffective, the individual tends to fall back on responses learned and used effectively in earlier developmental stages. It is consistent with Freud's emphasis on conscious, logical thought as the key to the control of one's behavior that most defense mechanisms should involve some modification or substitution of thoughts as a means of avoiding or terminating anxious responses.

THE DEVELOPMENT OF BEHAVIOR DISORDER

Freud developed two different theories of pathology. The first might be called the trauma theory and the second the conflict theory. In fact, however, the second theory did not replace the first but encompassed it. Freud did not reject the trauma theory as false, but rather as over-simplified. Trained in the natural sciences, Freud was a confirmed empiricist. He was also a careful, keen observer, and some of his work is a delight to read because of his careful reporting of observations and the generalizations derived from them. It is precisely because of this emphasis on careful observation that he reformulated his propositions several times, trying to find better ways to account for their inter-relationships. The data were not in error. The crucial responses *did occur* in his patients. One need not question his statements that patients told him of childhood seductions and sexual longings for parents. Rather his reformulations were attempts to explain the data better.

When Freud's writing is read in historical sequence, his theoretical reformulations seem partly related to the types of disorders he was trying to understand at the time. To put it differently, observations of patients with new kinds of symptoms required him to try to fit those observations into his theoretical framework. When he found he could not make them fit, he changed his theories rather than ignore the data. It is perhaps not so surprising to us today that at the time he was treating hysterical disorders he should formulate his trauma theory and emphasize sexual desires as an important factor in disorder. Similarly, as he began to deal with obsessive-compulsive behaviors, he struggled to develop an adequate explanation of the role of anxiety in behavior disorder. Thus, his observations, and therefore his theories, may well have been based on biased sampling. Since he was known to consider sexuality a normal and important part of life, it is probable that neurotics willing or wishing to talk about their sexual concerns would tend to choose him as their physician rather than some other. He once stated that patients in his private practice were "from an educated and well read social class" (1895). In addition, his own theoretical beliefs, and therefore his behavior in therapy interviews, undoubtedly influenced what his patients told him. The only time he acknowledged this latter possibility, to our knowledge, was in discussing his distressing discovery that patient memories of childhood seduction were usually fantasies (1925, p. 34). Even though there may have been serious deficiencies in his data, he always tried to be a "data man" in his theorizing.

Central Themes

Two classes of response provide the continuity in development from one formulation about pathology to another.

NEGATIVE AFFECT. From the very beginning, Freud observed that negative affect ("painful affect") seemed to play a central role in behavior disorder. Fear, anxiety, shame, and psychic pain were specified (1895, p. 3). Later he included hate or aggression; the currently popular terms among psychologists are anger, hostility, and guilt (1919). Throughout his formulations, anxiety (the "affect of fright") played the most crucial role. Fear is simply anxiety directed toward an external event of which the person is aware. At first, anxiety was interpreted as a manifestation of behavior disorder, but in his later reformulations he considered it to be the primary antecedent, that is, the chief cause.

THOUGHTS. In his early formulations Freud emphasized the importance of memories. When he realized, however, that many of the thoughts patients reported to him as memories were really fabrications which had little to do with real events, he began emphasizing a group of thoughts he called *fantasies* and *wishes*. Still later, when he became impressed with hate, guilt, and the self-punishing aspects of behavior, he emphasized still a third group, the self-evaluative responses (superego). Thus, thoughts always were significant in his explanation of behavior pathology, but the kinds of thoughts emphasized were not always the same. He never discarded any of these categories of thought as unimportant. He only changed his emphasis on them and his explanations of the roles they played in disorder.

SYMPTOM AND DISEASE. Freud was always quite clear about the differences between symptoms and their antecedents, or causes, as one might expect of a medically trained person. Although his earliest criterion of cure was symptom removal, his theories always emphasized subjectively observable responses (r) as the significant antecedent to symptom formation. Objectively observable responses (R) and situational events (S) played an important role in the original learning situation from which disordered behavior developed, but the disorder itself, after the learning has taken place, was entirely a function of subjectively observable responses (r). His theory of the functioning of pathological behavior is an r–r theory, and the most significant interrelationships are those among psychological energies, affective responses, and thoughts. In general, he proposed that disorders differed in their symptomatology but not in the basic process. In addition, he considered the disease to be constantly developing, rather than a static entity.

THE TRAUMA THEORY

This formulation was apparently worked out by Breuer and Freud jointly (1895). It is based upon an "investigation and treatment of hysterical phenomena." The discoveries were first made in the case of Anna O., treated by Breuer.

Learning of the Disorder

What are the conditions under which the disorder develops? Neurotic illness results from an incapacity to deal with an overpowering affective response. The individual, in a particular situation, experiences intense anxiety. If he makes extensive motoric responses (R) to dissipate, discharge, or terminate the anxiety responses, such as crying, talking about it, or revengeful acts, no future difficulties will develop (*abreaction*). On future occasions, when memories (thoughts) of that occasion and the responses made at the time recur, they will not elicit the same intense negative affect. The overt responses made at the time apparently serve to keep the affective response situation-specific and prevent it from becoming associated with the memories or thoughts of the situation. On the other hand, if, for some reason such as the social circumstances or his own state—for example, the twilight state of daydreaming—the person is unable to "act out" the negative affect, it will become associated with the thoughts and memories of the situation. On future occasions recall of the events will elicit the intense affective state. Since the affect cannot be terminated by "doing something about it," it must be terminated in some other way. This is accomplished by blocking it out of awareness. At that time, Breuer and Freud pointed to this phenomenon, but were unable to explain it.

Other response events occurring in awareness (1895, p. 126) simultaneously with the intense negative affect—muscle cramps, sensations such as smells, or visual difficulties—will also become associated with the memories, thoughts, and negative affective responses. This way of accounting for the formation of such interrelationships between responses is similar to classical conditioning circumstances based on simple contiguity. Freud suggested that there may be an hereditary predisposition toward learning such disorders. It is most likely to occur in childhood.

The intensity of the affect determines the intensity of the disorder. It is important to note that some of the responses occurring at the time of the intense anxiety may not have been elicited by the antecedent events, but were *accidentally* occurring at the time. They, too, may be blocked from awareness (dissociated) but become part of the pattern. The crucial condition is the occurrence of intense negative affect without effective motor responses to terminate them.

Responses associated with strong affect in one situation may also become associated with events in another situation that immediately follows. Freud cited the example of a young woman who served as the "protectress" of the children of her widowed uncle, a brutal man, very obnoxious with his children, and openly sexually involved with the servant girls. On occasion, her anger, her disgust, and perhaps her fear about his behavior, which she could not express openly, produced a choking sensation in her throat. Immediately following such scenes she sometimes had secret singing lessons during which the choking sensations continued and disrupted her singing. In later years, it continued to disrupt her singing, even though she no longer lived with the uncle's family (1895, pp. 122–123). Freud seems to have been describing what psychologists now call *stimulus generalization*. One especially important possibility in this regard is that on future occasions new thoughts may elicit the memories, which in turn elicit the negative affect. The new thoughts may then become associated with the previously learned pattern. Then, too, *any* occurrence of anxiety, no matter what elicited it, may come to elicit a symptom learned with the trauma.

The circumstances just cited provide the basis for the "growth of the disease." More and more situational and response events may become related to the occurrence of the negative affect. At first, Freud did not specify particular kinds of situations as being the source of trauma, for instance, sexual situations. This conclusion developed later because so many of his patients spoke of childhood sexual traumas.

The Learned Disorder

Occasionally, one very severe experience is sufficient to accomplish the learning, but more often a series of "partial traumas" occur which accumulate to give the same effect. Because a series of "learning trials" is involved, a whole set of memories may function as antecedents to the symptoms; that is, they may be overdetermined. After the learning has taken place, the occurrence of situational events which induce one response in the associated pattern, usually memories, will tend to arouse the other responses as well, although the person will typically not be aware of the connections. Thus, the responses seem inexplicable to them or are interpreted as the consequence of unrelated events. These responses, peculiarly out of context in the circumstances in which they occur, are characterized as symptoms. Freud thought they appeared because a quantity of affective energy was still waiting to be discharged. These learned patterns are particularly hard to change because: (1) they are avoidance responses functioning to prevent the occurrence of negative affect—the quantity of energy has not been discharged—and therefore the sequence of responses which must be modified do not occur so they can be modified; and (2) the memories of the frightening events cannot be thought about—they are prevented from associative elaboration—and through conscious thought be modified. The individual will be unable to recall the traumatic experience, an observation which led to the concepts of repression and resistance, and the memory traces remain undisturbed, as attested to by the vividness of the memories when attention does become directed to them.

Symptoms—that is, responses learned in association with the intense negative affect—may be conveniently classed as one of three types. Sometimes they are responses elicited in the original learning situation by situational events unrelated to those which produced the negative affect (accidental coincidences). Sometimes they were occurring in the original learning situation without any connection with that situation, such as a symptom of an actual physical illness (another type of accidental coincidence). And finally, they may be responses (such as nausea) that occurred in the original learning situation as a direct consequence of the events that produced the intense negative affect.

Thus, symptoms which are strongly inappropriate to present circumstances probably "made sense" in the original learning situation.

SOME EXAMPLES. The case of Anna O. (1895) provides several examples of coincidentally learned symptoms. She had acquired paralyses and contractures in the right arm and anesthesia, particularly in the elbow region. One night she was nursing her father and awoke with great anxiety about her very feverish patient. She sat near the sickbed holding her *right arm* over the back of the chair. She dozed, saw a black snake come out of the wall toward the patient as if to bite him, and wanted to drive it away, but felt paralyzed. "The right arm, which was hanging over the back of the chair, was 'asleep' and was anesthetic and paralyzed." She probably tried to defend with her paralyzed arm, "and thereby established the association of an anesthesia and paralysis with the snake hallucination." Her symptom of being able to speak and understand only English, even though German and French were more familiar to her, was originally an instrumental response. When the hallucination disappeared, she tried to pray, but was so frightened she could not talk until she remembered an English nursery rhyme, "and only in this language could she continue to think and pray" (1895, p. 26). Her disturbed vision (*convergent strabismus*) was similarly learned by trying to read her watch with tears in her eyes while severely fatigued and distressed (1895, pp. 26–27).

In a second example, Freud's case of Lucie R., the patient had lost all perception of smell, but was persistently bothered by the hallucinated odor of burned pastry (1895, p. 76). In this instance, Freud found that the odor was actually present on an occasion when she was experiencing intense distress about a decision she had made to return to her mother and leave the children she loved and had been caring for.

THE CONFLICT THEORY

In trying to account for the difficulties patients had in reporting memories of traumatic situations, Freud proposed they were blocked from consciousness. The question then became, what blocked them out? Since he assumed there was a quantity of energy associated with the traumatic memories (cathexis), he concluded there must be some other quantity of energy to oppose them and keep them out of consciousness (countercathexis). Thus, his theory of repression and resistance was really a kind of conflict theory—two response processes opposing one another. However, it was not until he recognized that many of his patient's memories were only fantasies or wishes that he made a definite and marked reformulation of his theory of pathology. If the trauma was "psychic" rather than "real," some other explanation was required. Thus, he shifted from a theory that leaned heavily on situational events to one that gave greater emphasis to subjectively observable responses (r).

Freud observed the phenomenon of conflict very early in his work. For example, in discussing the case of Miss Elizabeth von R., he spoke of "an erotic idea which came into conflict with all her moral conceptions" (1895, p. 118). The concept of conflict was used more extensively in his discussion of dreams (1900), and from that point on it progressively became the dominant theme in his theory of behavior disorder. It reached perhaps its fullest expression in his reformulation of his theory of anxiety (1925–1926) and in his division of subjective responses into three major classes (1923). Freud did not specifically refer to his position as a conflict theory, and never presented an integrated theory of behavior pathology in one publication. Four major publications, combined, probably represented his most complete and final position. These were his papers on metapsychology (1916), his paper relating the notions of death instinct and repetition-compulsion to the pleasure and reality principles (1919), his final theory of anxiety (1925), and his paper developing his classification of subjective responses into biological, learned, and self-evaluative thoughts, along with a revised statement of his theory of conscious-unconscious phenomena (1923). Jones' comment (1957, Vol. III, p. 266) that Freud was a "stubborn dualist" who struggled throughout his life to understand the two opposing forces in the mind supports the notion of a fundamental conflict. Freud himself stated that the problem of behavior was to reconcile the contradictory influences of psychological energies and responses (id), self-evaluative thoughts (superego), and conscious, thoughtful control of behavior in accord with situational influences (ego). In addition, he characterized all symptoms of behavior disorder as compromise responses representing conflicting "impulses" or "wishes." We shall summarize the learning sequence and then represent the functioning of the disorders after they are learned, although they never became completely stable. Freud believed a disorder was never learned in the sense of being a static entity. He considered it a constantly developing constellation of behaviors (1915, p. 386).

The Learning of Disordered Behavior

The learning fundamental to behavior disorder occurs in infancy and early childhood—ages one to six—and all later learnings are simply further elaborations. This assumption seems to have grown out of Freud's theories about childhood sexuality (1925, p. 55). If basic and *severe* or *intense* conflicts developed during this early learning, progressive behavior disorder was likely to occur (p. 154). One may crudely characterize these conflicts as between: (1) natural or reflex reduction of psychological tension (primary process—id) and conscious, thoughtfully selected behavior to achieve tension reduction without painful situational consequences (secondary process—ego); (2) thoughts about what one wants to do (wishes—id and ego) and what one should not do (super-ego); or (3) the unrestrained satisfaction of psychological tensions (id-primary process) and a negative and punishing environmental reaction to such unrestrained activity (reality). There are two attributes common to all three conflicts. One arm of each represents the active seeking of some kind of positive satisfaction, such as tension reduction or wish fulfillment. Here the emphasis is on active responding to situational events associated with the occurrence of or anticipation of pleasurable or positive consequences; one might call these *approach behaviors*. The other arm of each conflict represents either an attempt to avoid negative consequences through thoughtful control, or the actual occurrence of negative consequences, namely, negative self-evaluation, or a painful environmental reaction. The emphasis here is on not making certain responses because they led to negative consequences; one might call these *avoidance behaviors*.

Thus, the common core of all behavior pathology would appear to be conflicts between approach and avoidance. The *kinds* of responses involved in the conflict and the attempts to resolve it may vary, however. Any grouping of behavior disorders such as hysteria, anxiety neurosis, obsessive-compulsive neurosis, or schizophrenia would simply represent a subclassification of the kinds of responses involved in the conflict and in the attempts at resolution. As Freud would put it, the disease process is the same, but it may be manifested in different symptoms (1900, p. 573).

To understand behavior disorder, then, one must ask what responses are in conflict and what responses are being used to attempt to resolve the conflict. But why is it that some conflicts lead to behavior disorder and others do not? It is not because of the kinds of responses involved, but because of their intensity. *Behavior disorder develops out of intense approach-avoidance conflicts* (1900, p. 583; 1915e, p. 326; 1925b, p. 159). In neuroses there are many such conflicts, not just one. "Neuroses (unlike infectious diseases, for instance) have no specific determinants"; there is no single pathogenic factor (1938, p. 81).

THE LEARNING OF APPROACH-AVOIDANCE CONFLICTS. It will be recalled that in the sequence of normal development, psychological energies (instinctual drives) lead to motor responses which reduce the tension. At first this motor activity is reflexive and not always effective. The development of attending responses, the consequent awareness of images of the external world, and the development of symbolic thought all lead to co-ordinated patterns of motor responses which are more effective in producing prompt tension reduction. This represents what we have referred to as approach responses, that is, the individual approaches situational events to produce desired results.

Sometimes the sequence just described may involve situational events that elicit anxiety. The reader will recall that anxiety is an innate response occurring automatically under circumstances in which: (1) the person is overwhelmed with intense stimulation; (2) the situational consequences prevent tension reduction, and the intensity of the tension accumulates to an unbearable degree; or (3) the situational events resulting from the motor responses lead to pain (1932, p. 120). Thus, certain kinds of situational events function recurrently as antecedents to anxiety. The most important part of this kind of learning occurs in early childhood. Then the conditions of biological helplessness and dependence on the love and care of the parents to reduce his tensions and to gain protection from painful situational events make it impossible for the child to control and avoid anxiety elicitors. Infants and small children are more susceptible to emotional traumas (1925b, p. 153).

Responses occurring simultaneously with the intense anxiety may become antecedents to that anxiety, independent of the situational events. Thoughts are the most important such responses—for example, memories of the frightening situations. In addition, self-evaluative thoughts may become learned anxiety elicitors. Because of his dependence on parents for satisfaction and protection, the small child is exposed to the expectations and prohibitions of his parents at the same time that other situational events provoke anxiety—for instance, spanking. Because the small child requires the parents' attention for his own self-preservation and satisfaction, he begins saying some of these prohibitions and expectations to himself as a means of avoiding behaviors that lead to painful situations. Thus, self-evaluative thoughts are learned and may serve to produce anxiety. The kinds of "self-regarding" responses learned depend on "love" and differ in neurotics and normals (1914, p. 98). Freud believed the most important self-evaluative thoughts were learned in early childhood and functioned outside adult awareness; for example, much of the super-ego is unconscious. Although some evaluative thoughts may be learned in noninterpersonal situations ("it's bad to do that because I injured myself"), the crucial ones, moral and ethical judgments, are learned from other people, particularly the parents. Freud did propose that some evaluative thoughts were inherited, such as incest taboos.

Avoidance is the automatic reaction to anxiety. Situational events can usually be physically avoided. Where they cannot be avoided, or where responses are the events leading to anxiety, avoidance can occur only by actively disregarding (repressing) the situational and response events that are arousing the anxiety. Thus, the anxiety followed by avoidance of situational events which precipitate the anxiety, or their response representatives, signifies the development of the avoidance portion of the conflict.

THE LEARNED CONFLICT. We may now summarize the basic scheme of the learned approach-avoidance conflicts as follows. On the one hand, psychological energy accumulates and stimulates behavior aimed at reducing it. As this behavior occurs, it elicits memories and self-evaluative thoughts which have become learned elicitors of anxiety, of which some representative enters awareness. Signal anxiety occurs and is followed by ignoring responses, which block the antecedent events from awareness and terminate the whole sequence before energy reduction is achieved and before the major antecedents to extreme anxiety occur.

This avoidance, however, does not solve the problem, because the psychological energy continues to increase in intensity. Since the avoidance is seldom successful in "bottling up" the accumulated energy completely, some of it is diverted into other responses which appear as symptoms. These symptoms are always compromises expressing both the unconscious manifestations of the psychological energy (wish) and the negative evaluation of it (repressing idea). It should be noted that the learned conflict functions on a direct response-response basis. No situational events are necessary to set it off.

CONTENT OF THE CONFLICT. What kinds of psychological energies and what kinds of learned thoughts compose the conflict? Freud's answer was conclusive: the content is sexual! He considered this discovery one of his most astonishing and important contributions. At various times he characterized the approach side of the conflict as an immense sexual desire (1900, p. 538), infantile sexual wishes (1900, p. 538), sexual drive (1915e, p. 264), incestuous sexual wishful fantasies (1925a, p. 34) and sexual instinct (1915e, p. 360). The avoidance side of the conflict he characterized as sexual prohibitions (1900, p. 538), exaggerated sexual rejection (1900, p. 574); no sexual object available (1915e, p. 264); instinctual prohibitions; self-preservative instincts (1915e, p. 360) and opposing force (1925a, p. 34).

It now becomes apparent why Freud considered his concept of the Oedipal complex to be so crucial. This is the "nucleus" of neurosis (1925, p. 155). It will be recalled that the Oedipal complex represents a wish for or fantasy of sexual relationships with the opposite sex parent, on the one hand, and anxiety and guilt resulting from learned or inherited tabooing thoughts on the other. Thus, the fundamental conflict in all neurosis is between psychological sexual energy expressed through wishes for and thoughts about sexual relationships with the parent, and the affective energy of fear and guilt resulting from critical thoughts, which declare such a relationship taboo.

This conflict develops between the ages of three to six. Man's first choice of a sexual object is always incestual (1915e, p. 284). In the normal individual the quantity of energy involved in the conflict is not great and, therefore, does not lead to repression. The conflict is resolved by the child's adopting the masculine role of the father or the feminine role of the mother in all other ways and in seeking a different sexual object with the onset of puberty. For the person who later develops a severe neurosis or psychosis, however, excessive energy is involved; the sexual desire is intense, and so is the negative affect produced by excessively severe self-evaluative thoughts. Accidental early traumatic experiences such as childhood seduction probably contribute to the intensity of the conflict, thus predisposing people toward behavior disorder.

Similarly, Freud suggested there were probably hereditary predispositions which made individuals vulnerable. Because the affect is intense, it leads to avoidance rather than resolution of the conflict. Since the avoidance takes the form of active inattention, that is, repression, the conflict is never subjected to conscious modification in later years. During adolescence or adulthood, psychological sexuality reappears with renewed intensity. If the individual then encounters traumatic adult experiences which severely increase the intensity of the previously learned conflict, the repression breaks down, the forbidden sexual urges begin to provoke consummative responses, and symptom formation occurs as an attempted compromise between the arms of the conflict. This process may be repeated many times with new symptom formations each time.

When Freud introduced his notion of an aggressive instinct as basic as the sexual drive, the possibility became apparent that the content of the conflict could be between the aggressive drive on the one hand and the taboos against it on the other. However, he did not develop this possibility extensively. Instead he proposed that aggressive energy was blocked from overt expression through learning and manifested itself through punitive and derogatory self-evaluative thoughts (superego). Thus, the excessively critical self-evaluations found in people with severe neurosis resulted from the blocking of normal overt expression of the aggression. He then explained that anxiety was the consequence of potential aggression expressed through the self-evaluative thoughts.

An individual may have an extended series of traumatic experiences, which bring other wishes and other negative taboos into association with this basic conflict formation. This is apparently why Freud said there was no specific determinant of neuroses. Thus, the disorder may grow, with more and more behavior occurring outside the control of awareness, additional symptoms developing as compromises, and more situations and responses becoming provocations of anxiety and therefore being avoided. Thus, behavior becomes impoverished as the number and kinds of avoided situations increase. The amount of behavior occurring which seems inappropriate, stupid, or useless, and for which the individual cannot account, will also progressively increase. These are the general symptoms of disorder. Anything that increases the intensity of the psychological energy may produce new symptoms to accommodate the increase. These later experiences, however, are traumatic for the neurotic precisely because of the intense, repressed sexual conflict. There can be no neurosis where the sex life is normal (1915, p. 335). This helps account for the fact that "neurotics break down at the same difficulties that are successfully overcome by normal people" (1925, pp. 55–56).

CHARACTERISTICS OF SYMPTOMS. Freud suggested that neurosis is the result of conflict between the ego and id *(r-r* conflict), and psychosis the result of an analogous conflict between the ego and situational events. The neurotic is incapable of enjoyment or achievement. There is no enjoyment because responses that will effectively reduce sexual tension without guilt have not been learned. Achievement is restricted because so much behavior is tied up in avoidance responses (repression) that there is little room for positive accomplishment. Perhaps the most important characteristic of symptoms is that they are compromise formations; each symptom satisfies a part of both the approach and avoidance arms of the conflict it manifests (1900, p. 511). As such they never fully satisfy either side of the conflict, thus leaving the individual vulnerable to future difficulty.

A careful examination of a symptom should enable one to infer the nature of the conflict behind it. For example, a woman is deathly afraid to go out alone at night but is not afraid if there is a man with her. One might infer this symptom represented her sexual desires, on the one hand, and her fear of their expression, on the other. Every symptom has a purpose or function. No symptom is accidental. Actually symptoms are responses that were a part of the individual's earlier behavior but were not considered pathological at the time, either because they were not intense or chronic or because they were a part of the typical and perhaps even appropriate behavior for that developmental stage. For example, Freud proposed that perverse sexual behavior was nothing but a magnified fragment of infantile sexual behavior. He pointed out that individuals experiencing a trauma may fall back upon responses that were developed and appropriate at an earlier stage of development (regression). Which responses develop as symptoms ("choice of neurosis") depends on what responses were available in the repertoire at the time the avoidance pattern began developing (1911, p. 24).

Why is it that symptoms are so rigidly repetitive, so hard to change? Freud gave several reasons. First, symptoms are responses whose purpose it is to control conflicting stimulation or energies. Freud proposed that there is a fundamental principle in human life to repeat an earlier experience and one of the purposes of this innate tendency is to "master" or "bind" excessive stimulation (repetition-compulsion) (1925a). Second, every symptom is "overdetermined": during the course of learning a great many different kinds of events become antecedents to the conflict which the symptom expresses. The more antecedents, the harder it is to modify (1895). Since a symptom expresses *both* sides of a conflict, it is held in force by both. Changing one side of the conflict may only exacerbate the symptom. And finally, there is his notion of *secondary gains*. Because it is a tendency of conscious, thoughtful directing of behavior (ego) to organize and synthesize events, once a symptom becomes an established response, one gets what good one can out of it, perhaps by eliciting sympathy and attention from others because of the disability.

In both psychosis and neurosis there is an "impairment of reality"; certain kinds of situational events are avoided. The two differ in symptomatology. The neurotic still makes active attempts to deal with situational events and to control his behavior according to the requirements of society, that is, the ego is still partially intact; whereas the psychotic has abandoned attempts to control certain impulses in accord with external reality and has invented a false reality or delusion all his own: the ego has abandoned reality. In addition, the various kinds of situational events avoided are more extensive for the psychotic than the neurotic. Since neurotics are still more able than psychotics to relate to their environment, therapy with them is more likely to be successful.

Freud's work was primarily with neurotic patients. Although some of his followers have tried to apply his ideas to psychotic behavior as well, Freud's last belief was that psychoanalysis was unable to modify psychotic behaviors (1938). Now we may ask how Freud proposed that these behavior disorders might be modified.

THE GOALS OF THERAPY

Who Should Choose the Goals

The analyst is the doctor, and the person being analyzed is the patient. The doctor's task is to discover the nature of the conflicts and the responses related to them and to establish conditions that will bring about a change. The patient cannot do this, because repression keeps him unaware of his troublesome ideas. Actually, the objectives of treatment are set forth in Freud's description of normal and disordered behavior. The individual is troubled; he has symptoms because there are certain crucial thoughts to which he cannot attend. As a consequence, the symptomatic response sequences cannot be brought under the conscious control of thoughtful analysis. It is the occurrence of negative affect which leads to the chronic habits of inattention. Thus, the goal of analysis is to reduce the negative affect which maintains the avoidance of the ideas (repression). When this is accomplished, the thoughts will return to awareness automatically. Overt responding in speech or motoric movement will permit a discharge of all the affect associated with the traumatic experience which had not been released because of the repression. Then the conflicting ideas, the wishes and the prohibitions can be reconciled through logical thought, and a course of action consciously selected. Conscious control of affect and motility (motor activity) are the characteristics of the well-adjusted person. The purpose of analysis is not to free the individual from the conflicts of living. This is impossible, because an individual must live in his society where his psychological impulses and the demands of the world will frequently clash. Rather, the purpose is to extend his self-awareness so that he recognizes his psychologically determined wishes, his self-evaluative thoughts, and the demands of reality, and is able to apply the power and logic of his conscious thought to the choice of an effective course of action.

Should the analyst do anything to influence such choices? Freud indicated that when the "developmental inhibition" was resolved the physician would have the opportunity "to indicate new aims for the trends that have been liberated," for the goal is not only to terminate the avoidance (repression) but also to develop new responses (1915e, p. 395). He warned, however, that the analyst should avoid prescribing "high aims" and should "take the patient's capacities rather than his own desires as guide." In effect, he said that telling the patient what to do with his new freedom—what new behaviors to substitute for the old ones—is a risky business. While in some cases it might be desirable, it is "far from being in every case advisable" (1912–1915, pp. 118–119).

The therapist, then, decides what behaviors are disordered and should be modified; his theory tells him that. The patient plays a more active role in consciously selecting new behaviors to perform once the avoidance patterns have been modified. Because of his emphasis on sex, Freud asserted that free sexual indulgence is not therapeutic. A good adjustment is not characterized by uninhibited indulgence of one's impulses but by their control and expression according to the demands of situations. The key emphasis is on the conscious control of behavior, without self-disapproval, to achieve satisfying consequences from the environment—to "strengthen the ego." "Where id was, there shall ego be. It is reclamation work, like the draining of the Zuyder Zee" (1932, pp. 111–112).

CONDITIONS FOR PRODUCING BEHAVIOR CHANGE

Since Freud's treatment techniques represented the means by which he obtained his observational data, it is not surprising to discover that changes in treatment procedure generally seemed to precede or parallel his theoretical revisions. Before presenting the treatment procedures applicable to his conflict theory, let us present a brief summary of the early methods used and the reasons for their modifications.

EARLY PROCEDURES. The first procedure was actually developed by Breuer and adopted by Freud. Problems were conceived to be the result of the recollective thoughts (memories) of a traumatic experience, along with all the intense affective responses which had occurred at the time and had remained inaccessible to the person's awareness. The aim was to bring the memory and affect to consciousness and to discharge the affect by talking about it and perhaps even performing motoric actions (abreaction and associative elaboration). The technique hit upon to elicit these hidden memories was hypnosis. It appeared that in an hypnotic or hypnoticlike state the patient could recall the troublesome memories that were unavailable to him under other conditions. However, "Recollections without affects are almost utterly useless" (1895, pp. 3–4).

There proved to be major limitations in this "cathartic" method, however. Although it was effective in removing individual symptoms, it failed to modify the antecedents, so that new symptoms sometimes appeared to replace the old. An additional technique employed was hypnotic suggestion; it was used to implant counterideas intended to control the troublesome idea—for example, "you will no longer be troubled by that." Freud rather quickly discovered that only a small proportion of his patients could be hypnotized, and he has given an amusing account of the difficulties he experienced as a consequence (1895, p. 78). In addition, the results were unstable and would disappear quickly if the patient lost confidence in the therapist.

If, however, hypnosis were to be abandoned, how could one elicit the repressed memories? Freud decided to assume that his patient could recall the memories if only the therapist could lead him to impart them. Freud instructed the patient to relax and close his eyes and assured him something would come to mind. Memories frequently did. When they did not, Freud repeated with great confidence that something would occur. If that failed to work, he said he would put his hands on the patient's head, exert pressure, and afterwards a memory or image would occur which the patient was to report. He used this "pressure" technique with the case of Elizabeth von R., and stated enthusiastically that he "won perfect confidence in my technique through this analysis" (1895, p. 109). He considered the "pressure" technique a "trick," which served to "surprise the defensive ego." When the therapist discovered the hidden memories he told the patient about them, reasoning that they should be troublesome no longer, once the patient attended to them.

The abandonment of hypnosis and the use of the pressure technique led to two major discoveries which profoundly influenced his later procedures. First, he observed there seemed to be some kind of "resistance" to the recall of troublesome memories, which had to be overcome. This presented an important problem of technique. In addition, he observed that thoughts occurred in series, and that the patient's first idea led to a lengthy sequence at the end of which he found the pathogenic idea. Armed with these two discoveries, Freud proceeded to develop his techniques of free association and interpretation. The objective of searching for specific memories proved fruitless, however, and it was subsequently abandoned. In his final technique, the emphasis was on "removing resistances" and working through the "transference neurosis."

Although Freud stated on several occasions he was preparing a General Methodology of Psycho-Analysis, he never did so. Several specific papers were written on the topic (e.g., 1912–1915, 1937), but they do not represent a systematic and detailed presentation of treatment technique. Comments about technique are scattered throughout his case histories and some of his other papers. Two factors seemed to influence his reluctance to make public statements about technique. One was that if patients read such material, it might make treatment more difficult. More important, however, he seemed to feel strongly that treatment procedures were a somewhat personal instrument and might vary somewhat from one therapist to another (1912–1915, p. 111). He emphasized that considerable clinical experience with patients was essential to proficiency in conducting psychoanalysis. He also urged experience from one's own analysis as an essential part of preparation. In fact, in his final paper on this topic, he recommended periodic reanalysis to insure that the therapist remained adequately prepared to do therapy (1938)—a "5,000-hour check-up," so to speak.

Principles by Which Behavior Change Occurs

Freud's early descriptions of symptom development suggests that symptoms are learned when occurring at the time of intense anxiety, guilt, or other negative affect, if they are *contiguous to the arousal* of certain classes of responses. In one patient, anesthesia of the right arm developed, as we have seen, because the arm had "gone to sleep" while hanging over the back of a chair and the patient became aware of this during a period of intense anxiety. The contiguity had to occur in awareness, that is, in "the focus of attention." Another patient, we noted, was distressed by the hallucinated odor of burned pastry which had originally been noticed during a period of severe guilt feelings. The events and response associations learned need not be logically or causally related; they need not be instrumental in response arousal. Frequently they were simply fortuitous associations.

Later, the crucial learning principle became one of *contiguity with response termination* (pleasure principle). The individual's behavior is impelled by psychological energies. At first the energy is reduced by reflex responses. These responses are ineffective, however, and new ones must be developed. Those learned are instrumental in reducing the psychological energy. Apparently anxiety also functions as a kind of energy, because repressions are learned which avoid or reduce anxiety. Apparently, some traumatic memories were still learned according to the first principle. Thus, all responses, even the most inconsequential, must be considered as "motivated," in the sense that they must serve to reduce energy of some kind. Symptoms reduce two conflicting energies simultaneously and are therefore doubly "motivated." Learning is not the consequence of conscious purpose. Consciousness only selects the behaviors to be tried, which will become acquired only if they "work," that is, reduce a drive.

Sensory images (primarily pictorial or visual) and thoughts, which were originally auditory images, Freud proposed to be learned by simple contiguity; they left memory traces and could be recalled to consciousness, if they had been once attended to or had entered awareness. Self-evaluative thoughts (superego), however, were apparently learned from anxiety reduction, from the resolution or repression of the oedipal conflict, although some were considered innate, namely, instinctual taboos. Considering the detailed complexity of his theories, one is not surprised to find that Freud proposed these three learning principles which are distinctly different. In this theory, different kinds of responses are learned in different ways.

Patient Behaviors That Must Occur in Therapy

WHO SHOULD BE ACCEPTED FOR TREATMENT. Freud (1905) went into some detail about criteria for accepting patients and commented on this issue occasionally in other papers. Perhaps the most important distinction he made was that psychoanalysis is effective for neurotics but not psychotics, though he hoped that some day this would not be so. Psychoanalysis requires the patient to form a relationship with the therapist in order to be able to invest objects with libido. Freud believed psychotics could not respond in this way, so that they were not accessible to the therapist. He recommended a one- or two-week trial period before agreeing to accept a patient, to give the therapist an opportunity to observe the patient and determine if symptoms of a psychotic and prepsychotic nature were occurring. He also cautioned against treating relatives, friends, and the family of friends, indicating that one would probably lose the friendship as a result. He recommended treating only those who could pay for it. He noted that taking one free patient would consume 15 to 20 per cent of the analyst's earning power, and analysts' earnings were lower than other doctors, anyhow. He did take some free patients early in his career, however. Free treatment was also said to produce feelings of guilt and obligation, which were to be avoided. The patient should have a "minimum" of intellectual capacity. If at all possible, the patient should be independent of others "in all essentials of life," to avoid the interference of relatives. Where family pressures are too strong, it is impossible to carry out treatment. On the other hand, it is best if the patient continues to live under his usual life circumstances during treatment, rather than being hospitalized. One wants the patient to learn to deal with the demands of his real life, not those of the hospital.

ESSENTIAL RESPONSE CHARACTERISTICS. The patient's suffering and his wish to be cured is the primary motive force in the analysis. It is not important that he believe or disbelieve in the efficacy of psychoanalysis; only that he be willing to make the necessary effort and observe the fundamental rule of free association. He must still be able to form some kind of interpersonal relationship with the therapist. Without this, therapy cannot be successful. He must still be able to attend to situational events and think logically about them; the ego must still be somewhat intact and in touch with reality. He must be able to observe and report on his subjective responses. It is not expected that such observations will always be accurate or complete. "He must have the courage to direct his attention to the phenomena of his illness" (1912–1915, p. 152).

Conditions and Techniques for Eliciting Responses

PATIENT. The patient must follow the "fundamental rule" of free association. His task is to observe his subjective responses—thoughts, memories, affect—and report them accurately to the therapist. No screening of what is reported, no discarding of observations as unimportant or shameful should occur. The patient should not organize his report logically. He should attend his sessions regularly, once a day, six days a week, although with less severe disorders Freud found three times a week adequate.

THERAPIST'S TRAINING AND KNOWLEDGE REQUIREMENTS. Freud implied the analyst should be medically trained, but late in his life he seems to have dropped this requirement (1926). Three characteristics typify the training of a psychoanalyst. First, he must have a theoretical understanding as to how behavior works, including the psychological energies and the way they function. He must understand the organization of "mental life." He must understand the functioning of unconscious responses, the general nature of approach-avoidance conflicts (repression-resistance), the symbolism of screen memories both in dreams and waking life, and the phenomena of the intense emotional relationship which develops during therapy (transference). He can acquire some of this knowledge by *reading about* psychoanalytic theory, but he can best learn by *undergoing analysis* himself.

A second benefit of personal analysis is an extensive understanding of himself and removal of *his* avoidance behaviors, so that his observations and understanding of his patients will not be distorted by his own behavioral deficiencies. He must be a persistent, careful observer with considerable powers of attention, because the process is "toilsome and wearisome for the physician." He should have a good memory, because Freud recommended against taking notes during the interview. Finally, he must conduct psychoanalysis to become proficient at it, and considerable experience is needed over several years to realize the "full possible achievements of analytic therapy."

THERAPIST BEHAVIORS. The initial procedure for eliciting the kinds of behavior one needs to focus on is instruction in free association and subjective observation. Freud had observed early that thoughts and memories occurred in associative chains. Those relating to recent events usually occurred first, followed by others which proceeded backward in time until reaching the central idea. This would occur, however, only if the patient did not guide or direct the sequence of thought. The problem was to get the patient to observe and report honestly. It helps to make this all-important rule concrete by paraphrasing Freud's typical instructions to his patients: In ordinary conversation, you usually try to keep a connecting thread running through your remarks, excluding any intrusive ideas or side issues, so as not to wander too far from the point, and rightly so. But in this case you must talk differently. As you talk, various thoughts will occur to you which you would like to ignore because of certain criticisms and objections. You will be tempted to think, "that is irrelevant, or unimportant, or nonsensical," and to avoid saying it. Do not give in to such criticisms. Report such thoughts in spite of your wish not to do so. Later, the reason for this injunction, the only one you have to follow, will become clear. Report whatever goes through your mind. Pretend you are a traveler, describing to someone beside you the changing views which you see outside the train window. Never forget your promise "to be absolutely honest, and never leave anything out" because it seems unpleasant to talk about (1912, p. 134).

Freud's purpose was to have the patient's responses stem entirely from the antecedent conflicts, as they manifested themselves in memory, thought, affective responses, and overt behavior. He did not want the behavior to be elicited by the therapist, but rather wanted to observe "emitted" behavior, somewhat in B. F. Skinner's sense (1953). The therapist sat behind the patient, out of sight, but in a position to observe the patient's features as he lay upon the couch. This was partly a matter of personal preference. Freud could not endure being stared at for twelve hours a day. Moreover, it also prevented his behavior from eliciting unwanted responses in the patient, and made it unnecessary for Freud to exert control over his expressive gestures, something which would have been exhausting for him. His report and explanation of his observations (interpretations) to the patient functioned both as behavior elicitors and modifiers, but since their main purpose was to modify behavior they will be discussed in the next section.

Conditions and Techniques for Modifying Responses

RESPONSES TO BE MODIFIED. The therapist first focuses on the avoidance side of the conflict, the manifestations of resistance. Once these have been reduced sufficiently so that the approach response sequences begin to show themselves, the therapist must focus on the development of new responses to reduce more adequately the psychological energy that produces the approach branch of the conflict; that is, the patient must develop new "aims" and "sublimations."

TECHNIQUES. The major technique used by the therapist is that of explanation or interpretation. The therapist, in effect, makes a series of statements which provide the patient with different ways of thinking about his behavior. However, it is not so simple as it sounds. The therapist must know what kinds of thoughts to provide the patient and when to provide them; he must know what to interpret and when. Beginning therapists, Freud felt, frequently made the mistake of giving the patient explanations as soon as *they* discovered them. He commented that some particularly sensitive therapists could recognize the basic elements of the conflict quickly. Interpretation at the wrong time simply gives the patient another set of thoughts, which lie *parallel to* the troublesome thoughts rather than becoming associated with them in the unconscious. As such they have no therapeutic value. Freud himself discovered intellectual knowledge was not curative of itself (1895). The content to be interpreted is clear from his theory of pathology. It is the sexual wish and the prohibitions opposing it in all their many forms. The timing of the interpretation depends on the manifestation of the avoidance aspect of the conflict in disrupting behavior.

Before discussing this issue, however, we should take note of the *conditions* of the relationship which the therapist establishes. The therapist should take a serious interest in the patient, giving him undivided attention. He should not reciprocate the patient's affectionate feelings, or presumably his hostile ones. He should not introduce conventional morality into his discussions. He should maintain *complete neutrality* both affectively and intellectually. This serves to keep his his own emotional life separate from the transaction and to prevent his observations from becoming biased by his own predilections (countertransference). It gives the patient a feeling of safety, for he need not fear that the therapist will retaliate, no matter what he says. The patient must find the therapist impervious to any temptation. These conditions make it possible for the therapist to interpret the patient's behavior toward him as inappropriate manifestations of old habits (transference), rather than as behavior genuinely elicited by the therapist. Finally, the therapist uses a special observational procedure. Rather than remaining alert for certain responses to occur, the therapist maintains an "evenly divided attention." In effect, this is an application of the "fundamental rule" to the therapist: do not select, criticize, or discard anything; observe it all; only in that way can one be sure to discover the full significance of the patient's responses. It has the advantage of permitting the therapist's unconscious thought processes also to work upon the observations.

How can the therapist tell when resistance is occurring? One of the rules is: whatever disturbs "the progress of the work" is a resistance. Such disturbances include long pauses which suggest the patient is arranging, distorting, or screening his observations; inability to bring any thoughts or memories to mind; long and circuitous chains of thoughts; and sudden changes of topic. The avoidance pattern will continually vary in intensity, increasing as a new topic is approached, reaching its height as the new topic is discussed, and declining when that theme has been dealt with (cf. the concept of avoidance gradients in psychology). As the avoidance responses begin to occur, the therapist identifies them, informs the patient of them, and explains why they are occurring; he uncovers and identifies the resistance.

Freud commented that beginners often thought this was all that was necessary to do, but typically the avoidance responses will continue after they are first made explicit. The patient usually disagrees at first. One can usually recognize whether the patient is being defensive by watching his facial expressions and gestures. If the therapist continues to point out the avoidance responses, he will prevent them from reducing the anxiety, which will actually increase. As this occurs, the patient will find it harder to continue to deny their occurrence and will finally recognize and acknowledge them. There follows a period of examination and discussion by the patient as to their significance, a period of *working through*. This may lead to the discovery of approach responses with which the avoidance responses were in conflict. The therapist should not tell the patient what these drives are but should wait for the patient to make the discovery himself.

The therapist *may tell* the patient the solution—that is, interpret—when the patient is only one step removed from the discovery himself. If such an interpretation is followed by patient acceptance and elaboration, it is probably accurate. The significant fact in the successful sequence just described is that the responses in the conflict *are actually occurring at the time*. It is only then that they can be modified. As Freud put it, one cannot fight an enemy who is absent. Discovery of the resistance at its height "convinces the patient of the existence and powers of such impulses" (1912–1915, p. 155).

There is a particularly important kind of resistance, however, called *transference*. The responses the patient makes toward the therapist, their personal relationship, is one of the most powerful propelling forces in psychoanalysis. Such responses may be grouped into three classes. First, there are simple friendly feelings toward the therapist which are a great help in therapy and keep the patient at his work. Second, there are strong affectionate feelings with sexual overtones—transference love or positive transference. Third, there are hostile, resentful feelings—negative transference—which typically follow the intense positive ones. The last two represent the focusing of the patient's sexual and aggressive psychological energies on the therapist. They are "transferred" because presumably the therapist has done nothing to elicit them and they were originally developed in relationship to the parents (oedipal complex). They are extremely delicate to handle, yet present the therapist with a powerful tool. The responses made toward the therapist represent the basic conflict and are infantile responses learned along with the conflict. They represent the ambivalent responses of love and hate first learned toward the parent. Now they are occurring under different circumstances, however, and the patient has different sequences with which to respond to them. Properly handled (and this is a very delicate matter, about which analysts have written a great deal) the old conflicting responses can be modified under the new circumstances and thus brought under control. Successful therapy interviews involve considerable patient emotion.

The therapist should be very careful not to respond to these affective attacks. Rather he should quietly and calmly point out that they are misdirected and lead the patient to discover their real origin and aim, thereby bringing them under conscious control, so that new responses for reconciling the conflict can be considered. The patient actually emits the responses toward the therapist, thus making them susceptible to modification. This is called *acting out*. It has a special advantage. The patient may be unable to recall certain significant events and how they affected him. However, he may unwittingly perform those responses toward the therapist and if the therapist can render them explicit, they can be brought under conscious control again.

"Acting out," by itself, is not therapeutic. There is a special disadvantage. The patient may not restrict the performance of these responses to the therapy hour, but they may also occur with other people, such as his wife, business acquaintances, friends, and family. This can lead to serious difficulty which the person later may regret. The therapist, therefore, tries to confine all important "acting out" to the therapy hour. This is the reason for the prohibition that the patient should make no important life decisions, such as those concerning divorce, marriage, or business arrangements, until the analysis has been completed. Freud thought it was safe, however, to permit less important and even foolish responses to be "acted out" outside of therapy, since they were unlikely to lead to serious difficulty, for it is only through "his own experience and mishaps that a person learns sense."

In this manner the disordered behaviors become specifically related to the situational events of therapy. The "real" neurosis becomes transformed into a "transference" neurosis, and thereby becomes accessible to modification. What particular kinds of responses does the therapist discuss with the patient? He must help the patient come to think about the psychological energies, particularly sexual, as they are manifest in his wishes and thoughts. He must help the patient become aware of his self-evaluative thoughts and the manner in which they produce negative affect and prohibit the expression of instinctual drives. The self-evaluative thoughts have to be modified, and Freud suggested that they may be either too severe or not severe enough. Freud paid most attention to the former possibility, and one gets the impression it is probably easier to reduce the severity of the self-evaluative thoughts than to enhance them in patients with a "weak superego." Finally, the therapist must help the patient learn to observe and think about the situational events which may be used to reduce the psychological energies within the limitations of his self-evaluations and environmental sanctions.

If avoidance patterns are modified and anxiety is reduced, the patient must acquire new responses to reduce the psychological energies that now recur. How does this come about? Primarily, the patient chooses the new forms of behavior, although he is likely to discuss various possibilities with the therapist. If conscious control of his own behavior is to be the outcome for the patient, the therapist must avoid making the patient dependent on him for solutions. Eventually the patient must learn to develop his own.

Freud asserted that people who thought "advice and guidance concerning conduct in life" were basic analytic techniques were misinformed. On the contrary, "we want nothing better than that the patient should find his own solutions for himself" (1915e, p. 376). Freud was quite concerned that ill-informed and badly trained analysts were damaging the reputation of psychoanalysis. Considerable thought was given to the development of a kind of certification procedure for practitioners to keep this from happening.

Transfer of Behavior Change

If the patient's behavior toward the therapist is modified, the changes are expected to transfer automatically to other situations. The conflicts involved in the neurosis all become directed toward the therapist during the "transference neurosis." They are not situation-specific. They are responses "looking for an object to happen to." Thus, if they are changed while they are occurring in relation to the therapist, they will be permanently changed, and can no longer attach themselves to any object in their old form. No special procedures are necessary to facilitate the transfer from the therapist to other situations, if the therapist has successfully resolved the transference pattern of behavior. "Acting out" to some extent may accomplish transfer, but to our knowledge Freud never encouraged the patient to perform trial behaviors outside of therapy. He specifically wished to keep the "acting out" confined to the therapy hour.

EVALUATION OF BEHAVIOR CHANGE

Appraisal of Behavior Change

In discussing his abandonment of hypnosis, Freud acknowledged that he had found the results capricious and unpredictable, although he had previously expressed considerable enthusiasm for it. Thus, he early acknowledged the necessity for establishing that the behavior changes observed were stable, but he never specified any solution to that problem. He seemed to have assumed that the judgment that permanent change had developed would occur as a matter of course. A patient knows when he is better, and the doctor can tell from his observations when the patient is better. Apparently, if the patient said he was better, if Freud observed through the patient's report that he seemed to be behaving differently and thinking differently about himself, then, apparently, the patient was considered to have changed.

Freud would not allow other observers into the therapeutic transaction, for he felt it would destroy one of its essential ingredients— that of privacy in a personal relationship. Quantitative measurement of the phenomena with which he was concerned was something he felt was not possible, at least at the time. Psychological testing was in its infancy during Freud's time, and the only test he mentioned was a word association test. Clinical judgment was apparently his criterion.

Verification of Therapy Theory

Freud built and sought to verify his propositions entirely on the basis of naturalistic observations. It is true that he controlled some of the influences on the patients while he was making his observations. For example, no one else was present in the room except Freud. The patient was required to lie on a couch, thus cutting down motoric movement and other activity which might distract from the behavior to be observed. In addition, Freud attempted to exert control over the behavior he was to observe by giving the patient verbal instructions as to how to respond. The observations were extensive. The patient was observed one hour a day, six days a week, over a period of months and years, thus providing an enormous amount of observational data from which to generalize.

There is little question about the brilliance of Freud's observational skills, particularly about sequential behavior. The extensive case studies he presented reveal this.

He developed his theories out of this mass of observational data. He started with data, and inductively developed the theory, rather than beginning with theoretical formulations and deducing the observational data which should appear if the theory were correct. Freud was explicit about the way he felt theory should be formulated, and defined concepts as higher-order abstractions representing observations and relationships among observations.

No science begins with clear and sharply defined basic concepts. Rather, scientific activity consists of "describing phenomena and then in proceeding to prove, classify and correlate them." Ideas are applied to help bring order from the data. These ideas must have "significant relations to the empirical material," relations which we "sense before we can clearly recognize and demonstrate them." Advancing knowledge "does not tolerate any rigidity even in definitions" (1915a, p. 117).

Freud followed this procedure throughout his life. When new observations developed, the conceptual abstractions he invented to encompass his data were modified to fit the new observations. He persistently avoided definition of terms because he felt such definitions had relatively little meaning until they expressed and were derived from generalities about observational data.

No measurement, however, is involved in Freud's procedures of verification. No careful controls are established so that others can reproduce the conditions under which Freud made his observations. In fact, although Freud may have been a careful observer, the accuracy of his data records must be suspect. He recommended against taking notes during the therapy hour because, he said, this would interfere with the kind of suspended attention he felt the therapist must maintain if he were to observe data in an unbiased fashion. Freud stated that his practice was to conduct his therapy cases, frequently numbering ten to twelve a day, and then, at the end of the day, he would write up summary notes on each case. Anyone who has done psychotherapy cannot help but suspect that under these conditions a great many of the observations Freud made about his individual patients could not have been recorded in his notes. Without a careful record of what has occurred, the phenomena of observer bias can easily operate. Freud's memory was undoubtedly selective, and important events which he could not recall might well have made a significant difference in his theoretical formulations. Without a careful record of the events as they occurred, no other scientist can start with exactly the same observations and determine whether or not the generalizations Freud made from them accurately represent the data.

Freud did use another type of procedure of verification. He made observations on a number of occasions, and within and between these occasions he made observations on different kinds of response phenomena. From observations of different kinds of events on the same occasion and the same kinds of events on different occasions, he attempted to formulate generalizations which were consistent with these various observations. Thus, the criterion of internal consistency seems to have been one of the tests applied to verify generalizations.

He recognized there was a special difficulty with his concepts because a great many of them referred to phenomena which were not directly available to an objective observer. As he put it, one has some knowledge of the biological base of behavior (the brain) at one end and the observable behavior such as motoric responses at the other. Everything in between is a matter of inference. Thus, he built concepts about phenomena that were inaccessible to the objective observer by starting with careful observation of sequences of events within which there were discontinuities, irregularities, and inconsistencies that could not be accounted for entirely on the basis of what he observed. Because "something must have gone on in between," he developed intervening concepts to account for the inconsistencies and irregularities in his observations. In a sense, then, he recognized he was building concepts of the kind that psychology has recently called intervening variables or hypothetical constructs.

In the final analysis, however, Freud was a pragmatist. He insisted that his theoretical formulations would not help him succeed in curing people if they were not valid. In one discussion he noted that because of the emphasis on the human relationship between the analyst and the patient (transference), the danger existed that the therapist's influence upon the patient might bias the consequences of the therapeutic action. Thus, what is useful in therapy may be disadvantageous in research. Freud acknowledged the possibility that events (memories and fantasies) patients recall may have occurred in response to the therapist's suggestion. The power of an emotional transference may be just as effective a media for producing responses in the patient through suggestion as hypnosis. He had a criterion, however, for deciding whether this had happened. It is easy to make a patient into "a disciple," but therapy succeeds only if what the patient "is told to look for in himself corresponds with what actually does exist in him" (1915e, p. 393). Thus, another very important criterion for the validation of his theories seems to have been that the patients found his explanations of their behavior accurately representative of what they could observe in themselves, and the result of the interpretations led to a resolution of the patient's disorder. The theory was verified if it worked; the patient's behavior changed.

COMMENTS

Much in contemporary psychology is relevant to Freud's brilliant observations. For example, Miller's (1959) analysis of approach-avoidance conflicts is highly similar to the picture of behavior pathology developed by Freud. Freud's observations of what happened when the individual's thoughts came near to emotionally laden material represents, at a subjective level, the kind of phenomena psychology has studied under the notion of generalization gradients. His proposal that symptoms are behaviors serving important functions in the emotional "economy" of the individual is another brilliant notion, widely accepted, for which there is considerable support, though not all symptoms serve this purpose. His emphasis on the significance of the patient's relationship with the therapist anticipated a popular theme in psychotherapy literature and research today. His ability to spell out some of the ways in which "the child is father to the man" prompted the growth of an extended literature on child development. Arranging for a patient to talk about events which are associated with intense emotional responses, and to do so in the presence of a therapist, who can then operate on those responses and modify them, is a technique that became the ancestor of all verbal psychotherapy techniques today. Subsequent theorists came to differ about which response events should be focused upon, but in spite of these variations, the fundamental medium is speech; the therapist operates on the patient's behavior, primarily upon his speech, in the expectation that modifications in the way the person speaks will produce modifications in the way he thinks. This, in turn, will produce modifications in other kinds of behavior as well. Verbal psychotherapy as it is conducted today is not remarkably different from that which Freud conducted in the early 1900's. It may differ in content, but not in format.

Freud's picture of man is basically an ugly one. Man is pushed by demonic, destructive, animalistic forces. Psychological energies of sex and aggression must be controlled. All the contributions of our complicated society are simply consequences of the controlled diversion of the two major instincts. The individual would be a far happier person, Freud's theory implies, if his sexual and aggressive energies could be directly expressed through uncontrolled reflexive behavior. It is only because this leads to unsatisfactory environmental consequents that the individual must control them, although when they are controlled and diverted, a portion of their influence is lost. Freud once commented that it was saddening to "know" that contributions of society had come at the expense of these primary events (instincts).

One of our students made the interesting contrast between Freud's picture of man as built upon negative affect and religion's picture of man as built upon positive affect. One is a theory of fear, anger, and lust; the other is a theory of love and the positive constructive activities of man. If one interpreted Freud's notion of sexuality to mean the arousal of pleasurable impulses in the individual or to mean the significance of interpersonal relations, it might be more acceptable to many readers. In fact, there are often places in some of his writings where he seems to treat the concept of sexuality in this way. In most instances, however, he is definite in stating that he refers to sex in its literal sense. Even when refusing to define sex, he stated, "on the whole, indeed, we know pretty well what is meant by sexual" (1915*e*, p. 267).

His assumption that all behavior has to be started by a reservoir of energy which exists in the individual, which becomes attached to various responses, and which can be expended by greater and greater attachments thereby impoverishing the individual's behavior, seems unreasonable in the light of today's knowledge. It seems doubtful that all of behavior is determined by a reservoir of psychological energy. Moreover, Freud's position is heir to all the problems which have recently been recognized in drive reduction theories. It seems far more parsimonious to think of behavior as appearing under certain conditions and not others. Situational events function as cues in Freud's system, as guiding influences, but they do not initiate behavior, they only serve to help mold it in certain directions. This seems somewhat inaccurate; at least in reflex behavior, it is clear that the response will occur following the application of situational events. Thus, some situational events do function as behavior elicitors.

His emphasis on the irrationality of behavior was a revolt against the picture of man extant at the time, which viewed man's logical thought processes as his principal characteristic. Freud redirected that stream and brought us to a more balanced picture of the human person. Man is "full" of emotion, of behavior of which he is not aware, of behavior directed toward ends which are not consciously intended, as well as of behavior consciously planned and intentionally directed toward certain goals. A complete account of human behavior must encompass both characteristics. Freud made an elaborate attempt to accomplish this goal.

Chapter 6

Modifications in Psychoanalysis:
The Ego-Analysts

The group of theorists collectively referred to as the *ego-analysts* has represented an important modern development of Freudian psychoanalysis and one of considerable interest. It is a group that accepts a major portion of Freudian theory, and whose contributions are presented as logical extensions of Freud's ideas, rather than as a complete and separate system. Although following the basic outline, this chapter does *not* attempt to present this position as a system that can stand alone. Rather, it should be read as a supplement to the Freudian system presented in Chapter 5. It is included partly because of the importance of this development to psychoanalysis and partly because it may represent the best rapprochement between psychoanalysis and the discipline of psychology.

It has been difficult to choose the theorists on whom this chapter should be based, since there is no single person acknowledged as the leader of this group. In addition, terminology is used so loosely by some writers that there is doubt about which ones are considered to be contributors to this stream of thought. We have selected those to whom most writers in this field typically refer.

MAJOR THEORISTS

If there is any major spokesman for ego-analysts, it appears to be *Heinz Hartmann*. Robert Holt (1959) described him as perhaps the most influential contemporary contributor to Freudian psychoanalytic theory and its ego-psychology. Hartmann has been president of the New York Psychoanalytic Society and of the International Psychoanalytic Association. Thus, as a practicing therapist and a theorist, his fellow analysts seem to view him with considerable respect.

To our knowledge, Hartmann has never written a major book on ego-psychology, but he has produced many articles and papers presented at professional meetings. His first major contribution to ego-psychology was a lengthy paper presented at a meeting of the Vienna Psychoanalytic Society in 1937, since translated by Rapaport (1951*c*) and published in book form (Hartmann, 1958). Many of his other papers have been published in *The Psychoanalytic Study of the Child* (1950*a*). He has consistently emphasized his respect of Freudian theory and his wish to build upon it. He modestly introduced most of his papers with the statement that he was not presenting a theory, but rather presenting ideas relevant to the development of more adequate psychoanalytic theories.

A second major figure in this stream of thought has been *David Rapaport*. Born in Hungary, he received his Ph.D. in psychology at Budapest in 1938. As a member of the staff at the Menninger Clinic (1940–1948), he began to make his major scholarly contributions, which he later continued at the Austin Riggs Foundation until his death in 1960. Rapaport is perhaps best known to American clinical psychology for his monumental research on diagnostic psychological testing (1946). But he has ranked with the major theorists in American psychology as well. He played the role of translator of ego-psychoanalytic theory for American psychologists, especially the work of Hartmann, with which he was much impressed. Moreover, he made significant additions and modifications in ego-analytic theory.

Anna Freud, Sigmund's daughter, is usually credited with being an early contributor to this stream of thought (1946). *Erikson* (1946, 1950),

Kris (1951), and *Lowenstein* (1953) are also considered to be major theorists in this group. This chapter represents an effort to piece together the ideas of most of these writers into a general stream of thought. There are serious risks in such a procedure, but we believe such a summary may prove useful. It is possible, however, that greater consensus has been imposed on the views of these men than actually exists.

MAJOR EMPHASES

Although the ego-analytic theorists have tended to subscribe to much in the Freudian position, there are several respects in which they differ. These seem to be more than extensions of Freudian theory. At the least, their ideas represent important changes in emphasis; in other respects, their proposals seem to represent major changes in conception.

As a group, they concluded that the classical Freudians had neglected the direct study of normal or healthy behavior. Freud's ideas about normal behavior were extrapolations and inferences from what he observed in the disordered behavior of his patients. In trying to account for ordinary behavior this group concluded that it was inappropriate and misleading to try to explain all of man's behavior as an expression of fear, anger, sexual responses, or other psychological events—that is, instinctual drives. Frequently these are key elements in behavior disorders, so it is understandable that Freud's view of normal behavior should give them a central role.

The ego-analysts argued that the antecedents to behavior are considerably more varied than the innate psychological events—instinctual drives—of Freud. If this is true, some behavior may be learned in relation to other events as well. Such reasoning led them to explore the complexity in behavior that each person develops and with which he directs his own activity and deals constructively with his environment. This group came to emphasize these instrumental behaviors, which were called the *ego-functions:* Hence, the title *ego-analysts*. They proposed that psychoanalysis must develop propositions to account for the development of these "functions"—physical motility, sensory and perceptual responses, thought and language—if it were to have a truly adequate theory of normal development. Thus this group has characteristically emphasized the learned development of behaviors, normal and abnormal, and therefore the direct study of children from the psychoanalytic view has been a prominent part of its evolution. Many of its theoretical papers have been published in various volumes of *The Psychoanalytic Study of the Child.*

This emphasis upon man's daily behaviors also led them to recognize the significance of situational events both in eliciting and modifying behavior. Interaction with situational events is not something forced upon man; he actively seeks it. He does so not only because he is impelled toward them by innate psychological energies but also because his biological evolution has provided him with behavioral equipment, such as vision, which responds to the environment independent of the internal psychological energies. The social milieu and the environmental circumstances surrounding a person are powerful behavior elicitors and modifiers, above and beyond the primary psychological energies (drives).

Analysis of learned behaviors (ego and ego functions) led to an emphasis upon two particular classes of response: thoughts and consciousness or attention. Man appears to direct his own behavior consciously, and various kinds of thoughts and thought sequences are said to play a crucial role in this regard. The ego-analysts acknowledge that at times man is an animal, driven by innate psychological energies and responses, thwarted by and compromising with a difficult environment. However, they argue there is much that is significant about human behavior that is quite independent of man's "instinctual urges." They have focused their attention on this latter category of behavior. Thus, by adding their conceptions to Freudian theory, the ego-analysts have contributed significant new dimensions to the psychoanalytic theory of human behavior.

INNATE CHARACTERISTICS OF NORMAL DEVELOPMENT

It will be recalled that, in Freud's view, all complex human behavior was ultimately reducible to a few primary sequences, namely, psychological energies and the built-in *essentially automatic* behaviors to terminate them. Hartmann, followed by other ego-analysts, has rejected this as an overly simplified view. As an alternative, they have proposed that the human infant begins life with a collection of response capabilities which are relatively unrelated to one another. This is referred to as the *undifferentiated phase* of behavior development. A number of kinds of responses are fundamental, and they are classified into three groups according to the way they are thought to operate. The first group is composed of the antecedents to or the elicitors of behavioral sequences and their manifestations. The second represents responses innately related to events in the outside world—situational events. The third includes responses innately related to other responses, which serve a controlling and directive function, enabling the individual to respond in terms of past and future events as well as present ones.

Innate Response Sequences

Ego-analysts have emphasized that there are many behavior elicitors in addition to Freud's "instinctual drives." Rapaport (1959) has discussed seven psychoanalytic assumptions concerning the determinants of behavior: (1) the individual is typically unaware, that is, unconscious, of the primary determinants of his behavior—the *topographic* point of view; (2) all behavior is the consequence of a developmental sequence regulated both by innate characteristics of the person and by cumulative experience—the *genetic* point of view; (3) all behavior is ultimately determined by psychological energies, although the influence may be greatly modified in its effects by the operation of other determinants—the *dynamic* point of view; (4) all behavior reduces and is regulated by psychological energy that is not equated with any known kind of biochemical or muscular energy—the *economic* point of view; (5) all behavior has determinants in habitual learned patterns of behavior—the *structural* point of view; (6) all behavior is determined by situational events, namely, reality—the *adaptive* point of view; and (7) all behavior is determined by the society in which one lives, namely, man and society form a unity in which each influences the other—the *psychosocial* point of view. In his efforts to reconcile these various points of view, Rapaport (1960) proposed that behavior elicitors be classified into *motives* and *causes*.

MOTIVES. Some behavior is not obviously the consequence of situational events or somatic conditions; it is "spontaneous." Certain pathological behaviors, irrational thoughts, and behaviors seemingly beyond self-control are examples. Assuming that all behavior must have some antecedent, Rapaport postulated the existence of appetitive internal forces or psychological energies, not directly equated with any specifiable biological process. These "motives" are distinguished from situational or physiological elicitors and are characterized by: (1) *pre-*

emptoriness—they elicit behaviors which one "cannot help doing" in contrast to "take it or leave it" behaviors; (2) *cyclicalness*—a periodic rise in intensity leading to consummatory activity, resulting in a fall of intensity, followed by a gradual rise; (3) *selectiveness*—specific objects are needed or preferred for their reduction; they are suggested by the apparent striving for some particular result in the environment; and (4) *displaceability*—if the appropriate object is not available, others may become its substitute. This group subsumes Freud's instinctual drives but is said to be broader. Although the most important drives are innate, apparently derivative ones can be learned, as we shall see later.

Emotions are considered important innate responses, which are manifestations of psychological energy, that is, motives or instinctual drives (Rapaport, 1950b; 1960). They indicate accumulating energy, but do not effectively reduce the energy; they do not satisfy the motive. The greater the accumulated energy, the stronger is the emotional response (Rapaport, 1951c). Emotions are considered consequences of behavior elicitors rather than elicitors themselves. Fear, a particularly important emotion, is a reflex response occurring under conditions of danger. The definition of dangerous conditions is not clear, although such conditions are referred to as situations that tend to evoke feelings of helplessness. Apparently, increases in the intensity of psychological energy (motives or instincts), as well as some kinds of situational events, may represent danger. Emotions are manifested in a variety of ways, such as peripheral physiological changes (palmar sweating or trembling), changes in habitual behavior patterns (a child's temper tantrum), disruptions of thought or recall (slips of the tongue), or permanent alterations in habits of thinking (schizophrenic autism). Rapaport suggests this variety of manifestations may be one of the reasons for the confusion surrounding the concept in the psychological literature.

CAUSES. Ego-analysts (Hartmann, 1939; Erikson, 1950; Rapaport, 1960) have emphasized that there are a number of other significant behavior elicitors besides psychological energy (instinctual drives). These include external physical conditions such as gravity, physiological or somatic responses such as chemical toxicity (r), and social stimuli such as attack by another person. Some learned responses—for example, thoughts—may become elicitors, but more of that when we discuss learning. Situational elicitors can be physically avoided, but not so responses; they must be dealt with. This imperative characteristic of innate eliciting responses is probably one of the reasons they have been overemphasized in the psychoanalytic literature prior to the ego-analysts.

The elaboration of innate behavior elicitors, beyond psychological energies (instinctual drives), has important consequences in analytic theory. In the first place, it means that a considerable amount of behavior can be learned in relation to antecedents that do not involve instinctual drives. This makes possible a much more elaborate and complicated theory of behavior development. Second, it leads to an emphasis on behaviors developed and maintained as instrumentalities for dealing with situational events relatively independent of physiological determinants. Third, it makes clear that any behavior sequence probably has several different kinds of antecedents—is "overdetermined."

Situationally Oriented Responses

In line with their emphasis on a variety of behavior elicitors, the ego-analysts emphasize that a significant portion of man's response characteristics are innately related to situational events rather than primarily to his own physiological responses. By evolution, the human has developed responses which serve to "adjust" the person to the kind of environment into which he is born. It is interesting to note that ego-analysts arrived at an emphasis on environmental factors similar to that of culturally oriented writers such as Horney, but from a biological position.

Rapaport (1958) lists four kinds of innate responses which have as their main purpose enabling the individual to maintain contact with and deal with his environment, although they may also facilitate the reduction of psychological energy (motive satisfaction). These are memory responses, motoric responses, sensory and perceptual responses, and threshold responses, including discharge thresholds for physiological energies and emotional responses. He encompasses both the kind of response and the physiological equipment which makes it possible under the term *apparatus*—for example, *memory apparatus*.

Controlling Responses

Two other sets of responses are considered innate and of considerable significance, the responses of attention (awareness) and thought.

Humans are capable of attending to their own behavior, to what goes on around them, and even to what they are, or have been, aware of (*reflective awareness*). This category of response assumed growing importance for Rapaport in his later years. Humans are also innately capable of thinking, although what they will think about is determined by their memories, by what they attend to, and by other learned factors. It is through the responses of attending and thinking that the individual becomes capable of controlling and directing his own responses. This will be discussed further in the section on learned development.

INNATE REGULATING PRINCIPLES. Hartmann (1948) challenged the innate regulating pleasure principle as far more complex than a simple instinctual phenomenon. He recognized that what is "pleasurable" differs at different developmental stages and as a consequence of learning. Pleasure follows from activity itself as well as from the effect that activity has in reducing psychological energy. It appears that ego-analysts encountered the same difficulties with this concept as have drive reduction learning theorists in academic psychology. Ego-analysts have developed the concept of *neutralization* to account for the fact that much of behavior does not seem directed at reduction of sexual or aggressive energies, the two major drives in Freudian theory. The energy behind much of behavior was once sexual (libido) or aggressive, but by being "neutralized" it could serve a variety of other ends.

Hartmann (1958) suggested there are probably several innate mechanisms for maintaining or establishing equilibrium, and it is assumed that is the function of behavior. We are not quite clear about what he meant by equilibrium. At times he seemed to follow Freud, considering it a matter of distribution of energies, and at times he seemed to imply it might be more than this. One such mechanism functioned to maintain equilibrium between behavior and situational events $(r, R-S)$. This would seem similar to Freud's reality principle. A second functioned to maintain equilibrium among intense responses or drives $(r-r)$. This was similar to Freud's pleasure principle. A third one maintained equilibrium among learned response patterns and might be similar to Freud's repetition-compulsion principle, although it would appear to be considerably more inclusive $(r, R-r, R)$. A final innate mechanism maintained equilibrium between the "synthetic function" and the rest of the "ego." In a sense, this was "a specific organ of equilibrium at the disposal of the person" (Hartmann, 1958). By this Hartmann seemed to mean that it is innately characteristic of a human to attempt consciously and thoughtfully to maintain some kind of compatible organization among all his behaviors. As we understand him, Hartmann has not proceeded to detail the operation and relationships of these principles. We can now examine the proposals of the ego-analysts as to how these innate response characteristics become combined through learning.

LEARNED CHARACTERISTICS OF NORMAL DEVELOPMENT

The development of learned behaviors by which the individual controls his own behavior and deals with his environment (ego functions) is the primary focus of the ego-analytic writers. Behavior is far less dependent on innate urges in man than it is in lower animals. "With man, adjustment is mainly entrusted to an independent organization" (Hartmann, Kris, and Loewenstein, 1946). That organization involves the innate responses and response apparatuses previously cited, and all the learned behavior built on them. Although very early in the infant's life residues of instinctual or automatic behaviors which adjust the infant to situational events may exist, for all practical purposes they rapidly disappear. Man's adjustment to situational events is not primarily instinctual, but learned.

Changes in the assumptions about the innate characteristics of behavior led to a change of emphasis in the propositions about the development of normal and disordered behavior. With behavior developing for reasons other than the reduction of the sexual and aggressive energies, it was no longer necessary for analysts to interpret all the effort a man devoted to becoming a skilled surgeon as fundamentally an outlet for innate aggressive energies. Similarly, the extensive effort of a serious painter need not be interpreted as simply a sublimation of innate sexual energies. Some surgeons may be sadists. Some painters may be sublimating sexual responses. Others, however, may be carrying out these activities from quite different "reasons." Behavior may be elicited by physiological events, or situational events, or learned responses. Thus, learned behavior is devoted as much to dealing with situational events as with innate energies. It is the kinds of relationships that develop among different classes of response and different classes of situational events that are most crucial.

The ego-analysts do not view man as an automaton pushed hither and yon by imperative innate energies on the one hand and by situational events on the other, constantly seeking some compromise among these conflicting influences. When behavior develops in a healthy fashion, man controls both it and the influence of situational events, selectively responding to seek consequences he has thoughtfully selected. Rapaport (1958) summarized this newer emphasis well, and continued to insist that it is inaccurate to overemphasize either innate energies or situational events as behavior antecedents. Man is not at the mercy of either. He can impose delay and thought between innate energies and action, thus postponing the reduction of such energies indefinitely. Learned responses, primarily thoughts, make this possible, and although originally they may be learned as a consequence of their energy reducing function, later they may become relatively independent of such influences (drives) and control them. Such learned behaviors are called *apparatuses of secondary autonomy,* and they represent a concept similar to Allport's functional autonomy. In some respects this notion is similar to learning theorists' concept of acquired drives. Similarly, although much of man's learned behavior is the consequence of responding to situational events, he is not totally at their mercy either. As with innate energies, man is capable of delaying his responses to situational events as well. To put it in the language of the ego-analysts, the ego is relatively autonomous from the environment as it is from the id. In fact, it is the very existence of a variety of behavior elicitors that represents man's best guarantee against "stimulus-response slavery," to use Rapaport's phrase. Thus, ego-analysts refuse to grant complete dominance of behavior to any particular category of response or situational events. The progressive independence of behavior from "instinctual drives" is called *ego-autonomy,* and increasing independence from external stimulation is referred to as *internalization* (Rapaport, 1960).

Behavior Organization

Out of these diverse kinds of unorganized responses, different constellations of complicated, habitual response patterns (structures) develop, which may be called id, ego, and superego. Ego-analysts emphasize that responses in the last two groups can be learned in relationship to any of the innate elicitors, not just the innate energies (instinctual drives). In their terms, ego functions should not be thought of as developing out of id responses, as Freud proposed, but both should develop from the undifferentiated stage of infancy. Those responses learned independently from reduction of psychological energy (instinctual drives), Hartmann (1958) encompassed under the concept *conflict free ego sphere*. For example, sensory responses such as vision develop relatively independently from other responses, although in pathology they may become involved in behavior patterns dominated by innate energies (drives). Particular response patterns which develop in this way are referred to as *autonomous ego functions,* or *apparatuses of primary autonomy*. They are autonomous in the sense that their acquisition or functioning does not depend on psychological energies (instinctual drives). Before discussing the developmental sequence, let us summarize the general response groupings (structures) that eventually develop.

ID. Automaticity, imperativeness, and unconsciousness seem to be primary characteristics of these behaviors. Responses in this grouping center around the innate psychological energies, the physiological and emotional responses which are their manifestations, and the automatic patterns of behavior innately directed toward energy reduction, such as the need for oxygen and the automatic response of breathing. Most innate bodily functions are apparently included. Every person needs to be able to surrender himself to his "id" at times, as in sleep and intercourse (Hartmann, 1952).

EGO. This is the primary class of responses that ego-analysts have attempted to analyze. As Hartmann said, any listing of "ego functions" would be far longer than that for "id" or "superego" functions. The behavioral phenomena included in this group represent most of those to which the discipline of psychology has directed its attention. It is not surprising, then, that a more complete representation of such responses is essential if psychoanalysis is to develop an adequate general theory of human behavior. All the phenomena mentioned as ego functions seem to fall into three groups: (1) kinds of responses, (2) patterns of behavior, and (3) functions, or the way responses come to be related.

Four major *subclasses or kinds of responses* are mentioned as "ego functions." These are motoric responses (action or motility), sensory and perceptual responses, verbal-symbolic responses (thinking and talking), and consciousness and attention. Physiological responses are not mentioned and are apparently considered to be in the id classification. Sensory and perceptual responses maintain the organism's contact with both situational events (S) and subjective responses (r), that is, the external and internal environment. Motoric responses (R) enable the individual to deal with the environment to achieve selected results.

Verbal-symbolic responses (r, R), consciousness (r), and attention (r) represent responses that control and direct the other kinds of responses. They mediate between "reality" and other "psychic organizations." Some thoughts are in terms of images, others in terms of verbal symbols. The latter are considered far more flexible and useful. Illustrative of the kinds of thoughts mentioned are memories, self-identifying thoughts, thoughts anticipating or predicting future events, thoughts comparing and evaluating perceptions, judgments, and thoughts differentiating oneself from the environment and from other people.

Some concepts in this group seem to represent *patterns* or *sequences of behavior,* frequently recurring over time. The most inclusive such concept mentioned is *character,* by which the ego-analysts seem to be referring to large constellations of behavior including many different kinds of responses consistently recurring in many situations and through time. Still another example is inhibition, delay, or postponement of behavior. Acquiring the capacity to delay behavior is considered a crucial stage in development, and seems to be primarily a function of attention and thought. Here they seem to be referring to sequences of responses in which one prevents or delays the occurrence of another.

Certain other concepts in this group refer not to kinds of events, or to arrangements of or relationships among events, but to some functional characteristic by which events come to be related. Phrases like "the synthetic, integrating, or organizing function"; "the co-ordination and integration of experience and behavior"; "the centralization of functional control"; or "achieving solutions and directing actions," represent such concepts. They seem to imply (1) that all learned behavior tends automatically to become organized and to function as a unit, and (2) thoughtful, conscious, intentional organization and direction of behavior is most characteristic of human behavior. This is perhaps the most important aspect of the concept of ego. Effective operation of the "synthetic function of the ego" is considered a most crucial characteristic of good adjustment. "We know that when this is achieved, play becomes freer, health radiant, sex more adult, and work more meaningful" (Erikson, 1946). It is in contrast to the involuntary, unconscious, automatic characteristics of behavior that Freud emphasized.

Most behavior is said to be intentionally directed toward consciously selected consequences and has gratifications unrelated to or far removed from the primary psychological energies. The mastery of difficulties, the solving of problems, and thinking itself all seem to yield

gratifications of their own (Hartmann, et al., 1946). With this emphasis, ego-analysts have rounded out their picture of human behavior
to include both automatic behaviors elicited by events of which the
individual is unaware and flexible instrumental behaviors initiated
through thoughtful, conscious planning. Man is sometimes driven by
forces from within and without, but not always—perhaps not even
usually. Freud certainly did not overlook this aspect of human
behavior, but he gave more emphasis to unconsciously determined
behavior.

SUPEREGO. Using Freud's definition, the ego-analysts say that the superego is a special class of thoughts with the power to elicit emotional
reactions. These self-evaluative thoughts are referred to as moral demands, self-criticism, self-punishment, and formation of ideals. They
are the individual's habitual thoughts about what is right and wrong
and his use of those thoughts to evaluate his own and other people's
behavior.

The Developmental Sequence

In general, ego-analysts seem to accept Freud's position that the basic
foundations for all later behavior patterns are developed during the
first five or six years of life. One might think of this as analogous to
the foundation of a building wherein the general contour and shape
become established early, but within those limits there remains a
great variety of structures which could be built. Developmental processes occurring after the age of five or six will elaborate, enrich,
modify, or perhaps even restrict the basic behavior patterns, but once
established, a fundamentally new structure cannot be formed. Ego-
analysts seem to believe, however, that there are greater possibilities
for modifying that basic structure during latency and adolescence
than had been implied in earlier psychoanalytic writings (Hartmann,
et al., 1946).

Ego-analysts focus their discussions of behavior development on
selected aspects of behavior, such as ego functions, and consider these
as additions to the Freudian theory of the developmental stages. They
suggest, however, that different kinds of responses and functions—id
and ego—may have different developmental phases, and that the relationships among these phases may be important to study. They also
emphasize that situational events that have little significance in one

phase of development may be of decisive significance in another. Sexual experience is perhaps the best-known example of this phenomenon.

INFANCY. Within the womb, there are extremely few situational events that elicit behavior. The infant's external environment remains quite constant, so that a constant adaptation to it is possible. In addition, the apparatuses for perceiving and responding to situational events are still maturing. Thus, until birth, the infant's behavior is almost entirely elicited by his own internal responses (r_i). In the womb, his existence is essentially automatic, with all biological requirements being consistently and automatically taken care of by the mother's body. Immediately following birth this automatic and effortless adjustment is abruptly terminated, and the infant becomes bombarded by a great variety of situational events. Of course, for a period, the automatic physiological patterns are predominant, and the objectively observable responses (R) are unco-ordinated with one another and with situational events. The behavior pattern of the womb continues immediately after birth, but it is inappropriate to the new circumstances surrounding the infant.

The very earliest stages of development are determined by the innate maturational sequences. The sensory responses develop into more effective respondents to situational events. During the first few weeks after birth, the child regularly undergoes periods of deprivation resulting in a periodic buildup of the intensity of innate energies (instinctual drives) followed by their termination. Feeding exemplifies this process. This shift from the effortless biological conditions of womb life to the periodic occurrence of increasingly intense physiological responses and their termination following birth establishes one of the conditions necessary for the infant to learn to discriminate between its own responses and situational events. A second condition is the maturation of the sensory and perceptual responses. Thus, during the first few weeks after birth, motoric responses begin to appear more specifically directed toward situational events, such as seeking the mother's breast or the bottle nipple. The beginning of discrimination between responses and situational events is one of the first steps toward the development of that group of behaviors called ego functions.

Around the fourth or fifth month the infant begins to anticipate the feeding situation. Learning to anticipate future events is a second crucial step. It may be related to the gradual maturation of memory response functions. The growing maturity of sensory-perceptual and motor responses makes it possible for the infant to direct some of his energy, all of which has been directed toward himself in the past (that is, has been *narcissistic*) toward situational events. Thus, discriminations between responses and situational events, anticipations of future events, and the directing of energies toward objects other than the self make possible the beginnings of habitual response patterns toward particular situational events—*object attachments.*

Because of the special role of the mother in terminating intense physiological responses, such as hunger, she is the earliest and most important "object attachment"; she represents the first significant set of situational events to which specific, habitual response patterns become related. As the infant begins to distinguish between itself and its mother and begins to develop the capacity to anticipate future events, it begins to attend to and respond to the mother's communications. Her behavior comes to serve as a signal of what is to come. This probably develops initially through bodily handling, facial expression, emotive responses, and expressive movements. The phenomenon of identification, which we shall discuss in a moment, begins to assume importance at this point.

LATE INFANCY AND EARLY CHILDHOOD. During the second six months of life, further maturing of the sensory-perceptual, memory, and motor response apparatuses occurs. These developments give the child increased control of his own body and enable him to manipulate and influence situational events around him. He not only reacts to his environment but is also able to elicit reactions from it and to manipulate situational events to produce reactions in himself, that is, self-stimulation. His behavior is no longer completely dominated by efforts to terminate intense innate energy (pleasure principle) but is directed toward situational events as well, sometimes without innate physiological energies being significantly involved (reality principle). Along with this is the development of *intentionality*. The child comes to aim his behavior at obtaining some future objective. This represents the first appearance of that special quality of human behavior so important in ego theory, the conscious, thoughtful selection and control of one's own responses. It cannot develop until the capacities to differentiate one's responses from situational events and to anticipate future events have begun to mature (Hartmann, 1952).

The earliest situation-response relationships (object attachments) are formed in the service of immediate termination of innate psychological energies (primary process, pleasure principle). Sometimes, however, the intensity of such responses increases to the point where they control major portions of behavior, directed at immediate response termination, but the necessary situational events necessary are not available. For example, the baby may become quite hungry, but the mother is not there just then to feed him. Thus, an involuntary delay of response termination occurs. Experiences of such involuntary delay, along with the development of memory, thoughts, anticipation of future events, and self-direction of behavior lay the groundwork on which self-control is built (Hartmann, 1952). The implication would seem to be that if immediate desired consequences were always available to the child any time they were demanded, self-control would not develop adequately. In lay language, this might be referred to as "spoiling the child" or "overindulgence."

Following the beginnings of differentiation of self from objects is the differentiation of subjective responses and situational events from instrumental motoric behavior. Thus, added to the "I am" and "that is" thoughts are the "I can do" conceptions. A new kind of deprivation becomes important here. Deprivation of conditions necessary for termination of intense responses such as instinctual drives was essential for the infant to learn to discriminate between situations and his own responses. Similarly, the *interruption of ongoing activity* provokes deprivation. It is the interruption of activity, rather than its prevention, that may be crucial. A frequent consequence of such interruption is aggressive behavior (Hartmann, et al., 1946).

The development of the capacities to delay the termination of increasingly intense responses, to recall past events and to anticipate future ones, and to direct behavior toward achieving selected objects or consequents provides the basis for the development of habitual responses to situational events (lasting object attachments). As long as the demand for immediate gratification prevails, any absence of the people to care for the child and provide the terminating conditions will produce emotional responses of fear, anxiety, or perhaps anger. However, gradually the child becomes less situation-bound. By *recalling* previous occasions when relief was provided after a brief period of deprivation, by *controlling* the psychological energies, by *anticipating* future events, and by making the necessary *responses*, such as looking for mother, the child can maintain some independence from the immediate situation, control his fears and tensions, and maintain habitual response patterns even though they are not always effective. It is these habitual response patterns, functioning effectively across a variety of situations and through extended periods of time, even in the face of occasional periods of deprivation, that are the basis of one's feelings of personal continuity and *identity* (Erikson, 1946).

All these behaviors are learned, however; hence, it is crucial to ask how they come to occur in the first place. The social or interpersonal context of learning is apparently the most important factor in developing self-control. In order to retain the "love of his environments," the infant learns to control his innate energies and to perform responses that win positive, approving behaviors from others. The social context is also crucial for learning instrumental behaviors. Beginning in infancy, the child imitates or adopts the behaviors of those around him (the process of *identification*), and as a consequence he acquires their "methods of solving problems and coping with emergencies" (Hartmann, et al., 1946). Early Freudian theory seemed to emphasize the ways in which organized social life interfered with human behavior and thus viewed society as playing essentially a negative role. (Perhaps it should be noted that Freud never argued for a completely self-indulgent, "living from day to day for immediate and direct physical gratifications" type of society, though he was never able to say why.) Ego-analysts emphasize the many positive aspects in the role of organized social life as it contributes to the individual's development; it keeps him alive, provides necessary and desirable gratifications, and in the process "seduces him to its particular life style" (Erikson, 1946).

The development of habitual thoughts identifying what one is and what one can do and the positive self-evaluations of these characteristics (*self-esteem* and *personal identity*) depend significantly on the social context. They emerge from the exercise of various skills and the performance of varied interpersonal behaviors. Because of the dominance of the social context of learning, there is significant continuity from one generation to another within a society. Such continuity is considered essential in some form. For example, even the unconscious "incestuous" choice of a husband or wife because they resemble the first childhood love, the mother or father, is not necessarily considered to be pathological. It may help to create a desirable continuity between the family in which one was reared and the family one later establishes (Erikson, 1946). Thus, although the first six years of life are considered the years during which are acquired the fundamental behavior patterns on which all later behavior develops, the social context in which one lives thereafter can be crucially important in later modifications.

The Development of Two Particular Classes of Response

FEAR. Fear is an innate response which becomes connected to many other responses through learning. When the child has developed thought habits of anticipating the future, fear or anxiety serves as a *signal,* and behaviors can be performed to avoid an increase in anxiety (Loewenstein, 1953). Habitual behavior patterns that are elicited by anxiety signals and serve to avoid an increase in anxiety are called *defense mechanisms.* Anna Freud's book (1946) is considered a classic in this regard. Rapaport (1951c) suggests that the response patterns that come to serve as defense mechanisms may have been learned originally under conditions in which they did not serve as fear reducers. This would suggest that when fear occurs, the individual uses those responses already in his repertoire to reduce it.

Defense mechanisms are not bad things to have. Everyone needs such habitual behaviors to control his fear responses. This implies, of course, that fear responses are a normal part of living. In addition, such habits frequently have instrumental as well as protective value. In other words, the avoidance of fear-producing circumstances may be pathological. Avoidance may have a "positive correlate," however, since it may result in a search for optional behavior patterns, a most effective adaptation process. Habitual behaviors developed in childhood as reactions to dangerous situations may continue to function as habitual response patterns throughout life, although the original situations may no longer apply. Why this should occur is not clearly specified, although it is implied that they continue to have some utility in dealing with new situations beyond their original function of reducing or avoiding fear.

THOUGHTS. This is a response class to which ego-analysts have given a great deal of attention, probably because of their emphasis on normal behavior development and on thoughtful, conscious self-control of behavior. Rapaport (1951c) has published a volume about this response class and participated in an important symposium on cognitive theory (Rapaport, 1957). Ego and Freudian psychoanalytic theory have been used as the framework for the interpretation of verbal responses to psychological tests (Rapaport, et al., 1945, 1946; Schafer, 1954).

The following summary of the development of thoughts is drawn primarily from the writings of Rapaport, who considered his formulations to be extensions of Freud's basic position. Rapaport's concern with thoughts and their development has been referred to as "the central preoccupation" binding together all his theoretical and empirical efforts throughout the years of his professional and scientific activity (Klein, et al., 1961). The central importance of this class of responses is that they can give the individual relative freedom from the influence of innate psychological energies and situational events through delaying and controlling responses to them. Man is more than an automaton, primarily because of his awareness and thoughts.

Thinking develops from two innate characteristics of humans. The first is the fact of *consciousness*. Consciousness exists in "a whole range of varieties," and each variety may have a somewhat different cognitive organization (Rapaport, 1957). At one extreme, thoughts are experienced as if they were the real thing. This is exemplified by the experience of waking from a dream and not being sure whether the events really happened or were only dreamed. At the other extreme is the stage of consciousness in which the individual is fully aware of distinctions between events observed and events thought of, between himself and other objects and events, between past, present, and future, and in which he recognizes what he is aware of. Such reflective awareness is considered an essential ingredient of logical thought. These stages, characteristics, or varieties of consciousness are considered to be given, and they are determining or limiting factors for the variety of habitual thought patterns (*cognitive structures*) that can and will develop in various stages of consciousness.

The second characteristic is the fact that humans can recall responses and situations of the past, of which they have been a part. This is called the *memory apparatus*. What kinds of experiences leave "memory traces" that can later be recalled is not clear. At times Rapaport seemed to imply that any response (r or R) made by a person, as well as any situation the individual encounters, leaves a memory trace. In his later writings, however, it would appear that he subscribed to two principles to account for the registration of a memory trace. First, any event (response or situational) which is of sufficient intensity, duration, or frequency to elicit attention (*attention cathexis*) will produce a concept, a relationship between concepts, or some "threshold structure" (Klein, et al., 1961, p. 25). Second, experiences that occur in relatively close temporal relationship to a reduction of psychological energies (before or after) are likely to leave memory traces. Infant memory traces are nonverbal. Sensory images and dream phenomena lead to the inference that visual images predominate.

Thought is defined as a conscious phenomenon, and a certain

amount of energy is necessary to bring memories to consciousness, Initially, this energy comes from innate energies (instinctual drives), and the primitive model of thought is based on the primitive model of action. The innate action sequence is: energy increases $(r) \rightarrow$ activity $(R) \rightarrow$ energy termination (r) and the establishment of memory traces (r) of the events involved. Frequently the activity cannot result in response termination, however, because the necessary objects are not available. Then the following primitive thought sequence occurs: energy increases $\rightarrow$ activity (R) $\not\rightarrow$ (does not lead) response termination $\rightarrow$ further energy increase $\rightarrow$ affective responses, thoughts of previous response termination events, or both $(r) \rightarrow$ partial reduction of the energy. The memories or thoughts are experienced *as if* they were the real thing; they are hallucinatory images and thus are partially reducing. Individuals differ in the thresholds of excitation necessary to trigger off these affective and memory responses.

All memory traces occurring before or after termination of psychological energy or intense responses become organized around such responses. Later, when the responses recur, they may arouse any of the associated memories, which are called *drive representations*. The only logic of their association is their relationship to a common intense energy or response—thus, the apparent illogical quality of dreams representing this kind of thought (primary process). Most such memories are visual images. Since they are organized around psychological energies with no other logical connections, increasing "drive" energy may shift "illogically" from one memory trace to another (*displacement*) and may activate several memory images at once, producing a compound image (*condensation*).

In addition to being aroused by the innate energy, however, the activated memory traces must be attended to if they are to become thoughts. This is considered as another type of energy, called *attention cathexis*, with which the memory trace must be invested if it is to become conscious. Since this kind of energy exists in limited quantity, only a limited number of memories (thoughts) may be present in consciousness at a given time.

The purpose of this primitive thought pattern is to produce reduction of intense psychological energies (instinctual drives) through memories which have the quality of the "real thing" (hallucinated) when the necessary situations are absent (*wish fulfillment*). However, if the intensity becomes so great that an adequate amount of reduction is not possible through memory traces and affective discharge, such responses become inhibited, with the person automatically or voluntarily disregarding them (withdrawing attention cathexis). This is called *primal repression* and is analogous to physical withdrawal or flight.

This kind of thought (*primary process*) is characteristic of that phase of consciousness in which discriminations among one's own responses, external objects or events, and subjective responses are very gross or nonexistent. The patterns of thoughts, the content of which is primarily imagistic rather than verbal, are determined entirely by innate energies, and their purpose is to provide direct reduction of such energies. This is the first kind of thought humans develop, and it predominates in infants. It is less characteristic in adults but occurs in dreams and certain states of behavior disorder.

As the memory responses and the function of consciousness develop, another kind of thought begins to evolve. Memory traces of experienced situational events and of the individual's own past responses begin to be organized, not around psychological energies but around other attributes such as space, time, similarity, and self-other discriminations. The memories occur in a different phase of consciousness in which they are experienced as memories rather than as "hallucinated realities." Although they may be related to psychological energies, they are not organized around them. It is important to note other developing capacities, which relate to this new kind of thought development. It will be recalled that the infant is beginning to acquire capacities to delay the discharge of energies, to anticipate future events as well as recall past ones, to direct his behavior toward selected objects or consequences, and to imitate the behavior of others. All these developments converge and provide the basis for the development of logically ordered or goal-directed thinking (*secondary process*). Although both kinds of thinking continue to occur, logical, situationally oriented, goal-directed thinking gradually comes to predominate. On the other hand, "drive-organized" thinking, which does not have the necessary relations to reality, represents a decreasing proportion of normal adult thinking.

Some logical thought is directly elicited by psychological energy. However, logical thought functions to delay the discharge of such energy while the individual tries out, in thought, potential courses of action (experimental action) and then chooses the most appropriate one to perform. Although some thinking is motivated by fundamental psychological energies such as sex, however, other thoughts occur as a consequence of different types of response elicitors. On the one hand, thinking gradually becomes independent of the innate psychological energies (ego autonomy), and on the other hand, such behaviors become less dependent on immediate external stimulation (internalization). It is important to note that thought plays both a response-inhibiting and a response-eliciting function.

The concept of *hierarchical structures* is given great emphasis. The term structure refers to habitual patterns of behavior, of which certain thought habits (cognitive structures) are particularly important. These patterns or organizations of behavior may originate in relationship to physiological energies or other antecedents, but once they become habitual they may operate independently of the original conditions. In fact they may serve as antecedents to other future behaviors; they become functionally autonomous.

These learned patterns of behavior tend to build one upon the other, forming a *hierarchy*. Those at the base of the hierarchy were developed earliest and those at the top of the hierarchy latest; the latter occur most frequently at the present. If for some reason behavior patterns (structures) at the top of the hierarchy cease to occur, behavior patterns lower in the hierarchy become more likely to occur (*regression*). Implied in this notion of hierarchical structures is the idea that once a behavior pattern becomes habitual (learned) it is not unlearned, but may cease to occur through the learning of a new behavior pattern that displaces it. Thoughts become organized into hierarchies, too, with the "drive-organized," imagistic thought patterns earliest in the hierarchy, and these become gradually replaced by logical thought sequences (Rapaport, 1951c).

Related to the concept of stable organizations of behavior (structures) is the concept of *automatization*. This means that a voluntary effort is required when one learns a new behavior pattern or organization, but that after extensive practice, such a behavior pattern tends to occur automatically with little conscious thought. In learning to drive a car one must think about each act in sequence, such as stepping on the clutch, shifting gears, and braking to a stop; however, an experienced driver may go through the intricate motions of driving his car while carrying on an involved conversation with his companions. The same thing occurs in the development of organizations of thoughts (Rapaport, 1951c). Newly developed thought patterns may come to function independently of the original conditions (become autonomous) and may serve as starting points for the development of still further thought patterns. When confronted with a situation to which he must respond (a "task"), the individual elicits a general thought pattern delimiting the ideas to be used in responding to the task.

This is a more general formulation of the role of "sets" or "attitudes" (particular kinds of conceptual structures) in determining which kinds of responses are likely to be made.

In this context, defense mechanisms can be seen as only one kind of habitual behavior pattern (automatized structure). Their antecedents are certain kinds of physiological responses (r) called drives. However, there are many other such stable behavior patterns which are not necessarily defense mechanisms, and whose antecedents may be primarily situational events or other subjective responses such as thoughts. Patterns originally learned to control physiological responses (r) later may come to be used as patterns of responding to situational events quite independent of the responses from which they originated.

Thus, ego-analysts have modified Freud's theories about the development of normal behavior to de-emphasize the role of innate psychological energies and to give increased importance to situational events and to the learning of adaptive behaviors for reasons other than to control or discharge instinctual psychological energies. They have emphasized the fact that man develops increasing independence from the automatic influence of both situational events and internal goads to action. Man increasingly selects and controls his own behaviors to achieve particular consequences. He consistently becomes more of a pilot of his behavior and less of a robot. The role of learned responses as antecedents to future behaviors is stressed. Not all of man's behavior is the result of a compromise of conflicting psychological responses and situational events. Much of it is instrumental, directed at achieving consequences, the relevance of which is quite independent of innate psychological energies. This means that the role of society is far more than just one of thwarting or obstructing the "natural" expression of such responses. Rather social rules and individual behavior are reciprocal influences, with society making possible the existence of the person and the full expression of innate characteristics other than instinctual psychological energies.

The Development of Behavior Disorder

The ego-analysts have elected to develop Freudian theory into a more adequate general psychology. Thus, they have been more concerned with the development of normal behavior since this was the least adequately developed aspect of Freudian theory. Extended treatment of behavior pathology was not found among the writings of the theorists on whose work this chapter is based. Some of the implications of their formulations have been pointed out, however, and these can be briefly summarized.

It will be recalled that the direction of normal development is toward the increasing independence of behavior from the imperative demands of instinctual psychological energies (emphasized by Freud) and automatic responding to situational events (emphasized by some psychological theories). This "relative autonomy" is achieved through the development of stable response patterns (structures), the contents of which are primarily conscious thoughts. Through them, the individual controls and directs his behavior rather than allows it to be automatically elicited by physiological responses or situational events. In all adults much normal behavior is not consciously controlled; it has become automatic. However, some of this can be made conscious and controlled if the individual desires to do so, for example, habitual car driving behavior which is usually not a consciously directed sequence of behavior. Even in "normal" people, however, some behaviors are not subject to conscious direction and control.

Whenever large portions of the behavior repertoire are not under conscious control, or when behavior in critical situations escapes self-control—such as the occurrence of uncontrollable rages when a person is threatened or thwarted—behavior pathology is considered to exist (Hartmann, et al., 1946; Rapaport, 1958). To use their terms, behavior disorder develops when the autonomy of ego from the id and from reality becomes seriously disrupted. Thus, predisposition to behavior disorder is present when the learned behavior patterns (structures) and their overall organization (ego) are in some important respects inadequate to the task of conscious, thoughtful control of behavior. Inappropriate ways of relating to other people (inadequate object attachments) may predispose an individual to the development of schizophrenia if he becomes exposed to the appropriate kinds of stress. A great variety of the stable patterns may be inadequate, but seldom are all of them inadequate. Since they are all interrelated, the pathological features of behavior cannot be understood fully without also understanding those stable behavior patterns (structures) which are still functioning effectively (Hartmann, 1953). In the face of the same stressful situations, such as the loss of a loved one, or the menopause, some individuals' behavior will become disordered, and others will not, because they differ in the kinds of stable behavior patterns they have developed to deal with such circumstances.

Since it is inadequacies in the conscious, thoughtful control of behavior—that is, the lack of autonomy from innate response and situational influences—that lead to behavior disorder, one must ask what conditions interfere with the stable behavior patterns (structures) which make self-control possible. Rapaport (1958) dealt with this issue in an interesting paper. He proposed that stable behavior patterns had to be maintained by a regular diet of *stimulus nutriment*. He seemed to mean that some kind of periodic consequents were necessary to maintain any behavior pattern. Incidentally, it is important to note that this concept would include disordered behavior patterns also. He used self-evaluative thoughts as an example. "The maintenance of conscience" required the "presence, opinions and memories" of other people, "who have always known the person and always will" (Rapaport, 1958).

If periodic approval of such evaluative thoughts and values by others does not occur, their controlling effectiveness may decline. A soldier, stationed in a foreign country where the statements and actions of his comrades encourage promiscuity, may participate in sexual adventures he would never have considered in his home community. However, the "nourishment" for the maintenance of such stable behavior patterns need not necessarily come from situational events. Under circumstances which are not clearly understood, the individual may provide his own approval through his own thoughts. It is apparently harder to maintain behavior this way, however, than through the effects of situational events. It may be important for an understanding of behavior disorder to recognize that behavior patterns may be maintained either by the periodic influence of situational events or by the influence of subjective responses such as physiological responses or thoughts.

It follows that behavior will become disordered when adequate consequents are unavailable to maintain the person's behavior or when existing response patterns are inadequate to control and direct intense events emanating from the environment or from within the person. One type of disruption occurs when behavior becomes dominated by subjective responses (r) such as physiological or affective responses. In such circumstances, behavior patterns, which depend on periodic consequences (nutriment) from situational events, will begin to disintegrate in the absence of such reinforcement. For example, studies of stimulus deprivation have shown that when external stimulation is markedly reduced, thoughts and images come to dominate awareness and may be responded to as if they were real situational events.

The fact that behavior can be disrupted through prolonged confinement in isolation (an ancient form of stimulus deprivation) is well-documented. Subjective responses may become so intense that they exceed the person's capacity to control them. Rapaport gives puberty as an example, wherein sexual responses may become much stronger and dominate behavior until new controlling behaviors are developed. In instances of extreme hunger or extreme fear, intense subjective responses may disrupt habitual behaviors. It also seems possible for individuals to impose a special kind of "stimulus deprivation" on themselves by disregarding situational events, thus limiting the effects of these events on their behavior (Rapaport, 1958).

Hartmann (1953) suggested that something like this probably occurred in schizophrenia and perhaps in other psychoses as well. Aggressive and sexual responses may "overwhelm" the controlling behaviors, eliciting intense subjective responses such as thoughts or images which are attended, while situational events which may evoke strong fear responses are ignored. The net result may be domination of behavior by subjective responses (r-r patterns) and ineffectiveness in responding to situational events (reality testing). Some aspects of schizophrenic thought can be described in this way. This fact would make it more likely that logical, goal-directed thinking would decrease, and those responses of the "primary process" would appear. Psychotics can attend to situational events, but avoid doing so in those situations that, if heeded, would be distressing to them. Psychosis represents a way of avoiding situational events (reality) that have become intolerable. In organic psychoses, the physiological structures—underlying memory, perception, and the like—are disrupted, and this in turn disrupts the learned patterns of behavior which entail these responses.

Still another way to disrupt behavior is to arrange conditions so that the individual's behavior becomes dominated by situational events. Response patterns that are maintained by subjective responses such as thoughts then begin to disintegrate in the absence of such maintaining consequences (*nutriment*). As an example, Rapaport (1958) mentions instances in which the occurrence or termination of intense psychological energy becomes completely blocked (*massive intrapsychic blocking*). He seems to refer to circumstances where mutually incompatible events occur within a person, each blocks the other, and neither may occur. In a conflict model of behavior, this would be represented by the point at which two response gradients intersect, that is, are of equal strength. When such massive blocking of subjective responses occurs, "stimulus-response slavery" results and the individual responds mechanically to situational events. Catatonic conditions of echopraxia, echolalia, and cerea flexibilitas are given as examples. Hypnosis is another way to produce a similar effect. Hypnosis is said to narrow the individual's attention to a very limited group of situational events—for example, to the hypnotist—and to remove the influence of subjective responses such as thoughts, although there is some disagreement about the extent to which this can be done. "Brain washing" is still another example. The techniques involved are: giving the individual no privacy, since privacy is a situation in which the events are reduced and therefore subjective responses become more dominant; removing all situational events (nutriment) which maintain the existing thought habits, values, and the like that one wishes to alter, by not permitting or punishing conversations among individuals who would reinforce one another's existing patterns; and exposing the individual to a constant stream of instructions and information and trying to force or seduce him to pay attention to them. In the absence of other situational events, they may overwhelm existing thought patterns and elicit new ones. Of course, the new patterns will also require continual reinforcement (nutriment) for their maintenance (Rapaport, 1958).

Here again, it appears that the individual can impose such conditions on himself to some extent. By learning habitually to "inattend"—that is, repress—large portions of his subjective responses and by developing habits of attending to selected situational events, one may find oneself more at the mercy of the influence of situational events. Hartmann (1953) suggested that something like this might occur in neurosis. He proposed that in neurosis "insight into inner reality" was disrupted. The neurotic does not carefully observe his subjective responses and examine their validity or their relationships with other responses and situational events. Thus, it is difficult for him to modify his responses, since he neither examines nor tests them.

In summary, ego-analysts have not attempted a major revision of Freudian theories of behavior pathology. They have suggested, however, that learned response patterns (structures), the conditions that maintain them, and the influence of situational events play a more prominent role in behavior pathology than Freudian theory represented. They acknowledge the role of psychological energies as important but reduce their importance by viewing them in the context of other significant influences on behavior as well.

THE GOALS OF THERAPY

No direct discussion of this issue was found in the writings examined. It seems implicit, however, that the basic Freudian position on the responsibilities of the therapist is accepted. Similarly, the general goals of treatment would appear to be the same. Their view of disorder would be expected to lead the ego-analysts to seek to change the learned behavior patterns (structures) that seem to be limiting the patient's ability to control his own behavior, and that make him subject to the control of either his psychological energies or of situational events.

CONDITIONS FOR PRODUCING BEHAVIOR CHANGE

Once again, this is a theoretical area about which ego-analysts appear to have done little writing, at least those whom this chapter represents. Hartmann (1951) has observed that many questions of technique remain unanswered. Orthodox Freudian techniques seem to be generally used. Hartmann expressed the belief that psychoanalytic theory has developed to the point where more is known about how behavior develops and functions than can be used in a technical manner. He felt that a rationale of therapeutic procedures was lagging seriously behind other theoretical developments in psychoanalysis, but expressed confidence that it would eventually be possible to develop a technique system.

In the same vein, Rapaport (Klein, et al., 1961) was convinced that the most crucial weakness in psychoanalytic theory was that it lacked a theory of learning. He was highly critical of contemporary learning theories in psychology, largely because he considered them "empty organism" theories. He believed them to be based on invalid assumptions about the innate characteristics of men. At the time of his death he was embarking on an attempt to develop a learning theory for psychoanalytic psychology. The key concept in his theory was that of attention.

Although it is not clear whether the changes in psychoanalytic theory suggested by the ego-analysts should lead to the use of different therapeutic procedures, there do seem to be important implications about the way the therapist should proceed to understand his patient's behavior and the kinds of events with which therapy should be concerned. Hartmann (1951) suggested several such implications. He pointed out that the therapist needed to understand not only the behaviors that were disordered but also those behavior patterns that were functioning effectively. The therapist should seek to discover the interrelationships between disordered and effective behavior—that is, between the conflict and nonconflict spheres of the ego. He should attempt to deal with the behavior patterns by which the person copes with his environment, since this is a crucial antecedent to both behavior disorder and effective behavior. The ego-analyst's attitude toward the importance of situational events would lead him to find the antecedents to the development of neurotic anxiety in frightening situations, since these must be its original source. And, of course, the ego-analyst would recognize that disordered behavior was not necessarily related to conflicts with psychological energies. This kind of orientation would lead the therapist to make more of his interpretations in terms of concrete, specific events rather, by implication, than in terms of abstract concepts of Freudian theory. His interpretations would be aimed at helping the patient become aware of relationships among specific aspects of his own behavior and between such behaviors and particular kinds of situational events.

Rapaport (Klein, et al., 1961) speculated that his idea of "stimulus nutriment" as essential in the maintenance of behavior might become the cornerstone of a psychoanalytic theory of technique. He pointed out, for example, that some of the traditional psychoanalytic treatment conditions, such as having the patient recline on a couch, having the analyst out of the patient's line of vision, and the prohibition against physically carrying out behaviors (acting out) amounted to a kind of stimulus-deprivation situation. The consequence of such conditions was for the patient's behavior to become more determined by his subjectively observable responses, and this was precisely what Freud wished in his technique of free association. This kind of stimulus deprivation, however, might not be appropriate for some patients who might need situational reinforcement regularly during their interviews. Rapaport noted that hospitalization also tended to reduce the situational events which might function to maintain behavior (nutriment). This might help the patient to recover if the events so avoided were those that were maintaining the pathological behaviors. There is the danger, however, that the events excluded from the patient's life through hospitalization might also be those maintaining necessary adaptive behaviors. If this is true, effective behavior patterns may be damaged by hospitalization.

Presumably, the therapist's technique for modifying a patient's behavior would be to gain an understanding of the disordered and instrumental behavior patterns and to determine what kinds of events maintain them, whether they were response events such as thoughts or situational events such as the behavior of other people. Having determined this, the therapist would proceed to manipulate the appropriate events to alter the disordered behaviors and introduce other events to strengthen the instrumental behaviors. The crucial question, of course, is: How can these manipulations be performed? What kinds of behavior elicitors and modifiers are to be used? When should they be used? What are the principles that govern their effectiveness? Psychoanalysis still awaits the formulation of an adequate theory of behavior modification.

APPRAISAL OF BEHAVIOR CHANGE
AND VERIFICATION OF THEORY

Very little was said about these issues in the writings examined. One important emphasis of theory verification seemed to be the study of children. One can speculate retrospectively as to what childhood development must be like from a study of adult behavior, as Freud did, but such hypotheses can be verified only through the direct observation of the behavior of children. In addition, since the formation of behavior patterns is considered to be a continuous development throughout life, and since new behaviors are thought to be built on patterns acquired earlier, the study of humans as they progress through various developmental phases is absolutely essential. The sticky problem of how to verify those hypotheses that refer to response phenomena occurring within the individual (drives, thoughts, affects) and that are not directly accessible to an objective observer receives no systematic treatment.

All possible approaches to verification (naturalistic observation, empirical and experimental research) appear to be encouraged. However, Hartmann (1952) made a strong point of the fact that systematic observation, whether naturalistic or in formal experiments, was not sufficient for verification. Systematic observation obtains facts, but facts must be interpreted. Thus, he emphasized the importance of a conceptual framework for *interpreting* the observations obtained, regardless of the procedure used. He pointed out that observations might "look different" when interpreted within a psychoanalytic framework than when interpreted within some other setting. The most significant research is that interpreted within some theoretical framework.

COMMENT

Perhaps the most important consequence of this stream of thought labeled ego-analysis has been to extend the conception of behavior presented by Freud. Man's behavior is far more than a by-product of instinctual energies of sex and aggression as they seek expression in a complicated world. There are many other "causes" of behavior as well. Man's complicated attempts to control his world and create new things are unlikely to be simply sexual and aggressive responses that have been sublimated. The current interest in rockets is probably not caused by the fact that they are magnificent phallic symbols. Rather, they are powerful tools by which man may extend his own behavior, discover new things, stimulate himself with new experiences, and gain fuller control over his environment.

Ego-analysts suggest that man does these things because he has evolved into a complicated organism with response sequences that are reasonably well suited to the kind of environment in which he is likely to live. Although innate psychological energies and responses are a part of these response sequences, there are other quite independent, innate response mechanisms upon which learned behavior also develops. Man is more than an angry, sexual animal whose attempts at self-gratification are continually thwarted or diverted by a hostile world. He has other capacities he seeks to exercise and develop, and he does many things simply for the satisfaction of doing them. He is not only partially controlled by his environment, but he also creates, in fact, his own environment to a significant extent. He guides and directs his own behavior to a great degree, rather than being primarily directed by powerful impulses and situational events.

Instinctual psychological energies have been demoted in importance, though not abolished, and the adaptive aspects of learned behaviors have been brought to the fore. The role of situational events in influencing behavior has been given added importance, though the group is quite explicit in emphasizing that it is as inaccurate to overemphasize the influence of situational events as it is to overemphasize the role of physiological response energies. The constructive influences of society and culture on man have been emphasized, as well as their role in obstructing the uncontrolled, animalistic expression of "instinctual drives." Behavior disorder is to be understood in the context of normal behavior development and as it relates to the individual's attempts to adapt to and mold his own environment.

All these modifications are in the direction of bringing psychoanalytic theory up to date in terms of developments in other fields of knowledge such as psychology, sociology, cultural anthropology, and biology. Just as many disciplines have been powerfully influenced by Freud's ideas, Freudian theory is being modified by the ideas and findings of other disciplines. One criterion for an effective and significantly growing theory is that its proponents continue to modify and develop it so as to encompass new ideas and new evidence as it becomes available. By this criterion, Freudian psychoanalysis as modified and elaborated by the ego-psychology theorists is still a lively and growing theory. However, it remains in need of theoretical formulations about how behavior is acquired and modified. Its impact on the various sciences of human behavior will be even greater if some psychoanalytic scholar could encompass and rigorously systematize into a full theory of human behavior all the concepts and propositions thus far developed.

Chapter 7

The Learning Theory Psycho-
therapy of Dollard and Miller

The point of view to be represented in this chapter results from
an interdisciplinary collaboration by two eminent scholars, Neal E.
Miller, an experimental psychologist, and John Dollard, a cultural
anthropologist, sociologist, and psychotherapist. Both men have been
deeply concerned, not only with theoretical and research contributions
to their own disciplines, but also with integrating knowledge in the
social sciences and in finding significant applications of such knowledge to the practical affairs of man.

Their book *Social Learning and Imitation* (1941) was the first major
product of their collaboration. In it they tried to integrate the theoretical formulations of Hullian learning theory and the evidence from
cultural anthropology and sociology about the social context of learning into one systematic scheme. This important book was the direct
antecedent of their second major collaborative effort, *Personality and*

Psychotherapy (1950). This latter work was based on three streams of thought wedded into a new synthesis. First, they drew on the work of Freud or, as they put it, those aspects of Freudian theory and practice that they understood best. Second, they made the theoretical formulations of Hull regarding learning and the acquisition of behavior a primary base for their point of view. Third, they took the ideas of Sumner, Murdock, Kluckhohn, and Warner, among others, concerning the relation of culture and human behavior as important foundations for their conceptions about social learning. The background of both men seems unusually appropriate for such a collaborative effort.

BIOGRAPHICAL INFORMATION

John Dollard was born in a small Wisconsin town in 1900. He acquired his A.B. at the University of Wisconsin in 1922, and pursued graduate study in sociology at the University of Chicago (A.M. 1930, Ph.D. 1931). In 1931–1932 he was a research fellow in social psychology in Germany, at the same time receiving training in psychoanalysis at the Berlin Institute. He worked for three years on the Memorial Union Building Committee at the University of Wisconsin (1923–1926), and for an additional three years as assistant to the President at the University of Chicago (1926–1929). In 1932 he joined the Institute of Human Relations staff at Yale University, where he has remained. He has published a large number of articles and books, which reflect the breadth of his scholarship. Viewed in sequence, they seem to represent a gradual shift in his interests from an emphasis on sociological and anthropological problems in the late 1930's, to psychological problems in the 1940's with his analysis of fear, to problems of psychotherapy in the 1950's. In addition to his scholarly contributions, he has been an active professional psychologist for years. He served as a consultant to the Secretary of War during the Second World War, is a certified professional psychologist, is a member of the Western New England Psychoanalytic Society, has participated in the training of psychotherapists, and personally has provided psychotherapy to a considerable number of persons. Thus, he brought to his collaboration with Miller an extensive knowledge of the cultural influences on behavior and considerable knowledge and experience in the theory and practice of psychotherapy.

Neal E. Miller is also a native of Wisconsin, having been born in Milwaukee in 1909. He was educated at the University of Washington

(B.S. 1931), Stanford University (M.A. 1932), and Yale University (Ph.D. 1935). He, too, joined the staff of the Institute of Human Relations at Yale in 1932, and has remained there except for a Social Science Research Council fellowship at the Vienna Institute of Psychoanalysis (1935–1936) and service during the Second World War as director of a psychological research project for the Army Air Force. His early training in the natural sciences has been influential in his approach to psychological theorizing. He has cited Smith and Guthrie at the University of Washington, Terman at Stanford, and Hull at Yale as important mentors. In addition, a brief psychoanalysis with Heinz Hartmann in Vienna was significant in stimulating his interest in psychoanalysis in particular and personality theory in general. His major theoretical and experimental contributions have been in the areas of conflict behavior, learned drives, and the circumstances of reinforcement. He has published extensively and is a widely honored scientist. He has received the American Psychological Association's Distinguished Scientist Award. Miller is noted for his efforts to apply the findings of experimental science to human behavior in concrete social settings. Thus, he brought to his collaboration with Dollard a background as an excellent scientist, some personal knowledge of psychoanalysis, and a set of values which viewed the application of psychological theory to important human problems as a challenging and worthwhile task.

DISTINCTIVE FEATURES

Dollard and Miller have been careful to specify that most of their propositions about psychotherapy are hypothetical and should be considered as a basis for research rather than as proven principles. Their approach followed their conviction that a sensible discussion of therapy depends in turn on the formulation of a theory of neurosis as well as a theory of normal behavior. Recognizing that the task was enormous and that insufficient data was available on many points, they presented their ideas as a "progress report," hoping it would prove valuable to the field. They explicitly recognized their formulations to be incomplete and full of unsolved problems. They further restricted their position by noting that the propositions about therapy pertain directly, at least in part, to twentieth century American culture.

This initial statement typifies the care with which these two writers have approached the task of theory construction. The ideas represented in their theories are not necessarily better than those of other theoreticians, but they have been formulated with more precision than most, reflecting the writers' sophistication about the task of developing concepts and propositions into a sound system. Thus, an outstanding feature of this therapy position is the orderly and systematic fashion in which it has been constructed. Miller in particular is highly knowledgeable about the requisites of theory construction, and this fact is revealed in several major publications (1950, 1952, and 1959). He asserts that all scientists (and we suspect he would include professionals) consciously or unconsciously use some kind of theory. "Pure empiricism is a delusion" (1959, p. 200).

Several characteristics of Dollard and Miller's concepts and propositions should be noted. They have taken concepts developed to summarize observations of animal behavior and have assumed they are valid for predicting human behavior in psychotherapy. They cite the observations of psychotherapists, primarily psychoanalysts, as being similar to the kinds of observtions they would predict from these principles. However, they explicitly recommend rigorous research to verify this assumption.

Moreover, learning theory, in their view, has tended to emphasize the development of principles to account for *consistencies* in behavior patterns, rather than for the different *kinds*. The focus has been upon the way in which habits are acquired and modified, rather than on the various kinds of habits developed. This has entailed an assumption that the same general principles will be found to govern the acquisition of behavior regardless of kind. For example, it is assumed that habits of thought are acquired in precisely the same way as motor skills. If this is true, many fewer propositions can be used to explain the acquisition and modification of the great variety of subjectively observable (r) and objectively observable (R) responses.

A further characteristic of their position is that most of the major concepts refer to *relationships among events* rather than to *kinds of events* themselves. For example, the concept label cue may refer either to situational events or to response events of any kind. Any kind of event can exert a *selective influence* on the kind of responses that will follow its occurrence; the term cue refers to the selective influence rather than to the kinds of events doing the influencing.

Miller is well aware of the fact that Hullian learning theory has paid more attention to the connections between events than to kinds of events and has jokingly said that it has paid more attention to the hyphen in S-R theory than to the S and R themselves. Dollard and Miller, however, clearly recognize that to understand a particular individual's behavior, it is necessary to determine the kinds of events, both response and situational, that are specific to that person. In a sense they are nomothetic in regard to the principles that govern behavior in general but are idiographic with respect to the kinds of behavior and situational events influential for any specific person. They propose that individuals differ in terms of the content of their behavior and the context in which they live; they do not differ in the way in which their various behaviors operate—that is, people differ in the "what" of behavior but not in the "how."

Moreover, this is a "liberalized" S-R theory in the sense that concepts pointing to subjectively observable responses (r) are used extensively. In this system of psychotherapy, the two major sets of concepts used are *fear* and *thoughts* (higher mental processes). These terms refer to events that are not directly accessible to an objective observer. As Miller has pointed out, treating "central" responses such as perception, imagery, and emotion as behavior brings S-R theory much closer to the general group of cognitive theories. However, they assume that the "central processes" follow the same laws that govern peripheral or objectively observable events, while many cognitive theories propose that such events follow laws that are particular to these events and are different from those that control objectively observable responses. Both agree that an adequate understanding of human behavior, particularly neurotic behavior, requires that subjectively observable responses (r) such as fear and thought be given a central role.

This system also emphasizes the importance of situational events in determining human behavior. Not only does society represent the source of rewards and punishments which will help to mold the individual's behavior, but it is also a reservoir of the most successful responses man has found to deal with particular kinds of situations in the past. Successful therapy cannot be effected unless the therapist has an extensive knowledge of the influential social and cultural factors, namely, situational events.

Dollard and Miller are not specific as to the size of units that their concepts entail, nor do they specify which units of behavior are most appropriately used within their theoretical system. They indicate that the concept of *response* may be used to refer to a very small unit of behavior such as an eyeblink as well as to a very elaborate unit such as driving an automobile. Even so, this position is considerably more atomistic than most, since it holds that complicated patterns of behavior can be analyzed in terms of the smaller units out of which they are built. For example, car driving may be thought of as a response—it functions as a unit—but in its acquisition more specific units such as thoughts, shifting gears, stepping on the clutch, noticing a stop sign, are all included, and each of these particular events come to be related through learning into a pattern sequence which then occurs as a consistent unit.

Finally, it seems apparent that behavior is thought to be learned and maintained in an automatic and involuntary fashion. Drives and cues function so as to cause the appropriate responses to occur (1950, p. 32). If the appropriate response is elicited and followed by reinforcing conditions, learning (a cue-response connection) will automatically occur. They state that their position is based on the assumption that reinforcement has a direct, unconscious effect (1950, p. 22). Although they asknowledge the possibility that all learning may not occur in this way, they proceed to develop their proposals assuming the automatic effects of reinforcement. Strictly speaking, such a position leaves the person at the mercy of the conditions he experiences. In that sense, the individual is like a machine. Conscious participation by the learner is not required. If one were to set up the appropriate conditions, the performances of the person could be controlled or determined. As will become apparent, however, their definition of reinforcement is sufficiently general to leave room for some qualification of this position. When they turn to the analysis of complex adult behavior, the notion of consciousness begins to play a central role. They make it clear that the conscious control of one's own behavior is most desirable, adaptive, and efficient. The person does this primarily through the use of learned sentences, but such sentences are learned through the drive-cue-response-reinforcement paradigm, and thus, "self-control" is simply a consequence of automatic, involuntary learning. Thoughts are given a central role in this formulation, but they, too, are acquired through automatic reinforcement under appropriate conditions. The purposiveness or self-directing aspects of human behavior are viewed as more apparent than real.

THE DEVELOPMENT OF NORMAL BEHAVIOR

Dollard and Miller have not attempted to present an extended discussion of the development of normal behavior. Rather, they have summarized what they believe to be the basic pattern of learning. They have focused not so much on what is learned in the course of normal development but on how it is learned. Moreover, they express their belief that one of mankind's greatest needs is for a "science of child rearing," for a theory about and techniques for developing normal behavior; such a "science" would make it possible to prevent the development of much serious behavior disorder.

INNATE CHARACTERISTICS

It is desirable to begin this section with a discussion of the two major concepts of response and stimulus, since many of the later concepts to be discussed are really subclasses of these.

Response

Dollard and Miller do not attempt to define the concept of response in terms of physical energy or anatomical location as have some other stimulus-response exponents. The present state of knowledge makes it preferable to begin with functional behavioral definitions of basic concepts; only later should efforts be made to relate these to other kinds of events, such as physical energy. Their definition of a response is considerably broader than the one characteristic of traditional behavioristic psychology, that is, "a muscular contraction or a glandular secretion" (1941, p. 59).

A response is distinguished from other kinds of events in that it is any "activity" which can become "functionally connected" with an antecedent event through training (1941, p. 59). The attribute of functional connection can be identified only after the fact, that is, after it has occurred. Miller pointed out that this definition is not circular when one uses that identification to predict that in future circumstances the same response can become connected to other antecedent events. It should also be noted that this use of the label *response* does not denote any specific kinds of events. Thus, it is an inclusive concept which can refer to subjectively observable responses, such as thoughts, as well as objectively observable response events, such as muscular movement. Nor is there any limit to the amount of behavior (size of unit) to which it can refer. It can denote a very limited event such as a muscle twitch, or a very complicated set of events such as the swimming pattern.

Stimulus

A stimulus is any event to which a response can become connected through learning. The concept is not specific as to the kinds of events involved. *Any kind of situational or response event can become a stimulus.* The concept simply refers to the fact that events can become functionally related to responses; it refers to the hyphen in *S-R* theory. It does not limit the nature of that functional relationship. Thus, it would appear that a stimulus may be either a response elicitor or a response modifier. It is important to recognize that a stimulus cannot be identified as such until it has become related functionally to a response. In this sense, the definition of stimulus is also circular. Miller argues, however, that it is not circular when one uses this information to predict that in future situations the same event (stimulus) can become similarly connected to other responses. Three concepts representing different kinds of functional relationships (subclasses of stimuli) will be discussed later. These are drive, cue, and reinforcement.

Dollard and Miller discuss two other attributes of the concept of stimulus which are quite important: "stimuli may vary quantitatively and qualitatively." By this they mean that different *kinds* of events— events that are qualitatively different—may become functionally related to responses. Moreover, the *strength* or *intensity* of the event— quantitative differences—is an important factor determining the kind of functional relationship that is likely to develop. The attribute of intensity will be important in differentiating between the concepts of drive and cue.

As with the concept of response, there is no limitation on the size of unit to which the term stimulus can refer. For example, either a relatively discrete event, such as a flash of light, or highly complicated patterns of events may become functionally related to a response. The latter is exemplified by the sound of a siren, the sight of a police car in the rear view mirror, and a companion's statement that it is the State Police that lead to the lifting of the foot from the accelerator of one's car. Dollard and Miller comment upon man's marvelous capacity to learn to respond to elaborate and subtle relationships or patterns of events.

In any situation there are a great variety of attributes to which the person might respond, such as the absolute position of an object, its relative position, its absolute brightness, its relative brightness, its color, its form, or its distinctiveness. Moreover, responses are also occurring within the individual which represent further events which can become functionally related to subsequent responses. Response events, as well as situational events, can function as stimuli. No principles are presented to enable one to know which attributes are most likely to be influential. Miller notes that some research with children suggests that the relative dominance of different types of events that may function as stimuli seems to change somewhat with age, although there may be a variety of other factors as well.

With the concepts of response and stimulus in mind we can now proceed to discuss the innate characteristics of human beings as stated or implied in Dollard and Miller's formulation.

Innate Response Characteristics

There are four general subclasses of innate response to which Dollard and Miller indirectly refer.

MOTORIC AND PHYSIOLOGICAL RESPONSES. These include visceral sensations as well as muscular activity or body movement. Infants are capable of a limited number of such responses, which are gross in character. However, they automatically occur under specific conditions; they might be considered automatic reflexes. Although mentioned, this class of responses received little direct attention in the body of their therapy theory.

PRIMARY DRIVES. These include pain, thirst, hunger, fatigue, cold, sexual excitement, and "perhaps others." They are particularly important in Dollard and Miller's system because they are invariably followed by a sequence of responses. For this reason, they are called *primary* or *innate drives*. Their primary significance is that they "force" the occurrence of, or "impel," behavior. They function as response elicitors, initiating a general *sequence of responses* but not specifically determining the occurrence of a particular kind of response. Thus, innate drives are considered to be a subclass under the general concept of stimulus.

There are two important attributes defining this class of events. The first is that of kind: pain is a different response event than fatigue. The second important attribute is that of intensity. Events function more effectively as behavior initiators the more intense they become. Some of these, such as hunger and sexual excitement, seem to occur as a consequence of innate physiological rhythms, somewhat independent of the situational events surrounding the person. Every individual will periodically become hungry. Such responses have a special urgency because the individual cannot escape their occurrence, nor can he arrange his life so that they do not occur. He can only attempt to terminate them once they have begun.

EMOTIONS. This group includes responses such as fear, anger, nausea, and disgust. In many respects, these responses have properties similar to innate drives. They are innate; they can become intense; and they can elicit behavior sequences. There is one important difference, however. They do not inevitably occur as a consequence of physiological rhythms of the body. Special conditions are required to elicit them.

Fear is an emotion to which considerable attention is given. For one thing, they propose that a great deal more is known about fear than about other emotional patterns. But, in addition, it seems to play an especially important role in the development of neurotic behavior because of the wide range of intensity that can characterize its occurrence, because of a great variety of conditions that may come to elicit it, and because of the particular consequences that automatically follow. They suggest that other responses in this group, such as anger, are likely to operate in a similar manner, although they acknowledge that the evidence for this suggestion is slim.

Dollard and Miller presume that certain conditions innately elicit a fear response. Evidence derived from research with infant animals and children suggests that any sudden and intense stimulation through any sense modality automatically produces fear. For example, a sudden loud noise, sudden changes in the infant's posture such as would be caused by a person's dropping it, or sudden bright flashes of light all seem to evoke fear. They also propose that there are innate differences between individuals, in the threshold of intensity sufficient to elicit fear as well as in the amplitude of the fear response itself.

Dollard and Miller propose that there are several behavioral consequences of fear which are innate as well. They discuss two seemingly contradictory overt patterns: (1) to remain motionless and mute or (2) to show startle, withdrawal, running, and screaming (1950, p. 76). Sometimes fear seems to interfere with the smooth occurrence of many other types of responses, producing effects such as stuttering, inability to think, or inability to move. At other times, it is followed by attempts to escape the circumstances that elicited the fear, such as avoidance or withdrawal. Finally, there appear to be additional physiological consequences of fear which are described as automatic and innate. Examples given include an increase in stomach acidity, alterations in the rate and the regularity of the heart beat, perspiration, excretion, and subjective feelings of fainting and nausea.

THOUGHTS. Dollard and Miller give primary attention to thoughts, or "the higher mental processes." They do not propose that certain *kinds* of thoughts are innate. The kinds of thoughts one thinks, or the content of one's thought, is said to be learned. They propose, however, that there is some "innate capacity" on which thought is based, and presume that there is some type of embryonic thought response, the nature of which is "still unknown" (1950). Dollard and Miller provide a detailed account of the manner in which thoughts are acquired and function by applying their general principles to this kind of response. It would appear that innate drives, fear, and the capacity for thought are the three most important kinds of innate responses of concern to the psychotherapist, judging by the amount of space accorded them by these two theorists.

Innate Principles of Behavior

The fundamental process of learning is also part of the innate equipment of man, and several innate principles of behavior are proposed to govern the process of learning. It is assumed that in order for the person to respond, some event must occur to initiate that activity. As has already been indicated, certain subjectively observable responses (r), such as hunger and pain, automatically produce behavior sequences; they are innate drive stimuli. In addition, *any* event, whether it be a response or a situational event, will evoke responses or initiate a behavior sequence if that event becomes sufficiently intense; it may function as a drive stimulus. These behavior elicitors—these drive stimuli—do not determine precisely which responses will occur, however. Several different kinds of responses may occur as a consequence of particular sets of behavior elicitors. Each response has a certain probability of occurrence under given conditions. When a behavior elicitor occurs, the response with the highest probability will occur first, the response with the next highest probability second, and so on. There are *innate response hierarchies*. Humans innately try to avoid or terminate any event that becomes intense enough to elicit behavior. Responses keep occurring in decreasing order of probability until one occurs which serves to reduce the intensity of the event that initiated the sequence. Any response which succeeds in reducing the intensity of the event that elicited it will become more likely to occur in future circumstances; it will become higher in the response hierarchy. This set of phenomena is called the *principle of reinforcement*.[1]

There are two additional principles controlling the reduction in the probability of occurrence of a response (lowering it in the response hierarchy). The likelihood that any response will occur will decrease if it is not used (*forgetting*) or if it no longer leads to a reduction in the intensity of the instigating event (*extinction*). The effects of extinction, however, are not necessarily permanent. If after the passage of time the original eliciting events recur, the extinguished response will be found to have increased automatically in probability of occurrence. This phenomenon is called *spontaneous recovery*, which seems to be the opposite of forgetting and, therefore, must interact, although Dollard and Miller do not discuss this possibility.

These principles are postulated to explain how the probability of a response occurring in a future similar situation changes. This is called learning. Although precisely the same situation never recurs, the response still occurs in new situations which are highly similar to the original one. To account for this fact, Dollard and Miller assume that there is a tendency for a response to be elicited by any event that is similar in some way to the original learning situation. This is the principle of *stimulus generalization*, which is an automatic occurrence, innately characteristic of the human person, and not the consequence of any conscious process on the part of the individual.

There is another type of generalization. The response that occurs immediately preceding or at the same time as the reduction of the intensity of the eliciting event will show an increase in probability of occurrence on a later similar occasion. However, not only that response but also other related responses occurring earlier in the sequence will show a similar increase in probability. The farther removed the response is in time or space from the reduction in the intensity of the

---

[1] Dollard and Miller are careful to state that for purposes of their position it is not necessary to assume that this is the only innate principle that governs learning. Rather it is only necessary to assume that some learning is governed by this principle; however, it is true that their entire exposition is built around this principle alone. Thus, it seems reasonable to interpret their position as being based on this principle and no other.

eliciting event, the smaller the change in response probability. This is referred to as the *gradient of reinforcement*. It, too, appears to be an automatic principle independent of any voluntary or conscious effort on the part of the individual. Both of these effects, stimulus generalization and the gradient of reinforcement, are more pronounced the more intense the eliciting event, that is, the drive stimulus.

In summary, these innate principles are assumed to be universal and general to all kinds of human behavior. Moreover, they function automatically and are independent of awareness or volitional effort on the part of the individual. The development of human behavior follows from the interaction of a finite number of innate responses occurring in various situations, according to a set of behavioral principles or laws. All responses in all persons are assumed to be acquired, maintained, or altered according to the same general sets of laws, all the way from the simple restricted response up to highly complex behavior patterns.

Learned Characteristics of Normal Development

As one might expect of a therapy system that utilizes learning theory as a primary base, there are extensive discussions about the acquisition of behavior. In effect, Dollard and Miller assume that the infant comes into the world with a limited number of responses. These are automatic, occur relatively independently of one another, and are only grossly related to situational events. Through learning, however, they become related to one another in elaborate patterns and sequences and come to be elicited by a great variety of situational and response events. All the intricate behaviors involved in putting a man into orbit around the earth represent the behavioral complexity that can be achieved as a result of such learned interconnections. In spite of the tremendous possible complexity, one must never lose sight of the fact that in this system, the ultimate purpose of behavior is to reduce or avoid intense events.

The Learning Process

At the simplest level of this system, four conditions must obtain if learning is to take place. First, some event must occur to *initiate a sequence of behavior* (there must be a drive). This, however, will not determine which specific responses are likely to occur. A second kind of event must occur, which has as its effect the eliciting of *particular kinds of responses* (a cue). Third, some kind of *response* must occur. Fourth, the consequence of that behavior must be a *reduction in the intensity* of the event that originated the sequence in the first place (reinforcement). When all these conditions are met, learning takes place.

The sequence may be very simple or very complicated and extend over long periods of time. A whole series of responses may occur over a period of minutes, hours, or even days, before it is possible to perform the response which has as its direct consequence the reduction of the originating event. We can examine these concepts in some detail and later illustrate how they function. The concept of response has already been discussed. The remaining three concepts of drive, cue, and reinforcement are subclasses of the general concept of stimulus which was earlier considered.

LEARNED DRIVE. It will be recalled that *any* kind of event may come to elicit a behavior sequence if it becomes sufficiently intense. Certain kinds of physiological responses are the primary elicitors of behavior sequences (*primary* or *innate drives*). Except in serious emergencies or in seriously underdeveloped societies, there is no deprivation so severe as to produce highly intense physiological responses. Few people in the United States experience severe hunger throughout their life, for example. Similarly, people seldom experience severe oxygen deprivation, although for asthmatics the occurrence or anticipation of severe oxygen deprivation can be a dominating behavior elicitor.

Because such severe conditions seldom occur in cultures in which psychotherapy is frequently practiced, they are rarely the predominant elicitors of human behavior. Rather, most human behavior is provoked by events that have *acquired* the power to elicit behavior through learning. *Learned* or *acquired drives* develop through contiguous association with the innately intense events (1950, p. 32). There are two differences between learned and innate responses which serve to produce behavior. First, innate responses vary in intensity primarily with the physiological condition of the individual and are relatively independent of other sets of conditions. On the other hand, learned responses vary in intensity according to the conditions that were present at the time of learning. Second, learned ones will automatically decrease in intensity if they are not periodically associated with the innate elicitor and thereby renew their "charge." Innate ones will not be weakened by such conditions.[2]

Many important behavior elicitors such as the desire for money, or the wish to succeed in college, derive their "motive power" through association with some intense innate responses. Ultimately, all such drives are reducible to the necessity for eating, sleeping, keeping warm, and the like. There is almost no limit to the number of different kinds of events that can acquire this power to impel behavior.

How intense must an event become before it will elicit a behavior sequence? That question is not answered. It seems implied that the most intense event occurring at a given time will determine the behavior, although it may itself be only moderately intense. In a sense the central purpose of behavior is to keep events from becoming too intense.

CUE. Dollard and Miller call the "strengthening of the cue-response connection" learning (1950, p. 30). Cues, like drives, operate as stimuli. Moreover, as is true of drives, any response or situational event may function as a cue. There are two important differences between the concepts of drive and cue. Drive refers to the attribute of events which we have called their intensity, while cue refers to an attribute called *distinctiveness*. Every event (stimulus) has a certain intensity (drive value) and a certain distinctiveness (cue value). The attribute of intensity (drive) initiates activity, but the attribute of distinctiveness (cue) determines *what* the person will do, as well as when and where he will do it. Intense events elicit *behavior sequences,* while distinctive events elicit *particular responses within a behavior sequence.* Thus, whether or not a specific event is distinctive (has cue value) seems to depend on the prior occurrence of a relatively intense behavior elicitor (drive). It must be clearly recognized that the concept of cue cannot be defined independently of that of drive. Which event will be distinctive enough to function as a cue will depend on the kind and intensity of the eliciting events at the time. It also depends on the attributes of the event itself.

If there are no distinctive events available in the situation, responses will occur according to their innate and learned probabilities of occur-

---

[2] Miller (1959) acknowledged that recent research raises serious question as to whether many learned drives are acquired in this way. He recognized that some modification of this principle may be essential. However, since a new position has not been explicitly formulated and applied to psychotherapy, we shall represent the ideas in the form in which they were presented in Dollard and Miller's book on psychotherapy (1950).

rence. If the first response is not effective, a second, third, or fourth will occur until one produces the necessary effect, the reduction of the intensity of a drive stimulus. This might be called random or trial-and-error behavior, and it is very inefficient.

For young children, the most frequent kind of distinctive event is the behavior of other people. A parent may demonstrate to the child how to print the letter "E." Then the child will attempt to copy the motions of the parent using the same tool, a pencil. This process is called *imitation*. Many responses that might have occurred are limited in favor of those most closely approximating the correct response. Of course, it may take considerable practice for the child to be able to reproduce exactly the response illustrated by the parent, but that is only an elaboration of the process. Our society "represents a storehouse of solutions to recurrent problems," and older members of our society teach younger members "to perform just those responses which are most likely to be rewarded" (1950, p. 38). This saves each individual the trouble of discovering for himself the most effective response for a particular situation. Once an effective solution to a problem is found, such as the discovery of a vaccine to prevent polio, all the elaborate sequences used by previous men "to find the correct response" no longer need be performed. Others can simply imitate the correct response without going through all the steps by which it was originally acquired.

When language has been acquired, it is no longer necessary to demonstrate to the individual the response to be performed. Words can be used to describe the "correct" response. Words come to play a significant role as distinctive events (cues) serving to elicit specific kinds of responses. One can tell a boy who has acquired language to turn on a light switch, rather than having to show him how to do it. In a sense, libraries are storehouses of words summarizing the responses mankind has made in the past. Although it may have taken a rare genius to formulate the theory of relativity, most others with a reasonable command of words can duplicate that set of responses in a very brief amount of time. An individual may also use words to instruct himself as to the appropriate responses to be made and then attempt to perform them correctly (thought). He can perform the correct response on the first try after having "thought it through" (*insight*). This brief discussion makes it clear why distinctive events which function to elicit particular responses from among the many which are possible are crucial in learning.

Unfortunately, we have been unable to find a discussion of how one distinguishes the attribute of intensity from the attribute of distinctiveness, and thus a clear distinction between the concepts of drive and cue is difficult, not only for the theorist but also for the practicing therapist. It does seem implicit in their discussion that the attribute of intensity is something the individual wants to get away from, avoid, or terminate, and all behavior has this goal. On the other hand, the attribute of distinctiveness does not seem to have that consequence. Despite the overlap, these two concepts are necessary in the system because they assume there must be some event to initiate behavior and then some other events to determine which kinds of behavior will occur.

REINFORCEMENT. The repetition of a response alone does not increase the probability that it will recur on future similar occasions. An additional condition is necessary. To be learned, a response must produce a consequence that reduces the intensity of the impelling event (drive). *Reinforcers,* then, are events that follow the occurrence of a response and have the effect of reducing the drive. They are response modifiers. *Reinforcement* is a label for the entire sequence.

What kinds of events may modify responses, that is, be reinforcers? Anything that will reduce the intensity of the event originating the response sequence will do so. This is called the *drive-reduction* principle, but, more specifically, might be called an intensity-reduction principle. Note once again that this concept is not specific as to kinds of events. Presumably, either situational or response events could suffice.

Dollard and Miller propose that certain conditions innately reduce the intensity of certain events. For example, the intensity of the hunger response can be reduced by eating some kind of food. It cannot be reduced by running. Many different events may *acquire* this capacity, however, and these are referred to as *learned reinforcers*. Not only will mother's milk reduce hunger, but so will hot dogs, pizza, fried snails, and roasted grasshoppers. As with learned drives, learned reinforcers acquire their power through association with circumstances that innately perform that function. An example of a learned reinforcer is money. Money is simply bits of paper and metal. A child may be given money for doing a task. He may be disappointed at first because he would prefer a candy bar instead. However, he trades the money for a candy bar which is eaten and reduces the intensity of a hunger response. After several repetitions of pairing money with candy and hunger reduction, the child will continue to work to receive money even though he can only put it in his purse and save it. He can be taught to perform many new responses, then, if he is given money after each correct performance. If the money is not periodically traded for something that can be used to reduce the intensity of some response elicitor, however, it will gradually cease to be effective. It must be "recharged" periodically, so to speak. With proper training, presumably any events, including thoughts, can do this. The child can be trained to work long and hard, sustained by thoughts of the money he will make or the praise he will later receive.

These, in brief, are the principles by which Dollard and Miller propose that behavior functions. All behavior, no matter how complicated, has as its objective the reduction in the intensity of some events impinging on the person. Thus, the behavior of a person over an extended period of time is one of constant ebb and flow, occasioned by the arousal-activity-termination sequences that follow one another in a never-ending series.

Two Crucial Responses

Dollard and Miller extensively discuss two kinds of responses which are affected by learning and which play crucial roles in both normal and disordered behavior. These are fear and thoughts.

FEAR. It will be recalled that fear is an innate response which occurs automatically under certain specific conditions, such as pain. It has three primary properties. First, it can become very intense, and the more intense it becomes the more active will the individual become in attempting to terminate the fear response; it functions as a drive. Second, it can come to be elicited by a great variety of other events; it is a learnable drive. Third, the automatic consequences are avoidance of the feared events and interference with the performance of other responses. Since fear is a normal innate response, it is less important "how afraid a man is than what fear motivates him to do" (Miller, 1959, p. 258). Anxiety and fear are similar responses, differing only with respect to the person's ability to identify what it is that elicits the fear.

How do events that have no innate capacity to induce fear acquire that function? Innately certain conditions, such as pain, will provoke fear. Thus, any event that produces pain will be followed by fear. If some other event is present or associated with the event that produces pain and thereby fear, it can acquire the capacity to induce fear through that association. A dog bite produces pain and elicits fear. The fear becomes attached to many other contiguous events; the child who has been bitten may respond with fear to the sight of the dog, the neighbor's yard, the sound of the dog growling, and perhaps several other events. The dog's bite is no longer necessary to elicit the fear. Thus, fear is learned in the sense that it can be attached to previously neutral events.

The fear response may then be intense enough to serve as an initiator of a behavior sequence (a learned drive), and a variety of responses may be learned to reduce the fear. The child may choose a different route home so that he can avoid seeing the yard or encountering the dog. If these responses are successful in reducing the fear or in preventing its occurrence altogether, they will become established in the person's repertoire.

Fear displays other characteristics. For example, the sight of a dog similar in appearance to the one that bit the child may produce intense fear, while the sight of a dog very different in appearance may produce mild fear (gradient of stimulus generalization). Avoiding the sight of the house just before the one which is the dog's domain may reduce the fear in part and contribute to learning, but avoiding the dog itself will produce more learning (gradient of reinforcement). Similarly, if the child goes by this house several times and the dog has become friendly and affectionate, the probability of any of the events eliciting fear will gradually decrease (extinction).

It is important to note that the fear response will remain unchanged unless the child is exposed to the feared situation and finds there is nothing to fear. For this reason fears are hard to eliminate. As the child leaves school he may think about passing the house and the dog; the thoughts may induce mild fear, which in turn leads the child to follow another route and avoid both. By avoiding the situation entirely the child never has the opportunity to unlearn (extinguish) the fear response.

A good bit of normal behavior is learned on this basis. For example, looking both ways before crossing a street may be learned to avoid pain and fear. Similarly, learning to drive carefully and getting regular medical checkups are examples of behaviors that are probably learned on the basis of some degree of fear.

Dollard and Miller propose that the effectiveness of punishment as a training device can be explained in terms of fear. It is not punishment itself that produces learning; rather punishment produces pain, which produces fear. Responses are learned which function to reduce the intensity of the pain and fear. Punishment will not be effective unless the responses one wants the child to learn lead to a reduction of the intensity of the pain and fear. Otherwise, the only effect will be teaching the child to be afraid of the person. On the other hand, if the child is punished at the time he is performing the undesired response, or while he is thinking of having performed it—for example, stealing— the next time he thinks of doing it, the thoughts will elicit fear and the fear in turn can be reduced by stopping the response.

In summary, then, fear is an innate human response which is originally elicited by limited events. Through learning, however, it can come to be elicited by many kinds of events. Any response that effectively reduces the intensity of fear will be learned, and thus, fear can motivate learning of socially desirable behaviors such as driving carefully, looking for the source of danger, and planning ways to avoid difficulties. It can also motivate the learning of undesirable behavior such as cheating, lying, and abandoning other human beings in danger. Responses learned on the basis of fear reduction are difficult to alter, because if they did not occur fear would increase. By learning to avoid situations that produce fear, the individual denies himself the opportunity of learning other responses to the same situations.

THOUGHTS. Where do thoughts come from, and how are they acquired? Thoughts are a consequence of social training, acquired by imitating the thoughts expressed by other people, either in speech or in writing. Some are acquired from people with whom one has direct contact; others are acquired through exposure to thoughts recorded in books. Thus, one may learn thoughts expressed by individuals long since dead.

What kinds of thoughts can be learned? Words are extremely flexible. With words, almost any kind of event can be represented symbolically whether it is physically present at the moment or not. There can be a word or sentence for any kind of response or situational event. There can be a word or sentence for any kind of relationship among events. Thus, the potential content of thoughts is as rich and varied as the multitude of events in the world. The implications of this fact for the enrichment and the efficiency of human behavior are tremendous. There are two major classes of thoughts. Some are *instrumental acts* whose function is to produce an immediate change in some other event which serves to reduce the intensity of the motivating event. In a sense they are the terminal responses in a response sequence and lead to response modifications. Other responses have as their function the eliciting of still further responses and have no direct effect on the intensity of the motivating events. Dollard and Miller called these *cue-producing responses*. In the thought sequences of the typical person there often is a chain of thought-producing thoughts (cue-producing responses) which ultimately lead to a terminal response.

How are such thoughts acquired? They are learned precisely as any other response is learned. Thoughts are not acquired simply by imitation of the verbal statements of others, but rather must lead to a reduction in the intensity of some impelling event if they are to be learned (reinforcement).

In addition to different kinds of thoughts, certain habits of thought are acquired in any given society. For example, in Western society: (1) Children are taught to inhibit the performance of instrumental responses while they "stop and think." (2) Social training teaches the individual to think thoughts according to certain logical rules— children who speak illogically are interrupted frequently with, "I don't understand you," or "That doesn't make sense." (3) Children learn to match words and sentences accurately with features of situational events and response events; they are admonished not to label a horse with "doggie." Similarly, children are frequently asked "Where does it hurt?" or "Were you frightened?" (4) Elimination of contradictions in their verbal statements and indirectly in their thoughts is strongly trained into children in social relationships. (5) There is a good deal of training to orient children in terms of time and space. (6) Social training teaches children to seek an explanation. Parents and teachers repeatedly ask questions such as "Why did you do that?" Thus, children are taught not only what to think, but also how.

Once habits of thoughts are acquired, they materially increase the efficiency and effectiveness of behavior. Since words can perform the same functions of impelling, eliciting, or terminating behavior as do the events they represent, the power of words is great. With the use of language and thought, a variety of new behavioral possibilities becomes available. First, thoughts can substitute for the performance of other responses. A scientist who wishes to find a filament for a light bulb need not laboriously try one substance after another as Edison did to discover an appropriate filament. He may think a series of thoughts he has learned in a course of physics and chemistry and arrive at a determination of which particular substances are more likely to be effective. He can then actually try out those selected substances. Obviously this is a much more efficient way of proceeding and enables him to take advantage of what previous humans have learned. Dollard and Miller called it *reasoning*.

An especially efficient kind of reasoning, called *creative thinking*, involves starting with the desired end result and reasoning backwards step by step until reaching a starting point. Still a third kind of reasoning is called *planning*. The individual thinks of a future situation in which he will have to respond, then considers the conditions that will influence the kinds of responses he can make in that situation, and tries to think of the most appropriate responses to perform when the situation occurs. Of course, effective reasoning, creative thinking, or planning is not possible if the individual does not have the appropriate thoughts in his repertoire, or if effective habits of thought have not been acquired. Many difficulties arise because people have faulty habits of thought, do not have the necessary thoughts (ideas) in their repertoire, or have thoughts that are inaccurate or inappropriate for a particular situation.

Thoughts also facilitate the *transfer of responses* from one situation to another. For example, one may have learned to think of particular situations as dangerous—the neighbor's dog is dangerous. An effective response may be learned to deal with that situation—avoid the dog. If some other situation is then labeled as dangerous, it is likely to elicit the same avoidance response: "That horse is dangerous" will lead to avoiding the horse. Even though the new situation may be very different in many respects, it can be made similar by the way one describes it to oneself.

Similarly, it is sometimes desirable to prevent responses from transferring to other situations. One may wish to teach *discriminations*. Words can greatly facilitate discrimination by labeling similar situations differently. When this is done, the labels summon different responses. For example, the neighbor's dog might be labeled "mean dog" and avoided, but another dog might be labeled "friendly dog" and petted. Where situations are highly similar and yet require different responses, labeling will facilitate discrimination by enhancing the subtle but important differences between the two. The language developed over the centuries in a particular society is a storehouse of discriminations and generalizations which have been found useful. Thus, each new person need not discover these discriminations and generalizations for himself. As a consequence of learning the language, he acquires these differentiations and thereby profits from the successful experiences of his predecessors as well as their errors.

Thoughts may be used to control emotional responses by interfering with other thoughts which elicit them. For example, a pain in the stomach may lead to the thought "I have appendicitis," which in turn may provoke fear. If the individual then thinks "No, it's not appendicitis, it's indigestion from that big dinner," the fear may be terminated. Such thoughts are response modifiers (learned reinforcers). Inappropriate labeling will facilitate the generalization of a fear response, whereas appropriate labeling will facilitate discrimination and the inhibition of a fear response, a fact that is important in behavior disorder.

ANTICIPATORY RESPONSES. Dollard and Miller propose one other very important feature of learning. As a response sequence is learned, responses occurring near the end of the sequence (immediately before reinforcement) tend to occur earlier in the sequence wherever possible. Responses occurring near the beginning of the sequence tend to drop out. Thus, after several learning occasions, the sequence becomes shortened. Such responses are called *anticipatory*.

This term does not refer to a response of anticipation, or to an anticipatory thought. Rather, it refers to *any* response of *any kind* that shows a tendency to occur earlier in a learned response sequence. This anticipatory tendency is involuntary and automatic and does not require any conscious process. It is explained in this way. Responses that occur near the end of a sequence acquire a greater increase in the probability of recurrence (reinforcement) than those occurring earlier in the sequence. The more frequently the sequence is repeated, the greater will be the difference in the probability of occurrence between the early and late responses in the sequence. Since responses with the highest probability of occurrence tend to occur first, it is obvious that those near the end of the sequence will become increasingly likely to occur sooner. The increase in efficiency thus produced is very evident. It shortens behavior sequences, making for economy in time and effort in achieving the desired consequences. Thus, old habits may appear to be far different than when first learned.

The anticipatory responses may be faulty, however. According to the principle of stimulus generalization, any similar situation will tend to generate the same sequence of responses. In the new situation, however, the responses may no longer be appropriate. For example, a man returning from work to his new home, may drive inadvertently to the house he has just moved from instead. Thought sequences may be similarly affected. "Jumping to a hasty conclusion" is a common illustration in everyday life.

To sum up, all behavior is learned as a means of terminating or avoiding the occurrence of relatively intense response events (drives). In the course of normal development, the majority of people develop habits of behavior which are relatively effective in reducing the intensity of all the innate events such as hunger and thirst, as well as those events which through learning acquire the power to impel behavior. It is normal and desirable that the individual should learn to fear certain things as a means of protecting himself from harm. Most people, however, will acquire habits of reducing the intensity or avoiding the occurrence of fear so that it does not disrupt other behavior sequences. The kinds of habits acquired to achieve these purposes will vary from person to person according to each one's own innate response characteristics and according to the situational events to which they are exposed. Among the most important kinds of responses learned are thoughts, which greatly increase the efficiency of behavior.

THE DEVELOPMENT OF BEHAVIOR DISORDER

Dollard and Miller take the position that most behavior disorder is learned according to the same principles as those governing the acquisition of normal behavior and is the consequence of faulty child-rearing practices. Responses considered to be disordered are similar in content to normal ones and differ only in terms of their intensity and frequency of occurrence. It is only that they are more apparent because they are extreme (1950, p. 5).

Although they do not explicitly limit the applicability of their ideas to particular kinds of disorder, Dollard and Miller consistently refer to neurotics. They advocate caution in generalizing propositions to other realms of disorder; for example, they indicate that certain psychotic disorders might require different treatment procedures than those they have developed. However, it remains implicit in their formulations that all behaviors are learned and unlearned according to the same general principles, and thus neurotic and psychotic disorders are in principle the same.

Antecedents to Disorder

Dollard and Miller build their propositions about the acquisition of disordered behavior on several necessary antecedents. First, disorders are a consequence of the occurrence of *conflict,* and thus this system retains a conflict model of disorder. Specific kinds of conflict are necessary, however, namely conflicts between events provoking responses—conflicts between drives—and more particularly, conflicts in which fear is a primary element. Moreover, if a conflict is to be productive of disorder, the person must have learned to repress and not to think about the conflict; it remains *unlabeled* or *unconscious. Symptoms* represent attempts to resolve the conflict but are only partially effective and productive of further difficulties.

CONFLICT. Building on Miller's detailed research on conflict behavior (1948), they begin with the proposition that "an intense emotional conflict is the necessary basis for neurotic behavior" (1950, p. 127). They appear to be using the term conflict in the usual sense, that of denoting a relationship between events wherein two or more mutually incompatible response sequences occur and cannot be simultaneously terminated. Of course, many different kinds of sequences can be in conflict, but in this view, the conflict between two or more of the initiators of behavior (two or more drives) is the crux of subsequent disorder. They note that a single event could become so very intense that it might lead to disordered behavior—to traumas—but they do not elaborate on this possibility and imply that relatively little disorder is of this type.

The reader will recall that drive is defined as the attribute of intensity of any event, and thus situational events could conceivably be in conflict with one another; drives are stimuli and drive stimuli include events external to the behaving person. However, Dollard and Miller appear to espouse a response-response conflict model. Most of their writing and virtually all their examples indicate that they conceive the incompatibility to reside within the response repertoire of the behaving person, not in the situation.

Most frequently they discuss conflict in terms of incompatibility between response sequences following some innate elicitor occurring as a consequence of physiological rhythm, such as hunger or sex, and emotions, such as fear and anger, which stem from learned connections with situations. Most of their examples of neurotic-type conflicts discuss the interaction between physiological response events (innate and primary drives) and emotional response sequences such as fear, anger, guilt, and the like. Their most frequent examples of conflict are those of hunger-fear, sex-fear, and sex-anger on the one hand, and anger-fear on the other.

Not only do they propose that the initial responses in the hunger sequence or the fear sequence conflict with one another—that the drives conflict—but also that in disordered behavior the responses elicited by the two sequences are likewise incompatible, as are the terminating responses appropriate to each. The conflicting response elicitors lead to incompatible consequents.

TYPES OF CONFLICT. All behavior sequences are placed in two major categories, *approach* and *avoidance*. Some events that initiate response sequences lead the individual to approach objects if the eliciting response is to be terminated—for example, sequences following hunger, thirst, or sex. By contrast, some lead the individual to avoid and remove himself from objects in order to terminate the response—for example, fear, nausea, and disgust.

If all events initiate or lead to two types of situation-response patterns, approach or withdrawal, several major kinds of conflicts are possible. Two approach sequences can be incompatible with each other, two avoidant sequences can compete, and finally an approach sequence can clash with an avoidant one.

In approach-approach conflicts, approach behavior toward two divergent objects may be elicited, and the individual cannot complete both simultaneously. For example, a person might wish to see a movie some evening and also be interested in attending a dance, although he cannot do both. This type of conflict is thought to have little significance for the development of behavior disorder, since no matter which alternative is chosen one of the two will be terminated. Moreover, it is often possible for persons to schedule their behavior so that they can terminate both sets of elicitors in series if not simultaneously.

In avoidance-avoidance conflicts two sequences are initiated, both of which lead to attempts to avoid two situations, and the person cannot do one without becoming committed to the other. In this instance, the person is "between the devil and the deep blue sea," or in currently popular therapy jargon, in a "double bind." A child may be afraid of water and yet also afraid of the ridicule of his peers. At a swimming class he would remain poised on the edge of the pool, fearing to jump in and yet fearing the laughter of his friends if he does not. In this example, both sets of elicitors are learned; the sight of water evokes fear, and the disapproving laughter of his friends does so, too. Ordinarily, the person in such a conflict seeks a third choice, which will permit him to avoid both frightening events. In this instance, the boy might feign illness and seek not only to avoid both sources of fear but also to arouse the sympathy of persons around him. Conflicts of this type may be the basis for subsequent disorder, but Dollard and Miller seem to consider it unlikely. In their judgment, it is infrequent that persons are placed in situations where there is no option other than one of the feared ones; usually persons are able to find "some way out." However, there are some alternatives that present intense dilemmas; for example, the choice between serious illness versus an expensive, painful, and frightening surgical operation.

In approach-avoidance conflicts, one response sequence leads the person to approach an object or situation, but at the same time another leads him to avoid it. For instance, a wife's sexual impulses (innate drive) might lead her toward intercourse with her husband, but the prospect of a fifth pregnancy might lead her to avoid it (fear of pregnancy a learned drive).

These represent Dollard and Miller's three major varieties of conflict. They are described in simple form, but ordinarily, at the level of complex human behavior, they are more intricate. For example, a variation of the third type of conflict is the *double approach-avoidance* situation. A young woman may be torn between marriage and a career, each of which have both attractive and unpleasant characteristics for her.

In general, the seeds of subsequent disorder usually lie in the conflicts in which response sequences of avoidance are aligned against those of approach. The principal kind of antecedent leading to avoidance behavior is proposed to be fear.

FEAR. Although Dollard and Miller suggest that events other than fear —for instance, disgust or revulsion—might lead to avoidance responses, they suggest that fear is the primary problem producer in so far as it contributes to conflict. They acknowledge that they may have over-emphasized the role of fear in behavior disorder because so much is known about it. However, they cite three reasons why they propose fear to be most important. (1) It can become so intense that most of the person's repertoire is devoted to reducing or terminating it; (2) it can become so generalized that it is elicited by a wide range of situations, and thus the person is frightened recurrently; and (3) it can be sufficiently pre-eminent that it interrupts and interferes with the occurrence of responses necessary to terminate other intense and urgent elicitors such as hunger or warmth. The person can be so afraid that he neglects to eat or take the usual precautions in wintry weather.

Of course, fear is part of everyone's repertoire, and many important responses are learned by the ordinary person in order to reduce, control, and deal constructively with it. When fear becomes aligned against other significant behaviors, however, the prospects of difficulty and possible disorder increase importantly. The seedbed of subsequent disorder is composed of such conflicts as hunger versus fear, sex versus fear, and anger versus fear. Such conflicts as sex versus guilt are also possible, but they follow the same general form since the guilt response is considered to be a variety of fear and to operate in the same fashion.

THE CONSEQUENTS OF CONFLICT. Dollard and Miller present principles to describe and therefore predict the kind of behavior that will occur when an individual is in a state of approach-avoidance conflict. These are based on several propositions. The intensity of the responses to approach or avoid is determined first by the intensity of the eliciting events (drives) and second by the proximity to the situation that would terminate it. Thus, an intense fear would lead to intense responses to avoid the situation prompting it. Moreover, the closer the person is to the situation that elicits the fear, the more intense the fear response will be (the gradient of avoidance). Similarly, with approach tendencies, the closer the person gets to the situation, the more intense his approach responses would be (gradient of approach). Thus, proximity to the situation increases the intensity of both approach and avoidance responses; however, fear increases at a faster rate. The gradient of avoidance is steeper and rises more sharply than the gradient of approach. If one were pitted against another, for example in an approach-avoidant conflict relative to the same situation, some predictions could be made.

At the beginning, instigators to approach and avoid the same object or situation are operative, and the events occasioning the approach behaviors are stronger than the fear eliciting the tendency to avoid. This leads the person to approach, since on previous occasions this has led to a reduction of the intense events that started the behavior sequence. The situation also elicits fear, however, and the closer the individual gets to the situation the more intense becomes the fear. At some point, the intensity of the avoidance responses will exceed that of the approach responses.

Responding to the fear, and thus avoiding the situation, the person backs away, progressively reducing the intensity of the fear as he does so. He continues until he reaches a point where it again becomes less intense than the original event that impelled him to approach. As the approach sequence predominates once more, he begins to approach the situation, only to have the series repeat itself again and again. Thus, in an approach-avoidance conflict, one can anticipate that the person will vacillate back and forth, approaching and avoiding the desired and feared object. He is caught and unable to terminate either of the intense events that elicit the two response sequences of approach and avoidance. Moreover, the pressure to do so remains high and perhaps even increases; the person is in a *state of heightened drive*. From the standpoint of the objective observer the individual will show vacillation and muscular restlessness and tension; from the standpoint of the subjective observer he will feel discomfort and distress, that is, *misery*. Very intense and unresolved conflicts produce intense suffering and misery (1950, p. 222).

Although their description of approach-avoidance conflicts is often presented in spatial terms, Dollard and Miller propose that the same principles apply in other dimensions as well. Thus, nearness means not only spatial proximity, but also approaching in terms of time, or of any similar "qualitative or culturally defined" dimension. Hence, approach responses as a term refers to nearing not only a physical object, but also a time, an event, a symbol, or an idea.

CONFLICT RESOLUTION. The person in conflict, who is undergoing the attendant muscular tension and subjective distress, has any one of several courses of action to follow: he can remain suspended, he can quit the field, he can approach, he can avoid, he can respond to terminate both the approach and the avoidance sequences partially (a compromise response), and so on. The possibilities are determined by the nature of the conflict situation; the simpler the conflict, the fewer are the possible resolutions.

In significant conflict areas—ones which are of physiological import to the person—the individual will be forced sooner or later to approach or avoid, since one element in the conflict inevitably becomes more intense than the other. Hunger responses may become sufficiently intense to lead a person to risk danger in order to eat. If he does, his fear is not sufficiently intense to interfere with the approach-response sequence. If, however, the fear remains the strongest, the person will continue to avoid the situation, and if it is intense enough, he may avoid it completely. If the events that elicit the fear response are situational, the person may terminate or avoid the occurrence of fear by removing himself physically from them; he may walk away from them. If they occur within the person's own responses, however, it is impossible to "run away" physically from them. He must do something else. His only recourse is to prevent the occurrence of the responses that evoke the fear. Thus, if sexual thoughts are the antecedents, the person can preclude that instance of fear by avoiding thinking sexual thoughts. The responses that persons use to interrupt and to block the occurrence of various kinds of thought sequences Dollard and Miller call suppression and repression.

REPRESSION AND SUPPRESSION AS CONFLICT RESOLUTIONS. Imagine a husband who has contracted a case of the "seven-year itch" and whose sexual appetites are being aroused by a variety of young ladies he sees each day. Suppose his training has taught him to think of such desires as extramarital and sinful, producing guilt responses in himself. This would be a sex-guilt conflict, in which sexual arousal would lead him to attempts at seduction which guilt would lead him to avoid.

Several types of responses might occur. He could cease to attend to the situational events leading to his sexual thoughts by ceasing to look at the girls, or by averting his eyes when they are around; he could misidentify the physiological aspect of his sexual responses when they occur; he could stop thinking the provocative thoughts which occur when he sees the girls and which trigger off his sexual response. All of these could be accomplished by two sets of responses. The set is called *suppression* when it is under the control of verbal cues and, thus, remains within the person's power to initiate and stop. The other set of responses which stops thinking is called *repression;* it is intense and automatic and, thus, outside the individual's control.

Dollard and Miller do not seek to account for the origin of such responses but imply that all persons have the capacity for them. Such responses are important in conflict resolution because of their capacity for preventing or terminating fear. Consistent with their position, repression is not considered a "process" but a response, subject to the same sets of response laws.

DIFFERENTIAL CONSEQUENTS OF SUPPRESSION AND REPRESSION. If our beleaguered husband consciously blocks the thoughts that produce his uncomfortable guilt, he is suppressing the difficulty. Such a "blocking response" is under his thoughtful control and is, therefore, reversible. If the occasion demands, he can revoke the suppressed responses and can think, plan, consider, and weigh optional courses of action at a later date; he can apply all of his "higher mental processes" to the solution of the conflict which is said to be "conscious."

On the other hand, if repression occurs, no such possibilities exist. The habit of not attending or stopping thinking is so automatic that the person is unaware of it and cannot think about the crucial events which are controlling his behavior. Verbal responses, primarily thoughts, are man's way of controlling and directing his own behavior, and without them he is at the mercy of the impelling events within and about him. His behaviors are automatic and beyond his verbal control. Without thoughts, he responds to the immediate present and cannot delay his behavior for more propitious circumstances; he cannot identify the significant factors that influence him, nor can he select the responses with which he can protect himself and reduce the intensity of the impelling events. Thus, repression produces deficit and renders the conflict unconscious.

The consequents of repression are not restricted to these difficulties, however, for the person is not only handicapped in resolving the conflict but also becomes impaired in other ways.

1. In situations similar to those represented in the conflict, he is likely to behave inappropriately. He is less able to discriminate between situations and thus is more likely to respond inappropriately.

2. He will be likely to behave shortsightedly. Thoughts enable a person to delay his behavior and to respond in terms of distant future goals, and their absence makes it more likely that he will respond "thoughtlessly" to current events without considering the future.

3. He is handicapped in problem solving. Without appropriate thoughts, he is less able to define or analyze the problems or to reason and plan his behavior and, thus, to work out satisfactory solutions.

4. He tends to be less effective in his interpersonal relationships. Lacking appropriate thoughts, he is less able to express himself clearly or to react appropriately in conversations with other people.

5. He becomes less able to differentiate between what occurs within his thoughts and what goes on in situations external to himself. Thoughts are used to appraise one's own behavior and are needed to distinguish between the "make believe" and the "real."

Of course, no single conflict produces an inhibition of all thoughts; only those thoughts associated with the conflict are likely to be blocked. Presumably the more conflicts that are rendered inaccessible to verbal awareness, the more extensively impaired the person tends to be.

Development of the Neurosis

With these concepts, Dollard and Miller's view of how such approach-fear conflicts come to be acquired and how the development continues into significant disorder can be considered.

POTENTIAL CONFLICT-LEARNING SITUATIONS. What are the characteristic learning conditions under which such conflicts are acquired? Incompatible response sequences (conflicts) must have been acquired under inconsistent and poorly arranged conditions of training. To them, the existence of neurosis is a serious criticism of child-rearing practices.

Several factors contribute to faulty and inappropriate learnings in small children: (1) the training is conducted by only partially effective teachers—often parents themselves have been subject to contradictory and ineffective training, and this renders them less able as teachers of their children; (2) the kinds of behavior taught often are inconsistent—modern society has built-in conflicts which are passed on from parent to child; for example, the attempt to train children to be meek and obedient on the one hand, but strong and competitive on the other; and (3) the subject of training, the child, is small and helpless, and he cannot participate effectively in decisions as to the appropriateness of the training he is receiving. Children are particularly vulnerable to harsh and confusing patterns of training, since they have not yet learned sufficient thoughts to be able to control their own behavior, to wait, to hope, to reason, and to plan. They tend to be rather "stimulus-bound" and thus readily influenced.

Many learning arrangements produce subsequent difficulty, but Dollard and Miller suggest four in particular that are especially likely to lead to emotional conflict of a major sort. These are the situations in which the child is being trained with respect to eating, elimination, sexual responses, and anger and aggressive behavior.

In the eating situation, the child is impelled by intense hunger responses. If the parent punishes or becomes angry with the child, a hunger-fear conflict may develop. Similarly, urination and defecation are impelled by powerful innate responses. If the parent elicits strong fear responses in relation to the eliminative processes and the learning of their control by punishing, by disapproving and rejecting, by impatience, and by his own emotional reactions to the eliminative products, he may teach the child an approach-avoidance conflict in relation to the total situation and the organs involved. Training to control anger becomes critical in a society which generally forbids angry and aggressive behavior. Incidentally, this may be related to the cleanliness training situation, since thwarting the automatic eliminative processes may produce anger and rebelliousness in the child; frustration tends to lead to aggression. If, when the child displays anger, the parent physically assaults the child, personally derogates him, or in some other way arouses intense fear in the child, an anger-fear conflict may be created. Sex training is a fourth crucial situation. Dollard and Miller note that sex seems to be frequently involved in neurotic conflicts, not so much because it is more intense, but because it is one of the most severely attacked and inhibited responses in our culture. Parents frequently punish incipient sexual responses severely, not only because sex is often labeled as bad in our society but also because the adults themselves have acquired sex-fear conflicts, and these are aroused by the sexual behavior in their children, prompting the parents to become angry. They unwittingly reproduce the conflict in their children by teaching them to be afraid in relation to sexual events.

Inappropriate handling of these and other training situations may establish the basis for later serious neurotic behavior, not only because of the intensity of the conflicts that may be elicited at the time, but also because the child has insufficient language to label what is occurring and, therefore, is unable to think about it in the future and control it—the conflicts are unconscious.

DETERMINANTS OF THE NEUROSIS. The ingredients of neurosis are learned conflicts that are inaccessible to verbal awareness. Such conflicts arise from two general sources. First, the child may have acquired the debilitating problems before he acquired language, prior to the time when he could identify and represent to himself what was occurring, or use reasoning and logical thought to correct it. Second, the conflict can arise in a person exposed to emotional conflicts of sufficient intensity that the repressive response was called into play automatically, and what was once accessible to his verbal and symbolic response sequences is no longer so. Either way, not only does the person become handicapped as regards the conflict itself, but also the problem becomes more generalized and begins to impair related aspects of his behavior.

What determines the development of the crystallized neurosis? "Unconscious emotional conflicts" involving sex, fear, and anger are common to everyone. The normal course of development includes the use of repression, and it entails the inevitable acquisition of conflicts of which the person is unaware. What makes the difference?

Dollard and Miller are unable to specify how one predicts the development of the neurosis itself. Although they feel that such conflicts are identifiable in the behavior of neurotics and are inaccessible to the patients themselves, they can propose only hypotheses to account for why one person with conflicts develops a neurosis and another does not.

The possibilities they have considered include the following. First of all, persons destined to develop a neurosis may have been struggling with conflicts of a much greater intensity than have others, and if so greater degrees of discomfort and distress would occur, and there would be a greater likelihood that the repressive response would be used. More intense conflicts could arise from two general sources. The situations to which the person was exposed may elicit much more intense responses such as fear or hunger. One person may have been subject to severe punishment which led to intense fear, as opposed to another who was similarly taught but developed only mild fear. Or those who are destined to become neurotic may be "predisposed" by virtue of birth or constitution to have intense responses—higher states of drive, for example. Thus, neurotic people may come from a "different basket."

Another major possibility depends on the situations to which the person with an underlying emotional conflict becomes exposed. One person with a conflict might be "lucky" in the sense that he does not encounter the provocative circumstances that would excite his conflict, whereas the same person might be forced into just those adverse conditions that would trigger the problem. Thus, the role of situational events might be important in determining whether the conflict will assume serious proportions. If the individual had "resolved" his conflict by implementing the tendencies to avoid, he might have no great difficulty unless the usual situational context in which he operates undergoes a change (1950, p. 225).

THE DEFINITION OF NEUROSIS. Three characteristics define the neurotic situation: misery, stupidity, and symptoms. When these are judged to be present, the label of neurosis becomes appropriate.

We have already considered the first of these. Misery is represented as the subjective consequent of conflict. Stupidity describes the ineffective and maladaptive responses the neurotic employs because he is unable to identify the source of his difficulty and cannot come up with appropriate responses by which to resolve it. Stupidity tends to be confined to areas of his behavior that are affected by the conflict and stems directly from the use of the repressive response. Repression causes stupidity (1950, p. 224). The effects of misery and stupidity correspond with one another and contribute to still further impairments in the person's capacity to behave effectively.

The final hallmark of the neurosis, however, is the development of symptoms. Symptoms are the outgrowth of the preceding occurrences:

an underlying conflict which is inaccessible to verbal awareness via habitual and automatic habits of "stopping thinking" (repression), which is characterized by the inhibition produced by fear and its consequents, which is sufficiently intense to produce subjective tension and distress, and which the person is poorly equipped to resolve because the necessary ingredients for the solution are not available to his thoughts.

Characteristics of Symptoms

Symptoms result from fear. They are learned and maintained because of their effectiveness in reducing the intensity of fear, even though they may lead to future difficulties, conflicts, and misery for the individual. Thus, the paradox of the neurotic who apparently creates difficulties for himself is explained. His symptoms are focused on an immediate reduction of fear without regard for future consequences.

What determines the kinds of symptoms an individual will develop? Since symptoms are responses, it is very possible they were acquired first in relation to situations for which they were adaptive and appropriate. Later they are tried in relation to the conflict and, if effective in reducing the fear, they will be retained. They are called symptoms because the patient complains of them and because an objective observer sees them as being inappropriate to the new situation and likely to create further difficulties for the individual. Often symptoms are *compromise responses* because they are effective in reducing not only some of the intense fear but also some of the intensity of the incompatible response. However, such compromise responses only partially reduce each of the conflicting behavior elicitors and, therefore, both sets of events continue to impel behavior and keep the person tense and in some misery. In addition, such responses, being only partially effective, often create new dilemmas for the individual. For example, a person who is very frightened of speed may avoid airplanes, trains, and buses, and drive his own car instead, but this may interfere with a successful business career if his occupation requires frequent travel over long distances.

Dollard and Miller divide symptoms into two classes. First there are innately determined physiological responses which occur as a direct result of intense physiological or emotional responses, such as stomach acidity. These can be terminated only when the intensity of the instigating response is terminated; they are not particularly subject to learning. On the other hand, any learned response can presumably be altered if the appropriate conditions for relearning can be created. It is the latter situation that psychotherapy may be able to affect directly.

Dollard and Miller select several symptoms as illustrations of how all symptomatic behavior may be said to operate. These include phobias, compulsions, hysterical symptoms, and delusions and hallucinations. They also treat the responses of regression, displacement, rationalization, projection, and reaction formation in the same vein. All neurotic symptoms have the characteristic of automaticity. Under the appropriate conditions they will occur without conscious intent or voluntary effort on the part of the individual. The symptoms differ, however, according to the characteristics of the antecedent events instigating them, according to the kinds of responses that are represented in the symptom, and according to the consequences of their emission.

There is an implication in this characterization of neurosis and disorder which should be clarified. The reader may have recognized that the conception of symptomatic behavior as instrumental to the reduction of fear and fear as the principal component in the underlying conflict leads to the conclusion that all neurotic symptomatology is of the nature of avoidance and that neuroses are characterized primarily as patterns of avoidance behaviors. This, of course, is to be contrasted with other views which allow for additional functions of neurotic responses as well.

THE GOALS OF THERAPY

Removal of the symptomatic responses is not considered to be effective treatment. Symptomatic responses have as their function the avoidance or termination of fear. If only the symptoms are removed, the fear will become more intense and a new response will have to be learned to terminate or avoid the fear, that is, new symptoms are likely to be formed. Treatment should be aimed at resolving the underlying conflict, although an alternate procedure would be to help the patient learn different compromise responses which are more effective in reducing the conflicting drives. Ideally, the patient should be helped to acquire conscious control of his own behavior through his own thoughts. It is difficult to overemphasize Dollard and Miller's stress on the role of conscious, thoughtful anticipation and planning of events in healthy behavior; it serves to make a person "free within his own mind to consider every possible alternative course of action" (1950, p. 249). Healthy behavior involves the conscious delay of responses and the determination of what situations are appropriate for which particular patterns of behavior. It is true that therapy aims to help the patient unlearn the consequences of the automatic responses of repression and inhibition, but the alternative is not completely uninhibited behavior. In place of the "crude" responses of repression and inhibition, the successful patient "learns to substitute the much more discriminative ones of suppression and restraint," thereby bringing the events under verbal control, and producing "all the advantages of the higher mental processes" (1950, p. 221).

Since all neuroses are built in essentially the same way, the goals of treatment are basically the same for all therapy subjects: (1) the reduction in the intensity of emotional conflicts, (2) the learning of conscious sentences enabling the individual to think about the events influencing him and thereby to control his own behavior, (3) the removal of blocks to the performance of important instrumental responses, and (4) the acquisition of appropriate responses for obtaining satisfactions in real life.

Who Should Choose the Goals

Although Dollard and Miller do not discuss this issue directly, it seems implicit in their writings that the therapist is the expert and thus should decide which behaviors should be modified and which procedures should be used to modify them. In a general sense, the theory defines the goals. Typically, the therapist seeks to reduce anxiety, extinguish the disrupting patterns of avoidance behavior, restore conscious, thoughtful self-direction, and help the patient acquire new instrumental responses. In a specific case, it is the therapist's task to discover what particular *kinds of events* are eliciting the anxiety and what particular *kinds of responses* are involved in the avoidance sequences. He must be able to specify the approach aspects of the conflict in a similar way. It is precisely because the patient cannot make these judgments that he is a patient. It takes an expert to be able to observe these crucial events and to arrange the conditions so that the patient can become aware of them and learn to control them.

It seems still more likely that Dollard and Miller consider it the therapist's task to identify and attempt to modify the various elements in the avoidance sequences of behavior, while it is the patient's task to choose which responses he will perform to attempt to satisfy the approach drives in his life as it exists. This seems to be implied when they discuss the fact that effective responses are not really learned in therapy but in real life. In therapy the patient can talk about the various responses he might try out, but he can only really test them in everyday life. "These are the great actions of the patient's life in the spheres of love, work, and social relations" (1950, p. 334). Thus, it would appear to be the therapist's responsibility to determine which behaviors should be modified so that the patient becomes able to choose and perform significant patterns of behavior outside of therapy. The actual choice of which kinds of new behavior to employ would seem to be made by the patient.

CONDITIONS FOR PRODUCING BEHAVIOR CHANGE

Dollard and Miller have not attempted to present a manual or cookbook of therapeutic technique; rather they have tried to formulate the principles by which behavior is acquired and modified and then to illustrate how they believe these principles can be applied in a particular case to achieve the desired behavior modification (Dollard and Miller, 1950; Dollard, et al., 1953). However, they repeatedly emphasize that a person's behavior is a function of the particular conditions of his life, both past and present. Thus, although they believe it is possible to specify the general principles to be followed in trying to modify a patient's behavior, they believe it is impossible to specify, except for a given patient, exactly which responses should be focused upon, in what order, or which situational events should be manipulated, at which points in therapy and in what sequence, to achieve behavior modification. All such judgments must be made by the therapist as he observes the patient's behavior and the conditions under which it was acquired and under which it currently operates. In this sense there remains a considerable degree of "art" to therapy, consisting of the therapist's ability to observe carefully and accurately, to identify the crucial behavior sequences, and to judge which events he can manipulate to achieve the behavioral modifications he intends.

Principles by Which Change Occurs

The import of the therapeutic situation is that it is a new and special learning setting in which old behaviors may be modified and new behaviors acquired. Therapy is no less a learning situation than the schoolroom, although it is a very special type of learning situation with a very special type of teacher.

Therapy has two general purposes. To put it crudely, the therapist wants to help the patient get rid of some responses to life situations and acquire others. It is probably inaccurate to speak of getting rid of responses, since it is doubtful that a response once acquired is ever lost. Similarly, adults have had occasion in their life to perform such a tremendous variety of responses that learning frequently does not involve acquiring a new response, but learning to use the ones they have in a different sequence. Getting rid of old responses probably means altering the relationship between specific events and the responses they elicit. Similarly, new learning means rearranging the connections between specific events and responses the person already has in his repertoire, that is, developing new cue-response connections. In general, they refer to the development of a new relationship between a behavior elicitor (cue) and a response as *learning*, and the removal of an old connection between a behavior elicitor (cue) and response as *extinction*. Since the principles governing learning and extinction are somewhat different, each will be summarized in turn.

EXTINCTION. One of the first tasks in therapy is to break old "cue-response" connections. For example, in most patients certain kinds of thoughts touch off fear. The therapist's task is to break that connection so that the patient can think the thoughts without eliciting anxiety in himself. This is referred to as extinguishing fear.

How is this aim accomplished? The event occasioning fear must first occur through thoughts verbalized to the therapist; of course, when it does occur, it will be followed by the fear response. If it is not followed by punishment, pain, and the like (the feared consequent), the probability of that response producing fear on the next occasion is decreased. After several such experiences, the event loses its power to elicit a fear response. In simple language, the individual is no longer afraid in that situation. The likelihood that the patient will speak his thoughts increases because the fear, which has been blocking this occurrence, has been unlearned (extinguished). The fear response is terminated, not by avoiding the learned elicitor (cue), but by removing the feared consequence when the response is performed.

NEW LEARNING. The second type of conditions the therapist attempts to create are those that will facilitate the acquisition of new event (cue)-response connections. To put it differently, the therapist wants to help the patient to acquire different responses to both old and new situations. Responses to different situations will be acquired if they lead to the reduction or termination of intense physiological responses (innate drives) or emotional patterns (learned drives). Each time this happens it increases the likelihood that that response will occur in future similar situations. The number of times necessary to render the response habitual in future situations is a function of the intensity of the impelling event (drive) and of the number of learning occasions, as well as of how the learning experiences are spaced over time. The product is a new arrangement between events and responses—that is, cue-response connections are learned when they are effective in reducing drives.

It is important to note that both in breaking old habits and in acquiring new ones, it is absolutely essential that the response to be learned or unlearned occurs in close temporal and spatial contiguity to the other crucial events. This point is re-emphasized because of its importance in Dollard and Miller's view of therapeutic technique.

Patient Behavior That Must Occur

WHO SHOULD BE ACCEPTED FOR THERAPY. Not all persons with behavioral difficulties are appropriate candidates for verbal psychotherapy, according to Dollard and Miller. First, only behavior disorders that are the consequence of learning should be accepted for their type of psychotherapy. Individuals with organic disorders may be helped to acquire responses that will compensate partially for their deficiencies. Individual verbal psychotherapy is not the appropriate type of learning experience for such people. A thorough medical examination is desirable to rule out the possibility of important organic antecedents to the disorder.

Second, since "motivation" is crucial in learning, some intense events such as fear or misery must be occurring, so that responses can be learned to reduce their intensity; otherwise no learning can occur. Several signs of strong motivation are that the patient seeks therapy on his own, that he is willing to make sacrifices to get treatment, that he is experiencing intense, subjective feelings which are very uncomfortable and which he wants to terminate, and that he recognizes that his symptoms are creating difficulties and putting him at a serious disadvantage in leading a happy and effective life. Finally, environmental circumstances which consistently produce unfavorable consequences for the patient help cause him to endure the exigencies of therapy.

It will be recalled that the strength of a habit is a function of the number of learning trials and the intensity of the behavior elicitors involved in learning it. Thus, symptoms that are the consequence of intense conflict, that have existed over long periods of time and therefore have had many learning trials, and that elicit a good many positive rewards such as sympathy, relief from distasteful work, or financial income will be harder to unlearn under the conditions of verbal psychotherapy.

In addition, the patient must be able to make appropriate responses. There are several pieces of evidence the therapist may weigh in making this judgment. Any habits that interfere with the kind of behavior required in therapy would make prognosis unfavorable, such as the inability to talk or listen or extreme suspiciousness and consequent inability to form a relationship. Certain social learnings are prerequisites, and without them prognosis is poor. Patients with basic deficits in childhood training—for example, psychopaths—will be poor prospects. The individual needs to have acquired fairly strong habits of trying to be logical and reasonable, since much of the therapeutic endeavor is based on such behavior. It may be inferred that patients who have had long periods of good adjustment prior to or between episodes in their behavior disorder are more likely to have learned useful responses and social skills upon which more effective behavior patterns can be built. The individual must have a minimal ability to speak and think with words; he must have a reasonable degree of intelligence.

Another consideration is whether the individual's current life situation is one from which he can obtain reasonable satisfactions as his behavior changes. The more the patient has experienced such satisfactions in the past, the easier it will be for the therapist to arouse anticipatory responses toward gaining satisfactions in the future, but the possibility for real satisfactions must exist. As Dollard and Miller put it, the more the patient has to live for, the more favorable is the therapy prognosis (1950, p. 235).

In summary, the therapist should select patients who can learn readily. The drives upon which learning is built must be strong enough to continue to impel the patient to learn. The patient must be able to think about and attend to the events (cues) in his environment and in himself which tell him how he should respond. He should have the response capabilities in his repertoire for making more effective responses, and his life should be one in which appropriate rewards are forthcoming if he does make correct ones.

RESPONSES REQUIRED OF THE PATIENT. It is possible to deduce from Dollard and Miller's principles of learning the patient's tasks in therapy. First, since learning cannot take place except through repeated experiences, the patient must agree to attend therapy sessions regularly and to meet any other requirements that are a part of that learning situation. He must admit there are behaviors he wishes to change and try to do so.

Second, learning cannot take place unless the responses occur in the appropriate context of other events, namely, cues and drives. However, one of the consequences of the patient's disorder is that he is unaware of which responses must be unlearned or relearned. For this reason the patient cannot behave as he usually does in most social situations, consciously selecting the responses he will make. Any selection he makes is likely to keep important responses from occurring, particularly those involved in the avoidance sequences. Rather, the patient must learn to emit different classes of response than are usual in social relationships, and to inhibit others. The focus will be on the subjectively observable responses. Thus, the patient must inhibit most motor and instrumental responses; he is not to strike the therapist, for example, nor to make sexual advances toward him. The patient's task is to cause the subjectively observable responses such as thoughts, emotions, or physiological responses to occur, and to report them to the therapist. This is accomplished by following the *rule of free association.*

It requires the patient to initiate thoughts but to avoid controlling their content or sequence. As the thoughts occur they will carry with them other responses such as fear, anger, sensory images, and physiological responses. The second aspect of the rule might be called the compulsion to utter. The patient must agree to tell the therapist of his thoughts and other responses as they occur, without attempting to screen out any that produce discomfort. It is particularly important that the patient tell the therapist events, that is, thoughts, images, and the like, that seem associated with negative emotion. Since most of the crucial response sequences that must occur in therapy may be directly observed only by the patient, the requirement that the patient report all such events is essential.

The rule of free association has two important purposes. One is to get the responses to be modified to occur in the therapy situation.

The other is to enable the therapist to become aware of the sequence of those responses as they occur.

Emitting responses without conscious, intentional self-control is contrary to most social learning and, therefore, a facility that the patient must acquire during the course of therapy. "The rule of free association, though rigorously stated, is gently and gradually taught" (1950, p. 243).

Dollard and Miller assume that thoughts and images elicit other responses just as do situational events which they represent. Recalling memories of previous situations will tend to draw out the same responses as had occurred in the remembered situation, though in less intense form. Not only do the sentences the patient utters evoke emotional responses, but so do fragments of sensory images, old instrumental responses, "lost symptoms," and descriptions of past occurrences or forgotten dreams (1950, p. 252). Of course, the patient may not always be able to identify and immediately label them, but it is important to recognize that these responses are assumed to be occasioned by verbal statements and thoughts. Sometimes these verbal statements are provided by the therapist, but more typically they are expected to be provided by the patient himself. Not only do they give information about circumstances under which present habits were learned in the past, but they also produce the crucial responses in the present and thus make them susceptible to modification.

Finally, new responses must eventually be performed in real-life situations to produce real-life rewards. However, they can also lead to undesired consequences (negative reinforcement) and to further misery which could reverse the effects of therapy. Therefore, the patient should agree not to make any drastic changes in his life until the completion of therapy, to avoid the unfortunate consequences of impulsive, emotionally determined, poorly planned action.

Characteristics of the Therapist

TRAINING. Dollard and Miller's therapist is an expert. Like any expert he must be intensively and extensively trained in the theory, substantive knowledge, and techniques of his profession. Therapists also need special training in practical knowledge about neurosis and conflict. Since his objective is to change behavior, he must be well informed about the principles of learning. To use his knowledge effectively, he must have special training in the rationale and use of therapeutic procedures. Adequate understanding and skill can be acquired only by practice. Thus, the therapist's training must include an appropriate apprenticeship. In addition, undergoing a didactic treatment himself will give the potential therapist additional understanding and skill in playing the role of therapist and will help insure that his personal behaviors will not interfere with his therapeutic effectiveness.

Because situational events are powerful determinants of behavior, a good therapist should have special training in the knowledge of the social conditions of various cultures, such as class structure and social mobility, and how they influence behavior. Dollard and Miller believe that most psychotherapists tend to err in the direction of too little knowledge of and insufficient emphasis on the influence of social conditions. Finally, physical disabilities and faulty learnings often produce similar symptomatology, so that psychotherapists should be trained to recognize possible organic involvement. Nonmedically trained therapists should always insist on a physical examination of every patient before assuming that the disorder can be modified by therapeutic learning.

PERSONAL ATTRIBUTES. Dollard and Miller propose four personal attributes necessary for an effective therapist. It is interesting that they do not include the factor of intelligence, since such great demands are placed upon the therapist's skill at observation, thought, and expression. Perhaps they feel this is insured if the therapist can meet the training requirements earlier specified.

If the therapist is to observe, think, and act effectively in therapy, he must be free of the fear usually elicited by discussions of sexuality, anger, and "disgusting" topics. He need not approve of the things he hears, but he must be able to think about them without becoming distressed. He must not have been committed to the use of the repressive response so that he cannot think about the topics essential for the patient's cure. It is this absence of automatic avoidance responses within his own thought habits that Dollard and Miller refer to as *mental freedom*.

If the therapist has acquired the conventional emotional responses to certain kinds of thoughts and statements, his own responses can serve as clues as to what he should look for in the patient's behavior. For example, when he thinks about situations described by a patient who is angered, a slight anger response should occur within himself. Moreover, when an emotional response occurs as a consequence of rehearsing patient's thoughts that the patient himself does not report, the therapist is alerted to the possibility that the patient does not have the appropriate emotional responses attached to those thoughts, he is not labeling them, or he is withholding a report of them. It is a clue that the patient's account is incomplete. Similarly, if the patient's account is disorderly or illogical, the therapist's own training in logical thinking should permit him to recognize the incompleteness of the patient's statement. Comparing a patient's reports with the kinds of responses the therapist experiences as a consequence of those reports Dollard and Miller call *empathy*.

The therapist has acquired a set of responses elicited by and appropriate to most interpersonal or social circumstances. Many of these normal social habits, however, are inappropriate in the therapy situation, and the therapist must learn to restrain them since his personal behaviors are the primary instrument of treatment. All of his responses in therapy should be subordinated to the strategy of cure (1950, p. 412). This capacity of the therapist to control his own behavior as an instrument of therapy is called *restraint*.

The fourth attribute the therapist must have is a *positive outlook*. He must be convinced that the patient can learn and change, and that he is competent to help the patient. Confidence in the patient is a most important requirement. If the therapist is too unsure of himself, too frightened of the consequences of real-life action, too doubtful that the patient can improve, or too conservative in holding his patient back, his therapeutic efforts are likely to be unsuccessful.

Conditions and Techniques for Eliciting Responses

We now turn to Dollard and Miller's proposals as to how to arrange conditions to get the necessary responses to occur in the therapy hour. The therapist's objective is to arrange for the occurrence of the troublesome, emotional responses which in turn are the deterrents to effective action. To do this he must elicit the appropriate thoughts and words from the patient, because these symbolic responses lead to the emotional responses. He cannot arrive at these by direct questioning, because he usually does not know what to ask. Thus he must keep the patient thinking and talking. Which particular responses occur stem from the patient's effort. A difficulty arises from the fact that the patient avoids talking about events that evoke uncomfortable negative emotions. The therapist's task is to keep the patient at his work, promoting discussion of the most discomforting of events so that therapy can progress. He must do this without allowing the patient's misery to become so high or his optimism so low that he avoids the treatment sessions.

These objectives are accomplished in two ways. First, the therapist behaves as a "nice guy" and thus avoids becoming a fear elicitor himself. Second, he says specific things to the patient in order to maintain the focus of attention on the relevant events. He may point out that the things the patient is talking about are not directly relevant or that the patient appears to be withholding certain thoughts, that is, interpreting resistance (Dollard, Auld, and White, 1953).

A great many of the patient's troublesome response patterns have been acquired in relation to other people. Thus, somewhat independently of what he does, the therapist will elicit certain kinds of responses simply because he is another human being. These "transferred" or "generalized" responses are significant phenomena because they cause important responses to occur in therapy as such, rather than to be represented in the form of words. They may represent habits the patient has never labeled and is therefore unable to speak about. Particularly important are unlabeled emotional responses. Often, transferred or generalized responses are thought of only as interfering or inappropriate responses. It is true that many are, and that fact enables the therapist to identify certain patterns of behavior of which the patient may be unaware and of which he may be unable to speak. A therapist should carefully avoid labeling any response as a transferred response unless he is sure he has not done something to elicit it himself. To facilitate this judgment, it is desirable for the therapist to keep himself as neutral and undefined a personality as possible.

But many valuable responses are transferred to therapy as well. For example, the patient transfers habits of being self-critical, of identifying his own behavior and the events that elicited it correctly, of giving a sensible account of himself, and of trying out behaviors that others suggest (imitation). He has also acquired certain comforting emotional responses which result from reassurance by experts and a wish to please someone he admires and respects. Undoubtedly many other such useful responses transfer to therapy.

One of the most important obstructive responses which seem to generalize automatically to therapy is fear. Many of the conditions of therapy are similar to situations that the person has learned to fear. For example, there is its newness, its uncertainty, its requirement to talk about things that have been severely punished in the past, and its effectiveness in eliciting discomforting responses. Similarly, the patient's habits for terminating fear responses typically generalize to the therapy situation. Dollard and Miller discuss the following six habits.

(1) Stopping talking is the most common avoidance response in therapy. Although the patient may be thinking about fearful events, that fear may be considerably less than if he were to say them aloud and risk the therapist's reaction. (2) Physical removal of himself from the anxiety-provoking circumstances appears in early termination of therapy, the desire to leave during a therapy interview, and breaking appointments. (3) Obfuscation is also used to avoid fear. Patients may obscure or confuse issues by arguing about theoretical points, or leading the discussion aside and talking about unimportant elements of situations rather than the elements that are anxiety-provoking. (4) Another way of terminating fear is to attack and destroy the events eliciting it. In many social situations, becoming angry and critical of the behavior of another person will cause the other to change his behavior in some way so that it no longer provokes fear. (5) Anger may have become an antecedent to fear. Being dependent and agreeable sometimes serves to avoid eliciting anger in others. Similarly the patient may have acquired habits of not thinking or talking about events that would induce anger in himself. (6) Sometimes the assumption of responsibility for determining his own behavior may be fear-producing. The patient can avoid evoking fear by placing the responsibility for his behavior and the content of therapy upon the therapist. These kinds of avoidance responses are usually referred to as *resistance*. They can be treated as inappropriate only if the therapist is sure that his own behavior does not make it essential for the patient to behave in avoidant ways, that he is not eliciting legitimate fear in the patient.

Conditions and Techniques for Modifying Responses

RESPONSES TO BE MODIFIED. The patient comes to therapy with a pattern of avoidance responses motivated by fear, which function to terminate or control the fear and which interfere with the occurrence of other effective instrumental responses. Thus, the first response on which the therapist must focus is the patient's fear or anxiety. He has three objectives: to reduce the number of different situations which elicit the fear, to reduce the intensity of the fear response itself, and to help the patient acquire thoughts that will enable him to control the occurrence of and generalization of the fear.

First, a discriminant response to the therapy situation must develop. In the beginning it will almost inevitably elicit some fear, and this should be reduced as quickly as possible. Second, responses obstructing the occurrence of important thoughts and instrumental acts must be modified. These are called habits of stopping thinking (repression). Since they are the automatic consequences of fear, however, their modification is an automatic consequence of the modification of the intensity of the fear response itself.

Third, symbolic responses or thoughts and verbal statements must be modified. An important component of his neurosis is the fact that the patient has acquired habits of not thinking about certain events and past occurrences. Some of this may be because they happened early in childhood before he acquired adequate verbal responses with which to label them, even though the other responses continue to occur in the present. The second possibility is that the patient can think about the events; he has the responses, but they have been blocked from occurring by the obstructive responses such as rationalization, motivated by fear. Here again, once the fear is reduced the likelihood of the obstructive responses is correspondingly reduced, and it becomes more likely that the patient can utilize constructive thoughts in their stead. Many of the therapist's techniques are focused on producing changes in these various habits of thought.

Finally, those instrumental acts necessary for the patient to achieve appropriate satisfactions in real-life circumstances must develop or be revived. There are problems in teaching such responses, however, since their occurrence and learning require that they be performed outside of therapy. This issue will be discussed shortly.

MODIFYING CONDITIONS AND TECHNIQUES. It will be recalled that the primary element in the patient's difficulties is a conflict between events leading to sequences of approach and avoidance behavior. Prior to therapy, a variety of procedures has been used by the patient and his friends to induce him to implement the approach pattern of behavior, despite the fear and its consequent avoidance sequences. Precisely because the fear and avoidance patterns are so strong, the typical social procedures have been ineffective and the patient has come to therapy. Therefore, the preferred strategy is for the therapist to operate on the avoidance patterns of behavior first in his efforts to modify the patient's conflict—that is, first lower the avoidance gradient rather than raise the approach gradient.

It will be recalled also that to unlearn (extinguish) a fear response to a particular event it is necessary to arrange conditions so that that event will occur and not be followed by the feared consequence. Thus, the therapist first attempts to evoke positive emotional responses in the therapy situation and avoid providing the feared consequences, that is, prohibit negative reinforcement. To accomplish this, he creates a *permissive* situation. He is friendly, understanding, and sympathetic. He devotes his entire attention to the patient during the interview. Not only does he listen to what the patient says, but he also remembers it. He does not display fear, anger, or other negative emotions in response to the patient's behavior. He is neither critical nor domineering. He does not evaluate or judge the patient's behavior. He becomes a confidant, assuring the patient that his utterances and behaviors are in complete privacy and confidence.

The intended effect is to teach the patient to discriminate between the therapy and other interpersonal situations, thereby preventing the transfer of learned fears from previous interpersonal situations to the therapeutic one. Moreover, if the therapist behaves in these ways, he facilitates the occurrence of positive feelings in the patient toward himself and the therapy situation.

In this emotional climate, the patient is urged to begin talking and to report everything he is aware of during the course of the interview, no matter how fearful he might be in doing so. As his thoughts and statements move closer and closer to fear-producing topics, his fear will mount and he will be in conflict, wanting to pursue the discussion (approach gradient) but also fearful (avoidance gradient). The benign conditions of the therapeutic relationship maintain the fear at a low intensity, however, and the therapist's calm assurance prompts the patient finally to utter the fearful thoughts. The conditions that follow their utterance are completely different from those in the original learning situation. Instead of meeting with anger, criticism, ridicule, or rejection, which would reinforce fear, the patient is met with calm acceptance, sympathetic understanding, and absence of censure. Such an event reduces the likelihood that the fear will recur, and this effect automatically generalizes to similar thoughts, thereby increasing the likelihood that they will occur and be reported. This process recurs again and again, particularly in the early portions of therapy, not only with thought-fear sequences but also with other sequences such as anger-fear.

With some patients and with certain kinds of disorders, this may be all that is necessary. It is quite possible, according to Dollard and Miller, that modification of some types of behavior disorder can occur entirely without the patient's awareness through this unlearning or extinction process. Such would be a limited success, however, since the patient would not have acquired conscious control over these behavior patterns, and he would be unable to control them if they recurred in the future. Dollard and Miller believe such a permissive relationship is only a necessary and not a sufficient condition of therapy. Patients with severe neuroses need more help than just a nonpunishing human relationship to overcome their powerful, behavior-blocking avoidance habits.

This is where the therapist's professional training and experience in the theory of human behavior become so important. He must not only attend to the responses occurring but also consider those responses that should be occurring but are not being reported by the subject. He knows of two possibilities: (1) they are occurring, but the subject is unaware of them; (2) they are not occurring, even though they should be, because their occurrence is being blocked by some other event. How does the therapist know? His theory of human behavior tells him they should be there and he looks for evidences of them; if he recognizes aspects of the response, he knows the patient is unaware. If he sees no evidence of the response at all, he can presume that its occurrence is being impeded by another response process. Thus, the therapist should be a diagnostician. He listens to and watches the behavioral events, and he begins to form hypotheses about how they interrelate. He infers what is conflicting with what—such as fear conflicting with anger or sexual sequences—which habits are preventing the fear from occurring, and which habits could occur if the avoidance pattern were altered. In this sense there is a separate diagnosis for each patient.

There is a variety of clues which a therapist may use to help him formulate such hypotheses: incompleteness or gaps in the patient's verbal reports, for example, absence of grief when discussing the death of a dearly loved parent; or illogical accounts of situations; or when the patient becomes blocked and unable to think of something to say may all be indicators of areas that are being avoided or repressed. Dreams and slips of the tongue may provide excellent clues to the material being avoided. Repeated unhappy outcomes of a major type of life situation may also indicate a conflict area; repeated divorces, for example, may suggest sexual anxieties. When the patient becomes completely blocked, the therapist should suspect that there is something about the interview situation and the patient's responses to it that the patient does not want to speak about.

The therapist's knowledge of these events and the behavior areas which the patient has habitually come to ignore and avoid thinking about—that is, they are unconscious—become important when the patient's own efforts to make progress are blocked. It is precisely because his conflicts and many of the avoidant behaviors are inaccessible to his verbal awareness that the patient needs the intervention of a therapist.

At this point, the therapist's objective is to assist the subject to attend to and appropriately verbalize those aspects of situations and behavior that he has been in the habit of avoiding. He helps the patient attach appropriate words (labels) to the events as they occur. Making events verbally explicit permits the patient to become aware of them and acquire control over his responses to them. "We believe, however, that the learning is more transferable, and therefore more efficient, when adequate labeling occurs" (1950, p. 303).

If these new verbal responses are going to be effective for identifying events and controlling their occurrence, they must take place in the patient's awareness at the same time as the events to which they refer. Of course, to be learned, they must not only be contiguous but also must reduce the intensity of whatever physiological or emotional response (drive) is operating—for instance, fear, anger, or sexual excitement.

There are three general ways in which these new verbal responses may occur. First, the patient may hit upon them himself. In the course of his spontaneous talking and thinking he may discover precisely the correct sentences and say them or think them at precisely the appropriate time to get them connected with other response or situational events. Second, new verbal responses may gradually be acquired as a consequence of selective repetition by the therapist. The therapist can select from the patient's verbal flow those statements that are appropriate and useful, and by restating or rephrasing them can focus the patient's attention on them and with repetition induce the patient to think similar sentences himself when similar conditions occur.

The third way of helping a patient acquire new verbal responses is to lead the patient to utilize the statements of the therapist. This is the traditional act of *therapeutic interpretation*. Dollard and Miller suggest a variety of ways in which the therapist can present new verbal units for the patient to rehearse.

There are several criteria to be observed in determining when to make an interpretation. First, interpretations are desirable only when the patient is unable to make further progress by himself on a particular problem. For example, the patient may have come close to talking about anger toward his mother on several occasions but always changed to a different topic without apparent awareness of his consistent avoidance. When the important response seems about to occur, but the therapist expects the patient to avoid labeling it again, an interpretation might be made. It is best to make an interpretation (a) "when the behavior in question is occurring," (b) "when the patient cannot recognize the events himself," but (c) "when he is near enough to it so that undue fear will not be aroused," as it is made explicit (1950, p. 402).

Because the therapist is making judgments as to when an interpretation is timely, there is the possibility of error. Therefore, interpretations should be offered in a tentative fashion so that the patient may reject or avoid the interpretation without becoming badly frightened or having to disagree directly with the therapist to protect himself. The therapist can watch for signs of intense fear (perspiration, muscular tension, and overt agitation) as well as sudden flareups of symptoms, expressions of a wish to leave therapy, and serious suicidal thoughts. Any such signs of greatly increased fear indicate that the therapist should temporarily stop making interpretations, and should use all the techniques at his disposal to temporarily reduce the intensity of the fear.

Interpretations can be offered in a variety of forms. Questions can serve to direct a patient's attention to crucial events which are occurring and thereby increase the likelihood that the patient will discover the significance of those events for himself. They can serve as a kind of hint as to what to look for. Interpretations can take the form of tentative statements, such as "I have been wondering if this tense feeling you have when you go to bed at night might be sexual excitement." They might be simple assertions such as "Did you know you have been avoiding talking about your wife?" They might be assertions with supporting evidence, as when the therapist notes to his patient that in a sequence of therapy interviews, the patient has consistently shown fear each time the topic of anger has been approached. They might serve to distinguish between two different situations to help the patient build discriminations, as when the therapist contrasts the kind of behavior it was appropriate for the patient to perform as a child with the kind that it is now permissible for him to perform as an adult. They may serve to help the process of generalization so that the patient will transfer responses from one situation to similar situations. Interpretations help the patient distinguish between the consequences of thoughts and of acts, as when he observes that society punishes the actual act of murder severely but has absolutely no sanctions against thoughts of killing someone.

The creation of an interpersonal relationship which elicits positive rather than negative emotions in a patient and the use of interpretive, verbal statements in a variety of forms are Dollard and Miller's two major procedures for modifying the patient's behavior. Of course, these procedures are effective only when they occur in appropriate sequences where intense events impelling behavior can be reduced or terminated, and where the responses or situational events to which the connections are to be made are occurring.

OTHER TECHNIQUES: *Suggesting, urging, commanding,* and *forbidding* are the most common everyday methods by which individuals attempt to influence the behavior of others. Dollard and Miller believe that these are generally ineffective in therapy for two reasons. First, they have already been tried on the patient and have not succeeded in altering the problem. Second, they are often used in an attempt to force the individual to perform the feared responses, and may increase the avoidance pattern and intensify the conflict. Occasionally they are used by the therapist, however. For example, the therapist commands free association; he insists that the patient avoid drastic decisions of an irreversible sort until therapy is completed; and he may request the patient to abstain temporarily from any symptom which appears to be too drive-reducing, such as excessive drinking.

Reward and *punishment, disapproval,* and *approval* are time-honored procedures for modifying behavior. Usually the therapist does not have control over the most powerful rewards and punishments in the individual's life and cannot use them effectively. In addition, neurotics have met with a great deal of disapproval, and if the therapist uses the procedure of disapproval he is likely to encourage the generalization to himself of fear responses learned with other people. On occasion he may use disapproval, however, particularly in an attempt to get the patient to avoid doing himself irreparable harm. Approvals may be used, but should be used sparingly because if used too often they lose their specific value.

Reassurance is another response common in social interaction. It amounts to giving the patient some ways to think that will have the effect of reducing his fear and giving him hope. Here again, patients have been reassured many times, and if it had proven effective they would not be in treatment. Sometimes it may be helpful in controlling anxiety, but it should be used cautiously. The patient may learn to come for more reassurance for temporary relief rather than to solve his own problems and maintain his own emotional equilibrium.

In summary, Dollard and Miller's therapy procedures are directed toward the blocking of certain responses as well as increasing the likelihood of the occurrence of others. Procedures are recommended for the termination or avoidance of anxiety and for the blocking of instrumental responses that might do the patient harm. Other procedures are recommended for developing connections between thought responses on the one hand and emotional and instrumental responses on the other so that conscious self-control becomes more complete. The primary emphasis of all the therapeutic interventions they discuss, however, are to reduce anxiety and decrease the occurrence of avoidance responses while helping the patient to identify and think more adequately about the events influencing him and the responses he is making or might effectively make.

SEQUENCE OF CHANGE. Dollard and Miller note that therapy actually has two phases. The first they call the talking phase, and that is the one that we have discussed so far. There is a general sequence of change which occurs in the talking phase. (1) Fear of talking becomes reduced. (2) Thoughts and sentences previously blocked from occurrence appear. (3) Words and thoughts are attached to events "within the body and without" which had previously been blocked, denied, or ignored. (4) With the new words and new ways of thinking about these events, the patient becomes better able to compare, contrast, abstract from, and in general to conceptualize what is happening within himself in relation to the world around him. (5) As the patient becomes less afraid of thinking and talking about these events, he also becomes less afraid of actually doing something about them—"these extinction effects generalize to, and reduce the fear motivating the inhibitions of instrumental and goal responses" (1950, p. 331).

Of course, the sequence recurs again and again. The resolution of the initial fears leads to further areas of difficulty wherein new fears are encountered, which must in turn be reduced. As more and more fear responses are extinguished and more and more extensive, conscious, thoughtful judgment occurs, the individual begins to analyze, think about, and plan instrumental responses in his life outside of therapy.

Transfer of Change

It is of relatively little consequence that a patient becomes unafraid, happy, and effective in his behavior in the therapy hour. Most of his life is lived outside the therapy hour, and the therapeutic relationship can seldom continue indefinitely. Thus, seen in proper context, therapeutic interviews are only a means of getting the patient to the point at which he will go out into his life and try new behaviors, achieve appropriate satisfactions without extensive fear, and thus learn new effective patterns of behavior for conducting his life. In the last analysis conflict and misery are reduced only in real life, and this reduction is the real test of successful treatment. Dollard and Miller refer to the practicing and learning of new responses outside the therapeutic interview as the "outside" or "real world aspect" (second phase) of psychotherapy.

The principle of generalization implies an automatic tendency for the patient to transfer the habits of feeling and thinking which he gradually develops during his therapy interviews to the significant problems and persons in his life outside of therapy. However, the therapist cannot rely entirely on the automatic process of generalization. He must actively facilitate such transfer by directing the patient's attention to the potential rewards that await him in his life situations if he tries new responses; by helping him to consider the kinds of responses that he might make and that would achieve the satisfactions he seeks in his life; and by helping him assess the potential consequences of various ways he might behave toward his wife, his job, and other significant circumstances in his life. Thus, a critical part of therapeutic technique involves getting the patient to go out and actually perform the behavior once he has decided how he ought to do it. Unless the thoughts lead to instrumental action and actually produce major satisfaction, namely, are reinforcing, they will not become associated with instrumental responses.

Another important consequence of thinking through potential courses of action in the therapy interview is that the patient is being taught to stop and think before acting.

The influences in the patient's life outside of therapy are extremely powerful in comparison with the mild rewards the therapist controls. If the patient's life circumstances are so unfavorable that anything he does leads to painful consequences, there is relatively little the therapist can do, unless the patient comes to the decision that he must make a very major change in his life such as divorcing his wife, obtaining a new job, moving to a different geographical location, or in effect starting an entirely different pattern of life under different circumstances.

The first instrumental responses the patient tries outside of therapy are likely to be only partially effective. Therefore, it is valuable for him to be able to discuss periodically with the therapist their effectiveness and how they might be improved. There is a kind of cyclical sequence called "approximation and correction" in which the patient thinks about the planned responses to be performed, goes out into a life situation and tries them, discusses the consequences in his next interview, and then plans modified behaviors which he hopes will be more effective.

This trying out of instrumental responses does not occur just at the end of therapy but periodically throughout therapy as different portions of patient's behavior patterns become modified and as different aspects of the situations influencing him are examined. There is no sharp delineation between the "talking" and the "real world" aspect of therapy. Patients are doing a great many things between therapy interviews, and it behooves the therapist to keep informed about the patient's behavior, its consequences, and the major and permanent changes that are resulting. When the patient's anxiety-avoidance patterns have been reduced, when his capacity to think, reason, plan, discriminate, and generalize has been restored, when he has tried out new instrumental responses in real-life situations and has found them to be effective, he will have less and less need for the therapist and will eventually terminate therapy with the reasonable conviction that he can now handle his life without assistante.

EVALUATION OF BEHAVIOR CHANGE

Appraisal of Behavior Change

Although detailed on many other points, Dollard and Miller have presented neither criteria nor techniques by which the therapist can determine whether the behavior changes he has attempted to produce have occurred. One might suppose they would advocate the use of objective measures of one kind or another, although they do not say so. In a book illustrating the application of this system to a therapy case, Dollard, Auld, and White (1953) discuss the use of psychological tests for purposes of identifying the conflicts and troublesome behaviors, but conclude that they are of doubtful utility at the present time. One might also assume they would prefer an objective opportunity to observe the patient behaving in significant life situations, but this is impractical in most therapy cases. The implication remains that the therapist's observations during the course of therapy and his judgments of the changes the patient reports as having occurred outside of therapy are the main evidences upon which an assessment about behavior change can be based.

VERIFICATION OF THERAPY THEORY

There is no doubt about Dollard and Miller's preference for the use of experimental and empirical procedures in verifying any theoretical formulation. They emphasize that they are presenting hypotheses, not confirmed principles. One of the major difficulties in objective verification of their theoretical formulations is that many of the most crucial response events involved cannot be observed directly by the therapist or any outside observer. They can only be inferred. More objective methods of observation and measurement are essential before rigorous experimental and empirical research can be formulated (1959, p. 228).

Direct observation of behavior in the therapy situation can be very useful for developing significant propositions about behavior in general as well as about therapy processes themselves. Patients reveal themselves more fully than others ordinarily do, and the condition provides a "window to higher mental life." Of course, there are serious limitations to building a theory of human behavior based solely on observations of such a limited and biased sample of persons. Moreover, it seems a firm belief, particularly of Neal Miller's, that experimental study and verification of principles can be done more rigorously outside of therapy than in the therapy setting itself. Thus, it would appear that Dollard and Miller would encourage any kind of experimental and empirical research, both in therapy situations and in any other types of situations, that would permit the general principles to be verified or denied.

COMMENTS

Dollard and Miller have succeeded in presenting a systematic statement which simultaneously represents a significant contribution to the applied field of individual verbal psychotherapy and to the basic science of behavior as well. Turning to the basic discipline of psychology as a resource in the analysis of the development of behavior and the procedures for effecting change, they have made a significant effort to apply such principles to the solution of practical problems in psychotherapy. They have dealt systematically with issues many other theorists avoid. Their system is based on a theory about how behavior is learned, in contrast to those of other theorists which focus primarily on what is learned. They have made an intriguing attempt to deduce a great variety of phenomena occurring in psychotherapy from a limited number of psychological principles. Even though they recognized from the outset that there would be many gaps in their presentation because of the partial state of knowledge about behavior, they also believed that their effort might eventually help to develop a more adequate therapeutic system. The attempt is indeed impressive.

Further, their formulation of a behavioristic position that incorporates both subjectively observable and objectively observable responses has considerable significance for the field of psychology as a whole. Their position that a response is a response whether it occurs within or on the surface of an organism represents a necessary broadening of traditional behavioristic response definitions. Their analysis of approach-avoidance conflicts and the way fear affects other kinds of behavior is a valuable contribution and has generated a considerable amount of useful research. Finally, their emphasis on social and cultural factors in relationship to learning enhances the study of the learning process itself, above and beyond its assistance in understanding the acquisition of normal and disordered behavior.

As with any system, however, a number of difficulties remain, and there are several that appear to be inherent in this position. Many of these difficulties seem to derive from an underlying set of assumptions upon which the system is based. Several arise from the attempt to maintain that learning is completely automatic and involuntary. In this view all responses have specific antecedents which automatically and completely control their occurrence. Ultimately all responses are connected to and under the control of situational events. By inference, then, control of human behavior is accomplished by situational control. If the experimenter, or the therapist, can discover the correct events to manipulate, he can automatically elicit particular response sequences in the individual. Consistent with the theoretical tradition from which this system grew, the learning postulates characterize man as a robot. At its base, all behavior is acquired and then continues to operate in a thoroughly automatic, involuntary, and situation-determined way.[3] We shall comment about their position on verbal control of behavior in a moment.

It is doubtful that all human learning occurs as they propose. They assume that responses are learned which accomplish some situational consequence and terminate intense physiological events (drives). Increasingly, evidence has accumulated to demonstrate that the concept of drive as they present it is inadequate to account for the *why* of human behavior (Hall, 1961). Moreover, the concept of drive reduction as a single principle has been challenged by the evidence that animals also learn responses so as to stimulate rather than to terminate other responses. Miller acknowledges that the concept of drive reduction will probably have to be discarded as inadequate, but he justifies its continued use because of its fruitfulness in stimulating significant research. There is also the implication that there is no better alternative at the moment, and Miller has suggested that an alternative principle could be substituted without producing extensive changes in the system. Some other explanation does seem necessary, but we should be very surprised if it failed to produce major changes.

At the same time that Dollard and Miller propose that the basic initiators of behavior occur in the physiological response patterns of the person, they recognize that many other events also impel behavior, for example, situational events and other responses. To account for this, they propose that any event, response or situational, may acquire the power to initiate behavior if it occurs in appropriate association with the innate physiological responses (drives). But there has been repeated difficulty in demonstrating empirically what sounds plausible in theory. Difficulty in consistently producing such learned drives in second-, third-, fourth-, and fifth-order conditioning procedures renders rather questionable the hypothesis that this is the way learning proceeds (Amsel, 1961).

The same problem occurs with the drive reducers of the situational

[3] This may well result from their use of principles originally formulated to explain the behavior of "nonarticulate organisms" and of humans behaving at "prearticulate and subarticulate levels"—Hull's learning theory (Amsel, 1961).

consequents terminating the sequences of behavior that have begun. Dollard and Miller note that many environmental consequences which seem to terminate response sequences (act as reinforcers) cannot by any stretch of the imagination be thought of as innately having the power. Again, they argue that such events acquire their "reinforcing power" through association with events that are innate reinforcers. Experimental demonstration of stable third-, fourth-, and fifth-order learned reinforcers have not been demonstrated, and since they acknowledge that most important reinforcers are learned rather than innate, the question of how and why particular behavioral consequences effect learning still seems to be a major theoretical and practical problem.

They propose that learning in the human occurs automatically and that the effects of reinforcement are correspondingly so. No conscious or volitional participation of the person is involved. According to this view, he does not even need to attend directly to, or be aware of, the contingencies involved. It is doubtful that all human learning proceeds in such robot fashion. Some undoubtedly does, as has been demonstrated in the automaticity of the conditioned response in the response classes of muscular and glandular behavior. But a great deal of human learning also seems to entail the person attending to and being aware of the events that confront him, of symbolically choosing various courses of action, and the like.

It is true that Dollard and Miller give consciousness—or perhaps more accurately, unconsciousness—a prominent role in their discussion of pathology. Lack of awareness of the factors influencing him (stupidity) is one characteristic of the neurotic and interferes with the learning of other behaviors. Similarly, in discussing therapy as such, they use phrases such as "focusing of attention," "therapist calls attention to," and "anxieties come to be focused on." But this is not woven into their characterization of the learning process. The phenomenon of human awareness and that of attention, although used in their analysis of human behavior and significantly employed in their discussion of pathology and treatment, has no place in their review of how and what the human learns and how he continues to behave. This is a significant inconsistency if it is true, as the present authors suspect, that as much human behavior is learned with awareness as without and that learning is more intricate and involved than is represented by the automatic and unconscious effect of situational reinforcers. A recent paper by Miller reveals his growing view of the complicated functions of the human brain as an "active organ" (1961, p. 752).

We shall conclude these comments with a few observations about the behavioral concepts employed in this system. It has been noted already that the concepts of stimulus, response, cue, and stimulus and response generalization, to take examples, differ from most behavioral concepts in that they refer to *kinds of relationships* among events rather than *kinds* of events as such. Thus, a stimulus is defined in terms of its relationship to a response; stimulus generalization is a label denoting the relationship between a response and some class of other events. It is perfectly legitimate to have concepts that refer not only to certain events but also to concepts that refer to the interconnections between those events. But a difficulty arises when you have the latter without the former, and Dollard and Miller's system tends to have this difficulty. To an extent they are aware of this when they state that more attention has been paid to the hyphen in *S-R* than to the *S* and *R* themselves.

The system would become more precise and useful if attention were paid to the classification of different kinds of situational occurrences and different kinds of responses. The term stimulus is so inclusive that it encompasses everything. The term response is used to refer to behavior as different in size and kind as the eyelid reflex and the taking of a mathematics examination.

One of the initial impressions a reader of this system develops is that the conceptual units are clear, simple, and powerful. On closer analysis, however, one finds the apparent simplicity is deceptive, and a series of fundamental questions arise. The concepts of stimulus and response generalization are significant ones in Dollard and Miller's analysis of the development of disordered behavior or its subsequent treatment. First, with each concept defined in terms of the other, the two classes are not mutually exclusive. Moreover, there are no propositions in this system by which one can determine along what attributes of stimuli responses can be expected to generalize. Nor is there any way to tell which of many similar responses are likely to appear. The practising therapist will therefore have considerable difficulty if he attempts to employ these concepts in his treatment procedures. As Dollard and Miller suggested, sufficient data are lacking on many points, and this system, like others, continues to require greater specification and perhaps important modifications.

Dollard and Miller would probably answer that since the same principles apply to every kind of response-response and situation-response relationship, one need not concern oneself with the question of specific kind of response involved. Two points should be made about this position. First, it is debatable whether all classes of response in the human organism operate in the same way and according to the same sets of laws; many would dispute such an assumption. Second, such a position leads one to a thoroughgoing idiographic procedure, where if no general principles are available for specifying which *kinds* of events are typically related to which *other kinds,* these have to be determined in each individual case. For each person, the therapist must identify what situations are eliciting what responses, what response sequences occur within the individual, and what reinforcers are maintaining his behavior. Actually, Dollard and Miller probably do not anticipate such a completely idiographic approach, for they write as if some patterns and sequences are culturally frequent. But the system requires extension along this line, including more propositions by which to predict the kinds of behavioral sequences and patterns that can be anticipated in a given culture and a given patient with particular patterns of presenting symptoms.

A final comment should be made. Perhaps it can be introduced by noting that this system cannot stand alone as a treatment procedure. By this, we mean that a practitioner could not pick up the volume *Personality and Psychotherapy* and proceed to practice techniques of verbal therapy. Although he would have a rationale by which to account for the general ways in which responses can be connected with other responses and to situational events, he would find scant information about which responses are likely to be encountered in what conditions, what kinds of response are likely to be related to which other ones, which particular ones tend to go together with others in recurrently encountered patterns, and the like. Other writers, such as Adler and Horney, have concentrated on precisely the content of human behavior. Dollard and Miller, on the other hand, have emphasized the *how* of behavior and paid correspondingly little attention to the kinds of response patterns and sequences that characterize disorder and its treatment.

In summary, in their effort to remedy a crucial weakness of most therapy systems, to wit, the absence of an adequate theory of learning, they have erred in the other direction and have inadequately represented the content or substance of behavior. They themselves recognized that their presentation was seriously limited by the lack of substantial knowledge on a number of crucial issues. Even so, it represented the first major attempt to build a bridge between basic psychological and psychotherapeutic theory and practice. We can only hope they, or some equally competent theorists, will make a similar attempt as biological, psychological, and sociological knowledge advances.

Chapter 8

The Reciprocal Inhibition

Psychotherapy of Joseph Wolpe

Joseph Wolpe's developing approach to psychotherapy constitutes a major break from the mainstream of psychotherapeutic techniques represented by the other systems examined in this volume. He has challenged some of the basic assumptions underlying traditional psychotherapy and has invented a variety of training procedures which he believes are valuable for modifying different types of behavior difficulties.

He is not the only practitioner and theorist who has attempted a radically different formulation of how to think about and treat disordered behavior. During the last decade there have been several, apparently because of a growing conviction among a good many therapists that existing approaches, even though of considerable value, have serious limitations. Although the other therapists discussed in this volume have developed somewhat different ways of thinking about behavior disorder, they all use fundamentally the same treatment approach. They sit and talk with the patient. They differ in the content they believe should be discussed, as well as when and how to discuss it, but they do not propose the extensive use of other procedures. By contrast, a distinctive feature of Wolpe's proposals, along with those of Salter (1950) and Eysenck (1957), is that he advocates the use of other techniques in addition to talking, and his use of conversation as a treatment procedure is very different. Wolpe was chosen for examination for several reasons: He presents a fairly detailed discussion of his therapeutic procedures; there has been some interest among American psychologists in his approach (Lang and Lazovik, 1961); and he has recently attempted a systematic presentation of his ideas (1958). Since Eysenck acknowledges that Wolpe's theory agrees with his own in its "major aspects" and in no way "runs counter to" it (1957, p. 272), Wolpe's system seems to be a representative choice for analysis. Although there have been attempts to apply some of B. F. Skinner's unique ideas about learning (1957) to psychotherapeutic problems, no systematic approach based on Skinner's ideas is as yet available.

BIOGRAPHICAL INFORMATION

Joseph Wolpe was born April 20, 1915, and spent his entire childhood in the Union of South Africa, where his parents had immigrated as children at the very beginning of the twentieth century. The family was Jewish, and his maternal grandmother tried hard to turn him into "a pious Jew." This led him to read and be influenced by certain Jewish writers, especially Maimonides. He and a cousin had many long arguments about Wolpe's belief in God which led, when he was 20, to a detailed study of Kant (especially the *Critique of Pure Reason*) to Hume, through several other philosophers, to Bertrand Russell. Slowly his theistic position became replaced by a physical monism.

After an initial skepticism, he adopted Freud's view of human behavior, for he considered Freud a rigorous materialist like himself. Doubts began developing in 1944 as a consequence of reading publications by Bartlett, Malinowski, and Valentine, showing that some of Freud's ideas did not agree with facts. His puzzling discovery that the Russians did not accept Freudian theory led him in 1945 to study Pavlov's *Conditioned Reflexes* (1927). He was impressed by the experiments, but not the theoretical formulations. Then, in 1945 while he was on holiday in Cape Town, a friend introduced him to Hull's *Principles of Behavior* (1943), and he adopted that theoretical framework. He now feels that though many of Hull's postulates may turn out to be incorrect, the form of the theory has lasting significance.[1]

Wolpe's M.D. thesis (University of Witwatersrand, Johannesburg, South Africa, 1948) was concerned with the relationship between conditioned responses and neurosis. In the ensuing decade he published a series of papers concerned with learning and neurosis, culminating in his book *Psychotherapy by Reciprocal Inhibition* (1958), made possible by a Fellowship at the Center for Advanced Study in Behavioral Science at Stanford, California. This chapter is based primarily on his book, since it represents his most complete, systematic, and up-to-date account of his ideas. For several years he was in private practice in Johannesburg and a lecturer at the University of Witwatersrand. Subsequently he became Research Professor of Psychiatry at the University of Virginia.

CENTRAL THEMES

Wolpe has limited his concern to what he calls neurotic behavior. By this he means any persistent, learned, unadaptive habits in a "physiologically normal" person. It includes the various types of behavior usually given the labels of anxiety state, phobia, depression, hysteria, neurasthenia, and obsessional state. He specifically excludes psychoses such as schizophrenia, because he assumes they stem from an "abnormal organic state" (1958, p. 34). Examples of other organically based disorders cited are behaviors deriving from hyperthyroidism, epilepsy, or beriberi. Thus, his proposals about therapy can be expected to apply only to the class of neurotic behavior disorders.

He assumes that neurotic habits are learned and can only be eliminated effectively through unlearning. His approach is based primarily on the drive-reduction conditioning model of Clark Hull. He considers his own view to be "a new theory of psychotherapy" and "a serious alternative to the repression theory" (1958, p. lx).

Wolpe uses neurological arguments and some experimental studies on animals to support his view, but he makes no detailed statement of his learning theory base. He includes a brief chapter on "the biological matrix" of learning theory and another on limited aspects of

[1] From a personal communication by Wolpe.

learning theory "most relevant to neurotic behavior." Some of his other papers (1950; 1952e) suggest he has a more complete understanding of Hullian learning theory than his book might suggest.

One kind of response—anxiety—is given a central role in his theory of neurosis. It is always a part of the original neurotic learning situation and usually a part of the eventual symptom pattern. The therapeutic task, then, is to alter learned connections between previously neutral situational or response events (stimuli) and these anxiety responses or the unadaptive habits following upon the anxiety responses. This is to be accomplished by presenting the anxiety-eliciting events, or symbolic representations of them, in temporal contiguity to responses that are *innately antagonistic* to anxiety responses. In this way, anxiety is prevented from occurring and the bond between the eliciting event and anxiety is weakened. After an adequate number of trials, it can be completely extinguished. Different types of responses and different training procedures can be opposed to anxiety, and the ones selected should be those most effective with the particular neurotic habit to be extinguished. Thus, differential diagnosis and differential treatment are features of this view.

He assumes that human behavior functions according to "causal laws," as do all "other phenomena" (1959, p. 3). Behavior refers simply to "a change of state" or of "spatial relationships" to other objects or events. These changes are to be understood as the result of a potentially identifiable sequence of antecedent events functioning according to natural laws. The sequence should eventually be reducible to neural phenomena.

Finally, consistent with conditioning theory, habits will be learned or unlearned automatically if the therapist can arrange appropriate conditions in contiguous temporal and spatial relationships. Thus, concepts such as insight, choice, unconscious processes, symbolic responses (thoughts), awareness, and so forth, are not significant in this system. Of course, the patient has to help create some of the conditions, but this is far different from the patient changing himself as a consequence of newly acquired understandings.

Wolpe considers it useful to distinguish conceptually between molar and molecular aspects of behavior. He considers a molecular response to be a change in "a relatively small physiologically differentiated unit" —a cell or group of cells. Molar responses are the "gross resultant" of a number of molecular responses. As examples, he cites swallowing, jumping, sweating, and thinking. He indicates that it is sometimes useful to treat sequences of molar responses—for example, walking, talking—as a conceptual unit, and to these he gives the term *act* (1959, p. 4). Thus, he uses conceptual units of varying sizes, depending on their utility. He considers "molar" responses or sequences as the most useful conceptual unit for the psychotherapist. His "explanation" of learning, however, relies on molecular neurological response sequences.

THE NORMAL COURSE OF BEHAVIOR DEVELOPMENT

Wolpe has little to say about the normal course of behavior development. Innate behavioral equipment, response-response relationships, and variations in developmental patterns caused by different cultures or training procedures receive little attention. Characteristics of the normal, healthy, or well-adjusted person are not presented, although his approach requires the therapist to decide which old habits should be unlearned and which responses should replace them.

What follows has been derived, on the one hand, from Wolpe's discussion of learning and inferred, on the other, from his discussion of behavior disorder and its treatment.

Innate Characteristics of Normal Development

Wolpe refers to a variety of responses such as sensory responses and motoric acts which he seems to view as innate, although there is no systematic treatment of their development or their interrelationships. Three fundamental concepts are need, drive, and anxiety; each is considered innate.

NEED. In ordinary language, the term need refers to the feeling of "wanting" something, a state of "unsatisfaction," and is usually identified by the event or activity that will "satisfy" it—food, sexual satisfaction, rest. More accurately, needs are physiological "states" or responses. Although much is yet unknown, their great diversity is already evident. As examples, he cites dryness of the mouth and throat as a consequence of diminished body fluid, metabolic changes in muscle tissue resulting from activity, the tension of a full bladder, and sexual reactivity due to increasing amounts of circulating sex hormones. All such physiological events function as antecedents to "neuro-effector" responses—motor activity. In this sense, however, they are similar to "ordinary" sensory responses. How can the two be distinguished? Innate physiological responses differ from usual sensory events in their strength or intensity, leading to stronger, more extensive, and more persistent motor responses.

DRIVE. Innate physiological responses are not the direct antecedent to overt behavior. Between the physiological responses (needs) and motor responses "there intervenes excitation of neurones in the central nervous system," which Wolpe refers to as drive (1958, p. 8). The more "excitation," that is, the more neurones stimulated to emit electrical impulses, the stronger the drive. When a threshold intensity is reached, "effector neurones" are excited if "other conditions are present," and motor responses result (1958, p. 9). Thus, strictly speaking, neuro-electrical activity, not physiological responses, elicits motor responses.

Wolpe is postulating an innate sequence: biochemical deficits such as lack of food or intrusions such as hormones occasion physiological responses, which generate patterns of electrical potentials of threshold intensity in the central nervous system which, in turn, induce motor activity. The motor activity is directed toward achieving consequences that terminate the sequence. This is called *drive reduction*. It is important to note that the electrical excitation leading to motor activity may be aroused by events other than innate physiological responses, thus making possible the acquisition of *learned drives*.

ANXIETY. For Wolpe, this important innate response is the essential antecedent to the learning of all neurotic disorders. Anxiety as fear is an autonomic response pattern which is characteristically a part of the individual's response to noxious stimulation. Noxious stimulation is any event causing "tissue disturbance" and tending to produce avoidance responses. It is important to his treatment procedures that anxiety responses are those usually associated with discharge from the sympathetic portions of the autonomic nervous system. A few parasympathetic responses—for example, bladder evacuation—may also occur. They are innately elicited not only by painful stimuli but also by very intense stimuli, by falling, and by ambivalent stimuli—stimuli that are equally strong but conflicting.

Other kinds of emotional responses, such as anger and love, are not discussed. Apparently, Wolpe does not consider them important in learning, in the development of disordered behavior, or in therapy, although occasional reference is made to them in his case histories, and they are used as responses antagonistic to fear, as "assertive responses."

CONSCIOUSNESS AND THOUGHTS. These are manifestations of innate neural functioning, but Wolpe gives them a far less important role in behavior than do most theorists. The "content of consciousness" (thoughts, images, sensations) occurs *in parallel and not in series* with their neural correlates," constituting "the unique reaction of a specially placed observer (the subject) to these neural events" (1958, p. 16). Thus, "neural activity" can lead to motor behavior whether or not conscious thoughts occur. He implies that images can elicit "neural activity" when, in discussing one of his treatment procedures, he states that it is necessary to assume that the image of a situation will arouse the same general responses as the situation itself. In this instance, conscious images are crucial elements in the behavior sequence. In general, however, conscious symbolic responses are given no systematic place in his proposals.

BEHAVIOR SEQUENCES. He conceives of situational and response events as occurring in interrelated sequences. Any response is the consequence of all the situational and response events preceding it in the sequence. Similarly, every response is an antecedent (stimulus) to every other response event following it in a sequence. Having established the notion of sequence as a fundamental type of interrelationship among events, he does not make use of it in his discussion of pathology or treatment. However, his procedures for reciprocal inhibition could be interpreted as substituting different responses in old behavior sequences to bring about changes in those sequences.

MATURATION. Wolpe notes that behavior sequences develop as a result of biological growth and differentiation. In his language, functional connections among neurones develop from maturation. Simple response sequences established in this way are called reflexes, while more elaborate ones are called instinctual behaviors. He proposes that the less complex an organism's nervous system, the more completely maturation determines complex response patterns. However, man probably has no such sequences "that are complex enough to be called instinctive" (1958, p. 19). Most human behavior is the consequence of learning.

REACTIVE INHIBITION. This principle is basic to Wolpe's treatment approach. Each time a response is elicited, regardless of its consequences (reinforcement), "a fatigue-associated state or substance" develops which has "an inhibitory effect upon a closely following evocation of the same response" (1958, p. 25). The more frequently a response occurs in a given period of time, the greater the quantity or intensity of the fatigue-like state which will develop, and the less likely the response is to recur. However, the fatigue-like state dissipates with time in the absence of the response, and the probability of the response recurring under appropriate circumstances will increase once more. This quantity of "fatigue," an inferred (r_i) response, occurs in the central nervous system. Like all "neural excitation," it can function as a drive and can serve as the antecedent to the learning of new responses. It is this proposition which Wolpe expands upon in his treatment approach.

Learned Characteristics of Normal Behavior

Wolpe contends that effective psychotherapy must be based on psychological learning theory, and he has chosen the Hullian model for his framework. However, Wolpe's focus is almost entirely upon *how* learning occurs, and he refers to *what* is learned only by way of illustrating the learning principles he espouses. For example, he does not discuss the acquisition of typical patterns of motor response, habits of attention, the development of habitual self-evaluative thoughts, or how certain habits acquired early in development may influence the acquisition of later behavior patterns. The basic learning principles enable one to understand the behavior of another person, how it came about, and how it can be changed. Therefore, the material to be summarized in this section pertains entirely to the sequence of learning, assumed to be the same for all people, and for all kinds of responses, while nothing can be reported about the content of normal learning.

THE LEARNING PROCESS. If a response is evoked by a situational or response event, that is, by a "sensory stimulus," and if that response is followed fairly quickly by a reduction in intensity of some neural excitation (drive reduction), learning will occur. It is not necessary that the response be instrumental in achieving the reduction, only that the several events be associated closely in time.

Several factors influence how much learning will take place. First, the further apart in time the elicitor, the response, and the excitation reduction occur, the less learning results. In general, the best results are said to be obtained when they occur no more than a few seconds apart. Second, the number and distribution of reductions (reinforcements) has a major influence. The amount of learning is greater the more times the learning sequence occurs—that is, the more reinforcements—and even more learning is obtained if the reinforcements have some time interval between them. Just how long the intervals should be for a particular learning task is not yet known, however. Finally, the more intense the response elicitor—the drive—the more learning will usually occur.

How does one know when learning has occurred? Wolpe presents two criteria: (1) a previously ineffective event now evokes the response, or (2) an event now evokes the response more strongly than before (1958, p. 19). It is important to recall that innate physiological responses (primary needs) are not the only events that may arouse central neural excitation and lead to learning. In fact, the reduction of *any* excitation in the central nervous system, regardless of its origin, will facilitate learning. Thus, he extends drive-reduction theory to encompass the "innumerable instances of learning" (verbal learning and "sensory preconditioning") that have no physiological responses (needs) as their antecedent (1958, p. 24).

Any situational or response event intense enough to elicit some central nervous system excitation can be considered a drive. With such an all-inclusive definition, however, the fundamental question of why an individual's behavior is more regularly directed toward some environmental consequences than toward others remains unanswered. Wolpe suggests that some events, such as innate physiological responses or primary needs, stimulate more intense neural excitation than others. In addition, he refers to "conditioned needs" such as those for prestige and money, but he does so in a footnote and fails to explain how these come about. He also notes recent research which seems to indicate that response arousal (drive increment) will facilitate learning, as will response termination (drive reduction). However, he seems to believe his position will not be affected seriously if such a principle is verified.

HABITS. What is the consequence of the learning sequence described? It is the formation of habits, or a "recurring manner of response to a given stimulus situation" (1958, p. 5). The strength of habitual responses differ, and this fact may be estimated in several ways: (1) amplitude or intensity of the response; (2) response velocity; (3) frequency of occurrence under specific conditions; and (4) persistence when efforts are made to eliminate it. Frequently, more than one habitual response is acquired for a given set of circumstances: a habit family exists for that particular stimulus. These several habitual responses will vary in their strength and are said to exist in a hierarchy. When somewhat similar responses, though they may differ in a number of respects, become habitual across different but similar situations, a general behavior pattern is said to exist. Gentleness with children, regardless of the children, situation, or other aspects of the responses toward them, would be an example. All habits, including "conscious associations," are acquired and function in the same way.

Wolpe's approach to therapy relies on the unlearning or extinction of learned response sequences. Hence, let us turn to that issue next.

UNLEARNING. Wolpe uses the terms unlearning and extinction synonymously. If a learned response occurs several times without leading to a reduction of the intensity of the antecedent events—if drive reduction does not occur—a progressive weakening of the strength of that response to those antecedents will result. Following Hull, Wolpe proposes that there are two separate but interrelated factors contributing to the weakening. The first is the accumulation of a neural inhibitory fatigue-like state varying with response frequency (reactive inhibition). This dissipates with time when the response does not occur, and the strength of the response itself is not permanently altered; that is, spontaneous recovery takes place.

The second factor does lead to a permanent weakening of the habitual response to that situation, however, and is therefore very important. The fatigue-like state (reactive inhibition) that develops is assumed to be a type of neural excitation (drive) and will also facilitate the learning of habitual responses when reduced. Situational and response events (stimuli) occurring at the time the neural fatigue-like state is reduced become related in such a way to the response being extinguished that they interfere with the occurrence of that response on future similar occasions. This may even include events which have previously served to elicit the response; they may become "conditioned to an inhibition of the response to which previously they were positively joined" (1958, p. 25). Wolpe explains this effect, not in terms of the learning of a competing response, but in terms of neural activity in which the conditioned inhibition represents a decrease in conductivity at crucial synaptic connections in the response sequence being extinguished. He believes this explanation makes reasonable the apparent specificity of the inhibiting effect.

RECIPROCAL INHIBITION. Wolpe considers reciprocal inhibition to be a special case of the principle of conditioned inhibition. Most of his therapy procedures are based on this principle. Stated simply, reciprocal inhibition involves associating a response antagonistic to the response to be extinguished with the events that elicit it. Both responses cannot occur simultaneously, for they are antagonistic. The new response will become connected through repeated trials with the events that previously produced the old response, because the prevention of the latter reduces the intensity of the neural fatigue state associated with it; drive reduction occurs. In Wolpe's terms, the reduction of reactive inhibition produces conditioned inhibition (1958, p. 30). The new response will tend to be elicited by the antecedent events, and the old one will become progressively less likely to occur.

For example, in research on cats, Wolpe opposed an eating response to a fear response. He argues that the neural and physiological responses associated with eating and those associated with fear are innately antagonistic and cannot occur simultaneously. When the cat was fed in a corner of the room distant from the apparatus in which the fear was learned, the fear response was made weaker than the eating pattern. In a sequence of training trials, the food was moved closer and closer to the apparatus until the animal was eating without fear in the training apparatus itself. If the extinction had begun in the apparatus, the fear would have been the stronger of the antagonistic responses and would have become increased while the eating pattern would not have occurred and a learned inhibition of the eating pattern would have developed. Thus, the response to be learned must be stronger in the learning situation than the one to be extinguished if the procedure is to be successful and if disruption of a desired response pattern is to be avoided.

Wolpe argues that this arrangement occurs over and over again in everyday living. An example would be a child who has acquired a fear of water. Although he is afraid to go swimming with his friends, his affection for them is greater than his fear, so he goes along and has fun. The next time, the child's anticipatory fear is less strong, and his positive feelings about going have increased. After several such experiences, the fear will have disappeared or at least subsided to an insignificant level. In addition, through generalization, the child's fear of water in other situations, for example, boating, will also decrease, although to a lesser extent. Wolpe considers that ordinary forgetting occurs in the same general way. Thus, with the principle of conditioned inhibition and its subsidiary, reciprocal inhibition, he tries to account for all types of unlearning and forgetting.

CHARACTERISTICS OF NORMAL BEHAVIOR. Wolpe does not discuss this issue; hence, what follows is inferred from his discussion of neurotic behavior. It seems clear that he would not make a sharp distinction between normal and neurotic behavior. Behavior is thought of as being adaptive or unadaptive. It is adaptive if it successfully reduces central neural excitation—reduces a drive or satisfies a need—or if it successfully avoids possible damage or deprivation. However, since many behaviors have a variety of consequences, some good and some bad, one can speak only of the net adaptiveness or unadaptiveness of any given behavior sequence.

A few concrete attributes of normal behavior seem clear. First, the individual is not afraid or anxious in situations in which there is no realistic reason to be afraid. Some fears are realistic and adaptive; others are not. Second, the individual has satisfactory interpersonal relationships in which he can behave assertively, that is, be angry, loving, or dominant when it is appropriate. Third, he can carry out his daily activities at home or at work without inappropriate fears occurring. Finally, satisfying sexual relationships can be consummated when appropriate opportunities offer themselves.

THE DEVELOPMENT OF BEHAVIOR DISORDER

Wolpe presents an anxiety theory of neurosis. He assumes that neuroses are learned behavior patterns which are "basically unadaptive conditioned anxiety reactions." They may be few or many, mild or intense. They may disrupt major aspects of an individual's life, or they may be restricted to limited and unimportant realms. Wolpe's concern is with what he calls neurotic behavior—*learned disorders*. Disorders with an organic base such as psychoses are ignored, since he assumes they are not learned.

Wolpe has not attempted to present a complete theory of behavior disorder. He plans to present a full exposition of the etiology of neurosis in a future volume. However, we shall summarize the ideas he has presented. He assumes that clinical (human) neuroses are fundamentally the same as the experimentally created animal neuroses that he and others have studied.

The Learning of Neurotic Behaviors

PREDISPOSING CONDITIONS. Why do some people develop neuroses and not others? Neurotic reactions develop as a consequence of intense anxiety. Thus, any conditions that make one individual more likely than others to respond with intense anxiety would make him more susceptible to the development of neurotic behaviors. Wolpe mentions several such conditions. Individuals are said to differ physiologically in their reactivity to anxiety-evoking circumstances. Some respond with intense anxiety to conditions that elicit only mild anxiety in others. In addition, emotional sensitivity may be increased by learning. Individuals who have already acquired many inappropriate anxiety responses are more likely than others to develop a severe neurosis. Thus, individuals with a childhood history of distressing experiences might have acquired more inappropriate anxiety responses and be more susceptible to severe disorder. Other factors, such as fatigue, drugs, hormones, or other chemical agents, and special conditions of consciousness such as hypnagogic states, might increase the likelihood of an individual's responding with intense anxiety.

PRECIPITATING CONDITIONS. The "keystone" of all neuroses is severe anxiety. Under what conditions is it likely to be elicited? Sometimes particular situations will evoke it directly. If the innate elicitors of anxiety mentioned earlier are severe enough, they can provoke intense anxiety. In humans, however, anxiety is far more likely to be caused by events that were once neutral, for "even at an early age, there are far more anxiety responses to conditioned cues than to unconditioned ones" (1958, p. 34). The anxiety-evoking situation may be really dangerous, such as a battle in war. The fear aroused may become associated with any events present at the time—gunfire, smell of gunpowder, blue sky, open spaces, thoughts of death, pains in the leg. On the other hand, situations in which there is no "objective" danger can also come to elicit severe anxiety—for example, fear elicited by genital sensations because of punitive childhood training in which sex was considered sinful.

Another type of circumstance that may evoke anxiety is one in which there are conflicting response sequences. Wolpe sees anxiety as the result rather than the cause of conflict (1958, p. 79). His example is of a woman engaged to a man she dislikes, but fearful of breaking the engagement because of anticipated criticism from friends. He notes the similarity between his example and Miller's avoidance-avoidance type of conflict. However, he adds one important hypothesis. When a person is on the borderline of shifting from one response sequence to another in such a conflict—of breaking the engagement and facing the criticism of friends—the anxiety from both sides accumulates, thereby creating much more intense anxiety. The "barrier" to shifting from one course of action to another which is feared is then a major increase in anxiety; *both sides* of the conflict contribute to it at that point. Pursuing a course of action is less fearful, because then only the anxiety related to one alternative is elicited. Wolpe does not specify whether anxiety is considered to be a consequent of all conflict, of conflict between two courses of action, both of which the individual wants very much, or whether it is restricted to the double-avoidance type of conflict he exemplified.

Another precipitating condition is a restriction of the responses an individual might make to the fear-inducing events. When the response possibilities are severely restricted, the anxiety is likely to be more intense. Sometimes the restriction is environmental. For example, the response possibilities for an individual in a concentration camp or in an airplane under attack during a bombing mission are very limited. More frequently, the restriction lies in the response repertoire the individual has acquired. His interpretation of the situation severely limits the responses he might make. Thoughts can become anxiety elicitors, and "neurotic responses are especially likely to become conditioned" to events represented in thoughts (1958, p. 81).

THE LEARNING SEQUENCE. If intense anxiety is evoked, any events occurring *at the same time* may become associated with the anxiety, either as elicitors or as concomitants. A restriction to this principle is implied in Wolpe's definition of environment. Only the events to which the individual responds or reacts are considered his environment, while the totality of events at the time are considered his surroundings. Apparently only events to which the individual "responds" can become associated with the anxiety.

Almost any event or attribute of events can become an anxiety elicitor: relatively specific, well-defined events such as sounds, odors, pictures, furniture, crowds, people in authority, being rejected, and being the center of attention; more pervasive situational attributes such as closed spaces, daylight, darkness, large shadowy objects, and relative silence; and other response events such as thoughts occurring at the time. These are accidental associations. The events need have no meaningful relationship to the original anxiety-eliciting event. They only need to occur at the same time and be reacted to by the individual. The nature of that reaction—sensory, motor, awareness— is not specified.

A variety of responses may be acquired as concomitants associated with the anxiety. These constitute part of the symptom complex of any neurosis. The most typical are those that are a part of the anxiety pattern itself—tachycardia, increased blood pressure and pulse rate, hyperpnea, pilo-erection, mydriasis, palmar hyperidrosis, dryness of the mouth, hyperventilation, increased irritability, and sometimes bladder and bowel evacuation. Individuals differ in which and how many of these effects they will manifest. Other responses, not a part of the anxiety pattern itself, may also become learned concomitants. The most typical of these Wolpe refers to as hysterical reactions involving the sensory system, motor system, and functional units involving imagery and consciousness—anesthesias, paresthesias, visual disturbances, paralyses, tremors, contractures, amnesias (1958, p. 85). The original occurrence of the response in the learning situation may be a consequence of intense anxiety such as motor tremors, or simply an accidental occurrence at the time, for instance, a paralysis resulting from an arm "going to sleep" because its position cut off circulation during the learning experience. Either arrangement can produce such associations.

The effectiveness of the learning is influenced by a variety of factors, including the intensity of the anxiety during each experience, the number of learning experiences, the degree of similarity among the experiences, and the response possibilities at the time.

SECONDARY LEARNED SYMPTOMS. Two types of secondary learnings may complicate the symptom picture once the primary learning has occurred. These are new responses related to the fears that result from previously learned symptoms and from learned anxiety avoidance or anxiety termination responses.

Once anxiety becomes a habitual occurrence, it may undermine or impair other aspects of the person's behavior. Motor co-ordination may be disrupted; tremors may occur; muscle tension may produce "fibrositis" or headaches; concentration, thinking, and recall may be disrupted; diminished registration of impressions (retrograde amnesia) may result; sexual performance may be disrupted (failure of erection, premature ejaculation, frigidity); bizarre experiences such as "feelings of unreality" may result; there may be consequences that follow from aspects of the anxiety pattern, such as hyperventilation (paresthesias, tremors, myalgia, and precordial pain). In addition, there appear to be individual differences in susceptibility to particular types of reactions For example, there are respiratory reactors, stomach reactors, skin reactors, blood pressure reactors, "and many others" (1958, p. 36).

Any such symptoms may themselves elicit anxiety because of their painfulness, their embarrassing social consequences, their association with learned fears of physical illness, insanity, or death, their innate anxiety-evoking characteristics, or other reasons. If they do produce anxiety, new learnings may be acquired in relationship to that anxiety, and a kind of "vicious circle" is created.

Responses may also be acquired to avoid or terminate the occurrence of anxiety. *Physical avoidance* of anxiety-evoking situations "may be expected to be the rule" when possible. It may become habitual as an automatic consequence of the anxiety termination which it produces (drive reduction). Examples would include avoiding elevators, staying away from superiors or authorities, not reading obituary notices, and remaining inconspicuous at parties. The avoidance may be somewhat more complicated. For example, a person may read obituary notices because, although thoughts of death are frightening, his anxiety is greatly relieved when he finds the dead person is much older than himself.

Another type of anxiety-avoidance response which parallels that of physical avoidance is *displacement of attention*. By devoting his attention to and directing his behavior toward nonanxiety-producing events, the individual may control his anxiety. Examples cited by Wolpe include becoming engrossed in some job, extensive involvement in social activities to avoid being alone, participation in sports, and playing cards. Such behaviors are not abnormal, but they can produce further difficulties for the person if they lead him to ignore other significant activities and commitments of life, such as a wife and family. On the other hand, they may have permanent beneficial effects because of the satisfactions they produce. These would appear to be similar to the concept of "compromise symptoms" of other theorists.

It appears some drugs can also be used to control anxiety. Among these Wolpe lists alcohol, narcotic alkaloids, barbiturates, and various "so-called" tranquilizers. These, too, may create further difficulties if the person becomes addicted to them.

Obsessions are also acquired, and persist because they alleviate anxiety. Obsessions are relatively complex habitual behaviors, usually of two types. Sometimes they are well-defined and elaborate thought sequences, such as a woman's persistent idea that she might throw her child from the balcony. Others are relatively intricate acts or motor sequences, such as exhibitionism or "handwashing." The word compulsive is sometimes used for motoric obsessions. Some may combine both, as with an individual who has to think "It's a nice day," turn around twice, and clap his hands before leaving his home. The most significant characteristic of obsessions is not their automaticity, but their intrusiveness. They represent an "encumbrance and an embarrassment" to patients. Sometimes obsessions, for example, the recurring impulse to hit someone, may be the antecedent to severe anxiety. Hysterical symptoms and obsessions differ: the former are typically physiological in content, more restricted in scope, and relatively invariate; the latter have more the character of instrumental acts, are likely to be more complicated, and are usually more variable in content, though there is a constant general theme.

A final category of response which individuals may acquire to avoid anxiety is to *inattend events* that might elicit anxiety, or to *forget the contents of emotional experiences,* the memory of which would lead to intense anxiety. Wolpe considers this to be a fairly frequent type of symptom and includes amnesias in this class as well as the simpler act of "not noticing" significant events. The complete forgetting of highly emotional experiences, which he equates with the Freudian concept of repression, he considers to be quite infrequent and relatively unimportant in neurosis or recovery from it (1950, p. 94). This is in line with his de-emphasis of symbolic responses and consciousness in his learning theory.

Wolpe has a special explanation of pervasive ("free-floating") anxiety. Anxiety is *always* the consequence of some elicitor. Thus, where anxiety is pervasive or continuous, seemingly independent of any specific elicitor, it is probably being aroused by some "omnipresent" characteristic of the environment or the individual's behavior. Thus, anxiety is pervasive because of the pervasiveness of the events that induce it. Examples cited include a patient whose anxiety was elicited by the presence of any large object; another who was upset by any sharp contrasts in his visual field; and another who felt overwhelmed by physical space. Two learning conditions may contribute to the development of pervasive anxiety. The more intense the anxiety in the learning situation, the more attributes are likely to become conditioned elicitors. A second possible factor is the absence of any clearly defined events at the time the learning occurs. He cited the example of an individual for whom the experience of learning anxiety occurred in a dark room in which all he could see was the dark outline of objects. The patient subsequently became anxious when confronted with any heavy, dark objects.

The pattern of neurotic symptomatology may vary over the course of time for several reasons. The range of events that arouse anxiety may increase or decrease. The increase may occur because new situations are similar to the original situation; because other events become elicitors as a consequence of additional anxiety-learning experiences; and because of symbolic generalization. They may decrease because of natural unlearning experiences in everyday life. The *intensity* of the responses may increase through repeated anxiety learning, or decrease through natural unlearning. Thus, the symptomatology may spread if repeated life experiences are anxiety-producing, or it may retract if the individual's life takes a favorable turn and he has many positive day-to-day experiences leading to the unlearning of anxiety responses. The latter circumstance would account for cases of spontaneous remission.

The Learned Disorder

What are the characteristics of neuroses once they are learned? They are highly varied. In most instances, characteristics of the anxiety pattern will be part of the symptom picture, but not always, even though anxiety is always involved in the learning situation. Wolpe does not speak about typical syndromes, but usually speaks of his cases in terms of the major symptomatology. For example, he refers to several cases as "severe interpersonal anxieties"; "peptic ulcer"; "paranoid obsessions"; "hysterical paresthesia and coldness, left hand"; "reactive depression"; and "severe agoraphobia, interpersonal anxiety." Judging from his case descriptions, it would appear that a persistent feature in most of his cases is fear elicited by other people—*interpersonal anxiety*.

One characteristic of all neurotic symptoms, however, is their persistence. For two reasons they are less likely than other responses to be extinguished in everyday living. First, apparently anxiety responses generate little reactive inhibition, and therefore there is little basis for conditioned inhibition of the response to develop. Second, since many symptoms are learned in relation to the occurrence of anxiety and its cessation, and since individuals tend to avoid situations that elicit anxiety, the individual is unlikely to repeat the experiences that would enable him to unlearn the symptoms.

Behavior disorder should be viewed, then, as a collection of behaviors learned concomitantly with unreasonable fears or as means of reducing unreasonable fears. These behaviors are not necessarily related to one another in one integrated pattern as some theorists suggest. Thus, different fears and different symptoms may be extinguished without necessarily expecting others to replace them. This assumption that not all symptoms are related in one pattern has important implications for treatment.

THE GOALS OF THERAPY

Although Wolpe does not directly deal with this issue, it seems clear from his writing that the therapist is an expert who determines what is wrong and decides how it should be remedied. In a general sense, therapy would appear to have two objectives. One is to alter or extinguish any troublesome behaviors (symptoms) that are related to anxiety and that are disrupting the individual's life. The other is to help the patient unlearn anxiety responses to inappropriate events so that he can go through his day-to-day life without being handicapped by the frequent, intense, or frequent *and* intense occurrence of anxiety or fear. It is the therapist's task to decide what is connected to what so that he can select procedures for breaking those connections.

CONDITIONS FOR PRODUCING BEHAVIOR CHANGE

Wolpe's therapy is focused on behavior as it presently occurs. The task, as he sees it, is to extinguish the connections between inappropriate anxiety responses, the events eliciting them, and the unadaptive responses associated with them. To accomplish this, the anxiety-eliciting situations must be presented to the patient under circumstances in which responses other than anxiety will occur. With sufficient repetitions of the learning situation devised for this purpose, the troublesome connections will be extinguished, the unadaptive behaviors will cease to occur, and more adaptive behaviors will take their place. The therapeutic approach is based essentially on one basic principle (reciprocal inhibition), which may be implemented with widely varying procedures. This principle, and the therapeutic procedures he proposes to implement it, will be discussed in this section.

TRAINING OF THERAPISTS AND KNOWLEDGE OF DISORDER. What kind of training does Wolpe believe a therapist should have to employ this approach? He does not say. However, he views the first step in treatment as one of identifying the troublesome anxiety sequences and selecting appropriate treatment procedures. Thus, it would appear that the therapist would at least need training in the learning theory Wolpe espouses and in procedures for applying it in a therapeutic setting. He would have to be able to identify which behavior sequences are troublesome for a particular patient, note how they are working, select the treatment procedure appropriate for that problem, and have the skill to apply the procedure effectively. Wolpe's approach emphasizes differential diagnosis and differential treatment. Although all neurotic disorder is based on intense anxiety, the forms it takes may be quite different. Although treatment is based on a single principle, the actual procedures for applying that principle vary depending on the nature of the problem.

Principles by which Behavior Change Occurs

Wolpe asserts there are only three known ways of producing lasting changes in an individual's responses to a given situation: growth, lesions, and learning. Habits produced by learning, including neurotic habits, can be changed by learning. His therapy procedures are based on the principle of *reciprocal inhibition* discussed under normal development. If anxiety responses can be prevented in the presence of their usual antecedents by eliciting a response "antagonistic to anxiety," the likelihood of anxiety occurring on the next occasion decreases; the "bond" is weakened (1958, p. 71). He acknowledges the possibility that there may be other ways of accomplishing the same result, but believes this to be the most effective where anxiety is concerned. He notes that simply placing an individual in the original situation with the original anxiety-producing event absent (simple extinction procedures) is a particularly ineffective way of unlearning anxiety responses, because other events in the situation have also acquired the capacity to occasion anxiety and will help to maintain the habit. Neurotic anxiety responses are seldom extinguished simply by repeated evocation.

Wolpe says his position is based on a response-termination (drive-reduction) principle. If the anxiety response is blocked or inhibited by an incompatible response, "and if a major drive reduction follows," the anxiety habit will be weakened. It would appear also that a new habit (the incompatible response) would be strengthened, although he does not elaborate this possibility. Some of his examples seem to rely on simple contiguity for learning to occur, although he never suggests such a principle.

What responses can be opposed to the anxiety response? Wolpe has been willing to try any that seemed to hold some prospect of utility. In general, he has been guided by the assumption that anxiety responses are predominantly a function of the sympathetic portion of the autonomic nervous system, and that any responses involving the parasympathetic portion of the system are likely to be innately antagonistic to anxiety responses. He cites clinical and physiological evidence to support his assumption. He lists eight categories of response which he believes are available to the control of the therapist, and by which therapeutic change deliberately can be brought about. These include: (1) assertive responses, or the overt expression of anger and resentment, as well as friendly, affectionate, and other nonanxious feelings; (2) sexual responses; (3) muscular relaxation responses; (4) respiratory responses using carbon dioxide; (5) competitively conditioned motor responses; (6) "anxiety-relief" responses; (7) "pleasant" responses in life situations (with drug enhancement); and (8) interview-induced emotional responses and abreaction. Of these, he seems to use the first three most frequently.

Patient Behavior That Must Occur in Therapy

Because the kinds of responses involved in a patient's neurosis and the antagonistic responses used in the therapeutic approach may vary considerably from patient to patient, it is not possible to specify particular kinds of responses which must occur in all cases. At a more general level, however, two types of circumstances may be specified. The patient must be confronted with events (situational or response), or symbolic representation of such events, which inappropriately elicit anxiety and symptoms. At the same time, the patient must be performing responses which are antagonistic to anxiety or to the symptoms. Then the learned connection between the eliciting events and the troublesome responses can be weakened. The therapist must determine which events are crucial for any given patient and arrange the therapeutic combination of circumstances.

Conditions Necessary to Elicit
Appropriate Patient Behaviors

CONDITIONS PROVIDED BY THE PATIENT. Wolpe places no limitation on the type of patient who might be helped by his therapy beyond specifying that the disorder must be learned ("neurotic"). Apparently there are no limitations in terms of age, intelligence, sex, and so forth. His procedures imply that patients would have to be willing and able to report accurately their troublesome responses and the situations in which they occur, particularly those that evoke anxiety. Patients would also have to be able to follow his instructions and perform the "antagonistic" responses in specified situations. For example, Wolpe cites a patient who was unable to learn to perform relaxation responses and another whose treatment failed because the patient was not reporting accurately to the therapist.

CONDITIONS PROVIDED BY THE THERAPIST. Wolpe's treatment consists of actively arranging conditions so that the troublesome responses are elicited or inhibited in therapeutic circumstances. To do this, however, the therapist must make judgments about what the troublesome responses are, the conditions that elicit them, and the responses that must be opposed to them in specifiable situations. The therapist's first task is to collect the data upon which such judgments can be based. The first few interviews are devoted to obtaining detailed information about the patient's behavior, the factors influencing it, the circumstances of his development, and the present conditions of his life.

The therapist seeks a detailed history of the patient's difficulties and symptoms. Special attention is devoted to identifying the original learning conditions (precipitating circumstances). If, after reasonable effort, the patient is unable to recall such circumstances, Wolpe does not press the point, "for to overcome his neurotic reaction it is of greater relevance to determine what stimuli do or can evoke them at the present time" (1958, p. 105). The value of the history is in helping to understand the interrelationships among the symptoms and the events likely to elicit them, and to give clues as to potentially useful techniques.

Wolpe then conducts a detailed investigation of the patient's developmental history. He systematically analyzes the patient's habitual responses to major situational contexts. These include family, with emphasis on training procedures used; other people; school and school personnel, including accomplishments; occupation, both "its technical and interpersonal aspects"; sexual relationships and responses; marital relationships; religious training; and finally "any other fearful or distressing experiences not previously mentioned." The order of these topics is varied with the natural flow of the discussion (1958, p. 106).

Throughout his inquiry there is particular emphasis on habitual emotional responses in each setting.

All of this information is obtained through a methodical procedure of inquiry. The therapist's general manner while conducting the questioning is another important condition. He accepts the patient's statements without question or criticism. He maintains a completely non-moralizing, objective approach, which aims to have as its natural outcome the patient's impression that the therapist is "unreservedly on his side."

Following this, the patient is given the Bernreuter self-sufficiency questionnaire. If the patient's score is lower than about 20, he will probably have difficulty in carrying out the active psychotherapeutic tasks the therapist will asign to him. Finally, the Willoughby Personality Schedule is presented as a kind of systematic interview to obtain evidence about the range of situations which inappropriately elicit anxiety.

Having obtained the evidence, the therapist explains to the patient the nature of his difficulties and how they can be overcome. Wolpe gives an example of the kind of statement he makes. In effect, he explains to the patient that all his difficulties can be traced back to inappropriate fear responses. Using concrete examples, he illustrates how such fears are learned. Then, using the patient's own history, he tries to show the patient how his inappropriate fears might have been acquired. Finally, he explains the rationale of treatment, emphasizing that the essence of all the techniques to be used is opposing other emotional states to the inappropriate anxiety responses. Apparently his purpose is to convince the patient of the sensibleness of his approach, in order to elicit the patient's co-operation in implementing the therapeutic procedures.

Conditions Necessary to Modify Patient Behaviors

The therapist's next step is to formulate and implement a therapeutic plan. There is nothing vague about Wolpe's approach. He formulates specific goals and selects particular techniques for achieving them (1958, p. 113). Several categories of techniques and situations to which they apply will be summarized.

THE THERAPY RELATIONSHIP AS A GENERAL PROCEDURE. Wolpe proposes that all therapies create a special type of human relationship in which potentially therapeutic emotional responses are evoked in patients. If such emotions are antagonistic to anxiety and of sufficient strength to inhibit the learned anxiety responses to the material discussed, some extinction of the anxiety will occur. For example, he cites a 30-year-old machinist who was cured of strong fear related to an inability to look people in the face when talking to them; the device was four diagnostic interviews in which no deliberate therapeutic techniques were used. He warns of the possibility that anxiety may also be strengthened in such interviews if it is stronger than the competing emotion. Abreaction, the symbolic re-evocation of a fearful past experience, is a special case. He proposes that no permanent effects are achieved from abreaction if unrelieved terror is the only emotional factor involved. Therapeutic effects are achieved only when the patient feels the impact of the friendly, sympathetic relationship during the experience. Wolpe prefers more precise techniques which give the therapist more "detailed control of the processes of change" and facilitate changes that will not occur simply as a consequence of the therapy relationship.

ASSERTIVE RESPONSES USED IN LIFE SITUATIONS. Wolpe illustrates the use of aggressive, relaxing, affectionate, and sexual responses as assertive responses. This technique is used to extinguish anxieties elicited by interpersonal situations and should be used *only* when the therapist is sure the anxiety touched off by the other person is inappropriate, that is, when he can predict that "unpleasant repercussions" from the other person are not likely to occur if the patient changes his behavior in that situation. Having identified the interpersonal situations in which inappropriate anxiety occurs, and having decided therapeutic results will accrue if the patient will behave differently in those situations, the therapist proceeds.

He first explains to the patient how unadaptive fears are the source of his difficulties in the specified situations. He uses extensive concrete examples to "sell" the idea. He and the patient then select the kinds of responses the patient should make in the situation to inhibit the occurrence of anxiety. The therapist applies "as much pressure as seems necessary" to get the patient to perform the responses in the appropriate circumstances. In subsequent interviews, the patient's performance will be discussed and corrected, and the patient will try again. If the patient has difficulty in knowing how to perform the prescribed responses, they may be practiced in the therapy session with the therapist pretending to be the other person involved. The success of the technique depends on the patient adequately performing the responses in the real life situation. Talking about it with the therapist is no adequate substitute. If the therapist's predictions have been accurate and the patient successfully performs the responses, the emotions he experiences as a result of achieving different behaviors from others will inhibit the occurrence of anxiety and contribute to its unlearning. Behavior is shaped by its consequences. Real-life consequences are most powerful in this regard.

SYSTEMATIC DESENSITIZATION DURING INTERVIEWS. This appears to be one of Wolpe's most frequently used techniques. He considers it comparable to the experimental procedure of extinguishing anxiety responses in cats by feeding them in the presence of increasing "doses" of anxiety-evoking events. The first step is to develop a list of circumstances to which the patient reacts with inappropriate anxiety. The list is arranged in descending order, so that the circumstance eliciting the strongest anxiety is at the top and the weakest at the bottom. Several lists may be developed from the patient's report based on different themes. Examples of lists he cites will clarify this point.

Fear of Hostility
1. Critical remarks by wife.
2. Critical remarks by friends.
3. Sarcasm from people in general.
4. Speaking before a group.
5. Large social gathering.
6. Nagging.
7. Boss giving instructions.
8. Conversations with co-workers.
9. Overly solicitous people.

The next step is to train the patient to relax his muscles. Wolpe seldom uses more than seven interviews for this. He focuses the patient's attention on a particular muscle group, for example, muscles in the left hand and forearm. The patient is instructed to tense those muscles and may be helped to do so; he may notice what it feels like, and then gradually relax them, still continuing to observe the sensations. Presumably, over several trials the patient gains some symbolic control over relaxing that muscle group. One by one, different muscle groups are trained in this way until the patient can relax most of his body. For patients who cannot learn to relax intentionally when so instructed, this therapeutic technique is ineffective.

The third step involves hypnotizing the patient and instructing him to relax as completely as possible. The patient is then told he will be asked to imagine some scenes which will appear vividly to him and to signal with a hand gesture if any of them disturb him. The therapist selects one of the lists previously constructed and asks the patient to imagine the bottom scene on the list, the weakest anxiety elicitor. After from three to five seconds, the patient is instructed to stop imagining the scene and to relax fully again. If the patient responds with considerable distress, a weaker scene must be manufactured and presented. Only a few scenes are presented in each interview, usually ranging from one to three, but each may be presented for several trials and in more than one interview. Once the therapist is relatively confident a scene is not eliciting anxiety, he moves up to the next strongest one on the hierarchy list. Gradually, through several sessions, anxiety responses to the entire list will be extinguished. It will then be found that these same real-life situations no longer elicit anxiety. It should be noted that the procedure assumes that the images elicit the same anxiety responses as the real situation. A similar result may be accomplished with patients who cannot be hypnotized by having them relax and simply asking them to imagine the scenes. Each interview is begun with a discussion of events that have taken place since the last interview, to determine if there has been any progress or relapse. New lists may have to be constructed as therapy progresses and additional fears are discovered.

RESPIRATORY RESPONSES WITH CARBON DIOXIDE THERAPY. Wolpe has found this technique useful with pervasive "free-floating" anxiety, "with results that are almost uniformly good and often dramatic" (1958, p. 157). Even there, he restricts its use to individuals who infrequently encounter specific events which elicit anxiety.

The patient lies down, completely exhausts the air from his lungs, and then takes one deep inhalation of a mixture of approximately 70 per cent carbon dioxide and 30 per cent oxygen. Wolpe reports the results are quite immediate, and in most of the patients on whom he has used the procedure, the course of treatment was from one to four inhalations spread over a period of time. He assumes that the intense stimulation of the respiratory system and the complete muscle relaxation produced by carbon dioxide are both antagonistic to anxiety.

COMPETITIVE MOTOR RESPONSES. This is a technique which Wolpe has used relatively little so far, but he finds its successful use in two cases encouraging. Briefly, he assumes the following rationale. If, in the presence of a situation or image which elicits neurotic anxiety, a mild shock is applied which produces a well-defined motor response, and if this process is repeated several times, the occurrence of the anxiety response will gradually decrease. He reports using the technique successfully to treat a girl whose hands trembled when eating in company and another who had an intense fear of falling.

ANXIETY-RELIEF RESPONSES. Wolpe has used this technique occasionally to alleviate symptoms, but he expects that much more use of it will be found in "fundamental psychotherapy." It is assumed that the responses following the termination of an uncomfortable electric shock are the opposite or the "negative" of anxiety and therefore will inhibit it. In his procedure, electrodes are attached to the patient's left forearm and the palm of his left hand. Through pretesting, an uncomfortable but not unbearable level of shock is selected. The shock is administered, and the patient endures it until his desire to have it stop becomes very strong. Then he says the word "calm" and the shock is immediately terminated. Shocks are administered at half- to one-minute intervals. Patients must be told they will be warned before each shock, or they may become very anxious between shocks. The procedure is repeated ten to twenty times a session. After two or three sessions, the patient usually begins reporting that the word "calm" can diminish day-to-day anxiety. The effect is very marked in about 15 per cent of the patients, and a few report no effect at all. Wolpe thinks it is most effective with patients in whom the shock elicits strong emotional responses as distinct from sensory discomfort.

TECHNIQUES FOR RESPONSES OTHER THAN ANXIETY. Sometimes, it seems desirable to extinguish responses other than anxiety. In such cases the principle of opposing an antagonistic response to the one to be extinguished is still followed, but the nature of the antagonistic response will differ. For example, certain obsessions are considered to be intense and excessive approach responses. To extinguish them, a very unpleasant electric shock is applied in the presence of the obsessional object or an image of that object. The procedure is repeated five to twenty times a session with sessions spaced a few days apart. Wolpe states the procedure was quite effective in one case, partially effective in two, and ineffective in one other. In the most successful case, a marked food obsession was extinguished using images of food associated with the shock. The effects generalized to avoidance tendencies toward some foods at mealtime, but the patient considered this "as trivial in comparison with her obsession."

Similarly, some hysterical symptoms occur in patients in whom there seems to be relatively little neurotic anxiety (1958, p. 184). For example, a long-standing automatic habit of mimicking any rhythmic movements by others was extinguished by using hypnotic suggestion to get the patient gradually to reduce the magnitude of the mimicking motor response. After three interviews held over a period of a few days, the patient reported the habit had ceased, and in that last interview the onset of the habit was recalled under hypnosis. Four years later the patient remained free of the habit. Similarly, a functional paresis of the right forearm, which interfered with an electrician's work, was extinguished by repeated visualization (imagistic), under hypnosis, of the events that precipitated the symptom. Wolpe rejects the argument that if hysterical symptoms are removed by conditioning procedures they will be replaced by other symptoms because the "repressed complexes" have not been effected. He cites several such cases in which the old symptoms did not reappear, nor did new ones arise.

SUBSIDIARY METHODS. Wolpe mentions several procedures which he believes have specific effects but which he does not consider to be examples of fundamental psychotherapy. Correction of wrong ideas is one. The impression given is that Wolpe simply tries to persuade the patient he has a wrong understanding. This is sometimes an essential precondition to other procedures. Stopping undesirable sequences of thoughts is another example. He proposes this might be accomplished by conditioning the word "stop" to the inhibition of the undesired thought sequence. Finally, he proposes that some drugs may be useful in inhibiting and extinguishing anxiety responses.

Clearly, his therapeutic techniques are varied, and are selected to effect the modification of specific responses or response sequences in identifiable situations. The precision of the approach has real appeal if the procedures are effective. This leads us to the question of the evaluation of his theory and techniques.

EVALUATION OF BEHAVIOR CHANGE

Wolpe does not discuss the manner in which he believes his theory can be validated. His frequent reference to animal experiments, including his own, suggests he would view this as one effective approach.

He simply acknowledges that the propositions of his theory require further validation.

However, he devotes an entire chapter to the issue of the evaluation of the effectiveness of his therapeutic techniques. He takes the firm position that symptomatic improvement, "lasting remission of undesirable reactions," is the only solid criterion of therapeutic effectiveness (1958, p. 204). He uses five general criteria to estimate the effectiveness of his treatment procedures. These are: (1) symptomatic improvement, (2) increased productiveness, (3) improved adjustment and pleasure in sex, (4) improved interpersonal relationships, and (5) ability to handle ordinary psychological conflicts and reasonable reality stresses. He notes that not all five criteria are relevant in every case. For example, in some patients there is no impairment of sexual behavior so naturally no improvement would be expected. The changes must be apparent in the situations that originally evoked the difficulties.

How are the changes assessed? Wolpe seems to rely on three kinds of data. First, the patient's report that changes have occurred is apparently accepted at face value. Occasionally he refers to the reports of others as verifying the patient's report. Second, his own clinical observation appears to be a source of data. Finally, changes in Willoughby scores from pre- to post-therapy tests are used as evidence. Based on his criteria and his evidence, he states that 90 per cent of 210 patients have been "apparently cured or much improved"; the average number of interviews per patient is only 31; patients frequently improve rapidly with him after prolonged and unsuccessful attempts with other therapies; and there is usually a direct relationship between amounts of treatment and amount of improvement (1958, p. 75). He recognizes that to be convincing, his results must be verified by others and hopes such verification will be forthcoming.

COMMENTS

Several emphases in Wolpe's approach are thought-provoking and worthy of further development and consideration. His emphasis on the analysis and treatment of behavior as it is presently occurring is valuable. The purpose of a study of the patient's developmental history is to obtain evidence on which to base selection of treatment procedures. However, treatment procedures can be selected simply on the basis of an understanding of how the behavior currently operates, completely ignoring its etiology. If this rationale is found to be correct, at least for a large proportion of patients, it gives clear specification of the events the therapist should focus on in his interviews.

Second, his attempt to detail particular troublesome response sequences and to devise treatment procedures specifically aimed at their modification is an approach with considerable appeal. Wolpe may be mistaken, but certainly the hypothesis seems well worth exploring. It is quite possible that everything is not related to everything else; individuals may not always function as an organized whole, as some theorists suggest. It may be that particular response sequences operate relatively independently of others and may, therefore, be modified without affecting others. Should this be verified, it would probably lead to a much more precise and efficient type of therapy.

Third, Wolpe's emphasis on the importance of clearly identifying and dealing with the situations, or responses, that elicit the troublesome behaviors is in sharp contrast to theorists who pay lip service to the importance of such antecedents but do not systematically work them into their therapeutic approach.

Finally, his willingness to reject traditional procedures and seek better ones seems to us a healthy attitude in the face of evidence on the limitations of exciting procedures. One can only hope that Wolpe and others who follow do not make the error of "throwing the baby out with the bath."

Of course, a number of serious criticisms can be directed at this position. Whole realms of theoretical problems are not dealt with. For example, he presents no theory of the development of normal behavior, even though assumptions about normal behavior are implicit in many of the therapist's decisions regarding treatment. His theory of disordered behavior is quite incomplete and seriously oversimplified. However, he has promised a more complete theoretical presentation of disordered behavior in a later volume. His statement of how humans learn seems grossly oversimplified and seriously inadequate. It does not seem to explain adequately the therapeutic effects he says he obtains. For example, he bases his position on drive reduction, a position rapidly being abandoned by learning theorists, even though he acknowledges the growing evidence that learning can equally well be based on response arousal. Some of his results, such as the learning of new responses antagonistic to anxiety in the same situations, might be accounted for more parsimoniously by a response-arousal principle. Moreover, his description of the acquisition of fear responses in relation to situational events follows the usual description of learning by contiguity rather than drive reduction. His theory has been helpful to him, however, in suggesting new techniques that might be considered.

One must be careful to consider his techniques separate from the theory. His theory may adequately represent the nature of certain types of disorder, or it may not. Even if it does not, his techniques would not necessarily be invalidated. One may develop effective techniques for the "wrong reasons." In any event, we think careful attention should be given to his techniques. We suspect there may be a good bit of value in them, but must confess to a considerable amount of skepticism as to their general applicability. Our experience with disordered human behavior leads us to believe he has not adequately considered or dealt with some crucial factors.

The most notable example is his inadequate analysis of symbolic responses. There seems to be much evidence that symbolic responses mediate both generalization of behavior and discrimination; that control of one's own behavior is powerfully aided by conscious symbolic responses; and that such responses are heavily involved in most kinds of disorder. Human behavior is far more efficient and effective than that of other living organisms because humans can substitute symbolic for overt responses. Finally, symbolic responses seem to function to give man a considerable degree of independence from the automatic influences of his physical and social environment. We would be surprised if any adequate therapeutic approach could avoid giving this crucial category of response a central place in its theory. Yet this is what Wolpe attempts to do. In fact, it seems to us that Wolpe's therapy techniques lean very heavily on conscious, symbolic responses although in a somewhat different way than other systems.

We hope this represents only Wolpe's first step toward the development of a much more complete and adequate theory. We think there is promise in his line of reasoning. He seems to be suggesting that the first step in recovery from neurotic disorder is not a changed way of thinking, but a changed way of acting. Such a hypothesis is certainly worth pursuing.

Chapter 9

Alfred Adler's Subjectivistic

System of Individual Psychology

Alfred Adler initiated a series of important developments in therapy theory. Since the Second World War, the importance of this man has been increasingly recognized. Not only was he the first to break openly from the Freudian system, but also he was the first to emphasize several other factors. These included the role of interpersonal experience in the development of the human being—the situational determinants of human behavior—and the building and maintenance of the self-image. Moreover, his was the first extensive statement of the subjectivistic, phenomenological position which has been so popular in more recent therapy theory.

The reasons for presenting Adler's system in some detail go well beyond mere historical interest or description. His concepts are sprinkled throughout the writings of others; his propositions as to how behavior operates are on the lips of many present-day practitioners.

It seems apparent that whole pieces of Adlerian psychology are implicit throughout modern-day clinical practice, although often not identified as such. Expressions such as feelings of inferiority and insecurity, sibling rivalry, the only child, compensatory behavior, the unity of the person, and empathic understanding are all part and parcel of the everyday language of the layman and professionals alike.

Most commentaries on Alfred Adler and his influence have concluded that his ideas have been widely accepted, whereas his system, *qua system*, has had a relatively restricted impact. This has probably resulted from Adler's style of writing. He wrote extensively and voluminously, but unsystematically. His ideas are scattered hither and yon throughout his writings. Thus, it is not surprising that other systems presenting similar ideas in a clearer and more orderly fashion have displaced Adler's.

Munroe (1955) believes that Adler has had a greater impact on the lay public than on a professional audience. Adler lectured extensively to the general public, constantly encouraged the application of his ideas in schools, clinics, and juvenile courts, and made a great point of phrasing his viewpoint in the language of the ordinary person. Thus, his ideas have held the strong appeal of "common sense," fitting nicely with those of the man in the street. Concepts like inferiority complex or sibling rivalry had immediate appeal and were readily comprehended and utilized on a day-to-day basis by laymen. Adler's distinctive optimism, his "positive" approach to behavior, was another appealing factor. Many people objected to what they viewed as the pessimistic and derogatory view of man propounded by Freud, and responded warmly to Adler's view of man as highly plastic and malleable, capable of extraordinary accomplishments, and potentially capable of arranging optimum conditions for living, creating, and building for the betterment of mankind.

There is some evidence of a renascence of interest in Adler's system. Not the least of the factors contributing to this "rediscovery" of Adler may have been an important volume prepared by the Ansbachers, *The Individual Psychology of Alfred Adler* (1956). Here two writers, each of whom studied under Adler, have done what Adler himself had been unable to do. They have successfully abstracted and systematically arranged Adler's most lucid statements on critical issues. The book is composed of direct quotations from Adler, interspersed with comments. It represents the Adlerian system at its best and, thus, has been the primary source for the present analysis. The Ansbachers' systematization has made it possible for others to examine the system, to polish, correct, or change it and, thus, has made it viable.

BIOGRAPHICAL NOTES

Alfred Adler was born in a suburb of Vienna in the year 1870, the second of six children. His father was a grain merchant, whose vocation permitted the family to enjoy a comfortable income. Adler subsequently wrote of his only moderately happy time within the family group, of his somewhat discordant relationships with his mother and his older brother, and of his recollections of his vigorous and quite athletic pursuits as a young boy, away from the family home.

A serious childhood illness produced an ambition to become a physician, and he went on to earn his medical degree from the University of Vienna in 1895. First he established himself as a specialist in ophthalmology, then turned to the practice of general medicine, and finally to psychiatry. In 1897 he married a young Russian woman, who bore him four children.

Adler first attracted Freud's attention when he wrote a spirited defense of Freud's monograph on dreams, which had been roundly criticized in a newspaper. Impressed with Adler's countercritique, Freud invited him to join his psychoanalytic circle, and in 1902 there began a close personal association between the two men, although Freud was Adler's senior by fourteen years.

Adler quickly became a leader of the Vienna Psychoanalytical Society, perhaps because of the high esteem with which he was regarded by Freud himself. Freud turned over many of his patients to Adler and was pleased to have Adler as his personal physician. It was during this time that Adler published a series of articles which were regarded as important contributions to Freudian drive psychology. Finally, he was named Freud's successor as President of the Society and coeditor, along with Wilhelm Stekel, of the Society's journal.

However, major theoretical differences gradually developed between Adler and Freud. There has been much commentary on the distress which these differences occasioned in the protagonists, each unhappy that they were occurring, but unable to do otherwise than to pursue his individual persuasions. Finally, the Society decided to hear a comprehensive presentation of Adler's views, so that the members could discuss them at length. Adler completed his third presentation on February 1, 1911. During this series, it became obvious to Freud and

Adler that their views were diametrically opposite, and Adler decided to resign his association with the Society. Stekel resigned along with him, as did nine other members.

Some, including Stekel, minimized the theoretical differences and characterized the break as primarily one of terminology aggravated by personal antagonisms. Others recognized, as did Adler and Freud themselves, that the differences were basic and, as the Ansbachers point out, "about as fundamental and far-reaching as is possible within a given area" (Ansbacher, 1956, p. 4).

Within the year, Adler developed the name of *Individual Psychology* for his point of view and founded the society and journal bearing this name. There followed a very active and productive period of years during which Adler lectured and wrote extensively and encouraged the development of chapters of Individual Psychology societies throughout Central Europe, taking time out during the First World War to serve as a physician in the Austrian Army. After the war he became interested in work with children and established the first of 30 child-guidance clinics in the Viennese school system. According to the Ansbachers, Individual Psychology appears to have reached its height just before the advent of Hitler, with 34 separate societies becoming established.

From 1925 onward, Adler made several trips to the United States, eventually settling in New York in 1935 as Professor of Medical Psychology at the Long Island College of Medicine. He continued his pattern of clinical and private practice, teaching, lecturing, and writing. He died in 1937 at the age of 67, while on a lecture tour in Scotland.

Adler impressed most of his contemporaries and biographers as an extremely energetic man who seemed indefatigable in his productivity and his interest in the behavior of his fellow man. His concern for the ordinary person seems to have been very pronounced. Beginning with his student years, he persistently worried about and worked for the betterment of social ills, as exemplified by his choosing a lower-middle-class neighborhood for his first medical practice. Of course, the preoccupation is most readily seen in his lectures and writings. Always something of a crusader, he set out to improve the health of tailors whose deplorable condition excited his sympathy; he aligned himself with the Social-Democratic movement, an Austrian reform group; he spoke out strongly for school reforms, for changes in child-rearing practices, for the annihilation of archaic stereotypes and false conceptions of man which persistently led to interpersonal strife and human misery. He did all this so forcefully that his writings might strike the present-day reader as biting, bombastic, and offensive. However, Munroe (1955) notes that Adler was writing at a specific point in history, and what were false generalizations to be attacked at that time, seem nowadays to be unnecessary belaboring of the obvious.

Despite his serious intent and his unyielding persistence in correcting social ills, Adler is represented as a fun-loving, affable, and congenial person, someone who thoroughly enjoyed good food, music, and the companionship of other people. He abhorred pomposity and explicitly eschewed technical jargon. It was partly his concern for the ordinary person which led him to speak so often to such varied lay audiences, and to represent his notions in the concepts and language of the everyday world. In the opinion of most reviewers, this turned out to be both a distinct advantage and a significant liability.

MAJOR EMPHASES

It has become a matter of form for Adler to be credited with introducing the notions of organ inferiority, compensation, the striving for superiority, and feelings of inferiority. Similarly, his disputes with Freud about the nature of the Oedipal conflict and the role of sex have been thoroughly recognized and described. However, the Ansbachers have emphasized several characteristics of Adler's system dealing with theory construction which are often overlooked.

In contrast to Sigmund Freud, Adler developed a point of view that sought to study behavior from the vantage point of the subjective rather than the objective observer; emphasized the goal-directed rather than the drive-impelled causation of behavior; stressed the unity and integration of behavior rather than the conflict of disparate elements; proposed the use of molar and holistic concepts rather than restricted units of analysis; held an idiographic rather than a nomothetic purpose in studying behavior; and in short, differed from Freud in the most fundamental and basic fashions possible. We shall consider most of these characteristics in the following paragraphs.

A Subjectivistic Psychology

Adler became convinced that the explanation of behavior could arise only from the analysis of the individual's own "inner nature." Rather than seeking for the antecedents of behavior in objective events outside the skin of the individual, Adler proposed that all behavior was immediately determined by events occurring "within the skin" (subjectively observable responses). Moreover, he proposed that the crucial internal determinants were values, attitudes, interests, and ideas. Thus, different kinds of thoughts, which are the individual's approximations of and interpretations of reality, are the primary determinants of the ways in which people behave.

Adler was much influenced by Vaihinger's philosophy of the "As If," and employed it as a philosophical underpinning of his theoretical position. Events as viewed by objective observers (objective factors) do not directly determine the ways an individual will respond. Rather, it is the perception of, thoughts about, and interpretations of these events by the individual that are the critical antecedents ("internal causation"). Adler called these perceptions and thoughts *fictions* to emphasize that they were not completely accurate representations of events. It is what the individual thinks is there and how he interprets or evaluates it (his fictions), rather than the "real" events, that directs his behavior (Ansbacher, 1956, p. 45).[1] Since thoughts and perceptions are the primary determinants, they must be identified and analyzed if behavior is to be understood and modified.

Adler, of course, did not omit attention to objective factors completely. He took them into account when he discussed such things as inborn potentialities, organ inferiorities, the child-rearing practices in the home, and the like. However, in his view they became decidedly "de-emphasized." An objective event, such as a broken leg, poverty in the home, or excessive and punitive discipline in a classroom, determined only indirectly how an individual would respond. In Adler's view such events provided probabilities only, making some attitudes more likely, others less so, favoring the development of some ideas in the child, making other notions improbable. That is what the Ansbachers refer to as "soft determinism"—situational events are necessary antecedents, but their "causal significance" is minimized (1956, p. 178).

It will be recognized that Adler's viewpoint can be considered to be primarily a *cognitive* theory, built on the general proposition that behavior can be understood and its events can become predictable if one determines how the individual "comes to know" and represent the world about him. Typical of such theories, the direct study of other

[1] Throughout the chapter, direct quotes from Adler's writings are employed. The reader will often be referred to the Ansbachers' volume, however, as a more readily available source.

response events, such as the affective, physiologic, and motoric behaviors, is correspondingly de-emphasized.

Behavior as Goal-Directed

Following the lead of Vaihinger, Adler concluded that behavior was guided and directed by thoughts that were symbolic representations of actual events, but which were not isomorphic with them; they were "fictional" rather than "real." Adler became convinced that truth was relative to the observer, that there were as many beliefs as there were believers. Such beliefs might be more or less accurate, and the degree of "error" was related to neurosis (1931, p. 4; 1929b, p. 62). All ideas, all constructions about events, then, were abstractions from the events and were subject to error. Truth, after Vaihinger, became the most expedient error. All persons developed ideas because this helped them to cope with events better than otherwise. The individual builds conceptions and develops objectives; these he creates in order to find his way in a chaos of life.

Thus, Adler combined the notion of "fiction" with that of goal and developed the notion of the *fictional goal, fictional finalism,* or the *guiding fiction.* People develop habitual thoughts (fictions) about consequences to be sought (goals) and orient their thoughts, feelings, and behavior toward achieving such goals. Behavior is determined by one's ideas about consequences to be obtained in the future. Correspondingly, if the analyst knows the person's goals, he can predict the behavior that will follow.

The future, in Adler's view, was not the objective future, but a present estimate—current thoughts about the future. He did not fall into the logical trap of thinking of a future event working backward upon a present occurrence. Thus, the analysis and prediction of human behavior includes the analysis of the goals toward which that behavior is directed. The cause of both the "healthy and the diseased mental life" lies in the question "not where but whither?" (Ansbacher, 1956, p. 90–91).

The Unity of Behavior

Adler was one of the first systematists to propose that a primary characteristic of human behavior was its integration and unity. He apparently became markedly impressed with the efforts at "self-consistency" in human affairs and concluded that apparently disparate and superficially incongruous responses really could be identified as interrelated and mutually consistent.

Behavior Is Lawfully Organized

It was Adler's notion that the particular guiding thoughts (fictional goals) that an individual develops become organized around a single, unifying, guiding thought aimed at a general consequence, and this ultimate objective provides the primary unifying character to all specific responses (Ansbacher, 1956, p. 358). It must be emphasized that when Adler said all, he meant *all* in a very literal sense. Perceptions, thoughts, dreams, actions, neurotic symptoms—all responses (surface phenomena) "are connected with the essential inner core," which he subsequently came to call the *life style* of the person (Ansbacher, 1956, p. 395). All behavior becomes determined by the general objective, and a general habitual pattern of behavior—life style—to achieve the objective is acquired.

It follows, then, that the general objective would be discernible in each set of responses. For Adler, at whatever point the individual was to be studied, in whatever situation he was to be observed, whichever set of responses were to become subject to analysis, all would be indicative of a single general consequence toward which his thoughts directed his behavior. Recognition of the consequences sought enabled an observer to understand the "hidden meaning" underlying the various separate acts and to recognize them as parts of a unified whole.

Social Embeddedness

Adler emphasized the fact that human behavior developed in a social context from the very beginnings of life. Born into a family, the child inevitably develops a set of interlocking relations with the mother and its other members. The situation, composed of other people, sets important conditions upon the kinds of behavior that could ultimately develop (Ansbacher, 1956, p. 128). No human could live effectively as an isolate, since Adler viewed present-day society as being so constructed that one man's behavior was inextricably intertwined in the behavior of others. There were inherent "rules of game" which each person had to learn and in terms of which he would have to play.

This view leads to the conclusion that human behavior cannot be studied effectively outside its social context (Ansbacher, 1956, p. 126). It was thus that Adler referred to Individual Psychology as a social psychology. The emphasis was upon man's social behaviors. His responses in relation to interpersonal situations were considered the most important. This emphasis will be readily apparent in Adler's concepts of social interest, co-operation, common sense, and the like.

THEORY CONSTRUCTION

Method of Observation

The primary data for the analysis of behavior from the "subjective standpoint" became the subjective report of the individual under review. Thus, Adler's method for studying behavior was primarily one of asking the individual to talk about his perceptions, thoughts, goals, and other subjectively observable responses. His approach would be labeled "phenomenological" in contemporary language. Adler was looking for the ways the individual perceived events, how he thought about and evaluated them, which consequences he sought, and how he evaluated himself in relation to others. The primary method for studying behavior, whether or not one wanted to treat it, was to view it from the vantage point of the subjective observer, not from the frame of reference of the behavior analyst. Thus, the analyst of behavior had to approximate the position of the subjective observer. He did this via *empathic understanding;* he had to try to see events as the individual saw them; he had to think, feel, and "act" as if he were the other person. "We must be able to see with his eyes and listen with his ears (Adler, 1931, p. 72). The title "Individual Psychology" aptly labels the study of behavior from the standpoint of the behaving individual.

Characteristics of Concepts and Propositions

Adler seemed to have had a keen sense of the continuing flow of behavioral events, holding firm to a view which has often earned the label "dynamic." Intentionally, he chose terms that would represent behavior as a continuous process—movement, tendency toward, and guidelines to be followed. As early as 1912 he objected to class concepts. He associated them with primitive and neurotic thought patterns and argued that such thinking was employed to produce a spurious sense of surety in the thinker.

Frequently, the same variety of behavior received multiple labels in Adler's efforts to avoid the "fixing" of ideas and labels to the flow of behavior. Particular responses are not important; it is the patterned sequences and direction of behavior over time that is crucial. He considered his *Law of Movement* one of his "strongest steps" (Ansbacher, 1956, p. 195).

His emphasis on the flow of behavior led to the use of molar units. The response concepts (classes) which Adler employed are large and inclusive; social interest, courage, and creative self are typical. There is probably no concept in therapy theory that is more encompassing than Adler's *style of life*—the entire personal repertoire of the individual stretched over the course of years. In this sense, Adler has been described as an "holistic" theorist.

Adler's subjectivistic position predisposed him to a particular sort of propositional statement. The objective of his approach was to analyze and understand behavior by an analysis of behavior preceding it, or as the Ansbachers put it: "understanding how a psychological process follows from a preceding psychological process" (Ansbacher, 1956, p. 13). For Adler, propositions about behavior should be cast in the form of response-response relationships, and the response elements in such propositions should be subjectively observable events. Stated in another way, Adler was proposing a theory composed of *"r-r* laws."

Finally, it was Adler's view that both *nomothetic* and *idiographic* propositions were essential, the first representing statements of general validity about behavior, the second representing principles governing the behavior of an individual case. For the first, he developed generalizations about feelings of inferiority, compensation, superiority strivings, and the like, which were held to be true for persons in general. Such generalizations, however, were to Adler only the initial approach to the study of behavior. Such nomothetic principles represented only statements of statistical probability and, thus, were of "only limited value": generalization may well be untrue for any specific case (Ansbacher, 1956, pp. 194–195). Adler's view of the uniqueness of each individual's response repertoire led him to doubt the single utility of general propositions. To Adler, no two persons ever "apprehended, worked over, digested, or responded" to the same environmental influences in precisely the same way.

It was Adler's belief, therefore, that general laws and propositions could never permit the understanding of the individual case. Only with a representation of the laws specific to the behavior of the particular subject himself could understanding and prediction of individual behavior become possible. To Adler, the capacity to predict became the acid test of understanding; it was the single, sole criterion. But Adler's idiographic purpose did not lead to propositions as such, in the sense of formally stated laws about how a particular person operated. Rather, it seemed to result more typically in some kind of composite "picture," or as he put it, a "Portrait" (Ansbacher, 1956, p. 179).

THE NORMAL COURSE OF BEHAVIOR DEVELOPMENT

As was emphasized earlier, events as such were a good deal less important to Adler than the person's "opinion" of those events. Occurrences in the environment (situational events) had less to do with how a person behaved than the thoughts such events elicited. Similarly, a person's constitutional make-up was decidedly less important to Adler than the attitude the person developed toward his physiological condition. Thus, Adler emphasized neither heredity nor environment. He held a subjectivistic position throughout.

As a consequence, Adler's explicit statements about heredity and physiological characteristics were limited. It was the person's thoughts or ideas about himself and his body which were important—his attitude toward, his response to, and his way of dealing with his physiological structure.

INNATE CHARACTERISTICS OF NORMAL DEVELOPMENT

Adler did sometimes refer to what he felt to be innately determined in the human organism. He recognized that *physical attributes,* such as size, weight, appearance, and the structure and function of the human body, were all primarily matters of genetic inheritance. He also discussed a series of *response potentialities* which he felt would inevitably make their appearance. Finally, Adler developed a *primary sequence of responses* which he proposed to be basic and universal and on which all subsequent human behavior depended. This is the *inferiority feeling → compensatory striving for superiority* sequence for which he is so well known.

Actually, in the case of the latter two, Adler was never clear on whether he regarded the responses to be primarily innate or inherent. He spoke of them in both terms. He described them as inherent when he labeled the human as inherently inferior in the face of nature; social interest (social responses) was inevitable because the child was operating in a social context. He labeled them innate when he called the inferiority feeling "a feeling given and made possible by nature, comparable to a painful tension that seeks relief." However, it seems difficult to conceive of how a child could feel inferior to reality or could emit a response to a social situation unless these responses were already in his repertoire. For this reason, the writers have elected to follow Adler's depiction of them as innate, rather than inherent.

Physical Attributes

Adler regarded it as obvious that persons begin life with a physical structure that functions in a definite fashion. He also noted that there were evident individual differences in an individual's physiological equipment. However, he considered such differences of minor importance since, except for mental defectives, "everyone can do everything that is necessary," and it is what "the individual does with the equipment he inherits" that counts (Ansbacher, 1956, p. 206).

Adler did emphasize innate physical attributes in the case of constitutional organic handicaps. He proposed that in some people, a specific defect in organic structure, in function, or in both could contribute significantly to their subsequent development. Under the general category of *organ inferiority* Adler bunched all the specific defects in physical structure with which a person might begin life. Thus, a congenital heart defect, or defects in visual refraction, were objective impairments. Similarly, small stature, puny musculature, distortions in physiognomy, or a predisposition to illness were all conditions that were to be attributed primarily to hereditary, or congenital, factors. Nevertheless, it is not the inheritance of such difficulties that is important, but how an individual reacts to them (Ansbacher, 1956, pp. 206–207).

Response Potentialities

Adler assumed that humans possessed "potentialities" that would inevitably make their appearance. Although he did not present them systematically, several that Adler seems to imply have been abstracted and are summarized in the following paragraphs.

Actually, Adler spoke of the response "potentialities" at two different levels of analysis at least: that is, he categorized behaviors into fairly general and "molar" units on the one hand—creative power and the capacities for social interest, courage, common sense, and reason—and limited units on the other—perception, learning, memory, attention, fantasy, feelings and emotions, and actions and movements. Although he did not say as much, it is clear from the manner in which he wrote that Adler considered the following types of responses to be inborn human characteristics.

ATTENDING RESPONSES. Adler's mention of this response class occurred in connection with his discussion of forgetfulness, which he regarded as brought about by a narrowing of attention. He seemed to conclude implicitly that it was an inborn response, that it was much influenced by learning, and that people varied with respect to the range and variety of events to which they learn to attend.

PERCEIVING RESPONSES. Adler was never very careful to specify what he meant by perception, but he did emphasize that these responses occurred early in the infant's behavior; that a perception was an active and interpretive type of response, rather than passive and sensory; and that perception came to be selective and, thus, personally determined. To Adler, a person saw everything from a perspective which was "his own creation."

CONCEPTUAL RESPONSES. Adler mentioned these responses only in passing. He specifically referred to "the abstracting form of apprehension of the human mind" (Ansbacher, 1956, pp. 98–99), suggesting that the capacity to form concepts, and thus to think abstractly, was an innate characteristic.

Adler did not distinguish clearly between what he would regard as perception and what would be considered to be conception (or thought). He seemed to use such terms as regard, appraise, judge, and evaluate as terms synonymous with perceptual interpretation on the one hand, but to use the same terms, for example valuing and self-evaluation, as synonymous with opinions, attitudes, and thoughts—all of which would appear to be more centrally occurring events and more conceptual in nature. Adler also emphasized "understanding" or comprehension. By this, he apparently meant recognition of the relationship between two or more sets of events or things, and he seems to have allowed for verbal and nonverbal forms of understanding. Again, it is unclear whether he would regard such recognitions as primarily perceptual or conceptual. One is inclined to believe that Adler would have dismissed such distinctions as unimportant.

RECOLLECTIVE RESPONSES. Adler discussed the phenomenon of remembering only briefly, considering it one of the sequels to learning (his position on learning will be discussed later). Adler viewed remembering, like perceiving, as a response possibility residing within each human, but again markedly affected by learning and selective in its operation, and he saw the person as recalling only those impressions that would fit the person's objectives.

VERBAL-SYMBOLIC RESPONSES. Adler viewed the capacity for language as the single most significant class of responses in the human repertoire. He stressed the importance of language in interpersonal communication and consensual validation, but he also seemed to have concluded that it was a necessary antecedent to logical thought.

FEELINGS AND EMOTIONS. Adler made no great effort to define these responses any more than any others. It is apparent, however, that he felt them to be innate response potentials, and he further subclassified them into two major types: *disjunctive* and *conjunctive*. Disjunctive emotions included such response patterns as anger, sorrow, and fear; the conjunctive group included such ones as joy, fondness, and affection. There was one set of feelings, of course, to which Adler devoted a great deal of attention: *feelings of inferiority*. His notions concerning this particular set of feelings will be dealt with in detail later.

One can see that Adler's approach resulted in very brief and cursory treatment of these response events with many omissions and overlaps. An example of an omission would be the motoric responses, which he mentioned repeatedly but did not characterize as innate response possibilities. Adler's aversion to precise classification and definition and his preference for discussing behavior at a much more inclusive level such as creative power and social interest may account for such omissions.

CREATIVE POWER. The human person, including the infant and child, is not a passive recipient of stimuli impinging upon him from the outside; nor is he the victim of a series of events (drives, impulses) which impel him from within. To Adler, the human had the innate capabilities to fabricate and fashion his own perceptions, actions, thoughts, and opinions, and to build these into a coherent representation of himself and the world around him. He attributed to the child a "force" or "creative power" (Ansbacher, 1956, p. 177).

SOCIAL INTEREST. A further set of responses, which Adler called social interest, he considered critical for the satisfactory adjustment of the normal person, and he believed that their relative absence was a primary characteristic of the disordered person. Moreover, therapeutic treatment, in Adler's opinion, had to be pointed directly at these responses. He never succeeded in defining them clearly. It may be possible, however, to determine what it was that he was attempting to denote by listing what he regarded as the attributes of social interest. First, he considered social interest to be innate, in the sense that it was a response complex of which all humans were capable and which was elicited in a social context. The response will first appear in the child's first social interaction, that is, with his mother.

Second, the response is one that begins in rudimentary form in the infant and grows with successive accretions as the person matures, until in the adult it is a very intricate and complex "evaluative attitude toward life." It is evidenced in the small infant who directs affectionate responses toward others as early as the first year of life; it is manifested in the sharing of toys, the small acts of helping which the child performs for his parents. Humans are potentially co-operative and friendly, and self-centeredness is an artifact which is forced upon the child in the course of his development; it is learned.

Third, Adler emphasized that social interest was a subjectively observable response (r). When Adler discussed these responses at the adult level, he referred to them as a complex attitude which included perceptions, thoughts, and feelings toward other people of a positive social nature. The overt instrumental responses of helping another person, saying kind things, and co-operating in tasks were considered to follow such an attitude or intervening "social interest" response.

It seems very doubtful that Adler meant to attribute all such responses to the infant and thereby regard them as innate. However, if the primary attributes are taken together—such as an innate response of a positive social nature elicited in interaction with the mother and falling within the subjective response realm—the affective pattern of love (affection) would seem to meet the criteria. Thus, we infer that by innate social interest Adler must have meant the innate response of *love*. Also, by adult social interest he meant something akin to what others have referred to as love-of-fellow-man, or brotherly love. On a few occasions, Adler appeared to say precisely this—that "the child's organically determined impulses of affection blossom forth"—suggesting this was the basis of friendly, co-operative human relationships (Ansbacher, 1956, p. 138).

It is difficult to determine whether this was all that Adler attributed to the infant, or whether he meant to imply perceptual and symbolic responses going along with the love responses. He often wrote about complex adult behavior, asserting that it began in infancy, but omitting to say how much of the adult pattern actually began in those early periods or by what process the pattern became complicated.

The Basic Response Sequence

We come now to what Adler believed to be the most significant of all innate human characteristics. It begins with a primary response event which Adler believed occurred in the very first part of life and continued thereafter.

THE "NORMAL" INFERIORITY FEELINGS. Adler assumed that "every psychological life begins" with a "deep inferiority feeling." Being human means "to feel inferior" (Ansbacher, 1956, p. 115). Not only is man inherently inferior in the face of natural forces, and it is inevitable that he will recognize it, but this feeling is especially keen in the small child who is even more inadequate in the face of problems than his adult counterpart. Feelings of inferiority are considered inevitable from the beginning, they are universal and occur in every person, and thus must be adjudged to be "normal." Such feelings are considered constant and continuous, characterizing the person until the day he dies (Ansbacher, 1956, pp. 115–116).

Adler realized that many people would deny such a feeling, or at least protest that they were unable to recall its occurrence. Further, he commented upon the likelihood that it would be denied because of its social undesirability. Actually it would appear that a judgmental or interpretive response should precede such inferiority feelings, and at one point Adler stated that "a *self-evaluation*" developed which produced "feelings of inferiority" (Ansbacher, 1956, p. 98). Adler appeared to feel that such perceptions or judgments were well within the response capabilities of the very small infant. He went on to conclude that these inferiority feelings were innately displeasurable, a "positive pain . . . comparable to a painful tension that seeks relief."

It seems, therefore, that by the term "feelings of inferiority" Adler meant to refer to a recurrent pattern sequence which was implied to be innate and constantly operative. It consisted of a combination of thought and affect, occurring either simultaneously or in sequential order: a self-evaluation of inferiority (a perception or a thought) and some variety of negative affective response (a pain, tension, or discomfort). The judgments of inferiority are made *vis à vis* situational events, which are its antecedents. Its consequent was something that Adler felt to be the driving force of behavior.

Striving for Superiority

Adler was much impressed by the apparently ceaseless way in which all living things behave to overcome a "minus state" and to arrive at a "plus state." He concluded this was a primary attribute of life itself and termed it a "striving for superiority" or a "striving to overcome." It was assumed to follow thoughts of inferiority and their concomitant negative affect. He considered it "the fundamental fact of our life" (Ansbacher, 1956, p. 103). Early in his writings (circa 1907), Adler employed the notion of *compensation* which he defined as an automatic attempt by an organism to re-establish an equilibrated state. It was a postulate analogous to the principle of homeostasis proposed by Cannon in 1932. It gradually became elided, however, and "striving for superiority" was assumed to be a direct consequent of "feelings of inferiority."

It should be emphasized that Adler considered this a superordinate concept under which all apparently motivated response sequences, such as the searching for food or the seeking of pleasure, could be grouped. It included all efforts to overcome external obstacles, to solve problems, to complete tasks, to achieve stature and prestige, to build and construct—in short, all efforts of mankind were classified under this one molar concept. Even mistakes and errors were viewed as misguided efforts at accomplishment. Again Adler's preference for all-inclusive concepts is apparent. Adler apparently meant to refer not only to all human instrumental responses (thoughts, feelings, perceptions, and overt motoric responses), but also to characterize the "goal" of such instrumental responses as being the reduction or terminating of the negative thought and affective responses (feelings of inferiority) to which they were related. In this respect, Adler was close to later drive-reduction theories of behavior. Adler assumed the negative thoughts and affect responses were never completely terminated or reduced; rather they continued throughout a person's life, rising and falling as the individual went about his "strivings to overcome."

Adler regarded this basic response sequence (self-evaluation of inferiority → feelings of inferiority → striving for superiority) as extremely valuable to mankind. Many deplore feelings of inferiority, but Adler viewed them as not only inevitable but also a necessity if man were to survive and develop. Vulnerable to cold, man developed clothing and shelter; discomfited by sickness and the peril of death, man invested extraordinary effort in developing the science of medicine and thereby safeguarding himself. Thus, it is upon a foundation of avoiding negative thoughts and feelings (inferiority) and expressing positive affection (social interest) that man's progress is built.

LEARNED CHARACTERISTICS OF NORMAL DEVELOPMENT

We come now to what Adler regarded as the most critical aspects of development, on the one hand the context in which the child learned and on the other the course which learning itself might take. As one would expect from his general position, Adler's attention is always upon the latter, the development from the standpoint of the maturing individual. Relatively less emphasis was placed on the situational determinants as they might be objectively described, since the manner in which these were viewed by the person was the significant factor.

Situational Events

Adler's treatment of situational events was conspicuously brief in comparison to the time he devoted to aspects of behavior. Most of his remarks in this realm were confined to features of the *social* situation which surrounded the child, and a corresponding neglect of the "physical," apparently sharing with other therapy theorists the basic assumption that the behavior of other people represents the primary events in the situational milieu. The reader will recall that Adler emphasized that every person was socially embedded in such a way that inevitably he developed a network of social relations with a large number of persons.

Beyond this general position, Adler went on to categorize situational events into several major groups as far as their effects upon a person's behavior were concerned: the family, the school, and events in later life. In the first of these, he had some things to say about parent-child relationships and relationships with siblings.

FAMILY: PARENTAL BEHAVIOR. Adler was one of the first to emphasize the important influence that the responses of others held for the growing child. It was clear to him that there were obvious relationships between the way in which parents behaved toward the child and the child's subsequent behavior. Although he wrote in generalities, he was able to specify some of the parental behaviors that he felt to be advantageous and several he proposed to have a deleterious effect. Specifically to be avoided were response patterns of overindulgence and overprotectiveness on the one hand, and hatred and acts of rejection on the other. Adler proposed that these tended to lead directly toward the pampered and the hated child, and Adler saw them as the behavioral antecedents to antisocial and disordered behavior.

Rather, the ideal parent responded with love, support, and encouragement when he wanted to elicit certain kinds of responses in the child instead of punishment and bribery. "Discipline" and punishment were possible to use, but Adler stressed the necessity for applying them judiciously—not to force the child to submit to authority, but rather to help shape the desired responses.

The remainder of Adler's admonitions about parental behavior had to do with the responses in the child that the parents should be prepared to identify and to recognize as socially desirable, and to which they should apply their support and encouragement—social interest and a concern for others, initiative and self-confidence in the face of tasks, "striving to overcome" when it developed along constructive and co-operative lines. Adler particularly stressed the importance of the mother, who represented the primary source of training in the family situation.

FAMILY: BIRTH ORDER. Adler seems to have been the first theorist to call attention to the other children in the family and their effects upon the child's development. It was Adler's proposal that the child's *position* in the family had considerable to do with the problems with which he had to cope and the kinds of behavior which were likely to ensue. These patterns were not judged to be inevitable, since each child could build his own view of the situation in which he found himself—he only said that the serial position in the family structure presented certain probabilities, making some behavior patterns more likely than others.

The oldest child. Initially the only child and displaced from this position by the appearance of younger siblings, the oldest child is placed in the status of the "dethroned king," as Munroe (1955) puts it. Having once been displaced from below, he is likely to fear recurrences of this; because of his age, greater demands are made from him; because of his strength and skill, he is the natural leader of the children in the family. Adler thought that such a position made it more likely that the child would become quite concerned over the attitudes of authority toward him, tend to emulate this authority, and would be defensively oriented against encroachments from younger competitors. Such an orientation could become generalized and represent all his interpersonal behavior patterns, that is, become his style of life.

The second child. With an older, stronger, and more knowledgeable sibling in front of him, and subject to competition from below as well, the second child has to cope with a different constellation of problems. Adler believed the second child was more likely to develop a deep conviction that he was not as able as others, as well as a more competitive attitude toward his peers. Moreover, Adler believed that early training was often less stringent for the second child than for the first, so that this child became a good deal less concerned with obedience to authority. Adler saw this constellation of factors as tending to produce either a nonconforming, perhaps rebellious orientation, or a defeatist and cynical one if the child proved inadequate to the family situation.

The youngest child. Often treated as the "baby" of the family, perhaps petted and indulged, never subjected to baby competition by the arrival of still another sibling, the youngest child is prone to develop along egocentric lines, but also to develop a deep-seated feeling of incompetence. In short, he may develop a self-appraisal which directly reflects the evaluation by those around him: a lovable baby, but still a baby.

The only child. The youngster reared alone does not have available to him the opportunities for give and take between siblings by which a child's social behavior becomes importantly shaped. Neither does he have the behavior of other siblings on which to pattern his own. Thus, he is handicapped by the characteristics of the situation in which he develops, and this will have its effects upon his interpersonal response skills. Moreover, he is likely to be spoiled and pampered and come to expect indulgence from others. Finally, if he is an only child by virtue of his parents' dislike of children, he runs the special hazard of becoming the unwanted or the hated child.

Our further discussion of situational events as represented by Adler will be brief, since he gave this question little attention.

SCHOOL SITUATION. Adler's interest in children and preventive psychiatry was manifest in his concern with school influences. Apparently, Adler saw the important effect that teachers' behavior had upon the development of their students. In a way analogous to his treatment of the family situation, Adler was interested primarily in the interpersonal transactions in the school setting, the teacher-student relationships. It is clear that he was attempting to affect pedagogical approaches to children, and his writings in this realm were devoted primarily to admonitions to teachers to behave less punitively and with more frequent instances of acceptance and encouragement, to reward individuality and creative nonconformity rather than insisting upon similarity between one student and another, to arrange for co-operative behavior rather than competitive responses between students. Most of his remarks in this vein were rather of a common-sense nature and will not be further elaborated.

LATER PROBLEMS OF LIFE. With this inclusive label, Adler called attention to the adjustments the person continued to face after and beyond his exposure to the family and school situations. To Adler, the three major tasks the adult person was destined to encounter were situations posed by society at large. Each person comes face to face with the communal life and the necessity for achieving a social adjustment, with work and the necessity for earning a livelihood, and finally with marriage and the corresponding love relationships it typically entails. Of course, Adler also discussed these problems in terms of the responses that each successful person had to develop in order to achieve the necessary social, work, and marital adjustments. Here we are noting Adler's contention that society posed such tasks for each of its members, and from this aspect they represented situational demands which each could expect to encounter.

Development of the Response Potentialities

Since it was Adler's contention that most of the significant features of a person's development occurred in the first four to five years of life, it is upon the very early stages that one's attention must be focused. We shall attempt to represent the chronology of events which Adler proposed to hold true. As we proceed, his consistent emphasis upon the primary significance of the "subjective" events will become readily apparent.

The reader will recall Adler's proposition that the judgment that one is incapable or incompetent and the negative affect that goes with it are the principal initiators of behavior and development. These were postulated to be innate and to arise from several sets of antecedents. To the child's helpless posture as an infant and man's genuine inadequacy in the face of nature might be added the fact of actual physical defect (organ inferiority). Adler proposed that the infant soon recognizes this inferiority (perceptual evaluation) and this results in subjective discomfort and distress. This evaluation does not become habitual immediately, but develops over time. Such feelings set into operation a second set of innate responses, Adler ventured, by which such negative perceptions and feelings can be terminated (collectively referred to as "striving to overcome"). Automatically the infant begins to cast about, trying to find ways to reduce these unpleasant feelings of distress occasioned by his evaluative judgment of himself as incompetent and helpless. He begins to strive to make sense out of and cope with the many events that flood in upon him.

THE DEVELOPMENT OF FICTIONS. The world of events, to Adler, was one of continuous dynamic flow. To the child it appeared chaotic. To render it comprehensible, the human parceled it up into sensible packages; he stabilized his world by building perceptions of events, by forming opinions, by building ideas about what was occurring. From the response capabilities of attending, perceiving, abstracting, and the like he proceeded to build his construction of the events by which he was surrounded.

All such perceptual and thought responses to events are *fictions*. Adler was careful to distinguish between an event and a perception of that event. The perception of a table is not the same as the table itself. Similarly, conceptions, ideas, thoughts, or attitudes about the table are not the same as the table itself. Thus, with the term fictions Adler seemed to be including all cognitive responses—sensory, perceptual, symbolic, and imagistic responses, and the like—all of the variety of (r) or (r_i). Innate "properties of the mind" led to the development of thoughts, which imposed an arbitrary order on the constant stimulation "which is chaotic, always in flux, and incomprehensible" (Ansbacher, 1956, p. 96).

THE APPERCEPTIVE SCHEMA. As such habitual cognitive responses develop, they are acquired in interrelationship with one another and gradually take on the form of larger and larger networks of perceptions and thoughts to the point where they can be termed as schema. Defining the apperceptive schema was a problem: the closest that Adler came to specifying this organization of responses was to refer to it as a "picture." The child organized a "picture of the world" according to what he thought it looked like and how he thought it operated. To the writers, the term seems to refer to a network or complex of sensory-perceptual-conceptual responses functioning somewhat as a unit to influence future behavior.

It is important to note not only that such a schema is subjective and approximate to reality, but also that in each instance it tends to be unique. A conception of a fact is never the same as the fact itself, and thus different individuals, although confronted by the same general world of facts, would mold themselves differently. Each schema, each picture, will vary from individual to individual, no two precisely alike. Further, some schemata are more erroneous (less expedient) than others; there can be varying degrees of correspondence between the event and the idea developed to represent that event. In view of the child's limited capabilities in the early years, it is quite possible for inexpedient interpretations (misinterpretations) to become developed.

The development of such a schema was considered important in several respects. First, it helped the person to orient himself in the world, in a way analogous to a cartographer who orients himself by dividing the earth with meridians and parallels. Such acts served to establish fixed points which permitted the person to locate himself and objects in space and in relationship to each other. By such means, the child and the cartographer alike came to find their way. Moreover, such responses were important in helping to reduce or terminate the primary judgment of inferiority and the concomitant negative affect by giving the person the impression that he knew where he was and by what he was surrounded. Finally, such a schema, once developed, served to determine subsequent behavior since it would be in terms of his conceptions of himself and the world that he would behave. It was within such a schema that he would try to achieve his goals.

THE DEVELOPMENT OF GOALS. A special group of thoughts (fictions) occur equally early and are intertwined with the other conceptual patterns the child is developing. These are thoughts about future consequences (objectives) to be sought, which are treated by the child as fixed points he can achieve, which once attained will permit him to judge himself as superior rather than inferior and to be free of the unpleasant emotions that the ideas of inferiority entail.

From his low self-evaluation, which is also conceptual and "unreal" and thought of as fixed, the child conceives of future conditions that he judges he can attain. He can think of himself as big or strong, a fireman or a policeman, and these thoughts become reified into "things" he tries to attain (Ansbacher, 1956, pp. 98–99). Once established, these thoughts (fictional goals) serve to determine how the child will behave. They are conceptual anticipations of future events (r) with the implicit prediction that once attained one can judge oneself as superior rather than inferior. They become "the guiding point of all wishes, fantasies, and tendencies" (Ansbacher, 1956, p. 99). Just thinking about these future accomplishments elicits positive feelings and somewhat reduces the negative feelings resulting from thoughts of inadequacy. In addition, the acts of planning for and trying to achieve the objectives further reduces the negative self-evaluations and emotion. Striving for accomplishment makes one think he is more adequate (Ansbacher, 1956, pp. 99–100).

THE DEVELOPMENT OF THE FINAL GOAL. Out of these discrete and separate objectives, the person then develops an overriding one. It was Adler's proposition that more and more of the person's behavior became organized around a single objective, and this was a process which contributed to the "unity of the personality." The person begins to behave as if he believed that most of his specific objectives could be accomplished in a single way, and, thus, he formulates an ultimate objective in his thinking, what Adler referred to as the *final goal*.

Adler seemed to feel that there were at least two aspects of such a desired consequence, its unverbalized and diffuse aspect and its concrete specification. These tended to be congruent, but not equivalent. The first aspect is difficult to describe, for Adler was not accustomed to providing specific examples of such final goals. It is, so to speak, an implicit desired consequence which determines an individual's line of development, but of which he is only dimly aware and which he can only partially verbalize. These cause it to be characterized as *unconscious* (noting that to Adler this term denoted primarily that which was unverbalized) and implicitly determinative, rather than verbal and explicit.

These abstract and implicit objectives of people are represented as attempts to be superior in some respect, trying to achieve perfection, struggling to be especially competent or accomplished in some way. However, such abstractions have to be made concrete in order to be implemented on a day-to-day basis. Thus, there are specific derivatives of which the individual is aware and toward which he can explicitly strive, such as the aspiration for prominence in the community, eminence in one's chosen career, success as a lover, and the like. Even where the objective is specific and there are apparently many who share the same aspiration, the goal of each person is still unique and "deeply his own." There are a "thousand" different ways of trying to become an accomplished physician, for example, because to become one means so many different things to different persons.

Thus, each person has his ultimate objective, specific to himself, which he adopts early in life and in terms of which his later behaviors become developed (fictional finalism). His aspiration will determine what he becomes interested in, to which situations he exposes himself, and which response possibilities he will develop. The boy who aspires to be a great athlete will be interested in sports, be attracted to games, and will devote his time to developing his muscles and his stamina. A boy with a bent toward music develops along an entirely different line.

THE DEVELOPMENT OF SOCIAL INTEREST. The ways in which the child learns to perceive events and to think about them, particularly those thoughts by which he can rate himself as a superior person and thereby reduce the discomfort arising from his evaluations of inferiority and helplessness, represent one of the three major aspects of the developmental stream. The second important aspect of development, a process which goes on concomitantly with the cognitive development, Adler termed *social interest*.

The reader will recall Adler's proposal that the child had the innate response pattern of love and affection in his repertoire, and that in the course of interactions with people, especially the mother, these inevitably would occur. Given a favorable reception by her and by the other family members, Adler proposed that the love responses became enhanced and increased ("blossomed forth"), leading to still further affectionate interactions between the child and others. The child listened to what others said and watched what others did; because he was fond of them he tended to emulate their actions and to copy their ideas. He learned to implement his objectives in association with and in co-operation with these other persons.

If things go well, then, these responses of fondness for and concern about the behaviors of other people become interrelated with the other response patterns that are developing simultaneously. At the same time that the child is becoming fond of others, he is also learning ways of perceiving and thinking, learning to set objectives toward which to direct his behavior, and learning instrumental responses by which to achieve these objectives. Both sets of response patterns develop simultaneously and become appropriately related to one another. In Adler's language, striving to overcome becomes fused with the growing social interest. The child learns to accomplish tasks and overcome obstacles in such a way as to benefit not only himself but also those around him. His objectives become established in relation to his love for others, taking their welfare into account. The behaviors used to achieve his objectives will be selected to be of help and assistance to other people. The child will learn to eschew efforts to attain his objectives when he learns that they result in hurt or damage to other people.

Thus, the child's attempts to attain a "point" where both he and others can evaluate him as superior are not necessarily antisocial. Adler did not view attempts to be better than another as inevitably damaging to the other, not when they were for the benefit of and in the interest of others; social interest became an integral part of the striving for superiority.

In contrast to the basic response sequence and the inevitable development of objectives and instrumental response patterns directed toward them, extended responses of love toward other people do not inevitably develop. Indeed, when speaking of disordered behavior, Adler explicitly referred to a *lack of social interest* as a cardinal feature of the problem. He seemed to have meant more properly an underdeveloped set of positive social patterns. He thought it quite possible that the child could become so abused, hated, and rejected that he would fail to develop the expected affection for and concern about others. He would, on the contrary, develop aspirations for personal superiority which are antagonistic to the welfare of other people. The goal to become a fine statesman in order to advance the cause of freedom or to diminish social ills would be an instance of the former; the wish to become a dictator and to attain the gratification of personal power would illustrate the latter. Such egocentricity and "selfishness" was a social artifact, according to Adler, not a biological fact as Freud had suggested. It would have been forced on a child by the behavior of those around him. A certain amount of effort is required to block the development of normal love responses. Given any reasonable treatment in the social group, Adler would expect some measure of affection for and concern about others to develop.

The behavior of most humans, Adler felt, reflected some degree of love, although individuals would vary considerably in how restricted or extended it would be. The range of a person's affectionate interest and concern could include only family or friends, or be broadened to include fellow citizens, similar peoples, or mankind as a whole. It could be restricted to humans alone, or it could include animals, plants, or even physical objects. It was, of course, the human dimension that Adler felt to be crucial, and the ideal fusion would be an extended and abstract concept of some future ideal society developed by the person toward which he and his fellow man might strive and which he would actively seek to implement.

Such responses represented to Adler the general class of effective resolutions to underlying self-evaluations of inferiority. Since man is by nature an inferior being, he can maintain himself only when placed under favorable conditions and specifically when he has the aid of his fellow man. Just as the child cannot survive without his parent, man cannot survive without being social. Finding an avenue through which he can struggle toward objectives of social as well as personal advantage is the soundest "compensation for all the natural weaknesses of individual human beings" (Ansbacher, 1956, p. 154). The most effective way to minimize the intensity of discomfort arising from evaluations of inferiority is to develop the conviction that one is contributing to the common welfare and is therefore valuable (Ansbacher, 1956, p. 155).

Adler asserted that the normal person also developed *courage* and *common sense,* that the abnormal person did not, and that these would be expected benefits from a successful therapeutic course. These prove to be especially difficult concepts to specify, and they would not be mentioned were it not for the fact that they recur repeatedly in Adler's treatment of development, disorder, and therapy and are, therefore, important elements in his conception of behavior. By courage, Adler seemed to refer to the likelihood that a person would try to implement his objectives in relation to the interests and need of others. Thus, the person who was interested in the welfare of his fellow man and was active in expressing such an interest and took the initiative in doing so, would be one whom Adler would represent as courageous. By common sense, Adler seemed to mean thoughts and judgments that took account of characteristics and aspirations of others as well as of oneself. Here, common sense was to be differentiated from "private sense," or private view. Actions, efforts, and objectives were considered to represent common sense if they were designed with the interest of other people in mind; common-sense solutions are always socially oriented solutions. The person deficient in common sense was one who tended to hold an opinion of himself and the world which was particular to himself and reflected a desire for consequences of personal significance only. In the ordinary course of development then, individuals would be expected to learn actively to try to accomplish objectives which take into account the interests of others.

DEGREE OF ACTIVITY. A third primary factor which Adler considered important he called activity level. Although he labeled it primary, he gave it very brief attention, and it remained about the least well-developed concept in his system.

Apparently Adler was struck by the variability in the activity levels of individuals and by the relative consistency of activity level within a single individual over the course of time. He found it difficult to attribute this to innate factors, such as heredity or constitutional temperament. True to his general position, he decided that level of activity was something that the individual developed in early childhood, "fashioning" it from multiform impressions. He could not identify what determined that a high or low level would be acquired, and therefore he concluded the development was arbitrary (Ansbacher, 1956, p. 164).

He was attracted by the possibility of combining degree of activity and degree of social interest in a classificatory manner, yielding a 2×2 contingency classification. Each of the four resulting categories was then proposed as a behavioral type. Adler recognized that this could become a basis for a characterological approach. For example, someone low on social interest and low on activity level was considered to be the avoiding type (escapist character). This possibility, however, he pursued only partially, and it did not become a major aspect of his system.

The reader will recognize social interest, degree of activity, courage, and common sense as labels that cut across subclassifications of response types, such as perceiving, thinking, or acting. That is, some kinds of thoughts could be considered to show social interest, and this would be true of some kinds of perceptions and actions as well. This serves to illustrate the superordinate position of these concepts; they stand at a higher level in the hierarchy of abstraction, encompassing large constellations of different kinds of responses. They are molar concepts.

THE DEVELOPMENT OF THE LIFE STYLE. We come now to the most inclusive level of behavior analysis developed by Adler, what he referred to as the *style of life*. With this label he encompassed all of the foregoing response units into one general concept.

Adler proposed that it was out of the foregoing lines of development that a pattern of behavior gradually emerged which came to be unique to the individual. Looked at from the standpoint of the objective observer, it took on the appearance of a plan of life. It included the individual's objectives, his opinion of himself and the world, and his habitual behaviors for achieving desired consequences in his particular situation. Adler thought that ultimately each person came to develop a single generalized pattern of response to most situations. True to his habit, Adler resisted specification, and he provided at least eight differing definitions and synonyms for this concept. He variously equated it with self or ego, personality, total attitude, general method of problem solving, and the like. However, it is possible to characterize his notion of life style to some degree in terms of what he thought to be its attributes.

First, the life style is thought to be an organization of behavioral pieces, some kind of system that resulted from the integration of behavioral components. It is a product of learning, "created" by the individual child. It becomes formed by the time the child is five and remains relatively constant and unchanging from that point onward. Its content cannot be predicted from previous situational experiences because of the "creative power" of the individual. It is unique to the individual and is never quite duplicated by another person. It tends to achieve internal consistency, and once established it, in turn, determines all subsequent responses. Once fashioned, it becomes "sovereign"; everything a person does from then on is dictated by his style of life; "the whole commands the parts." It is from this that behavior becomes unified—the unity of the personality (Ansbacher, 1956, pp. 174–175).

Adler thus spoke of the *psychology of use*. In brief, he proposed that *all* behavior became organized in terms of the life style. A person's values, interests, intellective skills, instrumental motoric habits, perceptual responses, fantasy sequences, eating, sleeping, and sexual patterns—all became employed in the service of the principal objective and in the context of his habitual ways of thinking about and perceiving the world. What a person saw, how he thought, with whom he interacted, what he listened to—everything became instrumental (life style) to the general life objectives (fictional final goal). This process was all inclusive, since he proposed that even the innate potentialities, such as feelings and emotions, came under the general law of the psychology of use. Fear and anxiety, for example, were discussed in terms of the manner in which they became employed in the service of the individual's style of life (Ansbacher, 1956, pp. 266–267). No matter what was examined, one found a "confirmation of the melody of the total self." All behavior would be seen to be an infinite series of variations on the underlying theme.

The individual himself (the subjective observer) only vaguely apprehends that there are such generalized patterns in his behavior. Adler suggested that the person, although experiencing its operation, never could represent adequately to himself precisely what his life style might be. This was because it was built at a time when his language was only partially developed. Therefore, the total organization of one's behavior remained unverbalized and hence not understood (remained unconscious). It also remained withdrawn from the potential corrections of subsequent experience, tending in turn to render it constant and unchanging. Hence, by the time the child was five, his life style was usually so fixed and mechanized that it proceeded in more or less the same direction for the rest of his life. Only in minor ways would it become modified.

THE MASCULINE PROTEST. This is one of Adler's well-known concepts. It is introduced at this point not only to describe the pattern to which he alluded but also to illustrate how he tried to apply his general principles to particular kinds of behaviors.

This pattern of behavior Adler decided was a product primarily of the situational context within which the child might be reared. Adler saw no essential differences between men and women as far as their inherent inferiority was concerned. However, Western societies, in common with most patriarchal ones, seem to place a heavy premium on males and behaviors associated with the male status—the masculine roles. By contrast, the woman and what she does is often derogated and regarded as inferior in countless small ways. It seemed evident to Adler that little girls were regarded as inferior more often than boys, and as a consequence, females generally had more intense feelings of distress to cope with than did males, or as he put it, had an additional "burden of inferiority feelings" to carry. In the usual course of development, this, like any other problem, can be managed successfully by the growing child. If, however, the girl receives extra-heavy doses of derogation of herself and others like her, she may try to disown her own sex and the behaviors appropriate to it and try to copy the male response patterns instead, since these are the ones to be preferred. She thinks that she will be more acceptable by doing so; often she does not realize that these responses are praised if they are emitted by males, but even more severely derogated if a female uses them.

This was not the only way in which the pattern could be developed. Adler also used the same label to refer to the woman who reacted against such derogation of herself by asserting her feminine patterns even more extensively, by using her sex and her position to damage males, and by taking advantage of them in a revengeful way. He thought it could apply to men also; for example, the youth who was derogated as being unable to live up to the masculine role and perhaps taunted with the label of "sissy," being relegated to the inferior status of girls. Adler thought it likely that some would react by still more intense efforts to be adequately masculine. If any of these were to try to become an aggressive he-man, Adler would label this also as a masculine protest.

Adler believed that he saw many such patterns of behavior operative in the lives of the individuals he studied. This particular one, labeled the masculine protest, was only one such pattern which could become generalized enough so as to pervade a person's entire behavioral repertoire, that is, become his life style. Or again, if things did not proceed so smoothly, the same general sets of ingredients could combine in such a way that a neurotic disposition could become formed and various kinds of disorder could result. It is to the latter possibility which we now turn, the ways in which Adler proposed that disordered behavior (faulty life styles) developed.

THE DEVELOPMENT OF DISORDERED BEHAVIOR

In seeking to account for the evolution of disordered response patterns, Adler remained consistent with his general approach, attempting to do so by means of a few cardinal concepts and propositions. With the phrase "unity of mental disorders," Adler emphasized his conviction that the same underlying principles of analysis could account for the apparent diversity of all "failures or abnormalities." As a consequence, he paid little attention to the task of differentiating various types of disordered behavior and, thus, made no effort to classify the response patterns with which he was concerned. The following general classification was one which he seems to have used implicitly, but rarely did he go beyond a simple listing of what he regarded as the kinds of disordered behavior that might be developed: problem children, neurotics and psychotics, suicides, criminals, alcoholics and drug addicts, sexual perverts, and prostitutes.

Although he recognized the variability ("diversity") that was apparent in various patterns of disorder, Adler considered the significant variability to be individual. In other words, above and beyond the very general principles by which disorder could become acquired, the remaining variability between one disordered person and another was to be attributed to his own unique patterns of behavior which he had acquired and which he shared with no other person.

In general, Adler felt that there were two sets of things that distinguished the disordered person from his normal counterpart. First of all, the disordered person was subject to a greater degree of "feelings of inferiority," particularly in the early stages; this included both judgments of greater degrees of inferiority and more intense emotional distress as a consequence. Secondly, he acquired a set of faulty responses in his compensatory efforts to reduce this increased state of discomfort. Disordered behavior, thus, was described as differing both in degree and in kind from normal behavior. The difference in degree stemmed from the greater and more crippling antecedent feelings; the difference in kind followed from the fact that he acquired an erroneous set of responses which are inappropriate to the effective resolution of these inferiorities.

ABNORMAL FEELINGS OF INFERIORITY

The neurotic has experienced the distress occasioned by the inevitable judgments of inferiority inherent in the human situation. But for several reasons, these feelings were proposed to be of much greater intensity than those undergone by the ordinary person. Adler spoke of the potential neurotic as "overburdened" with such feelings. This resulted in a greater compensatory swing, giving rise to exaggerated responses whereby the person can see himself as superior. Adler was quite explicit on this point, postulating a direct and inverse relationship between the intensity of the antecedent distress (inferiority feelings) and the corresponding struggles to become superior—or as he put it, "between higher goal-setting and increased inferiority feelings" (Ansbacher, 1956, p. 245).

Antecedents to Abnormal Feelings of Inferiority

Adler proposed that three basic conditions contributed to the development of such high levels of negative affect responses. The first arises from the properties of the person, and the latter two are situational.

ORGAN INFERIORITY. Adler contended that children born with defective structures and functional anomalies of the body were likely to develop more intense distress than ordinary children. Such a relationship was not considered to be inevitable, merely probable. Some defective children would not construe the defect as a serious handicap, and if others in his surrounding did not do so either, the expected feelings of an exaggerated degree would not develop.

If both the child and others labeled it as a serious infirmity or personal liability which made him inferior to other persons, however, he could decide that he was a great deal more inferior than others and become much more distressed as a result. The responses directed toward the objective of superiority in his case would be correspondingly stronger. Apparently by "stronger" Adler meant that not only would the instrumental responses be more intense—the greater the intensity of emotional distress, the greater would be the amplitude of the instrumental responses—but also more frequent. Adler felt that often the instrumental responses would be directly related to the physical handicap. Excessively intense or frequent responses, whose objective appeared to be to arrive at a self-evaluation of superiority, could later point to the organ inferiority itself. Thus, a child who felt himself to be muscularly weak might attempt by great effort to become a weight lifter. It was to this sort of relationship that Adler pointed when he used the phrase the *language of the organs*.

PAMPERING. The child who is treated as a baby and is pampered, spoiled, and indulged becomes particularly prone to thoughts of inferiority, because implicitly he is being treated as such. The mother, worried that the child cannot take care of himself adequately, cannot make good judgments, cannot remember to wear his galoshes or cross the street unaided, can succeed in causing the child to fear the same situations. He, too, can become convinced that he is inadequate to stand on his own or that he is weak and prone to fatigue and illness. He can come to fear change in his routine or the loss of his protector. Again, a situation of pampering makes it probable, although not inevitable, that the child will judge himself to be more inferior than others and respond with more intense emotional distress as a result.

NEGLECT. Hatred, punishment, rejection, and neglect are conditions that characterize the situation to which Adler gave the name of the *hated child*. In one way or another, the child can be treated as unwanted, undesirable, bad, stupid, or unattractive. It would be difficult, Adler thought, for the child to remain unaffected by such treatment, and a self-appraisal of marked inferiority would be extremely probable; if this were to occur, intense emotional distress would be expected to follow.

Actually, these did not exhaust the various kinds of conditions that Adler wrote about as contributing to such intense feelings. He made mention of several specific kinds of mistakes that mothers make in child rearing, as well as the ways in which the behavior of his father and his siblings affect the child. However, these three were listed explicitly by Adler as the primary antecedents, the three principal conditions which "overburden" the child and most often set in motion the train of events leading to the development of the neurotic disposition.

CHARACTERISTICS OF DISORDERED BEHAVIOR

Disordered response sequences and patterns represent different response content, and Adler considered this a second defining characteristic.

Again, Adler discussed these events at least at two levels of conceptualization, and we shall review both levels of description. At the more molar level, he attempted to define the outstanding characteristics of the neurotic life style, or what he referred to as the *neurotic disposition*. In keeping with his analysis of the major dimensions of the life style, Adler proposed that disordered behavior could be distinguished from the normal in terms of the three primary aspects of behavior: (*a*) the kinds of instrumental responses which the child developed— the nature of the strivings for superiority; (*b*) the frequency and intensity of love feelings which he held toward other people—the degree of social interest developed; and (*c*) the relative likelihood of overt behavior—the degree of response activity.

EXAGGERATED STRIVINGS FOR SUPERIORITY. A prominent characteristic of the neurotic behavior patterns was excessively intense behavior directed toward imaginary conditions of superiority, resulting in the setting of extremely high standards of accomplishment and less flexible instrumental methods for achieving such objectives. Adler proposed that the neurotic characteristically selected ultimate objectives for himself which were "accentuated" and "dogmatized." The person implicitly struggled after godlike states which were impossible of attainment.

In a word, the neurotic wants to be perfect in some respect. Moreover, his efforts to become so tend to be rigid and unalterable. He becomes more strongly attached to his ideas and to his ideals and principles. For example, the neurotic boy who wants to be a leader will quit and take his football home if the other boys will not let him play quarterback. He is in contrast to the normal youth who has objectives which are reasonable of attainment and about which he can be flexible if the occasion warrants it.

UNDERDEVELOPED SOCIAL INTEREST. It seemed apparent to Adler that the neurotically disposed individual characteristically showed insufficient affection for and concern about other people around him, and this was particularly true of the pampered or hated child. Thus, Adler was stating implicitly that, in general, the same sets of conditions that led to increased self-evaluations of inferiority and increased negative emotions also tended to lead to disruptions in interpersonal relationships.

An underdevelopment in affection and concern for others has several facets. First of all, it tends to result in the building of an erroneous set of thoughts and perceptions about the self, people, and the world (apperceptive schema). If a child is at odds with people around him, if he is neglected, if he is treated differently than other children, he is unlikely to see and think about things as others do. The pampered child is not accustomed to taking into account the opinions or the ideas of those around him. The isolated child does not have as many opportunities to acquire ideas similar to others. Each of these tends to develop a "private view of the world"; he comes to see things differently, to construe events in an idiosyncratic way. He develops his own individual conceptions; his perceptions, his thought sequences, his "understanding and his reasoning" all come to reflect a "private sense" but not common sense. The hated child, for example, is likely to build a pessimistic set of ideas about the world of people. He is likely to think of people as hateful, punitive, and dangerous.

Second, it comes to affect the individual's patterns of interpersonal contact. Unfortunate interactions in the early years influence the child's anticipations of what he can do in a world of humans. The neurotically disposed child "approaches the problems of occupation, friendship, and sex without the confidence that they can be solved by cooperation" (Ansbacher, 1956, p. 156). The pampered child fails to be trained effectively in co-operation, and the hated child learns to avoid others as far as he can. These faulty patterns come to be generalized in such a way that they characterize almost all of their behavior; they become their "style of life."

Finally, the imaginary states that are selected as objectives become personally rather than socially determined. Because the child has had unsatisfactory relations with other people and cannot anticipate being able to attain social acclaim of superiority if he were to collaborate with others, he gives up striving for common objectives and directs his efforts toward his own ends. His aspirations become "selfish." The responses he tries to use to reduce his distress, in order to be able to regard himself as superior rather than inferior, become egocentric. He begins to strive for *personal superiority*, independent of or at the cost of the needs of other people. He begins to want personal power and mastery over others. The criminal wants money and power regardless of the cost to others; the suicidal act is committed in spite of the hardships inflicted on a family of dependents. The obsessive-compulsive strives to demonstrate his intellectual superiority by arguing, criticizing, and finding fault, and he shows a comparative unconcern for the ideas or wishes of others whom he is assailing. The neurotic, in trying to be superior in a selfish way over those around him, will run afoul of his fellow humans; inevitably he will fail, and he is doomed to continue to struggle on the "socially useless" side of life. He will find himself unable to attain the imaginary and antisocial state of personal superiority for which he strives. He will not earn the responses of respect from others for which he is working so hard.

DEGREE OF ACTIVITY. Adler failed to be very definitive in what he felt to be the characteristic outcome as far as the person's activity level was concerned. He stated merely that each case shows both qualitative and quantitative differences. But he seems to have been impressed with the relative inactivity of many disordered persons. Often he wrote as if it were an implicit proposition that the neurotic disposition was characterized by a general reduction in degree of activity. One way in which this would show itself was in connection with the individual's patterns of interpersonal interaction. Adler characterized the neurotic as lacking in active efforts to achieve socially co-operative goals (courage). Thus, it may have been the frequent social inactivity of the neurotic to which Adler was referring.

The primary bases of the neurotic disposition, then, begin with excessively intense levels of emotional distress, and these lead to correspondingly intense instrumental response sequences by the neurotic personality to get himself labeled superior, both by himself and by other people. His "wishes for superiority" become necessities; he *must* be *very* superior. He selects objectives that are excessively high, and he resists changing these ideals. Because of defective interpersonal relationships which contributed to the problem in the first place, he tends to avoid people so that he does not share a common view of events, and he fails to integrate his wishes to be superior with the needs and objectives of other people. He sets goals that are at odds with the goals of others around him. He develops exaggerated and unrealistic wishes for personal importance. He alienates others and isolates himself from them. Moreover, these are the primary characteristics of the individual's generalized behavioral patterns (his life style). Adler believed that the *entire* behavioral arrangement of the person became disordered, another reflection of his principle of the unity of behavioral organization. Thus, Adler classed the neurotic and the criminal in the same general grouping because he considered both to be oriented in an antisocial direction.

It should be understood that the neurotically disposed person is clearly aware neither of these happenings nor of the nature of his responses to them. The entire orientation toward the useless side of life was built in early childhood when language and reasoning were only rudimentary. The consequences (goals) toward which his behavior is directed remain implicit, unverbalized, and not readily understood. He is *unconscious* of them. This is true of the normal person, also, but he avoids difficulty because he has developed more effective patterns of behavior to achieve his unverbalized but socially co-operative goals.

Specific Attributes of Disorder

Adler's concepts of specific manifestations of the neurotic disposition refer to more restricted units of behavior and are somewhat more denotative in type.

PERCEPTION. Adler spoke of two characteristics of this aspect of the apperceptive schema:

Perceptual selectivity. In the development of his "private view of the world," the neurotic does not recognize events as others do, does not respond to events which would be antithetic to his view, and selects out those parts of events that fit with his prior conceptions.

Perceptual sensitivity. This is perhaps one aspect of perceptual selectivity. He is overly ready to make certain interpretations, whether or not they are appropriate.

THOUGHT. *Rigidity.* The neurotic's thought sequences are in general more rigid and consequently less alterable than those of the normal person. Rigidity can be seen in the neurotic's habits of employing:

1. *Antithetical modes of apperception.* He deals in categorical and dichotomous terms. He freezes events into black and white pigeon-holes.

2. *Analogical thought patterns.* He has the habit of engaging in erroneous "as if" equations, for example, responding to an examination *as if* it were a matter of life and death.

3. *Metaphorical thinking.* He frequently associates a relatively innocuous event with a very dangerous one, for example, thinking of the necessity for making a decision as similar to stepping off the brink of a precipice; the anxiety or fear thus derived forces him to avoid the enterprise.

Excessive abstraction. He tends to think with highly abstract concepts (good, bad) rather than more denotative ones (an angry act).

Egocentric ideation. He thinks with idiosyncratic ideas, assumptions, and values, which do not correspond with the ideas of other people.

Excessively high standards of conduct. His values and goals tend to be set higher than those set by others, and he is more stubbornly attached to "fictions." He insists upon absolute and moralistic principles and ideals.

Inappropriate evaluations of own behavior. He is inclined to make errors of judgment concerning his inferiority-superiority as compared with other people, for example, grossly overestimating his own superiority or inferiority.

Inaccurate characterization of own behavior. He typically describes his own behavior inappropriately—as humble and helpless when it would be more accurate to say aggressively demanding.

FEELINGS AND EMOTIONS. *Overly intense.* In general, emotions tend to be exaggerated.

Frequently occurring fear. Excessive evaluation of inferiority and inappropriate attempts to overcome it lead to recurring fears of things which are new and different, fears of defeat, fears of decisions, tests, and requirements, and fears of being unmasked and recognized as inferior. He especially fears any negative evaluation by others.

INTERPERSONAL SKILLS. *Egocentric.* He behaves in a "selfish" way, failing to take into account the needs or goals of others.

Vacillation. He tends to alternate between periods of interaction with others and trying to demonstrate his superiority, and avoidance of others and accompanying self-judgments of inferiority (Adler's *hesitation tendency*).

Dependent. Typically, the neurotic's interpersonal behavior is implicitly dependent; he spends time trying to get others to perform his tasks for him, to be excused for difficulties and the like.

The foregoing list exemplifies the many kinds of specific responses to which Adler referred when he utilized such inclusive concepts as the "neurotic apperceptive schema" or "underdeveloped social interest."

It seems particularly clear that the notion of *efficiency* played a strong part in Adler's conception of disordered behavior. "Appropriate," "healthy," "normal" behavior was focused on dealing effectively with situational events, with the "overcoming of normal, external, oppositional factors" (Ansbacher, 1956, p. 240). Adler conceived of the human person as being faced with a continual progression of problems, and hence of the neurotic as someone who was poorly equipped to arrive at effective solutions. The development of faulty compensatory behaviors resulted in the impairment of the individual's problem-solving repertoire. Effective living required a certain degree of activity, but the neurotic was often less active. Solving problems required a certain degree of flexibility in thought patterns; the neurotic was committed to certain rigid, antithetical, sharply schematized ideas. The neurotic would fail repeatedly at certain types of tasks because he was afraid of them and because he would be unable to solve them.

The Safeguarding Tendencies

The unfortunate person who has developed a neurotic disposition lives constantly under the danger that his self-evaluations of superiority will be exposed (unmasked) and that he will run into situations he cannot handle, where the evaluations of himself as inferior will be inevitable. He will be unable either to maintain the "fiction" that he is superior or to prevent others from judging him inferior. If such were to occur, he would be thrust back on the intense and painful distress which all of the superstructure has been acquired to prevent. Thus, he engages in still further maneuvers and stratagems to protect his particular self-judgments of superiority. These stratagems were labeled by Adler *neurotic safeguards* or the *safeguarding tendencies*.

Individuals acquire different neurotic responses, and the particular ones chosen will determine the type of disorder which develops. Some characteristics of disordered behavior are typical of all neurotics, but the safeguarding tendencies are the "essential character traits," the idiosyncratic manifestations of each person's disorder. Different kinds of disorders are built on different kinds of safeguarding responses.

In Adler's view, the person's selection or development of his protective response patterns is "a creative act." He chooses them because they help him to reduce the distress occasioned by judgments of personal inferiority and because they help increase his feelings of satisfaction which follow when he thinks of himself as superior.

Adler conceived of the safeguarding responses as falling into two large subgroups, those characterized by *aggression* and others characterized by *seeking distance*. This classification has many elements in common with the binary classifications of approach-avoidance and aggression-withdrawal present in other psychological theories.

AGGRESSION. *Depreciation.* Patterns of behavior in which the person enhances his own self-reactions of superiority by derogating others.

Idealization. A type of depreciation in which the individual holding unattainable ideals can thereby disparage everybody since they cannot live up to his ideals, and he can disparage and criticize the world "as it is"—"reality."

Solicitude. A further pattern of depreciation in which the individual can disparage others by feigning concern for their welfare and frequently offering advice, behaving as if others were incapable of caring for themselves.

Accusation. The response of blaming others, most often focused upon some member of the immediate family; "I would have been a marvelous person were it not for my father."

Self-accusation. A response which is the inversion of depreciation, and a subtle device. For example, labeling self as inferior in mathematics and indirectly blaming the instructor.

SEEKING DISTANCE. *Moving backward.* Responses of avoiding and escaping situational dilemmas (suicide, agoraphobia).

Standing still. Responses of refusal to act, failure to decide, procrastination.

Hesitation and backing off. Vacillation, moving backward and forward in relation to the situation or task.

Construction of obstacles. The search for reasons, excuses, or alternative tasks to perform to avoid a particular situation.

Exclusion tendency. The restriction of spheres of action to those wherein he can maintain his self-reactions of superiority.

Although this classification of Adler's is imperfectly drawn, one can recognize that he was identifying these responses in terms of their relationship to situational events. Adler's notion of neurotic safeguards must not be confused with the apparently similar classes of defense mechanisms or security operations of other therapy systems, which are ordinarily proposed to be fear-reducing in function. These response patterns which Adler was pointing to are acquired in relation to outside demands and problems of life, and thus the antecedent is not routinely the fear pattern.

Symptoms and Symptom Formation

Adler considered symptoms special kinds of instrumental responses chosen or acquired by the individual according to the same principles as other instrumental responses. They represented stratagems which served to increase the individual's positive evaluations of himself and to reduce the derogatory ones. Adler viewed symptom formation as an *unconscious* process, usually proceeding independently of the individual's self-awareness, even though it was a "creation" by the person. Thus, symptoms had an unconscious and implicit function and typically occurred in a far-flung network of safeguarding behaviors.

Sometimes the individual is aware of his symptoms and can speak about them. Here they are used as *excuses,* represented as obstacles, and constitute the verbally expressed reasons for failure, inadequacy, seeking distance from obstacles, and the like.

Symptoms often take on the nature of an *arrangement* on the part of the disordered person. He frequently provokes events and then exploits them. If part of his safeguarding procedures is to picture himself as slighted, cheated, or unappreciated, he may arrange his contacts with other persons so that he is snubbed; this will provide him with the justification for aggression, and he can proceed to derogate the other as impolite, congratulating himself on his superior virtue.

Symptoms are typically formed at points of crisis in the individual's situation. Thus, Adler wrote of the *onset of the neurosis*. The neurotically disposed person was considered to be especially vulnerable to failure at life tasks. Symptom neuroses occur in individuals with neurotic dispositions and are precipitated by situational crises. Adler presented a list of ten common situations (precipitating exogenous factors) which included such occurrences as marriage and embarking on a career. These he proposed were typical antecedents to symptom formation, for they represented demands for a readjustment and carried the dangers of failure and the public negative evaluations. He was also inclined to view symptoms as extreme responses, representing the last line of defense that the beleaguered neurotic has open to him after he has tried "all better ways of co-operation."

Adler frequently used the term "misguided" in his descriptions of the disordered person's efforts to resolve his dilemmas. Disordered behavior in all its manifestations represented mistaken answers to the tasks of life, exemplified by striving for "increased possession, power, and influence, and for the disparagement and cheating of other persons" (Ansbacher, 1956, p. 112).

THE TECHNIQUE OF THERAPY

Several major emphases characterized Adler's ideas about treatment. First of all, Adler's approach to the modification of disordered behavior was a generalized one. He proposed that his therapeutic approach was applicable to all forms of disordered behavior. This idea derived from his principle of the "unity of the disorders." If all behavioral difficulties followed the same general lines of development, differential diagnoses between types of disorder would be of no great significance, and a generalized therapeutic approach would become possible.

Adler was one of the first to emphasize the fundamental importance of the essentially social relationship that occurred between the therapist and his patient, a view he considered quite different from Freud's. He regarded its social nature to be a given factor and, thus, a defining characteristic of therapy; but it was also critically significant for the conduct of the therapy itself. Because of it, the patient brings to the treatment sessions and directs toward the therapist his habitual modes of response to significant persons in his life. This process permits an important source of data to be directly accessible to the observations of the therapist. But, more importantly, Adler proposed that it was by means of this interrelationship that therapy could proceed and by which changes could become effected. It was this social relationship through which the therapist could bring about a reduction in the patient's feelings of distress over his inferiority and increase his tendencies to approach and interact with others.

The attention of an Adlerian therapist is focused primarily upon the patient's subjectively observable responses. He is interested in the ways in which the person perceives events, his judgments about himself and about other people, his values, his opinions, his anticipations, his objectives, and the kind and intensity of emotional distress the person experiences.

Adler proposed two general ways in which the therapist could learn about such subjectively observable responses. First, the therapist could elicit the patient's report about them. Second, the therapist could observe the interrelationships among situational events and objectively observable responses, particularly those which occurred directly in the presence of the therapist, and infer the intervening responses.

Adler referred to these two ways of understanding the patient's difficulties as *empathy* and *intuitive guessing*. Later they will be discussed at greater length.

Finally, let us call attention to Adler's persistent advocacy of the idiographic approach. To Adler, the uniqueness of each person's behavior patterns was the primary factor to be kept in mind. His general principles about therapy procedures were reported by him, but only as suggestive guidelines for the therapist to follow. His writings about the technique of therapy were in no way proportional to the attention he gave to the questions of theory construction, normal development, and the neurotic disposition. This paucity of specification may have resulted from his idiographic emphasis, and may be an important reason why Adlerian methods of treatment have failed to obtain widespread support.

The Goals of Therapy

WHO DETERMINES THE GOALS? It appears to be implicit in Adler's general position that the therapist primarily decides what is wrong and determines the therapeutic objectives. The goals of therapy are derived from the nature of disordered behavior and, in general, represent the antithesis of the characteristics of the neurotic disposition. Moreover, Adler's view suggests that subjects are typically unaware of what is faulty in their response patterns and, thus, cannot be expected to know what would be required for their alteration. Finally, it is the therapist who guides the patient, first in an analysis of his particular difficulties, and second in effecting a change in them. The therapist is "always one step ahead" of the subject, as it were, and leading him in the direction of more appropriate behavior.

CHARACTERISTICS OF THE GOALS. Adler seems to have made some effort to relate therapeutic objectives to his analysis of the nature of disorder. The reader will recall Adler's generalized characterization of the neurotic disposition: excessive degrees of distress occasioned by excessive self-evaluations of inferiority and inadequacy; inappropriately chosen objectives, reflecting unrealistically and essentially unattainable aspirations; insufficient interest in, affection toward, and concern about other people; behavioral sequences directed toward personal power and superiority rather than toward objectives that would be constructive for both self and others; idiosyncratic and erroneous habits of interpreting and thinking about events; and deficient initiative in interacting in social situations. The goals of therapy, therefore, were considered to be the converse of each of these, namely:

1. Reduction in the intensity of the negative feelings that follow excessive self-derogation (feelings of inferiority).

2. Correction of the erroneous habits of perceiving and thinking about events (alteration of the apperceptive schema).

3. Alteration of the objectives toward which the individual directs his behavior by developing new ones which would permit judgments of adequacy and, at the same time, would represent a contribution to the welfare of others.

4. Development of greater affection for others, greater empathic concern for their welfare, more frequent affiliation with groups, better skills of interpersonal interaction, and increased co-operation with others in achieving one's objectives (increase social interest).

5. Increase in the person's initiative (activity) and the efforts to act in a social context (courage).

Arranging these treatment objectives in list form should not carry the implication that they have an order of importance or that they be sought in any necessary sequence. Neither of these were questions to which Adler addressed himself.

Occasionally Adler mentioned more concrete subsidiary or intermediate objectives. However, he did not discuss these in any systematic way, and they have not been abstracted for the purpose of this analysis.

Adler emphasized one common underlying denominator, the necessity for effecting an increase in the person's positive feelings toward other humans (social interest), for he felt that most of the other therapeutic objectives hinged upon and would entail this. The patient's "malady" lies in his "lack of co-operation," and as soon as he can relate to other people "on an equal and co-operative footing, he is cured" (Ansbacher, 1956, p. 347). To render the patient an adequate and effective social being was Adler's principal therapeutic objective.

Principles by Which Behavioral Change Occurs

Adler did not specify the processes by which learning occurs, and this omission is a very large and critical one. The time at which he wrote and the background out of which his thinking grew undoubtedly had something to do with this omission. Adler viewed most of the behaviors with which he was concerned as learning products. But he seemed to be quite unaware of the necessity for specifying the ways in which behaviors were acquired, how they were maintained, and under what conditions they became altered. It seems possible, too, that his aversion to specification led him to neglect this task. As was his habit, he treated the phenomena loosely. To Adler, the individual learned, imitated, realized, saw, interpreted, construed, acquired the habit, developed an opinion—each of these terms was used interchangeably. The implication was that each was a synonym for the other and that they did not refer to different response events.

Finally, Adler was so impressed with the "creative power" of the individual that at one point he wrote, "Everybody can accomplish anything"—an extreme remark for which he is famous and from which he retreated in the face of considerable attack. In general, however, Adler did feel that the extent to which an individual could alter his behavior had extremely broad limits.

Adler did propose that change in therapy was accomplished through the development of *understanding,* a term he used in both a restricted and a generalized sense. At several points he defined it as a recognition of "the relationship between things" (Ansbacher, 1956, p. 14). In this sense, understanding has occurred when the person recognizes that *a* leads to *b,* or that *a* covaries with *b*—for example, when he identifies the interconnections between situations and his perceptions of those situations, between his thoughts and the way he feels, and between the attribution of hatred to others and his own counterhatred and aggressive acts.

At the same time, Adler seemed to employ *understanding* to connote the complex processes of thought in the larger sense. The words recognize, realize, guess, become reoriented—all were used interchangeably with the term understanding: "unjustified wishes must be recognized as violating social feeling." Adler may have employed this term much as the concept of insight is employed by other writers. The Ansbachers propose that by *understanding* Adler meant the "insightful reorganization of dynamic factors" (Ansbacher, 1956, p. 294).

Adler also seemed to propose that by the very act of understanding, change had to occur, that understanding was a sufficient precondition (Ansbacher, 1956, p. 335). He specified his conviction that the lack of behavior change, that is, therapeutic failure, could be traced to spurious or incomplete understanding. When patients or therapists told him everything was understood but therapeutic change had not occurred, he considered their statements ridiculous (Ansbacher, 1956, p. 335). The changes that followed correct understanding were considered by Adler to be virtually automatic. When a person changed his habits of thinking and perceiving and developed new modes of conception about events in the world, he was expected simultaneously to change the ways in which he could behave. No longer could he behave as he had in the past.

The preponderance of Adler's writings on the conduct of therapy were devoted to the activities of the therapist. Adler wrote as if understanding occurred initially in the therapist, who subsequently communicated it to the patient so that the patient could share the understanding. Thus, most of his statements about the development of understanding in the therapist should be considered to apply to the patient as well.

Patient Behavior That Must Occur in Therapy

Adler paid no systematic attention to the kind or sequence of responses which the patient had to be led to emit. Virtually all his attention centered upon how the therapist should behave. What follows was pieced together from scattered comments about the patient in different contexts.

1. *Presumably, the patient must recognize that his behavior requires change and that he cannot effect such changes alone.*

2. *Presumably, he must agree to collaborate with the therapist in the resolution of his difficulties and to accept the treatment arrangements.* Adler wrote as if all of these patient responses had already occurred. He devoted virtually no attention to the problem of how to deal with patients unwilling or unable to initiate attempts at change. One suspects that his general optimism would have led him to conclude that almost everyone could be helped and to ignore the possibility of prohibitive conditions.

3. *The patient must agree to accept the initiative for the content of the therapy discussions.* Therapy conditions should encourage the patient to engage in free and friendly conversation in which "it is always indicated that the patient take the initiative" (Ansbacher, 1956, p. 334). Apparently, it is the patient who is responsible for selecting the topics to be discussed, for identifying the difficulties which need attention, and the like.

4. *The patient must accept responsibility for his behavior within and without the therapy session.* From the inception of treatment, the therapist "must try to make it clear that the responsibility for his cure

is the patient's business" (Ansbacher, 1956, p. 334). He represents himself to the patient as an adviser who may help to clarify his behavior and identify his mistakes, but the patient has to agree that the difficulties are his and that it is primarily his task to correct them. Presumably, if the patient does not agree to this the course of the therapy cannot be expected to advance, and the therapist may be faced with the patient's attempting to disown the responsibility or to thrust it upon another, such as the therapist. Should the treatment prove successful, the patient is given the primary credit.

5. *The patient must come to trust the therapist.* Adler expected most patients to begin their contact with the therapist in a cautious and apprehensive manner, to hold the anticipation of being hurt or damaged by him. The patient has to come to feel safe, to fear no longer that the therapist wants to dominate him, coerce him, or force harmful changes upon him. He has to conclude that the therapist can be trusted, and that he is "free" and at liberty to discuss what he wishes.

6. *The patient must come to like the therapist.* Perhaps in relation to his reduced fear of the therapist, the patient ideally comes to feel fond of the therapist. Only by the development of fondness toward this one person will it become possible for the patient to develop interest in others. It will also lead to a set of efforts on his part to understand and to co-operate with the therapist in the solution of his difficulties.

7. *The patient must recognize that he cannot succeed in his efforts to conceal and dissemble.* Adler felt it to be inevitable that the patient would attempt to maintain his self-evaluations of superiority, even though they were fictional and imaginary, by utilizing his established ways of responding (safeguards). Adler cautioned the therapist to expect the patient to raise distracting obstructions, to employ evasive devices, to erect counterinterpretations of his difficulties which were faulty and inaccurate, and to employ delays and excuses in his efforts to keep his ideas and objectives private and free from the observation and analysis of the therapist. But the desired response is the recognition of their failure and the relinquishing of them when faced with clear and consistent explanations of them by the therapist. The recognition of such failures should not be accompanied, however, by a feeling of defeat, as if the patient has lost in a contest with a superior antagonist.

8. *The patient must begin to adopt the therapist's conceptualizations about behavior.* Having relinquished his own, the patient will be more inclined now to accept the therapist's manner of interpreting events,

to employ his method of explanation, and to be more persuaded of their utility. The acceptance of a less erroneous representation of events will lead to the necessary corrections in his perceptual and thought sequences, which are the essential changes upon which successful treatment rests.

Once the patient has developed some facility at identifying events more accurately and thinking more appropriately about them, that is, with smaller degree of error, other desired responses begin to occur, including those listed earlier under the heading of the goals of therapy. The patient recognizes his self-evaluations of inferiority, modifies his objectives, extends his concern to other people, and becomes more active and "courageous" in his interpersonal relationships. If such responses were forthcoming, Adler would consider the therapy to have arrived at its terminal stage.

The Behaviors Required of the Therapist

Again, the whole of Adler's writings must be scanned in order to indicate the specific types of therapist responses he felt were necessary. Although he did not enumerate the qualifications of a good therapist, at scattered intervals he made the following observations.

The therapist must be able to remain alert and attentive. He must be a sympathetic yet "unemotionalized outsider"; presumably the therapist himself should have a goodly degree of "social interest" and, thus, feel and communicate a liking for and a concern about the patient. He must be tactful, that is, be able to find acceptable forms in which to express his ideas without eliciting annoyance in the patient. He must be persistent and resourceful, finding alternative ways to express ideas so as to induce the patient to accept them—a kind of ideational fluency, perhaps. He must be able to maintain patience and tolerance in the face of resistance and hostility. Of course, the therapist should be thoroughly conversant with the principles and observations of Individual Psychology.

Moreover, the therapist must be able to withhold certain other responses, to exercise "reserve." The patient is under no circumstances to be offended. Thus, the therapist must be careful not to employ criticism or hostility in his dealings with the patient. Neither should he engage in moral judgments about what he hears and sees.

Finally, he must be able to implement the major objectives of therapy, to perform the appropriate therapy operations.

Therapeutic Objectives and Operations

In Adler's account of the course of therapy, he was accustomed to divide it into three major parts which he labeled: (1) understanding the patient, (2) explaining the patient to himself, and (3) strengthening social interest. These can be rendered as: analysis of the problem, changing the patient's conception of the problem, and changing the patient's interpersonal response patterns.

ANALYSIS OF THE PROBLEM (UNDERSTANDING THE PATIENT). The first and most important task of therapy is to arrive at an effective representation of the patient's behavior. The task here is to "uncover the neurotic style of life." Unless the therapist identifies the specific events in the patient's situation and recognizes how they interrelate with one another, he cannot proceed to assist the patient in understanding them.

The analysis is accomplished in terms of the aspects of behavior Adler had proposed to be important (Ansbacher, 1956, p. 157). Thus, the Adlerian therapist examines for the physiological and situational antecedents likely to result in self-derogation and judgments of the self as inadequate; evidences of interpersonal alienation and an avoidance of social interactions—perhaps even antagonisms toward other people; and signs pointing to the implicit objectives of personal mastery, power, and superiority over others. Adler assumed that the patient's difficulties were precipitated by the occurrence of a current *dilemma,* which conflicted with the patient's habits of social interaction or challenged his private representation of himself as superior. Adler would try to identify the dilemma, along with the responses the patient was using to avoid the problem and to prevent the self-derogation and acute feelings of distress which would follow the "puncturing" of his inappropriate view of himself as superior.

The therapist does not attend to symptoms as such. Symptoms were represented by Adler as instrumental responses in the service of the individual's thoughts about what he hoped to accomplish (goals) and how he might be superior.

Analysis of symptoms permits inferences about what the person is trying to accomplish. The therapist should look behind the fact that the individual has headaches, anxiety symptoms, obsessive ideas, or is "a thief or a loafer in school." Symptoms reflect an "individual's struggle to reach a chosen goal" (Ansbacher, 1956, p. 330). Symptoms make sense when understood as attempts to achieve objectives. To Adler, every problem child, every neurotic, every drunkard, criminal, or sexual pervert made what he considered appropriate responses to attain some kind of superiority. Symptoms, and all other responses, provide data from which to infer the common underlying objective toward which all seem to be directed. In Adler's language this is the "fictional final goal" around which all the person's behavior is organized and which represents the guideline for his entire "life style."

Initially the therapist seeks to establish a tentative conception of the patient and the situation in which he is operating. From the ways in which the individual reports about himself and the events in his life and from his manner of response in the session itself, the therapist forms an initial hypothesis about the manner in which the patient perceives and thinks, and the objectives toward which his behavior is directed. Adler referred to this as the *general diagnosis*. In the beginning the therapist guesses, but through reasoning and inference he seeks to build up a "total picture" by successive interpretations of the verbal and expressive productions of the patient; the concrete responses —fantasies, dreams, opinions, activities, interests—are all expected to show an inner consistency, which can be "understood" if their common underlying denominator is identified.

The therapist must next accomplish a *special diagnosis,* which to Adler represented a series of "tests." The therapist examines the successive responses as they occur, making interpretations of each to determine what bearing it has on the initial conclusion. The initial hypothesis must be confirmed, or it must be discarded and another conceptual analysis must be developed in its place.

A series of discussion topics are used to elicit patient behaviors and reports to test this total picture. Adler referred to this as the *Individualizing Examination.*

1. Childhood recollections. The therapist examines for childhood response patterns similar to the presenting problem.

2. Childhood disorders.

3. Aggravating life conditions. (*a*) Past—for example, "organ inferiorities, pressure in the family, pampering, rivalry, or a neurotic family tradition" (Ansbacher, 1956, p. 328). (*b*) Present—exogenous facts precipitating the disorder.

4. Position of the child in the birth order.

5. Content of day and night dreams.

6. All expressive movements accessible to the therapist's observation.

Adler presented this list describing the topics as "the most trustworthy approaches to the exploration of personality," and he also developed an informal list of questions as a guide in a diagnostic interview for use with adult patients.

Adler also paid attention to the task of making inferences about the person's thoughts and objectives based on his behavior in the therapeutic hour itself. The free atmosphere was established not only to improve the subject's capacity to relate to a person but also to permit the therapist to observe the patient's spontaneous behavior, thus providing data of diagnostic utility. The act of one patient who went to sleep, for example, would lead Adler to infer underlying hostility and resentment, and also to develop the hypothesis that this was a generalized manner of response toward others as well as the therapist. He proposed that the therapist cease to attend to the patient's words occasionally, and focus instead on his motoric movements, feeling that these would be more indicative of the patient's manner of approach than the content of his words. Especially important to recognize were incongruities and sharp contradictions within simultaneous sets of responses in the subject.

Adler identified two skills, *empathy* and *intuitive guessing*, with which the therapist had to be particularly adept in this stage of work. Adler felt that the therapist had not only to elicit the subject's report of how he sees and thinks but also to empathize in order to identify these subjectively observable events more closely: one has to be able to "see" with the patient's eyes and "hear" with his ears. The therapist has to be able to take the role of the other and approximate in his own responses those which seem to be occurring in the patient. The therapist's representation of these subjective events to himself would never be precisely the same as the patient's, of course, but it is a necessary procedure if the therapist is to identify the significant response events.

Second, the therapist infers (guesses) from the way the patient describes events and from the way he responds to the therapy situation what might be occurring within the patient's intervening response sequences. He cannot rely entirely on what the patient reports. Ordinarily the patient has little understanding of the nature of his actions and could not represent them verbally with great accuracy. Thus, the act of inference becomes necessary. The therapist is especially interested in forming satisfactory inferences as to the patient's thoughts about his objectives (goal of personal superiority), because subsequent work will entail the clarification of those thoughts to the patient himself, helping him to recognize their inappropriateness and to modify them in a more socially appropriate direction.

CHANGING THE PATIENT'S CONCEPTION OF THE PROBLEM (EXPLAINING THE PATIENT TO HIMSELF). The next task of therapy is the communication of the therapist's understanding to the patient in such a way that he can reasonably accept it. The objective is to grasp the special structure and development of the individual's behavior and to express it with such lucidity that the patient "knows he is understood and recognizes his own mistake."

How is this accomplished? Adler was not clear, but he discussed this task in a variety of ways (for example, Ansbacher, 1956, pp. 334–335). He advocated the use of persuasion and the giving of information; he specified that references to fables and historical characters and quotations from poets and philosophers were often of use to the therapist. Particular assignments are made to the patient—"Never do anything you don't like," or again, "Try to think every day how you can please someone"—as ways to demonstrate to the patient his faulty ways of responding and to teach him the advantages of a different set of responses. Munroe (1955) reported one therapy session conducted by Adler in which he "bedeviled" a delinquent boy into admitting to some undesirable pattern of behavior. Clearly, the general phrase "explaining the patient to himself" encompasses an array of different types of specific verbal responses by the therapist.

It is clear from Adler's general "flexibility" of technique that a variety of procedures other than verbal methods were pressed into service whenever their use appeared to be indicated. In one instance, he discussed the hostile expressions used to the therapist by the patient's relatives as being of advantage in therapy. In some instances, he carefully attempted to stir up hostile expressions on their part, and then disclosed and explained this to the patient as a way of helping the patient to identify what was happening in his family situation. Adler's suggestion of specific actions for the patient to perform outside of therapy demonstrated the use of events other than verbal transactions to assist in the accomplishment of change. In another instance, he reported the manner in which he bound up a patient's injured arm after he had smashed a window, and his description of the friendly and kindly manner in which he accomplished this task implied that he believed affection could be fostered in other than verbal ways. However, such techniques were not detailed by him in any orderly fashion.

Unfortunately, the concrete details of the therapeutic process are obscured by the use of such an inclusive concept as "explaining."

Clearly "explaining" involves many techniques: the application of more effective concepts and labels in describing the person's behavior patterns; the rendering explicit of the unverbalized and unsymbolized events and developing a verbal representation of their interrelationships; the altering of faulty perceptions based on overgeneralizations (analogical thinking) through the use of challenges, questions, and the like (discrimination); or the attempt to break down the individual's dichotomous and categorical habits of thought by quizzical expressions, questions, or the presenting of analogies (generalization).

Finally, with the phrase *training the patient* to develop understanding, Adler implied that the therapist sought to facilitate the patient's imitation of the therapist's patterns of thought. With such an approach it is contingent upon the system to specify quite clearly just how the therapist is to think as well as how the patient is to be led to duplicate it.

Disarming the patient is a technique repeatedly mentioned by Adler. Although unclear, Adler seemed to be referring to the therapist obstructing the patient's neurotic habits of preventing the exposure of his underlying feelings and thoughts. The technique is composed of such precepts as: never let the patient force one into a superior role; do not make specific suggestions if you have reason to believe the patient will fail at them in order to defeat the therapist; do not permit the patient to perceive you as his last hope; do not continue to indulge a spoiled patient; and the like. This whole class of operations designed to interrupt or to stop habitual response sequences requires greater specification before others can use them effectively.

CHANGING THE PATIENT'S SOCIAL RESPONSE PATTERNS (DEVELOPING SOCIAL INTEREST). The final general objective and the operations for its accomplishment followed from Adler's conception of disorder as an instance of social disarticulation. Adler tried to get the patient to interact and co-operate with other people, to implement his objectives in social contexts, and to behave in ways nonantagonistic to the interests and purposes of other people.

The therapy relationship was the means through which to accomplish this, but Adler only described the relationship, rather than telling how to establish it. The therapist arranges for a relationship of friendly collaboration, helping the patient to view him as a co-worker who is interested in trying to help. He does not promise a cure, even in the most promising cases; rather he holds out the possibility of a cure following a fruitful collaboration. He earns the patient's "good will" to the point where the patient develops the conviction that he is truly free to say and do as he pleases.

In general, the therapist does this by permitting a wide latitude of behavior. Adler permitted his patients to sit where they pleased, to walk around, to smoke, or even to go to sleep on occasion. Finally, the therapist is careful to ascribe the work and the success of the therapy to the patient, thereby providing him with respect and a modicum of acclaim.

He conceived of this relationship as analogous to the relationship between the patient and an ideal mother. The therapist's role is "a belated assumption of the maternal function" (Ansbacher, 1956, p. 341). Adler thought of the mother as being the primary agent in the person's life for the acquisition of effective social behavior. With the therapist performing what the person's mother had failed to do, the person can engage in an appropriate and affectionate relationship with one individual, and this can become extended or generalized to persons at large. Apparently he expected the love responses toward the therapist to generalize automatically to other people. Indeed, Adler expected extensive changes in behavior to follow from the change in the individual's perceptions of, ideas about, feelings toward, and interactions with other people. Intellectual functioning would improve, feelings of worth increase, an optimistic view of the future develop, a kindlier view of others emerge, and interpersonal relationships improve (Ansbacher, 1956, p. 155).

The Transfer of Changes within Therapy to the External Situation

In Adler's view, if the individual's modes of thought became altered, if his orientation to the world underwent change, the transfer to other situations in his life would be accomplished automatically, since the patient carried the change with him as he went through the office door. Thus, Adler's theory did not require techniques for this purpose.

The reader will recall, however, that Adler provided several examples of therapist response which deal specifically with transfer. He advised his patients how to behave, he made suggestions as to what they should do, how they should think, and the attitudes that they should retain during the intervals between therapy sessions. It seems apparent that Adler did not remain consistent with his general notion that "altering his (the patient's) private picture of the world" was sufficient for the changing of behaviors dependent on that picture. The implication is that he did engage in techniques for effecting such transfer and did not recognize them as such.

EVALUATION OF CHANGE AND VERIFICATION OF THEORY

Adler described his system as an understanding psychology and an individual one. In these terms he asserted that the primary data of his psychology was subjective "experience," that his method of observation involved primarily introspective self-report by the subject under study, and that the purpose of his analysis was the explication of the personal behavior patterns characterizing the individual, to which he collectively gave the name life style.

In such a system, Adler proposed that there were several sources of "validation," with which the therapist could assess the adequacy of his observations of the person's behavior and whereby he could "verify" the propositions that were developed to account for each individual case. These included agreement by an outside observer, agreement by the patient, and agreement of one proposition with another (internal consistency).

Assessment of Behavior Change

In what way is the decision reached that therapy has been completed, that its objectives have been reached, that the necessary changes have become accomplished? Adler did not deal extensively with the problem of duration of treatment, other than to remark that it represented a difficult question to answer and to express his confidence that, properly carried out, the method of Individual Psychology should begin to yield dividends—show at least partial success—within three months and often sooner. He did specify that judgments on the patient's progress should be made during each session and presumably the question of prospective termination would be involved at each interview. The behavioral events observed for this evaluation were not specified, beyond a general reference to *degree of co-operation* (Ansbacher, 1956, p. 344). Presumably, the therapist also paid attention to all those responses to which Adler made repeated reference in discussing "abnormality" and neurotic "mistakes," statements by the subject which represented more appropriate ways of thinking about himself and his world, and behavioral evidences of fondness and concern for the therapist and other people.

Adler not only failed to be explicit about the behavioral events to be assessed, he also did not specify the conceptual steps through which the evaluation was accomplished. It is probable that if he were queried about the act of evaluation, he would have answered in much the same fashion as he did with the term "understanding," that is, by using a very global designation for what was actually a whole realm of complex and intricate procedures.

The Locus of Evaluation

Again, as with other evaluative issues, Adler did not explicitly deal with the question as to who was the instrument of evaluation. It is unclear not only when treatment was considered finished, but also which of the participants made the decision. In one sense, it might be argued from the manner in which Adler wrote that it was the therapist who decided, since his comments repeatedly set up the therapist's conception of the difficulty as primary and one that became taught to the patient. Perhaps therapy was finished when the patient "learned his lesson."

In another respect it could also be argued that the patient had to be the instrument of decision, since Adler stressed the idea that the responsibility for the "actual cure" resided in the patient himself. The therapist could only help to identify the mistakes; the patient had to "make the truth living," apply his learnings to the life-situation, and, therefore, test the adequacy of his reorientation.

In addition, it might be presumed that the decision for termination had to be arrived at in some mutual fashion, since Adler placed such great importance on the co-operative and collaborative efforts of therapist and patient in the analysis and solution of his difficulties.

Verification of Theory

INTEROBSERVER AGREEMENT. In this instance Adler advocated that the patient be examined in the presence of the family physician, without being asked leading questions or without any systematic inquiry being conducted. The test involves determining whether the uninstructed observer agrees with the therapist in the conceptualization of the difficulty. Adler expressed his confidence that this independent observer would recognize "coherence which comes to light," whereas the patient would be unlikely to do so (Ansbacher, 1956, p. 331).

AGREEMENT BETWEEN OBJECTIVE AND SUBJECTIVE OBSERVERS. Although he did not refer to this as a criterion of validity, it seems apparent that Adler operated in terms of patient agreement. At one point, in discussing what constituted a "real" explanation, he specified it to be one which was so clear that the patient "knows and feels his own experience instantly" (Ansbacher, 1956, p. 335). Again, when he spoke of explaining erroneous mechanisms to patients, he implied that explanation continued until such time as the patient came to agree. Adler made the bold assertion that he had "never yet" found this impossible (Ansbacher, 1956, p. 335). Finally, he acknowledged the necessity for a consensus of at least two observers, noting that even if the therapist understood, "we should have no witness that we were right unless the patient also understood" (Ansbacher, 1956, p. 335).

TESTS OF INTERNAL CONSISTENCY. Adler devoted primary attention to this method of verification. He was confident that behavior patterns were built consistently around a central theme and that, therefore, all behavioral patterns and sequences could be viewed as an implementation of this central theme. The therapist could start with any set of observations and check them against others since "every word, thought, feeling, or gesture" expressed one "melody" (Ansbacher, 1956, p. 332). Thus, to take an example, the analysis of a symptom would not be considered to be complete until it was conceived of as an instrumentality for some set of intervening thought sequences, thought sequences which could account equally well for most other response sequences comprising the person's habitual modes of behavior.

COMMENTS

In retrospect, it certainly would appear that Adler's reviewers are quite correct in emphasizing the importance of the system of Individual Psychology in the development of the field of verbal psychotherapy. Let us first note what appear to be significant and praiseworthy emphases in this particular system.

Adler's was perhaps the first phenomenological therapy system and still remains a major one. His advocacy of the study of the way a person sees situations, thinks about them, and feels toward them are emphases that other systems have repeated. Having identified such events to be important, however, Adler seemed to overgeneralize and assert that they were the *only* important events to study. Thus, he can be criticized for exclusive attention on such occurrences; focusing upon "subjective" events should not carry with it a corresponding neglect of objectively observable phenomena. Not all overt behavior is determined by the way a person sees a situation or thinks about it; some behavior is directly determined by the parameters of the situational stimuli themselves.

Adler is to be commended also for having called attention to another set of phenomena of great significance in human behavior, that of "goal-directed" behavior. In contrast to many psychological theorists who conceive of all behaviors as being pulled out of the organism by situational events, or being pushed out by endogenous pressures, Adler emphasized the importance of each person's thoughts about future events (goals). From a phenomenal point of view, it seems very apparent that humans do engage in anticipatory thoughts about the consequences of their behavior; that they do conceive of consequents which they might obtain and which they can anticipate would lead to satisfactions; and that they can estimate the results of certain courses of action. Furthermore, humans appear to guide or select their behavior according to these anticipated outcomes.

Another important set of events which Adler pointed to were the self-evaluations of inadequacy and inferiority on the one hand and those of comparative superiority on the other, although he called these "feelings." Again, Adler seemed to fall into the trap of generalizing about some critical types of events by asserting that they were the primary events around which all other responses developed. Certainly both self-doubts and positive self-appraisals are important types of thoughts, but people sometimes engage in eating when they are hungry, or go to a movie when they are satiated with their day-to-day work, without the implication that they are superior or inferior even entering their thoughts.

In addition to what seems to us to be excessive over-generalization, several more specific weaknesses may be mentioned. Let us note first of all the fact that Adler's overemphasis on thought responses led to a corresponding neglect of other responses. For example, the affective or the physiological response patterns are of great significance in the study of behavior, but these receive virtually no attention in this system. There are few concepts at the more restricted level of analysis (at the lower level of the conceptual hierarchy). Moreover, the relationship between these concepts and the concrete behaviors to which they refer are not carefully worked out. For example, the concept of perception is often used, but not so that one knows precisely to what it refers and in what way a perception differs from a thought or an attitude.

There is a corresponding excessive commitment to large and inclusive (molar) units of behavioral analysis. The concepts of *social interest* and *apperceptive schema,* for example, are not specified in such a way that the student of this system can identify precisely which lower-order concepts are to be covered and which concrete behavioral events are, therefore, to be included. Does the concept of social interest include only interpersonal perceptions and thoughts, or feelings and overt acts as well? If only thoughts, for example, precisely which ones? Thus, the relationships between behavioral event and concept, and also between concept and concept, are spelled out inadequately. Global and inclusive units of analysis, such as characterize this system, are useful when extended amounts of behavior are to be described and studied. But they can perform their function only when the conceptual hierarchy is laid out in a systematic fashion. In general, Adler's avoidance of careful delineation of response units, his use of multiple labels for the "same" events, his use of the same labels for different events, and his attempts to avoid classificatory analyses only compounded the foregoing problems and cannot be applauded as a method for building a theoretic system.

The same types of observations can be made about Adler's management of situational events. Adler is to be credited again for calling attention to the importance of situational events in relation to human behavior, especially interpersonal interactions. However, his system involved few concepts characterizing such interpersonal situations.

When it comes to viewing the propositions of the system, many analogous faults are evident. Adler's insistence upon idiographic propositions appeared rarely to have led to propositional statements at all. The propositions about the ways human behavior developed were significantly limited. First and foremost was the neglect of the principles of learning. But beyond that, his characterization of the sequence of events in the course of development was only very grossly drawn. The propositions were not tailored to known differences in the developmental sequence as a function of age.

Further, Adler can probably be charged with the error of *endelicomorphism*—attributing adult characteristics to the behavior of infants and children. It is undoubtedly true that the adult human makes judgments of inferiority-superiority about himself in relation to others around him and in relation to the tasks that he sets himself. But to assume that the small infant does the same, as Adler did, requires one to attribute more complex perceptual and symbolic capacities to the child than the ordinary observer is willing to allow. It appears very much as if Adler took important events in the adult human and simply extrapolated them backward, assuming their occurrence in pretty much the same general form in both infants and children.

Adler has been accused of reductionism and oversimplification. What seems to have been meant by this charge is that he sought to account for all the complexities of adult human behavior by means of a few large concepts and a small number of principles. All behavior of a person was "handled" through the use of the term life style; all behavior was ultimately reducible to a single basic response sequence, and in the final analysis, the entire superstructure of the human was built on the primary "feelings of inferiority." A search for simplicity seemed to lead Adler to identify far more consistency and integration in human behavior than was warranted by the facts. It seems very doubtful that all a person's behavior is oriented so nicely around a single objective and that all of his behavior can be legitimately interpreted in the light of this single "fictional final goal." Most observers of behavior agree that inconsistencies, incongruities, and poorly integrated patterns are as much a characteristic of human behavior as are their opposites. The overall proposition of the "unity of behavior" must be seriously called into question. Similarly, Adler's insistence on the current adaptive quality of every single act of the human person denied the possibility of errors, poorly chosen behavior, faulty instrumental sequences—in short, ineffective behavior in general.

When it came to the technique of therapy itself, Adler's system left the practitioner at something of a loss. He made no great effort to deal systematically with the conduct of psychotherapy; what was represented earlier was pieced together from discursive writings. Thus, he had comparatively little to say about the concrete operations a therapist should perform; and in addition, what he did have to say seems to have been greatly oversimplified.

If one reduces his point of view concerning technique to its barest essentials one finds that Adler discussed therapy technique mostly in terms of the *consequences* to be achieved rather than the *procedures* to be used in achieving those consequences. An adequate characterization of technique would include considerably more specification as to *how* the analysis is to be done, *how* it is that "persuasion" is to be effected, *in what ways* the affectionate feelings toward the therapist are to be facilitated, and so forth. To characterize all these specific tasks with the inclusive labels of "explaining" and "understanding" is to leave the practicing therapist at a loss as to what to do. It is clear that the therapist was expected to be quite active, and one can readily see why Adler's proposals concerning technique were labeled as didactic procedures, since the entire operation had the appearance of the teacher role.

In general, this system is to be highly regarded for its contributions to the developing field of therapy theory. Sophistication concerning theory construction and therapeutic practice has progressed considerably since the time in which Adler worked, however, and if the system is to continue to be viable, its deficiencies must be repaired and the theory considerably elaborated. Otherwise one can expect its fate to be that of most systems with such deficiencies: valuable elements will be absorbed into others, and the system as a system will lose out in competition to those that utilize better concepts, make more explicit and precise the propositions that account for the operation of these behavioral units, and can be more specific in denoting the therapeutic operations which are to be used on different response events. Even were this to happen, however, Adler would deserve an important place in the history of therapy theory.

Chapter 10

The Will Therapy of
Otto Rank

Otto Rank occupies a rather distinctive position in the history of therapy theory. In contrast to various other workers, he was explicitly philosophic and anti-scientific in his approach. To the systematist his work presents several kinds of problems, for his writings are suffused with a philosophical, literary, and artistic language which renders him difficult to understand and obscure on many points. Nor was he in the habit of writing in a systematic and orderly way. This chapter attempts to abstract as much of a systematic position from his writings as is possible.[1]

Rank would not have approved of the present analysis. He would have argued that it is inappropriate to subject his therapeutic con-

[1] Summaries of Rank's ideas about psychotherapy and personality development as he himself represented them are available in Karpf (1953), Mullahy (1948), and Munroe (1955).

ceptions to empirical or experimental test. He believed that an "intellectual ideology" which presumes human behavior to be predictable and subject to control through the acquisition of knowledge is quite contrary to the "purely human" factor in psychotherapy. His approach was clearly and firmly idiographic. Like Adler, he emphasized that psychology should deal not with "facts," but with individuals' "attitudes" (responses) toward "facts." He asserted that interpretations of, or reactions to, events differed from person to person and from situation to situation for each person. To Rank, scientific analysis did violence to the phenomena of behavior.

BIOGRAPHICAL INFORMATION

As Taft's biographical study (1958) revealed, Rank was always a deeply introspective man. Generally, he was also a lonely and somewhat unhappy person who formed close personal attachments with relatively few people. He had strong philosophical, artistic, and literary interests. It seems that by interest, by nature, and by self-instruction, Rank tended strongly toward philosophy. He attempted to satisfy his family by preparing for a trade during his youth, but he became so dissatisfied that he left the trade and withdrew to live by himself. During this period he lived a rather meager existence and devoted himself to extensive reading. Schopenhauer and Nietzsche were among the philosophers who seemed to have had a strong influence upon him. His early interests appeared to continue as a prominent theme in his later writing. The language he chose to employ makes him exceedingly difficult to comprehend, and his mode of expression has undoubtedly helped to restrict the influence of his ideas. As a result of his personal study, Rank wrote a brief manuscript in which he attempted to analyze the artistic person. The manuscript came to Freud's attention and stimulated his interest in Rank, and it was Freud who helped him to arrange and finance a university education.

Stimulated by Freud's powerful intellect and his personal interest, Rank developed an interpersonal relationship he had apparently been seeking and had not found in his earlier years. He became a happy and prodigious worker. During this period he became married and remained rather happily so for some 30 years. As Freud's protégé and personal secretary, Rank became quite close to the master. Following the pattern of several other of Freud's associates, Rank made a trip to the United States after completing his formal education. Upon his return to Europe, however, a gulf began to develop in the personal and intellectual relationship with Freud, since the student's ideas had begun to diverge from those of his teacher.

Subsequently Rank returned to the United States for a lecture series at the School of Social Work in Philadelphia, where he settled after a final and very painful break with Freud. His location at the school helps account for the fact that his ideas have been more influential among social workers than in other groups. He was never highly successful or popular in the United States. On occasion he had opportunities to deliver lectures, and it was in this way that Carl Rogers became acquainted with Rank's work. Rank sometimes offered seminars, which a limited number of people attended. He failed to develop any appreciable group of followers, however, and only a few seem to have become genuine advocates of his point of view. His major influence appears to have been through his writings. In addition, Taft (1948) and Allen (1942) did much to translate his ideas for other theorists and practitioners, particularly social workers. Following his painful separation from Freud, Rank's marriage began to dissolve, and eventually he and his wife were divorced. He married his personal secretary and died a few months thereafter.

Rank's propositions appear to have grown from at least four major sources. First, his philosophical background undoubtedly had a primary influence. Second, his ideas appear to have been strongly determined by his personal introspection and acute sensitivity to his own reactions. Third, Rank insisted that one got a different conception of neurosis when one approached it through the study of the "creative" (healthy) person. It was his original interest in studying the "artist" which initially led Rank to psychology. Finally, Rank's experience with psychotherapy itself played a part in the development of his ideas. However, his own comments about neurosis (1945) and Taft's biography (1958) suggest that the range of his experience was limited. Apparently he had very little to do with the psychoses and character disorders in his therapeutic practice. The only disorders to which direct reference was found were those that he labeled compulsion neurosis and conversion hysteria. His clinical experience appears to have been restricted primarily to neurotic disorders which did not require hospitalization. Therefore, one should not expect Rank's ideas to apply equally well to all types of behavior disorder, since they have a greater chance of verification with those types with which he worked.

From among the references examined, Rank's *Will Therapy and*

Truth and Reality (1945) has been the primary source of the ideas summarized in this chapter. Because Rank was quite sketchy and unsystematic, it is to be expected that this presentation of his ideas will be briefer than that of some other theorists. Moreover, it has been necessary to piece his ideas together into what appears to be their most systematic form. Finally, the authors have been forced to make definitional choices, in view of Rank's proclivity for using terms in a variety of ways. The attempt has been made to select the most important meaning for analysis, after indicating the various other uses at the hands of Rank himself.

MAJOR EMPHASES

A review of some of the central ideas underlying Rank's position will be helpful in providing a background for understanding the concepts to be discussed later.

Rank developed a response-response type of conceptual framework. Few, if any, of his major concepts included situational events. He seemed to conclude that situational events played an important role in behavior, but said little about *how* they were important. However, his theories gave fundamental emphasis to a person's relationships with other people, suggesting innate patterns of reaction to interpersonal stimuli.

Objectively observable responses (R) were also considered important but again were given little emphasis in his major concepts. The subjectively observable responses (r), available to the therapist only by inference, played the major role in Rank's theorizing. Emotions and thoughts were the crucial determinants and controllers of human behavior. Behavior was directed from within. To Rank, humans were not mechanisms. They were more like the flame of a candle than an automobile engine. They had an active relationship with their environment and did not merely react to the events that impinged upon them. He believed people *chose* both the events to which they responded and the responses they would make; they created and modified their environment to serve their purposes and desires.

Man enters this world, Rank held, with a number of response potentialities. There are appetites or impulses such as hunger, sex, and thirst. There are emotional responses such as fear, guilt, and love. All these response potentialities must find expression in behavior, but there is nothing innately healthy or unhealthy about them. It is the way they are expressed in behavior that is judged to be good or bad. Thus, when one is angry, he may strike someone, walk away, swear, or chop wood to express the anger. The anger response is assumed to be the same in all people, but the manner in which they learn to express it may be very different. Through learning, an individual comes to express his response potentialities in relationship to his environment.

Rank developed a volitional psychology. It is man's awareness of himself and his surroundings that is of crucial importance, since this permits man to make choices. Again, the angry person may choose what responses to use to express his anger in a fashion appropriate to the situational events occurring at the time. This active, choice-making characteristic of human behavior was of central importance to Rank and led to his concept of *will*.

Rank conceived of adjustment as a dynamic equilibrium constantly shifting as new experiences occurred. Thus, specific habits or behavior patterns were not the key to healthy development. Rather, effectiveness in solving new adjustment problems as they arose was the key to a happy life. This led him to emphasize that the focus of analysis was behavior as it occurred in the present rather than its historical antecedents. Each new situation represented a new adjustment problem for the individual and would reveal more clearly than any historical study the individual's habitual patterns of behavior in all their effectiveness and ineffectiveness.

THE NORMAL COURSE OF BEHAVIOR DEVELOPMENT

Innate Characteristics of Normal Development

Rank proposed that infants entered the world with a basic set of responses or response tendencies. One group of these Rank called *impulses*. The term referred to physiological responses which in turn led to further behavior. These included such response patterns as hunger, sex, and thirst (biological drives) which instigated the person to respond. However, the kinds of responses to which they led were highly varied and determined by learning. These primary response events (impulses) caused people to behave, but learning determined how they behaved. These impulses could not be judged as good or evil, but the responses required to implement them could.

Rank sometimes used the term "impulse" to refer to a pair of conflicting, innate responses as well. Every impulse "implies an inherent opposite impulse" (1945, p. 113). He observed that humans sometimes behaved in an independent, assertive, confident, self-determining, and individualistic way; at other times they responded in a dependent, conforming, submissive, and helpless way. These two patterns seemed universal to him, and he inferred that they must be innate response patterns. At first he proposed that the conflicting patterns of dependence or submissiveness—the effortless existence in the mother's womb—and independence or individualistic behavior—the biological separation from the mother—originated from the *trauma of birth*. Later, he seemed to consider birth as symbolic of the crucial conflict in relationships with other people without considering it as the source of the difficulty.

A second group of innate responses were emotions or affects. He used the term *affect* for negative responses such as fear, guilt, and anger. Fear and guilt, in particular, were crucial affective responses in his theories. Although proposing that fear was an innate response, he believed it could become associated with any set of situational events. At times, he seemed to think of fear as a chronic subjective state, but more frequently he seemed to consider it to be a response that occurred under certain conditions. He believed fear generally functioned to restrict or inhibit behavior, that it led to avoidance behavior, but that it might also serve the useful purpose of instigating productive instrumental responses. Rank used the term *emotion* to refer to friendly, loving, affectionate emotional responses. He seemed to view them as important ingredients in healthy behavior and considered them to be in direct conflict with the fearful, angry affective responses. *Consciousness* or *awareness* was another crucial innate characteristic in Rank's position, the importance of which will become apparent when learned behavior is discussed.

Each individual comes into the world with the basic conflicting patterns of dependence or submission and independence or self-determination. Birth symbolizes these conflicting responses since it represents leaving the comfort and security of effortless adjustment where one is completely dependent on another and entering a life in which adjustment requires a more personal effort because one is a separate individual and responsible for one's own acts. The response sequences of hunger-eating or thirst-drinking become part of these patterns, and thus become related to the basic conflict; they do not cause it. Rank seemed to suggest that all subsequent behavior is a manifestation of the basic conflict.

Learned Characteristics of Normal Development

Rank viewed the course of learning as deriving from the innate condition of response conflict. People differ in the responses they learn as a means of controlling or resolving the basic conflict. Thus, *what one learns determines whether one develops a healthy or pathological adjustment.* Another aspect of Rank's notion of innate conflict was that behavior was always in a dynamic balance and this balance might change as one or another part of the conflict changed, that is, became stronger or weaker. Adjustment was not something retained once achieved but had to be sought continually, since the response sequences had to alter as the balance between the basic conflicting responses changed. For this reason, habitual response patterns developed, which served, with varying degrees of effectiveness, the purpose of achieving a balance between opposing reactions and allowing all such reactions to find expression. Thus, adjustment mechanisms or habitual patterns of response were fundamentally good and necessary in human behavior.

As a consequence of the innate patterns of independence and dependence,[2] two further contradictory patterns of behavior begin to develop. On the one hand, the individual begins to behave in an assertive, self-directing, individualistic, self-centered manner—doing what he wants to, when he wants to, as he wants to. When self-assertive patterns of behavior begin to predominate, the innate conflict becomes unbalanced, for one aspect is being more fully expressed than the other. *Fear* results. The individual becomes fearful of being isolated from others, of being alone, of being rejected because he is different from others, of losing love, of failing at being successfully self-directing. Rank called this *life fear,* literally meaning that one is afraid to live his own life. In addition, *guilt* results, since in being independent the individual is inevitably rejecting others. At times, Rank seemed to imply that these emotional responses were automatic consequences of independent behavior, and did not depend upon the situational consequences that followed. In his discussion of guilt, however, he also implied that guilt might develop as a consequence of the reactions of others toward the behavior of the individual, that is, guilt might result from disapproval by others or from self-disapproval.

2 The terms independence and dependence will be used to refer to the basic conflicting impulses, but the reader should be aware that Rank's description of the conflict was somewhat broader than these terms frequently connote.

The latter interpretation will be used, since it seems the more reasonable.

Fear and guilt tend to lead to termination or avoidance of the independent, individualistic, self-determining responses, and the individual then responds in a dependent, submissive, conforming manner as dictated by the opposite side of the conflict.

Similarly, on the basis of the innate pattern of dependence, the individual begins to behave in a helpless, conforming, submissive way. The individual seeks the effortless comfort and security produced by having someone else care for and take responsibility for him. This causes the basic conflict to become unbalanced, with fear and guilt resulting. The individual becomes fearful of losing his individuality, of being dominated and overwhelmed by his parents, or a larger social group and thereby becoming completely helpless. Rank called this *death fear*, literally fear of the death of one's individuality. The fear tends to terminate or lead to avoidance of the dependent behavior and to elicit independent, self-reliant behavior.

Rank proposed that all behavior, regardless of its kind—or content, as he put it—could be understood within this basic conflict. To Rank it made relatively little difference whether the patient talked about his parents, friends, therapist, or himself; whether he talked about past, current, or future events. The basic conflict would be represented in whatever kind of behavior the patient chose to present, because all behavior developed as a consequence of this conflict. In his proposal that fear could be constructive as well as destructive, Rank was apparently referring to his belief that fear could be followed by approach as well as avoidance responses, and thus could facilitate instrumental behavior as well as interfere with it. Fear seemed to function as a limiting factor, preventing the individual from behaving excessively dependently or independently. His conflict model represented a kind of self-perpetuating system of response sequences which were continually changing to maintain a balance in the expression of conflicting responses. It was in this sense that Rank called his system dynamic.

AWARENESS, ATTENTION, AND THOUGHT. How does the individual reach some mode of adjustment so that he may live with his conflicts in reasonable comfort? He does it through the development of his *will*, perhaps the most crucial concept in Rank's theorizing. Unfortunately, Rank used the concept in at least three different ways, thereby making it difficult to understand, since one is never sure in which sense he was using the term. First, he used it to refer to the general direction of behavior. One may behave in a "positive, constructive, creative" way (will), or in a "negative, rebellious, oppositional" way (counterwill). In this sense, it is very grossly descriptive of broad, sweeping pattern sequences of behavior and has relatively little theoretical utility. Second, he used it to refer to the fact that human behavior occurred in complicated, integrated, self-evaluative, and self-controlling response systems (1945, p. 111). He seemed to be referring to something similar to the concepts of the self of other theorists. Third, Rank used it to refer to functional relationships which develop between emotional responses and symbolic responses or thoughts. These functional relationships appear to be of two types. They may either direct and release or inhibit and control affective responses. It is in the second and third usages that the concept plays an important role in Rank's theorizing.

With the concept of will, Rank emphasized his conception of humans as being purposive—volitional, conscious, choosing, self-determining individuals. The individual himself is "a moving, effective cause" (1945, p. xx). Thus, the person is not the helpless pawn of powerful biologically determined drives on the one hand and situational events on the other. Rather, these events provide the raw data, in a sense, on which the individual bases his choice of a pattern of behavior. It is thoughtfully guided behavior, adequately expressing all emotions and responses (drives) and appropriate to the situational events under which it occurs, which is characteristic of the healthy, creative person.

Apparently Rank was proposing that behavior was not instigated by "will," but by the primary instinctual responses (drives). The crucial characteristic of his concept of will was that of guiding, directing, and integrating behavior. One function was to inhibit and control the primary physiological responses, while another was to select constructive, "creative" responses which would be effective in terminating the primary responses (drives) or affect (fear, guilt). The manner and effectiveness with which this was accomplished were apparently determined by learning. Rank's concept of will involved subjectively observable responses (r), but it excluded affective responses, such as fear, as well as sensory and perceptual responses arising from interoceptive, proprioceptive, and exteroceptive sources. Thus, it would appear that the most accurate translation of this concept is in terms of habitual, complicated patterns of thoughts, which are acquired through learning, combined with the responses of attention or awareness.

THE DEVELOPMENTAL SEQUENCE. How does this come about? As near as we can tell, Rank seemed to view the development as follows: The infant comes into the world as a responding organism, his responses determined largely by innate biological mechanisms. He responds automatically to the people and events around him. The infant's responses are followed by reactions from the environment, the reactions of other people being the most important. For example, the infant's cry of pain may bring mother. Such reactions are situational events which elicit sensory responses in the infant. Vague "connections" begin to develop: infant responses (R) leading to situational events (S) to sensory responses (r) to new infant responses (R).

As maturation proceeds, the infant becomes aware of himself as a separate person. He also begins to use symbols (images or thoughts) to represent his responses and situational events. With the awareness that he is something different than the world around him, the child begins to experiment with manipulating and controlling the external world and other people, particularly the parents. This appears to be the first step in the development of "will," and Rank considered these first efforts negative or resistive: a "not wanting to" or "counterwill." They are manipulative rather than co-operative. Such efforts produce consequences in the environment and the responses of other people which serve further to define the child as a separate person. For example, a child's inability to perform motorically as other children do would be followed by thoughts that he was weak and ineffective at motor skills. In addition, this might be followed by thoughts that others did not like him because of it. On the other hand, if he were unusually skillful motorically, he might develop thoughts that he had fine motoric competence, and perhaps that he was deserving of respect.

Such consequences following from the child's interaction with the people and objects around him provide the basis for the gradual development of habitual patterns of self-identifying and self-evaluative thoughts, which become important antecedents to future responses. Somewhere along the way, these habitual thoughts become independent of circumstances under which they first developed—somewhat like Allport's notion of functional autonomy (1937). This organized pattern of thoughts defining what the individual is, what he can do, how he approves or disapproves of it, and what others are likely to think of it serves the purpose of directing and controlling the individual's physiological, sensory, affective, motoric, and other responses.

Thus, the habitual patterns of self-defining thoughts serve to resolve the innate, conflicting dependence and independence patterns by determining (choosing) behavior patterns which allow for adequate resolution (termination) of all physiological and affective responses in a manner appropriate to the situational events under which they occur. The behavior patterns that follow from this normal course of development have several characteristics. Behavior varies according to the circumstances with which one is confronted. There are a variety of habitual response patterns (mechanisms) for resolving conflicting responses effectively. There is awareness and utilization of new situational events and the responses which follow thereform. The individual discriminates between and among situational events and related responses and thus evaluates them differently. Affective and emotional responses are moderate and occasional, but they run the full range from fear and anger to love. Thought processes are logical and organized. The individual places himself in new situational contexts, seeking new experience, developing new response patterns.

This representation of behavior development is extremely sketchy, and of course innumerable questions remain unanswered. It is, however, all that it was possible to derive from Rank's discursive writings.

THE DEVELOPMENT OF BEHAVIOR DISORDER

Rank proposed a few basic ingredients in behavior disorder. "The sufferings of neurotics are emotional" (1945, p. 1); "all symptoms in the last analysis mean fear" (1945, p. 157); and "on this very conflict, the inability to submit and the inability to put over his will positively, his whole neurosis depends" (1945, p. 16). In other words, when the affective responses (primarily fear and guilt) become too strong, too chronic, or uncontrollable, and when the self-defining and directing patterns of thought are inadequately developed so that affective and other responses are not adequately controlled and directed, neurotic behavior develops.

Fear and Guilt Are Basic

According to Rank, as noted, the affective responses of fear and guilt are a part of every human's experience. Moreover they are useful, since they serve to prevent a person from behaving too dependently or too independently. The typical consequence of fear and guilt is to avoid the response patterns that lead up to such affective responses. Alternate response patterns are likely to occur, which would be relevant to (or satisfy) the opposite side of the basic conflict. Thus, approach-avoidance patterns in relationship to physiological responses and negative affect normally develop in all people. Behavior disorder develops when fear and guilt become excessive and cause the development of extensive avoidance patterns of behavior. It is not just the intensity of fear, but its antecedents ("quality") and what it leads one to do ("direction"), which are important (1945, p. 157). Guilt is as significant as fear in this respect. Rank stated that the inability to assert oneself and direct one's own behavior (will) without subsequent guilt was the real psychological problem.

It seems reasonable to conclude that Rank considered the behavior of other people as the crucial class of situational events antecedent to the development of behavior disorder. Certainly the relationship with the mother was emphasized. The basic dependence-independence conflict also seemed to gain much of its significance from the interpersonal context. The basic conflict leading to disorder occurred between the interpersonal patterns of submitting to others or being dependent, rather than dominating, and exploiting others or being independent. Finally, he proposed that guilt developed in relation to (as a consequence of) the reactions of others. He specifically rejected the notion that guilt or fear was the consequence of basic response patterns such as sex. He believed there was nothing innately good or bad about such events. Rather, the manner in which the individual learned to implement them and the reactions of others toward that behavior were the crucial antecedents of guilt.

To understand behavior disorder, then, one must know the antecedents to the fear—what the neurotic is afraid of—and whether the fear follows independent, self-assertive behavior (life fear) or dependent, submissive, helpless behavior (death fear). In addition, the consequences of fear and guilt must be studied. A great variety of responses is possible. The individual may avoid the fear by withdrawing, inhibiting, or restricting his behavior, or by focusing his attention on the past to avoid the present. On the other hand, he may avoid the fear by fantasy about the future, thus momentarily avoiding uncomfortable events in the present.

Thoughts and Action

Since fear and guilt may lead to the avoidance of any type of response pattern, it follows that neurotics are not people of action. They tend to substitute thoughts for deeds. They think a great deal about themselves and about what they should do, but they tend not to follow their thoughts and plans with constructive action. They struggle with thoughts of what they *ought* and *ought not* to do on the one hand, and what they *want* and *do not want* to do on the other. Frequently this is resolved with thoughts of "I cannot," which are really a distortion of "I will not try." Crucial among the neurotic's habitual thoughts are those "representing an extreme judgment, a condemnation of himself" (1945, p. 193). His self-evaluations are mainly negative. Rank believed that it was not specific acts but the evaluation (thoughts) of them as good or evil which was the source of difficulty. The neurotic "torments" himself; does not "accept" himself; and thus is "fighting" himself.

One important consequence of the development of avoidance behavior patterns may be a "destruction" of the associations in thinking and feeling. Thoughts may have been associated with affective responses, either as antecedents or consequences. In the neurotic, the affective responses continue to occur, but the associated thoughts drop out of the response sequence. It is this phenomenon which Rank believed to be the *unconscious*. He believed the individual's affective responses could not be stopped; they "demanded" expression, but the individual could repress them and not think about them, thereby somewhat reducing his discomfort. He seemed to believe that the particularly troublesome emotional responses were those once thought about but presently ignored or denied (1945, p. 35). Rank strongly rejected the Freudian "psychology of the unconscious" as another of man's attempts to avoid assuming responsibility for his own behavior by attributing his difficulties to events beyond his control.

Symptoms of Disordered Behavior

It is the response patterns of avoidance that represent what are typically called neurotic symptoms. The following are neurotic symptoms which Rank mentioned at various times. The neurotic seems to perceive situations in a personalized way, with little discrimination as to what concerns him and what does not. He tends to overgeneralize his responses, to respond in an "all or none" fashion. He tends to interpret every situation as a total acceptance or rejection of himself. There is typically either an inhibition of overt behavior, a restriction of living, or an aggressive driving to control the circumstances that cause the fear rather than to control one's own responses. The neurotic frequently expresses his inability to do things or cope with situations. However, this "not being able to" is actually "not wanting to," or "fearing" to try. The neurotic does not view himself as responsible for his behavior, because he believes himself to be compelled by inner (r) or outer (S) events over which he has no control. There tends to be a denial of affective responses and the symbols or thoughts associated with them. The neurotic is overwhelmed with negative affect such as anger and guilt. In addition, the neurotic has great difficulty recognizing positive affect such as love. Emotional responses continue to appear because emotions are automatic responses which cannot be completely inhibited, but they are disguised through rationalization and misinterpretation so that their real significance is not evident. Rational, conscious control or direction of behavior is ineffective. Thus, the neurotic may appear to be either impulsive or greatly constricted. The neurotic is excessively introspective and too concerned about himself. He is also excessively critical of himself, thinking that he is little, weak, bad, and worthless. Consequently, the neurotic goes to great pains to conceal this bad evaluation from himself and others, or continually torments himself with the knowledge of his worthlessness. He suffers a severe restriction of action in many realms. He is too concerned about his actions, the potential consequences, and what others will think of him. As a consequence, the evaluation of his behavior by others carries great import. The neurotic is either unable to assert himself with others or is far too impulsive, demanding, and aggressive in his behavior toward them.

Once again, Rank's unsystematic writings have made it impossible to assemble more than a gross outline of a theory of behavior disorder. The basic threads, however, seem to be clear. The behavior of other people appears to be the crucial kind of situational event antecedent to the development of behavior disorder. Behavior disorder develops as a means of terminating and avoiding negative affective responses occurring in relation to such interpersonal relationships. The key to disordered patterns and sequences are the affective responses and the self-referent, self-defining, and self-evaluative thoughts.

THE GOALS OF THERAPY

General Characteristics of the Goals

WHO DETERMINES THE GOALS. Rank did not specify who should determine the goals of therapy. At times he implied that it must be the therapist. For example, he stated that success depended on the proper management of the therapeutic situation and the patient's responses. On the other hand, his primary concern with the development of self-confidence and self-direction in the patient and his specification that it was within the therapeutic situation that this development had to occur, seems to support the notion that it is the patient who determines the objectives of therapy. The most adequate conclusion appears to be that the therapist broadly determines the goals; that is, fear must be reduced and controlled and the self-response system (will) must be strengthened. However, within those several objectives, it would seem that Rank would have expected the patient to choose the specific direction of his development.

ATTRIBUTES OF GOALS. Two generalizations can characterize the goals of therapy from Rank's point of view. The first is represented in his proposal that every personality has within it many potentially constructive responses. Even the most seriously disordered person has some affective responses occurring in his repertoire. One goal of therapy is to identify and capitalize on existing response patterns that are effective and desirable rather than to elicit new responses or extinguish old ones. A second characteristic of Rank's proposals about therapeutic goals is seen in his view that adjustment is continuous and dynamic. One is never "adjusted," but one may develop habits of effective "adjusting." The objective is to help the patient achieve a *method* of continuing adjustment rather than a particular *kind* of adjustment. Thus, therapy focuses, in general, not upon a permanent removal or extinction of pathological response sequences, but upon the development of existing responses by which the individual continually and effectively resolves life problems as they arise.

Rank suggested that the goals of therapy had to be determined "morally" or at least "normatively," although the therapy itself should not involve moral evaluation. By this he meant that the standards and demands of society had to be considered in establishing the goals of therapy. Finally, the primary goals of therapy seem to involve the subjectively observable responses (r) such as feelings and thoughts.

Rank's Goals

Rank saw the chief therapeutic goal as "the acceptance of the self with its individual ego and its volitional and emotional autonomy"

(1945, p. 97). Thoughts about the self should change from being critical and rejecting to approving and accepting. In addition, the patient should come to think of himself as capable of directing his own life, capable of making sound decisions, capable of doing things, and responsible for his behavior. The affective responses related to thoughts about the self should be less negative and more positive.

VARIED AND MODERATE AFFECTIVE RESPONSES The first major goal is to modify affective responses. Both the intensity and frequency of fear and guilt responses must be reduced. The occurrence of positive affective responses such as love must be increased. The patient must learn to behave affectionately and unselfishly toward others as well as to seek to elicit affectionate responses from them. Being able to utilize "the rich state" of all emotions "in small doses" is a guarantee for "remaining well and being happy" (1945, p. 165).

CONSCIOUS CONTROL OF BEHAVIOR. The second major goal is for the patient to become able to think about himself and his behavior in relationship to the world around him (situational events) without associated fear and guilt responses. When this "self-acceptance" occurs, "then self and ideal coincide." He must stop repressing, denying, and mislabeling his emotions, because only if he does can he deal with them effectively (1945, p. 35). One important aspect of this awareness and acceptance of one's own behavior is that one plans, makes decisions, chooses courses of action, and thinks of one's self as a self-determining individual, guided from within by thoughts (r) rather than from without by situational events (S) and the opinions of others (positive will).

When fear and guilt are reduced, and when self-directing thoughts are occurring, the overt responses that occur will be instrumental rather than avoidant. The individual will attempt to "create," through his interaction with his environment, the most desirable kind of environment for himself. The actions and statements of other people will produce less fear and guilt, and the individual will notice and accept differences in other people as well as in himself. He will respond more specifically and discriminatively to situational events, and he will be less self-conscious or introspective about his own behavior. He will be able to tell others of his own beliefs, accomplishments, and feelings without fear or guilt following. In Rank's eyes, man needed some kind of belief to be happy, and Rank's psychotherapy attempted to give man faith in himself, the most desirable of all beliefs.

CONDITIONS FOR PRODUCING BEHAVIOR CHANGE

Principles by Which Behavior Change Occurs

It has been impossible to find a clear statement of any principles of learning in Rank's writing. At intervals, however, he mentioned some characteristics of learning, and these have been abstracted and brought together at this point. It appears that emotion plays an important role in learning. Implicit in Rank's writing is the notion that fear and guilt lead to avoidance learning, but he failed to specify how this occurs. In addition, the occurrence of emotions in the therapy interview he considered to be a necessary condition for therapeutic change. A second characteristic of the learning situation seems to be that the behavior to be changed has to occur in the learning setting. The therapy interview is an "experience in living," not just a "discussion of living." Thus, it would appear that at least simple contiguity is a necessity for learning. Finally, the therapist's behavior is a necessary situational event antecedent to change. The internal instigators of behavior (impulses and the dependence-independence conflict) are innate and therefore not subject to learning. However, the behaviors by which the innate drives are expressed are learned, and subject to modification.

Therapy Techniques: Patient Behaviors

PRECONDITIONS FOR THERAPY. The only clear precondition for therapy which Rank specified was that the patient had to want some of his response patterns modified and had to have some confidence in the therapeutic procedure as a way of achieving the desired change. Rank apparently did not mean that the patient at the outset had to want to produce the change himself. Initially, he might place the responsibility on the therapist. Regardless of who was to be held responsible for producing the change, the patient had to want some aspect of his behavior changed badly enough to exert the necessary effort to initiate change and had to be willing to attempt to meet the therapeutic conditions. Behavior change could not take place in therapy without the patient's consent and co-operation.

BEHAVIORS REQUIRED OF THE PATIENT. There were two general propositions in Rank's approach to therapy: first, behavior to be modified must occur in the therapy situation (it is behavior as it is presently occurring that is crucial); and second, the assumption by the patient of responsibility for his own behavior is a necessary condition for therapeutic change.

The patient must *respond actively* during the interview if change is to occur. Responses cannot be changed unless they occur. It makes no real difference where the patient originally learned the responses, whether from unkind parents or unreasonable peers. Regardless of the conditions that resulted in the learning of a response pattern, the responses can be modified in the therapeutic relationship if they occur. The patient reacts in the therapy situation with all his old patterns, particularly those relevant to an interpersonal setting. Fears, guilt, love, denials, and distortions will occur in the relationship with the therapist if the patient will respond to him. The key to change is that the therapy situation is a new situation and therefore can result in new learning.

The patient should attend to and talk openly to the therapist about his responses as they occur in the therapy hour. However, the patient should consider such responses in terms of the therapist not as a person but as a representative of people in general. The patient should be led to discuss those behaviors of which he is proud, ashamed, and fearful, because as he does so the associated affective responses will occur and become susceptible to modification. Rank called this the *confessional* aspect of therapy, emphasizing that the patient was really confessing to himself. In other words, the patient should strive continually to avoid self-deception and self-rejection. The patient should talk frankly about his emotional responses and the thoughts associated with them as they occur during the interview, so as to bring them under control. This is important, for it is not only a means by which he becomes increasingly aware of the interpersonal events, but it also represents his taking the responsibility—a kind of "self-guidance" (1945, p. 23).

Rank emphasized the verbalization of conscious emotion because he believed that a patient was typically aware of most of his current responses. If he was not aware of some, he could quickly become aware of them by talking about his current behavior. Rank asserted it was "astonishing how much the patient knows and how relatively little is unconscious" if he were not given "this convenient excuse for refusing responsibility" (1945, p. 24). Discussion of dreams and their symbols could be used as an indirect way of discussing responses which were already conscious in another form. It was important that the patient discuss his affective and emotional responses as they occurred in the therapy relationship, because in this way they became associated with controlling thoughts (became conscious).

The patient *must take the responsibility* for changing himself! Because the central problem is one of "will," or becoming a self-confident, self-directed individual, the therapeutic endeavor will not be effective if the therapist accepts the responsibility for change. The desired behaviors must begin to occur during therapy if they are to be learned. Although he may be unable to do so in the early stages of therapy, the patient should strive consistently for self-direction, and assume responsibility for changing himself as soon as possible. This means the patient should focus his attention on his own responses and seek to understand and control them. He should stop thinking "I cannot," "it is beyond my control," and "others will not let me," and should assume the attitude "I can" and "I will." Rank recognized that this dictum of responsibility was a very difficult one for some patients and commented that some might not be able to accept his type of therapy because it demanded so much of them.

Therapy Techniques: Therapist Behaviors

THERE IS NO TECHNIQUE. Rank proposed that successful therapy depended entirely upon the proper management of the therapeutic situation itself and on the guiding of the individual reactions of the patient within the therapeutic hour. Even so, he doubted that there could be any generally applicable technique because of the nature of human behavior. He rejected "technical rules" which could be applied "ideologically" (1945, p. 105). One can know what to do only in a general way. In a sense, one must develop a new technique with each patient. Clearly, Rank belonged to that school of thought which advocates the therapist having no advance plan of action, but rather deciding as treatment proceeds what he will do.

Not only is there no formal technique, but neither is it possible to train practitioners in the conduct of psychotherapy through traditional methods of teaching. The therapist must use his "own knowledge," gained through his "own personal experience" (1945, p. 150). Apparently, one learns therapy by doing it. The whole purpose of

Rank's therapy is to bring the patient to self-help, in contrast to the analytic methods which Rank believed forced the patient to accept help from another. Even though Rank insisted there could be no technique, there are "suggestions" scattered through his writings about how to do therapy. We have organized them in a more systematic fashion, as the best indication of his ideas of technique. It will become apparent that he emphasized the present, not the past; behavior, not knowledge of behavior; and self-development, not instruction, guidance, or treatment "by the doctor."

NECESSARY KNOWLEDGE OF BEHAVIOR DISORDER. Rank emphasized that it was the knowledge of the behavioral sequences as they occurred *in the present* which was important. He did not believe that knowledge of the conditions under which they developed was particularly useful in understanding their current nature or in doing effective therapy. A discussion of past events might sometimes be helpful merely as a setting in which the current disordered patterns could become apparent, but he argued that historic-causal explanation did not promote behavior changes, for it enabled the patient to continue to deny responsibility for his *present* behavior. Similarly investigation of the *development* of responses was appropriate only if its purpose was to contribute to a knowledge of the current behavior. The major requirement for the therapist is a knowledge of the disordered response sequences as they occur and the ways in which they relate to other continuing behaviors. For the patient, a search for "actual truth" in relation to the past or even the present is dubious because the only historical document available is memory. Rank believed the individual often lived better with his conception of the past than in the knowledge of actual fact.

THERAPIST BEHAVIOR. The therapist represents the situational condition by which therapeutic change may be accomplished. Although Rank did not pursue the issue in detail, his position implied that the behaviors of other people in response to the individual were the crucial factors in the development of the individual's troublesome behaviors—fear, guilt, and self-derogatory thoughts. It follows, then, that other interpersonal events might be expected to be most effective in eliciting such response sequences anew and subjecting them to change. Rank concluded that this was the essential ingredient in psychotherapy; the only means of "healing" which psychotherapy had learned to use was another human being. He indicated there was probably a special type of personality that would be ideal for a particular therapist, but he failed to elaborate this point. His emphasis on the importance of the interpersonal relationship between patient and therapist is one of Rank's distinctive and important contributions. Rank's second reason for attributing a central role to the relationship stemmed from his belief that behavior change could be accomplished only by dealing with the patient's responses as they occurred in the present. But it is also primarily the affective responses which must be modified, and Rank proposed that interpersonal events were particularly effective in eliciting and modifying them.

The therapist has three objectives. *First,* he must elicit emotional responses. *Second,* he must facilitate the patient's awareness of the emotional responses and the development of thoughts which will control and channel the emotional responses in a fashion appropriate to other situational events and responses. *Third,* he must facilitate the development of assertive, self-reliant, independent response sequences in the patient without correlated negative emotional responses. What therapist behaviors may serve as appropriate events for achieving each of the objectives? Unfortunately, Rank was never very specific on this point. He typically wrote about the therapist in terms of the *effects* the therapist should attempt to produce rather than describing the therapist *responses* which would achieve the desired effects. One clear principle of therapist behavior did appear in Rank's discussion of the therapeutic relationship: The therapist does not punish (criticize, evaluate, derogate) undesirable responses to get rid of them. Rather, Rank emphasized the reinforcement (encouragement, development) of alternative desirable response patterns as the therapist's guiding rule.

EMOTIONAL RESPONSES. These are elicited by interpersonal behaviors. Thus, the therapist's first task is to create a significant personal relationship between himself and the patient. Emotional responses inevitably will occur because of the interpersonal situation; the relationship produces an "actual feeling experience." Moreover, these emotional responses are always "true" no matter how much the patient may seek to conceal them or to deny their existence. The therapeutic task is "to show him how he tries to destroy the connections" with these responses in relation to the therapist, just as he does in relation to others (1945, p. 37). Rank's emphasis on "direct experiencing"—the occurrence of feeling together with awareness of that feeling—was a reaction, in part, to what he believed to be a Freudian overemphasis on thoughts and talking.

What does the therapist do? He should refrain from any kind of moral evaluation. He should not take the part of the authority at any time. In every way possible, he should share with, encourage, or permit the patient to take the lead in the interview. He should prevent the patient from developing excessively intense affectionate responses toward himself. (He believed psychoanalytic transference problems were created because of the authoritarian, "love giving" role the therapist played.) All of these expressed Rank's belief that the locus of responsibility and evaluation had to be in the patient.

The patient is likely to react automatically to the therapist with emotional responses because of the interpersonal situation. However, to facilitate the eliciting of emotional responses from the patient in the situational context basic to the disorder (the dependence-independence conflict), Rank devised his *end setting technique.* The therapist, he held, in consultation with the patient, establishes a tentative date for termination of treatment. This date may be altered as therapy progresses. The reference point in time makes concrete for the patient the fact that some day he has to give up the therapist and become self-reliant. Fear of separation is a basic problem of man. By setting a termination date, Rank was attempting to use the issue of separation from the therapist to generate the broader problem of self-direction or dependence. The impending termination of therapy arouses in the patient emotional responses surrounding the central conflict. The first emotional responses are likely to be negative, because the patient first projects upon the therapist the most disturbing part of the basic conflict, the counterwill, and then reacts to that aspect of the therapist. Rank believed that proper handling of the patient's reaction to the impending termination of therapy would lead to a final resolution of the basic conflict.

AWARENESS AND CONTROL OF EMOTIONAL RESPONSES. This crucial objective is achieved by causing the patient to attend to and talk about the responses as they are occurring. This "permits living and understanding to become one" (1945, p. 26). It appears that if the verbal responses are focused on the emotional responses *at the time they occur,* they will become connected in such a fashion that the verbal responses can acquire a controlling function. Thus, the "unconscious" becomes "conscious."

It is the patient's verbalization rather than the therapist's explanations or interpretations which are therapeutic. The process is not a "making conscious" but a "becoming conscious." Thus, the therapist's verbalizations should be aimed at stimulating the patient to talk further about the emotional responses occurring rather than at presenting the patient with a conclusion that might terminate such talk. At first, the therapist's statements should not focus on the situational events producing the responses or toward which the responses are directed—the mother, brother, or therapist—(Rank called this *content*), but upon the responses themselves, particularly the emotional responses and the sequence in which they occur (Rank called this *form*). The therapeutic interview has the characteristics of restricting action and eliciting emotions. Thus it is "in essence a learning to feel," to experience emotion and to control it (1945, p. 156).

ASSERTIVE, SELF-RELIANT RESPONSES. All signs of self-direction should be encouraged. Rank believed the patient came to therapy with one side of the basic dependence-independence conflict denied. Therefore, by his statements, the therapist attempts to stimulate the patient to talk about the denied aspect of the conflict so as to bring about a reevaluation of this "condemned" side of the personality. The associated negative emotional responses should be verbalized and then reduced so that the behavior could be brought under thoughtful, conscious control. In this regard Rank suggested the proposition that the stronger the fear and avoidance pattern observed, the stronger would be the attraction toward that which was feared or avoided—the opposing impulse (1945, p. 157).

Rank's position concerning resistance is pertinent here. To him the Freudian view of resistance was a sterile one, actually representing the analyst's resentment that the patient would not co-operate, that he was not doing what he was "supposed" to be doing. Rank suggested that resistance might be the first sign of progress, because it represented response sequences through which the patient exercised some degree of independence, that is, manifested his will.

The therapist should encourage responses that indicate the patient is accepting the responsibility for becoming well. Responses that indicate the patient is doing things because he wants to, or because he believes them right rather than because he is forced to, should be confirmed. Rank recognized that patients might not like to assume too much responsibility for their own "cure."

Self-assertive behavior toward the therapist should be responded to favorably by the therapist rather than considered an interference or "resistance." The end setting technique establishes a deadline which keeps the patient constantly aware that at some definite time he can no longer lean on the therapist. This tends to stimulate the patient toward self-direction as the deadline approaches, behavior which the therapist can then encourage.

It is important to note that Rank believed therapeutic behavior change did not necessarily require some change in the patient's thoughts ("a new understanding"). The actual development of the appropriate response patterns in relationship to the therapist ("freeing through experience") is the crucial occurrence. The development of thoughts accurately characterizing what is happening (insight) may not be essential, although ideally it is apparently better if conscious control does develop.

TECHNIQUES REJECTED. Rank continually contrasted his position to Freudian psychoanalysis, rejecting a number of the classical techniques. He felt the technique of free association required the patient to completely abandon any responsibility for self-direction (will), and thereby worked in direct opposition to a major goal of therapy. Patients find free association difficult, he believed, because they innately resist giving up their self-direction (will). Great *attention to content* was rejected by Rank. He apparently did not feel there were any particular topics that patient and therapist should discuss. Rather, any topics that represented the basic independence-dependence conflict and brought forth the troublesome affective responses were satisfactory to work with. The disordered behavior could be represented in discussions about relationships with parents, with peers, or with the therapist, for example. *Tracing the historical antecedents* to the behavior disorder was rejected by Rank unless it was used as a way of representing the basic conflict. Memory of historical events was highly inaccurate. Discussion of the past permitted the patient to avoid attending to the difficulties in the present. By blaming historical antecedents, for example, criticizing the parents for their child-rearing, the patient might avoid responsibility for his current behavior. The disordered responses could be identified as they presently operated and be modified in present situations without attention to the past. Rank believed much time was frequently wasted by analysts in the belief there was much "new material" which had not yet been worked through. Finally, *insight* or thoughtful understanding was considered valuable only if discovered by the patient after observing his own responses. Knowledge or insight provided by the therapist was not important to him. Thus, explanation or interpretation would appear to be undesirable techniques.

SEQUENCE OF CHANGE. The first step in therapy is to reduce the fear to a controllable level. Since fear is the original motive for seeking help in therapy, however, the fear should not be reduced completely in the early stages of therapy or the force driving the patient forward out of the neurosis may be lost.

Once the fear is under control the patient should be led to experience a full range of affective responses during the therapy hour. As the responses occur, they should be discussed so that the patient becomes aware of them and the circumstances under which they occur. Any fear responses associated with the occurrence of other affective responses should be extinguished. This seems to be what Rank meant when he referred to accepting one's feelings as a part of oneself. Once the full range of affective responses occurs, the individual becomes aware of them, verbal responses become associated with them, and their control (not denial) of emotional responses will be a natural consequence.

It is particularly important that emotional reactions to other people (the therapist) come to be acceptable and controllable. As more varied but controllable emotional responsiveness develops, the patient should be led through verbalization to an explicit acknowledgment of the response sequences previously denied, so that their occurrence no longer elicits fear. As this re-evaluation takes place and the fear is extinguished, conflicting self-reactions and other conflicting response sequences will begin to disappear. As such responses are reduced, the patient should be helped to be more sensitive to situational events, to react to them more in terms of their characteristics than of his own dynamics; discrimination should be encouraged.

As the fear and conflicts are reduced and come under more conscious control, the individual should be encouraged to become more confident of his own evaluative responses, both toward his own behavior and toward situational events. This will lead to his overt actions occurring more confidently with less self-doubt and less self-consciousness, and he will be more willing to accept responsibility for the consequences of his own behavior. The termination of therapy symbolizes the patient's decision to chart his own course. Thus, the final goal of therapy is a "new birth," a new life in which the patient discards the therapist and assumes complete authority and responsibility for continually directing and modifying his own behavior.

Transfer of Behavior

Rank indicated that it was crucial that patients become enabled to relinquish therapy and accept reality, but he did not say how this was to be accomplished. Apparently working through the end setting process was thought to contribute to the objective. He did say that during the last stages of therapy he might postpone, omit, lengthen, shorten, or alter the treatment hour as a means of helping the patient "adapt to reality." Actually Rank seemed to assume that the transfer of behavioral changes outside of therapy would occur spontaneously. This followed from Rank's attitude that the patient's reactions toward reality depended entirely on the patient's acceptance and control of his own behavior. The central therapeutic objective was to produce changes in the patient's subjective responses ("adjust him to himself"). If this were accomplished, more effective behavior outside the therapy setting "follows thereupon spontaneously without further effort" (1945, p. 266).

THEORY VERIFICATION AND EVALUATION
OF BEHAVIOR CHANGE

Appraisal of Behavior Change

Rank said virtually nothing about how to evaluate whether desirable changes had occurred in a patient. It would appear to follow, since Rank proposed to make the patient his own healer, that the patient is the person who would evaluate whether appropriate changes had occurred. If the patient is to be the judge, then the patient's report of his subjective observations of change would become the process by which the therapist became informed.

Verification of Therapy Theory

As far as evaluation and validation of the propositions of "will therapy" is concerned, Rank made it very clear that he believed therapeutic procedures could be verified only through clinical experience and not through "scientific" justification. He would appear to have believed that his notions concerning human behavior in therapy were logically compelling or verifiable only through clinical observation.

COMMENTS

Otto Rank was undoubtedly a sensitive observer of human behavior, but he apparently knew little about formal theory building. In his writings, he jumped from point to point, assumption to assumption, in a casual fashion with no apparent realization of the great theoretical gaps that remained. The writers' attempt to make an orderly presentation of Rank's ideas in this chapter should not mislead the reader into believing Rank himself was orderly and systematic. In fact, Rank's position is hardly a system at all. It is more in the nature of a point of view, with a few major ideas loosely connected. His major concepts are loosely defined and carelessly used. Many important issues are completely ignored or only briefly commented upon. Despite the lack of any reasonably adequate system, however, his work is included here because some of his ideas were unique at the time, influential, and in our judgment, important.

Rank's emphasis on affective responses is important. Similarly, his de-emphasis of instinctual urges, in contrast to Freud, represented a change in emphasis of kinds of concepts. He considered verbal symbolic responses important, but he considered affective responses more crucial for therapeutic concern. Conscious, thoughtful control of behavior is desirable but not always essential for therapeutic change. He warned that the therapist had to be careful to avoid producing changes in the patient's thoughts and speech unless these changes became related to other aspects of the patient's behavior, especially the emotional patterns. Once again, Rank criticized Freud's therapy in this regard. At the time, his emphasis on independent and dependent behavior patterns was unique. With his concepts of will and counterwill, life fear and death fear, birth trauma, and end setting, he focused attention upon an important aspect of human behavior. Some people do have difficulty making decisions, are afraid to try new things, are unwilling to oppose the opinions of others, are afraid and unable to assume responsibility for themselves, and are dependent. Similarly, some people do rebel against authority, make excessive demands that their rights and wishes always be observed, and reject the rules and demands of the world around them. Rank saw the struggle to balance these two ways of behaving toward others and toward oneself as the crucial adjustment problem for humans, and most of his concepts reflected this assumption. He was deeply concerned with people's difficulty in forming close relationships with other humans without submitting or dominating—in his terms, "separation" and "union." This is a concern perhaps even more prevalent in our current society.

His deep concern with this one aspect of human behavior, however, apparently led to certain conceptual difficulties. Most importantly, it led him to overgeneralize and to assume that all human difficulties were of this form. His concepts dealt primarily with subjectively observable responses (r). Although he seemed to consider objectively observable responses (R) and situational events (S) important, they played a minor role in his conceptions. Thus, the realm of events to which his concepts referred seemed to be unfortunately restricted. Second, many of his concepts were not clearly defined, and some were used with several meanings, as exemplified by the discussion of will and counterwill. Third, the majority of his major concepts were molar, referring to a great amount and variety of behavior over a long period of time. Some, such as feelings of fear and guilt which held a very prominent place in his thinking, were more restricted. However, his concepts of will, counterwill, life and death fears, and birth trauma were involved, complicated, and highly inclusive concepts, which were only poorly related to lower-order concepts and to observable events. Finally, his belief in the universality of the dependence-independence problem apparently led him to assume biologically innate "impulses," drives, or motives toward each of these patterns of behavior. This concept of impulse seemed to be defined, however, by its *consequences,* and which pattern prevailed at a given time seemed dependent on the evaluative responses of others toward the behavior as well as the person's own evaluative responses. Thus, the assumption of an innate impulse had little, if any, utility in his theorizing. It seems to have been an unnecessary concept.

Perhaps Rank's most important contribution was his emphasis on behavior as it occurs in the present. He seemed to believe that behavior could be acquired under almost any arrangement of conditions and that what developed was dependent on this learning. However, one does not need to know the conditions under which the original learning occurred to modify such learnings. One does need to recog-

nize the behavior as it occurs in the present and to arrange the necessary learning conditions to bring about modification. This position
is in accord with current learning theory, which suggests that responses
must occur in reasonably close temporal and spatial contiguity to the
events that might modify them, if change is to occur. A related emphasis was on the behavior of other people as a powerful modifying
influence. He believed this to be the key to the effectiveness of therapy.
In a sense, Rank and Adler presented the first "interpersonal" systems
of therapy.

His emphasis on behavior disorder as a consequence of learning,
particularly avoidance learning, also seems to coincide with some
current psychological literature. His use of a conflict model of
pathology is also consistent with much current thinking. Unfortunately, his view of behavior pathology seems to be highly restricted,
based as it is on only one type of conflict. In addition, he never
spelled out the circumstances under which disorder developed.

Related to his emphasis on the present was his assumption that
humans were in active relationship with the world. Not only were
they modified by but also they modified the events around them, thus
controlling to some extent what happened to them. It followed from
this that psychotherapy should produce a *method* of adjustment, not
a *kind* of adjustment. The most effective method of adjustment he
believed to be self-conscious self-direction, without persistently intense
affect.

Unfortunately, the grossness and looseness of Rank's theorizing was
apparent once again in his propositions. He was not at all precise
about the types of relationships that could develop among his concepts or the conditions under which such relationships would develop.
Thus, he asserted the importance of fear and guilt responses in
behavior pathology, but he did not specify whether these responses
automatically occurred under given circumstances or whether they
were learned. He placed great emphasis on learning as the source of
behavior disorder and healthy adjustment but never dealt with how
learning came about. He referred to the importance of situational
events but ignored the how and why of their effects on behavior. He
emphasized that the patient had to assume responsibility for his own
cure. In fact it was precisely the assumption of that responsibility
that was an important part of the cure. However, he never specified
in any precise way how this was to result. He referred to his "end
setting technique," but careful explication of the propositions govern-

ing its effectiveness was absent. There was almost no apparent effort to relate his notions to those of others except psychoanalytic theorists. Some of Rank's ideas seem very important and deserve careful study. As a system, however, his point of view remains gross and undeveloped, and a great deal of work would be necessary to develop it into a reasonably comprehensive system.

Chapter 11

The "Client-Centered" Psycho-
therapy of Carl Rogers

The ideas of Carl Rogers have proven to be both controversial and influential. These are complimentary things to say about a theoretical position. His point of view has been controversial partly because his presentation has been clear enough to provide a reference point against which other theorists could direct their arguments. It has been influential because many people have tried to follow his suggestions for the conduct of therapy.

Rogers' conceptions have been characterized by constant change and revision. His initial volume concerning individual verbal psychotherapy, *Counseling and Psychotherapy*, appeared in 1942. His second treatment, *Client-Centered Therapy* (1951), reported upon a number of important changes in his position, representing almost a decade of consistent work. A third relatively complete statement of his theoretical position, *A Theory of Therapy, Personality, and Interpersonal*

Relationships, as Developed in the Client-Centered Framework, was published almost another decade later (1959) and represented still further changes, major in scope.

In all three presentations Rogers has sought consistently to avoid treating the postulates he has developed as statements of fact, and he has warned others against committing this frequent error. He has openly expressed distress over the manner in which "small-caliber minds" turn what is frankly offered as theory into "a dogma of truth." He considers theory "a fallible, changing attempt to construct a network of gossamer threads which will contain the solid facts" and "a stimulus to further creative thinking" (1959, p. 191). He notes that some "insecure disciples" translated Freud's proposals into "iron chains of dogma" to the detriment of dynamic psychology. Some of Rogers' own followers seem to have committed this same error. Therefore, Rogers has stressed the tentative status of his formulations, the necessity for their revision and improvement, and the desirability of submitting them to empirical and experimental test. Rogers is a significant theorist because he has emphasized therapy as an orderly process which must be scientifically investigated and has given an impetus to empirical research in psychotherapy. Both have been contributions of tremendous import, quite independent of his theoretical views.

BIOGRAPHICAL INFORMATION

Carl Rogers began his life in the state of Illinois as a middle child in a large closely knit family. Hard work and an almost fundamentalist Protestant Christianity were strong family values. The family moved to a farm, and as an adolescent he became interested in scientific agriculture, followed by a later interest in the physical and biological sciences at the University of Wisconsin. Unable to adopt his family's conservative religious beliefs, Rogers explored a more liberal religious view at Union Theological Seminary. Later, he enrolled as a graduate student at Teachers College, Columbia University, where he was stimulated by Kilpatrick's presentation of John Dewey's pragmatism and became acquainted with clinical psychology through Leta S. Hollingsworth's "warmly human and common sense" approach to the study of behavior. He was exposed to a Freudian orientation during his internship, and received a Ph.D. in Clinical Psychology from Columbia in 1931.

For twelve years he was a staff psychologist at a community child guidance clinic in Rochester, New York. The staff was eclectic, and clinical experience was the knowledge base for their work. It is impressive that during this period Rogers wrote his first book, *The Clinical Treatment of the Problem Child* (1939). Careful thought and reflection is necessary for systematic analysis, but it consumes time which is seldom available in a service setting.

Here, also, Rogers became familiar with the "controversial therapeutic views" of Otto Rank and the Philadelphia group of social workers, psychologists, and psychiatrists whom Rank had influenced. The writings of Taft, Allen, and Robinson made a particular impression upon him. Apparently, Rank's thinking closely paralleled his own, and it exerted a strong influence upon his later formulations.

In 1940 Rogers moved to Ohio State University. There he discovered that graduate students were unwilling to accept his therapy ideas on the basis of his clinical experience alone. It was the influence of his "intellectually curious, often theoretically oriented" graduate students at Ohio State and later at the University of Chicago, where he moved in 1945,[1] that stimulated Rogers to more careful theoretic formulation and research investigation, both of which have characterized his work since. In fact, his students contributed a number of important ideas to his theories.

His continuing clinical experience, however, remained the most important influence on his theories. Since 1928, he reports having spent an average of 15 to 20 hours per week in conducting psychotherapy, excluding vacation periods, and thus he must have spent 20,000 hours in therapy interviews in the last three decades. Rogers certainly seems to be qualified, by virtue of his experience in therapy, teaching, and research, to write authoritatively about psychotherapy.

CENTRAL THEMES

Rogers has developed a subjectivistic or phenomenological point of view. A patient's behavior can be understood only from the patient's observational vantage point (the subjective observer), and this is a necessary condition for effective therapy. Since his theories are based primarily on his therapeutic observations, it is not surprising to

[1] Since 1957, Rogers has been professor of psychology and psychiatry at the University of Wisconsin.

discover that all his concepts and propositions refer to subjectively observable responses (r). Because he has minimized the vantage point of the objective observer except for research purposes, he excludes concepts involving situational events (S) and objectively observable responses (R). He does not ignore the importance of these events, but they are represented by the subjectively observable responses (r) that intervene between them, that is, by the individual's subjective responses to them. The "perception" of events, rather than the events themselves, is crucial in determining how a person responds.

The concepts he presents emphasize sensory and visceral responses, affective or emotional responses, awareness, attending, and perceptual responses, and thoughts, particularly evaluative thoughts. Rogers' point of view is most frequently thought of in terms of its emphasis on affective responses, on the "irrational" aspects of behavior. Perhaps even more important and less well recognized is his major emphasis on the phenomena of human awareness and symbolic responses and their function in the development of effective human behavior, of the "rational" aspects of behavior. He speaks of that special human characteristic "the gift of a free and undistorted awareness," which produces "not a beast who must be controlled" but a person capable of achieving "a balanced, realistic, self-enhancing, other-enhancing behavior" (1961, p. 105).

The healthy person is aware of all his behavior, and in any given situation he consciously chooses response patterns that are most instrumental in effectively achieving the consequences he seeks. Since the individual is aware and actively chooses among available courses, he must continually make judgments. These evaluative judgments are the antecedents to the behaviors he chooses. Others evaluate him also, a fact of considerable importance.

A second characteristic of Rogers' position is a faith, a fundamental conviction, about the nature of man which is both the driving force of his therapy and a crucial assumption underlying his theories. It is "one of the most revolutionary concepts to grow out of our clinical experience" (1961, p. 91). Man's behavior is innately good and effective in dealing with his environment if it follows the normal course of development. Man becomes hateful, self-centered, ineffective, and antagonistic to his fellow man only because of the learning experiences he undergoes during the course of his development. All these negative attributes of his behavior are the consequence of learning. If inappropriate learning conditions do not occur, man will develop as a kind, friendly, self-accepting, socialized human being, although not always conventional or conforming (1961, p. 105).

A third assumption is that behavior is purposive and goal-directed. Individuals are not passive respondents to their environment. When they are aware of the influences upon them and the nature of their responses to such influences, they choose their course of action rather than responding automatically. They actively seek to manipulate and to arrange the world around them to achieve consciously selected consequences. Moreover, there is a single, common goal toward which all people strive. They make choices aimed at achieving the same general consequences. All particular behavior elicitors (motives and drives) are parts of or manifestations of this single master motive which is innately characteristic of all humans. It follows that since all behavior patterns are acquired to serve the same general objective, they will become interrelated. Consequently, human behavior occurs in a unitary and holistic fashion and should be understood as such. Because of this set of assumptions, the reader will find all of Rogers' major concepts to be large and inclusive. His units of behavioral analysis are not defined in terms of a particular response like a motoric gesture or an emotional response. Rather, they are defined by a variety of responses occurring in patterns and sequences, usually over extended periods of time.

A fourth characteristic is derived partially from the three just discussed. An effective therapist does not manipulate events to produce specific changes in the patient's behavior. He does not change the patient, the patient changes himself. At the most, the therapist creates a set of conditions under which it becomes possible for the patient to overcome faulty learnings and acquire new ones. The learning that occurs in therapy is self-discovery (1961, pp. 204–205).

Finally, Rogers' attitude toward the use of scientific procedures for the verification of theory should be noted. At one time it seemed to Rogers that there was a serious conflict between his position that an individual could be understood only by adopting his vantage point of observation, as subject, and his belief in the utility of science where the individual is studied as an object. In a paper entitled *Persons or Science* (1961, pp. 199–255), he attempted to reconcile his two convictions, concluding that the ends served in therapy and in scientific investigation were different and, therefore, the procedures were different. When the objective is to create conditions within which an individual can change his own behavior, the therapist must maintain a subjective point of view. However, when his purpose is to validate his hypotheses and to study the orderliness in behavior, the therapist may abstract himself from the situation and view the patient as an object. The first point of view helps one to understand the principles, which differ from individual to individual, by which a particular person's behavior operates—the *idiographic* principles. The second observational vantage point enables one to establish principles which govern human behavior in general—the *nomothetic* propositions. Rogers believes, however, that both start from the same base, the subjective experience of the observer. As therapist he attends to one set of subjective experiences, as scientist another (1961, p. 222).

Rogers emphasizes that science is characterized by careful observation and thought, not instrumentation, and thus one can be scientific in the natural clinical setting as well as in the laboratory. He believes that in any new scientific field, such as psychotherapy represents, observations will initially be gross, hypotheses speculative and error-laden, and measurements crude. The crucial requirement is that one continually seek greater degrees of refinement, specification, and verification. "Truth is unitary," and thus one may start with almost any segment of experience, if the original experience is "complete and completely accurate," and build a sound conception of behavior (1959, p. 191). This belief, for example, leads Rogers to attempt to formulate a theory of personality from his observations in psychotherapy.

In analyzing a growing theory such as Rogers', a choice must be made. This analysis is based primarily on Rogers' latest writings, although reference will be made to his earlier views at appropriate intervals. Not only is his theory a constantly evolving thing, but also his latest statement (1959) is by far his most systematic, consistent, and complete formulation. It includes: (1) a theory of therapy and personality change; (2) a theory of personality; (3) a theory of the fully functioning person, the healthy personality; and (4) a theory of interpersonal relationships, all of which are conceptually interwoven. Rogers emphasizes that the theory of psychotherapy and personality change is most closely related to the realm of observed fact and most heavily supported by research evidence. His three other points are derived from the theory of therapy and change, and thus stand less closely related to an empirical base. He anticipates a greater degree of error wherever the extrapolation from this base is increased.

THE NORMAL COURSE OF BEHAVIOR DEVELOPMENT

Rogers proposes that there is a natural course of behavior development, which will result in a healthy, well-adjusted (fully functioning) person, unless this course is interfered with by faulty learnings, although the particular behaviors that develop will vary widely among individuals. Persons are unique because of the *kinds* of behavioral patterns they acquire, not because of the *way* they acquire them. They differ in what they have learned, not in how or why they have learned it.

Innate Characteristics of Normal Development

In discussing the kinds of responses or response potentials which are a part of each individual's innate equipment, Rogers does not attempt a complete analysis. For example, he acknowledges the existence and importance of motoric responses but pays relatively little attention to them in his theorizing. Rather, his concern has been with those subjectively observable responses (*r*) which are the crucial antecedents to overt behavior, and all of his concepts have been translated into those terms. There are six concepts which play an important role in his view of the innate characteristics of human development. Each will be discussed, and the propositions by which they are interrelated will be described.

EXPERIENCE. Rogers recognizes that the individual is in a constant transaction with a changeable world which produces a variety of responses within him. In addition, processes going on within the individual also produce responses. The aggregate of these subjectively observable responses (*r*), potentially available to awareness at any point in time, is identified by the label *experience* (1959, p. 197). Rogers subdivides this great inclusive class of responses into two categories: essentially, nonsymbolic responses, on the one hand, and awareness and symbolic responses on the other. It is important to note that no objectively observable responses (*R*) are included under this concept. Such responses are represented in experience by their response correlates or consequences, such as visual sensations, kinesthetic sensations, and so on. Thus, the infant is capable of a great variety of responses.

ORGANISMIC EXPERIENCE. This concept represents the nonsymbolic sub-class of responses under the concept of experience. Although he does not specify the kinds of responses involved in this large class, Rogers' descriptive comments mention emotional or feeling responses, visceral sensations, and auditory sensations. Also included under this concept appear to be all interoceptive, proprioceptive, exteroceptive, and af-fective responses, which represent the raw data by which the environ-ment and its effects on the individual become available to the indi-vidual's awareness and thought. Rogers specifically omits physiological responses not potentially available to the subject's awareness, since he considers them more properly in the domain of physiology.

We should recall in this context Rogers' lack of concepts involving situational events. He recognizes they elicit responses such as seeing and hearing. However, situational events are important only insofar as they evoke responses. Strictly speaking, it is not the fact that an-other person is present that is crucial, but it is the individual's percep-tion of that person that is important. Within his system, then, situa-tional events are represented by the subjective responses they elicit, by organismic experiences.

AWARENESS AND SYMBOLIZATION. The second subclass of subjective responses is attending and symbolic responses. The capacity to be aware of events is a critical attribute of human behavior. It is "the gift of a free and undistorted awareness" that significantly distinguishes man from other members of the animal kingdom. All individuals innately have the capacity to be aware of all events both externally impinging and internally produced. One does not learn to attend or be aware. However, *what* one learns to focus attention on or be aware of is a product of learning, and a significant one. As we shall see, healthy behavior depends upon adequate awareness, and those things that interfere with the individual's awareness of significant events will jeopardize "healthy development."

Rogers considers *perception* to be a subconcept of awareness, a "syn-onymous" but "narrower" term. Perception refers to awareness of situational events, and awareness includes this as well as "symboliza-tions and meanings which arise from such purely internal stimuli as memory traces, visceral changes and the like" (1959, p. 199). Thus, the term perception is Rogers' way of talking about situational events.

He recognizes that individuals appear to discriminate among situa-tional events even though they are not aware of doing so, and he terms this innate "capacity" *subception*. It is an important factor in the development of behavior disorder, as we shall see later.

Rogers also proposes an innate human capacity to represent in symbolic form the events of which persons are aware. In other words, awareness either requires or automatically leads to some variety of symbolizing responses. In fact, Rogers uses awareness, symbolization, and consciousness as synonymous terms. One can be aware only of what is symbolized, though there may be widely varying degrees of awareness (1959, p. 199). Both imagistic and verbal symbols are possible. Rogers' writings imply that not only does the human innately tend to symbolize, but also that the images and thoughts will represent the antecedent events accurately unless certain kinds of learnings occur which produce distortions. Healthy behavior depends on experiences being "clearly perceived" and "accurately symbolized." The individual must be aware of and able to think about his behavior and the events influencing him if he is to be able to direct and control his own behavior. However, the *kinds* of symbols acquired are not innate but are the consequence of learning and, therefore, may be inaccurate and interfere with effective behavior.

THE ORGANIZING PRINCIPLE. Rogers refers to the human capacity to resolve discrepancies or incongruities among responses—for example, through thoughts and emotions. He speaks of behavior as being organized in a holistic fashion so that new experiences have to be fitted into the existing organization in some manner. Although he does not explicitly formulate this as a principle, it is implicit throughout his system. The implication is that an individual not only learns new responses in new situations but also automatically tries to fit these into existing response patterns so that they are neither conflicting nor discrepant. A corollary principle is that the organization of behavior is changing constantly because new behaviors (experiences) are occurring constantly and must be assimilated. This seems to be what he means when referring to behavior as a "process." A second corollary is that at any given point in time, the organization tends to function as a single unit, rather than in pieces. This principle might be interpreted as a manifestation of the actualizing tendency (next paragraph), but we have chosen what seems to us the more appropriate interpretation.

THE ACTUALIZING TENDENCY. In this theory, the prime initiator of behavior resides within the person. All more specific drives or motivational events such as "need reduction, tension reduction, drive reduction," and the like are manifestations of this "master motive." It includes not only hunger and thirst but also differentiation of organs and functions, expansion through growth, the use of tools and reproduction, and development toward "autonomy" and away from "control by external forces" (Rogers, 1959, p. 196). It is important to note that with this concept Rogers is referring not only to the events that elicit behavior but also to the fact that behavior seems to have a directional trend—"the urge to expand. extend, develop, mature" (1961, p. 351).

Rogers has also referred to this as the tendency to *maintain* or *enhance* oneself. This concept seems to be an abstraction from a great variety of particular events. In many ways individuals appear to seek to protect their physical integrity through eating, drinking, and avoiding being physically damaged or hurt; they try to *maintain* themselves. Similarly, individuals seem to seek events that result in new and pleasant experiences: for example, they try new tasks, learn new skills, and seek foods that taste good; they try to *enhance* themselves. In order to conceptualize about this great variety of behavior, Rogers apparently identified what he believed was an underlying theme and assumed it represented an innate characteristic. The direction of every man's life is not just to keep himself alive but to accomplish something, to exercise his talents, to attempt to mold and shape his environment into achievements that induce "pleasurable tension" in himself. Rogers specifically states that there are no other "sources of energy or action" in his theory. Thus, behavior may be thought of as one functional unit, for it all serves the same purpose. All behavior should be understood as directed toward such consequences.

Since all individuals innately seek certain kinds of behavioral consequences (maintenance and enhancement), how do they decide whether their behavior is effective? To put it differently, why do some responses become habitual and others not? Some judgment or evaluation of each series of responses must occur. Rogers postulates an innate process of making such judgments. He calls it the organismic valuing process.

Rogers assumes that humans are innately evaluative or inherently capable of differentiating between effective or ineffective, desirable or undesirable responses. But what is the criterion for such evaluations? Behaviors whose concomitants or consequences are visceral and sensory responses having the characteristics of comfort, pleasure, or satisfaction are "evaluated positively," while behaviors having the characteristics of discomfort, pain, or dissatisfaction are "evaluated negatively." The only kinds of responses in general psychology that appear to have such characteristics are affective responses, including the possibility of pain.[2] This interpretation is consistent with Rogers' earlier writings, where great emphasis was placed on emotions. Thus, we will assume that the affective responses associated with the behavior being evaluated provide the criterion data. The term "organismic" would then refer to the data or evidence on which the evaluative judgment is based. The individual "knows" whether a particular behavior effectively expresses the innate elicitor (actualizing tendency) by the type of affect that follows or is associated with it. If the affect is "positive" the behavior is effective, and if "negative" it is not effective. The "valuing process" is a cognitive act utilizing conscious symbolization of the "evidence" (subjective responses) on which the individual can base his judgment; "experiences are being accurately symbolized and continually and freshly valued in terms of the satisfactions organismically experienced" (1959, p. 210). Even in the infant, conscious symbolization of experience—admittedly less clear and precise than in the adult—and a judgment about that experience, determines whether it will recur.

Innate Sequences

Rogers proposes that there is an innate sequence in which the innate characteristics occur. The master motive (actualizing tendency) initiates overt responses to obtain situational consequents (purposive behavior). This behavior and its related consequences produce sensory and visceral responses within the individual (organismic experience). These subjective responses lead to or have related to them affective responses (organismic experience). The individual attends to and thinks about the subjective responses (perceives). He makes conscious judgments about them (organismic valuation). If the responses (r) are judged to be positive (actualize, maintain, or enhance the organism), the behavior is likely to continue or recur. If the responses are judged to be negative (do not actualize, maintain, or enhance), the behavior

[2] Rogers may also be referring to some attribute of sensory and visceral responses, such as intensity, which may have positive or negative connotations in subjective experience. We include that possibility under the notion of affect.

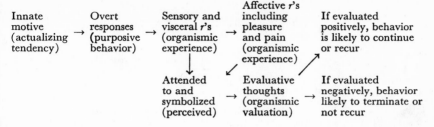

Figure 4. *A schematic summary of the innate sequence of behavior development as represented by Rogers.*

is likely to terminate or not to recur. As Rogers puts it, "He behaves with adience [approach] toward positively valued *experiences* and with avoidance toward those negatively valued" (1959, p. 222). This innate sequence is summarized schematically in Figure 4.

A simple example may be helpful. A person is hungry (a manifestation of the actualizing tendency). He goes into a cafeteria, selects a few foods from among the wide variety available, and eats them (purposive behavior). Eating the food produces sensory and visceral responses (organismic experiences). If the individual notices the food produces pleasurable or satisfying tastes and sensations (is evaluated positively) he may go back for more, or he will tend to select the same sorts of food the next time he eats, if they are available. On the other hand, if the food tastes bad or disgusts him (is evaluated negatively), he will be unlikely to finish the food or to select it on the next occasion.

Note that, in this conception, behavior is not elicited by situational events, but is impelled by a set of innate responses (the actualizing tendency). Situational events are important as consequences because they produce sensory, visceral, and emotional responses which follow the instrumental behavior, thus providing data for evaluation; that is, evaluation requires feedback. Rogers argues that the habitual behaviors that develop as a consequence of the innate sequences will be personally and socially effective and satisfying. *These inherent sequence do not lead to behavior disorder.* This abiding faith in the capacity of humans to make personally and socially satisfactory responses unless their behavior is distorted by inappropriate learnings is the cornerstone of Rogers' point of view and the driving force in his therapy.

Learned Characteristics of Normal Development

The innate sequence just described recurs continually. In Rogers' terms, behavior is a continuous process, not a static entity. Through it, habitual patterns of behavior are acquired. We must now ask what is learned and how do the products of learning affect future behavior? Rogers does not concern himself with certain products of learning, such as the acquisition of overt instrumental responses. It is implied that these will follow quite readily if certain antecedent subjective responses occur. Similarly, learned connections between situational events and subjective responses such as affect are ignored, even though the conditioning of affect to situational events is a well-established phenomenon. These may be ignored because, unless distorted by unfortunate learning situations, the "natural" connections that develop between situational and response events will be appropriate and not troublesome. In his view, the important consequences of learning are habits of attending to and thinking about crucial events (perceptions, self-conceptions, and evaluative thoughts). It is these thoughtful self-awarenesses that determine the instrumental responses to be performed, that evaluate their consequences, and by which the individual controls his own behavior. Therefore, the acquisition of habits of awareness and different kinds of thought will be discussed, including the concepts of self-experience, self, openness to experience, and the self-actualizing tendency. Two other products of learning reflect Rogers' emphasis on one type of situation, the interpersonal one. Every individual learns a need for positive regard from others and, as a derivative, a need for positive self-regard. Finally, the concept of congruence refers to the relationships among various categories of subjective responses. Each of these will be discussed in turn.

SELF-EXPERIENCE AND THE CONCEPT OF SELF. As soon as the infant begins to interact with his environment, he begins to be aware of himself as an entity separate from the events around him. He begins to notice or attend to and think about attributes of himself and the things he does. Events become symbolized in awareness in images and words. Rogers calls awareness of such events *self-experience* (1959, p. 223).

These awarenesses are the "raw material" out of which habitual patterns of attending to and thinking about self-characteristics develop. These habitual patterns of thought about the self Rogers refers to as *concept of self*, one of his major constructs. It includes not only thoughts such as "I am tall" or "I am smart," but thoughts relating oneself to others, such as "Other people like me," and thoughts identifying one's relationship with other kinds of events, such as "I am a skillful water skier." Important characteristics of these habits of self-thought will appear as several other concepts are analyzed. They are not simply a collection of self-referent thoughts, however, but are organized into a "consistent conceptual gestalt" and "the alteration of one minor aspect could completely alter the whole pattern." Rogers considered this an important discovery (1959, p. 201).

SELF-ACTUALIZING TENDENCY. What are the effects of the unit-functioning of thought patterns concerning the attributes of oneself which one has learned to attend to, think about, remember, and value? There are three important ones. First, this response organization determines which thoughts about oneself will become habitual. Only new images and thoughts that are consistent with the existing "unit" can become a part of it. Second, it functions as a unit in influencing the behaviors one will perform. People choose to perform behaviors that are consistent with and expressions of one's self-conceptions, and to reject others. For example, a person who considers himself a good musician and poor athlete may try out for the band but not the team. Rogers refers to this as the *self-actualizing tendency*—another manifestation of the actualizing tendency. Third, a change in self-conception may produce an important change in one's entire organization for each aspect is related to the other aspects in an "organized gestalt." The implications for psychotherapy are obvious, since a successful change in the person's habit of evaluating his responses to his mother, for example, is very likely to produce a change in his total pattern of self-evaluative thoughts.

Rogers also speaks of the "self as process." By this he seems to mean that these habitual self-conceptions are undergoing continual change and modification as well as continually and actively influencing the occurrence of other responses.

CONGRUENCE AND OPENNESS TO EXPERIENCE. Rogers seems to be proposing that once the habitual patterns of thoughts about oneself become established as a functioning unit they influence the subsequent situational events and responses which will be attended to and symbolized (perceived), remembered, and thought about. The broader and more inclusive the patterns of self-conception, the greater the variety of events one will attend to and symbolize, and the more adaptive will be the resulting behavior. Only those new response patterns (experiences) of which the individual is aware and which are consistent with the existing unit of self-conceptions, that is, the congruence of the self and experience, will become a part of the pattern of self-thoughts. New experiences that are inconsistent will tend to be ignored, not remembered, not thought about, and disowned. Rogers invented this way of thinking to account for the fact that the positive feelings of love or tenderness or confidence in oneself can be denied just as easily as feelings of anger or sexual desires. It is not these responses *per se* that lead the individual to ignore them—repress them—but it is the way he thinks about himself that makes these responses acceptable or unacceptable to him. If his habits of self-thoughts are very broad and inclusive, any of his responses such as anger, fear, love, or sexual excitement are consistent with his self-conceptions; he is *open to his experience*. The more the individual is able to attend to, think about, and accept as part of himself the whole range of his responses, the better adjusted he is likely to be.

Where do these habits of self-evaluation come from? They are clearly the consequence of learning. They result from the individual noticing his reactions to all kinds of situations. He learns that he can read well, but is not good with mathematics; that he is a skillful musician, but a poor athlete; that he is strong enough to do some things, but not others. Apparently these are learned if the individual notices them and symbolizes them, that is, if he thinks about them. Thus, thoughts identifying both "positive" and "negative" characteristics can be acquired. For example, the thought "I am smaller than other children" is just as likely to become a part of the system of self-thoughts as "I am stronger than other children." The thought "I am frightened" can be as acceptable as "I love her." However, many of the most important self-conceptions are learned through interaction with other people. If other people consistently react toward one as if one were handsome, one will come to think of oneself in that way. This pattern of self-conceptions is constantly changing, from day to day and moment to moment, as a consequence of new experiences.

NEED FOR POSITIVE REGARD AND SELF-REGARD. The consequences of learning discussed so far might be thought of as primarily cognitive in nature, that is, involving awareness and thought. However, another important product of learning involves habits of seeking certain kinds of consequences and affective responses related to them. Here the emphasis is on interpersonal situations and the behavior of other people toward the individual. As the infant becomes aware of himself as an entity different from others, he begins to notice differences in their responses to him and his to them. One important category of such responses Rogers calls *positive regard*. This includes such responses "as warmth, liking, respect, sympathy, acceptance," all of which seem to have a common denominator of positive affect, an apparently innately desired response which one seeks to create in oneself. It is proposed that when the individual notices that others are responding toward him with positive affect, it elicits positive affect in him—it is satisfying.

To put it differently, when others evaluate a child's responses negatively by displaying anger or disapproval, discomforting affective responses are produced in the child. Positive evaluation by others through smiles, approvals, or affectionate responses, however, produce "satisfying" affect in the child. The child gradually comes to seek the latter and avoid the former.[3] In Rogers' terms he acquires a *need for positive regard*. The infant learns to need and seek love and affection from others because such affectionate responses are innately satisfying; they fulfill the actualizing motive. When an individual consistently experiences positive affection toward others or when others always respond toward him in positive terms, even though not all specific behaviors are viewed in that way, it is called *unconditional positive regard*. Thus, not only will sensory and visceral responses produce positive or negative affect (organismic experience), but so will the evaluations of one's behavior by others. Since affective responses provide the evidence upon which one evaluates his behavior, this phenomenon is obviously very important. Consistent positive evaluation by other people (unconditional positive regard) is the most desirable social learning situation and the one in which the healthy personality develops.

Consistent with the innate learning sequence, the individual will tend to learn from others those evaluative thoughts that lead to positive affect. He acquires a set of habitual self-evaluative thoughts based on the evaluations of others rather than on what his own sensory experience tells him. He acquires a *need for self-regard*. He learns to judge his behavior as bad because others dislike it even though the behavior itself may be quite pleasant to him. The person applies the learned social criteria or values to himself *as if* they were based on the satisfactions he derives. Thus, the individual acquires a second

---

[3] Rogers believes this is a universal motive and, therefore, possibly innate. However, he suggests it is more likely to be learned, even though universal, as a consequence of the fact that all humans exist in a social context.

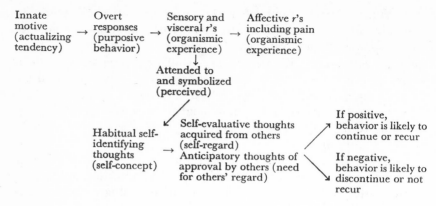

Figure 5. The learned evaluational sequence which provides an alternate to the innate sequence for choosing appropriate behaviors.

basis for evaluating his behavior and choosing his courses of action, which is independent of the innate sequence. Figure 5 represents this learned evaluational sequence. Note that the affective quality of the sensory and visceral responses are not a part of the data in this learned evaluation, even though they still occur.

In the healthy person, these learned habits of self-evaluation and strivings for the approvals of others coincide with the direct evaluation of his own subjective responses (organismic evaluation), and no difficulty develops. If in the course of development other people consistently show they like and approve of the child even though they may refuse to permit specific behaviors—they show unconditional positive regard—the child will not have to struggle for their approval, but can choose his behavior on the basis of its innate satisfying or dissatisfying qualities. Therefore, in the healthy individual, the innate and learned evaluational sequences operate together and lead to the same choices. To put it differently, the same instrumental responses will be innately satisfying and will please others as well. Figure 6 represents the two sequences operating jointly and effectively. Clearly, the most important consequences of learning are the learned self-identifying and self-evaluative thoughts.

If an infant develops in an interpersonal climate in which he experiences constant positive evaluation, even though limits are placed on him, he will learn to attend to and think about all aspects of his behavior, choosing first one source of satisfaction and then another but never finding it necessary to ignore and disregard any of them.

He becomes confident that he is loved, even though specific behaviors may be prohibited, and consequently need not continually seek the approval of others. His evaluative judgments of his own behavior—all of which he can attend to and think about—will rely primarily on the direct awareness of whether it leads to positive or negative affect rather than on whether others dislike it (1959, p. 25). Since behaviors whose consequences "naturally" elicit positive affect will be learned and those that "naturally" induce negative affect will be avoided, and since what is "naturally" personally satisfying is also generally socially adaptive, the consequence of this normal learning sequence will be a well-adjusted socialized individual (1959, p. 224).

CHARACTERISTICS OF THE FULLY FUNCTIONING PERSON. If the child grows, develops, and learns under the ideal set of circumstances we have been discussing, the consequence will be a happy, creative, socially effective individual. Rogers avoids the term "well-adjusted" because he believes adjustment is not something acquired but something continually occurring, a process. For this reason he speaks of the fully functioning person. If the developmental conditions that we have just described "are met to a maximum degree," the resulting behavior patterns will have several characteristics.

The individual will be able to attend to and think about all his sensory, visceral, and affective responses as they occur. His thoughts about such responses will be accurate within the limits of the avail-

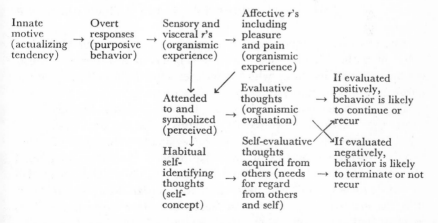

Figure 6. A schematic summary of the innate sequence of behavior development as modified by a system of learned self-identifying and self-evaluative thoughts.

able subjective response data. The habitual pattern of self-identifying and self-evaluative thoughts he has learned will not contradict any of his behavior, and he will be able to acknowledge all of it as a part of himself. He will choose his own courses of action on the basis of his judgments of what is desirable and undesirable rather than because of the evaluations of others, and he will be aware that he is actively making such choices. He will continually observe the subjective responses resulting from his instrumental behaviors and will base his judgments on whether the consequences of his behaviors are genuinely satisfying or dissatisfying, rather than on whether others approve. He will think of himself as being liked by others as well as himself. Because he has not acquired any habitual patterns of inattention, he will be able to attend to all the crucial aspects of each new situation and choose a course of action which is unique and appropriate to it. The choices he makes will be personally satisfying and socially effective because they are based on all the available sensory, visceral, and affective responses which are the data for making such choices. He will not have to exclude any of this evidence because of faulty learnings. He will be able to observe the consequences of the course of action he chooses and to evaluate them, incorporating the results into his habitual self-thoughts so that they can be used in making future choices. His social behaviors will generally be effective and approved by others (1961, p. 191).

THE DEVELOPMENT OF BEHAVIOR DISORDER

How can this sequence of normal development go awry? How does behavior pathology develop? Rogers sees behavior disorder as a consequence of faulty learning, which interferes with the functioning of the natural developmental sequence.

His is a conflict model of disorder. The fundamental conflict is between the individual's evaluative thoughts based on his sensory, visceral, and affective responses and the evaluative thoughts of other people which he adopts as his own. He believes that behavior guided by the "values of others" may lead to disorder, while behavior guided by "one's own values" will never lead to disorder. More particularly, it is the evaluative thoughts one learns—it is bad to be angry, it is good to be kind to others, or more generally, I am a good person or I am a bad person—that are the core of disorder. Learned evaluative thoughts control what one will notice and what one will ignore; they control what and how it will be symbolized in awareness and what will not be symbolized; they control what one will say and do and determine the acts one will avoid. The consequence of the conflict is anxiety. Responses are then learned to avoid or terminate the anxiety. These responses may lead to further difficulties, however, because they restrict the individual's habits of attention and thought and thereby restrict the actions he may perform. This further exaggerates the difficulties.

Rogerian concepts relevant to the development of behavior disorder include conditions of worth, incongruence, selective and distorted perception, discrepant behaviors, anxiety, vulnerability, threat, defense, and breakdown and disorganization.

The Learning of the Conflict

The ideal learning situation described in the section on normal development seldom if ever occurs. People characteristically behave inconsistently toward one another. Sometimes they act as if they like one another, and at others they are critical. Sometimes they are kind, and at others abusive. At times they are understanding, and at others domineering. Few individuals learn "I know other people like and respect me despite my weaknesses." They are more likely to learn "Other people like me sometimes and sometimes they dislike me." As a consequence of this inconsistent behavior by others, the individual learns that other people like certain aspects of his behavior but dislike others. He learns to apply these evaluations to his own behavior so that he comes to approve of certain aspects of his own behavior and not others, whether or not they are innately satisfying. The result is that the individual avoids behaviors because he has learned to think of them as bad, or performs others simply because he has learned to think of them as good. Choosing to attend to and perform behaviors for these reasons Rogers refers to as a *condition of worth* somewhat like the statistical notion of degrees of freedom. Thus, the individual may learn a few or a great many such interpersonally based evaluations; he may have few or many conditions of worth.

There is no problem if the socially acquired values coincide with the individual's judgment of the behavior regardless of what others might think of it, that is, if self-concept and experience are congruent. However, if the "learned" and "innate" evaluative sequences are contradictory, a response-response (r-r) conflict exists. Responses occur (overt or subjective), which have as their natural consequence positive affect—they would be organismically valued as maintaining and enhancing the organism—but which the person has learned to think of as bad because others have taught him to do so. For example, a child may find the experience of nudity pleasurable but thinks of it as bad because his mother became angry about it. He may, therefore, think of himself as bad because he enjoys the experience of nudity. Or an adult may have learned to think of sexual intercourse as bad, even though his bodily experiences during the act might be pleasurable. Such a contradiction between what the individual has learned to think of as good or bad and the positive and negative nature of the experiences themselves Rogers refers to as *incongruence between self and experience*. The fundamental conflict could be crudely characterized as "It feels good, but other people disapprove of it. Since I want them to like me, I'll disapprove of it too." This is man's "basic estrangement," "he has not been true to himself" (1959, p. 226). Unfortunately, such learnings are characteristic of all human beings in an imperfect society, and, thus, everyone is at least a bit maladjusted.

When are these conflicts learned? Rogers does not thoroughly discuss this issue, but he suggests that many are learned in infancy and early childhood (1959, p. 226). However, his emphasis on "process" suggests it is possible to learn such conflicts at any stage in life.

The Consequences of the Learned Conflict

Several consequences follow from the learned conflict. The individual's overt behaviors will be discrepant or contradictory. Sometimes he will behave to achieve certain innately satisfying consequences, for example, have sexual intercourse. At other times he will behave in accord with the evaluative thoughts that conflict with the innate qualities of the experience, for example, avoid sexual intercourse. A second and perhaps more important consequence is that *anxiety* results. An individual who has learned to think of a particular experience as bad when it is actually innately satisfying, or vice versa, will be likely to experience anxiety whenever he is in circumstances that arouse the conflict—he is *vulnerable*.

The characteristics of a learned conflict are exemplified in Figure 7. *Anxiety* is defined as a state of uneasiness or tension (presumably an

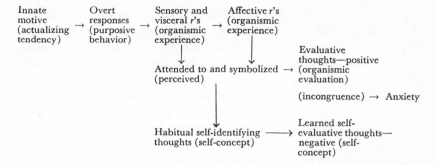

Figure 7. *A schematic summary of a learned conflict between the innate and learned evaluative sequences.*

innate response pattern). If the discrepant responses were fully attended and symbolized in awareness, acute tension would result.

Once the conflict is learned, it tends to function automatically, outside of awareness, when appropriate conditions exist. In other words, when responses (sensations and affects) that elicit both positive and negative self-evaluative thoughts are aroused within the individual, anxiety automatically ensues. However, clinical experience divulges that the individual often is unaware of the events preceding the anxiety. This presents a theoretical problem. Since anxiety is the consequence of conflicting evaluative thoughts, and since these thoughts are the result of awareness of responses occurring at the time, why should anxiety appear at all when awareness is absent? Rogers introduces the concept of *subception* to solve the problem. He draws on evidence from perceptual research to assert that individuals can and do discriminate among responses, even though they are not aware of doing so. Therefore, when subjective responses occur that would lead to conflicting self-thoughts (incongruence between self-concept and experience) if the individual were to attend to and think about them, an anticipatory discrimination develops, of which the individual is unaware. He is said to *subceive them as threatening*.

The "threat" is that if he attends to and thinks accurately about them, anxiety will occur. To avoid anxiety the individual will use two types of *defense*. The key to the occurrence of anxiety, according to Rogers, is that the individual becomes aware of responses that contradict his habitual ways of thinking about himself. Thus, to avoid anxiety, all the individual needs to do is prevent himself from becoming aware of the contradictory responses. He can do this in two ways. He can ignore the crucial responses, even though they may be occurring (*denial to awareness*), or he can attend to the crucial responses, but think about them inaccurately so that they can be in accord with the habitual self-thoughts rather than contradict them (*distortion in awareness*). The second type of defense is most likely to operate when a person's behavior is so obvious he cannot pretend it did not occur. Then, his only recourse is to misinterpret it to make it acceptable to himself.

Rogers believes most, if not all, neurotic and psychotic symptom patterns can be understood as one of these two types of habits. Ignoring one's anger responses when unfairly criticized would be an example of denial. Rationalization would be an example of distortion. Often, the two may occur in combination. For example, an individual may ignore his own sexual responses and at the same time attribute "dirty" sexual responses and thoughts to everyone else (projection). Rogers believes his dichotomous classification of habitual defensive behaviors is more fundamental and useful than other classifications (1959, p. 228).

The role of these two types of behaviors in preventing anxiety may be clarified by examining Figure 7. If the section of the summary in Figure 7 labeled "attended to and symbolized" is completely omitted, obviously all the rest of the sequence would also be omitted and anxiety could not occur. This is what Rogers calls *denial*. If the symbolization in Figure 7 is inaccurate so that the individual thinks only about the things that coincide with his habitual self-thoughts, the conflict can also be avoided and anxiety will not occur. This is what Rogers calls *distortion*. In behavior disorder, then, the crucial problems are inappropriate habits of attending to significant events, inaccurate ways of thinking about them, and habitual self-evaluative thoughts which reject "natural" or "organically satisfying" experiences. It would appear that any effective therapy would have to change these three categories of responses. We shall see later whether Rogers proposes techniques for doing this.

Breakdown and Disorganization

As noted earlier, human beings are inconsistent in their evaluations and affective responses toward one another. Thus, everyone develops some habits of: ignoring some of his own behavior; thinking inaccurately about some of it; and approving or disapproving some of it simply because others have taught him to, not because it is personally satisfying. Therefore, each person has some pieces of disordered behavior in his repertoire. However, people vary greatly in the extent to which they have acquired such habits.

Severely maladjusted individuals have acquired habits of ignoring and thinking inaccurately about great portions of their sensations, images, and emotions (organismic experience). They deny themselves much of the data on which their evaluations should be based. As a consequence, they are unable to make sound judgments about their behavior and sound predictions about the consequences to which it leads. In a sense, they are evaluating false or incomplete data, which will lead to inaccurate conclusions and the selection of instrumental behaviors that will be seriously inappropriate at times and frequently ineffective.

However, under extreme conditions the behavior patterns we have been describing fail, including the controls on the disordered behavior (denial and distortion), and the person loses a major portion of the control of his behavior. In Rogers' terms the behavioral sequences *break down* and *behavior becomes disorganized*. Under these conditions, "irrational" and "acute" psychotic behaviors can be observed.

What are the conditions? If the individual has acquired extensive habits of ignoring, or inattending, and inaccurately thinking about major portions of his behavior because he has learned a great variety of inaccurate self-evaluations, if there is a significant degree of discrepancy between what he thinks of himself and what he does (self and experience), and if subjective responses occur which the individual cannot avoid noticing and thinking about, because of surprise or because the behavior is so obvious, anxiety will develop. The greater the proportion of self-conceptions that are contradicted by the recognized responses, the greater will be the resulting anxiety. Under these conditions, when the anxiety is intense, the system of self-identifying and self-evaluative thoughts will break apart and the relationships among them will at least temporarily be destroyed; the self-concept will become disorganized. Since the thoughts with which the individual has been controlling and selectively choosing his behavior are disorganized, the behavior itself will become disorganized. Under these circumstances, the individual will sometimes behave in ways which he has previously denied himself; he may, for example, become sexually promiscuous when previously he led a restricted and socially acceptable sexual life. At other times the learned self-evaluative thoughts will function and the behavior will be in accord with those socially acceptable thoughts. When behavior is disorganized, the patterns of behavior that will occur are unpredictable by both the person and others around him (1959, p. 229). These conditions and consequences characterize what is called a psychotic break. In addition, Rogers states that patients in therapy report experiencing similar but less severe disorganizations as they approach recognition of behaviors they have been inattending or thinking inaccurately about before therapy.

Rogers notes that in acute psychoses, the dominant behaviors often appear to be those that the individual has been avoiding or prohibiting for himself in his previous life. Individuals who have seldom expressed open aggression in the past may be aggressive and perhaps even assaultive in the midst of a psychosis. In other words, the aspects of behavior previously denied tend to become dominant. Rogers tentatively suggests that once a psychosis has begun, a new "process of defense" probably sets in to enable the individual to achieve the most adequate adjustment possible under the circumstances. He proposes one very likely possibility to be that the various branches of the conflict reverse roles so that the previously denied behaviors become dominant and those self-identifying and self-evaluative thoughts that once were dominant become repressed and thought about inaccurately. Another possibility is that the self-identifying and self-evaluative thoughts gradually become dominant again, but in a seriously changed way, including the theme "I am a crazy, inadequate, unreliable person who contains impulses and forces beyond my control" (1959, p. 230). Patients develop an adjustment to their illness, resigning themselves to it and accepting it as a permanent part of themselves. Of course, this would be an adjustment which might require hospitalization throughout a lifetime, a consequence that occurs for many seriously disturbed people.

Symptoms of Behavior Disorder

Rogers did not detail the symptoms of disordered behavior. In a sense these may be thought of as the opposite of the characteristics of the fully functioning person which were discussed earlier. We have pieced together the following summary from various portions of Rogers' writings. The individual suffers from an excess of tension or negative affect, particularly anxiety. He tends to think about his subjective responses—his perceptions of situational events as well as his responses to them—in absolute and unconditional terms, that is, to overgeneralize. His responses are not specific, nor are they appropriate to the situations under which they occur. He tends to confuse fact and evaluation of fact. He tends not to "check out" his thoughts about himself and the world around him to make sure that they fit the realities of the situations. He ignores or thinks erroneously about many aspects of situations and his own responses. He avoids a great variety of new situations which would produce new patterns of responses (new experiences) within himself. He is unaware of much of his behavior and feels that some of it is out of his control. His behavior is erratic, characterized by behavioral impoverishment, and frequent inappropriate responses. Of course, as a consequence of all this, the behavior of other people toward him is likely to be unsatisfactory to him, and thus further difficulties may be created.

THE GOALS OF THERAPY

What are the objectives toward which the therapeutic efforts should be directed so that the individual can once again become a truly effective and happy person?

General Characteristics of the Goals

WHO DETERMINES THE GOALS. The therapist must allow the patient to determine the specific goals of therapy. This is true both because it fits Rogers' picture of the nature of man and because it is an effective therapeutic procedure. The reader will recall that Rogers sees the psychologically adjusted individual as one who chooses his own courses of action based on his own observations and evaluations rather than on what other people think he should do. Rogers believes there is an innate response pattern which elicits behavior (the actualizing tendency) and an innate regulatory mechanism (organismic valuing) which will lead to sound, socially acceptable choices if permitted to operate without interference. Thus, if the therapist were to choose the goals for his patients, he would be interfering with the essential nature of man and could not possibly establish the conditions by which the individual might once again find his essential nature and lead a satisfying life.

Even if one were to reject the assumption of these mechanisms as being innate, the permitting of the patient to choose his own goals would remain an essential therapeutic technique *if* Rogers' view of the nature of the psychologically adjusted individual were accepted. How could one help another person come to rely on his own judgment in planning his course of action if the therapeutic procedures did not permit him that opportunity? To become able to make sound judgments about one's own behavior, one must practice such responses. The therapist creates conditions in which the patient can do so without fear.

At another level, however, it would appear the therapist has the same general goals for all patients. These general goals are described in his theory of the fully functioning person (1959). He does not speak of these as goals, however. Rather he refers to his purpose as being to free the patient of his faulty learnings so that he can be what he was innately built to be. In a sense, the therapist selects objectives involving the modification of behaviors obstructing the patient's natural behavior development, such as distortions, and the patient selects objectives involving the new patterns of behavior he will adopt. One wonders whether Rogers would consider psychologically adjusted an individual who chooses a life for himself which contradicts Rogers' view of the innate characteristics of man, or whether he would consider this still to be a pattern of defensive behavior of which the individual is unaware. He does insist that if one confidently relies on the innate characteristics of the individual in observing and choosing his own behavior, he will find that the patient will always choose adaptive, mature, socially constructive behavior. Yet he has also suggested that if one never fully relies on these innate characteristics in patients, one will never discover their existence. Such a position is a bit disconcerting since it suggests that one cannot see the phenomena unless one believes they are there, or, perhaps in a more restricted sense, unless one looks for them. The danger is, of course, that one may interpret one's observations to fit one's beliefs if the phenomena are approached with that point of view.

ATTRIBUTES OF GOALS. Several general characteristics of the goals may be noted. First, the primary purpose of therapy is to bring about changes in the ways in which the person attends to, thinks about, and thoughtfully evaluates himself and the world around him. Since these habits of attending to and thinking about events control all other behavior, changes in them will produce different behavior patterns. Second, Rogers believes that when a patient completes therapy, only the pattern of change has been laid down. Thus, the goals for therapy itself may be somewhat more limited than the goals for an effective life, in that therapy is not expected to produce an optimally adjusted person but only to start the development of a new pattern of adjustment. In Rogers' terms, the purpose of psychotherapy is to "release an already existing capacity in a potentially competent individual," and when that is done, the process of adjustment can proceed along its typically normal course without the aid of psychotherapy. Finally, Rogers' goals characteristically define adjustment as a process rather than a state. The well-adjusted person is changing continually, revising his thoughts about himself in the light of new experiences, using all available observations for effectively choosing a course of action in each new situation, and continually obtaining satisfaction out of solving new problems rather than in not having any problems to solve. In a sense, the purpose of therapy is to help the individual to become aware of all the events influencing him and to help him use more freely his capacities for conscious thought in solving his problems.

Summary of Rogers' Goals

We have chosen to summarize Rogers' statements about the outcomes of therapy as his goals rather than his description of the fully functioning person, because he believes his therapy theory is most closely related to his observational base. In addition, his theory of the fully functioning person represents an ideal which he does not expect to be achieved, at least as the immediate consequence of therapy. Finally, it seems most appropriate to concern ourselves here with the outcomes the therapist may hope to observe in the course of treatment. Rogers speaks about the *outcomes* of therapy and the *process* of therapy. He indicates, however, that he does not mean to imply a clear distinction between the two. By outcomes he seems to mean the major changes in the patient's behavior which result from therapy, and by process he seems to mean the small steps by which the patient progresses toward these major changes as well as the sequence in which such steps are taken. We shall talk about the sequence of change later, following our discussion of technique. For the moment we shall attempt to summarize his ideas about outcomes. No meaningful sequence is intended in the order in which the goals are summarized.

The patient's observations about his behavior and his thoughts about himself come to be in much closer agreement (congruent). He learns to attend to and think about all aspects of his behavior, he becomes open to his experience, and his habits of repressing and inaccurately thinking about his behavior cease to occur; he becomes less defensive. His thoughts about his behavior and his responses to events become more concrete and less pervaded by abstract concepts. He makes finer discriminations among events. He seeks to verify his inferences about the relationships among the events he sees by submitting them to test; his thoughts about himself change flexibly. Because his observations and his thoughts about himself correspond with one another, fewer things make him anxious; he is less vulnerable to threat. The things he would like to accomplish become more attainable, and his thoughts about himself and what he would like to be become more similar to one another; the self becomes more congruent with ideal self.

Because his observations and thoughts about himself and what he would like to be are less discrepant (self-concept and ideal self-concept more congruent), physiological tension, psychological tension, and anxiety are all greatly reduced. The patient has a great many more favorable thoughts about himself. He directs his behavior on the basis of what he judges is right for himself (the organismic valuing process) rather than on the basis of what other people believe he should do, and he recognizes that he is directing his own behavior; he perceives that the locus of evaluation resides within himself. His observations about others are more accurate, and he has many more friendly feelings and sympathetic thoughts about others. He acknowledges many more attributes of himself than he did previously. He is far more confident of his ability to control his own future behavior. His responses to each new situation are more specific to the situation and more carefully chosen to obtain the best results from it. His habits of decision making change so that he relies less on the advice, belief, and evaluations of others and more on his own observations and thoughts. He observes that other people seem to like and respect him more (1961, p. 90). As a consequence of a greater awareness of and liking for himself, all the changes just summarized will eventuate.

CONDITIONS FOR PRODUCING BEHAVIOR CHANGE

Rogers' first therapy book (1942) was primarily a handbook of technique, which had grown out of his extensive therapy experience. His clear exposition of concrete procedures the therapist should use, along with illustrations from actual therapy recordings, caused the book to have a tremendous influence. In his second volume (1951) he rejected this earlier approach to the question of technique. He had observed that precisely the same therapist statements could be presented in differing fashions to produce entirely different effects on the patient. The responses of two therapists might be identical with respect to content but differ markedly in the *way* in which they were expressed. Thus, it was possible for a therapist to observe the "letter" of technique and yet be unsuccessful in effecting behavioral change. As with his analysis of patient behavior, Rogers turned to the thoughts and feelings the therapist held toward the patient as the most crucial antecedents to effective therapist behavior. He now assumed that if the therapist holds the "right attitude," if he has a fundamental faith in the patient, the appropriate statements and expressive gestures by the therapist will follow. He has emphasized this position about therapist technique by stating that the trend in the training of client-centered psychotherapists has been away from technique and toward attitudinal orientation. He has moved toward greater and greater freedom for the therapist in his interview behavior, and he has come to emphasize the evaluational aspects of the therapist's thoughts and emotional responses toward the patient, rather than what the therapist says or the expressive movements or gestures he makes.

As Rogers sees it, the therapist's task is to create certain conditions which make it possible for the subject to change himself. *If* the therapist is successful in creating the conditions, *then* the patient will change himself. He says his theory does not try to explain *why* the process occurs, only to *describe* it. He notes that it is not unusual in science for one to be able to describe orderly relationships among events and to utilize that knowledge to achieve predictable consequences, even though an adequate explanation of why things work that way may not yet have been developed. His emphasis on process represents his recognition that there is a predictable *sequence* of change in his therapy. In the description of therapist behavior which follows, therefore, one should not expect a statement of operations to be performed by the therapist. Rather, Rogers presents a description of the conditions to be created, regardless of the nature of the behavior disorder, which are likely to be followed by specifiable changes in patient behavior.

NECESSARY ATTRIBUTES AND TRAINING OF THERAPISTS. Rogers has frequently emphasized the rudimentary knowledge we have about the process of therapy, and he encourages the continued search for more information and evidence. He consistently asks that his proposals about therapeutic conditions be subjected to evaluation and alteration in the light of new evidence. He has tentatively listed several characteristics that he considers useful in the effective counselor. He does not propose that student therapists be selected in terms of these behavioral characteristics, since he believes that many of them can become acquired. Nor does he propose that these behaviors must be general and occur in all situations. It is only required that they have a high likelihood of occurrence under the conditions of therapeutic interviewing.

He believes the therapist should be sensitive to a variety of human relationships; be objective and yet also to be able to adopt the point of view of another; have respect for individual dignity and worth; have patience and self-restraint; be able sympathetically to understand the thoughts and feelings of others; and be aware of and be able to accept all his own behaviors. Apparently, he wants his therapist in the therapy interview to be able to adopt the vantage point of both the objective and subjective observer, though the latter is most important; to be able to observe and think about all the kinds of events which are occurring without having fear, anger, or negative affect aroused as a consequence. In addition, he wishes his therapist to hold a particular belief about the fundamental nature of man.

In regard to the training of psychotherapists, Rogers earlier believed it to be essential for the trainee to be grounded thoroughly in the data of psychology, whence he could derive effective ways of thinking about and dealing with patients' behavior. Rogers still believes such training to be valuable for those therapists who also wish to advance the knowledge of psychotherapy through research. However, in the training of practicing therapists as such, he no longer feels that training in psychology is a crucial antecedent. Indeed, he has expressed the belief that such training sometimes makes it more difficult to become a good therapist because it encourages habits of thinking of people as *objects* for study. He currently seems to believe the most valuable training background would be an extensive experience with people, either in direct contacts with a great variety in many cultural settings or acquaintance with this through reading. In addition, practice in trying to think, feel, and act as if one were someone else, as in drama or role playing, is considered helpful. The most valuable type of training for a therapist arises from direct and concrete interview experiences with great varieties of individuals. The experience of personal therapy might also be helpful. However, Rogers does not believe that the operation of deviant response patterns in the therapist will necessarily interfere with the effective conduct of therapy. At least such responses are not likely to damage client-centered therapy, because such deviations exert their most detrimental effect when the therapist plays the role of an evaluator, a role he should deny himself in Rogerian therapy.

NECESSARY KNOWLEDGE OF BEHAVIOR DISORDER. A knowledge of the nature and etiology of a patient's disorder (a diagnosis) is considered unnecessary in Rogerian psychotherapy. He acknowledges that a pretherapy evaluation might be useful in other treatment procedures, such as foster home placement of maladjusted children, but for his type of psychotherapy a pretherapy evaluation is considered not only unnecessary but also potentially antitherapeutic. His position concerning diagnosis is a logical outgrowth from his proposition that the fundamental nature of behavior disorder is the same regardless of how it is manifested; thus, no selection of patients or behaviors to be treated is required, and the same therapeutic approach is used regardless of the manifestations of the disorder. No selection of techniques is required.

There are two general sets of reasons why pretherapy analysis is held to be both unnecessary and undesirable. First, it is objected to on philosophic and ethical grounds. The attitude behind diagnosis is considered to be socially dangerous, since it is said to carry the connotation of the control of the many by a few and violates the ethic of self-determination. Second, it is argued that both the attitude implied and the diagnostic act itself are likely to interfere with the achievement of the therapy objectives. Rogers believes it is incompatible with the major objective of freeing the subject to rely on his own judgments and evaluations to guide his behavior. More practically, since disorder lies in responses which can be directly observed only by the patient, accurate and effective diagnosis by an objective observer (the therapist) is difficult if not impossible. The patient is in the best position to observe and diagnose the thoughts and emotional responses that are the source of his difficulties.

Principles by Which Behavior Change Occurs

Rogers seems to have three principles by which behavior is acquired: response arousal, response termination or response avoidance, and simple contiguity in awareness. Behavior sequences that are followed by positive affect (response arousal), whether they be thoughts, sensations, or acts, tend to recur or become habitual; they satisfy the actualizing tendency. Those that are followed by negative affect tend not to be repeated, and one seems to learn responses that avoid or terminate (response termination) negative feeling; they do not satisfy the actualizing tendency. Thoughtful judgment helps determine what behavior will occur in a particular situation, but it is the affective consequence of that behavior that appears to influence whether that same thoughtful judgment or same behavior will recur in the future. The crucial situational events which seem most likely to be followed by affective responses are the behaviors of other people, particularly their approvals and disapprovals. Thus, interpersonal situations represent a powerful learning situation. In addition, any event that is attended to and symbolized in awareness can result in a learned thought (contiguity in awareness).

All learned behavior—the self-concept, the learned valuing, the needs for positive regard and positive self-regard—can be modified by these learning principles. The innate motives and valuing cannot be modified by learning and indeed should not be, since they innately lead to healthy functioning. (It should be noted that the preceding comments about learning are inferences by the authors. Rogers' theories do not include a theory of learning, and this is, of course, a serious weakness.)

Patient Behavior That Must Occur in Therapy

Rogers' theory of behavior pathology makes it clear he believes evaluative thoughts learned from others and associated affective responses are the key elements in behavior disorder. These learned responses conflict with innate responses. The consequence is anxiety. Anxiety leads to inattention toward or failure to think about the events which lead to it; or it leads to inaccurate attending to or thinking about the anxiety-producing events as a means of controlling the anxiety. For example, a patient may have learned to think about himself as bad because he has sexual fantasies and masturbates. Thinking of himself as bad leads to negative affect (guilt). On the other hand, the sexual fantasies and masturbation produce exciting and pleasurable sensations in his body. These two response sequences are incongruent or in conflict. Anxiety results. To control the anxiety, the person attempts to avoid thinking about sexual themes, and if he masturbates he tries to forget it quickly or pretend it did not occur. In addition, when sexual sensations occur he will think about them in a distorted fashion, perhaps as intestinal distress rather than as sexual sensations.

The patient has acquired faulty habits of attending to, identifying, thinking about, and evaluating the raw data of his experience, his sensations and images (organismic experience). To correct this, the patient has to start over with the raw data and rebuild more accurate habits of awareness and thought. He should attend to, think about, and talk about his habits of evaluating himself and other people or events, including the affective responses associated with his evaluations. He should pay attention to how he naturally responds to events, both in terms of actions and in terms of the sensations and affect which follow. By noticing and thinking accurately about such events, the patient can reconcile the contradictions and thus remove, reduce, or control the antecedents to anxiety. If anxiety does not occur, the symptomatic consequences will disappear.

Necessary Conditions to Elicit Appropriate Patient Behaviors

CONDITIONS PROVIDED BY THE PATIENT. Rogers specifies three essential conditions for beginning therapy. First, anxiety responses must be occurring, or at least a considerable amount of the patient's learned behavior must be contradictory and, thus, make it very likely that anxiety responses will occur (there must be incongruence making the patient vulnerable or anxious). Therefore, anxiety appears to be the basic discomforting response which leads a patient to make the therapeutic effort. Second, the patient must at least tentatively believe (think thoughts) that the therapist respects him, will be kind and not hurt him, and understands how he feels and thinks. Associated with these thoughts should be positive rather than negative affective responses, for example, trust rather than fear (the patient must *perceive* the therapist's unconditional positive regard and empathic understanding). Third, the patient must meet with the therapist; there must be contact. Unless the patient regularly meets with the therapist, the therapist cannot affect the patient's behavior. If the patient does present himself for help, it may be inferred that the first and second conditions exist unless the individual has been coerced into coming through such devices as court referrals, threat of divorce unless he comes, or hospital procedure. The degree to which these three conditions are present will vary, but they must always be present to some minimal degree, which Rogers says he is as yet unable to specify.

In his earlier work (1942, 1951), Rogers mentioned several additional conditions, which he seems to have dropped in his recent work. These included a minimum degree of intelligence, genuine control over his own life situation including some independence of family control, and a desire to change stronger than the fear of trying to change. He also held that the responses to be changed should be inappropriate learnings rather than appropriate responses to real, highly stressful situations. In the latter instance he once proposed it would be better to change the situation. Rogers now seems to believe that while his psychotherapy might not produce marked changes in all people and with all types of disorders, it is a good climate for personal growth and extremely unlikely to hurt anybody. Therefore, it can be applied appropriately to everyone, if only to make a "good" adjustment "better." He seems to believe that his therapy may be helpful for almost any kind of learned behavior disorder.

CONDITIONS PROVIDED BY THE THERAPIST. Rogers' latest statement of therapeutic technique is simple and brief. The therapist's task is to feel friendly toward the patient, to think kind and approving thoughts toward him (experience unconditional positive regard), to understand how things look from the patient's observational vantage point (experience empathic understanding of his internal frame of reference), and finally to be aware of and honest with himself about the responses the patient is eliciting in him (to be congruent in the relationship). Of course, these are all subjective responses (r) in the therapist. When such r's exist, the verbal, motoric, and physiological responses (R) will automatically be gentle, kind, and encouraging, that is, noncritical, nonthreatening. In addition, the therapist should periodically tell the patient his understanding of how things look from the patient's vantage point (he should convey understanding and acceptance to the patient). The words chosen to express this understanding should be quietly, gently, and sympathetically spoken, but should neither approve nor disapprove of the patient's behavior. The therapist does not question or in other ways try to elicit particular responses from patients. In effect, the patient is expected to talk about anything that concerns him, and it is believed the patient's choices will lead to the central difficulties.

This set of therapist techniques is aimed at creating the second condition in the patient—his belief in the therapist's acceptance and understanding and his positive feelings toward the therapist. Thus, true to his phenomenological position, Rogers emphasizes what the therapist thinks and feels rather than what he does.

Necessary Conditions to Modify Patient Behaviors

The therapist's behavior should not produce fear in the patient. It seems implicit in Rogers' position that critical, angry, fearful, unfriendly, or inattentive behaviors on the part of other people provoke anxiety or fear in patients. Thus, the therapist should avoid such behaviors and convey exactly their opposite, which Rogers seems to believe typically elicit positive affect in patients. It is recognized that therapists cannot maintain this attitude perfectly, but when they deviate they should be aware of that fact and perhaps sometimes even share it with the patient. It will be noted that these modifying conditions are identical with those for *eliciting* the appropriate behaviors; they are both necessary and sufficient. Rogers seems to be saying that if the therapist is consistently friendly, attentive, understanding, and nonevaluative the patient not only will be unafraid of him and willing to speak about private thoughts and feelings which he has been disregarding or thinking about inaccurately, but also will change. This probably represents a kind of extinction procedure. Since the sequences—evaluative thoughts which engender negative affect, which produce symptoms—were learned in a punitive social context, the occurrence of those same thoughts as verbal statements in a nonpunitive, friendly, understanding social context which elicits positive rather than negative affect would seem to provide the conditions for extinction or unlearning.

In addition, the therapist helps to focus the patient's attention on the troublesome events. Thus, from among all the things a patient speaks about, the therapist responds primarily to the evaluative thoughts the patient reports about himself, other people, and other events as well as the associated affect. The therapist's function here, however, is not to try to change such thoughts by interpreting or explaining them and their false bases to the patient, but rather simply to direct the patient's attention to them. Thus, a Rogerian therapist may summarize some of a patient's conversation with the statement "You are angry with yourself, but you are puzzled as to why you should be so." He would not continue and say "of course, you are angry with yourself because . . . etc." In some ways this resembles the Skinnerian procedure for shaping emitted behavior.

In summary, Rogerian procedures for modifying behavior involve attempts to extinguish anxiety which is a consequent of evaluative thoughts and associated affect and to direct the patient's attention to the crucial thoughts and other r's which the patient has learned to disregard or think about inaccurately. It is assumed that once the anxiety is reduced and the patient pays attention to and thinks correctly about the crucial events, the patient can and will proceed to reorganize his own thoughts so that in the future they produce less anxiety and lead to more effective and personally satisfying behavior.

Rogers does not specify different techniques for use with different behavioral difficulties. If the therapist creates an interpersonal situation in which positive affect consistently occurs, and if he conveys his understanding of the way the patient evaluates and feels about himself and others, the patient will proceed to change whatever behaviors are troublesome. One treatment fits all ills! He acknowledges that the generality of his approach may seem surprising to "conventional therapists" (1959, p. 213). He has noted a recent study that indicated that patients who externalize their problems and feel little self-responsibility for them are more likely than others to be a "failure" in client-centered therapy. He acknowledges that different therapy procedures may be necessary for such patients if the finding is verified (1959, p. 213). This raises the possibility that other types of subjects, who are as yet unidentified, also may require different procedures.

THE SEQUENCE OF BEHAVIORAL CHANGE. The sequence of change is an issue of long-standing interest to Rogers, and it is referred to by the term *process*. However, his concern with sequence has not been with the order in which the therapist should try to *produce* changes, but rather with the order in which changes occur when the therapist creates the appropriate therapeutic conditions. In his first presentation (1942), Rogers defined the following sequence as characteristic of his therapy. (1) The individual seeks help; (2) the helping situation becomes defined; (3) the counselor encourages free verbalization and symbolization of emotional responses; (4) he accepts, recognizes, and clarifies negative emotional responses; (5) full symbolization of negative emotional responses is followed invariably by symbolization of positive emotion; (6) the therapist accepts and clarifies positive emotional responses; (7) congruence of self-evaluative and emotional responses in the patient results; (8) the patient begins to consider the possible courses of action; (9) he gradually initiates positive actions; (10) positive actions are followed by more complete and accurate discriminations and symbolization of situational events and responses; (11) increasingly integrated positive actions occur, and although certain symptoms remain they are no longer disconcerting; and (12) the patient feels a decreasing need for help.

His latest conception of the sequence of change (1959) is quite similar, except that it places complete emphasis on subjectively observable responses and has no reference to instrumental acts. At first, the patient will talk about situational events, events in the past, the behavior of other people, and his troublesome symptoms which are the consequence of anxiety or are behaviors which prevent the occurrence of anxiety. These are the first things discussed because they are less likely to be followed by the anxiety responses. As the patient talks, assuming that the therapist is providing the necessary conditions, he gradually begins to speak of his own feelings more frequently, and overt emotional responses in the form of motoric and physiological patterns of response begin to occur more often. For example, the patient may begin to talk about feeling angry toward his mother or afraid of his boss and at the same time make agitated hand movements, become flushed, and sweat. As feelings are discussed, he begins to talk about the feelings that occur when he observes his own behavior, such as "I get angry with myself for being so stupid," or "When I have to make decisions on my own, I get afraid." (The reader should recall that, for Rogers, the term feeling includes thoughts about the events observed as well as the affective responses associated with those thoughts.) As he talks about his feelings, the associated thoughts, and the events that preceded and follow them, the patient begins to learn or relearn discriminations. For example, he may discover the sequence "When mother criticizes, I get angry, then I think thoughts about how terrible I am, and then I get headaches," where previously he may have only realized he got headaches but was not aware of the antecedent conditions. Thus, these discriminations may involve attending to things previously ignored, thinking about events previously disregarded, and entertaining thoughts involving comparisons and judgments. As a consequence, events previously neglected and not thought about, or thought about in an inaccurate fashion, become more accurately conceived. With this new awareness, the patient also recognizes the discrepancies between the thoughts he thinks about himself and the responses he actually makes. As he begins to pay attention to and think about such discrepancies, associated negative affective responses occur and the patient observes and thinks about them rather than avoiding them as in the past. These thoughts and emotions frequently seem new and surprising to him because he has been ignoring them or thinking incorrectly about them, thereby preventing them from occurring. Once he attends to and thinks about—and preferably talks about—the conflicting thoughts and self-evaluations, he can reorganize his self-identifying and self-evaluative thoughts to reconcile the conflicting aspects. When this is done, the anxiety responses that resulted from the conflict no longer appear.

As he comes to think differently about himself, more events can be attended to and thought about without anxiety. He attends to more of the therapist's behavior without anxiety, and he relies more on his own thoughts and affective responses as guides to his decisions, rather than relying so much on the opinions of others. With new habits of thought about himself and with fewer responses leading to anxiety, his instrumental behaviors toward other people, toward his work, and so forth, become more variable, more appropriate and specific to the situations in which they occur, and his thoughts about himself change flexibly when necessary. His behavior becomes more spontaneous, because his new-found confidence in himself makes it unnecessary for him to anticipate and plan carefully for the reactions of others.

Of course, this sequence occurs in a halting fashion, with the various phases overlapping and taking different amounts of time in different patients. However, the general sequence is said to be typical of all patients if only the therapist provides the necessary conditions. Rogers notes that all the phases described may not be necessary in every client.

Transfer of Behavior Change

Rogers assumes that changes in behaviors outside of the therapy interview will follow automatically upon changes in the self-evaluative thoughts and associated emotions during the therapy hour. Changes in the self-evaluative thoughts and their emotional concomitants result in reduced anxiety, improved discrimination among situational events and responses, more accurate symbolization of them, and greater confidence in one's own decisions. These provide the conditions from which more appropriate instrumental and interpersonal responses will naturally grow.

In his earlier writings, Rogers discussed two conditions which appeared to facilitate the transfer of behavior to nontherapeutic situations. First, Rogers noted that the response difficulties the patient attempted to resolve during the interview were only a small fraction of what he worked out between interviews. A related observation was that during the latter part of therapy, an increasing portion of the patient's talk referred to plans and behavioral steps to be taken outside of therapy, along with discussion of their possible outcomes. This suggested to him that patients in Rogerian therapy symbolically "rehearsed" potential nontherapy behaviors, actually tried them out in nontherapeutic situations, and then discussed the consequences in the therapy interview. If this, in fact, occurs in Rogerian therapy, then it would appear to provide the means by which transfer may take place.

EVALUATION OF BEHAVIOR CHANGE

One of Rogers' unique and most influential contributions has been his continued insistence that the theory and techniques of psychotherapy must be evaluated by rigorous research and his convincing and frequent demonstrations that such research is possible (1954). Not only have he and his students completed a large number of studies, but also their work has stimulated similar attempts by therapists of other persuasions. Rogers' influence in advocating the principle that therapy is an orderly, lawful process which can be subjected to public and repeatable observational procedures, the consequences of which are expected to be verifiable principles, is difficult to overemphasize. Evaluation has two main aspects: (1) to determine when behavior changes have occurred in a patient, and (2) to determine the validity of the principles under which the therapy proceeds.

Appraisal of Behavior Change

It is consistent with Rogers' position that the patient determines when sufficient change has been achieved. The patient sets his own objectives and decides when they have been sufficiently reached. Rogers expects that the innate evaluative responses will lead to an accurate decision by the patient.

Verification of Therapy Theory

Rogers has been steadfast in his position that therapy theory should be tested and reformulated via carefully designed research. Rogers' stream of research began with careful analyses of complete protocols of recorded therapy interviews. With this start, studies of his theory and therapy have used almost every means of evaluation available in clinical psychology. For example, there have been studies utilizing projective tests, GSR scores, ratings by expert observers, ratings by patients, the Discomfort-Relief Quotient, paper and pencil tests such as the Minnesota Multiphasic Personality Inventory, and questionnaires. The discovery of Q-sort Technique stimulated an extensive stream of research because it fit the study of Rogers' perceptual and self-evaluative variables so nicely. There has been no "strait jacket" on the research of Rogers' group; its members have been innovators and have been willing to use any legitimate approach which seemed to hold promise. The reader interested in greater detail concerning research on this therapy system will find several bibliographies available (e.g., 1961). Rogers has expressed the opinion that nearly all the research evidence has tended to confirm his theory and that few of the findings have been flatly contradictory.

Most of the research to which Rogers refers as supporting his position is based on the verbal report of the patient. This is a necessity since the kinds of responses believed to be crucial, that is, thoughts and affective responses, can be observed directly only by the patient. The difficulties related to reliance on introspective or verbal report are well known. Even so, the research of the Rogerian group has been provocative and has encouraged many other people to believe that research on psychotherapy is feasible, ethical, or desirable.

COMMENTS

Carl Rogers' system has significantly influenced the development of therapy theory and practice. Several of its emphases deserve special attention, since they should be considered strengths in his view.

Attention should be called first to his unfailing commitment to the use of scientific procedures in the study of therapy. Beginning with the assumption that therapy must represent a lawful sequence of events, he has made consistent efforts toward systematization and has sought to represent his propositions in as clear and concise a fashion as he could. He has also continued to be faithful to the scientific method in his insistence on research as the means by which propositions are tested. Rogers himself has not only formulated and subjected his ideas to test but has also continued to revise them in the light of new evidence. His research productivity and the appearance of three theoretic revisions in 17 years bear testimony to this. In these respects he has done a great deal to contribute to the maturation of therapy theorizing.

Allied to this have been his useful emphasis upon therapy as a "process" and his initial success in demonstrating some of the features that characterize therapy sequences. His realization that specifiable situational events represented in what the therapist says and does tend to be followed by specifiable response sequences in the patient constitutes a basic step toward formulating systematic procedures which can in turn be subjected to verification. It has been characteristic of his later work that he has focused on the general pattern of patient responses through the successive therapy stages.

Rogers is to be credited also for his efforts to manage conceptually the subjectively observable responses (r), such as thoughts and feelings, to specify the conditions under which they may be modified and to begin to elaborate some of their interrelationships. This crucial set of events is so difficult to manage theoretically that some psychologists have chosen to proceed by ignoring them, or else to assume that behavior can be rendered intelligible and predictable without them, that is, that account need not be taken of them. Rogers insists upon their importance and seeks to demonstrate their lawfulness. The self-identifying and self-evaluative thoughts along with associated affects which Rogers emphasizes seem to the writers to be very important response classes. Rogers' attempts to map out interrelationships among these response classes and to specify how they might be modified are certainly important.

And finally, the appearance of Rogers' theoretic statements has performed an invaluable service in that they have for some time provided the major alternative in the United States to the popular stream of psychoanalytic theorists. This is true, even though some of his ideas are highly similar to psychoanalytic predecessors such as Rank and Adler. Rogers has helped the field of therapy theory immeasurably; all the advantages that follow from the confronting of differences have resulted from the theoretic contrasts he has developed so well.

In contrast to these several strengths, the writers believe there are important gaps and inadequacies in this system, which need to be remedied. These critical comments have to do with the kinds of events upon which his theory is focused, the types of concepts employed to treat them, and the variety of propositional statements developed to explain their interaction.

Concepts

First, Rogers' system is notable for its emphasis on subjectively observable events and its corresponding de-emphasis of events accessible to the objective observer. In his initial work (1942) he had sought to specify some of the objective situational events, particularly when he set out to study the interrelationships between what a therapist says and its effect upon the way the patient spoke about himself. Certainly the effort to study subjectively observed events is very important. It is regrettable that his more recent emphasis on this class was not *in addition to,* rather than *instead of,* his earlier attention to the interrelationships among situational (S) and response (R and r) events.

His argument that an individual's perception of, or subjective response to, situations is a critical antecedent to much subsequent behavior is undoubtedly sound. As he uses it, perception represents a very broad class of events and needs considerable subclassification for therapeutic, and perhaps theoretic, utility. However, his position seems inadequate because it does not consider systematically the antecedents to perceptions. There is considerable experimental evidence that many perceptions *vary directly* as a function of properties of situational events. In fact, Rogers' position implies that patients' perceptions vary as a function of conditions or situational events provided by the therapist. He has treated this problem somewhat along the lines of: if the therapist has unconditional positive regard (S) then the patient will . . . However, the writers believe it needs considerably more extensive treatment. For example, why must he treat his situational event classes in terms of the therapist's *subjective* responses such as unconditional positive regard?

His neglect of the patient's objectively observable responses (R) is equally serious. It would appear that this neglect stems from his implicit assumption that there is a direct correspondence between R responses and the r responses which are their antecedents; that is, that "appropriate" overt responses (R) will occur automatically as a consequence of appropriate mediating responses (r). Such an assumption seems questionable and at the least deserves experimental test. Most football coaches would agree not only that a player does need to memorize plays, but also that he needs practice in running them off, for example. Both (r) and (R) behaviors must be modified, and although they are interrelated, changes in one do not *always* bring the appropriate changes in the other. Another reason for believing Rogers could improve his theory through systematic treatment of objectively observable responses (R) lies in the problem of inference. He wishes the therapist to focus on the patient's self-evaluative thoughts and feelings. However, these are available to the therapist *only* through observation of the patient's objectively observable behavior, such as talking. Since the patient's thoughts and feelings are always to be inferred by the therapist, a knowledge of propositions concerning the correspondence between subjective thoughts and overt actions $(r \rightarrow R$ relationships) would seem virtually essential.

One of the difficulties involved in Rogers' concepts is their level of abstraction. For example, in his concept of organismic experience he seems to include all subjective response events such as intestinal sensations, sensations arising from movement, and auditory sensations. His concept of organismic valuing seems to encompass all kinds of emotion such as guilt, fear, anger, love, and "feeling good." Similarly, his notion of the self-concept includes a tremendous variety of thoughts. Subclassification would seem essential for theoretical and therapeutic precision. Examination of protocol material reveals that Rogerian therapists do respond to more particular events. For example, they discuss fear of mother, guilt over actions, self-derogatory thoughts, and so forth. There is considerable information in the literature on physiological psychology, sensation and perception, motivation and emotion, and psychopathology, to name a few examples, which is relevant to subclasses of Rogers' major concepts. Most of the concepts in this system are highly abstract. The correspondence between them and lower-order concepts as well as observable events is insufficiently detailed. The conceptual hierarchy of this system seems to need considerable development and perhaps elaboration.

Not only are the concepts of Rogers' system highly inclusive with respect to the *kinds* of events to which they refer but also with respect to different combinations of events at any one point in time and to series of events proceeding through time. Nothing could be more inclusive than the attempt to view the individual as behaving as an organized whole at any one point in time—treating the entirety of events as a single unit. Certainly behavior is continuous, but it cannot be studied or treated all at once. Similarly, the self-concept refers not only to complicated combinations of events but also to these combinations over lengthy time periods of weeks and years. Rogers has very few concepts which refer to discrete events, or to discrete event sequences, or to discrete event patterns. The reader will recall the position held by the writers. Concepts such as these are quite legitimate as long as their interrelationships with other concepts and with observable events are carefully treated. When one fails to do this, one is left with a collection of highly abstract concepts whose utility is markedly impaired. For research purposes, Rogers states that he has operational definitions for all his concepts. It would seem to us that the therapist needs "operational definitions" also for his work.

Some of the concepts themselves need careful attention. In the writers' judgment, one of the most awkward parts of the definitions in the system are the concepts of the "actualizing tendency" and the "organismic valuing process." Rogers acknowledges several of the difficulties entailed in such concepts and recognizes the objections that have been raised. But he continues to feel that these are appropriate ways to identify certain kinds of events, and he has developed propositions as to how he thinks they work. Submitting these concepts and their related propositions to empirical test seems virtually impossible at this point. Rogers has held that the more deeply one believes in and relies on this innate strength of the patient, the more fully one will "discover" it. Thus, therapists who do not find such events occurring in their patients fail to do so because they do not believe strongly enough in their existence. This is hardly an adequate form of validation; on the contrary it carries the distinct ring of dogma and faith. It has occurred to us that Rogers' use of the term valuing may be similar to a typical philosophical usage: any discrimination or judgment is a value. If this is what he intends, he starts from discrimination learning, and it seems to us it would be more helpful if Rogers were to tie his concepts to that research base and psychological language, rather than the language of philosophy.

Second, the concept is defined by its consequences. The most important of these consequences are interpersonal. What "maintains and enhances" people involves learned value judgments which vary from group to group. Therefore, it would appear that the inference of an innate sequence is not essential in the theory. What is enhancing appears to be primarily a learned interpretation based on the nature of affective responses. Since it has been fully demonstrated, using conditioning procedures, that affective responses can become associated with almost any kind of situational or response event, Rogers' assumption of an innate organismic valuation based on natural affective consequences to behavior seems questionable. It would seem closer to the data to speak of different kinds of learned values, of learned associations among various events, and affective responses. We wonder if Rogers may have allowed his ethics—man should be permitted to make his own choices—to become his psychology: man has innate mechanisms for making the right choices.

Propositions

Turning to the propositions developed by the system, one should note that virtually all of them have to do with response-response interrelationships. In addition, most are formal propositions, relating concept to concept, rather than empirical, relating concepts to observable events. The hazards entailed by a neglect of situation-response propositions have already been noted; here it should be emphasized that the exclusive attention paid by the system to very high-order concepts has led to a corresponding omission of propositions that deal with the interrelationships between classes of events at lower levels of abstraction, and most critical of all, at the level of observable events themselves.

A good example of the theoretical dangers involved in omitting important classes of events from one's thinking and in conceptualizing at an abstract level may be drawn from descriptions of the process of "Client-Centered Therapy." On the basis of a number of studies,

Rogers has been able to describe a general sequence of change in patient behavior during therapy interviews which seems consistent from patient to patient and therapist to therapist. Rogers has been careful to acknowledge that this sequence may not characterize other therapies, although he seems to feel that generally it may characterize effective therapy. A comparison of therapy protocols by different theorists will reveal a good many differences. The topics of discussion vary, as well as the order in which they are discussed. For example, Rogers would respond consistently to self-evaluative thoughts and feelings, an orthodox Freudian might devote considerable attention to early sexual experiences, while Whitaker and Malone might devote attention to reporting their own subjectively observable responses. The point is that what happens in a therapy session is a function of what the therapist does. One set of operations elicits certain types of patient-responses; another set induces still different behaviors. For example, certain learning experiments should lead one to expect a patient to show a steady increase in his reports of his subjectively experienced feelings and an increase in statements about his own evaluative judgments of events rather than those of others, if the therapist is repeatedly making statements prefaced by *"You feel . . ."* as opposed to making statements such as "Your mother thinks . . . ," "Everyone agrees . . . ," or "As your therapist, I conclude. . . ."

Here, then, is an instance in which the behaviors that are felt, thought, and emitted are probably strongly influenced by situational events (the therapist's behavior). If this is true of the within-therapy sequences, the "process" of therapy may vary as a function of the treatment operations employed. And if the *process* is situationally specific, could it also be true of the therapeutic *outcomes?* By deemphasizing situational events and by conceptualizing therapy with large inclusive concepts and units, the likelihood of overgeneralizing about the consequences one observes is increased.

Concepts and propositions could have been drawn from the work of other researchers. But Rogers at times has appeared to believe that certain related disciplines have little to offer. For example, he seems to doubt the relevance of present-day learning theory to psychotherapy. Yet, if the system is to grow and develop, it must evolve a great deal more in the way of detailed formulations as to the conditions that determine how responses are learned.

Rogers now proposes that responses are learned if they satisfy the master motive or its subsidiaries. How can conditions be arranged so that the consequents of a response are in fact satisfying? How can one determine which events are congruent with and which are contradictory to the master motive? So far, his answer to such questions appears to be, "When the patient says so." In addition, if the behavior acquired as a consequence of his innate regulatory principle will always be good, why does the individual learn the conflicting values of other people? Is there another article of learning? Even though he might not wish to adopt any current system of learning theory, surely the extensive body of research would be of considerable help in formulating a more adequate and complete set of propositions. For example, since Rogers' learning principles seem to involve the arousal or termination of affective responses, it would seem that the extensive literature on avoidance-learning, as well as the developing literature about learning related to stimulating or arousing responses in oneself, would be highly relevant to his theory. Similarly, Rogers proposes that the consequences of behavior influence learning. So do learning theorists. For Rogers the crucial consequences are "evaluations"; for learning theorists they are "reinforcements." What consequents to behavior are the crucial ones for learning?

Similarly, any complete theory of personality must account for the development of disordered response sequences as well as "healthy, integrated" behavior. Yet Rogers apparently does not consider it essential or desirable to question whether his personality theory growing from his therapy observations is congruent with the evidence in the extensive literature on psychopathology or developmental psychology. A concrete example may help clarify this point. Rogers assumes an innate "organismic valuing process." He further assumes that this innate process will result automatically in the development of healthy, socially adaptive behavior unless handicapping, competing evaluative responses (conditions of worth) have been learned. These assumptions do not seem congruent with other observations. For example, the self-centered, exploitive, psychopathic behaviors which have frequently been observed to follow upon a highly indulged, undisciplined childhood are difficult to reconcile with this point of view. There is considerable evidence that learned negative self-evaluative responses (conditions of worth) are essential for adequate development in a societal context.

Rogers' belief that "truth is unitary" and that, therefore, a theory builder may start from a restricted observational base, such as human behavior in therapy interviews, may be valid. Even if this were so, it is likely to be much more *efficient* to build a theory from the larger observational base of human behavior in therapy *and* in groups *and* in laboratory settings *and* in physically distressing circumstances, and so forth. Rogers has been an effective observer but apparently has not appreciated the limited nature of the observational base from which his theory is built. For example, little in his theory would help to account for the complicated thought patterns of an Einstein, the fine performance of an Olympic athlete, or the exceptional skill of a concert pianist.

In conclusion, it may be worth noting that the very extent of these critical comments is a compliment to Rogers. It is precisely because he has been so conscientious in trying to make his ideas explicit and testable that the present writers have been able to formulate pointed criticisms. Situational events influence critics as well as patients.

Chapter 12

Existential Analysis

or *Daseinsanalyse*

Existential psychoanalysis is a development in European psychiatry which attempts to combine the assumptions of existential philosophy about the nature of man with the phenomenological method, to achieve a more effective understanding and psychotherapeutic treatment of patients. It has enjoyed increasing appeal in recent years, partly because of its concern with the dilemmas of the twentieth-century man, and partly because it is seen as a way of bridging what some view to be a serious gap between the scientific theories of psychology and psychiatry and the essential concerns of mankind.

Throughout much of the twentieth century, Europe has been in turmoil, war, and crisis. First came the First World War, then economic chaos, followed by the Second World War and the Cold War. Accompanying this has been a rapidly accelerating industrial and scientific revolution, a growing emphasis on a naturalistic rather than a religious view of man, an increasing urbanization of western society, and the development of an economic, social, and political philosophy actively promoted by powerful nations, which subordinates individual man to the welfare of the group or state. All this is said to have led to a renewed questioning of old values and explanations, and of the "meaning of life," and to a concern about whether modern man has not been deceiving himself with his conceptions about his nature. With new discoveries uncovering the immensity of the universe and the infinitesimal portion of time and space occupied by each human life, the value one can attach to an "insignificant thing" such as the individual person has acquired renewed urgency. These developments are said to have reduced man to a cog in a machine, important only as a part of some whole, with a corresponding loss of individual significance and identity.

Within this context, several sets of psychotherapists in various parts of the world noted that fewer patients came to them with difficulties such as those which constituted most of Freud's early practice, for example, hysterias, but many more complained of feelings of loneliness, depersonalization, alienation, isolation, detachment, and a lack of significant relationships with other people. They characterized their lives as empty and meaningless. These psychotherapists found the emphasis in current Western thought to be inadequate for providing an understanding of their patients: it was an emphasis on the naturalistic view of man, exemplified in Freudian theory and American behaviorism, and on the procedures of science to analyze and explain man as a natural object like any other. They felt this view eliminated the most essential characteristic of man, namely, his awareness of himself (his existence) and his self-directed, goal-oriented strivings (his continual becoming). Seeking assumptions about the nature of man which would be more acceptable, they turned to the existential philosophers. Seeking a new method for investigating the attributes of man they considered most important, and for which the procedures of natural science were considered inadequate, they turned to phenomenology.

BIOGRAPHICAL INFORMATION

Although existential writers note that some of their views may be found in philosophy and religion throughout man's history, most agree the philosophical "tap root" of the present psychotherapeutic applications lies in the writings of the Dane, Soren Kierkegaard. He died in 1855 at the age of 42, and his writings were little noticed until the turn of the century. Similarly, although the phenomenological movement has an extended history (Spiegelberg, 1960), Edmund Husserl (1859–1938) was the German philosopher whose phenomenological method directly influenced the present developments. Martin Heidegger (1899–   ) is considered the godfather of *Daseinsanalyse* (existential analysis). He was a student of Husserl's, his successor as professor in Freiburg, and a great admirer of Kirkegaard's work. He brought these two streams of thought together in his 1927 book, *Sein und Zeit (Being and Time,* 1962).

Ludwig Binswanger, a Swiss psychiatrist, was tremendously impressed by Heidegger's book and attempted to apply the ideas to psychiatry. He considered Heidegger's existential analytics a "philosophic-phenomenological clarification" of the innate "structure of existence," and his existential analysis as "the empirical-phenomenological scientific analysis of the actual ways and *Gestalten* of human existence." His work has been in a professional setting. He was an intern under Eugen Bleuler and resident at Jena University at the Psychiatric Clinic for Nervous Diseases. He succeeded his father as Chief Medical Director of the Sanatorium Bellevue at Kreuzlingen in 1911, and remained in that position until 1956. He retained a warm, lifelong friendship with Freud, despite their theoretical disagreements.

Medard Boss also worked under Eugen Bleuler at the Psychiatric Clinic at Zürich and studied under Freud and Jung. He is presently at the University of Zürich as professor of Psychoanalysis in the School of Medicine. He has been enthused both about the techniques of psychoanalysis and the ideas of Heidegger, and has tried to combine the two. He attempts to follow Heidegger more closely than Binswanger. His book on the technique of therapy, *Daseinsanalyse and Psychoanalysis,* was published in the United States in the spring of 1963. He and Binswanger have been major proponents of this point of view, but apparently several others developed similar notions relatively independently of one another, including A. Storch, G. Bally, and Roland Kuhn in Switzerland; J. H. Van Den Berg and F. J. Buytendijk in Holland; Eugene Minkowski in France; V. E. von Gebsattel in Germany; and Erwin Straus first in Germany and later in the United States. Binswanger, Van Den Berg, and Buytendijk are considered leaders in the attempt to develop a "phenomenological context for a science of man" (cf. May, in Ruitenbeek, 1962).

There are important disagreements among both the philosophers and psychotherapists involved in this stream of thought (cf. Kahn in Ruitenbeek, 1962). In addition, existential psychoanalysis is represented by its proponents as a point of view rather than a system. Moreover, there is no one person considered to be the foremost spokesman for the group. Finally there has been to date only a limited publication of their work in English. All these factors have made it difficult to select sources for the present analysis. We have relied primarily on the volumes edited by May, Angel, and Ellenberger (1958) and Ruitenbeek (1962), supplemented by a few other sources. We have also relied on the work of Rollo May as one prominent American analyst who has attempted to bring this point of view to the attention of American psychologists. It is an active stream of thought, retaining within it many divergent points of view, and a stream of publications by its proponents has already begun in the United States. Some of those currently in press will undoubtedly clarify issues upon which we can comment only briefly on the basis of those publications available to the writers.

MAJOR EMPHASIS

Existentialism has concentrated its attention so far upon the presuppositions underlying therapy, rather than the development of a therapy system or set of techniques. Thus, its first distinguishing characteristic is a set of assumptions about the nature of man. Man has the capacity for being aware of himself, of what he is doing, and of what is happening to him. As a consequence, he is capable of making decisions about these things and of taking responsibility for himself. He can also become aware of the possibility of becoming completely isolated and alone, that is, nothing, symbolized by the ultimate nothingness of death. This is innately feared. He is not a static entity but in a constant state of transition. He does not exist; he is not *a* being; rather he is coming into being, emerging, becoming, evolving toward something. His ways of behaving toward himself and other events are changing constantly. His significance lies not in what he has been in the past, but in what he is now and the direction of his development, which is toward the fulfilment of his innate potentialities.

A second emphasis is the special character of the concepts utilized. One cannot identify man's development, the significance of his behavior, without reference to the conditions under which the behavior occurs. There is no meaning to behavior except with reference to the events towards which the behavior is directed. For example, a smile has no meaning except as a gesture toward someone; a hand gesture is significant only as a wave goodbye or the manipulation of a tool. Objectively observable behavior (R) is a function of the situations toward which it is directed (S) and the subjectively observable responses (r), the intents, which guide it. If any of these facets are omitted from consideration, the behavior (R) cannot be understood. As a consequence, most of their concepts or units of analysis reject the classification of events as situational and behavioral, as subject and object, and emphasize that the behaving person and his environment are "all of a piece." Therefore, the "subject-object split" typical of Western thought is inapplicable to understanding human behavior. Their concepts include subjectively and objectively observable responses $(r$ and $R)$ and situational events (S) as a unit. This is apparent in their many hyphenated labels for concepts, such as being-in-the-world, which literally means the-person-who-is-behaving-with-intent-in-this-situation-now-and-knows-it. The typical concepts in this point of view represent large, molar units of analysis.

A third characteristic is their adoption of the "phenomenological research method" as a means of gaining a "new scientific knowledge" of the concerns of psychiatry which cannot be obtained through using the procedures of natural science (cf. Ellenberger in May, et al., 1958, and Binswanger in Ruitenbeek, 1962). Unfortunately, phenomenology is a term which has been used in several ways (Spiegelberg, 1960), and this is apparent among the existentialists (Ellenberger, in May, et al., 1958). Generally speaking, it refers to understanding events as "seen" from the vantage point of the subjective observer. The purpose is to get at what is "existentially real" rather than "abstractly true" about a person. They appeal to "a reality underlying both subjectivity and objectivity," to "reality as immediately experienced," emphasizing the "inner, personal character of man's immediate experience." They reject theory, "be it a mechanistic, a biological, or a psychological one" (Binswanger, in May, et al., 1958), because it leads the therapist to try to make the patient's behavior fit his theories, and perhaps leads him to attend to only those behavioral phenomena that fit his categories of analysis. A full understanding of the patient will thereby be obstructed.

Of course, the therapist cannot "immediately experience" the patient's subjective thoughts, feelings, aspirations, and so forth, although some of the more extreme existentialists seem to imply that the therapist goes "beyond language and symbolic imagery." Even capable scholars like Binswanger, Boss, and Kuhn sometimes treat their "intuitions" about the patient as the patient's reality rather than their own (cf. their chapters in May, et al., 1958 and Kuhn in Ruitenbeek, 1962). How does the therapist get at these important data? Rollo May (1961 and in Ruitenbeek, 1962) presents what appears to be the approach of the less extreme participants in this stream of thought. The therapist can never overcome the "subject-object split" in the sense that he can never have direct access to the patient's subjective experience. Binswanger (May, et al., 1958) seems to recognize this when he states that the content of language is the crucial data of therapy.

May (1961) seems to extend this to include other objectively observable responses as well. "Phenomenological reality" may be immediately given for the patient, but for the therapist it must always remain an abstraction, an inference based on the responses the patient produces in him—his observations, emotional responses. Therefore, the phenomenological method represents an *observational attitude* in which the therapist knows his own thought habits or concepts with which he "listens" to the patient and thereby controls his own biases, keeping his way of thinking sufficiently flexible so that he can listen and think in terms of the patient's constructs or language as well as his own (May, 1961, p. 27). If he does not listen to the patient's depiction of events, he may jump to false conclusions. However, with this attitude the therapist not only listens, he "experiences" the patient's communications "at many different levels" (an aspect of *presence*). We interpret this to mean that the patient's behavior elicits subjective responses in the therapist, such as emotions, which, if the therapist notices them, give added meaning to the statements heard. Finally, the emphasis in this approach is on understanding man as an individual (ideographic), rather than on identifying the ways in which men are alike (nomothetic), except for the initial assumptions about the nature of man.

THE NORMAL COURSE OF BEHAVIOR DEVELOPMENT

The writings examined suggest that the actual observations (experiences) upon which the existentialist conceptions have been built derive primarily from work with adults, especially those seriously disturbed. Almost no reference to children or the development of children has been found, except as an inference from the study of adult cases. Consistent with their emphasis on understanding the individual from the vantage point of the subjective observer, they say little about the course of behavior development in general, since each individual's development is considered unique. In a sense they build a developmental theory for each patient.

INNATE CHARACTERISTICS OF NORMAL DEVELOPMENT

Emphasis on an understanding of the "nature" of man as a basis for effective psychotherapy is characteristic of existential writers. May (1961) has presented six such "principles," and Tillich (Ruitenbeek, 1962) has discussed the existential assumptions in this regard. Several such attributes have been abstracted from the writings reviewed.

Being

The central fact is that man is a living, behaving individual, whose behavior is changing continuously and constantly, and who has the unique capacity for being aware of that fact. But awareness has significance only as one is aware *of* something (*consciousness*). Man's capacity for being conscious of himself, the events that influence him, and his influence on events leads to the ability to make choices and decisions. Of course, his behavior is powerfully influenced by many events beyond his control, but these typically limit how he can respond rather than requiring a particular response. Man's significant freedom lies in his capacity to choose from among the options available (May, 1961; Van Dusen in Ruitenbeek, 1962; Binswanger in May, et al., 1958), and in this sense he creates himself and his "worlds" (Tillich in Ruitenbeek, 1962), or is responsible for his behavior (May, 1961). The terms *being* or *becoming* comprise this group of innate attributes. The terms *Dasein* and *Existence* encompass the same phenomena for a particular individual at a particular point in time and space. One implication of these terms is that man is to understand himself in terms of his subjectively observable responses, of which thoughts are only one, and not the most important, part. *Dasein choosing* is sometimes used to imply the individual's responsibility for himself—the-person-who-is-responsible-for-his-existence-choosing. The direction of the choices seems toward the development or manifestation of the person's *innate potentialities* (cf. May, 1961; Hora, in Ruitenbeek, 1962; and various case reports in May, et al., 1958 and Ruitenbeek, 1962). The infant rather quickly begins to experience this sense of being real, alive, an entity (Laing, in Ruitenbeek, 1962). Concepts representing events which "get behavior started" are unnecessary, since it is always occurring. The directions or forms it takes are the things at issue.

Man's consciousness is not just a matter of verbal symbols, however. They are important, but only as part of a pattern of thinking-sensing-feeling-acting in relationship to other events. He does not just think, he *experiences*. His thoughts are not his reality, as some philosophers have suggested, but simply represent and summarize the raw data of sensations, feelings, images, motor movements, and so forth in relationship to other events (cf. Boss, in Ruitenbeek, 1962). It is the latter which are "reality" for any individual.

Being-With

Man always exists in a context, and his sense of being a living, growing entity (existing) results "only *in* his relations and *as* his relations to the objects and fellowmen of his world" (Boss, in Ruitenbeek, 1962). It is from this fact that language and consciousness acquire their significance. It is "existence-with which makes man; only on this basis do language and self-consciousness become possible" (Kahn, in Ruitenbeek, 1962). Like other living organisms such as plants, man can exist only if certain conditions are present. Change his body temperature by a few degrees, deprive him of water, or modify the shielding atmosphere so that he is exposed to particular kinds of radiation, and he will die. One necessary condition for his existence is other humans. Man might exist as an animal without relationships with others, but his humanness is a consequence of living with people. Man's awareness of himself results from his interaction with other events, particularly people.

Nonbeing

One consequence of the kind of awareness we have just summarized (awareness of *being*) is that it leads to the awareness of the possibility of its opposite, *nonbeing* or *nothingness*. This concept appears to be used in two ways. Sometimes, it refers to the awareness of the possibility of physical death, the ultimate nothingness. More frequently, it refers to feelings of emptiness, loneliness, and isolation from others for which death is the symbol (Ruitenbeek, 1962). In this usage, man is said to be innately isolated, in the sense that his personal awareness can never be directly experienced by others nor theirs by him. At the same time, his self-consciousness and feelings of personal identity result from his interaction with other events. Without such interaction, his sense of identity, his self-awareness, cannot exist. Subjectively, without this, he is a nothing, though objectively, to other people, he may still appear to be a person. His communications with and relationships to other events prevent this isolation. His language, particularly, is his liberation as far as sharing his subjective world with others and sharing in theirs (*authentic being*).

Awareness of the possibility of loss of self-awareness or identity innately leads to *ontological anxiety* or *dread*. The fear sometimes reported by people subjected to conditions of stimulus deprivation might exemplify this. Such anxiety is innately human and therefore cannot be avoided, but it must be dealt with. It can be controlled by interaction with other events which continually develop one's self-awareness and identity. If the anxiety is followed by an avoidance of significant interactions with events (denial of potentialities), guilt naturally follows. Thus, guilt is an innate response.

Experience and Thought

Certain characteristics of the general pattern of man's behavior also appear to be innate. Sensory responses elicited both by attributes of the person and by situational events have the characteristic of being immediately recognizable and independent of any interpretive response. Sensory responses from all the various sensory modalities are occurring continuously and simultaneously. The child *innately knows* it is possible to relate to events or objects in different ways because of the immediacy of sensory experience from different modalities. For example, looking at an event produces a different response than touching or tasting. A person is aware of himself and situational events simultaneously as one complex experience, and thus there is no subject-object split for him. Sensory responses are considered the basic unit from which all others are developed, and have the quality of being "of the present," since they must be elicited by some immediate antecedent. "Thinking, remembering, imagining" are all similar subjective responses, are all derived from the basic "sensory experiencing," and may be understood by referring to their sensory origin (Straus, in May, et al., 1958).

To summarize, existentialists seem to hold several assumptions about the innate characteristics of man. (1) Behavior is continuously occurring and changing in interaction with surrounding events. (2) Man is aware of that fact in himself, and this self-awareness gives him his personal sense of identity, of *being*. (3) Because of his self-awareness, he is capable of being selective in what he responds to and how he responds. (4) By his selective responding he is continually expressing his innate behavioral possibilities, molding his environment to himself and himself to his environment. (5) He responds to the natural world, other people, and himself continuously and simultaneously. Variability in responding is initially a natural consequence of different sensory modalities. (6) Self-awareness leads to the recognition that he could lose his identity by losing all significant relationships with his environment. This leads to innate anxiety, a response characteristic of all men and therefore not necessarily a basis for pathology. It occurs when the person sees a threat to his existence, importance, or welfare. (7) Anxiety leads to a restriction of behavior, that is, avoidance, which has guilt as a consequence. Thus, guilt is also a normal affective response in all humans.

LEARNED CHARACTERISTICS OF NORMAL DEVELOPMENT

We have found little about learning or learned behavior patterns as such in existential writings, which leads one to wonder where the "nature of man" ends and his "acquired behavior" begins. The existentialists apparently recognize the importance of learned behaviors. For example, they generally acknowledge behavior mechanisms as postulated by Freud and consider this an important finding. Such mechanisms are considered quite specific, however, and of far less significance than what they have called *modes of being-in-the-world, modes-of-world, world-design, and basic forms of existence,* among other terms. These represent large and inclusive patterns of interaction with complexes of events, somewhat on the order of Adler's life style. A study of existential case reports (May, et al., 1958) has led to the conclusion that these modes begin developing very early in life and continue developing throughout life. Therefore, they will be interpreted as learned.

Being-in-the-World

Binswanger (in Ruitenbeek, 1962) has stated that this concept encompasses both "the individual's own world and the simultaneous and coextensive relationships with and to other people and things." Behavior can be understood accurately only as a function of the simultaneous interaction of response (R, r) and situational (S) events. Behavior cannot be understood correctly independent of the situations under which it occurs or of the person's intents or self-evaluations. Thus, the basic behavioral unit to be analyzed is quite inclusive $(S-r-R$ units). The individual's behavior at any given moment is to be understood as the product of his self-awarenesses and his habitual ways and intents of relating with and to situations, objects, and people. Behavior apparently functions as a unitary whole.

Apparently, this global concept may be thought of as including several subconcepts or kinds of behavior patterns in classes of situational contexts. Three frequently mentioned are *Umwelt, Mitwelt,* and *Eigenwelt* (May, et al., 1958, pp. 61–66). An objective observer might think of these as the world of nature, the world of people, and one's subjective world, three neat categories of different kinds of events. That is not what the existentialists mean, however, because in using the phenomenological method, they have adopted the vantage point of the subjective observer, wherein one asks "What is *his* objective in behaving that way toward those events, now?"

UMWELT. This represents the natural world of behavior, the biological patterns of behavior that would still exist if one had no self-awareness. In May's terms, "It is the world of natural law and natural cycles, of sleep and awakeness, of being born and dying, desire and relief"; these are behaviors functioning according to the laws of biological determinism. Sometimes they are called *being-at-hand*. People living in *Umwelt* choose their behaviors in relation to their biological urges and sensations, such as the sex drive, rather than on the basis of other criteria. Their objective in responding to situational events and to themselves is to utilize such events to maintain their biological existence and to produce satisfaction. (One can see why it is said that Freud developed a theory primarily about *Umwelt*.) The terms adjustment and adaptation fit this category. One adapts to a change in the weather and adjusts to his periodic hunger pangs. Such things function according to natural laws, and one can only do his best to become comfortable with them. One cannot prevent hunger or change the weather, but only alleviate hunger or protect himself from the weather. In this "mode of being," man is little different from other animals.

MITWELT. This category of behavior involves other people, but in a special way. The objective is to enlarge one's private experience by forming genuinely significant relationships with another through sharing private sensations, feelings, and thoughts in the context of some emotion aroused by the situation itself. Such a relationship is called an *encounter*, always involves mutual awareness, and serves to prevent feelings of isolation and loneliness because each participant is sharing vicariously in the private experiences of the other and thereby gaining new self-awarenesses and an increased sense of his own identity. This is something like Sullivan's notion of consensual validation (cf. Chapter 14). It is a relationship, rather than an adjustment or adaptation, because each person changes as a consequence of interacting with the other. But people can respond to one another as "its" rather than as human. One person can manipulate another for his own biological gratification rather than try to create a human relationship—as in the contrast between rape and intercourse between lovers. In existential terms, such a person is behaving in *Umwelt* rather than *Mitwelt*. Of course, the extent to which a person succeeds in forming such relationships may vary in degree, but his *intent* is important. Similarly, an individual may behave toward others in such a way that they can respond toward him only as an "it," another object like a car, a chair, or a rug. Significant, shared relationships (*encounters*) are peculiarly human and are greatly facilitated by language, but are accomplished in part by nonverbal communications as well. The emphasis is on a *shared* experience (Boss in Ruitenbeek, 1962), and this mode of behavior is sometimes called *being-with-others*.

EIGENWELT. This is a category of behavior which existentialists believe psychological science and depth psychology have both ignored. Humans have the unique quality of self-awareness. This leads to the development of a feeling of self-identity which, though it is changing constantly, we interpret to be an habitual set of patterns of self-identifying and self-evaluative responses, sometimes called *being-in-itself*. The person responds to events, then, in terms of what that interaction means with reference to his identity, his habitual self-identifying and self-evaluative responses. Through this "mode of behavior" the person "sees the world in its true perspective," in terms of the personal (self-referent) meanings guiding his responses to the events around him. For example, I buy that picture because *I* think it is pretty, or I go to school because *I* want to learn. All behavior, then, has the quality of "for-me-ness."

EXISTENTIAL MODES. Man's ways of interacting with other people as well as himself have been of special concern to existentialists, and several types of such patterns have been proposed (types of *Mitwelt*). Ellenberger (May, et al., 1958, p. 121) attributed the development of four such modes to Binswanger. In the *anonymous mode,* the individual obscures his identity with the result that neither he nor others can consider him responsible for his acts. The individual lives and acts "in an anonymous collectivity," thereby destroying his own individuality, as might be exemplified by the conforming person, the masked dancer, or the soldier "who kills and is killed by individuals whom he does not know." He uses his anonymity to perform acts for which he need not assume responsibility as an identifiable individual.

The *singular mode* refers to all the ways in which a person relates to (evaluates, identifies) himself, including his ways of responding to and evaluating his own body, as exemplified by self-congratulatory, self-punishing, or self-destructive statements and actions. The *plural mode* identifies all those ways of relating to others in which they are treated as "its" to be used or dealt with to obtain one's satisfactions or goals. It is exemplified by all "formal" relationships in which people are competing, serving, exploiting, and submitting to one another—relationships in which one person hopes "to get something out of it" and in which there is no personal concern, consideration, or emotional involvement with the other people.

The *dual mode* is the most desirable, forming "the core of the normal existential experience." In such a relationship, each thinks of himself, not as a separate person, but as "we," two lives intertwined in a significant and mutually satisfying relationship. It is characterized by concern about and consideration for the other person, affectionate responses toward him, interest in his private feelings and thoughts as well as willingness to share one's own with him, and mutually chosen and valued objectives. Such relationships are exemplified by intimate, affectionate, parent-child relationships, close friendships with confidants, and lover-beloved relationships. *Love* is a particular instance which is so powerful and meaningful that it cannot be disrupted by time, separation, or even death.

One can see in these concepts the consistent existential emphasis on the fundamental significance of human relationships—without them we are not human—and the multiple forms and purposes of such relationships. Every instance of behavior may be thought of as simultaneously manifesting a way of and purpose in relating to other people (*Mitwelt*), to oneself (*Eigenwelt*), and to the natural world (*Umwelt*). For example, autism may be thought of as representing not only a lack of relations with other people but a means of dealing with one's biological urges and of maintaining some semblance of personal identity. The same behavioral situation can serve a variety of purposes. For example, a normal marriage would be expected to be characterized by love, mutual concern and consideration, shared experiences and objectives (dual mode), but could be characterized by the partners simply using one another (plural mode), or by so much self-concern that the other is ignored (singular mode). Although it seems clearly implied that such patterns of behavior are learned, the how of the learning is not discussed, and the why is discussed only in individual cases.

Note should be taken of the second way in which the term existential is sometimes used, that is, to mean critical or significant. An individual's behavior is to be understood by discovering the stable patterns of response that he has developed. It is especially important to discover the particular "modes of relating" which are most significant, in the sense that they influence many responses in many situations.

Characteristics of Subjective Experience

In their efforts to analyze human behavior from the point of view of the individual's subjective experience, existentialists have proposed several attributes, dimensions, or "primary structures of human existence." These are not *kinds* of response events, but more like attributes such as intensity. Two of these, temporality and spatiality, will be discussed by way of illustration. These are categories independent of kinds of subjective events, such as thoughts, sensations, and affects.

Temporality is considered to be one attribute of subjective experience. This is not the same as objective, measurable time, although it is not completely unrelated. It is modifiable through experience (learning), although it is apparently an innate characteristic. The subjective experience of time is the "flowing of life," the awareness of a continuous stream of ever-changing experiences (*r*). This awareness is independent of the particular events occurring at any given point in time. There is a certain "speed," or rate of change, experienced. The judgment of the rate at which time is passing will vary under specifiable conditions such as excitement or boredom. It is "automatically constructed" in irreversible sequences. The past is something we "leave behind" but may remember. The present is experienced as awareness of one's own behavior in relationship to other events at the time the behavior is occurring. The future is experienced in expectation and activity (*immediate future*), wish and hope (*mediate future*), or prayer and ethical action (*remote future*). Habits of responding to the various phases of subjective time may develop. For example, individuals forced into extended unemployment may cease to engage in any expectations or activity directed toward the immediate future. Sometimes individuals are characterized as oriented toward the future (prospective) or toward the past (retrospective). These patterns are believed to change with age. A person's estimate of the passage of time leads to habitual ways of responding, just as he does to other events; one must fill up every minute, or "kill time," or one may procrastinate.

Spatiality is considered a second basic attribute of subjective experience. This, too, has to do with the subjective estimate of space rather than physical space or even responses to physical space. It is modifiable through experience (learning), though apparently an innate characteristic. Individuals can experience spatiality in different ways. *Oriented space* is the most common, and is apparently most closely related to physical space. It is experienced as having a vertical axis (up and down) and horizontal axes (before, behind, right, left). The vertical axis is thought to be the axis to which the most crucial responses are related. In this spatial experience, definite limitations and objects (with an inside and outside) are experienced. *Attuned space* is a special quality of experience determined by one's affective responses at the time. Terms such as "fullness or emptiness," "expanding or constricting," "hollow or rich" are used to characterize this experience. For example, "Sorrow constricts attuned space, and despair makes it empty" (May, et al., 1958, p. 110). Other characteristics of attuned space are "clear," "dark," and "luminous." Other attributes of spatiality are "historical," "mythical," "aesthetic," and "technical." Thus, at times the concept seems to refer to the patterning of sensory experience as one is aware of it, and at times to the patterning of affective responses as one is aware of them.

Other attributes of subjective experience are *causality*, experienced as determinism, chance, and intentionality, and *materiality or substance* represented in the experience of the physical qualities of the world.[1]

The Healthy Individual

Nowhere in the writings examined did we encounter a characterization of the behavior of the healthy person. We must infer what some of the behavioral attributes are likely to be. From the foregoing it would appear that the healthy person is one who is accustomed to interacting with a wide range of situations and is alert to all major aspects of events; he is continually aware of himself, of his behavior, and of the events to which he is responding. Moreover, he actively selects the way in which he responds to situations, rather than passively responding under pressure of events. He can analyze what a situation requires, select an appropriate objective, decide how best to implement that goal, and proceed to carry out his plan. Not only is he capable of responding to a wide range of situations, but he also has a wide range of effective behaviors, permitting him to be flexible when he encounters difficulty. "If it is threatened in one region, other regions will emerge and offer a foothold" (May, et al., 1958, p. 205). Finally, his responses to other people are of a special character, since he is capable of forming significantly intimate relationships with them, wherein private thoughts and feelings become shared (*Mitwelt*) and in which there is mutual consideration for the other person as well as feelings of love (dual mode).

[1] The present writers are impressed with the similarities between existential ideas and those of E. B. Titchener (1913). For Titchener, the subject matter of psychology was "experience dependent on an experiencing person," or "the world with man left in." Terms applied to his position have included introspectionism, structuralism, Titchenerism, and existentialism. He, too, was concerned with the dimensions of subjective experience, and his discussion of attributes such as quality, intensity, duration, clearness, and insistence sounds much like some of the existential discussions. Furthermore, he, too, assumed sensation to be the basic unit of subjective response from which all else was built. Existentialists do not cite his work.

Summary

It is clear from the preceding material that it has been impossible for the present writers to abstract anything approaching a description of the pattern of development of normal behavior, even characterized phenomenologically. All that could be done was to abstract some features proposed to be characteristic of humans, and to point to some of these as modifiable by learning. One presumes that, in this system, learning functions to develop stable patterns of relationships among response and situational events (modes-of-being-in-the-world) and to shape the subjective estimates of temporality, spatiality, and the like. The existentialists' view of the normal, healthy man seems to be that he has developed a great variety of ways of responding to himself, to other people, and to the natural world; that he actively and consciously deals with the present in an attempt to create something new and better in the future; that he develops intimate relationships with other people characterized by positive affect; and that a full range of behavior is acceptable in himself without extensive anxiety, guilt, fear, or anger.

THE DEVELOPMENT OF BEHAVIOR DISORDER

In one sense, existentialists have no theory of behavior pathology. They wish to avoid pouring patients into some theoretical or diagnostic mold, but rather propose to discover the mold the patient has created for himself. In this sense, they are idiographic, insisting that behavior disorder can be understood only from the vantage point of the behaving individual; a separate theory of behavior disorder is necessary for each patient.

In a second sense however, they do have some general propositions about behavior disorder which would seem to provide a basis for a general theory. Throughout existential writings one finds behavior difficulties characterized in terms of conflicting factors, as exemplified in May, et al. (1958): they destroy man's capacity to fulfill his own being (May, p. 35); becoming is blocked (V. E. von Gebsattel, p. 176); love of father conflicts with rebellion over his tyranny (Binswanger, p. 222). Similar examples may be found in Ruitenbeek (1962): disorder is the product of man's essential nature conflicting with demands made upon him by self or others (Tillich, p. 14; Binswanger, p. 19; Hora, p. 139). Thus, their theory of disorder would seem to start with the assumption that man is confronted with two alternatives, "being" or "nothingness," "becoming" or "nonbecoming." The alternative of "becoming" is characterized by intentional and assertive interaction with other people and the natural world in a continuous effort to live a satisfying meaningful life, free of excessive amounts of anxiety, guilt, or anger. The alternative of "nothingness" or "nonbecoming" is characterized by an absence or decrease in habits of self-awareness, little active engagement of the world to accomplish chosen objectives, and a cessation of efforts to achieve a satisfying life. Related to, or as a consequence of this pattern, excessive amounts of anxiety and guilt are present. The alternative of "nothingness" would thus seem to be the avenue toward disorder, since these are outcomes that are opposite to those of the "healthy" individual. Finally, since each person is the result of self-creation, the alternative is the result of choice; the person "chooses" disordered behaviors as his best course for dealing with his dilemmas.

The Sequence of Development of Disorder

The reader should be reminded that what follows has been pieced together from the writings of existentialists, since they have made no systematic effort in this regard. Considerable reliance has been placed on their case analyses, since these represent the primary source of evidence.

The infant has to develop ways of relating to the natural world, other people, and himself. In the beginning, he tries out a variety of ways of relating to everything, and these may be tried again and again throughout life (May, et al., 1958, p. 225). When the consequences of such attempts elicit anxiety or fear in the individual, he will tend to avoid similar attempts at relating in the future; anxiety "paralyzes action" and "destroys communication." Hostility is said to have the same effect; both are considered as ways of relating to self and others which "curtail or destroy being." Events that produce physical pain followed by fear are not too troublesome, apparently because individuals can learn to avoid or control them relatively easily. However, any circumstance—actions of other people, events in the natural world, or one's own reactions to or thoughts about oneself—that leads the person to conclude he has lost his personal value and respect produces anxiety and is much more difficult to cope with. If the anxiety-producing events are of great significance to the individual—for example, a parent who is critical—he will try one pattern of response after another in search of an effective way of relating to the desired but anxiety-producing events. He will relate in whatever way may be effective or has become habitual. All disorders, neuroses and psychoses alike, are thought of as a set of patterns for relating to events to reduce anxiety; they retain some of the individual's sense of personal identity, worth, and continuity as an individual (another form of "being-in-the-world"), no matter how ineffective they may appear to the objective observer.

The sequence of event → anxiety → avoidance → new attempt at relating starts in connection with particular events, such as the father's behavior. However, if an effective pattern of response is not found and anxiety continues over an extended period of time, the anxiety may generalize to similar events, such as other men, and the range of situations involved in the anxiety leads to increases in the avoidance pattern (cf. the case of Ilse, in May, et al., 1958). The difficulty may remain restricted to a particular class of events, such as father or men, and the behavior patterns (modes-of-being-in-the-world) related to other kinds of events may be quite effective. The anxiety → avoidance pattern can generalize, however, so that it follows upon events of many different kinds. In the extreme case, events in the natural world, the behavior of other people, and one's own behavior all become antecedents to anxiety (cf. the case of Ellen West, Binswanger, in May, et al., 1958). In such a case, an individual's entire behavior repertoire may be composed of attempts to reduce or avoid the occurrence of anxiety which is so pervasively generated. If certain classes of events do not lead to anxiety (for example, animals and natural phenomena), the individual may restrict his responses to that class: "being rigidly confined to a specific world." Similarly, it is possible for habitual patterns of response to events to be incompatible; one may "live in conflicting worlds." One's habits of relating to other people may be quite contradictory to one's thoughts and fantasies about one's relationships. This is exemplified in Binswanger's analysis of Ellen West where her thoughts of accomplishments ("ideal world") were incongruent with her actual achievements ("world of practical action").

Since it is behavior in relationship to events in the present which is crucial ("existence"), current events must be continuing to induce the anxiety. These may be situational events (S), but often they are self-reactions or self-evaluative thoughts. Thus, the pattern of behavior may be perpetuated through response-response (r-r) sequences in which anxiety plays a part (*Eigenwelt* guilt). *Behavior ("existence") must always be thought of as an attempt to cope successfully with an immediate situation,* that is, with present events.

However, an individual changes, other people change, the world changes, and new patterns of behavior must continually develop. In a sense, life is one crisis of "existence" after another. Old habits of behavior once effective no longer may be so, as with the aging dowager whose coquetry attracted men at the age of 17 but earns her ridicule at the age of 60. The reverse also is possible, as with the youth whose boyhood friends derogated his intellectual interests, but whose college teachers give him attention and admiration for his scholastic accomplishments. Thus, life is always "becoming," and never settled until death. Similarly, one's "potentialities," hopes, and aspirations change. Thus, new thoughts about oneself, new self-evaluations, new talents developed or old ones lost may come into conflict or in contradiction to current habitual ways of relating to events and thereby elicit anxiety. Behavior disorder may develop at any age.

But all persons must consistently meet new life crises. Why do some become disordered and others not? Early in childhood most persons develop an awareness of themselves as "a real, alive, whole, and in a temporal sense, continuous person" (Laing in Ruitenbeek, 1962). Some do not achieve this confident self-awareness and evaluation. They must constantly defend what little identity they have acquired, and events that are commonplace to others may threaten their self-conceptions and cause anxiety. Constantly defending what they have, they cannot "live out into the world" and thereby expand their self-awareness or identity, nor establish new and mutually satisfactory relationships with others (Laing in Ruitenbeek, 1962).

Thus, disorder constitutes learned behaviors which interfere with the innate tendency to establish mutually significant relationships with others or with the "realization of his inherent potentialities" (Hora in Ruitenbeek, 1962). As May (1961) puts it, disorder serves learned values more than innate security or survival satisfactions because man is the only organism that "makes certain values—prestige, power, tenderness, love—more important than pleasure" or even "survival itself."

Symptoms of Disordered Behavior

Symptoms are to be understood as specific attempts to resolve immediate problems of living. There are likely to be a variety of symptoms in any one person, particularly in more severe disorders, because the individual will try one pattern of behavior after another in an attempt to resolve his difficulties. The symptom pattern may also change over time because an individual may drop one extensive pattern which has been used over a considerable period of time (a form of "being-in-the-world") and adopt a rather extensive new one. Symptoms reveal the kinds of events involved in the disorder as well as the way the individual is trying to deal with those events. Thus, not all the following symptoms would be expected to appear in every disorder.

Typical symptoms are: an inability to take practical action, to begin or to complete something; an impoverishment in the variety of responses employed by the person and a restriction of the kinds of events to which the individual will make approach responses; a generalization so that many events become antecedents to anxiety and many responses become involved with the attempts to cope with anxiety; subjectively observable responses coming into conflict, particularly affect and thought responses; self-evaluative thoughts and associated affect tending to become less positive and more negative; a decrease in the kinds of events the person will attend to; a decline and avoidance of anticipatory thoughts, such as plans for the future, as the individual tends to respond from moment to moment; behavior becoming idiosyncratic, the individual responding with affect, thought, or overt behavior to many events in an inappropriate fashion; and conceptual or abstract thinking becoming less accurately related to the raw data of experience, for example, sensations, perceptions.

THE GOALS OF THERAPY

Who Determines the Goals?

In one sense, the patient chooses his own goals through the selection of the particular kinds of events to which he will respond and through the kinds of response patterns (modes of "being-in-the-world") developed to do so. Many existentialists emphasize the patient's choice of goals, and Binswanger's study of the case of Ellen West (May, et al., 1958), who committed suicide, in a sense defends the contention that death might be a legitimate goal chosen by a patient.

In another sense, existential assumptions about the nature of man define the therapeutic goals. The goal is to open up to the patient's awareness the possibilities for choice, self-direction, and self-responsibility, so that he can find his way back "into the freedom of being able to utilize his own capacities for existence" (Binswanger, and May, in Ruitenbeek, 1962). Thus, the therapist's objective would seem to be to help the patient make his own choices based on an awareness of the significant events, such as his own beliefs, sensations, values, and in terms of the possibilities available to him in his environment, particularly the behavior of other people.

What Are the Goals?

The initial objective is for the patient to adopt a fundamental attitude; he must take some responsibility for himself (May, et al., 1958, p. 87). He must recognize that despite all the conditions imposed upon him, such as mistreatment by parents, impoverished economic conditions, or limitations of physique, some degree of choice remains open to him, and he continues to be responsible for himself. He needs to realize that he does not have to be what is forced on him but can choose to be what he wishes within the limits of the conditions imposed on him (May, 1961, p. 41). To be able to assume such an attitude and make such choices, he needs to have available adequate data. Thus, the habitual response sequences of negative emotion leading to avoidance need to be modified; he should learn neither to avoid situations nor to ignore the raw data of his sensory, affective, and perceptual responses (experience) as representative of the conditions to which he may choose to respond. He must be confident enough of his "own identity" to risk it and expand it in new significant relationships with others (encounters) and with the natural world. Not only must he acquire habits of attending to the raw data of his own senses and to his values, and begin to think that he can make decisions, but also these should lead to a choice, a commitment to act. Doing concrete things in an effective way is also part of "becoming" (May, et al., 1958, p. 85).

The choices made and the behaviors that implement those choices will vary from person to person according to their characteristics, previous "life history," and also from culture to culture in terms of the opportunities available (May, et al., 1958, p. 228). The goals include not so much the altering or removal of unwanted or disordered behavior (symptoms) but rather the development of constructive, effective behavior patterns (being-in-the-world). Alleviation of symptoms will be a by-product of helping the patient "experience his existence."

CONDITIONS FOR PRODUCING BEHAVIOR CHANGE

Principles by Which Behavior Change Occurs

Although it is reasonable to infer that existential psychotherapists propose a person's "modes-of-existence" to be modifiable through learning, the present writers have not found any explicit principles stating how such learning occurs. The basic dichotomy of "being" and "nothingness" appears in many respects to be analogous to the classes of "approach" and "avoidance." The "being" person makes choices, decisions, and does things—characteristics of approach patterns—while the "nothingness" person does not choose, does not act, is restricted in his behavior, and the antecedent is anxiety—characteristics of avoidance patterns. However, the conditions under which various patterns of behavior may develop are not discussed, nor is it clear whether anxiety is an antecedent or consequent of "nothingness," or both. One cannot tell whether the conditions under which each person learns are thought to be different, or whether it is believed that general principles governing learning exist.

THERAPY TECHNIQUES

Preconditions

No preconditions for entering therapy with a patient are mentioned. The general enthusiasm and case illustrations of these writers give one the impression that they believe their approach has very wide applicability and utility.

Patient Behavior Required

Nothing was found to reveal what the patient is supposed to do in therapy. Obviously, he must talk about himself and his subjective experiences, but beyond that, the details of his behavior in therapy are unspecified in the sources studied.

THERAPY TECHNIQUES

Necessary Attributes and Training of Therapists

While technique is given second place to "understanding the patient," which in a sense is a pattern of responding to another person, technical skill is considered important, and the implication is that extensive training is necessary (Binswanger in Ruitenbeek, 1962). Rollo May (1961, p. 28) comments about the danger of "wild eclecticism" in existential and phenomenological approaches when used "without the rigorous clinical study and thought" necessary for any expertness. Rigorous training in dynamics and techniques should be considered essential. He considers diagnosis a legitimate and necessary function, particularly at the beginning of therapy. But the manner of thinking involved is considered different from that utilized in therapy itself. When used in the therapy task, the techniques should be so automatic that the therapist need not think about them.

Therapist Behavior

Systematic presentations of what the therapist should do in therapy have not been available. This may stem in part from the conviction that it is detrimental to therapy to treat the patient as an object, which is something they feel one does when one talks about therapy technique. Medard Boss's book (to be published in 1963) may give additional information. Some (e.g., Boss in May, et al., 1958) indicate they use orthodox Freudian techniques, proposing that the methods are effective in spite of the incorrectness of the Freudian rationale. Still others argue that any emphasis on technique treats the patient as an object, thereby interfering with "understanding the patient." Although critical of the "American" interest in technique because he thinks it is pursued at the expense of theory, May (1958, p. 77) went to some trouble to try to find out what existential therapists do in therapy. He concluded that existential therapists do not derogate disciplined technique but make it subordinate to "understanding." One might infer that they have developed a new way of *thinking about* patients, but it does not lead them to *do anything different* in treatment. Although there may be some truth to this, we believe technique differences are apparent. A good many comments about the approach to therapy have been found in the books, articles, and cases examined, so that an outline of the approach seems clear. Included are the therapist's special attitude and observational approach, a special type of human relationship, and a focus on particular kinds of events.

THE THERAPEUTIC ATTITUDE. The therapist must approach therapy with the conviction that the patient is an individual of worth, "with possibilities for self-respect" and the basic freedom "to choose his own way of life" (May and Boss, in Ruitenbeek, 1962). He must assume that the only way to understand and be helpful to the patient is to become a part of the patient's way of living during the interviews, to seek to understand the values that guide the patient and the special ways he has acquired for communicating them. He adopts special observational attitudes for this purpose. The therapist must realize that he is using his own habits of thought to try to understand things as the patient sees them, thus running the danger of imposing his biases of perception and understanding on the patient. To avoid this as far as possible, the therapist must recognize them, discipline himself to keep their influence to a minimum, and seek to adopt the patient's way of perceiving and thinking so that a full understanding of the patient's behavior can be developed, unbiased by the therapist's theoretical molds. This is not just an intellectual act. Communication may occur on "many levels," and the therapist should expect to respond to the patient in terms of his combined sensory-affective-thought responses (May, in Ruitenbeek, 1962).

THE HUMAN RELATIONSHIP. As has become apparent in the previous discussion, it is through certain kinds of human relationships that man becomes human. Therefore, it is consistent to find the relationship between patient and therapist one of the fundamental treatment procedures emphasized. The term *encounter* is used to refer to such a relationship in which there is a "decisive inner experience resulting from it for one (sometimes for both) of the two individuals" (May, et al., 1958, p. 119). Thus, therapy is fundamentally an emotion-arousing human relationship in which each person tries to communicate honestly with the other both verbally and nonverbally.

The therapeutic situation tends to be one of superior (therapist) and subordinate (patient), thus "inviting the patient to relinquish his position as the deciding agent." The existential psychotherapist tries to create a relationship which requires the patient to be responsible for himself rather than taking a "passive" attitude toward the causes of his difficulties (May, 1961). This is accomplished by approaching therapy as a partnership in which the therapist dares "to risk his own existence," to commit himself to a significant relationship with the patient, as a means of helping him (Binswanger, in Ruitenbeek, 1962). The patient is encouraged to be himself in the relationship rather than forced to behave according to the therapist's preconceptions—a "being-together in an attitude of letting-be," which is not the same as "leaving alone" (Hora, in Ruitenbeek, 1962).

Such a relationship represents a model for all significant human interactions and therefore becomes a setting in which the patient's habitual behaviors (modes-of-being) may occur, be understood, and be changed. As May (1961) puts it, the basic therapeutic unit is "two-persons-existing-in-a-world, the world at the moment being represented by the consulting room of the therapist." Both help to produce and then to understand the patient's behavior in that situation by their mutual interaction. But significant change will not follow simply from the ability to describe verbally what is happening. The objective is not merely to show the patient "where, when, and to what extent he has failed to realize the fullness of his humanity," but to "make him experience this as radically as possible" (*genuine presence*) in the therapy relationship (Binswanger, in Ruitenbeek, 1962). For therapeutic behavior change to occur, "it is *essential* that all psychological phenomena shall be *experienced*" in the patient-therapist relationship (Ruitenbeek, 1962). Presumably, the way the therapist responds to the patient represents a set of consequences which contributes to change.

SIGNIFICANT EVENTS AND THEIR REPRESENTATION. Language phenomena and attributes of awareness (such as temporalization) are central to therapy. Binswanger (May, et al., 1958, p. 201) emphasizes that it is impossible to recognize the "organized structure" underlying specific behaviors unless the therapist learns the "personal meaning" of the words the patient uses to speak of his experiences. He notes that patients may use different labels for the same kinds of events (experiences) and the same label for different kinds of events. Thus, to understand and predict the behavior of a particular patient, one must be sure of the events to which the patient refers with the words he uses. Communication with the patient also requires that the therapist be able to translate his understanding into the patient's language.

The therapist must interpret what a person says in the context of his other behavior. It is not just what he says, but *how* he talks; his meanings, tone, gestures, and the "whole world" surrounding the talk. Rollo May [2] has noted that viewing the patient's talk in terms of the nonverbal behaviors occurring at the time and in the full context of the therapy relationship has helped him and other existential therapists break through the "continual chatter that characterizes so much psychoanalysis" with sophisticated patients (like psychologists and psychiatrists), who use talk to conceal and evade problems, rather than to communicate them.

According to Van Dusen (Ruitenbeek, 1962), existential therapists focus upon subjectively observable responses (r). Situational events (S) and overt behaviors (R) are important in terms of their private meanings to the patient. They attend to the "most existential or crucial" experiences, behavior patterns that most widely influence other behaviors. They look for the patterns (modes-of-existence) within which the bits and pieces of patient behavior from moment to moment (comments, gestures, symptoms, dreams, fantasies, defense mechanisms) can be understood as attempts to achieve some purpose, as expressions of some decision made or being faced. The focus is on the "now events," those things actually occurring in therapy rather than remembered or anticipated events; past and future are important only as present behavioral events such as thoughts or memories. They will attend to "the patient's experiences as they occur," avoiding theoretical categorizing. From this emphasis on "immediate experiencing" rather than "intellectualizing," we take them to mean that the patient has acquired habits of misidentifying or misinterpreting the "raw data of his experience"—his sensations, emotions, perceptions. By redirecting the patient's attention to these raw data and helping him to compare his new observations with the inaccurate ways he had been interpreting and thinking about them, the therapist can help correct inadequate thought habits, and "thoughts and experience can become one."

Finally, the emphasis is on the patient's own capacity to choose how

[2] Personal communication, 1962.

to react to the conditions influencing him. Presumably, then, the therapist directs attention to those conditions during the interview in which the patient is confronted with making some choice (big or small); to the ways the patient handles such decision-making tasks; and to their consequences, thus helping the patient "to relearn and use his own freedom of choice."

The use of the therapist's "intuition" and the notion of "communication at several levels" is emphasized (cf. Kahn, in Ruitenbeek, 1962). We take this to mean that the therapist's responses to the patient are determined partly by factors he has identified, such as recognition of a consistent theme within the patient's behavior, and partly by subjective responses engendered by the patient, such as subtle emotions and sensations of which he may or may not be aware. His therapy operations are not carefully planned acts of intellect, since that would destroy the genuineness of the relationship. Within the context of the general treatment rationale just described, a great variety of specific procedures are apparently employed, such as couch or chair, dream interpretation, free association, and these are varied from patient to patient and from one phase of treatment to another. Some criteria for selecting specific procedures must be employed, but no discussion of this problem was encountered.

The Sequence of Behavior Change

Little discussion of this issue was found. Apparently, one of the first steps is for the patient to form a significant relationship with the therapist (encounter), and a later step is to take more responsibility for his own behavior and manifest this in actively making choices.

EVALUATION OF BEHAVIOR CHANGE

Appraisal of Behavior Change

Only a few scattered comments about how to determine when the desired behavior change has occurred were found. The task, from this approach, would be to determine whether changes in the subjectively observable responses (r-r patterns) to specifiable situations have occurred, and also whether these have led to choices about and instrumental acts (r-R) toward such situations. Two possible ways are suggested by which these judgments can be made: (1) the patient can report directly on them, and (2) the therapist can gain information indirectly from the patient's thoughts, feelings, and sensations as manifested in observable motoric, physiological, and vocal responses, fantasies, dreams, writings, and reactions to ambiguous stimuli such as the Rorschach. The context of the patient's verbal report is important in judging its validity, a kind of internal consistency criterion.

Verification of Theory

To Americans, the phenomenological approach to the verification of theory appears to be nonscientific, and to European phenomenologists the American demand for exactitude and certainty "seems to squeeze the life out of things" (Van Dusen, in Ruitenbeek, 1962). As Hora (Ruitenbeek, 1962) put it, the total of the parts of a man do not add up "to a whole human being." What alternative do they propose? Binswanger (May, et al., 1958, p. 192) asserts that existential analysis is an empirical science but has a method of investigation peculiarly its own. He distinguishes between the method of objective science ("discursive inductive") and the phenomenological method. He argues that the latter is just as exact and methodical, and that it requires the same degree of criticality. It seeks to interpret the "phenomenal contents" of a person's behavior. A detailed discussion of the phenomenological approach can be found in Spiegelberg (1960). Van Den Berg (Ruitenbeek, 1962) discusses some of the propositions that seem to him to make the phenomenological approach essential. For example, objects are defined by the way they affect and can be affected by behavior; the behaviors possible are defined by the conditions available at the time, and among the most important of these are the person's awareness and his self-conceptions; observations have significance only within their context; perception is in part the object and in part the person's responses to the object.

If procedures for verifying this therapy theory and techniques are to be judged on the basis of what is published, however, the individual case study by one investigator is the standard approach (cf. May, et al., 1958). Buytendijk (Ruitenbeek, 1962) states that verification lies in "the affirmation of everyone who, without prejudice, directs himself to the phenomenon in question." Verification rests upon agreement among observers. A minimal requirement would be the demonstration that different existentialists would obtain the same basic type of "phenomenal content" from the same patient, and that the "existential understanding" arrived at would be the same. If such agreement cannot be demonstrated, the method and its findings are called into question. As Binswanger himself stated, "In this, as in every science, everything depends upon the method of approach and inquiry" (May, et al., p. 192).

COMMENTS

Rollo May (Ruitenbeek, 1962) has noted that existential psychotherapy in the United States is currently a "Tower of Babel," troubled with some "faddist and bandwagon tendencies." This makes it difficult to present comments which will be generally applicable to the many proponents of this viewpoint. For each comment that we make, the reader might find an individual writer who is an exception.

In our view, existential psychotherapy contains several emphases which are significant and justify its current popularity. Its writers, who generally appear to be sensitive observers and skilled therapists, judging from their case analyses, have emphasized important aspects of behavior. They share with others, such as Adler and Rogers, an emphasis on the importance of subjectively observable responses (sensations, images, feelings, and thoughts); attention and awareness are fundamental, not only as they affect a person's present behavior but also as they determine what he will learn and how he will change in the future. These writers share with Adler the notion that how a person represents future events to himself (goals and objectives) has much to do with the way he can behave in the present. They have not missed the critical purpose of psychotherapy, and they stress the importance of the patient actually performing new and constructive responses in the everyday world; these concrete patterns of interaction (R) become the ultimate test of the success of psychotherapy. The analysis of behavior in terms of all the conditions under which it occurs including the characteristics of the situation and of the person is fundamental, as well as the dictum that behavior is determined by the conditions under which it appears. This leads to the analysis of the behavior in terms of "the present." They point to a pattern of difficulties frequent in present-day patients, isolation and loneliness, which they interpret to result from the person's learned avoidance of significant interactions with people. They emphasize a person's identity, or awareness of himself, as a basic antecedent to human behavior.

It is in the systematic aspects of this point of view that difficulties are apparent. Most proponents stress that they are emphasizing a special view of the nature of man and have not attempted to build a system. They do propose that their new view makes a difference in how one does therapy, however, and therefore, with assumptions about how behavior works and proposals about the consequences for therapy, they have begun a system.

Methodology of Analysis

Existentialists assert that they have a new approach to the study of behavior, which is different from the methodology of the natural sciences. They refer to their approach as phenomenological empiricism and say that it lends itself to rigor and exactness and will yield scientific facts—that is, conclusions that are repeatable, verifiable, and communicable to many persons.

The phenomenological approach is not new, but it is a familiar one to American psychologists (cf. Spiegelberg, 1960; Titchener, 1913; Snygg and Coombs, 1949; and Carl Rogers). Unfortunately, some existential writers sometimes misrepresent the approach in their enthusiasm (cf. Kahn, in Ruitenbeek, 1962). Some naively consider that they deal with what is "existentially real" about a person and can escape the development of abstractions about his behavior. But the therapist, an objective observer, does not "have access" to "reality as immediately experienced" by his patient. He cannot see the patient's thoughts, he cannot hear his feelings or hit them with a stick. Only through the patient's description of them, supported by inferences from other nonverbal behaviors, can he gain some notion as to what they might be like. Words are abstracts, however, and if the therapist does not form abstracts of his own, he is merely substituting the patient's abstracts. Unfortunately, words are often used to conceal as well as to reveal, and the correspondence between what a person says he feels and what is actually occurring can be small indeed.

On occasion, existentialists propose that they eschew *both* the subject's conceptions of his "immediate experience" and any conceptions about the subject that the therapist might develop from what the patient says. They appeal to a "reality underlying *both* subjectivity and objectivity," not to events as experienced but rather to the "inner personal character" of the immediate experience. The observer, in this instance, is apparently conceiving of a common denominator underlying the specific events reported by his subject. Were he to do this, we would have another construction by an observer, an abstraction about data, rather than a direct observation of the data themselves.

Thus, there seems to be considerable uncertainty about just what it is that therapists see as opposed to what they conceive to be in the behavior of the subject being analyzed. There are a series of occurrences going on: subjective events occur (sensations and feelings), the subject's conception of them, his report of them, the therapist's understanding of the report, and the therapist's conception of the report in the context of other responses and situational events he observes. Clear-cut distinctions have to be made between these because the correspondence is not exact between any two of them. It is not always clear that these distinctions are maintained, even by sophisticated proponents like Binswanger, Boss, and Kahn (cf. May, et al., 1958). As Kahn notes in his critical appraisal, "the cheerful subjectivity with which allegedly phenomenologically immediate data appear" and are "juggled around" is disconcerting. He notes that interpretations "obviously shaped in the writer's mind according to the pattern of Heidegger's thought" seem too often "to be taken as reality and as originating with the patient." It is inevitable that therapists use someone's abstractions about the patient's behavior. Rollo May [3] recognizes that the therapist needs to distinguish clearly between his conceptions and those of his patient and to utilize both.

When the existentialists complain that the "objectivity" of the natural sciences has led to a neglect of man's subjective behavior ("direct experience"), they are making a telling point. However, the correction of this problem does not require a reversion to its opposite, namely, exclusive reliance on the phenomenological method of analysis which presents methodological problems of its own. For example, Roland Kahn (May, et al., 1958) analyzes a patient's report of a church picture smiling at him. He concluded that the smile in the picture was the same as that characteristic of the patient, which in turn was similar to that of his mother. The therapist, however, had apparently not seen the picture nor the mother, who died when the patient was three or four years old. One must be a little bit uncomfortable with the outcomes of such analyses. Phenomenological data are important for study, but the method of study needs safeguards against error in such highly personal analyses.

[3] Personal communication.

Concepts

The concepts developed from the existential point of view show some interesting emphases but some formal weaknesses as well. Molar units of analysis characterize this position, such as *Mitwelt, Umwelt,* and *Eigenwelt.* Some way of representing enduring response patterns characteristic of a person across different kinds of situations were apparently sought, yielding such concepts as *Dasein,* being-in-the-world, and the existential modes. Also, many were designed intentionally to include both situational and response events under a single rubric, as represented in the many hyphenated concept labels—being-in-the-world, being-beyond-the-world, being-with-others. This latter effort stems from the insistence that somehow behavior is always related to the situation in which it occurs. Molar concepts have considerable utility for certain purposes, but this utility is diminished considerably if these higher-order abstractions are not well related to those lower in the hierarchy or even to the observations from which they are drawn. Such a statement seems true of many concepts in the existential point of view. This may be the consequence of their emphasis on individual behavior, where each person's behavior is considered unique. However, this emphasis should not exclude attention to commonalities as well. The situation is not helped when a number of key concepts are used in a variety of ways and when different concept labels are used for what appear to be the same phenomena, for example, world-design or being-in-the-world.

An emphasis on the importance of situation-response relationships (*S-r-R*) strikes us as very appropriate. But such an emphasis does not require one to encompass everything into one massive unit. There is the conceptual alternative of carefully studying such interrelationships.

We applaud these writers for emphasizing the responses of attention and awareness, both positive and negative affect, that is, love, fear, guilt, anxiety, loneliness, and dread, and the relationship between one's interpersonal patterns and one's self-awareness. The concepts utilized, however, need considerable clarification and specification.

Propositions

Little attention is given to propositional statements in the writings reviewed. Of course, some of this stems from the nature of the concepts employed. In general, the larger the concepts in a system, the fewer the propositions needed. The existentialists propose that everything is related and should be thought of in that way. Because everything is related, one must deal with the whole man, and thus every particular behavioral event is to be understood as a manifestation of underlying habitual patterns. Thus, what would be propositions in another system are taken care of by concepts in this one. An occasional propositional statement appears in a case analysis, for example, "pluralization of the thou." However, the comparative absence of propositions defining how the various aspects of behavior and situations interrelate is an important deficiency.

It is doubtful that all behavior occurs "as a piece." Even if all responses ultimately come to be interrelated with each other, some propositions are needed by which to account for how this eventuates. Under what conditions will one patient develop a "big-mouthed form of existence" or another an "existential emptiness"? The answer that it is a product of their life experiences and the choices they have made is a start, but grossly insufficient.

Propositions about behavior acquisition and modification are not mentioned. In spite of the emphasis on the "essential nature of man," it remains unclear as to how to separate "nature" from the products of learning. Frequent reference is made to the development of innate "potentialities," but what these are, how one determines them, and under what conditions they develop is unclear. There is the likelihood that they may treat learned behaviors as "innate potentialities." For example, Boss (Ruitenbeek, 1962, p. 228) reported that a patient improved when she renounced "enough of her attitude as a conventional lady, which was not in harmony with her real nature." The specifics of behavioral development should not be elided by a general comment such as that by Straus: "Thinking, remembering, imagining" are all derived from basic "sensory experiencing" (May, et al., 1958). Without criteria for determining what is learned and what is innate, a therapist's assumptions about the nature of man may turn out to represent the learned behaviors valued by the therapist.

Operational Procedures

Existential psychotherapy has not as yet formalized a set of procedures for the conduct of therapy. In fact, some writers might choose to argue against their development and specification. However, we expect more proposals about technique to appear from such a lively point of view.

There has been some emphasis on how the therapist is to think about what he hears and sees, on his view of the nature of man, and on the observational attitude a therapist should maintain. An appropriate "relationship" is said to be necessary, and some of the characteristics of that relationship are specified, in terms of the responses the patient should be led to make to the therapist, and vice versa. One can specify a relationship in terms of the desired outcome, but the problem of how one is to go about producing it remains.

Some writers may be of the opinion that if the therapist learns to think appropriately about the behavior of the patient, he will know how to speak and how to respond to the patient appropriately. Again, one might wish that things were that simple. Other writers make a point of stressing flexibility of technique, and point to their habits of varying the procedure from patient to patient and occasion to occasion. Criteria for deciding when to use different procedures are thereby clearly implied, and need to be specified.

May (1962) expresses concern over the position of many existentialists with respect to the problems of evaluation and verification. He notes that current enthusiasm for existential psychotherapy in America has, for some, become related to an antiscientific and anti-intellectual trend, which he deplores. Citing the serious errors to which this can lead, he espouses a search for "new scientific methods which will be more adequate for revealing the nature of man." We echo May's concern, hoping that the proverbial bath water may be discarded and the budding infant retained.

Their emphases on understanding behavior as a function of presently occurring events, as oriented toward the future, as being continually developing, and as being significantly determined by one's feelings of self-responsibility we consider important and worth careful development. We think it unfortunate that their presentations have the aura of a new faith. Some speak of developing a "new discipline," and they write with certainty, using such phrases as "no doubt," "because it is so," "of course," and "naturally." They are committing the error of excessive overgeneralization and abstraction, against which their philosophical ancestors rebelled. As Rollo May (1958) has so kindly put it, there is some tendency for them to get lost in philosophical abstraction.

Because existential psychotherapy is put forward as something new, because the language of its concepts is novel, and because its proponents are enthusiastic, it is likely to enjoy a period of popularity among some psychotherapists. Unless it develops along more systematic lines, however, it is likely to become displaced by other systems that can treat the same data in more explicit and useful fashion.

Chapter 13

Karen Horney's
Character Analysis

The work of Karen Horney represents something of an enigma in the field of psychotherapy. Many consider her an important figure, and she had extensive influence upon conceptions of neurosis and its treatment throughout the two decades 1940–1960. On the one hand she enjoyed an extensive following among nonprofessionals; it was jokingly remarked that a person was a social illiterate at a New York cocktail party if he could not participate intelligently in the discussions of her ideas and her recent publications. On the other hand, she had a considerable effect on the thought and practice of professional psychologists, psychiatrists, and social workers in the United States. Many of her basic propositions seemed to hold a strong appeal. Her socio-cultural emphases, for example, were welcomed as antidotes to the biological orientation of Sigmund Freud. Parts of her approach to the analysis of complex human behavior, her con-

481

ceptualizations about the intricacies of neurotic behavior patterns, and her proposals as to the techniques of therapy have become a part of everyday clinical language among many practitioners, though the ideas are often not attributed to her.

Among the factors contributing to the impact of her ideas was her writing style. Karen Horney appeared to have succeeded at a task to which many of her colleagues aspired; she captured the "clinical richness" of human behavior in all its complex patterns and interrelationships. Also the fact that she wrote extensively and published frequently may have helped to attract individuals to her writings and to render them increasingly familiar with her point of view.

At the same time, the writings of Karen Horney have been under considerable attack from many quarters. The primary complaints seem to have centered on the formal and systematic failings in her theories. It is typical of reviewers to call attention to the various lapses and inconsistencies in her descriptive propositions and to criticize the ambiguity of definition in some of her concepts. These contrasts among the views of Karen Horney's work is somewhat analogous to the fate of a Broadway play which enjoys an extended run in the face of negative reviews by the drama critics. It seems likely in such an instance that despite formal lacks of one kind or another, there is much in the production that viewers can find of value, and which they can put to some good use.

BIOGRAPHICAL NOTES

Karen Horney was born in Hamburg, Germany, in the year 1885. Her mother was a native German; her father was a Norwegian sea captain, and his occupation resulted in the family's moving extensively throughout her childhood. Later in her career, the fact of cross-cultural differences loomed large in her thinking and contributed to her break from the classical Freudian position. Perhaps her early familiarity with many different countries contributed to her realization of such differences and their pronounced effect on human behavior.

She earned her medical degree at the University of Berlin in 1913. Subsequently she turned to psychiatry, which she studied for four additional years, and this culminated in a teaching appointment at the Berlin Psychoanalytic Institute. Her training in Freudian psychoanalysis was thorough, and it included didactic analyses by two of the foremost training analysts of the day, Karl Abraham and Hans Sachs.

For a period of more than 15 years, she remained a practicing analyst in the orthodox Freudian tradition. However, she gradually became increasingly disenchanted with the Freudian viewpoint and developed the desire to make a "critical re-evaluation of psychoanalytic theories," because the classical approach led to a discouraging number of treatment failures. She found that "almost every patient" offered problems that psychoanalytic theory did not fit (1939, p. 7). This was a significant judgment by one who was considered to be a fine clinician and quite versed in the application of the standard Freudian technique. But Horney also was dissatisfied with the theoretical propositions of the system, at first attributing her uncertainty to a lack of experience but gradually coming to the conclusion that the fault lay more in the theory than in her own conceptual inadequacies. There was much that she felt to be in error. She found Freud's analysis of the behavior of women difficult to accept, as was his hypothesis of an instinct toward death. The latter struck her as an implausible inference to draw from the observations of behavior at hand. Her "dimly perceived doubts" were encouraged by two colleagues at the Institute, Harold Schultz-Hencke and Wilhelm Reich. It was Schultz-Hencke who helped Horney make explicit their mutual doubts of the curative value of infantile memories and, by contrast, of the necessity for an analysis of the actual conflict situation which the patient was facing. Reich's repeated emphasis on the necessity for analysis of the entire neurotic character pattern struck a responsive chord in Horney's thinking.

In 1932 Horney accepted an invitation by Franz Alexander to come to the United States and assist him at the Psychoanalytic Institute of Chicago. There she remained for a period of two years before moving to New York City to accept a teaching position with the New York Psychoanalytic Institute, where her major publications were prepared.

In her first major theoretical statement, *The Neurotic Personality of Our Times* (1937), she presented the contention that neurotic behavior was brought about by cultural factors, and more specifically by disturbances in human relationships. She presented her views only as modifications of Freudian theory. However, as she pursued her lines of thought, the discrepancies became increasingly apparent, and her effort to clarify where she stood in relation to Freud resulted in her second volume, *New Ways in Psychoanalysis* (1939). Here she took issue with what she regarded as the instinctivist and genetic psychology of Freud, proposing instead a remarkably different view as to the acquisition and function of neurotic behavior. A rejection of the "libido theory" led to entirely different interpretations of the oedipus complex, the concept of narcissism, anxiety, and even more to the conception of therapy events such as resistance and transference. Even the objectives of psychoanalytic therapy became different in her reanalysis of the neurotic's problem.

In *Self-Analysis* (1942), she asked the intriguing question: If in psychoanalysis the crucial steps are various thought sequences which the patient must make and thus the patient's "mental activity is the source of change," what is the possibility that he can make at least some of these in the absence of the therapist? In the light of the scarcity of practicing psychoanalysts, this possibility assumed importance. Since she took the position that a self-analysis should approximate as closely as possible the conduct of a formal psychoanalysis, a major portion of the volume became a statement as to the psychoanalytic procedure itself. She also took the occasion to bring up to date the changes in her conceptions of pathogenesis.

Modifications in her analysis of neurotic behavior continued, and two additional volumes, *Our Inner Conflicts* (1945) and *Neurosis and Human Growth* (1950), reported the successive changes she had felt to be necessary. At this stage, her position was so far removed from that of Freud that she could no longer present her view as an improvement of traditional psychoanalysis. Although there remained agreement as to many clinical observations, she recognized that her interpretations of their "dynamics and meaning" had become entirely different (1950, p. 375). Her conceptions had emerged into a distinctive point of view about human behavior.

Karen Horney maintained an active practice and was reputed to be an excellent professional practitioner. She continued her interest in the training of psychotherapists and in the formation of professional groups, helping to found both the Association for the Advancement of Psychoanalysis and the American Institute of Psychoanalysis, of which she was also Dean. She became the editor of the American Journal of Psychoanalysis. She died in New York City in 1952 at the end of a full and productive career.

This representation of Horney's views has been built primarily on her 1945 publication, *Our Inner Conflicts,* following the pattern of most reviewers who regard this volume as the culmination of her writings and the major statement of her theory of disordered behavior. These ideas were considerably different from those presented in her earlier writings, and quite a different view of her theoretical position would be evident were those earlier ideas chosen as her main contribution. We relied on the volume *Self-Analysis* (1942) for the majority of her observations about the details of the treatment process.

DISTINCTIVE FEATURES

Karen Horney is recognized for having laid stress on the learned aspects of disordered behavior and on the fact that disorders represented patterns of interpersonal behavior acquired in relation to situations in the family.

Reacting against Freud's position that most behavior was determined by innate physiological events which he called instincts, Horney proposed that the vast majority of human behavior was learned, and learned in relation to a socio-cultural environment. This opened the door to a study of the relationship between one person's behavior and that of another, people to parent (culture to member) and parent to child. This view led Horney to search for the antecedents of disorder in social situations, and she found them within the interpersonal relationships that occurred within the family during the early formative years. For Horney, biological and physiological determinants receded into the background, and situational determinants were correspondingly emphasized.

Consistent with her emphasis on cultural and social factors was Horney's view that complex human behavior was most readily conceptualized in terms of the organized patterns of interpersonal responses which the person developed. Beginning with relatively discrete sets of responses acquired in relationship to other people, larger and larger organizations of these responses become formed, until by the time the person is an adult his patterns of response to interpersonal situations are very intricate indeed. Thus, virtually all of Horney's descriptions and representations of human behavior followed the form of detailing the interrelationships among the perceptions, feelings, opinions, judgments, values, goals, etc., which are typically encountered as concomitants of one another. The description of *trends* and *patterns* is a hallmark of Horney's system.

Still another important emphasis was her commitment to the study of behavior as it operated within the present. In the Freudian point of view an historical analysis of behavior was considered essential since later behaviors in the adult were considered to be repetitions of, or subsequent expressions of, underlying infantile response sequences. Horney argued that, even if this were true, the significance of any bit of behavior depended on how it operated and was maintained in the present—on what functions it *currently* performed. Her position did not deny that neurotic behavior had historical antecedents, or that an analysis of the early childhood influences might not be required for a thorough understanding of the development of behavior. But she anticipated no simple relationship between adult reactions and childhood ones because so much had intervened. Moreover, in the analysis of any particular case, the utility of an historical analysis would be determined by the light it would shed on the adaptive functions which the response sequence currently performed.

Finally, Horney was one of the few therapy theorists to analyze in detail the possibility that certain behavioral changes ordinarily thought to be possible only under the conditions of psychotherapy could conceivably be reproduced in another context—through self-analysis. Although she cautioned, that there were limitations to the effectiveness of self-analysis, she concluded that it was not only feasible but also desirable, and indeed sometimes the only possibility left open for some individual circumstances.

THE NORMAL COURSE OF BEHAVIOR DEVELOPMENT

Karen Horney devoted her attention almost exclusively to accounting for the development of disordered behavior. This focus is apparent in each of her writings. The relative absence of any propositions as to the innate equipment with which each human child begins his life, the process of maturation, or the characteristic ways in which behavior becomes acquired through learning is consistent. We must content ourselves, therefore, with only a few comments concerning her view of healthy behavior development.

INNATE CHARACTERISTICS OF NORMAL DEVELOPMENT

As did many writers in the therapy field during the period 1930–1950, Karen Horney acknowledged the fact of innate differences in behavior from subject to subject and recognized that some behavior was determined by such innate events, but she gave such factors only brief attention.

Why did she accept the fact of innate determinants of behavior, yet de-emphasize their significance for a system of psychotherapy? She apparently felt that little was known about such constitutional determinants on the one hand, and that by contrast considerably more was known about factors involved in learning. Moreover, she seemed to believe that innately determined responses, tending to be relatively immune to change, were not a matter for attention in a system concerned with effecting changes in a person's behavior. Thus, although she recognized that a child begins with "given qualities" such as the degree of his "vitality" and the "relative softness or hardness of his nature," yet she chose to comment only about those characteristics "susceptible to change" (1942, p. 43). She seemed to perceive that the therapist elected to change some response relationships (those that were learned) and did not seek to change others (those that were innate), but she did not seem to recognize the necessity for specifying which were which.

Then, too, Horney was conscious of an explicit reaction against the position of Sigmund Freud, feeling that he accorded biological and genetic factors an excessive role. Not only did she feel this to be in error, but she also regarded it as pessimistic. She shared with Adler the contrary view that man's behavior, rather than being instinctive, was primarily learned, and hence remarkably susceptible to change "as long as he lives" (1945, p. 19). Although she paid no systematic attention to the question of the innate characteristics of normal development, it is clear in two types of contexts that such a view was *implicit* in her position.

First of all, Horney dealt with the problem of the basic antecedents to human behavior and proposed several ways of conceptualizing the reasons that humans respond. In her earlier writings (1937, 1942) she suggested that humans begin life with two primary sets of response sequences: those that relate to *satisfaction* and those having to do with *security*. She seemed to assume that humans had a built-in response pattern of a positive affective sort, and that this pattern occurred at the conclusion of some response sequences—perhaps after eating or after sexual intercourse. But she was impressed also with how much neurotic behavior seemed to have "security" as its objective, and when she discussed security she apparently meant the reduction or avoidance of fear, more generally, basic anxiety. Presumably, therefore, she was proposing that two primary response patterns were present in the human and tended to determine his behavior, that humans behaved in such a way as to arouse and maintain a positive emotional response pattern (satisfaction) and also to terminate or to reduce a negative emotional pattern (security).

Later, however, she extended her thinking to postulate a "search for unity." As the concept of conflict became more prominent in her view of neurosis, and as she obtained frequent reports from neurotics of a fear of being "split apart" by their conflicting feelings and responses, she proposed that there was an inherent (or innate?) averse response to the fact of response conflict, and that one of the features of neurotic—and presumably of normal—persons was the tendency to terminate or to change responses that contributed to such a conflict. If a person was "continually driven in opposite directions," he faced the "supreme terror of being split apart" (1945, pp. 56–57).

Finally, in her last publication (1950) she conceptualized the antecedents to behavior in considerably more abstract terms. At this point she postulated the presence of innate "forces," whose occurrence led to the emission of behavior, and also determined which responses would tend to occur and which would subsequently undergo development. Earlier (1942) she had considered the feasibility of therapeutic change in those persons who had an "incentive to grow." By 1950 she had apparently concluded that such response tendencies were universal. As an analogy, she noted that an acorn, given appropriate conditions, would grow into an oak, thus realizing its intrinsic nature. Similarly, she argued, each person has intrinsic potentialities and given appropriate conditions will grow "toward self-realization" directed by that "central inner force" (1950, p. 17). It is not possible to determine what it is Horney meant to refer to when she utilized the concept of force. In physics, the term is ordinarily used to refer to events having the characteristics of energy and directionality. One wonders if Horney was implicitly proposing: (1) some factor of innately determined energy, (2) an innately determined direction in which maturation would proceed, (3) an innately determined sequence of responses, one appearing after another in a developmental chain, as in the analogy of the oak, or (4) all of these. Until such specification of the concept is made, it has the unfortunate characteristics of a negative hypothesis. In an attempt to answer the question of the *why* of behavior, an undefined event is proposed; thus one unknown is merely replaced by another.

There is an additional set of factors which reflects the fact that Horney implicitly thought in terms of innate response events. When discussing particular responses, such as fear and repression, she defined them almost in passing as innate. In her early review of the concept of anxiety and its relation to fear, she proposed that they were comparable responses, both innate but differentially elicited. The antecedents to fear she proposed to be events external to the person (situational), whereas the antecedents to anxiety resided in the subject's own behavior and hence were "subjective" and "psychological" (1937, pp. 63–64). *Basic anxiety* is a concept which we shall subsequently consider. From Horney's writings the authors would conclude that she viewed anxiety or fear as an emotional response pattern, which was an innate response capability in the human child, and one that was inevitably elicited by a certain pattern of situational events. This seems to be a logical necessity, since it is not possible to determine in her writing whence such a response could otherwise arise. Again, Horney was not explicit; indeed, she rarely considered the question of response origin with respect to behavior in general.

The concept of *repression* is another instance of the same sort. In her earlier analyses of disordered behavior Horney made more use of this response "event" than she did in her later publications. In 1937 she characterized it as a "reflex-like process," the occurrence of which was automatic and beyond symbolic control. Whenever the emotional pattern of fear or distress reached a certain level of intensity, repression automatically occurred. The response of repression, then, became an innate human response, which would inevitably happen whenever certain behavioral conditions obtained. Thus, although she discussed some responses "as if" they were innate, she made almost no systematic use of this idea in her theories.

THE LEARNED COURSE OF NORMAL DEVELOPMENT

Although Horney emphasized environmental influence in behavior development, she had little to say about how learning occurs. Her statements can be summarized briefly.

First, Horney subscribed to the general view that the vast majority of man's behavior was acquired through learning and that this rendered most of his behavior potentially modifiable. Secondly, she proposed that there were two major sets of events, the combined effect of which determines the course of learned development. These she labeled *temperamental* and *environmental influences* (1942). We have already reviewed the brief comments she had to make about the first of these, the innately determined response events with which the human begins. Among them are the growth lines laid down by his structure (the central inner force toward self-realization).

The situational events (environment) to which the child is called upon to respond were viewed as the more important class of determinants as to how his learning would proceed. And the most important subclass of such events are the behaviors of other people. Thus, Horney emphasized interpersonal relationships: what a person learns is most significantly influenced by the way in which he is treated by other people.

Horney believed that there was a collection of behaviors that would facilitate the unfolding of the various responses which would follow from the child's innately established developmental sequence, and that there were others which would hamper or impede it. At this point, Horney was content to be very general. The child's responses could emerge appropriately if his behavior were met by *warmth, respect,* and *consideration* (1942) on the part of others, as well as *good-will, guidance, encouragement,* and *healthy friction* (1950). Apparently she took these descriptive labels as self-evident, since she failed to specify in any more concrete fashion the particular responses by others to which such labels referred. But the parental behaviors that would foster and encourage natural development (self-realization) entailed not only the occurrence of such positive events as love, encouragement, or respect, but also the avoidance of others such as domination, over-indulgence, indifference, excessive demands, and the like. Again, as with the positive situational determinants, Horney merely alluded to the many possible *adverse influences,* regarding them as too "manifold" to specify.

Finally, Horney laid stress on the fact that each of these events considered singly would not help in an attempt to represent how an individual might develop. Rather it is the *pattern* of such events, positive and negative, as indicated by the phrase "whole constellation of factors," that determines whether the person's development will proceed primarily in the direction of normal and healthy behavior or in the direction of neurosis and disorder. Unfortunately, Horney did not attempt to represent the various possible patterns that could occur in any greater detail.

Actually, Horney tended to discuss these facets of development in two general ways, on the one hand identifying and pointing to the actual responses by others (situational events) as being the crucial occurrences to observe, and on the other hand pointing to the child's responses which such events elicited as being the more important to study. When she wrote in the latter vein, she spoke of loving and considerate behavior as producing little in the way of fear of other people (inner security) and few anticipations of punishment for what the child might say about his thoughts or for what he might do (inner freedom). Apparently, too, such positive behaviors by family members were seen as eliciting affectionate responses in the child, which are necessary for him to develop still further interpersonal responses. Horney seemed to be emphasizing that there were sequences that had to be studied, sequences which included situational events (the way the parents behaved), the child's subjectively observable responses (how they led the child to think or to feel), and the effects which these in turn had upon subsequent behavior (his further thoughts, actions, or both).

Horney's comments about the relationship between culture and personality should be included in this section. It was Horney's thesis that cultures had resident within them conflicting prescriptions and proscriptions as to what responses should be developed in each of their members; and that cultures differed in their definitions of what constituted acceptable behavior. Thus, Horney anticipated a correlation between culture conflicts and intrapersonal ones, proposing that whatever conflicts were resident within a culture would be reflected in the behavior of its members. Hence, each child should acquire these incompatible responses from the purveyors of his culture, his parents and other teachers.

In the American culture, Horney identified what seemed to her to be a collection of such inconsistencies. She recognized conflicting standards with regard to affection, competition, positive self-evaluation, self-assertion, aggression, and sexuality (1937). She perceived inconsistent statements as to whether these were appropriate responses and under what conditions they could acceptably occur. For example, the demands for "brotherly love" often conflict with competition and aggressive self-assertion in the world of business, with vague definitions of the conditions under which one is appropriate and the other not. Individuals are often punished for evaluating themselves negatively (being too modest) and on the other hand punished for its opposite (being vain or conceited). Sexual expression versus sexual inhibition was another built-in conflict that Horney perceived as recurring repeatedly in Americans, neurotic and normal alike.

Therefore, conflict is culturally determined to a considerable extent, and the existence of conflict is not a defining characteristic of the disordered person. Neither the presence of conflict nor its content distinguishes the normal from the abnormal, but rather the way in which the person proceeds to deal with it. Normal resolutions of conflict are different in kind from those employed by the neurotic, and they are more effective. Horney did not continue beyond this point in characterizing normal behavior, however, or in specifying what would constitute effective conflict resolution or how such responses were acquired.

The foregoing paragraphs encompass most of Horney's comments about the course of normal development. Apparently she felt no theoretical constraint to proceed any further with such an analysis. In general, with her attention continually focused on the course of disordered development, she was content to say that in the absence of adverse influences, normal development would "proceed along its natural course."

THE DEVELOPMENT OF DISORDERED BEHAVIOR

In discussing Horney's views concerning the acquisition of disordered behavior, we shall be presenting her propositions about the development of *neuroses,* since with this term she referred to all patterns of deviant behavior. To Horney the term neurosis was virtually equivalent to pathology in general, and she apparently held to several implicit assumptions: that all disordered behavior develops in essentially the same fashion; that the symptomatic differences between one disorder and another are secondary to the neurotic process; and that symptomatic differences do not imply essentially different etiologies. As had Adler before her, Horney de-emphasized the significance of symptomatology, and indeed devoted no effort to its description or classification, or to a study of its functional relationships with other aspects of behavior.

THE DEFINITION OF DISORDER

But what is it that characterizes a neurosis, and in what way does neurotic behavior differ from the normal? Horney's notions about *character* become important at this point. She began with the observation that neurotic people not only had manifest symptoms but were also disturbed in their everyday dealings with life, and that although symptom behaviors might or might not be present in a particular instance, the generalized difficulties with people and events always were (1942). She then went on to assert that every neurosis, no matter what the symptomatic picture might be, was a *character neurosis* (1945). By character, Horney appeared to mean all the extensive organizations of thoughts, feelings, and habits of thinking and perceiving a person has developed over the course of his life, although characteristically she did not define it explicitly. The primary characteristics of a neurosis, then, were the subjectively observable responses—the neurotic's perceptions, thoughts, and feelings. It is such mediational events which determine the way a person behaves in general and the symptom behaviors that he develops in particular.

Thus, the study of neurotic behavior entails the analysis of the complex patterns of perceiving, thinking, and feeling that the person has acquired toward various people and things. These are what Horney referred to collectively as his *attitudes*. She proposed that such patterns of behavior (attitudes) resulted from an insidious and chronic process, beginning in the person's childhood and involving extended realms of the person's behavior. Again, it was not the symptoms (if present) that represented the neurotic's problem; rather his entire personal orientation was at fault.

Horney thus ruled out of consideration the temporary lapses in behavioral efficiency that occur when a person is faced with a given situation which is difficult for him. She did not regard these as very intricate types of problems, and saw their resolution as relatively simple and straightforward. Even though she referred to these as *situation neuroses*, it is clear that she did not mean to consider them as neuroses in the same sense.

Disordered behavior, then, is to be traced to disordered patterns of perceptions, thoughts, affects, and other subjectively observable responses. How does one determine which of these patterns are to be considered neurotic and hence abnormal? Horney recognized that this was a problem and prepared what she regarded as only a tentative answer (1937). She suggested that the conception of what is neurotic is relative, varying from culture to culture, from time to time, and from class to class; also it varies by sex, since what is regarded as normal for one sex can be defined as abnormal for the other. Thus, neurotic responses are first of all deviations from the usual patterns of behavior appropriate to a given culture at a given point in time. They are both culturally determined and culturally relative.

Horney felt that a second characteristic was the relative invariability with which such responses occurred. Neurotic behavior is characterized by *rigidity* and *compulsiveness*. She seemed to mean that such responses were often overgeneralized, occurred indiscriminately, and were applied without variation—all without regard to their appropriateness to a given situation.

Horney proposed that neurotic responses were events which seemed incongruent with the person's capabilities, his background, and his other attributes. Neurotic behavior in general represents an *impairment*, in the sense that the responses are less than one would expect ordinarily from the subject. The person is judged to be less productive, less enthusiastic, less spontaneous, or less accomplished than he is expected to be (1937, p. 26).

Thus, Horney was thinking in terms of multiple criteria of disorder, implying that it differed both in degree and in kind from that of the normal. Not only does the neurotic think and perceive differently from the normal—the content of his responses is different—but also the frequency of his responses differs. Perhaps he also differs from the normal in that certain of his responses are a great deal more intense; later we shall see that she felt the neurotic to have more "basic anxiety" than the normal. Moreover, he has more inappropriate relationships established between his responses and the situations in which they occur; he is more apt to produce the same, and thus inappropriate, response to entirely different situations. Finally, he has inappropriate relationships established between one set of responses and another; he will select ineffective responses with which to deal with his difficulties, and one set of inappropriate thoughts will lead inevitably to others.

With this general characterization of disorder, we can next discuss what Horney conceived to be the content and sequence in which such behaviors developed.

THE SEQUENCE OF DEVELOPMENT

Horney proposed that disorder begins with severe, predominantly negative behavior toward the child by others, which elicited *basic anxiety*. The child develops conflicting neurotic trends, or habitual patterns of behavior for dealing with such interpersonal difficulties. *Neurotic solutions,* or behavior patterns, are acquired to resolve the conflicts. These solutions are only partially effective, however, and lead to additional difficulties and *symptoms*. Often they produced the very consequent they were designed to forestall; a *vicious circle* became established. The core of behavior disorder lies in conflicting response patterns for dealing with individuals who evoke fear and anger responses in the individual.

THE SITUATIONAL ANTECEDENTS TO BEHAVIOR DISORDER. Horney was clear in proposing that disordered behavior was learned, and that it was initially acquired in relationship to other people and their behavior. In contrast to the conditions that were said to favor normal development were those contributing to neurotic development, which Horney grouped together under the label *adverse influences* (1950). Horney failed to subcategorize these interpersonal events in any systematic way, merely listing various groups of behaviors under such titles as: domineering, overprotective, intimidating, irritable, overexacting, overindulgent, erratic, indifferent, and the like. She proposed that they held in common the absence of responses of love and respect, and by implication the presence of rejecting and critical responses by the parents, others, or both toward the child.

Whether open and direct, or veiled and subtle, such events are said to lead inevitably to subsequent difficulty if they represent the prevailing pattern. One might expect the indirect and subtle to present even greater difficulties for the child because of their ambiguity, although Horney did not elaborate this possibility.

THE OCCURRENCE OF BASIC ANXIETY. A direct sequel to such situational events was a response pattern that Horney referred to as *basic anxiety*. It is a concept which is distinctive to her position, and has become one of its hallmarks. Some approximation of what Horney was referring to can be made by examining what she felt to be its attributes.

She characterized this pattern as: "a terrible feeling of being isolated and helpless in a potentially hostile world." She proposed that it had three "elements": feelings of helplessness, hostility, and isolation. Together with these went another set of responses, "a child's sense of lurking hypocrisy in the environment" (1945, p. 41).

Clearly, Horney was not referring to one kind of response, such as fear, but rather to a pattern of different kinds of responses. Further, the responses that make up this pattern (or recurrent pattern) are not directly accessible to an objective observer. Some are affective in nature, namely, feelings of anger and feelings of fear. It seems probable that thoughts and perception are also entailed, since the term "feelings of isolation" would seem to denote more particularly the recognition or thought "no one wants me" and some distressing affect which would follow. Similarly with the notion of "lurking hypocrisy," which would seem to imply some judgment or evaluation by the child of the behavior of others around him.

Here, again, we see Horney's predilection for molar concepts with scant specification of their attributes. She did not specify how such a pattern came to be in the child's repertoire, but only made reference to what it was and under what conditions it was elicited, although the writers have earlier assumed that Horney implicitly viewed the pattern, or at least its elements, to be innate. Nor did she indicate at what stage of development such a pattern could occur; it was implied that it appears in early childhood, but no effort was made to specify when it could be anticipated, whether in the infant, the toddler, or the preschool child. Neither is there reference to whether such events are accessible to the awareness of the child in whom they might occur, or to what extent they could be represented verbally by the child. Finally, there is some doubt whether this pattern of events was thought to occur in unit fashion and operate as a pattern, or whether the term basic anxiety was used to refer to similar types of responses which occurred at discrete points in time and were abstracted by the observer into a single descriptive class. Thus, when punished, derogated, and rejected, is the child supposed to respond with the entire repertoire of fear, anger, helplessness, and isolation? or does he on one occasion feel angry, on another afraid, and so forth? And if the events are discrete, does the objective observer place them into one class because they seem to hold elements in common with one another, for example, negative thoughts and feelings?

The Development of Neurotic Trends

Horney proposed that the next stage of disordered development represented attempts by the child to cope with this pattern of inner events (basic anxiety) on the one hand and the frightening people in his surroundings on the other. In her view, the child learns to employ various strategies which are "ad hoc" in the sense that they are developed in response to the inconsistent and fear-producing behaviors of others and are acquired without foresight and symbolic planning. Thus, she regarded them as *unconscious* and unrelated to the usual contents of awareness or to the habitual verbal language of the child.

There are many specific patterns of response which are possible, and in her earlier writings Horney listed ten such interpersonal patterns (neurotic trends) which the child might acquire, and which she felt to be readily identifiable and also significant. They represented clusters of responses directed toward people and were composed of thoughts, feelings, expectations, and needs; the concept of need remained undefined in her writings. An example of such a pattern of interpersonal behavior (a neurotic trend) is the *Neurotic Need for Perfection and Unassailability,* which was number ten on her list. The types of responses which she felt were typical of such a pattern included: (1) Relentless efforts for perfection in general; (2) ruminations and self-recriminations regarding possible flaws in own behavior; (3) feelings of superiority over others because of self-evaluation of perfection; (4) dread (fear) of finding flaws within the self, or of making mistakes; (5) dread (fear) of criticism or reproaches (1942, pp. 59-60). Subsequently Horney decided that all such patterns of behavior were reducible to three groupings, each following from one of the primary elements which she had proposed make up the basic pattern of emotional distress (basic anxiety).

MOVING TOWARD PEOPLE. In response to his judgments that he is helpless, the child can adopt a pattern of compliance and dependence. Horney proposed that this entailed a recognition and acceptance of inadequacy on the part of the child. It was her notion that if such behavior by the child was successful in eliciting love and support from the parents, then it became an established pattern. Such overt love would lead to satisfying feelings—he gains a feeling of belonging and support—and to a reduction in his fear—feels less weak and isolated.

MOVING AGAINST PEOPLE. In response to the aspect of hostility, the child can develop a pattern of behavior which is antagonistic to the people who surround him. His angry feelings can lead to acts of rebellion against the commands and dictates of his parents, to defiant and destructive behavior, and to other aggressive responses. Again, Horney proposed that this involved the recognition of angry affect in himself, the perceptual identification of anger in others, and the implicit decision to fight. With such hostile responses proceeding within, the child finds multiple ways to rebel. This interpersonal pattern becomes established if several consequents are forthcoming: if he succeeds in beating or overcoming others and derives satisfaction therefrom; if he experiences satisfaction following acts of revenge; and if his fear subsides after the aggressive acts have succeeded in fending off frightening persons. In Horney's language he does it partly for his own protection, partly for revenge, and partly for the feeling of strength that he derives.

MOVING AWAY FROM PEOPLE. The isolative aspect of the basic pattern of distress can lead to an avoidance pattern. Rather than patterns of compliance or aggression, the child can develop a pattern of withdrawal from people, and turn to other objects and events in the situation. Thus, avoidance of people entails an approach to something else, to the "world" of nature, dolls, books, dreams, and so forth. Although Horney did not emphasize the consequents of such a pattern, to remain consistent one would expect it to become stable if it were to contribute to a proportionate increase in responses of positive emotionality, and also to a reduction of or a termination of fear.

On the occasion of their first occurrence, each of these would appear as appropriate responses to specific situations. After all, they are, in content, the same responses as those employed by the child who is destined to be normal. Everyone will on occasion give in to others, fight them, or keep to oneself. However, in the case of the child who is in the process of pathogenesis, Horney asserted that he "cannot be flexible." In his instance, the responses are related to the intense emotional pattern of distress (basic anxiety), and Horney proposed that it was this antecedent that differed from the normal and determined a more intense response of compliance, aggression, or avoidance. Each child develops a preferred pattern of response; which one of these he acquires will be determined by the situational context in which he operates—that is, which responses are permitted, encouraged, or both, by the parents—and thus which serve to maximize positive emotion and minimize negative. But because they are acquired in relation to the intense emotion of distress, these preferences in the case of the disturbed child are presumably much more intense. Further, if some circumstance prevents the occurrence of the preferred interpersonal pattern, Horney proposed that this would revive the primary distress; severe panic would ensue. A preference develops for one of the three, though not to the complete exclusion of the others, and thus it becomes possible to characterize any one person in terms of the stratagems which he predominately employs. Moreover, since they were acquired in relation to intense emotional distress, they themselves are more intense; they have become "compulsive."

THE FORMATION OF INTERPERSONAL ATTITUDES. The next phase of disordered development Horney proposed was one in which the discrete patterns of interpersonal interaction begin to generalize and to "pervade the entire personality." She believed human relationships molded the "qualities we develop," the "goals" we acquire, and our "values." These in turn influence how we behave toward others and thus are "inextricably interwoven" (1945, pp. 46–47). Specific behaviors towards others inevitably tend to extend if they have been acquired in response to the general pattern of emotional distress. Presumably they not only generalize to other humans but involve other responses as well, so that larger and larger behavioral patterns develop, in which the theme of submission, hostility, or avoidance is apparent. This extension occurs in all response realms, influencing how the child typically sees others (perceptions), the way he conceives events (thoughts), the way he feels in the presence of others (emotions), and the overt instrumental behaviors he employs. Such a general pattern of response Horney referred to as an *attitude,* and since she felt these to be fundamental to the development of disorder, she labeled them the *primary attitudes.* She avoided the use of such terms as submissive or dependent to refer to these attributes, considering them inadequate to describe something so all-inclusive as to reflect a "whole way of life" (1945, p. 55). Such patterns need not occur only to the behavior of others, either, since the generalization could occur to animals, nature, and events of all kinds—indeed, to life in general. Thus, a child who developed a generalized pattern of hatred could readily come to conceive of the entire world as a case of "eat or be eaten."

THE BASIC CONFLICT. From the foregoing we arrive at what Horney regarded as the "core" of disorder and her "new theory of neurosis." If a person developed the various sets of interpersonal patterns, each of them of intense amplitude, and if all three were to become elicited at one point in time, the person would be caught in severe conflict; he would be drawn simultaneously to being compliant, aggressive, and avoidant. The conflict is occasioned by the fact that these global patterns are mutually incompatible with one another in the potential neurotic, since they are of sufficient intensity that he must behave in terms of one and only one. If all are equally strong, he cannot behave at all.

Horney cautioned against thinking of this conflict in oversimplified terms such as love versus hate, compliance versus rebellion, submissiveness versus dominance. Although such elements are present, she feared that such terms would lead one to overlook the crucial fact that these are highly generalized patterns (attitudes) involving many other kinds of responses as well.

Horney proposed that several consequents follow such a conflict. On the one hand, the individual would be under the exigency of having to do something—on the other, the cumulative effect of the unterminated distress would become sufficiently high that the person would become agitated and subjectively feel as if he were literally being split apart. The efforts to terminate the distress resulting from such conflict constitute the next group of disordered response patterns, the *neurotic solutions.*

The Four Major Conflict Resolutions

There are four principal patterns of response which Horney proposed are typically employed to "dispose" of the crippling conflict between equally strong sets of interpersonal patterns. She emphasized these above several subsidiary patterns because of their presumed frequency, because they tended to lead to extensive changes in other behaviors (produced extensive personality changes), and because they usually produced further difficulties.

THE SELECTION OF ONE PATTERN AND THE REPRESSION OF ITS OPPOSITE. One of the things a person could do when faced with such a response conflict is to enhance and facilitate the development of one of these patterns and to deny and remove from symbolic awareness all behavior perceived as inconsistent with it. If the development is in the direction of obtaining love and compliance, this will yield what Horney referred to as the *compliant neurotic* character; if on the other hand it developed in the direction of hostility and rebellion, it would result in the *aggressive neurotic character.* Once this development is under way, it proceeds to generalize throughout the person's behavior so that all of his responses, mediating and socially instrumental responses alike, become oriented in a similar direction (1942, p. 49).

We can illustrate briefly what Horney meant by referring to the characteristics of one of these neurotic life patterns, the compliant one. In the interest of reducing fear, this choice involves extensive reliance on others. Whenever he is in interaction with people, they prompt his feelings of fear and anger, and he has learned to become submissive and compliant in order to cope with them. He becomes alert to the wishes of others, conciliatory in his manner, generous in his actions, appeasing in the face of anger from others. He develops a corresponding overevalution of the worth of others, regarding them as kind and trustworthy, attractive and able. By contrast he derogates and underestimates himself, rating himself as inferior and helpless. Thinking in this fashion leads him to depend on the approval of others, judging his actions in terms of what others think; his self-esteem rises or falls with the degree of approval he obtains. His values are developed along corresponding lines. To him goodness includes sympathy, love, generosity, unselfishness, and humility. Any behaviors that could be labeled as egotistic, ambitious, callous, unscrupulous, and hateful are considered to be bad. Horney pointed out that this pattern of thinking about the world of people leads the individual to develop an inappropriate evaluation of love and sex. He conceives of love as the sure cure of everything, and sexual intercourse as the epitome of love. Both are sought as the ultimate objective with which to solve all problems, and they come to occupy his attention and his thoughts; much of his day-to-day behavior is determined by this way of thinking.

On the other hand, the adoption of such thoughts and values entails the simultaneous denial of anger and resentment, since the occurrence of anger would endanger the person's pattern of pleasing others and eliciting their love and respect. This necessitates the repression of any and all angry responses in his own behavior, as well as responses similar to it, such as ambitious ideas, thoughts of power, or incipient acts of assertiveness. There develops a whole series of inhibitions against such responses and a corresponding pattern of avoidance to situations that are likely to elicit them. Thus an "entire philosophy of life" becomes elaborated.

The reasons for the maintenance of such a pattern are several: it serves to reduce the person's fears about the prospects of hostile interaction with other people; it increases the frequency with which he elicits loving and kindly responses from others; and finally, with such a pattern, the paralysis of conflict is interrupted.

Difficulties arise, however, because this is a misrepresentation of events. Not only does the individual misidentify what is going on with respect to his own behavior, but he also has a roseate view of the behavior of others. He will encounter frequent disappointments, since people are often not as he pictures them. His aspirations are faulty—love and sex will prove ineffective in resolving the many difficulties that characterize his interpersonal affairs. The pattern as a whole is a faulty way of trying to interact with people, one which will lead to many derivative types of problems.

Horney proceeded at length to describe the many other thoughts, expectations, opinions, and the like which she observed to recur in such a compliant pattern. Indeed, Horney was at her best when describing the intricate organizations of such mediational and socially instrumental behaviors in the patients she studied. The *aggressive character pattern* could be described similarly, but the example given is sufficient to illustrate how Horney believed disordered behavior should be studied.

DETACHMENT. The pattern of interpersonal avoidance—moving away from people—can become further developed into a more widespread personality orientation called the *detached character structure*. This concept does not refer simply to responses of physical isolation, but more to a pervasive emotional withdrawal from other people. Implicitly, as well as by deliberate planning, this person elects to avoid emotionalized interactions with others in any way, whether to love them, fight with them, co-operate, or compete. Superficially, he may appear to "get along" with others, but this obscures a generalized tendency to suppress all feelings (primarily love and hate) with a corresponding emphasis upon intellective pursuits. Often he values self-sufficiency and seeks to be self-sufficient, avoiding any obligation to other people, making it a matter of principle not to accept help. He seeks privacy, preferring to work, eat, and sleep alone. He refuses to divulge the details of his private affairs to other people, whether they be shame-producing or not. He often insists on independence in a negative fashion, resenting and avoiding what he interprets as any attempt by others to influence, coerce, or obligate him. As with other disordered behaviors, all of these responses are intense, overgeneralized, and hence indiscriminate (compulsive). However, Horney believed that for such persons it had become the only possible way of living. Moreover, it provides certain advantages: it makes for a measure of serenity and an absence of acute periods of emotional distress; it permits the opportunity for some measure of originality in thought and feeling, and thus, it can contribute to the development of creative abilities. Horney was impressed with how many "creative persons" also reflected this pattern of generalized detachment from emotionalized interactions with other people.

This, then, is a "solution" in the sense that it serves to maximize the positive emotional responses of satisfaction and also serves to keep the major conflicts from awareness. However, the intense emotional patterns of love and hate remain; they have not been extirpated, merely repressed. These continue to be strong and continue to harass the detached person. Moreover, he is represented as more vulnerable to decompensation than the earlier two patterns of adjustment, since he does not even have the techniques of interpersonal interaction that they enjoy. If he were exposed to a situation where his privacy became invaded—for example, an economic necessity for earning a living when his life had previously been sheltered—his entire pattern could become disrupted, and intense fear and distress would occur. This decompensation would appear primarily in the form of intense fears (panic): a fear of becoming submerged in the mass of humanity and losing his claims to distinction; a fear of helpless exposure to aggressive persons; and a fear of impending insanity.

THE IDEALIZED SELF-IMAGE. A third solution to the conflicts is to deny (negate) their existence and build a conception of what the disordered person believes himself to be, what he can be in the future, or what he ought to be. He can begin to misrepresent to himself what his behaviors and his attributes are; rather than consider himself to be weak, hostile, frightened or unwanted, he can describe himself as strong, powerful, virtuous, and the like. One person may perceive himself to be a genius, another a saint, still a third a Don Juan. Each of these constitute groups of self-congratulatory thoughts and is instrumental in increasing feelings of satisfaction and stopping feelings of fear.

Horney felt that all disordered persons tended to build such images of themselves to a greater or lesser degree. In each case the series of thoughts is routinely flattering. Often the development of such habits of thinking is implicit and unverbalized, and thus, although the self-inflation might be obvious to an objective observer, the person himself would not recognize it. It is always positive in content and inaccurate, although not completely so since it is a set of abstractions composed of both inaccurate and appropriate observations of one's own behavior. Such inappropriate self-conceptions are established and maintained because they permit a person to judge himself as superior rather than weak and contemptible—the former leads to positive affective responses, the latter to fear and distress.

The development of such a conception is ineffective in the long run. The person attributes to himself qualities he does not have, and he fails to perceive accurately his real feelings, thoughts, and actions. If he takes his inaccurate self-descriptions as fact, he becomes vulnerable to mistakes and errors in his interactions with people. Moreover, since the conceptions are unrealistic, he cannot possibly live up to his expectations. As a result, there is an increase in anticipatory fear, anger toward oneself, and fear and anger toward others. New conflicts appear. An especially important set of conflicts are those between the accurate thoughts about his behavior and the idealized ones—conflict between the real self and the idealized image. In her latest publication (1950) Horney had come round to viewing this particular conflict to be the central one in all neuroses. In addition, the result is behavioral impoverishment, since such a conflict leads the person to restrict his life lest he be exposed as a fake. He avoids those situations in which he fears he would not be respected and admired and those tasks that he is uncertain he could master. But worst of all, this false representation of himself is built on pretense rather than fact. The person cannot behave effectively, since he so badly misjudges and misrepresents what he really feels and values. In Horney's words, he becomes *alienated from the real self*, "caught in a spider's web of unconscious pretense and rationalization," producing "precarious living" (1942, p. 111).

EXTERNALIZATION. When the construction of a network of self-congratulatory thoughts fails as a solution to the multiplicity of conflicts that have accumulated, the person may resort to *externalization*. This Horney defined as attributing internal responses to an outside source and blaming the latter for one's difficulties. She included not only the responses of blame avoidance, as in the concept of projection, but others as well. For example, a person utilizing these response mechanisms could, without being aware that he feels profoundly oppressed, still be very disturbed by oppression of small countries. Moreover, he could become so habituated to interpreting situational events as the "cause" of his behavior that he could ascribe not only his disturbances but also his good fortune to external events.

As a form of conflict resolution, this response pattern entails a denial of conflict within one's own responses and the perception of conflicts as occasioned by other people; external conflicts replace internal ones. Because he comes to think that his life, for good or ill, is now determined by others, he becomes preoccupied with trying to change, reform, punish, coerce, or impress them. His anger toward them is increased, as is his fear, for he considers that he must protect himself from the interference of others. Thus, his difficulties with others become exaggerated even further and antagonism increases.

CONSEQUENTS OF NEUROTIC SOLUTIONS. Although we have touched upon some of the consequences, there is a group that Horney felt to be generally characteristic of all neurotic solutions. First, a group of fears seems to emerge routinely from such adjustment patterns. Specifically she mentioned fears of insanity, of exposure, of any form of behavioral change, and of anything expected to disrupt the established patterns of behavior. Second, behavioral impoverishment typically occurs, together with feelings of hopelessness, despair, and futility. Moreover, these patterns can often become self-perpetuating, in the sense that they continuously reproduce the behavior in others which initiates the neurotic patterns. Such vicious circles are likely. A further complication arises when sadistic trends become developed. Symptoms are the final gross manifestation of these long-established and intricately organized patterns of interpersonal behavior.

THE GOALS OF THERAPY

Who Determines the Goals?

Horney seemed to be of two minds about this issue. Writing in 1942, she stated that the patient established the objectives, and that the therapist's task was to help the patient recognize and modify behavior patterns to the extent the patient desired (1942, p. 123). Indeed this was necessary since the therapist could not induce changes beyond those the patient himself wanted to effect (1942, p. 19). She proposed that the therapist take advantage of the patient's efforts to develop whatever capabilities he might have and to live as "full a life" as his given circumstances would permit.

And yet, in writing just three years later, she began to specify the goals of therapy, independent of the requests of a particular patient. She outlined four ideal therapeutic objectives which the therapist should attempt to attain, proposing that these were directly derived from her theory of the development of disordered behavior and that they constituted appropriate counters to the disordered patterns themselves (1945). Since the objectives she listed hardly seemed to represent objectives as a patient would define them, she would appear either to be contradicting herself or changing her position.

The Nature of the Goals

At different points in her writing, Horney stated: the goal of therapy is to change behavior; the task of therapy is to achieve self-recognition and change; any successful treatment increases self-confidence; the goal of treatment is the analysis and understanding of the entire neurotic character; and the objectives of treatment are twofold—a modification of the distress occasioned by neuroses, and helping people toward their best possible further development.

Taking all her comments into account, the following summary would seem to represent her view. The patient reports symptoms, emotional distress, or both. The alleviation of these is one of the objectives of treatment. However, complaints derive from the fact that the patient has acquired a set of generalized patterns of interacting with people which are ineffective, which contribute to his difficulties, and of which he is usually unaware. In order to achieve a change in symptoms or distress, a change must be effected in these general and basic patterns. This will entail a careful analysis of all the person's habits of perceiving, thinking, valuing, behaving, and so forth, with an eye toward helping the patient recognize them and understand how they operate. Particularly important will be the discovery of behaviors of which the patient is unaware. Once he recognizes how his habits of thinking, valuing, and responding to others affect his behavior, he will be able to make changes in his behavior according to his personal goals and will be proceeding in the direction of his best possible further development.

Above and beyond these considerations, Horney proposed a set of four general goals: responsibility, inner dependence, spontaneity of feeling, and wholeheartedness (1945). By the term *responsibility,* Horney appears to have meant the following kinds of behaviors: the person judges himself to be capable of making decisions and accepting the consequences of them; he considers himself to be the primary source of control over what happens to him; he accepts the proposition that to some extent he is responsible for the welfare of others. Responses reflecting *inner dependence* would include the recognition and endorsement of his own hierarchy of values by the patient and the application of these values to his everyday behavior. In terms of interpersonal relations, it implies a respect for the values of other people. *Spontaneity of feeling* to Horney meant the recognition, acceptance, appropriate expression of, and effective responses of control over one's affective responses of all kinds—hate, fear, love, elation, or sadness. She proposed that interpersonal interactions in which affective responses occurred in free and appropriate fashion were relationships characterized by love and friendship. The final objective, *wholeheartedness,* can be approximated only as conflicts are resolved. Horney did not specify it clearly. It includes being "without pretense," "emotionally sincere," and committing oneself fully to one's feelings, one's work, and one's beliefs (1954, p. 242).

PRINCIPLES BY WHICH BEHAVIORAL CHANGE OCCURS

Horney did not tackle systematically the question of how relearning proceeds within therapy. The following ideas have been pieced together from her writings.

First, the reader should be reminded of what the writers concluded was an implicit set of statements about the learning process. Horney had written that two factors determine whether a disordered pattern will be acquired and maintained: (1) if it reduces fear (produces security) and (2) if it produces positive emotion (satisfaction). Assuming that the normal person learns in the same way as the disordered person, responses that terminate fear or elicit or arouse some pattern of positive affect will be learned. Thus, she seemed to utilize both response termination and response arousal principles.

Beyond this, however, Horney suggested that change could be, and was, mediated by symbolic responses. Change is accomplished through *recognition, insight,* and *understanding.* Although these terms are not clearly defined, the gist of Horney's writings indicates that she used them in synonymous fashion. Recognition refers to a cognitive and affective response pattern, an "intellectual and an emotional experience" (1942, p. 111). The cognitive aspect seemed to include a combination of perception and thought, for example, when a patient identifies and labels behavior of which he had hitherto been unaware. But it also included the perception of relationships between events, how situations evoke certain responses, and how they in turn habitually generate other sequences of behavior. Such perceptions and thoughts are always accompanied, however, by emotional responses, both positive and negative, such as relief and gratification or pain and fear. Both aspects of recognition are necessary for behavioral change to occur.

Occasionally, Horney wrote, behavioral change occurs as a direct result of simply identifying an event or a series of events to be occurring within one's behavior. Patients often hope it will be this simple. but complicated neuroses are no more likely to disappear this way than is a "social calamity such as unemployment" simply because it is identified as a problem (1942, p. 53). Identification of what needs to be changed does not constitute the ability to change it.

Horney asserted that ability to change inappropriate behaviors can only follow a decrease in the intensity of their emotional determinants. She noted the necessity for the patient to become less afraid, less hostile, less isolated—the three elements in the basic anxiety pattern. These first of all reduce the intensity of the inappropriate neurotic responses, since there is a direct correlation between intensity of the emotional antecedent (anxiety and distress) and the strength of the resulting response. Also, as this occurs, the patient's relationships with others improve, and presumably new responses begin to occur.

But what produces the alterations in response intensity in these particular responses of fear, hostility, and the like? The answer is further analysis and understanding of the relationships between his various behaviors. He "works through" the implications of his faulty patterns, he "realizes more profoundly" the unfortunate consequences to which they lead. The ability is gradually increased as one manifestation after another is clearly recognized and understood. Understanding of their interconnections reduces their intensity and renders them susceptible to change. Accurately thinking about the crucial events is prerequisite to more extensive behavior change. Thus, there is a possibility that Horney was implying still a third learning principle: attention to events can lead to conceptions as to how they occur, and these in turn can lead to further changes in thought and action.

Patient Behaviors That Must Occur in Therapy

Horney conceived of the therapy relationship as a mutual enterprise in which a division of labor existed between patient and therapist. She did not elaborate at any great length on the responses the patient must bring to treatment. Writing in 1942, she seemed to feel that a certain set of responses was a necessary prerequisite, having to do with whether the patient was "motivated" for treatment. She proposed that treatment was feasible if the patient had some emotionalized commitment to an objective which would entail a change in his behavior. She referred to this as an *incentive* to arrive at some goal, or the *incentive to grow*. Later, however, she proposed that this characterized all humans, so that it was no longer viewed as a selective factor in the question of treatment (1950). She also made note of the necessity for the patient to seek to change his behavior, hence remanding himself for professional treatment. Again, this was not considered to be a limiting factor, since she proposed that every disordered person at some level knows that something is wrong, even though he might not like to think so and be even more averse to admitting it openly. If this were true, it leaves us with the assumption that Horney came to view all persons as potentially accessible to verbal psychotherapy.

Within the treatment sessions themselves, it is the patient's "constructive activity" which determines the length and outcome of therapy (1942, p. 14). Horney proposed that the patient had to proceed through three general tasks: (1) he must verbalize freely and frankly; (2) he must identify his inappropriate responses and their effects upon his life; and (3) he must change patterns that are disturbing his relationships between himself and the world of people around him.

The first task is acceptance of the *condition of free association*. In doing so, the patient must report to the analyst all his subjective responses as they occur—sensations, images, feelings, thoughts, and recollections—and he must report them in the sequence in which they occur. The second task is the identification of events hitherto inaccessible to him, the recognition of relationships between his thoughts and feelings and his overt social behavior. The third is that active efforts must be made for change to occur whenever change does not automatically follow from the understanding of his behavior and how it works. On occasion the patient will be confronted with the fact that his understanding has proceeded as far as it can go and that he is face to face with a conflict in which a decision has to be made. After a thorough clarification of the problems involved, the patient must eventually take a stand. He must in such an instance be willing to select a course of action and not remain content to allow the conflict to continue indefinitely.

Stated in this fashion, it might appear that the things the patient must perform are relatively simple. It is the second set of responses, however, which are in reality extremely intricate and detailed. The process of treatment Horney proposed involved the analysis of the "entire neurotic character structure," and thus it would entail:

1. Examining in detail all implicit attempts at resolving conflicts he has undertaken;

2. Identifying and studying all the implications of his predominant interpersonal patterns (attitude), his misrepresentations of himself and his behavior (idealized self-image);

3. Coming to recognize the effects of these upon his day-to-day behavior in interpersonal situations;

4. Recognizing the incompatibility between his various patterns and how they conflict with one another (the basic conflict);

5. Analyzing all the ineffective compromise responses the patient is trying to make;

6. Recognizing the relationship among these events, his symptoms, and the adverse consequences (1945, p. 230).

All this is referred to collectively as *working through*. Clearly, with such extensive things to be accomplished by the subject, treatment must necessarily be prolonged. Horney did not comment on length of treatment, although one gathers from the case illustrations in her books that it would characteristically take a number of years.

Two things are apparent here. The first is Horney's extensive emphasis on awareness and thought (cognitive responses). Although she frequently mentioned that affective responses were intricately involved, she did not attempt to detail their operation nearly as completely as the thought processes involved. The second is that although Horney is thought of as a theorist who emphasized the importance of situational (cultural) determinants in behavior, her discussion of therapy techniques was almost entirely in terms of response-response relationships.

Behaviors Required of the Therapist

Horney believed that there were two large groupings of behaviors which were necessary for the therapist to have in his repertoire and to be able to employ. The first of these had to do with the behavioral equipment of the therapist prior to the treatment operations themselves. In her view, a professional psychotherapist (analyst) should be able to meet three requirements, or else not assume the responsibility for treating others.

1. He should have extensive knowledge of those events that can determine behavior of which patients are not typically aware (unconscious forces). He should know the response forms in which they occur,

the reasons for their intensity, and the ways they determine other responses. He should be familiar with the procedures for identifying and eliciting them.

2. He should have a definite set of skills acquired through training and practice. He must be skilled at dealing with people. He should know what topics to discuss with a person, and which to postpone. He must be able imaginatively to take the role of the other, and to "project himself into a strange world" with its own peculiarities and laws (1942, p. 25).

3. He must have relatively effective patterns of interpersonal adjustment in his own private affairs; otherwise he will inadvertently misconstrue, mislead, and actually even harm the person he is attempting to assist.

The behaviors required of the therapist in the treatment process itself Horney cast into five main classes: "observation, understanding, interpretation, help in resistance, and general human help" (1942 p. 123).

OBSERVATION. The therapist has two sources of information concerning the patient's behavior: the patient's reports about his responses, and his own observation of the patient's behavior during the treatment sessions. Effective observation lets little go unnoticed. Horney felt that the therapist should absorb as many observations as possible about the subject's behavior, since he wishes to understand the entire personality structure, and he does not know offhand what may be most relevant. He notes everything the patient tells him of the content of his behavior, past and present, his relationships with himself and with others, his plans, wishes, fears, and thoughts. He takes note not only of what the patient says, but also of his manner and the intonations of his voice. No observation should be regarded as unimportant.

UNDERSTANDING. Among the seemingly disconnected maze of observations, the therapist tries to discover significant patterns, forming hypotheses about what is related to what, thereby forming a tentative picture of how the patient's behavior works. He repeatedly submits his hypotheses to test to determine whether they can account for the data in a satisfactory way. He is primarily interested, not in the obvious connections between responses which the patient can identify and report, but in the implicit relationships which have escaped the patient's attention and which he cannot identify by himself (the unconscious motivations and reactions). He does this by making inferences about the content implicit in what the patient is saying; by studying the context in which particular feelings and thoughts appear in the associative chain, asking himself why it comes up just now; by taking note of repetitive themes or sequences; by studying dreams and fantasies since these are proposed to be direct correlates of implicit (unconscious) feelings; by noting the, point at which sudden shifts in the patient's therapy behavior occur; and by noting the associations that arise in the therapist's own thought sequences. Each of these is described as a useful way of inference making, an act which Horney defined as partly reasoning from facts and partly intuitive guesswork.

INTERPRETATION. Once he has developed an understanding of the implicit (unconscious) events occurring, the therapist must decide if and when he will share his conclusions with the patient. They are put forward as tentative possibilities at those times when the therapist has judged that the patient can accept them without distress and can employ them to facilitate his own understanding. It is also done in terms of a *sequence,* since problems should not be tackled in a helter-skelter fashion.

In general, Horney suggested that the interpersonal patterns (neurotic trends) be examined one at a time—after each is discovered. Then analysis should proceed "into the depths," starting with aspects of the pattern that are more readily accessible and proceeding through the pattern, rendering explicit those that are increasingly removed from symbolic awareness. Patient and therapist proceed together, and for each major pattern they first identify and recognize the various features of the pattern, then identify its antecedents, manifestations, and consequents, and finally discover its interrelationships with other patterns in the patient's repertoire. Recognition of the circularity of the events is often an important part of this process. In general, the analysis of and interpretation of symptoms is the final step in these *stages of understanding* of each pattern. Horney repeatedly cautioned therapists not to focus on symptoms too early, since to do so would obscure and prevent the analysis of that which produced them, namely, the underlying patterns making up the personality. Horney (1942) cites a case in which there were three such patterns: compulsive deference, dependence, and efforts to coerce others into labeling the patient as superior. Thus, treatment was divided into three stages, representing the sequential analysis of these three patterns. The enterprise took two-and-one-half years of analysis stretched over a four-year period.

Other than making some comments about deferring the analysis of some patterns until late in the treatment sequence (sadistic patterns and the idealized image), Horney felt it was not possible to prescribe the sequence of therapy in any greater detail. As she put it, even if there were a finite number of discernible patterns in our culture, for example, fifteen, the number of possible combinations of these would be simply staggering. Beyond these very general guide lines the therapist pursues a sequence particular to his specific patient.

HELP IN RESISTANCE. The real difficulties arise as the patient develops *resistance*. With this term Horney was referring to all the manifold ways in which a patient could resist, reject, and evade the therapy tasks, reflecting his aversion to co-operating. When such a set of responses develops, the therapist must take the lead. His task is first to recognize the resistance as such and then to help the patient to recognize it. Resistant behavior appears when the patient is hurt, frightened, angry, and the like. It is the therapist's job to find out which it is and to help the patient to recognize it.

GENERAL HUMAN HELP. Added to the primarily conceptual responses which the therapist makes is another group, including personal concern, sympathy, interest in his welfare, encouragement, and praise, all of which are duplicated in any friendship relationship. Although she did not elaborate on this particular phase of the therapist's responses, Horney seemed to regard them as very important therapeutic operations. She proposed that if the therapist emitted responses reflecting a liking and respect for the patient, the patient could see that his fears and hates were inappropriate for at least one person, and this could lead to the discovery that others were trustworthy, too. It would help the patient to "retrieve his faith in others" (1942, p. 45).

The Transfer of Change

This was a question to which Horney made no reference. Preoccupied with effecting changes in the mediating processes, she neglected to remark on how changes in these became translated into overt behavior outside the therapy condition. Perhaps she implicitly assumed that changes in thought automatically led to changes in socially instrumental behavior. If this were true, the therapist needed to concentrate only on modifying the perceptions, thoughts, and feelings occurring during the interview.

THE VERIFICATION OF THEORY AND THE
ASSESSMENT OF CHANGE

It is unfortunate that Horney neglected to remark on how one arrived at a judgment that sufficient change had been effected to warrant a termination of treatment. Indeed she omitted a discussion of the termination procedures entirely. One is left with no notion of who is to decide and in what way the decision is to be reached.

A comparable failing appears in Horney's scant reference to the ways in which one might go about verifying the accuracy of observations and testing the validity of the theoretical propositions. Her only suggestion as to a way to proceed was to gather more observations by additional observers. At one point she proposed that the substantive features of her system were so obvious that even an untrained observer could verify the findings. Anyone "sufficiently experienced with children" or "with reconstructing their early development" could verify the theory for himself (1942, pp. 45–46). On another occasion she proposed that independent professional observers such as anthropologists and psychologists might be employed to verify her assumptions about "the relation between culture and neurosis" (1937, p. 35). Apparently she was unaware of or unimpressed with the importance of explicit procedures for verifying either her theories or the facts of therapeutic change.

COMMENTS

From a formal point of view, this system of psychotherapy leaves much to be desired. Its systematic weaknesses appear in sharp relief when subjected to the method of analysis employed in this volume. Comments were made about many of the shortcomings as they were encountered throughout the chapter. Here it might suffice to summarize some of them, in an attempt to clarify some of the ways in which improvement might be effected.

The definitional aspects of this system are particularly weak. The concepts employed have not been sufficiently well specified so that one can know precisely to what behaviors the class labels refer. The concept *basic anxiety* is one to which some attention was given in the chapter, revealing the various difficulties. What is true of this primary unit is equally true of the vast majority of other concepts in the system. Horney was apparently particularly prone to point to large and complex arrangements of events, lumping them together and regarding them as self-evident entities. Basic anxiety was something that to her was quite obvious, and she seemed to assume that it would be equally obvious to anyone who took the trouble to look. She was implicitly antireductionistic when she observed that there are wishes and strivings in the human person which are basic and defy further analysis (1942, p. 23). To take complicated sets of events and to treat them as self-understood and entities incapable of analysis is to fail to appreciate what is involved in the process of observation and the building of concepts with which to treat them.

The conceptual omissions in the system are equally serious; whole ranges of human behavior fail to be explicitly recognized and incorporated. The failure to make provision for classes of behavior such as the physiological and the motoric, or the sensory and imagistic responses, of course, is a deficiency of which some other approaches to psychotherapy have been equally guilty. There is almost an exclusive emphasis on the mediating events such as feelings, thoughts, and perceptions (attitudes), and this is one of the ways in which the system is open to the charge of oversimplification.

Especially neglected are the categories of innate responses and their interrelationships. Horney not only fails to specify what they might be, but also fails to provide any way of distinguishing between these and other learned events. This omission is particularly important, for she specified psychotherapy as a way of effecting changes in learned behavior but failed to provide ways by which one could identify unlearned aspects of behavior.

The propositional aspects of the system require considerable attention as well. Careful specification has not yet been made as to precisely what sets of conditions lead to what sets of events. What propositional statements occur are almost exclusively statements that relate very complex sets of occurrences to one another (patterns to patterns, and pattern sequences). The depiction of behavior is at such a high level of abstraction that it would be difficult to be specific. Thus, problems with the propositional aspect of the system stem directly from the nature of the units of analysis initially chosen.

Even more serious perhaps is the fact that there are extensive realms in which virtually no propositional statements are made at all. There is a neglect of a careful analysis of the development of behavior, which is seen in the failure to explicate the innate response equipment and its bearing on the development of both normal and disordered behavior. The system is sketchy about the situational determinants of behavior. For example, years of complex and intricate family events are compressed into simple gross characterizations; thus, the details of family influences are obscured by their depiction in terms of a general climate, whether positive or adverse. The growth process is treated as an entity, with no attempt to differentiate stages of development. In dealing with the development of disordered behavior there is no effort to deal systematically with the problem of differential classification of disordered events, and indeed the significance of differences in disorder is de-emphasized. Horney shared with Adler the general notion that all disorder is built along the same general lines, and thus came to view symptoms as a set of relatively unimportant differences. This is partly a function of which end of the telescope one peers into—whether one tends to see the similarities or the differences. There may be certain commonalities in the overall process of disordered development from one type of disorder to another, but recognition of this should not lead one to deny the very evident differences that do exist, nor should it prevent one from proceeding to try to account for the different etiological conditions that must precede them.

Horney was less inventive when it came to the question of the operations of therapy. Although her view of the development of disorder was in many respects quite different from those of Adler, Rank, and others, she does not seem to have approached the problem of therapy in any different fashion. Viewing Horney in relation to these others, one can wonder why it is that differing analyses of what goes wrong does not lead to very different prescriptions for its remedy.

In spite of these shortcomings Horney's system has had historical impact, and the writers believe that it has some contemporary utility as well. She has been an important champion of the emphasis on the learned characteristics of disordered behavior and on the importance of the interpersonal patterns in the development of disorder; particularly significant has been her emphasis on the acquisition of patterns of responses to interpersonal events and the necessity for one to analyze the functions such patterns perform in the individual's *current* life situation.

Indeed, it was Horney's attempt to deal with the patterning of complex human behavior that struck the authors as the single most important contribution of this system to the study of disorder. She will probably be found to have been in error in her attempt to find a few very large patterns of behavior by which all the person's interpersonal responses could be characterized, and this appears to be another respect in which her analysis is undoubtedly oversimplified. But the general notion that the acquisition of response *a* typically leads to the subsequent acquisition of responses *b, c,* and *d,* in such a manner that patterns of perceptions, thoughts, and feelings tend to become developed and employed in a highly generalized way to ranges of situations, would appear to be a very useful one. It seems likely that there are such describable patterns as Horney began to explicate, patterns of compliance, detachment, or both, for example. But the question is, first, whether they are built and operate as Horney said they do, and second, whether their alteration entails the extensive sets of operations that Horney proposes in her therapeutic suggestions. Assuming that extensive patterns of behavior get built pretty much as she proposed, with all kinds of thoughts, feelings, and attitudes interwoven with one another, does the individual need to learn to attend to and recognize each and every one of these and then identify their interrelationships, as well as their implications, for his life situation? Horney says he does, and that it takes a very long while to do so. There is room for doubt, however. There is the possibility, for example, that one can alter one or two primary responses, and whole constellations of behavior which depend on or have been learned in association with them can thereby be changed.

Finally, Horney's emphasis on the central role of situational events (culture), particularly the behavior of other humans, in the development and maintenance of behavior patterns is important. It is unfortunate that she did not extend this emphasis, which appeared so prominently in her discussions of behavior analysis, into her analysis of the conditions of therapy and specification of therapeutic technique. Had she done so, important modifications of traditional treatment procedures would probably have developed.

Chapter 14

Harry Stack Sullivan's Theory
of Interpersonal Relations

The work of Harry Stack Sullivan is in many respects very impressive to a person outside the field of psychiatry itself. It strikes one as both unusual and admirable that an investigator who had apparently received little formal training in the problems of theory building and system construction should have come to recognize so many essential requirements of a therapy system and to have developed his own work in relation to them. His influence on the field of therapy theory has stemmed from his personal popularity, from his reputation as a successful therapist, and from his dedication to the teaching of his colleagues in the intricacies of psychotherapy. But none of these would have proved sufficient if the nature of his ideas and their theoretic structure had not impressed his listeners with their clarity and prospective utility.

BIOGRAPHICAL NOTES

Born in Norwich, New York, February 21, 1892, Harry Stack Sullivan began his career in the fields of medicine and psychiatry following his graduation from the Chicago College of Medicine and Surgery (M.D., 1917). He proceeded through a number of staff appointments at neuropsychiatric facilities in the Washington, D.C. area. For approximately the first 20 years of his career he immersed himself in direct clinical investigations. It was later that his theoretical formulations began to take shape.

In the early years in Washington his attention was focused primarily on schizophrenic patients, and he became well-known for his clinical facility with this group of disorders. He spent some time in this initial period at St. Elizabeth's Hospital in Washington, where he worked in association with William Alanson White. They developed a personal relationship which is said to have had considerable influence on Sullivan's developing conceptions about disordered behavior. During a period of time at the Sheppard and Enoch Pratt Hospital in Maryland, Sullivan was able to devote his attention to investigating the difficulties of acutely disturbed and recently developed schizophrenic disorders under the conditions of a small hospital unit. During this period he published several influential articles, which held the germs of his later theoretical formulations.

Sullivan entered private practice in 1931. Treatment of neurotic disorders became increasingly prominent in his clinical practice. He spent perhaps another ten years on intensive investigation of these groups and seems to have been particularly admired for his work with the obsessional disorders.

Toward the end of this period, a formalization of his theoretical point of view began to emerge. The occasion for this seems to have been Sullivan's lecture series in 1939 at the Washington School of Psychiatry. His first volume, *Conceptions of Modern Psychiatry* (1947), represented his 1939 lectures. It was also in this period that the journal *Psychiatry* became established, with Sullivan as co-editor and a significant contributor.

Sullivan served briefly as a consultant to the National Selective Service system at the outbreak of the Second World War, but thereafter returned to his pattern of lecturing. The remainder of his life (eight years) was devoted to refining his point of view and communicating it to numerous groups. One of his most significant sets of lectures was delivered at Chestnut Lodge in Rockville, Maryland.

Late in his career, Sullivan became concerned with the contributions psychiatry and psychology might make to interpersonal relations at the international level. He was active in forming the World Federation for Mental Health and was an important participant in the UNESCO project studying tensions affecting international understanding. A significant and productive career was cut short by his untimely death in 1949.

Recognizing the importance of his system and technique in the growth of the field of therapy, a group of colleagues have carefully compiled and edited the lectures and personal notebooks which Sullivan himself had not yet crystallized into publishable form. Mabel Blake Cohen, Patrick Mullahy, and Otto Will are several of his significant posthumous editors and reviewers who have been responsible for the transformation of his influence from a handful of therapeutic students and practitioners to the field at large.

THEORY CONSTRUCTION

As most of his reviewers have emphasized, Sullivan was first and foremost a clinical psychiatrist. His primary objective was the development and application of successful therapeutic procedures. But he recognized that effective treatment required an adequate and systematic set of conceptions about behavior, and that the procedures of empirical science were essential in verifying such theories.

To develop specific therapeutic procedures Sullivan believed three general sets of propositions were imperative. His posthumous editors have carefully followed Sullivan's view of his contributions by editing his reports to present: (1) A conception of the course of normal development of behavior (*The Interpersonal Theory of Psychiatry,* 1953); (2) a statement of the development of disordered behavior (*Clinical Studies in Psychiatry,* 1956); and (3) a statement of the rationale and procedures for the conduct of the psychiatric and the psychotherapeutic interview (*The Psychiatric Interview,* 1954).

Sullivan consistently emphasized that the data of therapy and personality theory could and should be subjected to empirical investigation, and that the logical rules for the construction and validation of

hypotheses which the scientific method required were the only procedures upon which verification of therapy theory could depend. He
was eager to submit the events of concern, that is, patterns of interpersonal interaction, to the scrutiny of empirical test. He welcomed
the appearance of the scientist into the therapeutic operation itself,
anticipating that the patterns of action which occurred between therapist and patient could be identified, observed, and defined in a manner that would move the entire process from the obscurity of an art
to the clarity of a science. He did not attempt such research himself.

Sullivan was quick to see that one of the critical barriers to effective theory construction and implementation lay in the nature of the
concepts that therapy theorists used. He considered the concepts prevalent in the field seriously deficient. He was disturbed about their
vagueness of definition and resultant lack of clarity, as well as by the
rubbery fashion in which terms were employed in multiple ways. He
not only saw this as a barrier to communication between workers in
the field, but he also recognized that such habits of thought dictated
the kinds of data that therapists looked for, and encouraged faulty
theories. He was especially critical, perhaps downright hostile, to
concepts representing faulty generalizations. The classic diagnostic
categories are a case in point. He was troubled both by their poor construction and by their pervasive misuse. He thought that many of the
so-called differences between the behavioral classes of schizophrenia
or manic-depressive, for example, were neither carefully defined nor
empirically verified. Moreover, reliance upon such classes led to careless work and were often used as a means of saving oneself the dis-
comforts of rigorous thinking and precise research. Sullivan was not
setting himself in opposition to concepts of this order, since he himself employed them. However, he feared that characterization of a
person as belonging to a clinical category was running the danger of
overgeneralization (1947, p. 77). He believed that the practitioner who
diagnosed a set of behaviors as schizophrenic and then proceeded to
the implicit assumption that everything else about the patient's behavior was of a schizophrenic nature also made a serious error. On the
contrary, Sullivan's expectation would be that the majority of such
a patient's behaviors were more likely to be quite normal. "We are
all much more human than anything else," he was fond of saying.

Sullivan's solution to the problem of inadequate concepts was to
propose his own. Of course, this created problems of its own, but it
arose from his intent to develop a technical language appropriate to

a field of science. A series of precise terms was his objective, and he explicitly avoided the use of many current concepts that had acquired multiple meanings.

Sullivan was greatly influenced by the operationist position of P. W. Bridgman and others, and he sought to integrate their thinking into the fabric of his system. He is reputed to have been fond of puncturing colleagues who were careless about the relationship between observation and inference. A phrase characterizing a patient's behavior in a gross and overly generalized way was typically met with the rejoinder "As demonstrated by what?" This was Sullivan's way of drawing the ties between abstract concepts and their observational base. He worked hard at least to approximate the principles of operationism in his construction of concepts, although he recognized the difficulties occasioned by the subject matter of his theory.

Along with his efforts to formulate clearly defined concepts went comparable attempts to identify their interrelationships. His ultimate objective was a series of clearly stated, empirically verifiable propositions by which to account for the way behavior occurred and he referred to his propositions as "theorems." These were distributed at intervals throughout his lectures, and represented first steps toward a system of formal statements. Sullivan considered them rudimentary in nature, requiring further development and extension. He never lost sight of the fact that propositions were hypothetical and always required further scrutiny (1947, p. 55).

Finally, Sullivan's general approach to the question of treatment was to search for different treatment operations specific to the nature of the personal difficulties to be resolved. Sullivan rejected the idea that one set of therapy procedures was applicable to all types of problems. He argued that the choice of treatment method was dependent on the nature of the patient's difficulties. Objectives determined technique. Technique should be specific to the nature of the problem. He argued for example that the "rule of free-association" was inappropriate to the treatment of a manic, an obsessional, or a schizophrenic; that warm and sympathetic interest in the subject only frightened and alienated a paranoid; and that the use of a "following" or submissive role with an obsessional only produced a wandering, circuitous, and unproductive conversation. This point of view paved the way for his trial of a variety of techniques on different kinds of behaviors.

DISTINCTIVE FEATURES

As the reader proceeds, he will recognize several distinctive features about the viewpoint of Harry Stack Sullivan. The emphasis on interpersonal behaviors is perhaps most central. Sullivan regarded these as the primary data of concern for both the personality and the therapy theorist. Sullivan proposed that behavior be analyzed in terms of the kinds of response patterns acquired in relation to interpersonal situations. Behavior disorders were conceived as arising from within the context of interrelationships with people. Correspondingly, the treatment of such disorders requires interpersonal conditions. In simple terms, people make people sick; it takes people to make them well.

Moreover, to Sullivan, an outstanding and crucial aspect of interpersonal transactions is communication. Sullivan attributed his original interest in communication to the influence of the anthropologist, Edward Sapir, who emphasized the role of communication in interpersonal relationships and in the psychotherapeutic interview itself. Sullivan became convinced that interpersonal relationships were mediated primarily by verbal and nonverbal communications. Speech was critical for transactions between people; thought or "muted speech" was an important way in which a person "communicates" with himself. Finally, speech was the vehicle by which psychotherapy was conducted, and in this setting the question of communication became doubly important. Sullivan realized, for example, that speech was often employed to obscure and confuse as well as to clarify interpersonal events. Since speech is a major therapeutic procedure, its direct study becomes an important aspect of therapy. Thus, for Sullivan, the focus of psychotherapy was on difficulties in interpersonal interaction and communication, and this resulted in a strong emphasis on speech, thought, and other communicative acts.

This, in turn, led to Sullivan's distinctive approach to the psychotherapeutic session itself. Believing that a person's behavior was a function of interpersonal events, Sullivan explicitly eschewed the analysis of a person's behavior *in vacuo,* as it were. The unit of analysis was always more than the behavior of one individual. It was an interpersonal transaction. Sullivan would have avoided characterizing a subject as likely to become angry. He would, however, have spoken of a person as angry when spoken to harshly. Or again, the subject's response of weeping took on significance only when it was known that the antecedent had been a derogatory comment by the therapist. This, of course, led Sullivan to his well-known characterization of the therapist as an analyst of the subject's behavior but simultaneously a participant in a social exchange, a role he labeled *participant observer*. The therapist not only observed the patient's behavior, but his behavior was a highly significant antecedent *and* consequent to the patient behaviors being observed.

The concept of anxiety plays a central role in Sullivan's theories of behavior and therapy. Anxiety is represented as the critical antecedent; it is the "destructive commonplace in human living"; it is the event that renders intelligible all the myriad difficulties in relating to and communicating with people.

The reader will be struck by Sullivan's emphasis on the concept of attention. This is a concept with an established history in academic psychology and was often employed in the more traditional psychiatric viewpoints. Sullivan was one of the few therapy theorists, however, who gave it first-order prominence in his behavioral concepts.

THE NORMAL COURSE OF BEHAVIOR DEVELOPMENT

Characteristics of Concepts and Propositions

A detailed analysis of the concepts in Sullivan's system reveals a confusing situation. Not only did he invent his own terms, but also there were some clear-cut inconsistencies in the concepts and propositions of the system. Apparently it was impossible for Sullivan to maintain his ideal of conceptual consistency throughout the development of his system.

Two types of difficulties are apparent. The first occurs in the treatment of situational variables. At times, Sullivan clearly argued for an analysis of behavior in terms of interpersonal situations. The unit of analysis from this viewpoint is the complete interpersonal exchange between individuals A and B. Not A in relation to B, but rather A and B considered as a unit, including both A to B and B to A. Following this avenue, one would develop concepts by which different kinds of interpersonal situations could be classified and analyzed. Sullivan did this, for example, in classing situations as *conjunctive* or *disjunctive* in terms of whether the corresponding needs of the participants achieved satisfaction. He frequently abandoned this position, however, and used two other types of concepts. Sometimes his unit of analysis was the behavior of one individual in different situations, not an interpersonal unit. Examples included the more usual concepts such as projection, sublimation, need, personification, and the like. Still a third set of concepts were used, which referred to behavior independent of any situational contingency at all. This is most clear in his characterization of the prototaxic, parataxic, and syntactic modes of experience. It is not inconsistent to use three different types of unit, but it is inconsistent with his stated objective of using an interpersonal unit of analysis.

Contradictory emphasis on situational events appeared in another context. On the one hand, Sullivan argued against conceiving of behavior as endogenously produced, and he selected Freudian theory as the classic instance of this sort of error. He emphasized the necessity for conceiving of the individual as behaving in relation to situations, rather than in response to wishes, impulses, or other sorts of subjective events. At the same time, Sullivan proposed a set of primary "integrating tendencies" which he believed characterized human behavior, were the antecedents to other responses, and arose from a biological base. Thus, the role of situational events in his analysis of behavior was variable, and he did not specify how these different types of concepts fitted together.

Size of analytic unit creates another problem with a similar result. For example, the concept of *dynamism* is an important building block in Sullivan's system. Briefly represented, dynamisms are recurrent patterns of behavior which typify an individual in his relationships to people. And, according to Sullivan, such dynamisms represent the *smallest unit* of analysis that can be meaningfully employed in the study of an individual. But he went on to specify more concrete responses, such as an image, a stereotype, a parataxic distortion, or the perception of tension. Of course, the use of units of different size is appropriate. The confusion arises because Sullivan differed with himself as to which level of abstraction was to be preferred.

Such problems present the reviewer of Sullivan with a choice. In order to emphasize one theoretical line, he necessarily de-emphasizes another. In the face of this, we have represented what appeared to be the dominant stream of Sullivan's theory. The following discussion patterns itself after his treatment of the analysis of behavior as he presented it in a series of lectures, posthumously published as *The*

Interpersonal Theory of Psychiatry (1953). We can begin by following Sullivan's procedure of building from the level of specific to general events.

INNATE CHARACTERISTICS OF NORMAL DEVELOPMENT

For Sullivan, the level of raw data, and consequently the raw data of a science of behavior, is represented by *energy transformations*. All behavior is ultimately reducible to changes of energy in chemical or physical terms (1953, p. 368). Sullivan here was attempting to denote precisely what is meant by an event, and it is similar to our definition of a response. Behavior is continuous and never-ending and represents life; therefore, as a function of being alive, an infant is composed of a perpetual series of responses. The fact that such events occur in no way requires that the person be aware of them.

Sullivan paid a great deal of attention to the built-in response potentialities of the human, both those present at birth, and those which unfold in the process of maturation. The innate response repertoire is extremely intricate and complex, and it is considered markedly influential in the individual's later development.

The notion of patterns of events takes on great significance in Sullivan's system, and therefore is worthy of specific emphasis at this point. In his view, responses (energy transformations) and the situational events to which they are related occur in patterned form and must be analyzed in that way. Virtually all of his higher-order concepts are represented as intricate constellations of more primary parts. This is as true of his analysis of physiological events as it is of other behavioral events; it is the underlying theme in his conception of situations, whether physical or interpersonal. Patterns of responses occur in relation to patterns of situational events, and this is characteristic of the entire behavioral exchange.

Sullivan conceived of several distinct types of innate responses. He spoke first of the innate physiological patterns of behavior and of innate tension-reduction sequences. Later he turned to a characterization of innately determined responses such as attention, sentience and perception, the referential processes of images and thoughts, the emotional patterns, and finally overt actions such as movements and speech. Sullivan mentioned what he believed to be important inborn differences in the response equipment which had a great deal to do with subsequent behavior. He noted that people differed greatly in senses such as vision and hearing; in anatomical differences basic to various motor skills, including speech; and in complex factors such as those on which learning ability is based (1953, p. 22). Innate differences such as these he considered a major source of variability between one human and another.

Physiological Events and Patterns

As one might expect from his prior training in medicine, Sullivan was thoroughly familiar with physiological responses. He frequently referred to physiological events which were associated with behavior, recounted their operation, and sought to relate them to more complex behaviors. For example, he described the defecatory pattern from a physiological standpoint and illustrated how it might become interwoven with other responses, such as perceptions and recollections. This led him to his conception of a class of response patterns, primarily physiological, which he labeled *zones of interaction,* and which included zones such as the oral, anal, and urethral. These represent neuro-muscular organizations of behavior which are functionally interrelated through sharing common receptor-effector organs and tissues. The oral zone is "a remarkable organization," which is involved in breathing, ingesting, crying, smelling, and sucking. To Sullivan this represented an important anatomical fact which greatly influenced later development. He argued that experience acquired special characteristics from the zone of interaction that was primarily concerned in its occurrence (1953, pp. 64–65).

To illustrate further, Sullivan made much of the influence of the structure of the distance receptors on the perceptual behavior of the human, of the effect of deprivation of oxygen, water, or sugar on other responses, or of the structural interrelationships between vocalization and hearing in accounting for language development. Sullivan did not employ a classificatory approach to such events, since his attention was focused on events at higher orders of abstraction. Thus, his reference to physiological occurrences appeared "as needed" in his treatment of behavior. It is important to note his awareness of these occurrences, however, and his attempt to interweave the relationships between events conceived of in physiological terms and those more typically referred to as behavior.

TENSIONS. An important subcategory of built-in responses is characterized as *tensions*. Tensions have a directional quality to them; they represent tendencies toward overt action. This activating aspect of tensions is an intrinsic quality, and presumably different tensions tend to lead to different kinds of activity. They, too, may or may not be represented in subjective awareness.

Sullivan said that these responses operated virtually continuously, and rose and fell in intensity over the passage of time. The variation was said to range over a hypothetical continuum, extending from *absolute euphoria* at the one end to *absolute tension* on the other. These hypothetical extremes really never occurred, but they were postulated in order to aid in conceptualizing about the occurrence of behavior. Euphoria is equated to a total equilibrium of the organism, which is never attained but is approached at those intervals when tension is at a minimum. The closest approach to absolute tension is regarded as being something like the extreme state of *terror*.

It would appear that he was referring to some kinds of physiological responses or energies which functioned as behavior elicitors. He discussed three major groups of such responses.

Tension group I: Needs. Initially Sullivan considered there to be a set of physiological responses which arose as a consequence of physico-chemical events, and which episodically and recurrently increase in intensity. Although Sullivan did not proceed to a formal classification, he did enumerate several, such as those arising from lack of oxygen, lack of sugar, lack of water, and lack of adequate body temperature—states of deprivation. Sullivan suggested that there were certain inborn response patterns which tended automatically to follow such response conditions, such as the infant's breathing movements arising to remedy his oxygen needs or the sucking movements in the service of sugar or water needs.

A particularly important set of physiological responses later in the maturational sequence are those of *lust*. These response conditions do not become operative until the developmental period of early adolescence. The built-in response sequences appropriate to its satisfaction include the skeletal-copulatory movements and the actions that provide "cumulatively augmented sentience" resulting in orgasm (1953, p. 263).

The reduction in intensity of such responses he labeled *satisfaction,* a concept similar to drive reduction in other theories. Failure to terminate such responses presumably resulted in still further intense responses. Prolonged deprivation of physiological requirements led to the response pattern of *apathy* or complete lethargy.

Tension group II: Anxiety. A second class of physiological responses or energies are those Sullivan called anxiety. Anxiety is said to differ from physiological needs, both in terms of its antecedents and its consequents.

This particular group of responses is elicited by the *personal* environment as opposed to the physico-chemical. Anxiety is an innate response, elicited by the behavior of other people—the mother, for example. Sullivan proposed that the occurrence of anxiety was inevitable in the infant and arose when he was dealt with by an anxious parent. He expressed this in the form of a proposition, or what he referred to as a Theorem: *The tension of anxiety, when present in the mothering one, induces anxiety in the infant* (1953, p. 41). Sullivan initially suggested that this occurred as a function of *empathy,* a concept for which he was roundly attacked. Later he backtracked and spoke of the events in terms of *a* leading to *b*. However, he clearly considered anxiety to be the consequence of some kind of *interpersonal situation* (1953, p. 41). Therefore, anxiety is an innate response, inherent in the human situation, and an inevitable component of each person's response repertoire.

Anxiety also differs from physiological needs in terms of its consequents. Sullivan proposed that there were *no* innate responses automatically functioning to terminate anxiety; the human infant had no built-in responses by which anxiety reduction could be effected. For example, crying in relation to infantile anxiety is typically ineffective or worse. It usually increases the anxiety of the mothering one and thereby increases the infant's anxiety. Only a change in situational events can terminate anxiety during infancy, although in later years the person will acquire responses which serve to forestall, minimize, and avert anxiety responses as they might be elicited by situational events.

Anxiety also exercises a "paralyzing effect" on a great many other responses; it restricts the range of awareness, interferes with the effective operation of all the various cognitive processes, and in general exercises a disorganizing rather than a facilitating effect on the person's response capabilities. As Sullivan repeatedly remarked, anxiety has many effects comparable to a sharp blow on the head.

Reduction in the intensity of anxiety responses is referred to as *security,* to distinguish it from the termination of physiological needs.

If not terminated, the intensity of anxiety can cumulate and approach intense terror. Prolonged anxiety arousal can result in a pattern Sullivan labeled *somnolent detachment,* as distinct from apathy.

Sullivan proceeded to characterize the behavior of human beings as being organized in the service of two "primary goals," satisfaction or security. That is, the objective of all behavior is either to reduce the intensity of physiological needs or to avoid anxiety. Sullivan considered this basic differentiation of the consequences toward which behavior is directed one of the most important principles of living (1956, pp. 10–11). Physiological needs and anxiety are conceived to be noxious occurrences; their reduction (or termination) defines the direction that behavioral sequences will follow. This is also true of the tensions that lead to sleep.

Tension group III: Tensions of sleep. The third great category of physiological responses in human behavior are those that are "relaxed or remedied" by sleeping, which Sullivan called a *phasic* state of living. These differ from the preceding two categories, primarily in terms of the fact that the response pattern of sleep was the built-in and, therefore, "appropriate" consequent to such tensions.

There seem to be two general reasons why Sullivan introduced them. He believed that sleep and the responses that take place during sleep are a primary human activity in the normal, and extremely important in the analysis of disordered, behavior. In addition, he went on to develop the notion of antagonistic tensions.

Antagonistic tensions. Sullivan distinguished between these "genera" of tensions not only because there were discriminable differences in their antecedents and consequents, but also because there were important interrelationships among them. He considered them to be incompatible and antagonistic in the sense that they could not be simultaneously operative and effective. For example, the tensions of anxiety and the ensuing behaviors (avoidance) are typically antagonistic to the need-satisfaction sequences, and both the tensions of need and anxiety are opposed to the tensions toward sleep. On this base he developed his notions of sublimation, selective inattention, dissociation, and the like, as response procedures by which the person manages such conflicts. His entire point of view about the development of both normal and disordered behavior rested on this assumption.

INTERPERSONAL NEEDS. Sullivan recognized that physiological needs, anxiety, and sleep all became quickly embroiled in interpersonal transactions. This is because the infant's behavioral repertoire is insufficiently developed to carry out the appropriate need-satisfaction activities, and he is dependent on the co-operation of another person. Since these responses are terminated in the context of interpersonal transactions, they quickly take on the character of interpersonal needs. Thus, all infants learn to seek certain kinds of responses from others to control responses within themselves. From this Sullivan went on to characterize certain of these patterns as the *need for tenderness*, the *need for security*, the *need for intimacy*, the *need for compeers*, and the like (1953, p. 40). Since interpersonal events are inherent in the human situation, the patterns are inevitably acquired, and are presumed to be universal in humans, although not innate in the sense of inherited. Sullivan's position was quite analogous to that of other theorists who distinguish between primary and secondary (or acquired) needs or drives. In Sullivan's case all important "secondary" needs were interpersonal.

It is to be noted that these interpersonal needs are characterized in terms of behaviors in other people which the person seeks to elicit. For example, the need for tenderness refers to efforts on the part of the subject to evoke tender responses from others, seeking benign and kindly people, some of whom will be companionable, others who will behave as close friends, and still others who will be loving and intimate.

RESPONSE EVENTS. Sullivan was accustomed to thinking in terms of the triple classification of neurophysiology where responses in the human organism are categorized as receptors, eductors, and effectors. The next groups of behavioral events directly parallel these, and can be represented as attention, sensation and perception, the referential processes, and work (overt functional activity). All but the last of these he collectively referred to as the *cognitive processes*.

ATTENTION. It was by means of the concept of attention that Sullivan dealt with the question of awareness and consciousness. Attention and its opposite *inattention* were described as "a universal bit of human equipment," an innate response characteristic. Actually, the greater proportion of Sullivan's writing in this connection dealt with selective *in*attention, since apparently he tended to consider attention as being defined by whatever responses are occurring at a given time. At the same time, he spoke of the "focusing of awareness," of the "control of the contents of awareness," and of "the narrowing of attention" as if there were specific responses of attending which had the function of controlling awareness. Similarly he had the implicit concept of a "field" of awareness when he spoke of the focus as opposed to the "margin" of awareness (focal awareness), and tended to characterize concentration as the process of the narrowing of the span of attention, the maintenance of a restricted attention span, and the selective inattention to events irrelevant to the task at hand. And finally, he spoke of attention as becoming restricted, or suspended, or both under conditions of stress or emergency situations.

By selective *in*attention, on the other hand, Sullivan was referring to an active response by which an individual fails to notice or react to events or to his own responses. This proves to be a very critical explanatory concept in Sullivan's position on the development of normal and disordered behavior. Sullivan was clear and explicit in his recognition that awareness was a matter of inference and certainly not one of direct observation.

SENTIENCE, PREHENSION, AND PERCEPTION. For the next group of response events which are analogous to the physiological receptor apparatus, Sullivan followed the lead of Charles Spearman in making a distinction between response events proximal to the stimulus source and events that follow and are more "central" in their occurrence. Thus, he distinguished between *sentience* on the one hand and *perception* (and *prehension*) on the other. Prehension is a term Sullivan used to refer to rudimentary perceptions; thus prehensions are the ancestors to fully developed percepts.

Sullivan was clear in his characterization of perception as temporally consequent to sensory events (sentience) and including responses to both internal and external events; that is, one sensed and perceived one's own responses (r and R) as well as situational events. But he was less clear in characterizing precisely which kinds of responses were called perceptions, as opposed to other mediational events. He considered identification of events as perceptual responses and proposed that they began in infancy, more as vague images, of course, than sharply differentiable percepts. Similarly, he seemed to consider discriminative responses as perceptions, for example when the infant learned to identify and respond differentially to the smiling and angry expressions of his mother. Sullivan was apparently suggesting an innate capacity to identify differences and similarities among events as a primary response capacity of humans.

It would appear, therefore, that Sullivan conceived of the "receptive apparatus" of the infant as equipped innately with the capacity for raw sensory events (sensations) and certain rudimentary responses to these sensations (prehensions). Sullivan was less interested in the precise character of these rudimentary events than he was in pointing out that later habits of perception had to have historical antecedents in the behavior of the infant.

REFERENTIAL PROCESS: REVERY. Sullivan conceived of a second class of mediating events, which he called the referential processes, and in which he apparently included such response events as thoughts, revery, "unrefined thinking operations," and the like. These responses are analogous to the eductor functions in the receptor-eductor-effector representation of nervous system structure.

By *eduction*, Spearman and Sullivan meant the responses by which the person saw relationships between events, made connections between occurrences, and the like. Early ontogenetic operations of eduction Sullivan called *revery*. Revery responses occur prior to the acquisition of language symbols, and thus represent wordless or imagistic thought. Thought itself Sullivan conceived as being primarily in verbal and language symbols, and acquired in the course of familial training. Thus, he proposed that symbolic thought arose out of imagistic thought.

Sullivan's differentiation between verbal and nonverbal referential processes reflected his view of the importance of nonverbal events. He was impressed with how many of the day-to-day activities of the ordinary person were composed of these sequences of images (revery): he believed the "brute fact" was that most of living occurred that way (1953, p. 185). He was impressed also by the occurrence and significance of such events in sleeping, dreaming, and in pathological states, and he felt that attention to and analysis of them was important in understanding the ways in which both normal and disordered behavior occurred. For example, Sullivan's conception of the schizophrenic patterns included the occurrence of imagistic thought sequences either derived from or similar to the reveries of infancy and childhood.

It appears that all of these responses which have been considered so far can go on outside the focus of awareness. Indeed, in discussing selective inattention, Sullivan gave several examples in which the subject had been looking at and carefully examining an object without at the same time being aware that he had been doing so. He gave similar examples with imaginal sequences. Thus, Sullivan conceived these (sensations, prehensions, imagistic thoughts) to be responses which occurred and of which the person might or might not be aware, depending on whether or not he attended to them.

EMOTIONS. Still another group of subjective responses Sullivan alternately referred to as *feelings,* or *emotions.* It is difficult to represent his position with respect to this group of responses, for he treated them in several distinct ways. On the one hand, he spoke of them as tensions, such as the tension of fear, serving as behavior elicitors. In addition, he spoke of feeling or emotion as the *felt aspect* of tension, for example in his definition of fear as the felt aspect of tension resulting from danger to the person's biological integrity or existence (1953, p. 50). He also spoke of feelings as innate responses to certain kinds of events. These included *uncanny emotions,* of which the most commonly experienced were *awe* and anxiety. Rage was also considered innate. He characterized it as innate in the infant consequent to terror, which arises when certain types of physical restraint are imposed, especially restraint of breathing. Other groups of feelings, such as anger and resentment, he characterized as learned derivatives of the innate pattern of rage. *Disgust* was described as an innate, presumably biological reaction, representing the capacity to empty the stomach in the reverse direction. Shame, embarrassment, humiliation, and chagrin were thought of as learned elaborations of this basic response pattern. Response patterns such as hate, love, grief, and the like Sullivan represented as complex learned patterns of interpersonal interaction. Thus Sullivan seemed to propose a small group of innate emotional responses, including rage, fear, disgust, and the uncanny emotions, and to say that all other emotions were complex patterns of the innate ones.

WORK. Work referred to the effector aspect of behavior, not work in the usual sense, but all "functional activity" (1953, p. 92). Since such "actions" are described as physical, they are directly analogous to the objectively observable responses (R). Although Sullivan dealt with this class only in passing, his writings were full of references to overt actions of all kinds—for example, crying, shrieking, sucking, and kicking in infants.

Whereas Sullivan did not attempt to analyze all such responses, he did emphasize three sorts of "capabilities" which he felt to be of paramount importance: the interrelation of vision and the prehensile hands, which he considered a significant human tool; the interrelation of hearing and the speech apparatus, which is so "exquisitely refined" as to permit language development; and the relationships among these and all other receptor-effector systems in a complex forebrain, making possible effective functioning as with "abstracts of experience" (1953, p. 20). For example, humans can make manipulatory explorations into the world of objects (nursing activity, exploratory behavior), be violently active when restrained, and produce vocal intonations and repetitive syllables—all of which are basic building blocks from which later complex activities and skills become shaped. The subsequent development of language, for example, requires the innate response possibilities of facial movements, gestures, changes in posture, and sound-producing capabilities.

It is especially in connection with the effector apparatus that Sullivan emphasized the role of maturation. He referred to the "truly astounding" maturing of capabilities that characterizes the unfolding behavior of the infant during its first year of life. And he stressed the fact of "late maturation," in the sense that some response patterns, innately determined in the human, did not make their appearance until the latter phases of maturation, for example, in the patterns of motor behavior that characterize copulatory posture and movement. The maturing of innate response patterns, then, is an important part of the unending process of human development.

To understand the occurrence of actions, particularly in later years, Sullivan added the assumption that the execution of these innate response capabilities as they emerged was an interpersonal need and was inherently satisfying (1953, p. 193). What is satisfaction? Actually, Sullivan's writing was unclear on this point, sometimes referring to it as the occurrence of tension reduction, at others making reference to "feeling" satisfied. For example, once the child has learned to crawl, he derives pleasure from the act, and will continue to do it. In this instance he seemed to mean the arousal of some positive affective response. Presumably Sullivan felt he needed this addition to account for the why of locomotor rehearsal in the very young.

LEARNED CHARACTERISTICS OF NORMAL DEVELOPMENT

Thus, for Sullivan, the human is born with certain response potentialities, which are either present at birth or will unfold in the course of maturation. He also is embedded in an environment, so that not only is he dependent on other persons for the reduction of his intense physiological and emotional responses and the production of satisfaction, but it is also inevitable that everything that occurs and everything he learns will be influenced and determined by this interpersonal context. Sullivan's depiction of the developing human was thus one of attempting to trace the intricate interrelationships which occurred among innate, maturational, and learned factors in the growing child in relation to interpersonal situations. Also, in Sullivan's view, the operation of learning in the development of behavior was almost immediate, so that very quickly indeed the specific behaviors that the infant developed were a blend of innate possibility and learned experience.

It was the relative constancy provided by heredity and maturational factors (barring individual differences) and the relative constancy of the interpersonal conditions within the American culture which led Sullivan to develop the notion of a *course of development*. This was a series of phases through which the typical child would proceed, which could be characterized by the kinds of situations to which the child was exposed and the kinds of responses likely or typical during that phase. He proposed these "stages" as heuristic and convenient for the "organization of thought."

Stages in Development

Consistent with his emphasis on interpersonal relationships, many of the points of demarcation of these stages are changes in the kinds of relationships prominent at the time. The stages have several characteristics. They are not definite units, but phases of development. The age at which any phase might begin would vary from person to person. Moreover, there are transitional periods between phases, in which the individual's behavior may represent an amalgam of the behaviors of one stage with some of the next.

The stages themselves are listed here as Sullivan represented them, and discussion of the normal course of development will follow that outline.

Stage	*Up to*
1. Infancy (from birth)	
	The appearance of articulate speech (however uncommunicative).
2. Childhood	
	Incipient patterns of interaction with playmates and companions.

Stage	*Up to*
3. Juvenile	
	Incipient patterns of intimacy with another person of comparable status (one's own sex).
4. Preadolescence	
	The eruption of genital sexuality and shifting interest to person(s) of the opposite sex.
5. Early adolescence	
	Semistable patterns of sexual interaction.
6. Late adolescence	
	Establishment of relations of love for some other person.
7. Adulthood	

Sullivan also spoke of the occurrence of *arrest in development,* for example a person having become arrested in the preadolescent stage. By this he meant that a person might show delay in following the course of behavioral change which was statistically usual, not that the individual was "stuck" in one stage. He meant that the individual's capacity and opportunities for constructive change became markedly reduced, and that the person became handicapped in his subsequent behavior development. The maintenance of the pattern might preclude the development of a more advanced one.

Moreover, Sullivan regarded the entire sequence as crucial for evolving behaviors appropriate for the society. Explicitly he criticized the notion that enduring patterns were established by the age of seven, for example. He emphasized that extremely important behaviors were acquired after that time, which had marked influence on the type of personality that emerged. Sullivan noted the possibility of marked and drastic changes of pattern and direction occurring at ages well beyond the childhood era. He particularly emphasized the "therapeutic effect" of the preadolescent stage, and he described at some length how important and beneficial changes could occur then in reshaping behaviors that might have become "warped" at earlier stages.

INFANCY. Sullivan gave this phase extended treatment, partly because he felt that a great many crucial behavioral patterns began here. Many of his higher-order concepts were introduced in connection with the infantile stage.

The primary sets of interpersonal relationships which characterize the infant's behavior are in connection with "the mothering one." With this phrase, Sullivan was referring to the many responses which the "mother" makes toward her infant (holding, feeding, dressing, bathing), and he was emphasizing that many of the infant's responses are acquired with such human behavior as the important situational variable.

DEVELOPMENT OF INTERPERSONAL NEEDS FOR SATISFACTION AND SECURITY. It will be recalled that Sullivan conceived of the infant as beginning with a set of physiological responses related to the physico-chemical equilibrium of the infant (tensions or needs). These are accompanied by other innate responses such as crying, kicking, sucking, and the like. Through repeated contact with people, the mothering ones, whose behavior helps alleviate the physiological deficits, the infant soon begins to learn to seek such behavior from people; his needs take on an interpersonal aspect. Soon he not only needs milk, for example, but he needs mother holding him while giving milk. A need for tenderness develops, for example, out of the repeated experiences of the mother tenderly caring for the infant. Habits of seeking different kinds of interpersonal conditions (interpersonal needs) thus develop through association with "tension reduction." Sullivan uses the term *integrating tendencies* to refer collectively to all the response patterns of "satisfaction-seeking" behavior (1953, p. 93).

Concomitant with the acquisition of such habits, however, is the inevitable development of anxiety. It will be recalled that the response of anxiety appears in relation to anxious behavior on the part of the mother. The frequency and intensity of anxiety in the infant is thought to vary with the degree of anxiety displayed by the mother. Anxiety is itself a distressing response, disrupts the continuing behavioral sequences within the infant, and is characterized by a *tendency to avoid* the anxiety-producing situation. It may be manifested, for example, in the tendency to reduce nursing activity or to avoid the nursing situation altogether (1953, p. 97).

Thus one respect in which infantile behavior unfolds is in terms of the major patterns of approach and avoidance with respect to satisfaction-producing and anxiety-producing behavior on the part of the mother. Moreover, when these are simultaneously operative, they are directly incompatible. Since the infant has no repertoire for the resolution of such discrepancies, the tendencies to avoid take precedence over the integrating tendencies.

Development of the Cognitive Processes: Prehensions into Perceptions

Prehensions or primitive organizations of experience are operative at birth. Learning quickly comes to influence such primitive responses, and early in infancy perceptions start to become formed. Perceptions are symbolic responses and arise from the infant's built-in capability to discriminate and to differentiate among events (or sensory responses aroused by events). It is as a consequence of this potentiality that the child learns to distinguish between himself and external objects, between situations that lead to satisfaction or anxiety, and to develop the capacity to anticipate and also to recall events.

Sullivan used simple, discriminant responses to help account for the development of differentiations between the self and other objects. These, in turn, become the basis for the person's habitual thoughts about himself (personification of the self). The discrimination becomes possible because situational events and bodily events elicit quite different patterns of sensory responses. For example, the child sucks both a nipple and his thumb, but the difference is that in addition to the sensations in his mouth, *his thumb feels sucked.* Multiple and recurrent discriminations of this order gradually accumulate, permitting the infant to develop a collection of responses toward his body which are different from those he makes toward other objects.

Following the lead of Charles Morris, Sullivan proposed that out of the unceasing flow of events the infant also learned temporal discriminations. He began to learn that certain events consistently "herald" the coming of other events. Sullivan believed this to be one of the early perceptual responses and termed it *a sign.* All people learn to anticipate a frequently recurring sequence of events. For example, one may learn that event A typically precedes event B. Event A becomes a sign that event B is on its way. In Sullivan's system, these signs (perceptual responses) are of two kinds. Simple sequences, as in the example given, are referred to as *signals.* The human proceeds in his development to the point at which he can respond in terms of *signs of signs,* and Sullivan refers to these as *symbols.* Responding in terms of sequences of signs or interrelationships or patterns of signs represented symbolic activity to Sullivan. This would be illustrated by the situation where the infant learns that a ringing bell will be followed by his being set down by his mother, and then she will walk toward a black instrument and talk into it.

One can see that Sullivan considered symbolic responses to include most mediational responses. He considered covert and overt symbolic behavior central to psychiatric theory. Any activity influenced by the organization into signs of previous experience in terms of seeking satisfaction, or of avoiding or minimizing anxiety, Sullivan considered symbolic behavior. Other theorists who define symbolic behavior primarily in terms of language and number symbols are, thus, led to speak of nonsymbolic activity; whereas for Sullivan there was very little in either adult or infant behavior which was nonsymbolic (1953, pp. 186–187).

FORESIGHT AND RECALL. From such perceptions, the important capacity for *foresight* develops. Foresight, to Sullivan, was a particularly important response capability. Indeed, he could not conceive how complex human behavior could be understood without recognizing the importance of the capacity to anticipate events. He considered this a critical difference between humans and other animals (1953, p. 39). Learned signals and symbols enable the infant and later the adult to modify his behavior in the direction of situations likely to produce satisfaction and security, and to avoid situations likely to produce further tensions and anxiety. The early stages of successful foresight occur in infants. With signs and symbols events can be represented in the person's awareness, and the person can make "anticipant responses" to symbols of future events.

The infant can not only discriminate between current events, but he can also identify events which previously occurred; he can *re-cognize* them. Sullivan proposed that the important functions of *recall* developed from this capability. The mechanism of recall may be something like the following: in a particular situation, a whole series of responses occur. Some of these have occurred before to the same situation, or to situations very much like it. These recurrent responses are recognized by the person and identified as having occurred previously. When this happens, one speaks of recall. Sullivan believed the responses of foresight and recall became related to every critical human response pattern and became richer and more varied with increasing experiences. This phenomenon begins in infancy. For example, the infant's crying-when-hungry quickly becomes related backward (recall) to the producing of the lips-nipple experience and forward (foresight) to the desired consequents of sucking and swallowing (1953, p. 69).

DEVELOPMENT OF COMPLEX PATTERNS OF RESPONSES. In the later stages of infancy, Sullivan proposed that more complex response interrelationships became elaborated into *personifications, dynamisms,* and the beginnings of the *self-system.*

PERSONIFICATIONS. These are response patterns and are not to be confused with the persons themselves as they might be objectively viewed. They are groups of related symbolic responses (perceptions, recollections, images, thoughts) which have been acquired as abstracts from extended experiences with the person "personified." They are elicited when the individual comes into contact with the person, hears his name, thinks about him, and so forth. The term *personification of mother,* for example, is a shorthand way of referring to the composite pattern of mediating responses that occur when mother is either physically or symbolically present. In the infant they might be thought of as unlabeled concepts at the first stage of development. They develop in the course of social interaction. Among the significant personifications that develop in infancy are those of *good* and *bad* mothers, and the several personifications of the self which Sullivan referred to as the *good me,* the *bad me* and the *not me.* The good mother personification results from the satisfaction-producing and anxiety-reducing interactions with the mother. The personification of the bad mother results from experiences of the opposite sort. As the infant develops such personifications, he begins to respond to the actual comings and goings of his mother in terms of them. A large, complex, recurrent pattern of responses (habits) toward mothering persons develops.

Sullivan proposed that the infant gradually began developing self-referent responses built from the history of experiences with its own body. From this base, he proposed that a tripartite cleavage of self-referent responses was an inevitable consequence of the growth process. The *good-me* is a pattern of recurrent (habitual) responses (perceptions, images, recollections, thoughts) about the self, learned in situations where behavior has led to satisfactions, coupled with rewarding and tender behavior by the mother. The *bad-me,* on the other hand, is a recurrent pattern of self-referent responses learned in relationship to situations in which increasing degrees of anxiety were associated with behavior. The child can communicate these conceptions a year or so later, and Sullivan felt that it was reasonable to infer that they had their beginnings at an earlier stage. The *not-me* constellation of self-referent responses is typically very unclear and undifferentiated, since it relates to experiences of extreme tension, intense anxiety, horror and loathing, and the revelation of such response patterns only appears in an occasional dream while one is asleep, in acute schizophrenic episodes, and the like. Contrary to the response constellations of the good-me and the bad-me which later become invested with language, the not-me group is usually beyond discussion in communicative terms and virtually always continues to operate at the vague imagistic and nonverbalized level.

These patterns of symbolic responses (perceptions, images, etc.) later become fused with language symbols. The previously disparate response constellations representing the good and the bad mother will yield to a verbalizable single representation of the mother. Thus, when asked, the child can provide a description of his mother as a single composite. The dual representation of the mother will in time become manifested only in relatively obscure processes such as dreams. Similarly, the tripartite response groups relative to the body will become merged into a *personification of the self*. But the importance of these multiple patterns lies in the fact that they contribute importantly to the peculiarly inefficient and inappropriate interpersonal relations which constitute problems of mental disorder. In disorder the pattern of disparate and multiple response constellations associated with other humans reappears.

DYNAMISMS. In the later stages of infancy, also, Sullivan begins to utilize the concept of dynamism to represent interpersonal behaviors. Dynamisms are learned, habitual patterns of responses (1953, p. 103). While many such complex habits develop, the most important are those related to human interactions.

When Sullivan spoke of dynamisms, he explicitly meant complex associations of responses both concomitant and sequential in time. For example, he represented the sexual dynamism as including *all* the following covert and overt symbolic events:

1. Observation and identification of sexual feelings;
2. Observation and identification of a sexual object;
3. Judgment of the suitability of the situation for sexual satisfaction;
4. Foresight;
5. Activity in the pursuit of or in avoidance of the goal;
6. Covert accompaniments of various sorts;
7. Retrospective and prospective, witting and unwitting analysis of the particular experience;

8. Various subsequent complex processes associated with the events (1953, pp. 286–288).

Clearly, a dynamism involves a great many behavioral events intricately related to one another in a complex pattern through time. Of course, this particular dynamism is characteristic of a virtually mature human, and infantile dynamisms are much more simply patterned and less firmly established.

Sullivan conceived of two classes of dynamisms, two kinds of patterns which could be conceptualized. On the one hand, such extensive behavior patterns could be viewed in terms of the situations to which they were related, interpersonal situations being most important. The dynamisms of fear and lust are examples. On the other hand, one could analyze such patterns with reference to physiological patterns involved. An example of the latter would be the oral dynamism.

The complex habits (dynamisms) of particular interest in the infantile stage are those relating to the patterns of innate physiological responses. Sullivan did not subclassify the types of infantile patterns, but he spoke variously of the oral dynamism or the anal dynamism, meaning to refer to the complex of behaviors that the infant acquires surrounding these body areas.

DEVELOPMENT OF THE SELF-SYSTEM. This set of response patterns Sullivan also proposed develop during the infantile period. The *self-system*, to Sullivan, was clearly a high-order abstraction and did not refer to a particular kind of event. It referred to all the behaviors the child acquires in the course of his interpersonal relationships which perform the function of avoiding or minimizing the occurrence of anxiety. In other terms, the concept referred to the group of avoidance behaviors acquired in relation to people. Sullivan conceived of these behaviors as taking on the characteristics of an habitual pattern, and thus he referred to it as a system or an organization of behaviors.

Because anxiety-producing situations are inevitable, Sullivan felt that a person without such a pattern of responses was "beyond imagination." The pattern is learned, primarily in interpersonal situations. This notion should not be confused with the concept of the personification of the self, which refers to the composite of responses the person makes to his physical attributes and to his behavior. The latter concept is composed primarily of thoughts expressed in the form of language symbols.

Avoidance responses (the self-system) come to play an important role in Sullivan's conception of complex behavior, both normal and disordered. This stems from the fact that it is a group of behaviors that are deemed relatively resistant to change. This was sufficiently central a proposition to his system that he expressed it in the form of the *Theorem of Escape* (1953, p. 190). In it, he proposed that such avoidant behavior was unlikely to change because it kept the person from situations and responses likely to result in revised learning. The relative resistance to extinction of avoidance responses of all kinds as compared with approach responses has received considerable clinical validation and some experimental support.

The system of avoidances includes symbolic and overt actions which are acquired to avoid the occurrence of anxiety in interpersonal situations. Later on in the course of development it becomes the system of behaviors involved in the protection of the person's "self-esteem"—the responses by which the person avoids derogatory evaluations of himself which would lead to anxiety and maintains favorable evaluations of himself. Various subclasses of avoidance responses will be referred to later as specific *security operations,* analogous to Freudian defense mechanisms. The system of avoidance responses is basic to all inadequate and inappropriate living and is quite central to the whole problem of personality disorder and its remedy. In spite of its being central in the problem of disorder, one should not lose sight of the fact that Sullivan deemed this collection of behaviors to be universal to humans, and thus an important aspect of the repertoire of the normal as well as the disordered.

This completes the major developments that Sullivan associated with the infantile epoch. Clearly, many of these presumed events are not directly observable, and Sullivan was quite aware that they represented products of *inference* rather than of observation. He observed such behaviors in older children and adults; he saw their appearance during conditions of sleep and disorder, concluded they must have had historical antecedents, and assumed their incipient acquisition prior to their overt manifestation. For example, the child of four verbally reports several patterns of thought about himself. Sullivan did not feel it to be unreasonable to presuppose that the beginnings of these occurred prior to language acquisition.

CHILDHOOD. The major occurrences in the childhood stage relate to the expanding interpersonal relationships on the one hand and the maturation of skills on the other. In the first instance, the child becomes exposed to more people, and the childhood stage introduces the fact of age equals and companions. In the second case, many manipulatory and locomotor skills emerge, and the appearance of language and its derivative, thought, appears. A third factor becomes important, namely the use of rewards and punishments in an active fashion by the child's mentors, in the beginning of a long-term program to shape his behavior in the direction of social norms.

In general, the response patterns that occur during infancy undergo steady elaboration; the child continues to develop a greater variety of differentiated perceptions and an increased capacity to anticipate events, and to recall symbolically events from the past. He develops expanding private characterizations of people (personifications) and more intricate patterns of relating to people (dynamisms), and the avoidance patterns (self-system) become more and more extensive. The child acquires increased and more complex patterns of interpersonal integration, since with greater skills and more people he learns more effective patterns of interaction whereby he can engage in relationships that serve the needs of both participants (conjunctive relationships). Together with greater facility go more intricate and involved interpersonal needs. His ways of eliciting tender responses from others (the need for tenderness) become elaborated into patterns in which he seeks participants in his play, and still later he seeks attention and applause (need for an audience).

The application of rewards and punishments by the child's mentors begins to play a crucial role in this stage and, of course, will continue thereafter. The child's steadily developing motor skills and actions become progressively shaped in the direction of cultural requirements —the process of socializing the child—and his behaviors come to approximate more and more closely the prescriptions and proscriptions of the social environment in which he is reared. An important aspect of this stage is the progressive modification of the infantile emotions into more socially acceptable patterns. The child learns, for example, to moderate his rage in various circumstances and to display purposive anger in its stead, or he learns to withhold his anger and to maintain it covertly (resentment).

There were, however, several response capabilities which Sullivan felt to be very important and which he dated as beginning somewhere in the childhood epoch. These had to do with the child's acquisition of language and his developing proficiency for sublimation.

THE ACQUISITION OF LANGUAGE AND THE DEVELOPMENT OF THOUGHT. At several points in this treatment of the ideas of Sullivan, it has been noted that he attached tremendous importance to the role of language in human behavior. As a consequence, he gave this response realm extended treatment in the course of his writings. Only the salient features of his viewpoint can be briefly reviewed.

He proposed that it was out of the innately determined utterings of the small infant that language became shaped. Sullivan noted the emergence of sounds such as "lalling" in later stages of infancy, and remarked both that the infant apparently sought to approximate sounds made to him by persons in his surroundings and that social agents operated on his sounds with successive doses of praise and reward, to shape the sounds into acceptable cultural forms. Moreover, Sullivan emphasized that the learning of the *gestural* aspects of speech were often equally important to the acquisition of the words themselves. In a set of 1948 lectures he distinguished between the "expressive" as opposed to the "denotative" aspects of speech, referring to the myriad responses of facial expression, muscular gesture, and tonal inflection which he regarded as crucial and often-neglected features of communicative behavior. The acquisition of these aspects of language go hand in hand with the verbalizations themselves.

The significance of this developing capacity relates to several important things. First, the responses of language and gesture become interwoven with the earlier response patterns, and as a consequence the child starts developing his capacity for involved interpersonal relations. Ultimately his speech will be perhaps the single most important vehicle with which he manages the multiple interpersonal relations he encounters in his day-to-day living.

Second, language is the process whereby the person can proceed to acquire consensual responses to events. Syntaxic symbols are words that have been consensually validated. By progressive shaping of the verbalizations emitted by the child, he is gradually taught a repertoire of speech sequences that follow the rules of syntaxic logic. And this leads to the next significant import of language development.

Language is the antecedent to syntaxic thought. Sullivan proposed that what later becomes *covert* logical thought (r) was at an earlier point in time *overt* interpersonal speech (R). He regarded this as of paramount significance, since unless this were true, covert thought would not be particularly susceptible to outside influence (1953, p. 177). Precisely because of the connection between covert thought and overt language, influences on the latter have effects on private and "inaccessible" events. Thus, the acquisition of logical sequences of thought is accomplished through the acquisition of logical sequences of speech.

Once the child has acquired the media of communicative speech and thought, his perceptual situation becomes altered, since the way a person "sees" is partly determined by the way he thinks. Sullivan was calling attention here to the influence of verbal symbols on the organization and occurrence of perceptions. He did not say as much, but it seems implied that perceptions consequent to language acquisition are of a different order than perceptions without the mediation of verbal symbols.

Logical verbal symbols do not become related to all of the child's behavior, however, nor to all of the situational events to which he becomes exposed. Many of the mediating thoughts which Sullivan had earlier referred to as imagistic (revery) continue to operate and are in fact never fully absent. The development of language is a time at which the child is encouraged to develop effective discriminations between fact and fancy, thinking in terms of logic as opposed to the uncontrolled sequences of revery and imagery. Many of these earlier referential responses become replaced but not eliminated, since they can recur under certain later conditions such as sleep, schizophrenia, brain damage, and the like. Moreover, many continue to operate since they have never had occasion to have been related to logical thought sequences or have never undergone socializing influence.

This is, of course, no guarantee that the child will develop only consensually validated speech and thought, since under certain circumstances he can proceed to acquire verbal symbols which are quite idiosyncratic and have meaning only to himself. If this occurred, Sullivan referred to it as *autism*. Private and unshared speech and thought symbols, or autistic language, play a large part in certain behavioral problems later in life.

A fourth significance to the acquisition of language is the facility it provides for the development of the child's general behavioral repertoire. By means of symbols the child can organize and classify events more efficiently; language will promote his capacities to foresee and anticipate, and will multiply his capacity to recall. It will become the major sets of responses he utilizes to solve problems he encounters. Thus, symbolic thought or covert symbolic speech is the primary set of mediating events that characterizes the complex human.

But language is not always facilitative, since it can also be employed in the acts of *deception*. It is not long before the child learns not only that it can communicate, but also that it is satisfaction-producing or anxiety-reducing to deceive. He learns that some verbal sequences can be used to forestall anxiety, for example, when he lies to evade a spanking for breaking his mother's favorite vase. He learns that some verbalizations of his thoughts are punished and others rewarded; from this he can acquire verbalisms called *rationalizations,* which are a plausible series of words, regardless of their validity, which have the power to spare a person anxiety or punishment. Moreover, he will learn to talk to himself with extended verbal sequences in ways that will tend to make him feel satisfied and nonanxious. He will weave extensive *fantasies,* and he will engage in *dramatizations* in which he will think, speak, and act as if he were someone else. He can acquire roles which are used in ways that succeed in avoiding anxiety and punishment; extreme reliance on such dramatizations are, of course, seen in many situations of serious disorder. Such patterns of deception are acquired in the context of the interpersonal situation in which the child matures. If they are employed by his parent-teachers themselves, he is, of course, many times more likely to acquire them himself by means of both direct and indirect tuition.

The final influence of language has to do with the fusion of the several conceptions of himself and people (especially the mother), which Sullivan proposed had already begun during the infancy period. As soon as single symbols become associated with single persons, it becomes impossible for the child to continue to maintain his earliest impression of "two mothers." Discriminations among different persons requires the child to treat each as a unit (1953, p. 189). Sullivan was at pains to point out that this fusion was never complete, although at the level of awareness it might appear to have been so, since later under certain conditions multiple personifications of people could reappear.

THE DEVELOPMENT OF SUBLIMATION. Although incipient occurrences of the phenomenon of sublimation make their appearance in the stage of infancy, Sullivan thought it was not until the childhood period that these responses become especially significant.

The reader will recall Sullivan's proposition that physiological deficits (needs), such as hunger and thirst, lead to behavior which was antagonistic to the behavior resulting when anxiety was to be avoided or terminated. Sullivan believed that it was particularly in the childhood era that these tendencies collided, and the event of *sublimation* began to take on "very broad significance." This is because a "social censor" or an "acculturating person" more frequently produces anxiety. Sublimation, therefore, represents a compromise response, for it serves to implement both forces in the conflict. It simultaneously reduces the anxiety and provides a partial achievement of the other satisfactions sought. It is one of the more general class of substitution responses. Since satisfaction from sublimation is never complete, the "excess of tension" becomes discharged in relation to other overt and covert behaviors which do not collide with anxiety. A particularly important point of discharge is sleep, where symbol processes take care of the rest of the unsatisfied need in the ordinary person. Other avoidance behaviors are required in the case of the disordered individual. Sublimation is also considered an "unwitting substitution," not a conscious act, so that unawareness is one of its defining qualities (1953, p. 193).

Although such responses begin in later infancy, they assume conspicuous importance in the childhood era, the time when the child really begins to locomote, manipulate, speak, and the like, and when his initial behaviors are bound to conflict with the social pattern of the family. Thus, they become the occasion for forbidding gestures, punishment, deprivation—all of which serve to elicit anxiety.

Once instituted, sublimation as a response process steadily unfolds in such a way that at each major developmental stage the child must reformulate and modify his compromise into patterns deemed appropriate for his level of maturity. Therefore, the sublimations become increasingly complex as the child approaches the adult level. Conflicts between the child and others will continue through the years, but with each successive growth period the child is expected and encouraged to develop progressively more mature responses to resolve such conflicts.

THE JUVENILE ERA. At this stage, the child's interpersonal relations typically undergo another change. He ventures farther from his home base, and the changes in the nature of his playmates and his attendance at other homes and at school serve to expose him to a greater variety of social mentors. It is a time when the person's world really begins to be complicated by the presence of many other people.

These changes in the nature of his interpersonal relations introduce new factors in the developmental pattern. It is the developmental stage in which the limitations and peculiarities of the person's own home as a socializing influence first become apparent and subject to extensive competition. Healthy antidotes to familial eccentricities in the home itself now become possible. Perhaps adults who are effective socializers will now appear on the scene in the form of a kindly neighbor or a good school teacher. If so, they can operate to offset many eccentricities of attitude and behavior that the child's own home represents.

Sullivan, however, regarded the juvenile era as the time when the vast majority of social patterns become acquired; "it is the actual time for becoming social." In this light, he specifically referred to the myriad patterns of interpersonal relations the child acquires during this period. He develops patterns of subordination to authority, patterns of social accommodation wherein he learns to accommodate his own behavior to the needs and requests of other people, patterns of competition and compromise in his relationships with others. Of course, his patterns of sublimation undergo reformulation, and this is part of the general process in which he progressively relinquishes ideas and operations that had been appropriate to the childhood era. It is also the time when the person first encounters and has to learn to respond to social rejection and ostracism. It is a time when there occurs an incipient development of what Sullivan termed an *orientation to living*. This Sullivan conceived of as a set of symbolic formulations that the person held about himself, and which included: (1) his awareness of the interpersonal patterns he retained, (2) the general set of circumstances in the "here and now" which would produce satisfactions for him, and (3) a formulation of the general set of circumstances (long-range goals) which he could anticipate would yield a maximum of satisfaction along with a minimum of anxiety and discomfort. But, most important, the juvenile era is a stage at which the person begins to acquire skill over the control of the contents of awareness.

By *control of focal awareness* Sullivan referred to what he regarded as a very critical set of skills. To be able to manage what happens in the focus of one's attention is a gradually learned skill necessary both to achieve desired consequences (satisfaction) and to avoid anxiety (security).

To be able to perform tasks, to accomplish computational acts, to be able to read or write, a person must learn how to attend to the relevant and to screen out and ignore the irrelevant. He must learn how not to heed distracting situational events and how to disregard his own responses which might interfere with and derail the problem-solving thoughts underway.

By the same token, he must learn how to inattend situations and parts of situations that provoke anxieties in himself. These are not only unpleasant, but they also render him ineffective. He must learn how to shunt off and by-pass those thought sequences that characteristically lead to anxiety, through substitution of other responses that do not proceed to the same consequent.

Thus, the person gains control over the focus of his attention by means of selective sensitivity and response substitution. Further development of his efficiency as a behaving person depends on the facility with which he learns such skills.

THE PREADOLESCENT STAGE. A new type of interpersonal relationship characterizes this developmental era. The person begins to concentrate his interest on a particular member of his same sex and develops the pattern of a close friendship; he has a chum. Partly because of the recurrent restriction of interest to the one person, the way is open for the development of patterns of *intimacy*, which is in turn the early antecedent to what later comes to be called full-blown love.

The major element in this change is the fact that another person comes to be valued as much as the self. The preadolescent begins to respond in terms of "we" rather than as "X and me." Also, patterns of collaboration begin to replace those of co-operation only. The successful accomplishment of such patterns of interaction is considered the necessary antecedent to more intricate patterns that occur later in the course of development.

Important changes in the interpersonal patterns of the growing person develop as a consequence of such intimate relations with another. Sullivan believed the capacity for important change in the self-system became almost "fantastically important" in preadolescence (1953, p. 247). This follows from the fact that in an intimate relationship the person talks with his intimate friend about many stereotypes and conceptions of people and things which he had hitherto held only in his private thoughts. Thus, intimacy presents the potentiality for the correction of autistic, fantastic ideas about oneself and about others, which the person has acquired in the course of his earlier relationships. In this connection, Sullivan referred to a collection of specific "warps" which he thought could become remedied as a consequence of such "chumships." Such corrections are an essential part of the process of growing up. The youngster who misses such opportunities runs the risk of retaining misconceptions and faulty representations in his point of view and of not acquiring the skills for forming intimate relationships in the future.

Preadolescence is also the period responsible for the development of the pattern of *loneliness*, which Sullivan thought of as the response to failure to achieve satisfaction following efforts to establish an intimate relationship. He described loneliness as an "intimidating" experience, so terrible that it almost "baffles recall." When lonely, people seek companionships even though intensely anxious while doing so. Thus, loneliness can be more distressing than anxiety itself (1953, p. 262).

EARLY ADOLESCENCE. In this next stage, Sullivan begins to treat the problem of sexuality. In contrast to other theorists, Sullivan felt that sexuality made its first important appearance at puberty, and that it was this point in the maturational sequence that ushered in the stage of early adolescence. He defined this stage as occurring from the point of "eruption of true genital interest," felt as lust, up to the patterning of sexual behavior with a member of the opposite sex.

Sexual interest and efforts to achieve a satisfying interaction of a heterosexual nature (the dynamism of lust) is conceived to be the last of the major need-satisfaction sequences to emerge. Its appearance is dictated by maturational factors, but this occasions a marked shift in the interpersonal patterns of the developing individual. It ushers in a change in interest to a person of the opposite sex, which is reflected in pronounced changes in the mediational responses of thought and fantasy, as well as in the patterns of speech which the person uses in his contacts with people.

Not only is this a period of distinct change concerning normal development, but it is also one in which "collisions" between different interpersonal patterns can occur. Sullivan referred to such conflicting patterns as: genital interest in another person yet fear and avoidance of such an interaction (lust versus security); the wish to be friendly and intimate with a person of the opposite sex, yet fear of interacting with them in that fashion (security versus intimacy); or genital interest yet an inability to share a satisfying friendship (lust versus intimacy).

Sullivan here was identifying the fact that there may be no necessary integration of the emerging sexual patterns with those that are already operative in the person's behavior. Such conflicts lead to various compromise responses (sublimations) if they are not more directly resolved. The most usual at this stage are autosexual patterns, with masturbation the single most frequent one. Failure to effect such integrations of the genital with other interpersonal patterns can result in the individual having to develop separate response sequences for each set of needs, for example, in the classic madonna-prostitute complex; but in this case wherever they converge, he is ripe for the occurrence of anxiety and his habitual avoidant responses (security operations) quickly have to be called into play.

Thus, difficulties in sexual behavior, which Sullivan recognized to be very important, arise from an inability to effectively intertwine the various patterns of response toward the same set of people—those of the opposite sex. Homosexuality is conceived to be the result of the failure to effect a change from the preadolescent patterns of intimate interaction with members of the same sex, primarily caused by fear and avoidance of genital interaction with the other. Problems such as celibacy, gynephobia, misogyny, and the like are represented as results of the use of dissociation in the resolution of conflicts.

Sullivan stressed the importance of satisfactory interactions with the opposite sex for the successful acquisition of stable patterns which represent integrations of these different response patterns toward a heterosexual object. He also pointed to the more usual circumstance in our culture, where wretched experiences with the adolescents' first heterosexual attempts are legion, and result from the encounter of two persons who are at best fumbling and awkward and at worst badly, though differently, "warped." From this, one would expect a certain amount of sexual misadventure and anxiety to be the cultural norm.

LATE ADOLESCENCE. Sullivan spent little time in a treatment of this stage of development. Assuming the development to have been successful up to this point, he viewed the period of late adolescence as one wherein relatively stable and satisfaction-producing relationships with members of both sexes become established, including the important patterns of genital sexuality. But these are only part of the significant patterns formed. Sullivan was equally emphatic about the importance of the multiple learnings which persons acquired in the course of high school, vocational schools, and colleges. He was impressed with what he viewed as an astounding development of information about peoples, roles, and occupations, problem-solving skills, motoric skills, and capacities for engaging in logical thought, which occurred during late adolescence and early adulthood. It is not surprising, when one considers his general position about behavior and disorder, that he would regard the acquisition of such skills in interpersonal contexts to be of critical importance in determining the person's behavioral effectiveness.

FURTHER CONCEPTS. There are several large-order conceptions developed by Sullivan, which have often come to be thought of as "trademarks" of his system. Let us consider them at this juncture. These include his notions of *experience,* the several *modes of experiencing,* and *personality.* A review of these conceptions has been deferred until this point for reasons of exposition and to set them apart from the foregoing representation of behavior.

By *experience* Sullivan said he meant the "inner component of events" in which a person participates (1953, p. 26). He used it as a collective term to refer to "anything lived or undergone." This very vague definition leads to speculation, but the subclasses of events about which he spoke seem to occur along two general dimensions: kind of event and degree of development.

Within the domain of experience, Sullivan at least included sensations and perceptions which arise in the course of transactions with the environment. Looking at a dog gives rise to visual sensations and a perceptual experience of a dog. Similarly with events which go on within the skin, such as sensations and perceptions arising from the bodily tissues. Sullivan was careful to warn against the "stimulus error," calling attention to the frequent mistake of assuming that the perception of an event was the same as the event itself. Thus, experiences are clearly response events and are not to be confused with the situational events antecedent to them.

Sullivan went on to suggest that there were several varieties of experiencing, which could be cast in terms of developmental stages. The most primitive mode of experience was labeled the *prototaxic mode.* It was defined primarily in terms of the kinds of responses inferred to be operative in the early stages of growth. Sullivan proposed that the initial sensory and perceptual responses (prehensions) were gross and undifferentiated, and the infant could be represented as proceeding from one mass state to the next through the course of time. His felt experience was all of a piece, as Mullahy (1948) has described it. As maturation proceeds and learning occurs, Sullivan proposed that differentiated perceptions come to be formed, and the person begins not only to discriminate events one from another but also to respond to their temporal relationship. When this occurred, he spoke of responding in the *parataxic mode.* The essential characteristic of this mode is that the individual is aware that events go together, either through time (in sequences) or at the same time (in patterns). The person does not yet recognize any more complicated, logical, or orderly relationships, such as cause and effect (Mullahy, 1948). With the introduction of language and consensual use of symbols, the way is open for the development of the *syntaxic mode* of experience, in which reflection and comparison of events becomes possible through the use of language symbols. To the extent that the person acquires the conventional usage of the language and accepts the principles of logic which accompany it, he can engage in logical and consensual responding toward events as they occur around and within him (in the syntaxic mode).

Thus, Sullivan broadened his characterization of experience to include not only perceptions of events but conceptions and thoughts as well. At the syntaxic level of response, the person is not only identifying and interpreting what it is that occurs, but he is also operating on these perceptions in the manner of comparison, reflection, recall, and the like. It appears that when Sullivan spoke of the "inner elaboration of events" he meant virtually all of them, or what might be referred to as the subjectively observable sequences and patterns. In doing so, his concept of experience was a high-order concept, which denoted a large and inclusive set of responses.

His definition of *personality* is of the same order. By personality Sullivan meant "the relatively enduring pattern" of recurring interpersonal relationships characteristic of a human life (1953, pp. 110–111). It is clearly a concept, not an event. However, since all response patterns in Sullivan's system are of an interpersonal order, having been acquired in an interpersonal context, this renders the concept of personality synonymous with habitual behavior.

THE DEVELOPMENT OF DISORDERED BEHAVIOR

Sullivan began his representation of disordered behavior by emphasizing that such occurrences stemmed from the everyday transactions of human beings, and as a consequence did not show any differences in *kind* from those which characterized the normal. Disordered behavior differed only in degree. Thus, there were no peculiarities shown by the "morbid" that did not have their counterpart in the normal course of development.

He conceived disorders to be patterns of inadequate and inappropriate action in interpersonal relations. It was always in relation to other persons' behavior that disordered behavior occurred, so that disordered patterns were specific to this class of situational events. Sullivan, of course, recognized that some disorders arose from a physiological base, or what he referred to as "primary biological defect." Such defects could be apparent at birth, could occur as a function of

maturation, such as Huntingdon's Chorea, or could follow some fortuitous event, such as the ingestion of poison or cranial injury. However, it was the learned patterns of interpersonal reactions with which
Sullivan was primarily concerned.

He built his conception of disorder around the concept of anxiety.
His propositions, therefore, conveniently fall into two general classes,
the antecedents to anxiety, and the consequents. *In brief, disordered
behavior represents responses that have been acquired in an effort to
mitigate, control, or eliminate the disastrous effects of anxiety, which
has been elicited by other sets of events.*

ANXIETY

ANTECEDENTS TO ANXIETY. The primary group of antecedents is represented by the kinds of interpersonal situations in which a person has
come to be reared. In the main, it was the situations posed by the
child's teachers, especially his parents, which Sullivan identified as
the anxiety-producing events, but he also referred to the interpersonal
events encountered by the individual outside the home and with his
age equals as an important source of behavioral difficulty.

First and foremost is the possibility of excessive anxiety being
elicited by proximity to *anxious persons*. By the phenomenon of
empathy, the growing child is prone to excessive amounts of anxiety
tension if he is unfortunate enough to be in the hands of an anxious
mother or mother-surrogate. There is also the possibility of *malevolent
persons* in the role of the socializers: a mother, a nurse, a baby sitter—
any one of these can behave in such a way as to hurt or otherwise
provoke fear in the growing child. Again, there are the various occurrences of *ostracism* (Sullivan's term for rejection) which are responsible for provoking anxiety and insecurity in the youngster. *Ridicule*
also serves to foster anxiety and promote difficulty in the child. He
noted that ridicule from parents and others was one of the worst
techniques used on early adolescents (1953, p. 268).

Punishment is another technique, but Sullivan was quick to point
out that punishment in and of itself did not promote disordered behavior. In his view, it was punishment applied with malevolence, or
with anxiety, that engendered fear and anxiety in the child. A parent
who rails at his child and punishes to inflict pain can reasonably
expect the child to fear him. Or again, consider the disordered mother
who becomes distressed at the sight of her child's sexual explorations

or the appearance of his excretions on the floor, and who moves in on the youngster in an agitated fashion, punishing as she goes. This is a circumstance in which Sullivan would have predicted that intense anxiety is bound to occur.

Sullivan proceeded to cite whole groups of "insanities" which well-meaning parents inflicted upon their offspring. Not the least of these are the errors of *inconsistency* committed by uninformed parents as well as those who suffer from "unfortunate peculiarities of personality." Prescriptions that are glaringly contradictory to another adult represent confusions to a child, and confusion results not only in anxiety but also in an inability to devise ways in which to avert the anxieties that arise at intervals.

Sullivan did not neglect the possibility of disastrous encounters with persons other than the primary socializers. Particularly important here are the groups of age equals with whom the youngster must learn to cope, whose attacks of disparagement, ridicule, and ostracism can be especially crippling when they follow similar occurrences in the child's own home.

THE OCCURRENCE OF ANXIETY. The importance of anxiety is not only in terms of the event itself but also in terms of its consequents—what it impels the person to do. The reader will recall that Sullivan represented anxiety as a "disintegrating situation." Not only does it produce distress, but it also interferes with effective responses. The more severe its intensity, the greater will be the impairment. Severe anxiety has the effect of producing useless confusion and an equally useless disturbance of attention to the events immediately preceding its onset.

The instant reaction to anxiety is avoidance, and thus the child promptly learns to avoid situations which have been anxiety-producing to him, and to relinquish responses in his behavior which have produced or been related to anxiety in the past. He can do this through his perceptual responses whereby he learns to distinguish the events that signalize the imminence of anxiety. Thus, all persons develop anxieties related to certain kinds of things or acts, and they learn to avoid them. Cultural taboos of various kinds are acquired in this fashion.

Anxiety leads to the development of disorder: (a) when it occurs excessively frequently and at excessively intense levels—the disordered person has had to cope with more anxiety than the normal; (b) when the events that elicit it occur in a confused and inconsistent fashion so that the child is unable to acquire reliable and stable avoidances needed to forestall its occurrence; and (c) when it becomes attached to situations or to responses that are necessary for the termination of various physiological responses (need tensions). If (c) is true, a direct "collision" occurs. In this instance, the child is faced with a dilemma in which both tendencies to approach and tendencies to avoid are directed toward the same objects or events; he is in conflict.

In normal development, the child acquires appropriate compromise responses (sublimations) to resolve the conflict at least partially. In the development of a disorder, effective compromise responses are not developed, and the child either acquires ineffective resolutions of the dilemma or proceeds to avoid the situation and the responses appropriate to it altogether.

INEFFECTIVE RESOLUTIONS OF ANXIETY. In place of appropriate patterns which are hypothetically possible (integrated dynamisms), the child may develop what Sullivan sometimes referred to as *"dynamisms of difficulty."* By this term, which he later ceased to use, he meant that there was a certain collection of anxiety-reducing response patterns a person might employ which would prove to be ineffective. "At best they achieve only an unsatisfactory goal" (1956, p. 5). They are ineffective or inappropriate in the sense that they either directly interfere with the termination of basic physiological responses (with need satisfaction) or they simply predispose the individual to further anxiety and upset. *Disordered responses are avoidance patterns, which are inappropriately designed to accomplish the consistent avoidance of anxiety-producing events, and which conflict with other sequences that would lead to the response of satisfaction.*

The reader will recall that the collection or organization of avoidance behaviors in Sullivan's system is referred to as the self-system. Thus, another way to refer to the disordered person is to speak of him as having an extensively developed and far-reaching system of anxiety avoidances, which prove to be insufficient to keep his tensions of anxiety and needs at a minimum level. Disorder results from a faulty system of avoidance behavior.

The avoidances constituting the self-system are of two general types: (1) those by which the person manages to avoid and fend off situations that cause him to feel anxious and distressed; and (2) those by which the person manages to control the contents of his awareness so that anxiety-producing events, both situational and response, are unlikely to occur and unsettle him. Simple patterns of physical withdrawal and isolation from upsetting situations, as well as more complex patterns of altering interactions, such as changing the subject in a conversation, exemplify the first type. For situations where he cannot physically and spatially avoid anxiety-producing people, the person can learn to rationalize his behaviors, to talk his way around potentially punitive people, to engage in dramatizations and as-if performances, and to be deceptive and misrepresent in speech his private thoughts or his past actions. A man who hates his neighbor can feign an interest and behave as if he liked him by making those responses which he has learned that friendly neighbors make. Or again, a child may learn that going to her parents and chastising herself as bad and naughty proves to be an effective way to forestall punishment, since her parents are loath to spank if she appears tearful and sorry.

But Sullivan regarded the control of the contents of awareness as the more critical aspect of the self-system's avoidances. Here, the person is faced with the occurrence of anxiety-producing events in his own behavior, his own awareness. And Sullivan pointed to essentially two sets of behaviors the person could employ in order to maintain a tension-free awareness: (1) the person learns to be selectively inattentive to situations that will produce anxious thoughts, feelings, and the like; and (2) the person can learn to replace the anxiety-producing responses with others that do not have that effect. The first is, of course, *selective inattention;* his term for the second group of events was *substitutive processes.*

To circumstances the person cannot physically avoid, he can learn to be selectively inattentive and simply not to hear or see what it is that would elicit the anxiety. In situations he cannot avoid and to which he cannot be selectively inattentive, he can learn to substitute other responses so as to preclude those that would distress him. He learns to engage in preoccupations of various sorts. For example, he learns to engage in extended obsessive and verbal sequences and becomes committed to fantasy themes of various sorts, to patterns of self-disparagement and self-criticism resulting in "customary low self-esteem," to preoccupations with self-pity, to hypochondriacal preoccupations, or to paranoid projections to excuse or avoid blame.

All these are examples of substitute thought sequences which the individual learns to employ in place of responses whose terminus would be anxiety or fear. The "trick" is to occupy one's awareness with thoughts and percepts that obviate, while one is awake, the pattern of severe anxiety—uncanny emotion (1953, pp. 314–315).

Of course, selective inattention is an important response in all persons. Moreover, the substitutive responses are the mediators of dissociation, and thus everyone manifests dissociation. Ineffective and inappropriate uses of these patterns (dynamisms) follow from an excessive reliance on and an exaggerated application of them to wide ranges of situations and behavior.

THE CONSEQUENTS OF INEFFECTIVE RESOLUTIONS OF ANXIETY. Selection of inappropriate or poorly designed avoidance behaviors (security operations) or excessive reliance on selective inattention and the substitutive processes predispose a person to further behavioral difficulties. Several of these may be listed in order to represent the sort of "snowball effect" to which Sullivan was pointing.

1. Avoidance behaviors result in "restrictions in freedom of living." To the extent that a person has learned to avoid situations and to be selectively inattentive to others, he becomes the victim of a sort of behavioral impoverishment. Whole areas of potential satisfaction may be unavailable to him because of anxiety and his habitual avoidances. His security depends on his avoiding a particular field or a particular subject. A fear of authorities and anticipation of punishment can lead a child to avoid classroom situations, and this can result in extensive behavioral "loss." This effect is particularly important when viewed in the context of the developmental sequence. Failure to develop appropriate interpersonal patterns at one stage may preclude or handicap the acquisition of effective patterns at the stages to follow. This can result in disasters in development, for example in the case of delayed preadolescence. Great stress may be applied to a personality unable to move on the typical time schedule, and the unfortunate person may be thrust into situations that will provoke intense anxiety with which he is not prepared to cope.

2. Avoidance behaviors may interfere directly with the necessary interpersonal relations that must occur if the person is to obtain a satisfactory outcome to his important behavior. Sullivan was concerned here with what happens to the needs for satisfaction in a person whose behavior is heavily committed to avoidances (security operations) of various sorts. A case in point is the person who employs projection of blame as his preferred substitutive response. In doing so he makes it very difficult for himself to accomplish successful interactions with persons he also regards as his persecutors. Or again, the preoccupations of the hypochondriac with his ill health may cause him to forego many important satisfactions because he thinks of himself as too tired or too ill to engage in them. It would be difficult to

have adequate sexual relations with a wife to whom one had constantly complained of a lack of physical strength.

3. Substitutive thought sequences the person must use in order to avoid the occurrence of derogatory responses toward himself may in turn render him ineffective in situations where he tries to interact. If it proves necessary for the person to maintain a false set of thoughts about himself or his behavior, he will find himself exposed to awkward situations and will make many interpersonal blunders. If he is forced to retain inadequate and inappropriate conceptions of others, his stereotypes and prejudices about them will lead him into many unsatisfying and unsuitable interpersonal transactions. Such responses toward others are likely to elicit hostility, criticism, and rejection in others, making even more troublesome situations to which to respond. With selective inattention, one may deny himself much of the data necessary for choosing behavior appropriate to and effective in a situation.

4. The most serious consequent follows when important responses or interrelationships are deleted from the individual's repertoire altogether. This effect Sullivan dealt with in terms of the concept of *dissociation,* and he spoke of the dissociative process and the dissociated system. Dissociation is mediated by the occurrence of selective inattention and various substitutive responses. It is an instance where an important response system is effectively barred from any disturbing influence on personal awareness for a period of years and perhaps even for a lifetime.

Sullivan proposed that a predisposition to serious disorder arose from significant dissociations, massive avoidance of and inattention to interpersonal relationships critical for the person's "satisfaction and security." Dissociations of minor systems of behavior are to be expected in the course of development and are characteristic of the ordinary person. However, anyone who builds up an intricate dissociation of a major area, for example, anything to do with genital sexuality, Sullivan proposed, was in imminent danger of a schizophrenic collapse, for dissociations of that order are almost impossible to maintain.

ORIGIN OF INEFFECTIVE RESOLUTIONS TO ANXIETY. Occasionally Sullivan referred to what he believed to be the sources of such inappropriate ways of coping with intense anxieties. Selective inattention and the uses of substitutive processes, of course, he viewed as inborn *capabilities* of the human, but he also sought to answer the question of how an individual learns to *apply* his capacity for inattending, and also how it was that a person acquired some substitutive thought sequences and anxiety avoidances as opposed to others.

First and foremost is the possibility of direct teaching. The person may be trained directly in the use of certain responses by encouragement and reward at the hands of his parents or other significant adults. A compulsive father may train a son in duplicating his habits of checking because he regards them as valuable. Similarly, by imitation the son can acquire them if the same set of avoidance patterns are employed by the persons who surround him. An important source, therefore, for some of these anxiety-reducing responses are the parents themselves, who wittingly or unwittingly accomplish specific training in unfortunate and undesirable behaviors because they are disordered themselves. Following this, one might expect obsessive parents to produce obsessive children more often than nonobsessive parents do.

Sullivan also spoke of the possibility of a person "hitting upon" a way of resolving his anxieties as a function of "trial and success," or following progressive discovery on his own that certain things he did (his fantasy, or hypochondriacal thoughts) gradually and slowly took care of more and more distressing situations and more and more upsetting awarenesses. Thus, the source of many other habits of avoidance lies in the general repertoire of the culture, in the sense that they can come from any source (movies, books, playmates, etc.), can be elaborated upon and developed by the anxious person, and become progressively extensive within the intervening response sequences of the person himself.

Finally, the acquisition of ineffective resolutions to anxiety may occur when the opportunity for learning appropriate operations is not available. For example, the geographically isolated child in a rural area is much more likely to develop substitutive responses and ineffective sublimations of his genital sensations during the adolescent years, partly because the people he needs to interact with in order to learn how to implement his genital interests are simply not available.

THE DEVELOPMENT OF ADVANCED DISORDERS. Excessive anxiety occasioned by poor training conditions, heavy and persistent use of substitutive thought sequences to maintain critical dissociations, and extraordinary reliance on ineffective habits of avoidance (security operations) in order to keep anxiety to a minimum all conspire in time to produce advanced disorders of behavior. The particular kind of illness that develops is determined by the kind of behaviors habitually employed by the disordered person.

Thus, Sullivan proposed that "extraordinary dependence" of a person on a "particular dynamism" was the fundamental notion to have in mind when thinking about advanced behavior disorders (1956, p. 6). For example, the paranoid dynamism is characterized as the recurrent use of the projection of blame onto others in order to escape the awareness of inferiority. This would represent the paranoid trend. Misinterpretation of events to supplement and buttress the projection constitutes the next step in a full-blown paranoid state. Or again, dissociation is identified as the "security operation" upon which the schizophrenic places heavy reliance (the dynamism of emphasis).

In his discussions of the advanced disorders, Sullivan was often at his very best, and this fact stemmed from his extensive experience with and close observation of this group of behaviors. It is not possible to go into detail about each of the disordered groups. Thus, no convenient listing of the symptoms of disorder can be presented here, for the result would be a lexicon of pathology. We will content ourselves with noting that Sullivan was at some pains to identify and describe the differing behaviors that appeared to characterize each symptom, and to discuss the implications of such behaviors on the other aspects of the personality. In his volume of *Clinical Studies in Psychiatry* (1956), he examined each in turn, from his tripartite point of view of their behavior: (1) analysis of the patterns of avoidance—self-system and its various security operations; (2) analysis of the remainder of the personality, or what was occurring with respect to the rest of the individual's needs and satisfactions; and (3) the occurrences and disorganizations in sleep.

Sullivan's representations of the development of schizophrenic and obsessional states were particularly noteworthy and have received considerable acclaim. These cannot be discussed in detail. The essential elements of his conception of schizophrenia are worth noting in passing, however, since it represents a good example of his conception of the course of disorder. To Sullivan the schizophrenic episode occurred in an individual who had relied heavily on dissociation to resolve anxiety-producing situations (primarily sexual), and these proved insufficient to maintain him. No longer able to maintain a dissociation of anxiety-producing events, his avoidance behaviors became ineffective in controlling his awareness. He could no longer exclude the early perceptual responses and referential ideas or restrict his awareness to late, highly refined logical thought. Obscure, autistic, unrefined thinking operations characteristic of very early life would return—those excluded from awareness by the socialization process. The collapse was not complete, of course, and thus one encountered an admixture of highly refined referential processes along with much more primitive and general ones. However, it tended to progress in the direction of paranoid responses, or to deteriorate into a hebephrenic condition.

Sullivan's emphasis on the details of such disorders stemmed from his position that adequate analysis of the disordered behavior had to precede any attempt at effecting a change, and that treatment operations had to be tailored to, and accordingly vary with, the type of behavior on which they focused. Therapy procedures effective with certain kinds of behavior are relatively helpless in the face of others; a knowledge of the details of pathology and pathogenesis is part and parcel of Sullivan's system of therapy.

THE GOALS OF THERAPY

WHO DETERMINES THE GOALS? Sullivan did not approach the question of objectives in this form, but it is possible to derive his position from what he has written about the therapeutic transaction in general. He defined the psychiatric interview as involving a patient who sought out an expert on a more or less voluntary basis because he had patterns of behavior which he found particularly troublesome, or especially valuable, and who undertook a series of interviews from which he expected to derive benefit. In a sense, then, the patient defined the goals, and Sullivan made it clear that if the subject developed the conclusion that the expert was not assisting him in learning how and with whom he underwent the difficulties plaguing him, the course of interviewing became rough indeed.

On the other hand, the patient is consulting a person who is more adequately informed and better equipped to study and to make sense out of the interpersonal difficulties. In short, he is an expert. Ideally, the expert knows how to analyze the nature of the difficulties that the patient poses and how to effect a remedy. The expert's theories and experience give him some notion of what is relevant or irrelevant to the patient's problems, and of the appropriate order in which aspects of the problem can be treated most effectively. The subject does not have such equipment. Of the two, it is the expert who knows what has to be done in order to effect the changes the subject seeks. Thus, if he accepts the patient's general goals for the therapy, the expert still determines the procedure and the intermediary goals that must be accomplished in sequence before the ultimate wished-for change can be reached.

The expert should also know, however, whether the goals of the subject might be achieved with the means at hand. He can recognize, for example, when the patient's request for physiological changes cannot be achieved. He can judge certain patient goals as inappropriate because they involve new patterns as ineffective as those to be replaced. The expert in these instances would not undertake to pursue the objectives the patient requests.

Thus, the establishment of goals seems to occur as a function of negotiation. The patient states what he seeks. The therapist proceeds to evaluate the suitability of such goals and the feasibility of achieving them with his therapeutic procedures. A working objective is established which will support the interview series, in terms of which both the therapist and the subject can participate; subsequently, different goals could come to be established and made explicit by the same procedure. Shared, explicit goals seemed to be the basis on which Sullivan felt the therapeutic operation should proceed.

CHARACTERISTICS OF THE GOALS. The general objectives of a therapeutic series include the identification of the patient's difficulties, an analysis of how they operate, what has to be done to effect a remedy, and putting the remedial procedures into effect, with the outcome hopefully one of success. Thus, objectives will vary from patient to patient, depending on the nature of the difficulties to which the patient and therapist attend. They might prove to be small in number and readily achieved in one instance, extensive and intricate in another; they might entail a single interview for one subject, several years of interviews for another.

In connection with these general objectives, Sullivan represented his schema of major stages for the psychiatric interview (1954). These stages concerned intermediate objectives, each of which should be accomplished before the next stage was initiated.

In the first stage, *the inception,* the purpose is to arrive at a preliminary definition of the problem or problems to be dealt with and to get a clear understanding of the basis of the interview or series of interviews. In the second stage, *the reconnaissance,* the objective is to review the background of the problem and develop a summary statement of the difficulty. It consists of obtaining a "round outline" of the social or personal history of the person. At its conclusion, the expert prepares a definition of the difficulties as he sees them and checks it with the patient to insure consensus. He informs the patient whether the problems fall within the field of psychotherapeutic competence. When consensus is established, therapy can proceed to the next objective.

In the *detailed inquiry,* the third stage, the heart of therapy occurs. The intention here is to effect a painstaking, careful analysis and elucidation of the interpersonal patterns constituting the subject's difficulties. Assuming this goes well, one arrives at the final stage, *termination of the interview,* where the purpose and methods are designed to consolidate the progress that has been made in terms of some durable benefit to the patient. Typically, in this stage the expert makes a final statement, suggests a prescription for action, and makes a statement of expectation as to what is likely to follow—after which the transaction is completed.

This general outline was proposed by Sullivan as appropriate for the single interview, for a brief series of interviews, for an extended series, and for individual sessions within extended series. Sullivan consistently emphasized that the therapist should develop both long-range and intermediate goals, and should proceed methodically in order to implement them. His procedure, then, was what others have referred to as "planned" therapy. Moreover, he argued that efficient therapy entailed the recognition and acceptance by both participants of what was being done. The objectives, procedures, and evaluations of progress were to be open and *explicit.* Thus, the subject acquired a clear understanding of the purposes, steps, and gains throughout the treatment process, insofar as he was judged able to handle it. Sullivan believed that the subject could engage in the enterprise more effectively if he were kept informed of the process.

CONDITIONS FOR PRODUCING BEHAVIOR CHANGE

Consistent with his point of view as to how behavior operates and the ways in which disordered behavior becomes developed, Sullivan viewed individual verbal psychotherapy as another and a very crucial kind of interpersonal transaction. Thus, he considered the psychotherapeutic interview to be essentially an interpersonal situation in which two participants, a patient and an expert in interpersonal relations, engaged in a joint effort to elucidate and modify the difficulties in living that characterized the patient and his situation. Presumably the joint effort continued as long as both participants expected some desirable outcome to emerge.

Their attention focuses on interpersonal phenomena, since it is in response to interpersonal situations that the patient has developed his troublesome patterns of behavior or those he values and would like to reinforce and retain. Since the objective is to clarify and "elucidate" the patient's behavior in certain interpersonal situations, the therapy interview itself is a special instance of such situations, containing within it the essential qualities of all human interrelationships. What occurs between subject and expert is represented as a sample of the individual's typical behavior in social situations. Thus, data relevant to the subject's general pattern of response to people can be observed by the therapist himself. Sullivan did not view the therapy relationship as unique. It was simply another interpersonal relationship.

Viewed in this way, the therapist is not only an observer and behavior analyst, but he is also a participant in the social situation itself. He is a *participant observer*. Sullivan repudiated the notion that the therapist could be viewed as essentially neutral, and emphasized that the patient's behavior was importantly dependent on the interviewer's behavior. To Sullivan, the behavior of the therapist in the situation was as significant as was that of the patient himself.

The reader will observe a corresponding emphasis on method. Sullivan recognized that an absence of method predisposed both patient and therapist to becoming hopelessly entangled in the intricacies of extensive observational data about which adequate theory and knowledge are not yet available. Proceeding in a methodical fashion serves to help the therapist keep his bearings by reminding him of what information he needs to gain, what steps are next, and which areas he has not yet explored. It makes it less likely that he will overlook or ignore important interpersonal processes. Sullivan therefore suggested an overall schema which the therapist could employ as a guide.

He went further, however, in the direction of specifying particular "techniques" and his volume, *The Psychiatric Interview* (1954), is replete with examples of statements which Sullivan proposed the therapist should make at various times. In general, however, Sullivan believed that the choice of technique depended on what behaviors one wanted to effect in the subject: *objectives determine technique.* For example, some patients might be able to "free associate" and that might be an effective technique for the interview objectives with them. However, he considered it inappropriate for objectives with some other patients.

One can see that such an approach—defining the objective first, and then considering what methods must be employed to effect it—would pave the way for trying a variety of techniques. This was apparently true of Sullivan's own therapeutic techniques, since he is reputed to have yawned in the face of his patient's speech, walked out of an interview office, and criticized a patient's behavior on different occasions in order to elicit a response sequence that he deemed at the time to have been important to effect.

PRINCIPLES BY WHICH BEHAVIOR CHANGE OCCURS

From the foregoing sections it is clear that Sullivan viewed disordered behavior with which the psychotherapist was concerned as learned. The disordered patient has developed fears and anxieties which obstruct the learning of other effective and appropriate responses. Therapy, then, becomes a process whereby the blocks to further learning become removed. Sullivan emphasized that the patient would be progressively solving the problems he faced without a therapist, if he had not learned in the past that attending to his difficulties produced discomfort and anxiety, while ignoring them was comforting. His learned avoidance patterns prevent him from solving his problems himself.

Thus, successful change of the disordered behaviors hinges upon successful modification of anxiety-avoidance patterns. *Elucidation* is the term that Sullivan repeatedly employed to refer to the principle by which therapeutic change comes about. Sullivan seemed to conclude that learning to recognize one's own behavior accurately, represent it conceptually, and evaluate it honestly were the essential requirements for behavioral change. Mental health is characterized by contentment with one's utilization of one's opportunities, self-evaluation appropriate to one's conduct, knowledge of and frequent accomplishment of needed satisfactions, and infrequent anxiety (1947, p. 117).

Unfortunately, Sullivan did not seem to relate the propositions of learning he proposed to the original development of behavior, and his propositions about relearning and redevelopment in therapy. This failure may have been due, in part, to Sullivan's diffidence about his learning principles. He knew the mechanisms of learning were important for an understanding of how normal and disordered behavior is acquired, but he was hesitant to discuss this topic. For him, learning was "the organization of experience," and he decried "a form of craft union antagonism" by some theorists which Sullivan felt seriously interfered with a necessary "multi-disciplined" approach to a satisfactory theory (1953, p. 150). Despite this complaint toward psychologists and his self-acknowledged weakness in this area, Sullivan tackled this theoretical problem because of its "very great importance." One might say that Sullivan espoused in general a tension-reduction theory of learning. The following conditions are those he defined.

LEARNING IN TERMS OF THE ANXIETY GRADIENT. Consistent with his position concerning anxiety, Sullivan thought that persons learned to discriminate increasing from diminishing degrees of anxiety and altered their activity in the direction of the latter. Individuals avoid situations that increase anxiety and seek those that reduce it.

LEARNING IN TERMS OF TRIAL AND SUCCESS. Sullivan proposed that success, which he defined as satisfaction, had a "remarkable fixing power" and thus responses that led to satisfaction tended to recur.

LEARNING IN TERMS OF REWARDS AND PUNISHMENTS. In speaking of these conditions, Sullivan was thinking of the consequences that others apply to the person's behavior. Roughly speaking, Sullivan suggested that reward tended to lead to pleasurable responses and punishment to pain, with the former increasing the likelihood with which the response would recur and the latter acting to decrease it.

TRIAL AND ERROR LEARNING BY HUMAN EXAMPLE. Sullivan had in mind the possibility of a person's emulating or duplicating the responses he saw others make and tending to retain those responses that led to success (satisfaction).

LEARNING BY MEANS OF EDUCTION. Sullivan evidently wished to have some fashion in which he could refer to complex human learning in which thoughts were central. He proposed, therefore, that a final condition of learning followed the act of educing relationships between events, perceiving connections and interpreting cause and effect. It seems possible that Sullivan implicitly thought of the process of eluci- dation in therapy and the condition of learning by eduction as being comparable, that change in therapy was a consequence of coming to make more effective eductions, but he did not make this explicit.

However, it would seem legitimate to recharacterize the learning conditions which Sullivan posited in the following fashion. First, he seemed to propose that learning could occur as a consequence of *response termination,* this group including anxiety-reduction, the ter- mination of noxious physiological responses (needs), and the cessation of pain following punishment. Responses that produced the reduction of such noxious events would tend to recur or become acquired. In the second instance, he seemed to believe that learning could also occur as a consequence of *response arousal.* He seemed to imply the occurrence of some pleasant or desired emotion following such things as situational (interpersonal) rewards. Responses followed by "satis- faction" and "pleasure" tend to recur. Finally, Sullivan proposed that the modification of responses could occur through the *mediation of symbolic processes.* His principle of eduction appeared to involve changes effected through the identification of differences and similari- ties and the perception of relations between events.

It seems probable that Sullivan judged groups one and three to be most significant with respect to behavioral change in therapy. He re- ferred to the therapeutic process as the lessening of anxiety which had been acquired in relation to both situations (interpersonal) and re- sponses (the subject's own behavior). Anxiety termination makes pos- sible the effective use of the symbolic processes. One has to occur before the other will be rendered available. Presumably anxiety reduc- tion is a necessary but not sufficient condition for producing the de- sired change. Conceptual and symbolic response processes are also necessary. In contrast to other groups of theorists, Sullivan was clearly not referring to automatic behavioral change without attention and awareness, as exemplified by the classical conditioning paradigm. The role of group two, the occurrence of satisfaction and pleasurable re- sponse events, would be expected to follow the satisfactory accomplish- ment of anxiety reduction and conceptualization.

PATIENT BEHAVIOR THAT MUST OCCUR IN THERAPY

Sullivan's book on the process of interviewing represents a statement of the objectives and operations that define the therapist's role. It says relatively little about the patient behaviors that must occur. It implies that the therapeutic process begins once several basic prerequisites have been met.

The patient must be physically present, he must have settled on some working objective in collaboration with the therapist, he must believe some benefit will be forthcoming, and he must be able to talk about himself under the therapeutic conditions. Sullivan seemed to imply that given such conditions, and given careful and expert operations on the part of the therapist, one could anticipate a satisfactory outcome—the achievement of the objectives.

Sullivan did speak of several types of self-evaluative thoughts which patients often brought with them to therapy and which would act as sources of interference if not successfully handled. People are taught that they ought not to need help, they ought to know themselves and not have characteristics about their behavior for which they cannot account, they should be governed by logic, they should be ashamed of themselves if they have not been able to rise above the handicaps in their early lives, and finally they should be self-sufficient and independent. Presumably successful alteration of thoughts such as these is necessary for effective therapy to proceed.

As therapy continues, another set of responses must occur. As Sullivan said, the *quid pro quo* that keeps the subject an active participant in the necessarily disturbing business of therapy is the judgment that he is learning something that is, or promises to be, useful to him. This implies that the subject periodically evaluates the effectiveness of the therapy sessions, and the evaluation has to be positive if he is to continue. In the long run the investment of time and effort must result in some perceived "payoff."

What particular kind of patient responses must occur? Actually, since it is possible for something to have gone awry in virtually every response realm, the range of behaviors with which the therapy might become concerned is very broad. Difficulties can be operative in the realm of attention (important types of selective inattention), in the sensory and perceptual responses (parataxic distortions, dissociation), in the conceptual and symbolic realm (inaccurate representations of one's own behavior, false personifications, faulty sequences of logical thought), in the emotional and effective response domain (fear, anxiety, hatred), and finally in the entire arena of instrumental behaviors (actions). However, the particular responses in a specific subject which must be discussed are those directly relevant to the solution of the problem at hand. For example, a subject might have developed an unfortunate series of scatological habits in which he engaged in the privacy of his room. Attention is not necessarily focused on these, nor are efforts directed toward their correction, if the statement of the therapeutic objectives does not include them and if they are not relevant to the objectives agreed upon. The more extensive the objectives or the more involved the problems, the greater the variety of difficulties the therapist and patient are likely to become concerned with.

Because of their ubiquity, however, the therapist is likely to encounter certain responses in most therapy situations. These include inaccurate and inappropriate self-evaluations (inaccurate personifications of the self), inaccurate identifications of events (parataxic distortions), selective inattentions, various substitutive thought sequences, and the like. Moreover, certain types of avoidance patterns are characteristic of certain clinical groups, and thus the therapist might be particularly attentive to the patterns of perceptual distortions, denials, projections, and inaccuracies in the thought sequences which characterize the paranoid group.

Since Sullivan's conception of disorder was built on the notion that unfortunate behaviors were acquired in the service of anxiety and operate as avoidances, and in that fashion interfered with the remainder of the person's situation, patients should talk about: (1) the avoidance behaviors—the self-system; (2) the occurrence of anxiety, to which these behaviors are related and which represents their antecedent; and (3) the interpersonal situations in which they occur. The sequence of patient responses in therapy, then, should follow a course where:

a. He first commits himself to the therapy series and agrees to follow the pattern of inquiry to be set by the therapist (inception);

b. He then proceeds at the behest of the therapist to report on the ways in which he looks at, thinks about, feels toward, and acts with people and with himself (reconnaissance);

c. He focuses attention along with the therapist on those *particular* patterns of response to patterns of situations that are agreed to be the areas of difficulty. These will be the ones characterized by patterns of anxiety and anxiety avoidances, whichever have come to be preferred by the subject, and which will always occur in relation to patterns of interpersonal situations.

d. Once having identified the events of concern, the next step is to join with the therapist in the task of identifying and piecing together the interrelationships between these events (eduction) to develop a representation of them in effective symbolic form.

e. Once the patterns of anxiety and defense have become established and made explicit, the subject is in a position to develop further relationships. He can, together with the therapist, develop a "realization and understanding" of the ways these patterns have represented handicaps and barriers to the progress of his life, the ways they have directly interfered with other patterns of importance to the subject, and thus the ways they have produced deficiencies in his development. (Phases *c*, *d*, and *e* constitute the stage of detailed inquiry.)

f. Having arrived at this point, the subject begins to be ready to make appropriate changes in his behavior patterns outside the therapy condition itself. Some of these changes are planned, and these are discussed with the therapist during the terminal stages of the process.

BEHAVIORS REQUIRED OF THE THERAPIST

As was indicated earlier, the treatment by Sullivan of the therapist "role" was intricate and detailed. This section deals first with the general attributes of the therapist role and then turns to more specific behaviors required in the treatment process.

General Attributes of Therapist Role

Sullivan first spoke of the therapist behaviors essential throughout the entire course of psychiatric interviewing. He proposed that the characteristics of an expert in interpersonal relations would include the following ones.

CERTAIN CONCEPTUAL AND SYMBOLIC SKILLS. Sullivan believed that the expert should retain an excellent grasp of the field of interpersonal behavior, including a thorough familiarity with psychopathology as well as with the attributes of normal development and a familiarity with the variability of human behavior, or with practically everything that people do to one another. Formal training is required.

CERTAIN ATTENDING RESPONSES. Sullivan repeatedly emphasized the necessity for the therapist to be able to maintain constant attention to the phenomena of concern, to remain constantly alert, so that he continues to be able to observe, weigh, compare, and evaluate through out the behavioral transaction between the subject and himself.

CERTAIN PERCEPTUAL RESPONSES. To Sullivan, the expert was one who not only knew what to look for and was alert to its occurrence, but could also quickly identify and accurately label events once they appeared. He was someone who was "perceptive to the intricacies of interactions" with varieties of people; he was someone who could readily identify when the patient becomes anxious or ill at ease, and who therefore will not often frighten the patient or make him anxious through inadvertence or clumsiness.

CERTAIN AFFECTIVE AND EVALUATIONAL RESPONSES. Sullivan emphasized the necessity for the therapist to maintain an "objective attitude" by which he avoided becoming involved as a person and kept to the business of being an expert. The therapist does not have strong affectional or hostile responses toward his patients, nor does he respond as if he were superior and more worthy of respect than are they. He remains someone who deals with patients simply because he has had the advantage of certain unique training and experience which make him able to help them. It is a job, and his occupation is not necessarily any more worthy than anyone else's form of employment. These statements give a flavor of the evaluational responses that Sullivan proposed that the therapist should maintain toward the behavior of his patient and toward his own role in therapy.

CERTAIN VERBAL AND COMMUNICATIVE SKILLS. The therapist's primary procedure of treatment is talking. He must "readily produce fruitful communications" with varieties of people about varieties of topics. He must be able to speak easily, to have a variety of ways in which he can express an idea and a variety of gestures by which he can communicate. Sullivan was loath to have this interpreted to mean that the therapist became simply an actor. But he wanted to emphasize that the expert had command of a variety of responses, which he could call upon as needed.

Not only does the expert have such skills with which to perform his task, but he is also aware of and knows about as much of his own response repertoire as is possible. To the extent that the therapist is unaware of or unwitting about his participation in the interview, he does not know what is happening. The therapist should be aware of how he acts; he should know his typical "stimulus value" for subjects; he should have learned from previous observations the usual impres-

sion he makes on others, how he affects subjects under interview conditions, how he facilitates some things and retards others. Since he is
the instrument of change, he should, like any other craftsman, know
the properties of his tools.

Sullivan summed all this up by saying that it was synthesized into
an aptitude to do nothing exterior to awareness which would greatly
handicap the development of an interview or which would direct its
course along unnecessary lines. Thus, the ideal therapist is in command of and controls his own behavior. He knows what he is about,
he has the necessary tools, and he knows how and when to apply them.

Sullivan emphasized that the therapist select his techniques to
achieve particular objectives. His first task is to elicit patient responses
relevant to the objectives and to analyze them. His second task is to
modify the troublesome responses.

Behavior Elicitors

We shall first discuss the data to be obtained and then the procedures for obtaining them.

OBJECTIVE: DIAGNOSTIC AND PROGNOSTIC EVALUATION. In general, the
first objective is to accomplish a diagnostic and prognostic appraisal
of the subject's situation. Sullivan was strong on the point that an
adequate analysis of a problem had to precede any attempts by a
therapist to operate upon it. The therapist should avoid "expansive
promises" and treatment attempts before he knows the patient well
enough to judge whether therapy might have "any earthly constructive
influence" (1954, p. 81). The diagnostic approach which Sullivan
suggested was less in terms of the classical clinical entities than in
answering the following two questions: (1) What are the outstanding
difficulties in living, the liabilities of the patient, as opposed to his
assets? (2) What are the grounds for therapeutic operations—what can
be done by means of verbal psychotherapeutic procedures? No efforts
at modification should be made until workable tentative answers are
achieved (1956, p. 197).

Thus, Sullivan proposed that the expert, before he considers the
possibility of a detailed analysis, should accomplish an initial review
to determine the major handicaps and advantages in living which are
relatively durable characteristics of the subject. His knowledge of
behavioral development and disorder is essential, since it helps him

determine which areas need to be explored and how the data he gets is to be evaluated. He must know the signs and typical patterns of disorder and the evidence that distinguishes severe from mild conditions. His knowledge indicates which areas have to be investigated even if the subject does not spontaneously elect to do so.

OBJECTIVE: DETAILED ANALYSIS OF THE PATIENT RESPONSES. If he decides verbal psychotherapy may be effective, the therapist's next task is to inquire in a detailed fashion into the intricacies of the patient's difficulties. Methodical procedure is to be preferred, and thus Sullivan suggested an interview schedule to guide the detailed inquiry. This schedule is built around the developmental history and, if followed, will take the therapist through the various stages of development and into the different response realms. Such a schedule provides a framework within which to work, helps to define the objectives toward which the therapist can proceed, presents a conceptualization within which to place the myriad data uncovered, and prevents the therapist from inadvertently overlooking important areas of behavior. The last is particularly important, since the therapist must be concerned not only with response patterns and sequences that are currently operative and troublesome but also with those that are conspicuously and importantly absent from the subject's repertoire.

As he proceeds through the detailed inquiry, the therapist is particularly alert for certain classes of events: overt indices of anxiety, patterns of anxiety avoidance, and the situations under which each of these typically occur.

First of all, he looks for signs of anxiety itself. These can include a whole range of events, such as hesitations in speech, motoric tension, evasions of stimuli (selective inattention), and the like. Single instances of such events are not considered to be pathognomic; however, if after having tried several topical approaches to the same area the therapist repeatedly discerns this pattern, he can hypothesize that the topic is provoking anxiety, and he can then use more specific techniques to elucidate it.

He is also alert to any of the signs of avoidance responses, the security operations that constitute the self-system. A knowledge of behaviors people typically employ to forestall or reduce anxiety is essential for this purpose. Knowing the characteristics of selective disregard, the various substitutive thought sequences employed by individuals, the many roles they can play to fend off a threatening person, or what obsessional response sequences look like, he proceeds to make progressive inquiries into the response repertoire of the subject. He watches for such events, and as they appear and become explicit, both he and the patient try to understand them. Thus, the therapist gradually builds a picture of the individual's pattern of avoidances—his self-system.

Many of the habitual avoidance responses occur during therapy, revealing how the subject behaves in analogous interpersonal situations. The therapist permits these anxiety-reducing behaviors to go on long enough that he can develop a reasonable certainty about the conditions that arouse them. He uses them for clues to the underlying anxiety. For example, if he discovers that the subject is responding to him as if he had done him some harm, he recognizes it as an inappropriate response—assuming he has not actually done so—and can look for its antecedents.

Sullivan's next step was to identify the circumstances under which these avoidances and security operations occurred. A "much more practical" therapy results when the sources of patient anxieties are sought in interpersonal relations than when the symptoms as such are dealt with (1954, p. 11). By studying these avoidance responses in relation to the interpersonal situations in which they occur, he can then proceed to pin down "what the insecurity is about." He casts this in the form of a hypothesis, which he subjects to continuous testing and correction, either by the evaluation of further information or by clearly purposeful exploratory investigation.

ELICITING PROCEDURES. Questions of many kinds represent Sullivan's primary eliciting technique. The interviewer actively introduces "interrogations," not to reveal that he is "smart" or "skeptical" but to be sure "he knows what he is being told" (1954, p. 21).

The variety of questions which Sullivan proposed for eliciting appropriate responses is too great to be considered in detail. The questions range from simple direct probes (What was it your wife said to you last evening?), to presenting the subject with as-if situations (How do you suppose one might feel if . . . ?), or with response possibilities (I wonder if you might not have felt angry since . . .). On occasion the therapist might introduce a statement that was obviously incorrect, with the objective of eliciting a more explicit and accurate report of the events being discussed. An interesting method, which Sullivan discussed in some detail, was the use of various kinds of transitions and their effect on the subject's responses. One, for example, was the abrupt transition where the therapist engineered a quick change in topic in order to open up an area of inquiry without the subject having been forewarned and able to use evasive tactics to fend off the therapist. Sullivan was not reluctant to make out and out guesses as to what was happening and to check his suppositions with the patient.

Most of the examples of technique which he provided in his volume represent certain kinds of questions in certain sequences, designed to uncover and clarify particular response areas. An example might help to illustrate the method. It might happen that the therapist recognizes his patient beginning to display fear and distrust of him and, in effect, responding to him as if he were someone else; a parataxic situation exists. Sullivan would use a question or two to establish the basis of the patient's fear. Let us suppose that the patient responded by saying he expected the therapist to be critical and to dislike him. Sullivan would then ask whether the patient really feared he would be critical. If the patient answered yes, Sullivan would go on to inquire when he had begun to think of his therapist in that fashion. After rendering the anticipatory fears quite explicit, Sullivan would proceed to break down the generalized fear by pointing out that the patient's fears were in contradiction to what had actually happened in the therapy sessions. He would follow this up by noting that the obvious explanation must be that someone had actually treated the patient in that way in the past, and that the patient had unwittingly assumed that the therapist would treat him in the same way. Thus, Sullivan would wonder aloud who that significant person might have been and proceed to uncover the actual persons whom the patient dreads (1954, pp. 231–232).

One sees from the foregoing the style of investigation employed by Sullivan. Step by step, with questions at each point of the way, the therapist proceeds to draw the subject along, almost after the fashion of the Socratic dialogue. In the process, the *content* of the questions and their *sequence* become very important factors of interviewing. In general, Sullivan proposed that questions should proceed from the general to the specific, and that they were best expressed in concrete form. Moreover, questions and comments should be brief; no lengthy dissertations were advisable, since the subject only half listened to such speeches. He felt that the secret of good interviewing lay in the therapist being able to accomplish much by saying little. The use of brief questions by the therapist, which led to lengthy responses by the patient, was the preferred method of procedure.

Before the therapist can proceed to make effective inferences about anxiety and the interrelationships between situations and avoidance behaviors, he must have information about these two sets of events. But this is not possible if the subject's avoidances are complete, if the situations are thoroughly repressed, and if there is no representation in the subject's thoughts of the responses that occur in those particular situations; in other words, if the response area has become subject to dissociation. The uncovering of dissociated systems is a necessary antecedent to the elucidation of the various interrelationships, and this requires particular techniques, although these are not clearly specified. He did specify, however, that a slow and indirect inquiry was essential, since "frontal attacks" had long since become ineffective through the patient's having acquired automatic responses which simply "blunt the attack" or "brush it off" (1956, p. 181). Thus, the therapist specifies his objectives, employs his knowledge of behavior and psychopathology to provide himself with a set of *optional probabilities,* and by a series of adroit questions sets out to confirm one and to disprove the others.

PROCEDURES TO STOP INAPPROPRIATE RESPONSES. Just as he seeks to elicit relevant responses, the therapist also must exercise his skill in discouraging trivia, irrelevancies, graceful gestures by the patient which are intended for his amusement, or repetitions of things which both have heard. He does this gently and kindly, because attention to such events do not advance the course of inquiry. For example, it could be as simple as: "Yes, that is probably quite important, but perhaps you should tell me about . . ."; or it could be somewhat more complex, such as the use of smooth or abrupt transitions from one topic area to another. Sullivan actually made a great deal of this variety of technique. He was quite impressed with the ways people had learned to employ speech as means of hiding, evading, obscuring, and misrepresenting events. The obsessive, in particular, he described as a past master at engaging in circuitous and evasive tactics with the seeming appearance of co-operating with the direct search for the patterns of difficulty. Accurate identification of such tactics and appropriate ways to shunt them off are necessary, or else the course of therapy is destined to be unnecessarily long, painstaking, and inefficient.

It should be clear that Sullivan was concerned with the task of keeping the inquiry on the straightest and most direct course toward the uncovering of problems that the expert could manage. The task is to maintain the flow of relevant and appropriate responses and to minimize, divert, or prevent the occurrence of inappropriate ones. Keeping this flow in process also entails the adequate handling of breaks, stoppages, or interruptions. All this Sullivan referred to as the communication process. Difficulties in maintaining the response flow (retaining effective communication) are occasioned by the fact that the very objectives of the interview are in opposition to the patterns of avoidance the subject has developed. This is the problem of getting at the data despite the subject's anxiety associated with it. Sullivan also emphasized the possibility that the anxiety may arise from the interview situation itself, representing a fear caused by anticipation of hurt from the therapist, with a resulting stoppage or interference in the progress of the inquiry. Should this occur, further inquiry is handicapped if not virtually blocked. Sullivan proposed that whenever this occurred the therapist should concentrate on what in the immediate situation was blocking the verbal exchange. Identification of the anxiety and its relationship to what had passed in the therapy interview was necessary before a return to the general inquiry could effectively take place.

A special problem is presented when anxieties are mutual, that is, when the participants stimulate anxiety in each other and thereby promote their mutual withdrawal. If this occurs, it will obscure, if not disrupt, the therapeutic course, and thus Sullivan greatly emphasized the awareness on the part of the therapist of his own stimulus value in the situation.

Finally, it should be emphasized once again that Sullivan proposed that different styles of questioning were appropriate for some types of behavior as opposed to others. For example, he suggested that in dealing with paranoid patterns of relating to and speaking with people, the therapist should behave differently than he would with an hysteric. With paranoids, Sullivan felt that the therapist must be quite distant in the manner in which he questioned, careful to make the implications of each of his inquiries quite explicit—especially the unpleasant ones—and cautious lest his statements be interpreted as agreement with, or approval of, sequences of illogical thought which the patient might retain.

Behavior Modifiers

OBJECTIVE: MODIFICATION OF THE PATIENT'S RESPONSES. As the reader w ll recall, Sullivan was somewhat hazy about how behavior was learned or modified. Therefore, it was difficult for him to specify concrete procedures for modifying behaviors. Several ideas seem implicit in his writing, however.

Sullivan, as we have noted, stated at various junctures that anxiety reduction had to occur, since until this became accomplished the subject could not readily attend to the events (situational and behavioral) related to this anxiety, nor could he exercise his symbolic and conceptual responses in order to identify the interrelationships between events and their impact upon the rest of his behavior. He spoke of the process of "elucidation" following, or concomitant with, anxiety reduction.

But many questions remain. Are these processes inevitable consequents of the process of inquiry, or detailed analysis, which the therapist and subject jointly perform? One gets the distinct impression that Sullivan at times felt that the act of "elucidation" automatically produced anxiety reduction, perhaps because the subject's puzzling behaviors became intelligible and their analysis provided relief. Or a second question: does anxiety reduction follow from the explicit "labeling" of anxious feelings? If this is true, perhaps Sullivan was correct in implying that all the therapist had to do was to arrange to elicit verbalizations about anxiety patterns, and a lessening of anxiety would occur automatically. Again, does the identification of relationships between events and patterns of events occur automatically following anxiety reduction?

Modifying Procedures

In general, Sullivan seemed to feel that all that was required in the process of effecting change was progressively to uncover the various interrelationships that characterized the subject's interpersonal relations. He discussed the technique for effecting this as one of using questions, and perhaps because of this fact the use of behavioral consequents as modifiers of patient behavior did not come to be explicitly and systematically discussed.

And yet it is apparent that he implicitly referred to such procedures, and his examples of technique reveal the fact that he recurrently used them. In actuality, they seem to have been very critical parts of his technique, although he did not refer to them as such. Many examples can be found scattered through his writings. For example, what appear to be mildly punishing statements such as "I don't believe it" and "it sounds amazing" are used as modifiers.

Many other examples could readily be employed. Sullivan gave some consideration to the use of reassurance and to when it was appropriate to follow a subject's responses by such a technique. He also spoke of the necessity for the therapist to avoid displaying undue curiosity in what the subject might have said; nor should he ever display shock or surprise. If a report has been elicited by his questions, the therapist registers no emotional response, since an expert is not surprised to find the answers he expected to get. Or again, he calls attention to the effect of silence following a paranoid statement, stressing that it should be carefully avoided since it is often taken by the paranoid as tacit assent or approval. There is, of course, the strong suspicion that the consequents that follow the report by the patient of his anxiety-producing thoughts have a great deal to do with whether the anxiety becomes reduced or not.

Thus, it would appear that very critical situational consequents were being used by Sullivan, in addition to the response starters about which he spoke more often. Specification of operations by which to modify behaviors is essential to improve the system.

Sequence of Behavioral Change

The notion of sequence is implicit in all of Sullivan's discussion of therapy, although he did not discuss the question in this form. However, one has only to recall the suggestions he made about stages of interviewing, the outlines that should be followed in the pursuit of the detailed inquiry, and his cautions as to the necessary attention to the steps in which the succession of questions should be presented, to recognize that Sullivan was thinking of an orderly and methodical set of events through which the therapy should proceed. The actual development of explicit "programming" of interviews along this line would be an extended and painstaking task, and this fact makes very understandable why Sullivan did not go further in representing the order of events which should be effected.

One can derive a sequence, however, from the foregoing material. The overall process of therapy might entail something such as the following:

a. Initial review of the problem.

b. Reconnaissance of the behaviors relevant to the problem.

c. Decision as to general outlines of the difficulty and the course therapy shall pursue.

d. Careful and detailed study of the subject's response repertoire.

e. Identification of the anxieties, avoidance patterns, and the interpersonal situations in which they occur.

f. Rendering these patterns explicit to the subject.

g. Making explicit the fact of intervening anxiety.

h. Drawing out the effects of these anxiety patterns on the remainder of the subject's behavior.

i. All of the foregoing has the effect of reducing the intensity of anxiety and permitting the operation of other responses in their stead.

TRANSFER OF THE EFFECTS OF BEHAVIORAL CHANGE

Sullivan seemed to be of two minds about whether changes within the therapy situation could be expected to transfer automatically to outside therapy situations or whether they had to be explicitly planned for and arranged. On the one hand, he tended to argue that no direct effort toward such transfer was necessary. Patients were expected to "cure" themselves once he had helped them accomplish the "necessary brush clearing" by elucidating their "recurrent mistakes" of inappropriate anxiety and anxiety avoidances which have led to "ineffective and inappropriate action" in the past (1954, pp. 238–239).

On the other hand, in discussing the procedures involved in terminating a particular interview or the therapy series in general, Sullivan recommended stating a prescription for action, which the subject was encouraged to try. The interviewer indicates possible courses of action which in his opinion, in view of the data collected, would improve the patient's chances of success and satisfaction in life. In this case, transfer is very definitely being attempted, with the interviewer describing behaviors that he anticipates will produce a satisfying response in the subject if he is successful in emulating them.

The Evaluation of Behavior and of Behavior Change

With Sullivan's therapy approach, the importance of the therapist's evaluative operations is apparent. Sullivan's expert is proceeding along particular lines of inquiry, making judgments as to what to explore and what to avoid, how to proceed to do so, and deciding which of several possible analyses is the most appropriate. This requires almost constant evaluative responses and judgments on the part of the therapist.

Sullivan explicitly recognized this and presented a rule, which he thought an interviewer "might well engrave somewhere on his interior" (1954, p. 128). Throughout the course of therapy, even in the terminal phases, the therapist must continue to "verify his observations." He must be careful not to react unwittingly to what the patient says by word or gesture. He must check the habit of uncritical and "automatic" responding to events to which "all of us are prone"; such have "very little place" in the intricacies of therapeutic work (1954, p. 128). The therapist's evaluative judgments can be treated in terms of the operations which Sullivan suggested for the validation of observations, the verification of inferences, and the assessment of behavioral change.

OPERATIONS FOR THE VALIDATION OF OBSERVATIONS. The observations that the expert can make, more or less objectively, about the behavior of the patient are referred to as *signs;* reports by the subject about his troublesome behaviors are referred to as *symptoms.* Thus, only the patient can "experience" symptoms. When the therapist's observations and patient's report "coincide," an area "which warrants further investigation" has been found (1954, p. 184).

Thus, one primary criterion for validation is agreement between two observers; in the therapy situation the two observers are seeking concurrence of observations about one of the pair. When the observations of both participants coincide, a measure of confirmation has been achieved. This Sullivan referred to as *consensual validation,* and it is the primary criterion by which the therapist can determine whether his observations are in some measure correct.

Secondary procedures involve checking for the correspondence of one observation with that of other observations. Replication of the same observation by the same observer over a period of time, such as repeated identification of the same pattern of response to similar kinds of events, increases the therapist's confidence in the accuracy of his inferences. In addition, the therapist may judge whether his observations match his theoretical expectations. If they do, and if he has confidence in his theory, he may conclude that he is correct even though the patient is as yet unable or unwilling to provide confirmation.

The therapist must regard all observations as tentative and must keep in mind the necessity for finding ways in which they can be validated and confirmed. If, for example, he identifies a *sign*, such as apparent "loss of thought," he must not assume that this identification is necessarily correct without gaining confirmation from the patient or from some other procedure. It was apparent to Sullivan how readily an expert could be led astray if he did not constantly check his observations with that of the second observer. Sullivan referred to two general ways the expert could attempt a validation. On the one hand, he could look for further evidences, additional observations, which would tend to confirm or deny his initial judgment; on the other, he could engage in "clearly purposed exploratory activity of some kind" through framing of questions which were so designed that the response would indicate whether the observation was reasonably correct or adequate. The therapist had intentionally to arrange for validation.

THE VERIFICATION OF INFERENCES. The therapist continually formulates educated guesses, inferences, or hypotheses as to the events probably occurring in the patient's situation and about the likely interrelationships between events the subject has not yet recognized or reported. Sullivan saw the therapist as formulating sets of expectations, rather than single ones, and casting them in the form of optional probabilities. Then, just as in the case of objective observations, he had deliberately to arrange for the checking of these various hypotheses, looking for the most relevant evidence by which to confirm or deny them. An example might be useful to illustrate how the expert might proceed.

Suppose that in the course of discussion a sign of blocking of speech in the subject appears. Sullivan's first task was to make sure that it was blocking, rather than inattention or something else. Suppose further that he observed signs of anger to accompany the stopping of the subject's report, and he confirmed this by a series of questions, to which the subject answered that he was angry. Sullivan's next step might be to infer that the anger occurred as a consequence to anxiety, and he might set up a series of other possibilities as to what elicited the anxiety, such as a recollection that had been stimulated by the discussion, or an anticipatory response related to where the discussion was apt to lead. He also might examine whether it could be related to the therapy relationship itself, since he knows that what he said, or how he said it, may have been the precipitator of anxiety in the subject. With questions, he might provoke the subject's reports of the ways he was feeling and thinking at the time. Confirmations can come by way of subject's report, therefore, but presumably the most adequate confirmation will occur when the apparent signs of anxiety are diminished and the stream of the interview has become resumed.

OPERATIONS BY WHICH TO ASSESS BEHAVIORAL CHANGE. Sullivan was clear that evaluations of the ways in which the subject's behavior was proceeding is a constant task for the expert. The assessment of change, of course, requires a base rate against which differences can be compared. The "point of departure" is the "gross impressions" gained from the inception and reconnaissance phases of treatment (1954, p. 114). He advocated ratings of the subject's behavior and the interview process in terms of several dimensions or attributes: (1) degree of alertness—a rating of the patient with respect to attention, whether it seems to be focused, overly intent, distracted, or vague; (2) intelligence—a rating of the capacity for effective use of intellective skills; (3) responsiveness—a rating of the kinds of patterns the subject is employing in relation to the interview and the interviewer, whether understanding co-operation, obtuseness, unwillingness to be led, or deliberate obstructiveness; and (4) more specific ratings of the patient's habitual attitudes toward his recall and memory and his habitual feelings about answering questions. Moreover, Sullivan proposed that the therapist engage in constant evaluations of how the "communication process" was developing, being alert to any signs that it might be deteriorating or improving, watching for the things that seemed to interfere and the things that appeared to facilitate the exchange.

Although he recognized its importance, Sullivan did not spell out this process of evaluating behavior change. Moreover, the dimensions he mentioned, in terms of which change was to be rated, were not directly related to the interview objectives. From Sullivan's emphasis on establishing clear objectives it would seem that these would be the critical factors upon which to judge the effectiveness of therapy. Sullivan did not discuss changes external to therapy, nor did he concern himself with the question of how the therapist could gain information about such change.

Verification of Theory

Although Sullivan stressed the importance of empirical and experimental validation, he did no research himself and had no specific recommendations to make. He simply encouraged others to do it.

COMMENTS

The fact that this system has received space and attention in this volume equal to that accorded to Freud reflects the authors' judgment that in many respects this is a system of first rank. Although subject to weaknesses, as all must be in this stage of development of the field, it represents an excellent foundation upon which to build.

There is little need to recount its many virtues. A good many of these will have been apparent in the comments distributed throughout the chapter. Several major characteristics are especially important and bear re-emphasis at this point.

Perhaps first to be considered is the system's effort at a comprehensive representation of behavioral development in terms of stages of growth. One can hardly hope to account for acquisition of complex behavior without paying close attention to maturational patterns, to different behavioral opportunities available at different ages, to different situational factors, such as the way the individual is treated by others of different ages and to the fact of sequencing. There is a big question, of course, whether events occur in just the way that Sullivan said they do and at the stages of development which he proposed. But the system is valuable, perhaps both as an attempt at a factual statement of the sequences involved and as a model representing the kind of thing that can and should be done. Even more important, when doing so the system places itself in the position where it can take advantage of the range of information about behavioral development which has been acquired in such fields as developmental and educational psychology. The observational base of such a system need not rest on the narrow apex of the psychotherapeutic interview.

A second feature which deserves comment is the direct way the system attempts to represent the formation of complex behavior. Sullivan appears to be one of the few theorists who attempted to depict how intricate adult behavior developed from an essentially physiological base. He did this by trying to trace the formation of patterns and pattern sequences of behavior, through a study of the arrangements of more primary responses and their interrelationships. Further, he has been more successful than most in avoiding the temptations to find a few gross patterns by which he could conveniently, and probably spuriously, account for the myriad behaviors that humans perform.

Sullivan's emphasis upon the situational determinants of behavior was equally impressive, and the authors share his conviction that, of all the situational events, the interpersonal ones have the greatest significance for the study of personality. Sullivan's position is consistent with the Galilean dictum that the behavior of an object is a function of the conditions under which it occurs. One of the critical and often neglected set of conditions in personality theory are those which are external to the behaving organism. It is unfortunate that Sullivan did not proceed further in the systematic representation of these events. This system shares with others the failure to classify and study the details of situational events as they relate to behaviors. The focus of study has continued to be almost exclusively upon responses themselves. It becomes increasingly apparent that a study of behavior must include the analysis of the way kinds of response events occur in relation to kinds of situations, an emphasis which may be one of the reasons for the growing interest in America in social psychology. Such an extension would be compatible with Sullivan's system, although he himself failed to accomplish it.

Sullivan was one of the few theorists who attempted to represent some of the response mechanisms involved in the phenomenon of awareness. Freud accepted the fact of consciousness and thought that there was some automatic process (repression) which had something to do with what a person was aware of. Rogers refers to awareness as an innate given, says that persons learn to control it, but does not specify how. Dollard and Miller point to one possible response mechanism (stopping thinking), but this contributes more to an explanation of what does not go on within awareness than of what does. Sullivan's use of the attending responses is thus very important, and his notion of response substitution helps to account for what occurs within awareness, as well as what is absent.

The system explicitly recognizes the significance of language, and the advocacy of its direct study is a strong point which this system shares with that of Dollard and Miller. Speech is perhaps the single most important response mechanism in patterns of interpersonal interactions. The relationship between language and thought is not only critical for a general understanding of human behavior but is also of the utmost significance for the conduct of psychotherapy where changes in nonverbal behavior are sought through the interrelationships that are presumed to exist between speech, thought, and other nonverbal responses. Sullivan has further pointed to the necessity for a direct study of the correspondence between verbal report and the subjectively observable responses it often purports to represent. On reading many of the other systems, one gets the distinct impression that frequently such correspondence is assumed to be so great that the patient's reports of events are taken at face value. Judgments that improvement has occurred in the patient's situation often depend on the patient's word. Analyses of what is happening outside the therapeutic hour in the subject's transactions with other people often appears to depend exclusively on what the subject has observed and what he is able and willing to report. Sullivan expressed the conviction that there were categories of response events that words were inadequate to express (uncanny emotions), a conviction artists have held for centuries. Verbal report, by itself, is an inadequate observational base for understanding human behavior.

A corollary emphasis is Sullivan's beginning attempt to study the details of the vast realm of thought. Rather than lumping all such responses into one large class and treating them as if they were homogeneous, Sullivan began to specify some of the different kinds of symbolic responses—eduction, recognition, recall, foresight, and anticipation, imagistic as opposed to logical, and syntaxic thought. Of course, such specification was only a beginning. However, he was correct in calling attention to the necessity for studying the different kinds of mediating responses and their interrelationships with other responses in the same general class (thought), as well as with different response events such as perception, speech, affect, and instrumental action.

Finally, it should be observed that Sullivan was virtually the only theorist among our group explicitly to use the facts and observations from the fields of psychiatry and psychopathology in developing his theories. Adler and Horney, for example, were trained psychiatrists and knew some of the important differences between psychotic and neurotic, depressive and paranoid behavioral sequences. They are reputed to have pursued their individual practice with such information at hand, and to have made decisions as to whom they selected for psychotherapy, etc., in terms of such knowledge. They did not, however, incorporate such facts and principles into their systems. Sullivan knew that such impressive differences in behavior entail different developmental sequences, and this knowledge led him to a study of the differential etiologies of the various kinds of disorder. Similarly, such differences in habits of thought, manner of perception, and mode of interaction with other people lead to the implication of differential treatment depending on what aspects of what kinds of behavior the psychotherapist sets out to modify. Looked at in this fashion, the possibility of specifying the particular kinds of operations to be performed on particular kinds of behavioral problems is greatly enhanced.

There is also much in this system that needs careful attention and modification. Better delineation of many of the concepts needs to be effected. Since anxiety is reputed to be such an important response event, the difficulties observed to accompany the use of this concept should be resolved.

Greater attention needs to be placed on the category of emotions in general; better classification of the kinds of emotional patterns is a necessary first step. Advantage should be taken of the basic work in sensation and perception in order to improve the representation of this set of events and the way in which they operate and affect other sets of behaviors. In basic outline, the system has much to recommend it. However, a greater degree of specification is undoubtedly needed in each of its parts.

The greatest single lack in this point of view is an adequate set of principles by which to account for the precise manner in which different kinds of responses become related to situations and to other sets of responses and thereby form into patterns, namely, a theory of learning and therapeutic procedures based on such a theory. Sullivan knew this to be an important weakness and he attempted to repair it in spite of the fact that he had no formal training in the psychology of learning. His observations about learning are interesting, but, of course, they are extremely limited, as one might expect from the position of the naturalistic observer on the one hand and the armchair thinker on the other. The detailed study of the processes of learning is a problem for the laboratory and the experimental method. Sullivan was perhaps useful in joining the chorus of voices which emphasizes the importance to human behavior in general, and psychotherapy in particular, of the complex learning which entails awareness and the verbal symbolic processes. He, like others, complained that the study of the automatic acquisition of motoric and glandular responses without awareness was an inadequate base from which to seek to account for the complexities of human behavior and the phenomena of individual verbal psychotherapy.

Section III

A Comparative Analysis

Chapter 15

The Development

of Normal Behavior

Ten such major systems of verbal psychotherapy as we have examined in varying detail are certain to have their commonalities and differences. In this final section of the book, we shall address ourselves to these elements. Some students and "eclectics" have remarked that all therapy theories stress essentially the same things, while others have commented that comparison seems futile, if not impossible, because theories differ so much. Whether one elects to accent the similarities or the distinctions probably depends on which end of the telescope one selects for viewing. It is our conclusion that there are significant areas of agreement and disagreement, both of which we shall explore in the remaining chapters.[1]

[1] This conclusion is undoubtedly a function of the systems we chose to examine. A group could have been selected to accentuate commonalities (*e.g.* phenomenologists) or differences (*e.g.* Existentialists vs. Wolpe). Our criteria for selection were presented in the preface.

Of course, there are literally hundreds of ways in which the systems might be compared, and not all of these can be considered. Readers will have theoretical interests of their own and may be desirous of making additional comparisons. We hope they will find our analyses helpful in facilitating such efforts.

GENERAL SIMILARITIES AND DIFFERENCES

Personal Background

It is impressive that all of these theorists represent West European and American culture and are primarily of Anglo-Saxon background. None arise from the cultures of Asia, Scandinavia, Africa, the Near East, or South America. In the most general sense, therefore, all the systems have much in common, since they may reflect a view of man and an approach to the study of his behavior strongly influenced by the general themes of the Greco-Judaeo-Christian tradition. Therapy systems deriving from another tradition, such as that of the Asian cultures, might emerge with very different theories about human behavior and its treatment. This similarity in the personal background of the theorists suggests that the theories and the data upon which they are built may be somewhat culture-bound.

With the exception of Rank, Rogers, and Dollard and Miller, all of our theorists have been medically trained. It appears that few had formal training in theory construction or in research technique. This may account, in part, for some of the inadequacies encountered in the approaches to theorizing and for the frequent lack of attention to the problems of empirical validation. For the majority of these theorists, the principal methods of data gathering and verification were those of naturalistic observation.

With the exception of Neal Miller, all these theorists have been practicing therapists. Most of them have been employed in professional rather than academic or research settings, although many did participate in the training of other practitioners. These therapy theories have been developed largely by those regularly involved in trying to help patients, not by researchers or academicians.

Finally, it is our impression that there were important restrictions on the types of people each of the theorists characteristically treated. Most of them studied adults as opposed to children; disordered rather than healthy persons; neurotics rather than psychotics, criminals, or addicts; ambulatory rather than hospitalized patients; and probably persons drawn from the higher educational and socio-economic strata (Hollingshead and Redlich, 1958). Such restrictions limit the observational data and probably produce a biased view of human behavior, thereby placing limitations on the general applicability of the resultant theory.

Underlying Assumptions about the Nature of Man

A theorist's generalized image of man significantly influences the theories he develops. It determines what he considers important to study and therefore the kinds of behaviors he will seek to observe; the conditions he arranges and the procedures he selects for making his observations; and finally the concepts and propositions he develops from those observations. Few of the theorists were explicit about this issue, although the Existentialists gave it special emphasis. However, two general views about the nature of man appear to have been implicitly operative in most of the theories examined (Urban and Ford, 1962).

MAN AS A PILOT. Sometimes man is viewed as exercising control over his behavior and the situations he encounters. He pilots his craft through the sea of life, choosing his course from among those presented by the characteristics of his ship, the influences of the winds and waves present at the time, and the ports toward which he wishes to sail. He can be "responsible" for his own behavior.

Data emphasized. This view leads to an emphasis on the responses by which man appears to do his piloting. Awareness and acts of attending represent responses by which he obtains the raw data he needs for plotting his course. Different kinds of symbolic responses such as sensory images (simple percepts), judging, comparing, analyzing, choosing, and planning are used. Ways in which the individual evaluates data, both in terms of the external consequences likely to ensue and their potential effects on him, would be considered important. Conditions that might disrupt this pilot function—for example, negative affect—are emphasized. Situational events are de-emphasized, for it is the person's responses to them, that is, how he perceives and evaluates them, that is important. In addition, motor behavior tends to be ignored in such theories, as if setting the rudder were simple once the course has been chosen.

Observational settings and procedures. Since man is the only known organism capable of complicated patterns of symbolic thought and language, this view would lead one to restrict one's observations to human behavior. Since the data considered important are subjectively observable responses (r), such theorists adopt the vantage point of the subjective observer and minimize or actively reject that of the objective observer. They are interested in "phenomenal reality," not "objective reality." Therefore, they devise observational settings in which the person under study reports his observations of the important responses (for example, perceptions). Although such mediating responses might be revealed in other ways, for example, motor movements and physiological responses, verbal report is the most flexible and elaborate means, and thus two persons talking to one another constitute the basic observational paradigm. The therapist attempts to create conditions that avoid distortions and biases in such reports (a "relationship"), so that he can observe what the patient is attending to, the meanings he attributes to events, and how he perceives, thinks, and feels. Under such conditions, one might assume a high degree of correspondence between what the patient reports and what actually occurred, and therefore might tend to accept as accurate not only the patient's description of his present subjective responses, but also his recall of events in the immediate and the remote past.

Concepts and propositions. The "pilot" view assumes that subjectively observable responses (r) are of basic importance. Therefore, the concepts formed will represent such behaviors. Typical are self, experience, fictions, will. Situational events tend not to be involved in the concepts but are represented by the responses they elicit (for example, perceptions, ego functions). Although motor behavior tends to be ignored, it is implied in concepts representing the consequences such motor behavior is directed toward—such as, goals, maintenance, strivings for superiority. Also, since the patient's view of things is considered basic, there is a tendency to use his conceptual units in the fabric of the theory. Because subjectively observable responses (r) are emphasized, propositions will generally appear in the form of r-r laws; for example, incongruence of self and experience make the person vulnerable and lead to denial and distortion. Moreover, since the organizing and directing aspects of behavior are emphasized, one will usually find propositions about such functions as organismic evaluations, creative power, will, *Dasein* choosing. Propositions representing *S-r*, *S-R* or *R-r* relationships are seldom formulated.

The theories of Adler, Rank, Rogers, and the Existentialists generally have the characteristics we have been describing, and therefore we conclude that they are implicitly built largely upon a "pilot" view of man. Its most extreme form might be symbolized by Adler's enthusiastic statement to the effect that "anyone can do anything."

MAN AS A ROBOT. Another image of man is also implicit in several of the theories. In this view the automaticity of behavior is emphasized. Man's craft follows the currents in the sea of life. It is the direction of the wind, the power of the waves, the size of the ship's sail, and so forth that determine its direction. It only seems to be guided, but in reality it cannot help itself. Therefore, it is not responsible for its direction.

Data emphasized. This view leads to a study of the forces that push the ship around and to the characteristics of the ship, thereby making its course predictable. Physiological responses and energies, as well as situational events, which elicit behavior sequences, are considered basic (for example, urges, instincts, drives, stimuli). Rather than talking about goals, such theorists talk about the characteristics of events that determine in which direction behavior will proceed; they use concepts like cues and reinforcers. Responses in which the phenomenon of automaticity is more obvious tend to be emphasized (motoric, physiological, and emotional responses), and these tend to be objectively observable responses (R). In a sense, man is conceived of as something analogous to a programmed machine. Starting with given attributes, its programs are increased and become enormously elaborate via learning, but no matter how intricate it becomes, it is at base situationally determined. Control of human behavior is accomplished by situational control. If an operator could accomplish controlled manipulation of external events and their pattern of presentation, he could conceivably program and operate another person like a machine. Thus, situational events (S) and their manipulation are quite important in such theories. Responses such as awareness and thought tend to be deemphasized, because their participation is not considered crucial in automatic behavior sequences, although thoughts are considered to be automatically determined also.

Observational settings and procedures. This type of theory adopts the vantage point of the objective observer. What the patient says, as well as his physiological, motoric, and emotional behavior, are all data from which the therapist can infer the kinds of "programs" operating within the individual. The patient's verbalizations are not accepted as accurate representations of what is going on "inside," but as a basis for inference. Such theorists prefer observational settings in which they can manipulate situational events and observe their effects. Thus, they like to test their theories in experimental as well as clinical settings and are more willing to use observations of animal as well as human behavior, since they do not give thought responses the same central role in behavior. They are less concerned with arranging conditions to get accurate reports about subjective responses from patients than they are with arranging circumstances to elicit predictable responses in the patient—for example, systematic desensitization.

Concepts and propositions. The concepts developed reflect the emphasis on automaticity (such as habit and stimulus). Because the vantage point of the objective observer is adopted, it is the observer's conceptual units, rather than the patient's, which are likely to be used—for example, id, ego, superego. The propositions developed will include $R\text{-}r$, $S\text{-}r$, and $S\text{-}R$ laws as well as $r\text{-}r$ laws—for instance, any intense stimulus will elicit responses. Propositions about how behavior automatically becomes acquired, selective, and generalized have to be developed. Typical are reinforcement, reactive inhibition, generalization. Wolpe, Dollard and Miller, and Freud exemplify theorists for whom this image underlies at least part of their theories, in our judgment. Dollard and Miller's statement that their position about behavior acquisition and modification rests on the assumption of the "automatic and unconscious effects of reinforcement" exemplifies this view.

These two points of view can lead to different and quite important consequences. For example, Freud's emphasis on the unconscious (automatic) control of behavior resulting from childhood learnings powerfully contributed to a shift from emphasis on punishment—people responsible for their behavior must face the consequences—to rehabilitation—they are the victims of their childhood and must be retrained.

Both Are Needed

Neither of these images of man have appeared in any of the ten systems in pure form. All agree that behavior is characterized both by automaticity and by choice making: man is both "robot" and "pilot."

He not only responds "unconsciously," but he also "controls and directs" himself in accord with situational demands. Although agreement exists in principle, however, the theorists differ markedly in their emphasis on automaticity and choice making, as we have tried to illustrate in the preceding discussion.

It is our conclusion that an overemphasis of either alternative will lead to serious theoretical weaknesses. Excessive emphasis on the "pilot" image omits reference to and incorporation of the many facts established about physiological, motoric, and glandular responses, and their more complex organization into emotional patterns—something of immediate and direct relevance to psychotherapy. It neglects the many studies of behavior where automaticity is typical, such as conditioning phenomena and reinforcement procedures, which are especially effective with emotional responses. Exclusive emphasis upon the "robot" features of man leads to corresponding deficiencies. It can lead to a restriction of attention to those behaviors easily observed and manipulated, in which automaticity is typical. It may lead to erroneous generalizations from observations on one species to another, as from rats or pigeons to man, or from one response realm to another. Thus, one may assume prematurely that the laws that govern disc pecking, lever pushing, or maze running (all motoric behaviors) will apply equally to verbal and conceptual behaviors.

We believe more rapid progress will follow from assuming that behavior is both automatic and consciously determined, along with adopting both the corresponding subjective and objective vantage points of observation, thereby avoiding the pitfall of ignoring significant data. The question then becomes: Which kinds of behaviors function according to which laws?

General Characteristics of Concepts and Propositions

SIZE OF CONCEPT UNITS. As a group, our theorists have generally concentrated on the building blocks of their theory, developing concepts to represent groups of events or behavioral units. There is correspondingly less attention placed upon the task of developing propositions specifying how the different behavioral units become interrelated with one another and can be modified. Moreover, for most of the systems the concepts employed are typically large and inclusive (that is, molar). As we observed in Section I, such concepts have their uses, but much of their value is lost if they are not clearly related to lower-order concepts and observable events. Many of these theories suffer from that defect. Some theorists such as Dollard and Miller use one concept, but use it in such a way that it can encompass any size unit with any kind of content, for example, response. This seems to us a somewhat undesirable procedure, at least at the present stage of theory. It tends to obscure major differences between different kinds of behavior, for instance, an eye blink on the one hand and Adler's all inclusive life style on the other.

The size of the conceptual units chosen may have something to do with the tendency to develop a limited number of propositional statements. By treating large amounts and varieties of behavior occurring over extended periods of time as a single unit, such as Freud's ego or Rogers' self-concept, one tends to obscure the many interrelationships that develop and change among the kinds of events within that unit. Similarly, the extensive use of large molar units may be one reason for a lack of clear specification of treatment procedures. It is difficult to specify procedures for changing an individual's superego or life style, but somewhat easier to discuss changing a person's hatred toward himself.

CONTENT OF CONCEPTS. All the theorists acknowledge the operation of the three general classes of events: situational events (S), objectively observable responses (R), and subjectively observable responses (r). They differ widely, however, in the extent to which each is included in their concepts. Some (Dollard and Miller, Sullivan, Ego-Analysts, Wolpe) use situational events extensively in their theorizing, while others (Adler, Rogers, Rank) de-emphasize such events to such an extent that they are virtually absent in their conceptions about behavior. Some of the reasons for these differing emphases were discussed earlier. In the face of all the evidence of the situational dependence of behavior, however, it seems doubtful to us that a fully adequate theory can be developed without a detailed study of situational events and their relationship to behavior.

Few of these theorists make significant use of objectively observable responses (R) in their theorizing. The only subclass of responses in this group given much attention is speech (for example, Sullivan). But even here, most of the writers theorize about thoughts, but not about speech and its connections with thoughts. Since it is objectively observable behavior, along with the situational conditions under which it occurs, that provides the data for inferring the existence and operation of subjectively observable responses (r), lack of careful attention to this category of responses is a serious weakness.

Conceptually, the widest source of agreement among all ten theorists lies in their emphasis on subjectively observable responses (r) as the most important category of behavior. For many of them, the important *initiators* of behavior are responses which fall in this group. All of them consider *affective* responses, particularly negative ones, as crucial, especially in behavior disorder. All of them emphasize the responses of *awareness* and *thought* and their role in both disordered and healthy behavior, although the role given them varies considerably. If these theorists are right, we can never have a good science of human behavior until such responses as awareness, thoughts, feelings, perceptions, and value judgments are studied carefully and useful propositions about how they may be inferred and how they operate are made explicit and systematic.

This may be one of the reasons experimental psychology so far has had a limited impact on therapy theory. Until recently the responses considered most important by therapy theorists were not those to which researchers were devoting their primary efforts. What distinguishes "personality theory" from other "behavior theories" is the emphasis on subjectively observable responses and response content. Personality theories are largely theories about subjectively observable responses!

CHARACTERISTICS OF PROPOSITIONS. If therapy theorists could make one request of their research colleagues, it would undoubtedly be: "Please help us by studying and delineating the acquisition and operation of these crucial kinds of responses." Significant research leads may be found in these theories. For example, are such different kinds of responses as thoughts and motor activity acquired and modified according to the same principles (Dollard and Miller, Wolpe), or are there different principles governing the learning and modification of different responses (ego-analysts—memory traces are established when an experience attracts sufficient attention cathexis)? Most psychological learning theories develop their principles through a study of motoric and physiological responses of animals in a variety of situational contexts. By contrast, research on verbal learning reported in psychological literature seldom refers to the same principles. Most research on learning has been contrived to rule out awareness as a factor, yet it is precisely this response to which most therapy theorists give central emphasis. If psychotherapeutic modification occurs through a process of learning, explication of the issues just raised is essential for the formulation of more effective therapeutic techniques.

Not only have these therapy theorists been more successful in developing concepts about behavior than propositions about how it works, but also the propositions they have developed are typically formal rather than empirical. It seems likely that deficiencies in the propositional aspects of these systems are directly related to the nature of the concepts developed. If one's concepts represent high-order abstractions about concrete behavior, the statements by which one concept is related to another will necessarily be in the nature of a formal proposition: for example, the ego strives to control the id and superego. Such statements, in the absence of more primary empirical propositions, are open to the same hazards and limitations that characterize concepts that are not effectively tied to some observational base. Moreover, the larger and more inclusive the concepts one employs, the fewer the propositional statements needed to account for the interrelationships. This may be a second reason for the relative paucity in the number of such statements.

The emphasis on the subjectively observable events (r) by some theorists would naturally lead them to construct propositions of the form r-r and to neglect the development of other important types of statements such as S-r, S-R, and R-r. This is a general characteristic of most of these ten theories. Finally, although some theorists (Adler, Rank) frankly espoused an idiographic point of view, all the systems developed a set of propositions considered to have general validity and, thus, all built from a nomothetic base.

THE DEVELOPMENT OF NORMAL BEHAVIOR

Innate Characteristics

The ten systems differ in the extent to which assumptions concerning innate behavioral attributes have been made explicit. Some (for example, Horney) openly ignored them because "they can't be changed anyhow"; others (Sullivan, the Existentialists) have considered specification of the "nature of man" essential. Typically, each theorist tended to emphasize some characteristics and to ignore others. For example, Sullivan discussed many kinds of innate responses, whereas Dollard and Miller emphasized the innate principles by which response acquisition and modification occurred and devoted less emphasis to response content.

Both the different kinds of responses of which the individual is innately capable, and the built-in principles by which behavior operates are the building blocks from which complicated adult behavior patterns become constructed. All discussions of normal behavior, disorder, and treatment have implicit within them assumptions about innate behavioral principles and characteristics. Those systems that do not carefully explicate these in detail do not lend themselves to evaluation, and they should be subject to empirical verification. Untenable propositions can arise from inaccurate, excessively limited, or culture-bound assumptions about the way the human organism is innately built to function. This is particularly likely to be true of theories that depend entirely on subjectively observable response events (r).

The systems of Sullivan and the Ego-Analysts have made the most extensive attempt to meet this requirement of an adequate system, while the formulations of Horney and Rank are the most inadequate in this regard. It seems clear that therapy systems should take advantage of the information in developmental psychology and its related literature—particularly that which focuses on infancy and early childhood—for more adequate data about innate behavioral characteristics and the evidence concerning maturation. It is too easy for a theorist who depends on observation of troubled adults to interpret learned behaviors, which occur with high frequency, as innate. Most of the theories examined are built primarily on such data and may contain such errors.

Kinds of Concepts and Propositions

Of the response classes discussed in Chapter 2, these theorists unanimously emphasize innate subjectively observable (r) and unobservable (r_i) responses. Innate objectively observable responses (R) receive scant attention, with Sullivan and the Ego-Analysts showing more interest in them than the others. Similarly, situational events (S) are given minimal treatment and are usually represented by concepts involving the individual's responses to such events (for example, perception).[2]

[2] The question of whether there is a reality independent of one's perception of it represents a controversy of long standing. By proposing classes of situational events independent of responses, we are obviously assuming the theoretical and practical importance of recognizing the existence of a reality independent of one's perceptions. Simpson (1963) puts this question in evolutionary perspective.

Notable exceptions are the Existentialists, who have tried, though awkwardly, we think, to make them (S) an integral part of their conceptual framework; and Sullivan, Freud (cathexis, oedipal complex, reality principle), Dollard and Miller (stimuli), and Horney with her cultural emphasis also gave them varying degrees of consideration. Even here, attention was largely restricted to one category, the behavior of other people. If behavior is always a function of the situations under which it occurs, and if inferences about subjectively observable responses are heavily dependent on the situational context (Ranck, 1961), careful study of the interrelationships among various kinds of situations and responses is fundamental. The literature of sensory, social, and developmental psychology should provide a relevant starting point.

Among all the response possibilities, affect (r), awareness and attention (r), the capacity for thought, including perceptual identification (r), and biological or psychological energies (r) are emphasized by almost all the theorists.

Affects

Affects (r) are given the status of responses, although some (for example, Freud) suggested they might be simply the conscious manifestation of some biological or psychological energy. They are proposed to function both as important elicitors of behavior sequences and as behavioral consequents to be sought or avoided. Positive and negative affect are proposed to function somewhat differently.

POSITIVE AFFECTS. Generally, the ten theorists give far less attention to these than to negative affects. This may be an instance in which the source of data influenced theory construction, since the empirical base for most of the theories is the behavior of troubled people in therapy where negative affect is a salient feature. Although all ten mention positive affect in their case discussions, only Adler (social interest), the Existentialists (love), Rogers (innate valuing process), and perhaps Freud (eros and libido) give it a fundamental place in their theories. Others (for example, Sullivan, Horney) refer to satisfaction as a "pleasurable" response and may be thinking of some kind of positive affect, but this is confused by the use of the same term to refer to the termination of noxious events as well. Several (Adler, Horney, Rogers, Sullivan) emphasize the importance of loving, affectionate behavior by other people in the individual's development, but as situational events. The limited number of concept labels for positive affect (such as love, tenderness, affection) are in contrast to the great number suggested for its opposite, negative affect.

There is considerable agreement about some very general propositions concerning the operation of positive affect. As the term positive connotes, it is generally considered to be constructive and pleasurable. As an elicitor, it initiates "approach" behaviors, a seeking of new kinds of stimulation and experience, and friendly approaches to other people (for example, Adler, Sullivan, Horney, the Existentialists, Rogers). As a consequence, it serves as a "goal," and individuals may direct their behavior toward arousing positive affect in themselves (for example, satisfaction—Horney, Sullivan; positive self-regard—Rogers). Freud's usage involves these characteristics, but simultaneously he makes positive affect a manifestation of libido or the sexual instinct, psychological energies which the individual must learn to struggle with and control. This somewhat contradictory conception may result from his relating love to sex, an equation frequent in Western society but perhaps an erroneous one.

Positive affects are important innate responses according to these systems, and we believe this to be correct. It may well be one of the essential cornerstones for the development of healthy behavior. Unfortunately, the kinds of positive affect which occur, their possible derivatives, and the propositions by which they function are not yet well explicated. The discipline of psychology has also generally ignored this class of response as a recent review of research on motivation (Hall, 1961) discloses, with the notable exception of Harlow's research on monkey love (1958). Important advances in theory would result from careful analysis of the kinds of positive affect that exist and the manner in which they function, analogous to the extensive theorizing and research about fear which has been so productive during the last few decades. Studies of infants and small children, as well as monkeys, would be a useful starting point.

NEGATIVE AFFECTS. All theorists considered these to be basic and gave them extended consideration. Fear or anxiety are unanimously emphasized and generally considered to be the same kind of response, although some (for example, Sullivan) have tried unsuccessfully to distinguish between the two. Anger is also given primary status by some (for example, Freud). A variety of other negative affects, such as guilt, disgust, revulsion, terror, rage, and dread are mentioned, but careful distinctions are not made as to whether each is innately different or whether some are intense degrees or learned derivatives of others.

There is considerable agreement that anxiety may be innately elicited by intense bodily disturbances (for example, tissue damage, sudden dropping, pain), response conflict (for example, Rank, Rogers), and situations of "threat" or "danger" (for example, Rogers). There is almost complete agreement that it innately elicits response sequences directed at its termination, and that when excessively intense it may lead to restriction and disorganization and may interfere with other behaviors. It is also proposed that when it occurs consequent to a behavior sequence, it is innately avoided. Thus, anxiety leading to avoidance is a fundamental proposition in most of these theories. Extensive analyses of other negative affects were not made, although some (Dollard and Miller) suggested they might well function in the same general fashion.

Negative affect undoubtedly received extensive consideration because of its central role in behavior disorder. These hypotheses concerning the innate fear sequence nicely exemplify the provocative hypotheses researchers may find in therapy theories. Research in recent years has substantially verified the ideas about anxiety and its operation first developed by therapy theorists nearly 50 years ago. By the same token, therapy theorists should take advantage of the important research literature on fear. It appears that the experimental study of the concept of fear provides a model for similar analyses of other negative affects. Researchers can expose subjects to disgusting or guilt-producing situations as well as fearful ones. It may also be important to determine whether the response of pain is similar to these negative affects or whether it is sufficiently different to require its own distinctive sets of propositions.

Awareness and Attention

All ten theories consider these phenomena of fundamental importance. Two (Dollard and Miller, and Wolpe) explicitly exclude it from their theoretical formulations about learning but introduce it in discussions of behavior disorder and treatment. By contrast, Rapaport felt it sufficiently important that he began to develop a theory of learning with awareness. These theorists generally treat it as another kind of response: the act of attending (Freud), stopping thinking (Dollard and Miller), and "inattending" (Sullivan). Although some

treat the response of attending and the content of awareness as one—
for example, thoughts define awareness (Dollard and Miller)—more
prefer to separate the two.

As a response it may or may not be associated with other responses,
and thus sensations, feelings, and thoughts may occur independent
of awareness. Some (for example, Freud) think of it as a constantly
active response phenomenon becoming related to one kind of response
after another (for example, visual sensations, affects, kinesthetic sensations). There is considerable agreement about an innate fear-atten-
tion sequence. The individual innately avoids attending to events
that would evoke fear if he were to become aware of them—for instance,
fear leading to repression (Freud, Dollard and Miller). The Existentialists speak of awareness as having certain dimensions or attributes, such
as temporality and spatiality.

We think the unanimous agreement among these theorists concerning the importance of this set of responses indicates that it is a necessary cornerstone of any adequate theory of human behavior and therapy. Therapy theorists' proposals as to why and how one becomes
unaware need to be supplemented by equally extensive analyses of
why and how one becomes aware. Unfortunately the basic discipline
of psychology has insufficient research on which to build at this time,
although papers about attention and awareness are appearing with
increasing frequency, and the research on activation, vigilance, set,
and the like may be helpful (Gagné, 1962; Deutsch and Deutsch, 1963).
Careful analysis and empirical study of attention and awareness probably would result in another basic contribution to psychological theory, especially to learning theory. A significant point of departure
might be to study the conditions under which habits of attending and
inattending are learned and come to be modified. Such findings could
be of considerable value to therapists.

Thoughts

The innate capacity for thought is one of the most important characteristics of human behavior, according to these theorists. There is
general agreement that individuals are innately capable of two major
types of thinking: imagistic (sensory, primarily visual) and verbal or
symbolic. Some (for example, Freud and Sullivan) propose that different sets of laws govern these two different types of thought. The
former is considered more primitive, infantile, and emotionally de-

termined; the latter is considered more flexible, adaptive, and situationally oriented.

Many theorists concur in proposing that some kind of thought responses begin early in infancy and constantly recur thereafter. Some (for example, Adler, Horney, Rogers) seem to attribute fairly intricate judgments and evaluative thoughts to the infant. We are doubtful that infants can judge themselves to be inferior (Adler) or make evaluative judgments about the consequences of their behavior (Rogers). We suspect that such hypotheses developed partly because the theorists saw such judgments occur with great frequency among their adult patients, were impressed with their apparent universality, and inferred that there must be something innate or "instinctual" about such behavior. Of course, this is a possibility, but we suspect it exemplifies the kind of theoretical error that may result when one builds behavior theory on the restricted base of observations about adult therapy patients.

Most agree that it is the capacity for thought that is innate, and that the content of thought is learned, as are specific habits of thinking. We shall return to this category of response at several junctures in this section.

Biological or Psychological Energies or Deficits

Several systems employ some concept to refer to intervening events of a physiological nature, which are inferential but which are proposed to be innate and important antecedents to other behaviors. The concept of drive is used frequently, although terms such as need (Sullivan) and impulse (Rank) were also used. Collectively they refer to innate organic rhythms or periodic physiological deficits of the body, such as hunger, thirst, sexual appetites, and the like, which the individual must alleviate to maintain comfort and perhaps life. All ten theorists acknowledge the existence of such deficits, but several (for example, Rogers, Adler, the Existentialists) do not attempt to distinguish among them or to make them a basic theoretical concept.

The concept of drive is an instance of the way the same concept label may be used to represent quite different phenomena and, therefore, lead to confusion. For Freud and the Ego-Analysts, it referred to some kind of psychological energy (for instance libido) which might be consequent to a biological condition. Dollard and Miller used it to refer to intensity of the physiological events themselves, while Wolpe used it to refer to excitation of neurones. Although organic rhythms and physiological responses are clearly important innate factors, how they operate remains unclear despite extensive research (Hall, 1961).

Other Response Attributes

In general, response attributes other than kind, such as intensity, duration, and frequency, were not emphasized extensively by the theorists. Of this group, more was written about intensity than any other. Certain kinds of responses (such as emotions, drives, biological, psychological, or neural energies) are said to vary innately in terms of intensity or quantity, and this fact has important consequences in the development of both healthy and disordered behavior.

Propositions

A number of innate principles are proposed by these theorists and seem to be aimed at answering several questions.

WHY DOES BEHAVIOR OCCUR? There appear to be four general points of view. First, there is the assumption that behavior sequences are started by some kind of innate response events (for example, Freud, Rank, Rogers). From this point of view, all behavior is propelled from "inside," although such theorists differ considerably in their proposals as to the kind, variety, and functions of such innate elicitors.[3] Some assume one major instigator of all behavior (for instance, Adler—striv-

[3] Some proposals seem to us to represent a serious theoretical error. Rank's "impulses" toward "independence" and "dependence" are instructive examples. His theories are based primarily on observation of adult therapy patients. We suspect he noted that patients alternately behaved in a dependent, submissive, helpless way, and in an assertive, independent, self-directing manner. To account for these observed consistencies, he apparently assumed the existence of an innate "impulse" to behave that way. We suspect Horney with her final position regarding "self-realization" and Rogers with his notion of "enhancement" may have committed the same type of error, because these concepts seem clearly to imply value judgments, which it is hard for us to imagine as being characteristic of infants. Rogers may be referring to something like the response-arousal learning phenomena, but if so it is not clear, and a re-examination of that concept might improve his theory. We do not question that such behavior patterns exist and are significant. It is the assumption of an innate tendency to behave that way which is highly questionable and probably tautological, as exemplified by the instinct theories popular in psychology in the 1910's.

ing for superiority; Rogers—actualizing tendency; Horney—central force).

Second, Adler, Horney, and Sullivan agreed that some behavior seemed to have innate response antecedents, but they argued that much of behavior was elicited by situational events, primarily the behaviors of other people. They all proposed that situational events elicited negative affect (anxiety, basic anxiety, feelings of inferiority), and this in turn elicited an extended behavior sequence aimed at terminating the negative affect.

The Ego-Analysts, Wolpe, and Dollard and Miller go still further. In effect, they propose that behavior may be elicited by any kind of event if it becomes sufficiently distinctive or intense. Not only can physiological responses and the behavior of other people serve to elicit behavior, but so can other situational events, as well as learned responses such as thoughts. There is considerable evidence to support this position, but it leads to a number of sticky problems. For example, why does the same intensity of an event produce behavior on one occasion and not another? How can one identify this attribute of intensity?

Finally, the Existentialists propose that it is an attribute of human life that behavior is constantly occurring. Like Kelly (1955), they see no need to assume something to get behavior started; no "motor" is required. Their deceptively simple formulation has considerable appeal. However, it trades one question for another. Instead of asking "What starts behavior sequences?" they must ask "What causes variations in the content of the stream of behavior?" Clearly, the content of behavior is not always the same, and somehow we must account for its selectivity. Dollard and Miller, for example, proposed an energizer (drive) and a selective influence (cue). This fourth position states that no concept of energizing is needed, but the Existentialists still need to account for the selective influence, for the occurrence of one pattern of behavior rather than another under particular conditions.

In our opinion neither these systems, nor psychology in general, has yet evolved a satisfactory formulation of this most challenging problem of human behavior. We suspect the notions of motivation extant in experimental psychology are limited because research has focused primarily on trying to account for the occurrence of motoric and physiological responses. For example, in his review, Hall (1961) justifies the use of motivational concepts to predict something about "activity level," "direction of activity," and "persistence" in attempting to reach a "goal object." But note that the motorically quiescent animal is not "unmotivated," but is simply "motivated" to do something different from what the experimenter sought to produce.

CHOICE. It seems to us fruitful to assume that at any given point in time several "motives" or behavior elicitors are operative. The behavioral motor is always running. A person may be simultaneously too hot, hungry, thirsty, tired, frightened, and confronted with demands from other people to do productive work. If simultaneous operation of several motives is the typical circumstance, what determines which behaviors ensue? Several of these theorists agree that the crucial factors are: What is the individual attending to? Which behavioral opportunities does he recognize as possibilities? Which does he choose? (Existentialists, Adler, Rank, Rogers). The innate capacity to make choices is considered a fundamental human attribute by such theorists, something which may override urgent physiological demands. For example, a person may choose to undergo physical pain to protect his honor rather than have the satisfaction of eating. Others (such as Freud, Dollard and Miller) propose that the predominating behavior depends simply on whichever "motive" is the strongest. We suspect that a more adequate theory would represent some combination of these two and would encourage researchers to contrive situations in which several "triggers" to behavior are operative and several response possibilities exist, so as to study the relationship between behavior elicitors and choice-making behavior.

What Terminates Behavior Sequences?

There appear to be two general positions among these theorists on this question. For some (for example, Dollard and Miller, Freud, Wolpe) all behavior is innately aimed at the avoidance of, termination of, or reduction in intensity of noxious, discomforting, or painful events. Two kinds of noxious events are emphasized. The first are responses aroused by physiological deficits or biological functioning, such as hunger and sex. The second are negative affective responses, notably fear or anxiety.

Another group of theorists (for instance Adler, Horney, Sullivan, Ego-Analysts, Existentialists) acknowledges this principle but adds a second. It proposes that much behavior has as its objective the arousal of certain responses. It speaks of satisfaction, accomplishment, enhancement, creativity, self-realization, and the exercise of capabilities.

This is an important difference. If one takes the first position, all of man's behavior must be interpreted as avoidant behavior. One orbits a satellite, creates a painting, or writes a book to ease some pain or fear. The Freudian attempts to interpret all behavior as a manifestation of sexual energy (libido) or the aggressive instinct are illustrative. It is implied that the optimal condition is a state of quiescence or equilibrium, and Freud's death instinct exemplifies this way of thinking at its logical extreme.

The second group of theorists seems to have anticipated recent developments in experimental psychology which suggest that some response sequences are directed toward the arousal of responses rather than their termination. People seek to upset the state of equilibrium (boredom?) as much as to maintain it. If both response arousal and response termination can terminate sequences and contribute to learning, it would appear that an important stream of research should be devoted to determining which kinds of responses function in which way, and under what circumstances. It is important to note that apparently both principles usually require some situational consequences for their operation. It appears that response-response interrelationships are usually inadequate by themselves to achieve the end result.

Innate Organizing Principles

Most of these theorists propose that a further innate characteristic of humans is that their behaviors are organized (for example, control or bind excitation—Freud; maintain equilibrium—Freud, Hartmann; organize experience and resolve discrepancies—Rogers; creative power —Adler; will—Rank). These theorists could have arrived at such a proposition in several ways. They may have looked at complicated and highly organized adult behavior and made the error of assuming an innate tendency to organize. On the other hand, they may have identified a fundamental innate attribute. Some support for the latter view might be found in the research of Gestalt psychologists and evidence about sensory functioning. Certainly, many psychotherapists have reported that the feeling of losing behavioral control or "falling apart" is often terrifying to patients (for example, Horney). There is no doubt that adult behavior is highly organized and systematized. This seems to us to be a theoretical issue of basic importance, one which needs considerable thought and research. We need to know not only whether there are such innate principles but also whether they pre-dispose everyone to organize certain aspects of their behavior in par-ticular ways (for example, Rogers' ideas about the self-concept).

CONSISTENCY AND VARIABILITY. Dollard and Miller and Wolpe utilize explicit principles to deal with issues that were only implicit in the other theories. Why do old responses occur to new situations? Why do new responses occur to old situations? How do responses cease to occur once they have been learned? Their answers to the first two questions utilize the concept of generalization. To the first question, they an-swer that the new situation must somehow be similar to old situations in which the response was learned. To the second question, they answer that the new response must be similar to old responses learned in that situation. The effects generalize along lines of similarity. How-ever, they do not tell us how to determine the attribute of similarity. The phenomenologist would argue that what represents similarity for one individual would not do so for another. Although the phenomena of stimulus and response generalization are well established, research should be devoted to the question of what conditions determine the attributes of situations and responses along which generalization will take place. For example, does generalization take place more readily along some attributes than others? Do special responses such as aware-ness or unawareness play an important role in generalization?

UNLEARNING. Finally, Dollard and Miller propose that responses stop occurring either because of disuse or ineffectiveness in producing re-sponse termination. Others (for example, Rogers) suggest that response conflict may account for certain responses ceasing to occur. If there are innate principles governing the unlearning of responses, these theorists did not discover them. They had surprisingly little to say about the problem, despite the fact that much of therapy is focused on problems of "unlearning."

Innate Behavior Patterns and Sequences

This is a topic that most of these theorists acknowledged and then ignored, with the possible exception of the fear sequence discussed earlier. Sullivan (developmental stages), Freud (psychosexual stages), and the Ego-Analysts (maturation of sensory or motor apparatuses) were the only ones to give much attention to this question. These agree that there are definite maturational sequences which provide the basis for certain learnings at given ages and which make certain categories of situational events more crucial at one age than another. They suggest that certain patterns of adult behaviors may be the consequent of the interaction of situational influences at particular points in the innate maturational sequences. The phenomena of imprinting (Lorenz, 1952 and Jaynes, 1958) and some clinical examples (Eisen, 1962) lend support to this idea. Such a view suggests that certain patterns of behavior might be almost impossible to modify or to develop in adults because the necessary learnings did not occur at the critical maturational stages.

Comments

The innate characteristics are the building blocks on which all the complicated patterns of human behavior must develop. It is our conclusion that therapy theorists considered as a group have given far too little attention to this theoretical base. Moreover, what has been proposed appears to be largely a set of inferences from observations of a highly restricted sample of human behavior—adult therapy patients. Relatively little use seems to have been made of other types of observations (from zoology, physiology, genetics, endocrinology, perception, sensation, developmental and physiological psychology). Too often the error appears to have been made of observing complex patterns of adult behavior and imputing some innate tendency of human behavior as the cause. Careful distinctions between what is innate and how this influences future learning will help produce a more effective therapy theory.

LEARNED CHARACTERISTICS OF NORMAL DEVELOPMENT

The ten theorists varied considerably in terms of the amount of attention given to the process of normal development. Without exception they all regard it as the crucial antecedent to the adult behavior with which their theories were concerned, even though this was not always reflected in the extent to which they tried to account for the way it comes about. Thus, there are several theorists who paid virtually no attention to normal development at all (Rank and the Existentialists); others gave it only scant treatment (Horney). Still others, notably Freud and Sullivan, recognized the importance of a detailed study of the development of normal behavior and devoted extensive effort to the task.

The Outcomes of Learnea Development

In spite of their differing emphases, however, is it possible to discern any common attributes amongst this group of theorists as to what it is that they think becomes learned? We are concerned here with the products of learning as distinguished from the process by which they come about, a topic we shall discuss later.

They generally agree that *there are two principal outcomes to the process of learning:* (1) *learning serves to develop combinations of responses, derived from innate capabilities, into recurrent, efficient, and stable patterns, and chains; and* (2) *learning serves to extend and to modify the range of situations to which responses and patterns occur.*

All agree that adults are characterized by complex organizations of responses, occurring in intricate patterns and chains. For example, Freud emphasized that sets of instrumental responses developed in relation to intense physiological events or psychological energies, their function having been to terminate them. In addition, complicated "reaction formations" develop for mediating the interaction between these events on the one hand and the environment on the other. Rank spoke of patterns of behavior in relation to the basic conflict (dependence-independence). To Sullivan, the crucial sets of behaviors are the interpersonal dynamisms, patterns of response acquired in relation to other people. Horney, Adler, and Rogers as a group emphasize even more complex patterns and organizations of response (character, self, and style of life). Implicit in these systems is the notion that learning functions to form increasingly large behavioral arrangements, building on an innate base.

Similarly, all agree that the adults respond to an increasingly wide range of situations as a consequence of learning. Children come to fear other persons as well as immediate intense pain (Dollard and Miller); basic anxiety, learned in relation to the parents, becomes extended and occurs in relation to people in general (Horney); the growing child becomes exposed to and learns to relate to increasing numbers of people and things as he proceeds through the developmental stages (Sullivan).

Thus, there seems to be general agreement that the task of a developmental theory is to account for the way in which certain kinds of responses become intricately related to one another in broader and larger organizations of response, functioning to achieve particular consequents and occurring in relation to increasing ranges of situational events. With this statement of general consensus, we can proceed to exemplify its specific details.

The Relationship of Behavior Patterns to Other Events

We can begin with the most clearly evident aspect, that the adult comes to be characterized by increasingly complex patterns of response. We can ask the question: in relation to what do these patterns and sequences become acquired? As a group, these theorists propose that the patterns of response become acquired in relation to almost any kind of event, but three groupings are evident in their discussions: (1) *situational events*—the external world of objects and people; (2) *innate physiological events*—such as the response occurrences of hunger, fatigue, and sex; and (3) *other responses*—including those that are learned. Thus, Freud noted that the human person learned behaviors with which to reduce the intensity of instinctual drives as well as to control their expression in relation to the external world. The Ego-Analysts explicitly state that behavior is acquired in relationship to these three classes of events. The Existentialists stress three general types of behavior-situation patterns (*Umwelt, Mitwelt, Eigenwelt*), each of which relates to the three classes just listed. Wolpe regards behavior as successful if it results in a reduction of central neural excitation, avoids possible damage or deprivation, and results in satisfying sexual interactions and other interpersonal interrelationships.

Beneath this very general consensus, however, are wide differences in the relative emphasis placed on certain of these classes as opposed to others. For example, there is a group (Adler, Existentialists, Horney, and Sullivan) which proposes that the patterns of response to situational events are the most significant, and that the behavior of other people is the single most important subclass. For this group, the most important aspects of human behavior are the person's habitual patterns of interpersonal interaction. Sullivan and Horney go to the extent of saying that a person is to be described in terms of these habitual and enduring patterns of social interaction. The Existentialists also place primary emphasis upon man's relations with other men, through which his relationship with himself comes to exist.

All the theorists consider social responses of importance, but most do not emphasize them to this same extent. For example, Dollard and Miller regard the person as developing elaborate patterns and sequences of behavior which are specifically related to classes of situations, not just the interpersonal ones. Freud is noted for his emphasis on the innate response antecedents to behavior, but he, too, detailed some of the kinds of patterns acquired in relation to people—for example, the oedipal complex.

Most of the theorists emphasize two characteristics of interpersonal behavior that they consider to be crucial: the affective and evaluative response patterns directed toward the growing person. They say it makes a basic difference whether the child is responding to angry or loving persons, and whether significant people are evaluating the child as good or bad. Similarly, several theorists emphasize the affective, evaluative, and conceptual responses with which an individual learns to respond to his own behaviors. For example, Rank, Rogers, and Sullivan (self-concept, personification of the self) share the view that the responses a person learns to make to his own behavior become interrelated in patterns, and that these, in turn, become determinative of still further response patterns which come to be acquired. In Adler, for example, is the clear proposition that when the symbolic responses (fictions) are acquired, from then on the individual responds in terms of them—all subsequent behavior occurs in relation to these prior response events. Thus, there is considerable agreement that *the patterns of behavior which are of especial significance for personality and therapy theory are those affective, evaluative, and conceptual patterns that have been acquired in relation to* (1) *the behavior of other people, and* (2) *the behavior of oneself.*

The Composition of Learned Patterns of Behavior

Is there any agreement among the theorists as to what goes to make up these patterns of response? In very general terms, all implicitly, and some explicitly, agree that *such patterns of behavior represent organizations of more primary response-components: sensations, perceptions, feelings, thoughts, and motoric and instrumental responses.* For example, Sullivan, in discussing dynamisms, went to some pains to indicate explicitly that they were composed of arrangements of *all*

the more primary response units. However, the theorists more frequently restrict their emphasis to three classes of response, attention
or awareness, thought, and affect, in their characterization of the most
significant patterns. Thus, Adler's concept of feelings of inferiority
and Horney's notion of basic anxiety are two examples of the importance attached to certain types of thought and the affect accompanying
them. Similarly, the concepts of repression, the unconscious, stopping
thinking, and ego, to cite a few examples, all represent combinations
of awareness and thought (for example, perceptions).

Less often has this group of theorists concerned itself with the way
in which sensations, physiologic events, and motoric responses become
woven into the behavioral patterns. Even where such responses appear
to be emphasized (for example, Rogers' "organismic experience"), it
is the way the individual attends to, thinks, and feels about them—
"perceives" them—which is primary. Seldom are the instrumental
functions of such responses emphasized, although the Ego-Analysts
(for example, sensory apparatuses) and Sullivan (for example, dynamisms, work) exemplify theorists who have formulated concepts stressing instrumental response-situation linkages.

It is tempting to suggest that this emphasis on awareness, thought,
and feeling, and the corresponding de-emphasis of other classes of
events, partly stems from the observational base from which many of
these theorists worked. Typically, patients do not go to a therapist for
help in developing their intellective skills or to acquire proficiency
in some motoric pattern. Nor do therapists assume it is appropriate
to deal with such problems. Moreover, therapists who deal primarily
with *reports about* events rather than arranging for direct observation
of extratherapy behavior might well be prone to emphasize the way
a person felt toward and thought about such events, as distinct from
how he actually behaved. There is ample evidence in psychology that
situational events powerfully affect behavior, but if verbal report is
the only data at hand, it is easy to emphasize the word, or thought,
rather than the event it represents. Motoric responses and skills are
very critical events, however, and have to do with the efficacy with
which a person negotiates his way through his daily life.

The same thing is true of physiological events and their effects on
behavior. A number of theorists gave attention to these as initiators
of behavior sequences, but subsequently paid little heed to the way
in which physiological functioning is affected by and in turn affects
other responses. This becomes even more obvious in the neglect of
the "somatic" aspects of behavior disorder. Again, Sullivan is a notable

exception to these remarks. He tried to weave observations about physiological functioning into his discussions of learning and development, attempting to show its importance in complex behavior patterns. Theorists who tend to ignore such responses (for example, Adler, Horney) acknowledge that they are important to human life but do not consider them particularly relevant to the problem of therapy. His habits of attending, thinking, and feeling are the fundamental things, for example, his "fictions" or "attitudes." A complete theory will not omit the obvious, and we are sure that physicians such as Adler and Horney did consider whether organic illness might be causing a patient's difficulties before initiating psychotherapy.

The Developmental Course

In what way does the acquisition of such patterns proceed over the course of development? There seem to be two general answers to this question among the theorists. On the one hand, one group seems to assert that the overall course of development from birth to adulthood is, in principle, the same. With the same major elements involved at each step of the way, the patterns are said to grow and develop by successive accretions over the course of time. In this group are placed Dollard and Miller and Wolpe, who propose that all responses are acquired in essentially the same fashion. The primary difference between the child and adult must lie in the various combinations of responses acquired and the degree of complexity achieved. These theorists have concerned themselves with the *how* of development, the way learning occurs rather than with what becomes learned. Thus, they have nomothetic principles of development, but none that have to do with the kinds of behavioral patterns that are successively acquired in the developmental process. Similarly, there are a few theorists, such as Adler and Horney, who conceive of a common overall process that goes on from birth to adulthood. These theorists also eclipse differences from age to age in the developmental process.

A second group of theorists (Freud, Ego-Analysts, Sullivan) argue, however, that the development of human behavior occurs in terms of stages. Different responses appear at different ages (Sullivan); the person is faced with different situations at different stages (Sullivan, Ego-Analysts); there are inherent sequences in behavior acquisition— one cannot acquire response *b* unless *a* has been previously developed (Ego-Analysts, Freud, Sullivan). As a group these theorists emphasize that certain kinds of linkages form into patterns at different ages. This group attempted to formulate nomothetic principles with respect to the content of behavior.

It goes without saying that a combination of these two approaches is the more complete: *propositions are needed by which to account not only for how patterns of response are acquired but also for which patterns become acquired in what order.* This will not be possible without a careful study of the process of development, with attention to both its maturational and its learned characteristics. Developmental psychology has already established significant findings in this regard, and therapy theory needs to take them into account.

Critical Stages in Development

Is any aspect of the developmental course considered to be more significant than others? A number of theorists have followed the lead of Freud, asserting that the basic characteristics of these patterns are laid down in the first 4–6 years of life and that, once established, such patterns become relatively stable for the remainder of the person's life (for example, Ego-Analysts, Adler and Horney). On the other hand, Sullivan asserted that every stage of development had its own significance. If faulty patterns of response become acquired, this can have occurred at many stages in development, both early and late. By the same token, mistakes occurring in the early formative years can become corrected and undone in later developmental epochs. Naturalistic observation would lead one to expect that both positions are to some degree tenable: *some enduring patterns may become established and remain relatively unchanged; others may be more readily altered by changes in the developmental course.* The formulation should not be in terms of either-or. We *need to devise research to establish which response patterns tend to become established and relatively immune to change, which are relatively susceptible to change, and the conditions under which each occurs.*

Degrees of Organization

Up to what level of complexity do such patterns obtain? Theorists differ remarkably in relation to this question. At one extreme is a theorist such as Adler, who proposed that everything was interrelated with everything else. It was his view that responses became organized into one large and inclusive pattern, the style of life. The person's entire behavioral repertoire became integrated, including those aspects which were implicit and unverbalized. Even apparent inconsistencies were seen to be parts of the overall organization.

Next in order are theorists such as Horney, Rogers, and the Existentialists, who assert that several large pieces of a person's repertoire become organized—modes of existence, attitudes toward people, self-concept. The individual is represented as composed of a few large patterns; a lack of correspondence between patterns is an antecedent to difficulty.

Of the systems examined in this volume, Wolpe's is probably one that, although thinking in terms of patterns, is conceptualizing them in the most restricted sense. Wolpe proposes that individuals develop "a recurring manner of response to a given stimulus situation," that patterns of response are relatively situation-specific. Conceivably one could have as many different patterns of response as there are distinctive situations. Wolpe also allows for somewhat larger or more extensive patterns, however, when he says that individuals can develop a generalized pattern of behavior if somewhat similar responses become habitual across different but comparable situations.

As usual, Sullivan seemed to include both points of view. He seemed to assert that behavior could be organized into large inclusive units which were general across many situations, or into small and restricted units which were relatively situation-specific; that individuals varied in the degree to which their behaviors integrated with one another. He proposed that a favorable outcome to the developmental process was one wherein most of the person's significant behavior became well integrated into an "orientation to living." But degrees of incoordination between behavior patterns were also possible, and at the other extreme one could have relative disorganization, which would represent a pathological condition.

These differences among the theorists correspond with a dispute that once was lively in academic psychology, the generality-specificity of behavior. The former position was espoused by Allport (1937), and he was engaged by several who argued for situational specificity (Hartshorne and May, 1928). Sullivan's answer would appear to be the more plausible: *patterns of response may be both general and specific.* Again, the question should be reformulated for the purposes of study. *Under what conditions can behavior be acquired so that it is situation-specific, or general across many situations? Are some kinds*

*of behavior more likely to remain situation-specific, while other kinds
are more likely to generalize,* such as fear? The literature on discrimination learning, generalization, and vigilance may be good starting
points, although the response realms investigated in such research
have been relatively limited.

Rules Governing the Formation of Patterns

Is there any agreement as to how these patterns become formed?
This question deals with how interrelationships among responses are
developed, and the answer seems to be that there is little consensus
about the precise details. This is because the theorists vary so in the
degree to which they attempt to represent the how of learning. There
are some, like Dollard and Miller and Wolpe, who devote much of
their writing about development to this kind of question; there are
others like Adler who failed to deal with the question at all. He
simply asserted that it happened—interrelationships do become formed
—and that it could come about in almost any fashion. *It is not enough,
however, to assert that responses become integrated, and that patterns
do occur. If one is going to change complex human behavior, one must
know what relationships are present in the patient's repertoire, and
what conditions one can establish to rearrange them.*

SITUATIONAL GENERALIZATION. Although little agreement occurs as to
the precise details, an underlying theme appears to be general to
nearly all the theorists. As a group they seem to employ the notion
of *learned generalization.* For example, Horney proposed that initial
interactions with specific people, such as parents, could produce a
pattern of behavior which she labeled basic anxiety. Later, it could
become related to the class of humans at large. Actually, she proposed
that it did characteristically generalize to people and could generalize
beyond that class to the classes of animals, objects, or perhaps to virtually all situational events (the world). Moreover, she proposed that
the more *intense* the response, the wider the range of generalization
that could be expected.

Similarly, Freud proposed that the responses of resistance and anger
acquired during the period of toilet training could generalize and
come to occur in relationship to other events as well. It was with
such a rationale that he viewed the development of the anal-retentive
character, or correspondingly the oral-incorporative or the oral-aggres-

sive character types. Examples could be chosen from each theorist, but these are sufficient to demonstrate the similarity with the standard conception of stimulus generalization in psychology, one which is explicitly employed in the systems of Wolpe and of Dollard and Miller.

RESPONSE GENERALIZATION. By the same token, many of the theorists are using what appears to be some form of the principle of response generalization. Adler proposed that the way a person perceived an event would influence the way he thought about it; Sullivan proposed that a person's conceptions of people would determine how he perceived their behavior on later occasions; Horney asserted that a person tended to develop values, interests, objectives, and opinions that were similar to and consistent with his primary conceptions and thoughts about events. Theorists who write in this fashion seem to be implicitly proposing that once certain responses are acquired, others *similar to it* will tend to occur. By such a principle, patterns could tend to develop across response realms as well as across classes of situations. Again, the theorists seem to vary as to the degree of generality which such patterns attain, that is, the extent to which response generalization tends to occur.

SYMBOLICALLY MEDIATED GENERALIZATION. Finally, a good number of these theorists place strong emphasis on the symbolic processes as mediating generalization. Freud might explain the fear of a young boy over being deprived of his baseball bat as a symbolic act of castration. The two events are rendered functionally equivalent by means of the symbolic associations the boy had acquired earlier. If the boy's conception of a bat was associated with the notion of penis, a fear of castration could be elicited by the loss of his bat. Similarly, Rogers and Adler assert that the significance of an event is determined by what it "means" to the person, or rather, the interpretation he places on it. The interpretation of a novel situation as one of threat would result in the occurrence of the responses which he would ordinarily employ in threatening types of situations. Thus, it can be demonstrated that a number of theorists have used this vehicle for describing some of the ways in which responses and situational events become related to one another.

Actually, the notion of generalization (stimulus-, response-, and verbally mediated) is more in the nature of a descriptive principle than an explanatory one. The term stimulus generalization, for example, refers to the observation that a response related to one situation is later recognized to have occurred in a second. It does not represent an explanation of why that comes about. Further, none of the theories examined, including those of Dollard and Miller and of Wolpe, have developed any principles that permit one to predict along which dimensions stimulus generalization will occur, to which responses response generalization will materialize, and by which one can determine the classes of situations which are likely to be rendered conceptually, or verbally, equivalent. Wolpe presents a procedure for determining on a *post hoc* basis which gradients of stimulus generalization happen to have been developed in a particular patient but no principles by which one can predict this occurrence in advance. This is one realm in which we think a new approach is needed, and the proposal by Prokasy and Hall (1963) that stimulus generalization may be a function of discriminant learning may be a promising lead.

DISCRIMINATION. Again with the exception of Dollard and Miller and Wolpe, the theorists as a group seem to have been much more impressed with the question of how responses generalize and become patterns than of how they become discriminated. When someone like Freud takes the toilet pattern and from that jumps to the possibility that the person develops an overall pattern of response to people and objects of an anal-retentive character, he is glossing over all kinds of complications in the learning process. Further, it would appear that the notion of generalization necessarily implies the operation of an opposite phenomenon, discrimination; otherwise, there would be an inevitable spread of responses across situations and a never-ending process of development into larger and larger patterns of behavior. The only possible outcome would be that conceptualized by Adler. Dollard and Miller propose that discriminant patterns are formed via verbal mediation. When situations are rendered distinct by being labeled in different fashion, different patterns of response will occur in relationship to them. This becomes an important technique in the practice of therapy when the therapist is dealing with a behavior pattern which, through generalization, is occurring in inappropriate fashion to a particular situation—for instance, transference phenomena.

The notion of discrimination is implicit in many of the other systems' discussions of technique when they deal with showing the patient the difference between one situation and another, breaking up the pattern of transference by explicating the distinction between the therapist and the patient's father and mother, or by calling the patient's attention to the contrast between the way he responded on one occasion and on another. Thus, it would appear that the concept of discrimination is implicit rather than explicit in many of these discussions of behavior, that it appears in the discussions of treatment procedures, but that it is importantly omitted in the analysis of the ways in which behavior is acquired in the first place. It is apparent that *careful delineation of the phenomena of generalization (situational, response, and verbally mediated) and discrimination are needed if one is to account for the sequential acquisition of patterns and sequences in the growing person.*

BEHAVIOR VARIABILITY. The concepts developed by these theorists emphasize the consistencies of human behavior (life style, modes of existence, attitudes, self-concept), and by contrast underemphasize the variability in behavior to the same specific situational context. Given the same sets of events, persons do not always respond in precisely the same fashion; it seems doubtful that patterns of response are always reproduced from occasion to occasion in exactly the same form. Variability in response is probably as much a property of behavior as is reliability and consistency. It is true that several theorists emphasize the individuality of behavior, but they are often emphasizing variability among people—each person is different—rather than within a person. Why does the same response not always occur to the same situation, and why does the same response occur to what appears to be an entirely different situation? Notions basic to such variability are apparent. Dollard and Miller speak of response hierarchies; Wolpe utilizes the concepts of reactive and conditioned inhibition, and several theorists emphasize choice behavior (Existentialists).

Kinds of Relationships between Events

Before we leave the discussion of the formation of interrelationships among events, a few comments should be made about the nature of the interconnections themselves. We are speaking here of the hyphen in *S-R, R-R,* and *r-r* connections, to use the manner of speaking employed by Miller. It has been traditional in psychology to view such interrelationships in terms of their temporal connection. Thus, the hyphen is often translated to mean "leads to" or "goes with." The relationship expressed by the symbols *S-R* would be rendered as: a

situation leads to a response. Similarly, when describing the relation-
ship between events occurring simultaneous in time, $\genfrac{}{}{0pt}{}{R}{R}$, the translation is rendered: R_1 goes with R_2. Both of these express the fact that
the major kind of interrelationship considered is a temporal one. But
is this the only kind of functional relationship that can be developed?
Implied in many of these theories is the notion that there is more
than one kind of "hook-up" possible, that different types of hyphens
occur. There is the suspicion, for example, that the interconnections
between perceptual responses and emotional ones are different in kind
from the "hooks" that become formed between thoughts and actions.
For example, Rogers and others propose that certain kinds of thoughts
perform some kind of organizing function distinct from the interrelationships formed between any other sets of responses. Although Rogers
does not try to explicate what this organizing relationship might be,
it seems evident that it is viewed as of a different order from other
kinds of functional relationships which are formed.

Some Primary Types of Response and Their Interrelationships

The special emphasis in these systems on the response classes of
thought, affect, and attention warrants additional discussion of the
kinds of functional relationships in which they may become involved.

THOUGHTS. There would appear to be a great deal of agreement that
*thoughts as a group of responses are not only extremely important
but also have a rather distinctive set of functions in human behavior
and play a central role in therapy theory.* In Adler's view, for example,
everything in behavior depends on the fictions a person has acquired;
Sullivan regarded symbolic activity as the primary feature of the
human. Rank, Adler, and the Ego-Analysts attribute to thought characteristics which no other type of human response shares, such as
guiding, directing, controlling, synthetic, organizing, and co-ordinat-
ing functions.

When one studies the theorists' comments as to what thoughts are
and the interrelationships which become formed between thoughts
and other events, it can be seen that as a group they emphasize the

relationships between thoughts and situational events on the one hand and thoughts and other responses on the other.

Several theorists emphasize that *some patterns and sequences of thought are acquired in relationship to the external world.* The individual forms conceptions of events around him (forming abstractions —Adler); he applies labels to his concepts (Dollard and Miller); he recognizes various kinds of relationships between events (eduction— Sullivan). Some propose that these thoughts about the external world become elaborated into a network or an organization (apperceptive schema—Adler). Other theorists emphasize that these thoughts also become extended with respect to the temporal dimension; the person develops groups of thoughts relative to past events (memory and recall) but also relative to events of the future (anticipations and foresight). Anticipations of future events are particularly emphasized by theorists such as the Existentialists and Adler. Adler, for example, considers it a very important feature of human behavior that the person symbolically represents consequents (goals) to himself, and by doing so he can then consider various responses in terms of their relative contribution toward reaching that objective. This seems to be the type of behavior to which Rank was referring when he discussed the guiding and directing aspects of human behavior, and what Dollard and Miller discuss under the label of planning. Symbolic rehearsal of various possible responses in advance of their actual execution is said to be a critical feature of human behavior. Still other theorists emphasize the evaluational responses in the general class of thoughts, perhaps considering these to be a special variety. They call attention to the judgments in terms of good-bad, pleasant-unpleasant, etc., that the human makes; some like Rogers propose that the human is innately valuational, and every event is implicitly evaluated by the person who encounters it.

As a group, the theorists also propose that the *relationships* established between thoughts and all other kinds of response events are equally if not even more significant. Not the least are the relationships that become formed between thoughts and other thoughts. Further, *it is by taking advantage of such established relationships that the person can control the occurrence of his behavior; he does this by controlling the thought sequences in which he engages.* Hence, Freud spoke of the fact that through thought a person secured a postponement or a delay in the performance of certain motoric responses: thoughts intervene, and forestall, prevent, or inhibit the automatic sensorimotor sequences with which the young child is initially equipped. In the language of the layman, he stops and thinks before he acts. Sullivan and others emphasize that one can control the perception of events one will have by means of the antecedent thoughts one employs. Most of them emphasize that control of affect and feeling is accomplished by thought sequences of some kind. They propose that certain relationships become developed between thoughts and feelings—that some thoughts are associated with fear, love, hate, disgust, and the like. Thus, an individual can learn to control to some degree the way he feels by the thoughts he thinks. If he engages in certain thought sequences he will feel frightened, whereas if he stops these thoughts, or gets another sequence started, he can produce a different emotional consequent. Especially emphasized in this group are the sets of thoughts that people develop to forestall, to minimize, or actually to prevent the emotion of fear (anxiety) from occurring. The person learns to deny, to project, to rationalize, or to fantasy.

Thoughts, moreover, play a "middle" role, mediating between situational events on the one hand, and response sequences on the other (Ego-Analysts). Thoughts play important parts in the instrumental sequences leading to a termination of patterns of innate responses (instinct gratification—Freud).

Thoughts can be acquired in the form of elaborate chains and sequences. Because of the interrelationships established, an individual can control to some extent the subsequent thoughts that will occur by some form of selection of the antecedent ones. He learns thoughts by which to manipulate thoughts. In the language of Dollard and Miller, some thought responses are cue-producing; their main function is to elicit other responses.

Just as some theorists had proposed that the symbolic responses toward the external world become organized into a network or pattern, several theorists in this volume suggest that the symbolic responses one has toward one's own behavior also become organized and formed into a pattern. This proposal is embodied in the notion of the self-concept (Rank, Rogers), the idealized image (Horney), the personification of the self (Sullivan) and *Eigenwelt* (Existentialists). The self-identifying and self-evaluative thoughts one has toward one's physical attributes and toward one's own responses are said to become integrated and related to one another; or, as Rogers phrases it, they become a consistent "conceptual gestalt." Practically all theorists discuss such responses; however, some treat them in itemized fashion, simply referring to the occasions on which the evaluations of one's own response as good or bad, desirable or undesirable, influence the occurrence of that response. Thus, the Ego-Analysts refer to superego thoughts as habitual judgments of right and wrong, which are applied in the evaluation of the behavior of oneself and that of other people. Thus, a discussion of such thoughts can be referred to as an *aggregate* of responses, which are simply classed together because of their similarities. Or they can be represented as a *pattern* which becomes formed, and once formed continues to operate as a pattern, working in a selective fashion (guiding, determining) on other sets of responses (for example, self-concept).

The theorists do not seem in good agreement as to how all of these myriad kinds of thoughts become acquired. Some assert that thoughts are in principle the same as any other response, that they operate according to the same laws, and that they are altered according to the same procedures as any other kind of response in the human repertoire. Such a position is maintained by Dollard and Miller, and an attempt is made to represent how thoughts work from a study of other responses which are more objectively observable, that is, motoric responses.

Others assert not only that thoughts differ from other responses but also that there are different subcategories of thoughts and that there are probably different sets of principles which govern their operation. Freud subclassified thoughts into two sorts, which he labeled as primary and secondary process. Although he proposed that both were learned, the first of these was described as essentially imagistic, and learning occurred by contiguous pairing. Primary processes, then, were nonlogical relationships among imagistic responses. These were adjudged to be of a different order, and subject to different rules of operation than were those of a more logical sort acquired in relationship to instinct gratification and situational events. Similarly, Sullivan distinguished between various kinds of thought (protaxic, parataxic, and syntaxic): these were different kinds of symbolic responses, and they were said to work in differing fashions.

Beyond this, few of the theorists have proceeded very far. Freud, Sullivan, and the Ego-Analysts are probably the theorists who have attempted the most detailed analysis. Although they have identified what appears to be a highly significant category of response events, most of the systems have not succeeded in spelling out the factors that determine which thoughts one develops, or how the interrelationships between affect and idea, thoughts and actions, and thoughts and other thoughts become established.

If these theorists are correct, *a study of complex human behavior requires extensive investigation into the phenomena of thought*. A classification of the various kind of thought responses would appear to be an essential first step. Following this, one could proceed to determine the conditions under which various types of thought occurred, seeking to establish the interrelationships which become formed among them and with other categories of events. Only after careful delineation of classes of thoughts on the one hand, and classes of events on the other, could the interconnections be determined. Only then would it be possible to identify whether a single set of principles would suffice for all, or whether for certain classes of symbolic events one set of principles obtains, and for others a different set needs to be employed. Whatever the procedure, it is evident that if thought and symbolic behavior are indeed the primary and significant aspects of human responsivity that therapy theorists believe them to be, a direct study of this class of events is necessary. There has been a marked acceleration of interest and research on this category of behavior in psychology recently (Skinner, 1957; Bruner, et al., 1956; Osgood, et al., 1957; Underwood and Schulz, 1960; Mowrer, 1960). This would appear to be a hopeful sign of things to come.

AFFECT AND EMOTION. Affective responses are a second important class of responses in the eyes of this set of theorists. Some imply that affect is an inevitable accompaniment of all behavior: thus, all response sequences are said to have an affective undertone at some level of intensity. Others assert that affect plays a critical role in the learning process itself. Events such as pleasure or satisfaction are represented by some to be the after response which determines whether certain sets of behavior will be acquired. We cannot think of any other response group with which satisfaction can be placed, other than to group it with feelings or affects. The role of affect in learning is more clearly exemplified in those theories that propose that fear plays a critical role in the acquisition of other behaviors, and that many responses are acquired in order to terminate fear. Horney proposed that significant or important learnings, those that matter to a person, have a pronounced affective component (recognition and insight).

Again, while pointing to such events as significant and important, the systems have had relatively little success in really accounting for the ways in which affective responses operate, where they come from, how they become interrelated with other response events, and the like. There is virtually no agreement on any classification of kinds of emotional responses. Fear seems to be an agreed-upon term, but there are differences of opinion as to whether the term includes anxiety, or whether this is a particular form of affect distinct and separate from the fear pattern. Anger is another affective response to which frequent allusions are made, although surprisingly, some theorists make virtually no reference to it at all. There is a surprising omission in several of these systems of references about learning built on the response pattern of love, although in others it is represented as an affective pattern of equal importance to fear.

Although it is true that few of the details of emotional responses have been specified in these systems, they do seem, with a couple of exceptions, to share as a group the general point of view that *there are a finite number of affective response patterns with which an individual is born. These affective patterns have predetermined situations which will serve to elicit them, as well as built-in response events which follow. Learning operates in two general ways: (1) to extend the range of conditions that will serve to elicit the response, and (2) to modify the response pattern itself, via the addition of other responses to it, such as thoughts, or by altering component parts of the pattern and thereby varying the form or expression the pattern will take.* The way in which fear becomes attached to neutral situations and subsequently becomes generalized is apparently thought by several to occur as a function of contiguous pairing, perhaps after the fashion of respondent conditioning (Skinner, 1953). Response modification, or the changes in the affective pattern itself, apparently is often viewed as resulting from the consequents that follow their occurrence, and the way others behave toward the child and his emotional behavior is regarded as the most important set of consequents. Again, a most crucial feature of adult emotional behavior is the interconnections which become established between thought and affect, since emotional patterns in the adult are far more intricate than the simple affective patterns of the small child.

ATTENTION AND AWARENESS. Consciousness and awareness are two terms that are equally recurrent in this collection of systems. There seems little doubt that most of them regard the response of attention as being of primary significance. Together with thoughts, attention is viewed as an important instrumentality by which the human can respond more effectively in his interactions with events. There is a repeated theme throughout these systems that if a person can attend to the relevant events and conceptualize them in appropriate fashion, he can direct and control his response sequences so as to enhance himself, obtain satisfactions, avoid discomfort, attain objectives, and the like. *Being aware of, or being able to attend to, the relevant events is a critical component, then, of effective behavior.*

As was the case with thought and affective behavior, our theorists have succeeded in identifying a phenomenon of significance but have failed to specify in any detail what they propose this "awareness" to be, or how this response comes under the control of other events, that is, how it is affected by learning. Most of the theorists say in effect that attention is a set of responses with which the human is equipped. Such an observation is followed by the statement that one learns to control it. Freud thought of it in this fashion. To Rogers the response capability of attention is a given factor, and what one focuses on and is aware of is a product of learning. Only Sullivan spent any effort in trying to specify the way in which attention and awareness come under the control of the person, referring to two sets of responses that the individual learns to employ in order to "control the contents of focal awareness" (selective inattention and response substitution). Moreover, Sullivan was able to recognize the significance of such controlling behavior throughout an individual's behavior, not merely in relationship to the avoidance of negative affect which most of the other theorists had emphasized. Learning to control one's attention is important in the successful performance of arithmetic, just as it is important in the maintenance of personal comfort.

Freud is a theorist who devoted much discussion to the reverse side of the coin. He developed some propositions as to what occurred in the response sequences to which attention was not being directed—what goes on outside of awareness. He was thus very interested in the products of inattention, an interest which may have reflected a revolt against the rationalism of his day as well as the nature of the data from which his theories were built. He was dealing with disturbed persons in whom a lack of attention to important events was seen to be an important part of their problem. Intent upon solving the problems, he may have been insufficiently impressed with all that they were aware of and could direct their attention to. By contrast, someone who confined his study of behavior to the normal might well propose that the proportions of Freud's iceberg should be exactly reversed, since from a different vantage point it might appear that only a small proportion of a person's response sequences occur outside the domain of the normal person's attention (for example, Rank).

Several theorists emphasize that thoughts are not the only contents of awareness. For example, Rogers proposes that sensory responses (organismic experience) are the most important events to be attended to. These provide the data on which sound evaluative judgments can be based. In fact, attending to the evaluative thoughts learned from others may be misleading and troublesome.

How habits of attention become acquired, how they influence the thoughts one thinks and affect the acts one performs, are crucial questions for study. The literature on perception, a conglomeration of studies involving both awareness and thought, may be a good starting point.

Some Thoughts about Learning and Development

If one were to take these theorists as a group, a very gross outline of the nature of development could be evolved. Development would be represented as a combined product of the factors of heredity, maturation, and learning. The human organism begins life with a series of behaviors which comprise a built-in program of responses, patterns, and sequences of response. These built-in response organizations are of many types, ranging all the way from single-unit responses (the eyeblink) up to prolonged series of responses such as the ingestion-digestion-elimination sequence. All of these tend to have particular antecedents which evoke them, and these are of two major sorts: situational elicitors (puff of air on eye leads to eyeblink), and response elicitors (once food is ingested, the chain of mastication, swallowing, digestion, and elimination proceeds rather automatically). Not all innate responses occur with birth; some appear at later intervals, according to a maturational schedule which is species-constant.

Learning represents the complication in behavior introduced by the capacity of the human to have his behavior modified, depending on what situational factors he becomes exposed to. Generally speaking, the growing person becomes one who develops more and more complex patterns of responses and sequences of these patterns to an increasingly rich and varied range of situational events. Thus, by extending the range of situations to which the person comes to respond, and by modifying the responses which come to occur, learning entails the *rearranging* of the initial basic relationships which had been built into the organism and results in new and different arrangements of *S-R, S-r, r-R, r-r,* and *R-R* combinations. Complex human behavior consists of patterns and sequences (*interrelationships*), which are organizations of more primary response components: sensations, perceptions, emotions, thoughts, motor habits, speech, overt actions, and the like.

Although complex human behavior may ultimately be analyzable into more elemental components, such an analysis might not be useful for some purposes. Certainly these ten theorists showed a preference for complex units. The rationale for using complex units has often been that complex behavior is more than the "sum of its parts." Several points should be noted here. First, such a statement implies concept units of varying sizes—complex versus parts. We have pointed out earlier that the selection of concept units is an act of theoretical choice and, therefore, what is a "complex" behavior for one theorist may be only a "part" for another. Thus, if one theorist complained that another was "reducing" behavior into "elementary parts," it would be possible to show that he too employed concepts referring to pieces of behavior. Every theorist uses some "part" concepts, as our various analyses have shown. This finding transforms the question from parts versus wholes to a question of which parts.

There is a certain validity, however, to the statement. To explicate what we mean, we can begin with an analogy. Water "looks" quite different from hydrogen and oxygen, which are its components. Water is something "new" which "emerges" when H_2 and O are combined. The units from which water is built include (1) hydrogen, (2) oxygen, and (3) certain functional properties (smaller units such as electrons and protons could be used). By the same token, a behavior pattern often "looks different" once it is developed than it does during the course of development. For example, an attitude is something different than the specific experiences from which it is built. However, *if one could observe it in the process of development, the relationship between the specific experiences (parts) and the eventual general attitude might be more apparent.* Many responses originally involved in learning a habit have dropped out by the time the complex habit has been efficiently learned. Therefore, when one observes complex habits which are extensively overlearned, as these therapy theorists did, it is tempting to conclude that the analysis into parts is not necessary. For purposes of relearning, however, it may be crucial.

The ways in which response rearrangements come to occur vary, depending on which kind of response is involved. Perhaps the situation is analogous to biology where different structures of the body, such as the heart versus the stomach, function according to different operations. Thus, the way emotional response patterns become modified or attached to situations might be different in principle from the way perceptions or thoughts are learned.

The interrelationships that are of basic importance in the study of complex human behavior are the central mediating events, including attention, perception, thought, and affect. According to these ten theorists, the ultimate progress of therapy theory depends on the detailed analysis of how these responses operate and determine the way in which the person relates to situations and subsequently acts.

Chapter 16

The Development

of Disordered Behavior

In the preceding chapter, we pursued the idea that much of what these theorists had to say about the development of normal behavior might be thought of as the evolving of interrelationships among different kinds of responses and response attributes and different kinds of situations. Let us now examine their ideas about the development of behavior disorder, and if our conclusions about normal development are relevant, they should be describing disorder as something amiss in the relationships among: (*a*) responses and the situations in which they occur; and (*b*) various kinds of responses and response attributes.

This chapter is organized around four questions. First, how can disordered behavior be distinguished from normal behavior? Second, what kinds of events and interrelationships are involved in disorder?

Third, how does disorder become acquired? Fourth, what does disorder look like after it is learned?

THE DEFINITION OF DISORDERED BEHAVIOR

Specification of what constitutes disordered behavior is of primary importance. It provides the criteria by which the therapist can differentiate disordered from normal behavior and therefore know what to attempt to change. The general literature on psychopathology sometimes tries to distinguish disordered behavior from normal in terms of degree and at other times in terms of kind.

Disorder as a Difference in Degree

When disordered behavior is differentiated from the normal only in terms of degree, it is argued that the same kinds of behavior occur in both normal and disordered persons (Dollard and Miller). This definition of disorder begins to break down when one discovers that theorists do not always talk about differences in degree in precisely the same fashion.

Sometimes the term degree is used to refer to differences in response *amplitude* or *intensity*. For example, the neurotic is not only said to be afraid, but his fear is judged to attain higher levels of intensity when it occurs. The term degree has also been used to refer to frequency. The phrase, "he has more fear than the normal" often seems to be used to indicate that fear responses occur more frequently. A corollary is sometimes added: *more situations elicit fear,* and thus the response is not only expected to occur more frequently, but it is also described as showing a greater degree of generalization. At still other times it is used to refer to characteristics of the person's responses. For example, the disordered person not only is said to have "more" fear, but also more of his response repertoire is committed to fear-reducing (avoidance) behaviors of various kinds. Such descriptions seem to be referring to variables such as *extensity* or *pervasiveness* throughout the person's repertoire. Although we have confined our comments on "degree" to the response pattern of fear, and our illustrations all employed the notion of "more than," they also apply to observations of "less than" and to responses other than fear. Thus, the disordered person is said to have "more unconscious conflicts," "less social interest," and the like.

Disorder as a Difference in Kind

It is sometimes argued that disorder differs in kind from normal behavior. Here again, it is difficult to see precisely what the term kind refers to. On the surface, one might expect it to refer to response content. If so, the assertion is made that the disordered person performs particular responses which the normal person rarely, if ever, does. Horney perhaps came closest to this position, defining neurotic behavior as deviant. By this she meant that it is statistically infrequent in a particular culture at a particular point in time. One can see that the question of what defines a response would occur immediately, if one were to assert that the disordered person employed kinds of responses which the normal did not.

This distinction between degree and kind, while appealing, has not led to agreement about a definition of disorder. Often there has been little difficulty in labeling a behavior sequence as undesirable in a concrete instance, but to arrive at a general set of criteria which would hold true across a variety of cases has proved to be much more of a problem. Therefore, although distinction of degree and kind are necessary, they are apparently not sufficient criteria for the definition of disorder.

Disorder as a Set of Inappropriate Interrelationships

When the theorists discuss the possibility that the disordered person has excessive fear, or insufficient social interest (love), it seems probable that they are referring not so much to the response itself as to the way in which it is related to a particular situation. It seems unlikely that any of the theorists would assert that a fear pattern as such is undesirable, or that under certain conditions extremely high levels of fear are "unreasonable." What seems more likely is that the intense fear is judged to be *inappropriate* on that particular occasion. Intense fear of an onrushing flood after a dam has broken is to be distinguished from an intense fear of a small brooklet. The same is probably true with respect to other parameters of a response in addition to its amplitude—its latency, duration, or rate of emission—since it is possible to conceive of situations in which intense, delayed, or prolonged responses might well be judged to be appropriate.

The same might be true of the observation that disordered behavior differs in kind from the normal. Adler is one of the systematists who takes this position. He referred to misguided and mistaken solutions which the disordered person displayed in his approach to problems and pointed to the inefficiency of such solutions in resolving the difficulty faced by the person. Perhaps what is meant here is less the fact that the neurotic is performing discrete responses which the normal never would than that the ones which do occur are inappropriate to the situation at hand. The same sets of responses might well be considered legitimate, and might even be successful in another context.

The possibility arises, therefore, that *disordered behavior differs from the normal not so much with respect to the kinds of responses that have been acquired, or with respect to attributes such as intensity, duration, or frequency, but more in terms of the ways in which they have become arranged in relationship to one another and in relation to situational events. It is possible that the disordered person can be characterized as one in whom inappropriate situation-response and response-response relationships have become established.*

We should observe that the term inappropriate is being used in a very general fashion, and that the theorists themselves used many terms to refer to the significance for disorder of the interconnections among events; they used stupid, ineffective, mistaken, deviant, incongruous, conflicting, overgeneralized, rigid, to name a few. It is likely that various kinds of interrelationships can be developed among events, and that some of these can be judged to be faulty. The term inappropriate here refers to a general class of faulty interrelationships which could conceivably become developed.

Differentiating Appropriate from Inappropriate Behavior

From the point of view of the scientist, one need not concern oneself with what is good or bad, appropriate or inappropriate, valuable or invaluable. The objectivity of the scientist leads him to study the properties of the organism, what it can and cannot do, what conditions lead to one set of events, and what will follow from another. The position of the psychotherapist is very different, however, since he works in an applied fashion. He must be concerned with what is defined as appropriate or inappropriate in a particular situation or culture, what the consequents are for individuals of various kinds of behavior, and what range of satisfactions is available to persons in their cultural milieu.

CRITERIA. Every judgment of this kind is based on some assumptions, implicit or explicit, about what is considered desirable. Is an inability to think in logical sequences, as in schizophrenia, a set of inappropriate or disordered interconnections? Only if one assumes it is bad to be unable to do so. But if such an inability seriously interferes with the effective performance of life tasks, is that not inappropriate? Only if one assumes that the effective performance of life tasks is good. But if life tasks are ineffectively performed, the individual cannot survive; is that not inappropriate? Only if one assumes that survival is good.

If one wishes a person to survive, remain healthy, be productive in some kind of work, have intimate warm relationships with people, form a close love attachment to a member of the opposite sex, be a responsible provider, then a series of things follow. He cannot be paralyzed into inactivity by conflicting and incompatible responses; he must not be so frightened of situations that he begins to avoid large collections of them; he must not be so constructed that guilt and hate responses occur toward people instead of loving, affectionate ones. To be effective, he must be able to perceive events accurately, think through problems logically, love under appropriate conditions, fight under others, or engage in sex with the "right partners."

The kinds of criteria just cited are typical of Western culture, which requires a great deal of adaptiveness from its members. In these cultures, people are expected to be highly mobile so that they can enter most types of situations in case job demands change. They are expected to resolve the vast majority of day-to-day problems on their own. They are expected not only to be able to provide for themselves economically but also to be able to shoulder the economic support of a family. They must be able to fight under some conditions and not under others, since they must be both a reservist in time of war and a civilian in time of peace. The list of behaviors expected could be indefinitely extended and some could be demonstrated to be quite contradictory. But this is sufficient to indicate that an extensive set of behaviors is necessary.

In contrast, other cultures may value other things. For example, the Arapesh Indians are trained to value suspiciousness, acts of deception and trickery, and revenge. One might consider the values implicit in the Chinese Communists' attempts to manage the Chinese peasants' behavior as another example of such cultural differences. In developing the commune, their objective was a highly efficient productive unit, a person who would work industriously for sixteen hours a day, without question or complaint, at whatever task was assigned, on the smallest amount of food possible. At various times sexual behavior, independent thought, nonproductive work, and so forth were tabooed.

This may help to account for some of the agreement which appears among the systems. In the light of the Western tradition and its cultures, in which all these systems have been built, it is not surprising to see certain common features appear as to the unwanted consequents which are characterized as disordered: the occurrence of negative affects, such as hate and fear instead of affection and love; avoidance of situations, interpersonal and otherwise; inability to respond because of conflicting response sequences; or inaccuracies of conception as to what is occurring in the external world or within one's own behavioral repertoire. It should be apparent that such characterizations of what is good and bad are man-made and culture-bound; the psychotherapist must be intimately concerned with what they are and how he can assist a particular person in relation to them. He should not, however, slip into the error of defining what is appropriate for a particular culture and then conclude that what is ideal for that set of conditions is an absolute ideal for man at large (such as Rogers' fully functioning person).

THE JUDGE. Since different people in the same cultures, as well as those in different cultures, may value different behaviors, it is obviously important to ask who makes this judgment of inappropriateness. Recalling our earlier discussion about observers, it becomes obvious that there are two perspectives from which the judgment could be made, the person in whom the behavior is occurring (the subjective observer) and other people (the objective observer). Rogers, for one, makes a great deal of this distinction, and his proposals about the development of behavior pathology builds on the idea that there are different "evaluators." Two different observers are likely to differ in their judgments of what is disordered because they hold different values and because their judgments are based on different data, which will be discussed in a moment. For this reason Sullivan emphasized the importance of therapist and patient arriving at a mutual agreement as to what is disordered.

THE EVIDENCE. The reader will recall that the subjective and objective observers have somewhat different sets of behavioral events directly accessible to their observation. The objective observer has direct access to and can make observations about situational events and overt responses. The subjective observer has access to these, but also to other response events such as affect, thought, and sensations. Those systems built upon the observations of the subjective observer (such as Rogers) have generally relied on the judgment of the subjective observer (the patient) as to what was disordered. On the other hand, systems that emphasized the role of the objective observer (Freud, Sullivan) tend to rely on the objective observer's judgment as the criterion for what is disordered. In this second group, situational events played such a prominent role (Horney, Ego-Analysts, Sullivan) that cultural criteria of what was and was not disordered were emphasized.

In a sense, systems emphasizing the objective observer's judgment have tended to focus more on faulty situation-response interrelationships (S-r and S-R patterns). Thus, they speak of faulty interpersonal habits, habits of inattention, or inappropriate perceptions of situations. On the other hand, systems emphasizing the subjective observer's judgment have tended to focus more on response-response interrelationships (r-r and r-R patterns). They speak of conflicts between fear and anger, between different kinds of evaluative thoughts, or between physiological and affective responses.

It seems to us that any definition of disorder (judgments of inappropriate patterns) which relies on only one set of values as to what is good or bad, on only one observer or on only one class of evidence, restricts itself unnecessarily, making it less likely that one can account for all the different types of behavioral problems with which the psychotherapist or behavior pathologist is likely to be confronted.

COMPONENTS OF DISORDERED BEHAVIOR

There would appear to be several choices that are conceptually possible. First, it might be that the disordered person develops patterns and sequences of response just as does the normal, but that the patterns acquired are in some way judged to be related inappropriately to the situations in which they occur. A second possibility might be that the patterns which do become developed in the course of disorder are poorly put together in some fashion; something might be wrong with the way they are constructed, and thus there are said to be inappropriate relationships occurring between one set of responses and another. Finally, it might be that a disordered person fails to develop patterns that others do, and thus his behavior might be characterized as essentially unpatterned or disorganized. We can examine the group of systems to see whether they agree as to any of these possibilities.

DISORDER AS BEHAVIOR INAPPROPRIATELY RELATED TO SITUATIONS. It would appear that most of the theorists tend to view disorder as an orderly set of patterns, albeit undesirable ones, which are directed toward some consequent, such as the resolution of conflict or the termination of fear. Disorders are patterns of inadequate and inappropriate action in interpersonal relations (Sullivan); disorders are patterns of avoidance which serve to reduce fear but which are unadaptive (Wolpe); disorders are mistaken solutions to the problems of life and represent patterns (styles) which are inexpedient (Adler); disorders are rigid and overgeneralized sets of neurotic trends which occur in relation to people (Horney). These illustrate that *many of the theorists have often conceptualized disorder as patterns of behavior, whose elements are related appropriately to one another, but wherein something is wrong with the relationship between the entire pattern and the situations under which it is occurring.*

A recurrent theme among the systems is the specification of inappropriate "hookups" becoming formed between situational events, such as behavior of others, and certain patterns of behavior, such as fear or hate. Certain of the behaviors that follow are viewed as appropriate, legitimate, and quite intelligible if it is known that the individual is initially frightened. Thus, his pattern of withdrawal to his room or his habits of becoming engrossed in the world of books might be considered quite appropriate, given the initial fear. The subsequent behavior (isolation), then, is viewed as appropriately organized; what is inappropriate is the initial situation-fear relationship. Or to take an illustration from the field of pathology, it is often noted that the paranoid's thought sequences tend to be arranged in logical and orderly fashion, if one grants his initial premise. That initial assumption, or the initial perception of a situation, however, is the feature of his behavior that is judged inappropriate. From that point on, the thought sequences are said to be appropriately put together, and his delusion is described as an orderly pattern of thoughts.

A variant of this conception is described by Wolpe, who observes that *some aspects of disordered behavior are direct—innate and inevitable—consequents of certain events.* High levels of fear, for example, will produce physiological disfunctions of various kinds; impairments of attention and concentration, interruptions of thought and memory sequences, and an interference with various patterns of behavior which are dependent on the function of the parasympathetic nervous system, such as eating, sleeping, and sexual gratification. If these are direct and inevitable consequents, it would be incorrect to refer to them as inappropriately related to the fear. In this instance, Wolpe talks about the inappropriate interconnection between situation and fear, not between fear and its sequels.

We have been discussing this point in terms of patterns of response to situations, because these theorists generally used molar concepts, often including large amounts of behavior interrelated with extended classes of situations over prolonged periods of time. Examples include *Umwelt, Mitwelt, Eigenwelt* (Existentialists); moving toward, against, and away from people (Horney); ego (Freud); dynamism (Sullivan); and life style (Adler). It should be observed that situation-response interrelationships were often discussed in more specific terms, particularly in case illustrations, referring to the interconnections between a specific kind of response and situation. Thus, they comment on individual selectivity in thinking about and judging aspects of situations. They also comment on the fact that something is awry between an event which is going on and the likelihood that the individual will attend to it. The inappropriate "hookup" between event and the attending response is summed up in Sullivan's concept of selective inattention.

Most of the theorists note that sometimes patterns of behavior appropriate to a situation are missing. Behavioral impoverishment is an outcome of disorder which is frequently remarked upon. For example, an "absence" of affection for other people is something that Adler and Rank particularly emphasize. This, however, can be recognized as a special instance of the more general case. Thus, an observer can note the absence of active sexual patterns in a particular person and speak of the disorder in terms of what is missing. But it follows that if the person is not emitting sexual patterns, he must be doing something else when sexual situations occur. *Thus, the absence of one response pattern appropriate to a set of conditions entails the presence of another which is judged to be inappropriate—or less appropriate.*

DISORDER AS INAPPROPRIATE RESPONSE-RESPONSE INTERRELATIONSHIPS. Perhaps even more pronounced has been the theorists' discussion of the various kinds of inappropriate relationships that can become established between various sets of responses. *Some disordered behavior results from the fact that undesirable "hookups" have become established in the response-response interrelationships that characterize the person's behavior.* Patterns have become established as in the case of normal development, but these patterns are composed of poorly arranged elements.

Many of the theorists emphasized that instances in which two or more responses occur simultaneously in time, but are incompatible with one another (conflict), are basic to the development of disorder. Conflicts between several classes of responses have been noted. One kind of affective response can occur and be incompatible with another kind (for example, Dollard and Miller—an anger-fear conflict). Affective patterns can occur in conflict with physiological sequences of various sorts (Freud, Dollard and Miller, Sullivan); one can encounter situations in which fear is incompatible with the sexual sequence, or fear can conflict with the eliminative response sequence. Thoughts can conflict with thoughts and produce difficulty (Rogers, the Existentialists).

But other forms of inappropriate response-response relationships are also said to be possible. There seems to be general agreement that *it is possible for parallel response sequences which are not effectively related to one another to be operative; responses can be incongruous with one another even though they are not directly incompatible* (Rogers). Particular stress seems to have been placed upon the incongruous relationships between verbal-symbolic events (thoughts) on the one hand and all other classes of response on the other. As a group, the theorists seem agreed that it is possible for physiological events, motoric behaviors, affective patterns, and the like to occur without appropriate or effective conceptual representation of these same events by the person in whom they are occurring. For example, Dollard and Miller discuss ineffective labeling. Rank comments on the occurrence of emotions without appropriate symbolization of them. Rogers discusses the possibility that the individual can be inattentive to their occurrence (denial) but can also build inaccurate conceptions (distortions) about what is going on in the different response realms—in the sensations, feelings, actions of the person. The concepts of repression and dissociation are used by many (Freud, Sullivan) to refer to this lack of correspondence between thought sequences on the one hand and other sets of responses on the other. Incongruence between the way an individual thinks and feels and the way he speaks and acts also occur. Sullivan, for example, noted that a person could practice deceptions and engage in "as if" performances. He can think critical thoughts, feel hostile affect, and yet speak and behave toward a neighbor as if he were friendly.

Still further inappropriate interrelationships are possible, for example the sequential hookups in behavior. Thought sequences may be inappropriately arranged. Several theorists wrote extensively about the illogical, irrational, and overgeneralized habits of thought encountered in disorder, for example the extended ruminative sequences of the obsessive. These would be considered to be faulty sequential arrangements within the same response class (thought). But apparently it is also possible between classes of response as well. For example, critical thoughts occur following response events and in turn elicit fear, anger, or the like. These derogatory self-evaluations are said to be inappropriate judgments as to what the person just saw, felt, thought, or did (for example, Rogers). By the same token, one can have inappropriate self-congratulatory responses, according to Adler (Godlike states) and Horney (idealized image).

Some of the illustrations in the previous paragraphs refer to inappropriate relationships between relatively restricted units of behavior, and others point to those occurring between larger and more inclusive arrangements of responses. Horney is perhaps a useful theorist with whom to illustrate the latter point. She characterized disorder as stemming from the acquisition of mutually incompatible patterns of response in relation to interpersonal situations (moving toward, against, or away from people). In one sense, the patterns themselves (neurotic trends) were "sensibly" put together, but in addition to representing an exaggerated, overgeneralized response to the interpersonal situation in which they occurred, they conflicted with one another and were thus inappropriately related. And what is true of this particular system seems in large measure to be true of many: patterns of dependence conflict with patterns of independence (Rank); the self-concept is incongruent with organismic experience (Rogers). To a great extent, the theorists we have considered think that some of pathology at least represents the operation of inappropriate interrelationships between very large units of behavior.

DISORDER AS UNPATTERNED BEHAVIOR. It would appear that relatively few conceptualize disordered behavior as an instance of disorganization. More often they have tended to view disorder as an orderly set of patterns, albeit undesirable ones, which are directed toward some consequent, such as the resolution of conflict or the termination of fear. Rogers and Sullivan are exceptions, for they consider that some aspects of disorder are instances in which the patterns that the person has developed over the course of time become disjointed and fragmented. The stable patterns of response on which he has previously relied are no longer operative, and disorganization results. They tend to regard this as characteristic of end stages of disorder or advanced conditions which few individuals attain.

It would seem that this eventuality must be given considerable weight in any effort to understand behavior pathology. Taken at face value, some features of disorder look as if they were best conceptualized as disorganized rather than patterned. The condition of catatonic excitement and the Ganser Syndrome are two instances in which organized and stable patterns of behavior are difficult to detect. Of course, persons with such conditions are ordinarily hospitalized, and this fact may help to account for the comparative inattention given to this possibility by our group of theorists. However, it also seems likely that episodes of disorganization in the patterning of responses might occur within individuals who usually emit fairly stable and reliable behavior. Of course, it will be seen that disorder as unpatterned behavior would be a special instance, since disorganization refers to collections of response events that are regarded as highly unrelated or very inappropriately interconnected with one another.

We certaintly have not exhausted all the various kinds of faulty response-response and situation-response interrelationships that have been remarked on by this group of writers. Looked at in this fashion, however, there does seem to be an underlying source of agreement that *a study of disordered behavior entails the analysis of how such faulty and inappropriate relationships become developed and earn the label neurotic, undesirable, and the like.* Moreover, looked at from this vantage point, it would appear as if *faulty "hookups" between events can occur with respect to any conceivable situation, and between any sets of responses of which the human is capable.* Apparently something can go amiss in his habits of attending, sensing, perceiving, imaging, thinking, and feeling, and in any of his physiologic and motoric patterns as well. If the foregoing is true, each of the theorists, in emphasizing some faulty interrelationships and not remarking upon others, may have been viewing aspects of the range of pathology somewhat after the fashion of the classic group of men who stood at different points around the elephant; each has focused on certain of the kinds of faulty arrangements and has tended to be inattentive, or at least has not remarked upon, the others. Only by bringing them together as a group does one recognize the possibility that each may have been observing an important aspect of the problem.

Moreover, what seems to be true of particularized arrangements and interconnections between events (situation-response and response-response) may also be true of larger arrangements of behavior. Perhaps the question is not so much whether disordered behavior is patterned, unpatterned, or poorly patterned, as it is a question of the conditions under which it becomes one of the three. There are few of the systems that discuss the disordered person as one in whom the entire repertoire is inappropriately put together, or whose behavior patterns never occur at appropriate times or on appropiate occasions.

This leads to another set of comments which might well be made. It seems quite likely that *the kind of disorder that develops depends on the kinds of behaviors and situations that become interrelated.* This is Sullivan's position, and it seems to be a highly tenable one. Looking at it in this fashion, one is led to a differential study of these various kinds of interrelationships, how they are differentially acquired, and finally to a search for differential methods of effecting changes in them. Sullivan is one of the few theorists, however, who has attempted to draw such distinctions between various kinds of disorder. Of course, Freud was responsible for several original contributions to the classification of syndromes. However, the majority of the theorists, especially Horney, Adler, and the Existentialists, have de-emphasized the significance of "symptomatology" and made virtually no effort to describe, classify, or build into their systems any notion of the differential etiologies of such behaviors. *If different kinds of disorder represent different types of faulty interrelationships between different kinds of responses and significant life situations, any effort to effect changes in the disorder would require one to be able to specify precisely where in the behavioral sequences the difficulty lies, leading to differential treatment procedures.*

THE LEARNING OF DISORDERED BEHAVIOR

It is characteristic of most of these theorists that they had much more to say about the content of disordered behavior than about its acquisition—with the notable exception of Dollard and Miller. The theorists agree that much of it is learned, and some have gone so far as to assert that all of it is learned. More attention has been devoted to the description of what disordered behavior looks like and how it operates *after* it has been acquired, however, than to specifying the process of development in detail. This fact is not surprising when one recalls that most of the theorists dealt with adult patients in whom the process of development had already occurred. If one were to stick to the information that the patient could provide, one's reconstruction of the events would have to be based on one's recollections, and these necessarily would be sketchy and incomplete.

We have already discussed some of the observations the systematists have made about the way disordered behavior appears to be constructed. We can now ask whether there is any consensus among the group as to the ways in which these inappropriate interrelationships come to be established.

One generalization can be made at the outset. The theorists seem agreed that *inappropriate learnings are attributable directly to inappropriate conditions of training; this, in turn, is the consequence of the significant teachers who unwittingly or mistakenly train the growing person in undesirable, inappropriate, ineffective patterns of behavior.* In discussing the learning of disordered behavior, therefore, one begins with a discussion of the training conditions, the situational antecedents to disorder.

Situational Antecedents to Disorder

All of these theorists seem to agree that the situational conditions necessary for the development of behavior disorder are the ways other people behave toward the growing person. Although they all emphasize interpersonal events, they speak of these learning conditions in quite different ways.

Some assert that *the training error can lie in what the person is taught.* In effect, the growing child is taught the wrong things. For example, Dollard and Miller speak of conflicting demands being placed on the child and give many examples of how he may be taught two sets of mutually incompatible responses. Rogers emphasizes, as we have seen, how the child can be taught inappropriate values, and describes how sexual or other "organismic experiences" which are essentially satisfying become labeled as bad by the child's parents, and the child adopts their evaluation as his own. This produces a troublesome conflict between his primary (innate) judgment that it feels good and his learned judgment that it is bad. Freud speaks of the acquisition of the superego in similar terms, pointing to the inappropriate expectations and prohibitions of parents, which the child adopts and thereby acquires an "excessively strong superego." The Existentialists speak in the same vein when they exemplify disorder as the product of man's essential nature in conflict with the demands made on him by himself and others. Adler notes that the child need not feel excessively inferior because of physiological inadequacies unless he is judged to be so by others in his surroundings; he will learn to evaluate himself as inferior if others label him that way.

Some of these same theorists also emphasize that *the difficulty can lie not only in what the child is taught but also in the way the training is carried out*. In Horney's list of adverse influences, she spoke of erratic, intimidating, and domineering parents; the teacher's training conditions were variable or inconsistent, and hostility was used to produce fear. Adler listed neglect and pampering as well as hatred, punishment, and rejection as undesirable methods applied by parents to what their children were doing. Similarly, Dollard and Miller speak of harsh, confusing, or inconsistent conditions of training, and emphasize the inappropriate use of punishment. Sullivan added the factors of ridicule and ostracism.

With several theorists, it is clear that they were referring to both of these factors simultaneously. Thus, when Horney spoke of domineering parents she was pointing not only to the fact that the method was inappropriate, but also that an undesirable response was being taught the child, namely to be afraid of the parent. Similarly, with his concept of conditions of worth, Rogers seems to be describing a situation in which a parent not only defines a pattern as bad in the child but also seeks to correct it by rejecting him when he emits it. Thus, mistakes in training can follow not only from an injudicious choice of what the child is and is not to learn, but also from undesirable training procedures employed to produce that learning. The import of the first is that the child is directly encouraged to acquire inappropriate responses to situations or inappropriate relationships between what he does and thinks and how he feels and acts. The significance of the second is that undesirable or inappropriate responses are acquired as a function of the way he is treated; punishment may help the child to stop what is labeled an undesirable response, but it may have the unfortunate by-product of teaching him to fear the punisher and others like him.

It is interesting that so few of the theorists pointed to conditions other than interpersonal interactions as the antecedents to disorder, for instance, protracted states of physiological deprivation such as intense hunger or economic deprivations such as poverty. One wonders whether this results from the fact that they worked within reasonably affluent segments of Western cultures, or whether there lies within their observations a very useful conclusion, namely, that learned disorders (neuroses, psychoses) are a product of the way people interact with one another. If a person is deprived of food, he becomes hungry; if he is mistreated by others he can become neurotic. It is also possible that hungry and poor families can indirectly produce neurotic children, if those conditions cause them to hate, to neglect, and to punish each other unduly. This would appear to be a fruitful area for investigation by sociologists and social psychologists, since in several current societies—Sweden, for example—the fears and the concerns of its members regarding their physical and economic welfare have been remarkably reduced, and it would be interesting to establish whether there has been a corresponding reduction in the incidence of behavior disorder.

One striking thing about the characterization of disorder-producing training conditions is that they are situations thought likely to produce guilt, fear, anger, and the like. The possibility that excessive loving may create conditions of disorder seems to be ignored. In fact, it is implicit in many and made explicit by some (for example, Rogers) that unlimited amounts of loving are thought to be good. We think such an assumption needs careful examination. For example, it appears to the layman that some people become obnoxiously self-centered, excessively demanding, and unrealistically positive in their self-evaluations because they have been "spoiled" in a training climate of excessive indulgence, admiration, overprotection, and the like. Similarly, it appears that excessive "loving" stimulation through extensive and frequent hugging, kissing, caressing, and affectionate talk may lead to adult behavior that is excessively dominated by "love seeking." One might argue, as Rogers seems to, that one should consistently love the "person" but may disapprove of specific acts. But this begs the question, since it acknowledges that signs of disapproval are "good" and loving acceptance is "bad" under some conditions. The question still remains: under what conditions is each true? If it is true that behavior disorder is a consequence of the way people treat one another, particularly in childhood, adequate preventive steps probably depend on the development of an adequate "science of child rearing," as Dollard and Miller suggest.

The Critical Events in the Development of Disorder

Initially, one is impressed by the frequency with which terms such as anxiety, fear, tension, and conflict are used to describe the significant result of these inappropriate conditions of training. Sullivan and Wolpe assert that the primary difficulty follows when anxiety is elicited and through learning becomes excessively frequent, intense, or inappropriately related to the people, objects, and events in the situation. Dollard and Miller also use this term along with the label fear, and they and Wolpe agree that these become significant when acquired in inappropriate relationship to other responses, so that conflicts develop (sex versus fear, or eating versus anxiety). Rogers stresses the acquisition of conflicting responses (evaluations) and asserts that the critical consequent is also anxiety. Rank, speaking of the conflicts inherent in human behavior, asserts that the primary fact is that they lead to anxiety and fear on the one hand and guilt on the other.

Some of the systems, moreover, do not restrict their list of critical events to those of anxiety and fear and their role in relationship to other responses (conflict). Horney, the Existentialists, and Freud stress the fact that anger and hatred are response patterns which can also be inappropriately acquired and lead to subsequent difficulty. And Adler and Horney added what appear to be sets of inappropriate thoughts to the distressing feelings of anxiety and fear, when they spoke of the judgments of inferiority, helplessness, or both as critical components.

The repeated use of similar terms (anxiety, fear, conflict, negative self-evaluations) might lead one to think that these theorists "are really saying pretty much the same kind of thing." Actually close inspection reveals that they are not. Although sharing what appears to be a relatively common vocabulary, they are in point of fact referring to different sets of events with the concept labels they employ.

Anxiety, to Horney, was a complex pattern suffused with fear, anger, and a characteristic series of thoughts, for example, I am helpless. To Sullivan, anxiety was distinct from fear, not in terms of its subjective "feeling" but in terms of its observable antecedents and consequents. To Wolpe, however, fear and anxiety are synonymous. Others consider anxiety to be similar to but not the same response as fear—a learned derivative of fear, an anticipatory fear perhaps. And to Rogers, the term is synonymous with tension.

Perhaps it is true that among those theorists who have difficulty in agreeing on what anxiety "is," there still might be general consensus as to the role it plays in the development and the maintenance of disorder: what some of its interrelationships might be: what it follows from, what it leads to, what goes with it, and the like. In discussing its antecedents, some theorists emphasize that situational events of various kinds can serve to elicit anxiety: the behavior of other people (Existentialists); certain kinds of behavior emitted by others, such as rejection, hostility, punishment (Adler, Horney, Sullivan); situational events of all kinds, including concrete objects (Dollard and Miller, Wolpe). Other theorists point to the possibility that the antecedents of anxiety can reside in one's own responses: judgments of inferiority can lead to fear (generalized distress) according to Adler; certain thoughts may be the learned antecedents to fear (Dollard and Miller); the conception of nonbeing can produce anxiety (Existentialists); and incompatible responses (conflict) can lead to fear (Wolpe). Although some of the systematists point to several possibilities simultaneously, it remains true that for members of the group there are marked differences as to which of these antecedent-anxiety relationships they propose to occur, and to which they assign primary emphasis.

The situation is quite similar with respect to the concept of conflict, one which occurs and recurs throughout this group of systems. It will not have escaped the reader that those systems viewing conflict as a focal event differ considerably in what they consider to be its components. The critical conflict to one theorist is that between two sets of valuing responses, one innate and the other learned (Rogers). It is sets of interpersonal patterns which are incompatible with one another (Horney). Basic patterns of dependence and independence are in conflict (Rank). The problem-producing conflicts are primarily approach-avoidance conflicts to Dollard and Miller, but avoidance-avoidance conflicts to Wolpe.

The differences are only compounded further when one examines some of the interrelationships that are said to occur between anxiety and conflict. Rogers asserts that anxiety is a *consequence* of the attention to and symbolization of a certain kind of conflict. Sullivan, on the other hand, asserted that anxiety produced or *led to* conflict. Dollard and Miller conceive of anxiety (fear) as a *component part* of the pathogenic conflict. Freud thought of it as a consequence to conflict—the result of cathexis versus countercathexis—at one time, and as the antecedent motive producing conflict at another. Horney considered anxiety as an antecedent to the development of conflict, but once conflicts were acquired, she considered it possible that they, in turn, could lead to still further apprehensions and fears. Perhaps for this reason, she referred to the first as "basic" and sometimes referred to the others as "secondary." In any event, in her series of propositions, she considered that anxiety could be *both* an antecedent as well as a consequent of conflict.

Looked at in this fashion, the diversity of viewpoints becomes quite impressive. Many of the theorists are employing the same concept-labels—anxiety, conflict, negative self-evaluative thoughts, unawareness, to cite a few. Thus, they tend to sound the same, and therefore some might conclude that they are all saying the same thing about disorder and its development. But the similarity is sometimes found to be superficial, since analysis reveals that they are employing the same terms to refer to different combinations of events.

THE ACQUISITION OF DISORDER

In this section we must attempt to characterize how the systems propose that such complicated disorders like schizophrenia, manic-depressive psychoses, character disorders, and the like arise from the relatively simple beginnings that they have described. This is important, since they all agree that the disorder, when examined in the fully grown adult, looks very different from the way it probably appeared as it was becoming acquired.

As a group they have specified that the seedbed of subsequent pathology lies in the situational conditions that lead to noxious and distressing responses: fear, hate, distress, tension, anxiety, and misery. Some assert that these follow from conflict, others that they lead to conflict, still others say that both can occur. However, *most agree that when these negative emotions and affective states begin to occur, the person starts to do things to terminate them.*

Taken collectively, these systems agree that *there are literally hundreds of different responses by which the human can stop these negative affects from occurring.* He can physically avoid the situations that elicit them, or he can seek to destroy the elements in the situation that are distressing him (motoric); he can cease to pay attention to events that are frightening and become involved with other things; or by the same token he can inattend the distressing sensations and feelings themselves (attention); and he has optional ways for perceiving the situations and his responses to them, for how he comes to think about them and how he speaks to the various people involved (perception, thoughts, and symbolic communication). The *theorists agree that some sets of responses which come to occur are useful and lead to appropriate resolutions of the difficulty, whereas others are inappropriate and serve to worsen the problem.* Thus, the next step in the analysis of learned disorder is the specification of the kinds of situation-response and response-response relationships that prove to be ineffective and contribute to further difficulty.

The theorists seem agreed that certain classes of behavior are more likely to prove ineffective than others. *Thus, if certain kinds of responses come to be used in relation to "distressing situations," further trouble can be anticipated.* If the child learns to avoid people and situations in order to terminate his fear, several unfortunate sequels can develop. He will be deprived of the chance to develop skills of interrelating with different kinds of situations, and he may be prevented from developing more appropriate ways of responding since he cannot expose himself to the conditions (Dollard and Miller, Sullivan, Rank). It can lead to extensive patterns of avoidance to many ranges of situations (self-system—Sullivan) or to an avoidance of an engagement with the world (Existentialists). It can lead to behavioral impoverishment, or to an absence of a repertoire of responses through which to deal with situations with which he may become confronted (Rank, Sullivan, Dollard and Miller); it can lead to a corresponding overemphasis on other kinds of responses, such as the substitution of thoughts for action (Rank), or to the commitment to fictions and fantasy; and to a corresponding pattern of inactivity (Adler). He may be deprived of important kinds of satisfactions because he avoids the situations necessary for their occurrence; thus, if he learns to fear other people and learns to avoid them in order to remain comfortable, he may lose out on the opportunities for love, sexual gratification, cooperative play, and the like (Existentialists, Sullivan, Adler).

Other situation-response interrelationships are described as inappropriate as well. If the child tries to terminate his distress by attacking and destroying the conditions producing it, comparable difficulties arise. Horney (moving against people), Freud (destructive impulses), and Sullivan (pattern of malevolence) made special note of this. Sometimes the reason that these kinds of responses prove to be inappropriate is that they unfortunately tend to produce the very conditions they were designed to terminate. Vicious circles are possible (Horney) where the child attacks because he is angry, but his attack only serves to provoke others, who counterattack or reject; this only serves to enhance the distressing affect of anger in the child. The ways in which the child chooses to behave may be obnoxious to other people, so that parents and other children begin to label the child negatively, calling him bad, stupid, inferior, and unwanted. Since most of the theorists agree that the child's evaluations of himself are built on ("incorporations of") the evaluations of him by other people, this contributes to the development of extensive habits of self-derogation and self-criticism (Freud, Rogers, Sullivan).

The theorists have also emphasized several sets of response-response interrelationships which are said to be equally significant. Especially important in this connection is what the person learns to attend to, the way in which he learns to think about important events when trying to manage the intense and distressing affective responses occurring within him. If the child can neither physically avoid nor successfully ignore a situation (S) because he is continually confronted by it, one of the things he can do is fail to heed the distressing affects (r) evoked within him. He can deny his organismic experience (Rogers); he can stop thinking about or labeling the drive stimuli of fear (Dollard and Miller); he can dissociate the events and prevent them from entering the focus of his awareness (Sullivan); he can forget the contents of the emotional experience (Wolpe); he can repress (Freud). If the child becomes committed to sequences of behavior such as this, he renders himself seriously handicapped. He will be unaware of the events as they occur; they will happen implicitly, and thus he will be unconscious of them (Adler). This will make him stupid, since the information he needs in order to resolve the problem effectively will be inaccessible to his awareness, and it will remain unconscious (Dollard and Miller). He will not be able to think, plan, or conduct his affairs effectively in relation to those situations since being able to attend to the events is a necessary condition for being able to symbolize them appropriately (Rogers). Habits of restricted attention and thought lead to restraints on how a person can act. It produces ineffective rational control over one's behavior (Rank). And it can lead to the person becoming unwittingly exposed to very unsettling situations, since he has no way of knowing in advance that they lead to such distress (Sullivan).

All of the foregoing can result in the development of inappropriate habits of thought, which serve only to increase the impairment in the person's behavior. In order to prevent, forestall, or minimize the occurrence of distress, which is elicited continually and difficult to disregard, the person may proceed to develop thought sequences that are characterized as idiosyncratic and inappropriate. It is here that all the myriad conceptual difficulties are said to occur—the habits of rationalization and projection (Freud, Sullivan, Dollard and Miller), the inappropriate setting of objectives (Adler), inaccurate and idealized self-evaluations (Horney), distortions in awareness (Rogers), and the like. Inaccurate and inappropriate ways of thinking about events, both external and internal, are generally considered to be the stepping stones to further disorder.

We have been discussing a general position to which most of the systems subscribe, namely, that disordered behavior is comprised of various kinds of situation-response and response-response interrelationships acquired for the purpose of forestalling, minimizing, and terminating negative affects of various kinds. Disorder from this standpoint represents different kinds and combinations of avoidance behaviors. Some of the theorists, however, allow for a second possibility. They propose that *at least some behavior judged to be inappropriate is acquired not for the purpose of terminating a distressing state of affairs but rather to produce some kind of positive responses instead.* Several employ a concept such as satisfaction (Sullivan, Horney) to refer to this; others use comparable terms—pleasure (Freud), or feelings of superiority (Adler). Thus, the uncontrolled and impulsive gratification of urges is referred to as undesirable and inappropriate (violates the reality principle—Freud). Perhaps the alcoholic drinks because he likes the sensations it produces within him. Perhaps this is what the addict means when he says he takes heroin "just for kicks."

Still a third possibility is suggested. Some, such as Horney and Adler, conceived of *disordered sequences of response operating to produce both sets of consequents, resulting not only in the termination of responses such as fear (producing security or reducing feelings of inferiority) but also in the arousal of responses of the opposite sort (satisfaction or a feeling of superiority).* The alcoholic may drink both because he likes the feeling it produces and because it helps to allay tension, fear, or distress. Freud viewed much of disorder in this light, conceiving of it as a set of compromise-formations, which served to allay the fear or guilt arising from the superego and also to permit the indirect gratification of the instinctual energies. Such responses are viewed as markedly resistant to change, since they are doubly "determined."

It seems to us that all three conceptions are equally possible. Several systems restrict their characterizations of disordered behavior to patterns of avoidance, but it is clear that such a conception would account for only a portion of the range of pathology which is encountered on a day-to-day basis in the community clinic, the hospital ward, or the university counseling center. As some of our theorists have observed, not all disordered sequences appear to have as their function the termination of distressing affect. Some look as if they were operating to produce certain after-responses of satisfaction or gratification. Not all sexual promiscuity about which complaints are raised appears to occur as a pattern for reducing fear. Moreover, some of the behavior labeled disordered appears as if it were directed toward no obvious consequent at all, but looks rather more like a gross disorganized state. Finally, it seems quite doubtful that many of the physiological concomitants of disorder can be conceptualized in this fashion. It is rather impossible to consider the ulcerous condition of one patient or the intense asthmatic attacks of another as acquired responses because they lead to a termination of some negative affective pattern such as fear, rage, or shame. What would seem a good deal more profitable would be to seek an explanation for such events in terms of the built-in relationships existing in the response repertoire of the human, and in terms of the rearrangements that can be made in those interrelationships as a consequence of contiguous learning.

THE FORM OF THE LEARNED DISORDER

For describing how disordered behavior appears once it has been developed—at the adult level, for example—the theorists seem to have chosen one of two courses of action. Some were interested in discussing the characteristics held in common by the various kinds of advanced disorders. Others emphasized the symptomatic differences. One theorist (Sullivan) set out to do both.

General Characteristics

Adler, Rank, Rogers, Horney, and the Existentialists did not sort disorder into different types, except at a very gross level. They described what they saw as a unitary phenomenon. For example, Adler specified his notion of the unity of the disorders. Several labeled these general attributes with terms such as the "neurotic disposition" or the "neurotic character" (Adler, Horney). It is interesting that when one collects these general characteristics and places them in list fashion, one finds considerable agreement as to the salient types of difficulties in each of the principal response realms: attention, perception, affect, motor, physiological, symbolic, and conceptual behavior. Thus, disordered persons are said to have various impairments in their capacity to heed relevant and significant events (attention); inappropriate habits of recognition and identification, such as perceptual selectivity or distortions in awareness (perception); inappropriately intense or excessively recurrent affects of a negative sort, such as fear, anxiety, rage, tension, and distress, as well as infrequent occurrences of appropriate patterns such as love and affection (affect); habits of avoiding extensive ranges of situations, as well as restricting or impoverishing instrumental actions in concrete situations (motoric); and inappropriate habits of thinking, such as habits of overgeneralization, rigid, overly abstract, or egocentric thought sequences, "dogmatic objectives," incongruous relationships between thought and affect, inaccurate conceptions of external events, and inefficient planning (thought). Included under this last grouping would be the instances of inappropriate self-evaluations, both those that are excessively negative and derogatory and those that are inappropriately congratulatory. All of the foregoing are said to make the disordered person "ineffective" in interpersonal relationships—"stupid," "misguided," and the like.

It seems to us that efforts to find general characteristics of disorder in a fashion such as this cannot prove to be very successful. For every patient who is inhibited sexually one can find one whose problem is promiscuity; complaints of involuntary and excessive love attachments among teenagers occur, just as do those where the person complains of an inability to feel love or affection for others; some may "substitute thought for action," for example, the obsessive-compulsive, but others fail to reflect enough upon the consequents of their behavior, as illustrated by the impulsive "acting out" of the hysteric. Moreover, in trying to define common underlying characteristics, one must sometimes move to a level of abstraction that is not helpful; for example, it is said that the disordered person is perceptually selective, but this characterization is so general as to include the normal as well. Patterns of disorder may share the fact that they are inappropriate, but different kinds of behavior are inappropriate for different reasons.

Symptom Formation

Several theorists move in the opposite direction, seeking to define and describe specific kinds of symptoms and specific kinds of disorder. Freud's approach entailed this. Symptoms represent partial resolutions of both aspects of an underlying conflict, and from this fact an objective observer can infer the content of the conflict from inspecting the content of the symptom. In this view, different kinds of disorder are a function of different kinds of conflict, and thus the hysteric, the paranoid, or the obsessive patient were said to have oedipal, homosexual, or anal problems, and to have been fixated at different levels of psychosexual development.

A slightly different tack has been assumed by a systematist such as Sullivan. He shared with theorists such as Freud and Dollard and Miller the view that different symptoms represented different etiologies and thus came to be acquired in different fashion. From Sullivan's standpoint, however, disorder developed because of an excessive reliance upon or commitment to certain kinds of response patterns as opposed to others. The schizophrenic is said to have relied heavily upon the procedures of dissociation, whereas the obsessive-compulsive has been prone to use the substitutive response processes, such as obsessions, rationalizations, projections, and the like. In addition to Sullivan, others (for example, Freud's notion of regression) suggest that responses involved in disorder were originally acquired and practiced under other conditions. When the need for protective responses develop, the person uses those at which he is already skilled. For example, if fantasy is a significant part of the disorder, one might assume that fantasy play was a response pattern extensively practiced in childhood.

These are not idle differences because they have important implications for treatment. A theorist such as Rank, who saw different kinds of disorder as sharing the same general characteristics, was led to propose the same general procedures for their treatment. Differences in symptomatology were de-emphasized, and symptomatic treatment was deplored. On the other hand, a theorist such as Sullivan emphasized that symptomatic differences were important because they represented different kinds of responses in different kinds of interrelationships, and this led him to propose treatment operations specific to each. Of course, this latter view entails a great deal more in the way of detailed elaboration. It requires one to specify each of the "preferred responses" developed by people in order to cope with their distress—or to produce their satisfactions—and then to work out the syndromes or patterns of these responses that recur together. Following this one must spell out in detail the treatment operations appropriate for each.

We find ourselves in sympathy with this latter position. *It seems clear to us that the field of therapy should move in the direction of devising differential treatment procedures specific to the type of problem involved.* This is the general direction in which any science proceeds—toward increasing degrees of precision and specification, resulting in increased capacity to predict and to control. Physics has gone from the gross level of everyday mechanics to the exactitudes of nuclear structures. This is equally true of applied sciences; success in medicine has been coincident with the ability to devise specific, focal, or local-acting treatments in place of gross techniques with diffuse effects. Is there any reason to expect that the future of therapy theory and technique will be different?

Chapter 17

Principles and Procedures

of Psychotherapy

Behavior disorder is composed of responses that are inappropriately intense or inappropriately related to other sets of events. On this, the ten systems seem to agree. Differences of opinion exist about the kinds of events involved and the nature of the inappropriate relationships, but the general agreement makes the task of psychotherapy clear. *The conduct of psychotherapy facilitates rearranging the interrelationships between, and modifying the intensity of, different sets of responses on the one hand and responses to different kinds of situations on the other.* The purpose is not to add "new" responses and "remove" undesirable ones. Rather, it is to rearrange the conditions under which different kinds of behavior occur.

An example may clarify this. A patient who had felt excessively guilty about masturbation may, in the course of his psychotherapy, cease to feel guilty about it. But this does not mean that guilt re-

662

sponses have been removed from his repertoire. He may still feel quite guilty about stealing, or damaging others. What has happened is that the conditions under which guilt is likely to occur have become altered; the interrelationships between masturbation on the one hand and guilt on the other have been changed. Similar examples could be cited with reference to the "extinction" of other responses such as hate, fear, inappropriate thinking, misperceptions, and the like.

We have examined each theoretical position to discover how it decides what kinds of changes should be sought (goals), the principles by which it proposes that behavior changes occur, and the therapy procedures it considers useful in implementing those changes. As we pursued the results of these ten analyses, it seemed to us that the closer these theorists came to the arena of concrete action, that is, the practice of therapy, the less specific the suggestions became. Our analysis in this chapter will have a different flavor from the preceding ones, since we make a number of observations as to what has been omitted as well as included in the system statements. This is not meant to imply that there is not an extensive literature about the problems of technique, or that several of these systems have not been extended by other writers with respect to therapy procedures. There are hundreds of individual articles in the therapy literature, but there is a general lack of systematization of these pieces. Menninger (1958) has written about the theoretical rationale for psychoanalytic technique, extending Freud's system in this respect, and Fromm-Reichmann (1950) has carried through on many aspects of the Sullivan viewpoint. However, we have limited our analysis to the writings of the original theorists and have been obliged, unfortunately, to omit the elaborations of their systems by other writers.

THE GOALS OF THERAPY

Who Selects the Goals?

There appear to be three general opinions among these theorists on this issue. Freud, the Ego-Analysts, Dollard and Miller, Wolpe, and Adler all view the therapist as an expert whose task is to determine what is wrong and what is required to produce a change. Part of the patient's difficulties are seen to be caused by his lack of awareness of significant portions of his behavior and of the events that influence him. His disorder *prevents* him from making sound judgments about what is wrong and what the objectives of therapy should be. However, the first three theories in this group do give the patient an important role in determining certain of the goals. While the therapist determines which behavior patterns are disordered and should be changed, the patient is generally expected to select the new response patterns to take their place. Wolpe and Adler, however, suggest that the therapist should be active in selecting the alternate responses as well.

A second opinion (Rank, Rogers, Horney, Existentialists) argues that the patient must select the goals of treatment. In fact, it is implied or stated (Rank) that the act of the patient choosing his own goals is itself a significant aspect of treatment. Rogers and the Existentialists assume that man's innate nature involves choosing his own goals (organismically valuing); any learnings that interfere with this are undesirable. In a general sense, however, each theorist in this group has the same objectives for all patients, and thus the theorists also choose some goals. For Rogers, the modification of faulty learned self-evaluations is a goal for all patients since he considers it to be one of the basic conditions in all disorder. Such general goals are determined by what the therapist's theory of behavior disorder specifies to be amiss.

Sullivan represents the third opinion, with which we find ourselves in sympathy. He emphasizes that *the therapist and patient should agree explicitly on some goals toward which they both can work. Agreement about what they will try to accomplish is a precondition to effective therapy.* The therapist may privately formulate additional goals and seek to gain explicit agreement about them later in therapy when the patient is ready to consider them. Sometimes the therapist cannot, or should not, seek to achieve some goals proposed by the patient. He may not have the techniques to do so, or the objectives may be undesirable. Although some changes in the patient's behavior can be achieved without his awareness, they can be accomplished more efficiently if the patient explicitly agrees to them and can participate actively in the effort to realize them.

The Nature of the Goals

These theorists seem to emphasize two general sets of objectives. The major accent is on the modification or extinction of the disordered responses themselves, implying that more effective alternate responses will be developed by the patient without special effort by the therapist (Freud). Others stress the development of new, more effective behaviors as the primary task (Rank, Existentialists). Some propose that the therapist must attend to both (Adler).

We consider this to be an important theoretical and practical question. Should the therapist concentrate on modifying troublesome response relationships, such as making it less likely that the patient will fear the opposite sex, or should he be concerned with what other responses will occur in their stead, for example, effective sequences of behavior in relation to girls? *It is probably not a question of which; it seems more likely that the answer lies in careful study of the conditions under which each is appropriate.* Inquiry may establish that the quickest and most effective way to extinguish some fears is to help the patient develop new instrumental responses rather than to focus on the fear itself. Some (Rogers) express concern about the ethics involved and argue that no one should determine how another should lead his life. We agree that therapists are involved inextricably in problems of ethics and values, but we think it is important that clear distinctions be drawn between principles of behavior and ethical considerations. The question of whether the therapist should be active in developing new behavior patterns is not the same as the question of what those new patterns should be. The patient may be able to specify the latter, but need considerable help in developing them. In any event, we doubt that the therapist can avoid influencing the development of new behaviors, and we suggest that he be explicit about the procedures he will use and how he will determine the behaviors to which they will be applied.

MODIFYING DISORDERED RESPONSES. There seems to be some agreement as to what kinds of relationships in behavior should become changed. The therapist should reduce or extinguish negative affect inappropriately related to other responses or situational events (Freud, Ego-Analysts, Dollard and Miller, Wolpe, Adler, Rogers, Sullivan). This includes primarily fear and anxiety, but anger is also mentioned. Avoidance patterns developed as a consequence of the negative affect must become changed (Freud, Ego-Analysts, Dollard and Miller, Wolpe, Sullivan). Inappropriate habits of attending and inattending events—for example, repressions or distorted perceptions—must be altered (Freud, Ego-Analysts, Dollard and Miller, Adler, Rogers, Horney, Existentialists, Sullivan). Erroneous thought habits, both about oneself and about situational events, must be changed (Freud, Ego-Analysts, Dollard and Miller, Adler, Rank, Rogers, Horney, Existentialists, and Sullivan).

DEVELOPING ALTERNATIVE RESPONSES. Second, several objectives entail the development of alternative responses. Awareness of significant events, and conscious control over the responses one performs should be developed (Freud, Ego-Analysts, Dollard and Miller, Rogers, Horney, Sullivan). Positive evaluations in relation to his own behavior should be acquired by the patient, such as judging himself capable of making his own decisions and believing in his own values (Rank, Rogers, Existentialists, Horney). Affection for and more effective responses toward other people are essential (Adler, Rogers, Horney, Sullivan). Finally, most of the theorists say new instrumental responses are often necessary (Freud, Dollard and Miller), but fail to specify why, which ones, and how they can be developed. We think that too little attention has been given to this category of therapeutic objectives by these therapy theorists. We wonder how frequently personal difficulties are resolved or kept from recurring because of a loving wife, or by a satisfying job where the respect and affection of one's colleagues are readily apparent. How many therapists have wondered whether the extensive behavioral changes they observed in a patient resulted from the therapeutic effort or from a significant new set of friendships the patient acquired? Therapy theory should devote more attention to the study of instrumental patterns for achieving major life satisfactions outside the therapy condition itself.

CONDITIONS FOR PRODUCING BEHAVIOR CHANGE

Therapy theorists have written extensively about the "dynamics of behavior"—how behavior works, the patterns in which certain responses occur, the way one kind of response very often follows another, and how certain patterns and sequences of responses are typical of disordered behavior. When the issue of technique arises, however, as a group they have had far less to say. Problems of technique have been discussed in terms of the *effects* to be achieved, rather than in terms of the *procedures* to be used to achieve such effects. Frequently, therapists say that anxiety should be reduced, without any specification of how it can be done, or what situational events are to be manipulated to achieve the reduction. *Some arranging of situational events is always implied, since a therapist is considered essential in all ten systems!*

Why Are Techniques De-emphasized?

There are those who seem to consider the question of technique to be antitherapeutic, since it leads the therapist to think inappropriately about the patient (Existentialists), or else impossible to answer, since technique must differ for each patient (Rank). Still others seem to wish to maintain the position that they are not really doing anything to produce particular behavioral changes. For example, Rogers speaks of creating "conditions" in which the patient may change himself, as if the therapist's behaviors could not be considered operations or situational manipulations that would have specific effects.

One wonders why these theorists as a group have specified so little in the way of principles and techniques for producing behavioral change. Some have expressed concern that published techniques might come to be misused by uninformed people (Freud). Rogers started out by specifying technique but abandoned this when he realized that the same statements made by different therapists could have different effects. In his instance, we think he erred in concluding that further specification was not possible. A more appropriate conclusion would have been that since his original degree of specification was inadequate, certain other variables must be considered: tone of voice, or the context of statements. More specification, rather than less, was required. Several of the theorists have discussed in very general terms what the therapist should feel toward the patient and how he should think about the patient's problems. The issue is often dropped at this point, as if appropriate actions or techniques would follow automatically. We think such an assumption is untenable and encourages one to evade the difficult task of specifying technique. It is what the therapist does, not what he thinks and feels, that directly affects the patient. It is true that patients make inferences and guesses about the therapist's subjective responses, but one must assume that these are based on the therapist's objectively observable behavior. We consider these attitudes about technique to be unfortunate and misleading, and likely to retard, seriously the development of more effective therapies. A patient goes to a therapist precisely because he cannot modify his own behavior. By accepting a patient for treatment, a therapist implicitly agrees that some outside intervention is essential, and thus implicitly accepts responsibility for performing some manipulations intended to achieve behavioral changes. If this is true, a clear specification of principles and procedures for change is essential so that verification of their effectiveness becomes possible.

Theory and Technique Interrelated

In most instances the systems' view of technique seems to be influenced by their conception of how behavior works and how it becomes disordered. The reader will recall that for some who assume that all disorder is fundamentally the same, it follows that the same technique will suffice for all patients, regardless of their symptoms (Rogers, Horney). Others assume that all disorder is fundamentally the same, but different techniques must be selected, depending on the kinds of patterns of behavior involved and their relationship to situational events (Wolpe). By contrast, Sullivan emphasized that all disorder was not the same and pointed to the need for different techniques, selected after the behavior modifications to be achieved had been determined. Here we have a clear difference of opinion which needs to be subjected to extensive research scrutiny.

Learning Theory and Techniques

The lack of clear specification of therapy techniques probably stems from the absence in many systems of a theory of behavior change or a theory of learning. We agree with Hartmann and Rapaport, who consider this the greatest current weakness in therapy theory. A good many clinical psychologists seem to agree, if one can judge from the frequent proposals in the literature, that a wedding of learning and psychotherapy theories would be a most fruitful union. These hopes have not been realized, however, and we believe it is because present psychological learning theory is grossly inadequate to account for complicated human behavior. To date, principles have been demonstrated to be applicable to only very limited kinds of human behavior in very restricted situations. Major concepts such as drive are under serious attack because they do not adequately account for the available evidence. Fundamental aspects of human behavior, such as human awareness, are usually completely omitted from current learning theories and are considered troublesome and contaminating variables in much research.

There is general agreement among the therapy theorists that it is the consequences which follow a behavior sequence that influence its future occurrence—instinct gratification, drive reduction, satisfaction, organismic evaluation. However, what kind of responses are influenced by what consequences in which ways remains essentially undefined. The concept of reinforcement in psychology does *not* tell us which events will be reinforcing for what responses, under what conditions, and in what ways. The American literature on learning theory during the last three decades reflects an emphasis on certain classes of response: rat running, pigeon pecking, button or lever pushing, eye blinking, and certain autonomic and glandular responses such as salivating, sweating, and changes in electrical potentials on the skin. There has been considerable research on other responses, such as verbal learning, but often independent of the stream of popular learning theories. Most of the research on which current psychological learning theories are based has been performed with animals below the level of man.

It has been generally assumed by learning theorists that the same principles govern the modification of all responses regardless of kind, and that principles established with one animal (rats) will hold for another (man). Therefore, research on those responses most easily observed and manipulated experimentally is sensible. This may prove to be true, but not yet has it been demonstrated. We suspect a major modification of current learning theories will have to occur before they become generally applicable to practical human problems, such as those confronting the psychotherapist. The same feeling is apparent in other fields of application (Gagné, 1962). Apparently the wedding between psychotherapy and learning theories will have to be postponed until the bride and groom are more mature.

Principles of Behavior Change

Few of the theorists discussed the issue of learning in any detail, and many of our comments about their views were inferred or abstracted from their statements on related issues. Implicit in all the systems appears to be the assumption that if the behavior has been learned it can be unlearned, and therapy is a situation in which such learning and unlearning can take place. Some were careful to designate certain categories of disorder which they doubted could be changed by therapy (psychotic behavior—Freud), but others seemed to show increasing optimism as their thinking developed, seeing fewer and fewer limitations on the behaviors which they thought could be modified by their approach (Rogers).

Few gave attention to the possibility of irreversible learnings, or of learnings which could never be acquired if they did not occur in a certain developmental period. And several other important questions were typically omitted. For example, it may be technically possible to change certain behaviors by means of therapy, but it may not be feasible because it may take more time, money, resources, or effort than is considered reasonable to invest in the change. There may be behaviors which hypothetically might be changed, but for which no operations for doing so are known presently. Although certain behaviors may be modifiable by verbal psychotherapy, there may be other types of procedures still more economical or effective.

With these limitations in mind, we can summarize the several types of learning principles suggested by this group of theorists.

CONTIGUITY WITH RESPONSE TERMINATION. This principle appears to be present in most of these systems. In general, the systems propose that behavior is directed toward the termination of some response which is painful, distressing, or noxious in some way. Responses associated with the termination are likely to be learned. For Freud it is the pleasure principle and the discharge of instinctual drives; for Dollard and Miller as well as Wolpe it is drive reduction; for Rogers it is negatively valued responses; and for Horney and Sullivan it is striving for security. In general, it is applied to the acquisition of behavior whose antecedent is some innate physiological response (thirst, sex) or some negative affective response (fear). This principle has been prominent in psychological research for the last 30 years, and there is considerable evidence that some learning does seem to occur in this way.

CONTIGUITY WITH RESPONSE AROUSAL. A number of the theorists found it impossible to account in any satisfactory way for all behavior development on the basis of one principle. Several proposed that certain kinds of learning occurred when behavior led to response arousal. Typically, the response aroused is considered to have certain positive qualities to it. For example, this principle would suggest that people seek sexual intercourse, not because they seek to discharge sexual energy (Freud), but because they want to arouse the pleasurable sexual sensations. Sullivan and Horney seemed to suggest that it was some kind of positive affective response which they called satisfaction. Rogers seems to be combining positive affect and thought in his notion of positive evaluation. Wolpe requires the occurrence of some response (usually positive), which prevents the fear usually elicited in the situation. Freud proposed that if one were aware of some response—for example, muscle cramp—at the time intense anxiety occurred, that response was likely to be learned as a part of the anxiety pattern. Recently, such a principle has been attracting considerable attention in experimental psychology as a consequence of research on stimulation of the central nervous system.

These two principles combined would help to make sense out of therapists' discussions of compromise responses, conflict, and approach-avoidance behavior. Individuals may seek both to terminate noxious responses and to arouse positive ones. Thus, children may prefer soda pop to water, not only because it terminates thirst sensations but also because it tastes good. They may drink ten bottles at a picnic, not because they are thirsty, but because it continues to taste good. Any behavior which simultaneously terminates noxious responses and arouses pleasant ones would be doubly reinforced.

RESPONSES FROM OTHERS. Many of these theorists comment about the powerful influence of the behavior of other people, and all emphasize the importance of the therapist's behavior for the patient (Rogers, Sullivan). In general, they seem to agree that individuals seek positive, friendly, affectionate, and loving responses from others. Similarly, they are said to avoid negative, critical, angry, fearful behaviors in others. The theorists do not make it clear whether the effects are direct, or whether such interpersonal behaviors are simply categories of situational events that lead to positive or noxious responses and function according to the previous two principles. Taken as a group, however, there is considerable emphasis on evaluative behaviors as a crucial influence in the development of both normal and disordered behavior.

CONTIGUITY. Several of the theorists seem to propose a special principle governing the acquisition of thoughts. In effect, they suggest that awareness and thought produce learning (Horney, Rogers, Sullivan), that understanding produces behavior change (Adler), or that sensory images or thoughts leave memory traces if attended to or if they enter awareness (Freud). For example, a statement by the therapist could be expected to become a learned thought for a patient if the patient attended to or repeated it to himself. Of course, that would not mean that the learned thought necessarily would be related to other thoughts or responses. Not all theorists agree that such a principle may exist, but the primary disagreement comes from theorists like Wolpe and Dollard and Miller who try to account for all behavior with Hull's drive-reduction hypothesis.

UNLEARNING. As a group, they gave even less attention to this issue than to the acquisition of new response patterns. What little is said seems to represent the two classical notions of unlearning through disuse and through interference. Since much of therapy is devoted to the "unlearning" of disordered behaviors, it is unfortunate that a more thorough analysis was not given to this issue.

SUMMARY. It seems apparent that most therapy theorists do not agree that all learning can be accounted for by means of one set of principles. They seem to suggest that different kinds of behavior may function according to somewhat different sets of laws. Some principles may be specific to particular kinds of responses (thoughts). *Termination of "negative" affect and sensations, arousal of "positive" affect and sensations, and awareness are considered of fundamental importance in learning.* If one assumes there is value in the extensive naturalistic observations made by these theorists and in the theoretical abstractions derived therefrom, the following recommendations for research would seem to be well founded. *Careful study should be given to the conditions under which different kinds of responses become acquired, since there is a good possibility that they are not all learned according to the same principles. The kinds of responses individuals seek to elicit or arouse in themselves and the conditions which will do so need careful investigation. Further specification of the kinds of responses individuals seek to terminate within themselves is needed.* Extensive research on these three issues might well result in a very different psychology of learning.

Patient Characteristics

What are the response characteristics of patients for whom psychotherapy may be effective? The theorists varied considerably in the attention they gave to this issue. Some seem to believe that no selection of patients is required, since their procedures are applicable to anyone (Adler, Rogers). Others were far more cautious and believed certain patient responses were desirable or necessary for therapy to begin (Freud, Sullivan).

As a group, the theorists seem to be in agreement about certain points. The patient needs to be suffering, miserable, subject to anxiety, or unhappy and dissatisfied with at least some of his behavior. Apparently there is consensus that what the patient is thinking, feeling, and doing must terminate in a negative or dissatisfying state of affairs or he will not be interested in changing his habits. This implies that if his habitual sequences lead to "pleasure" or "satisfaction," the therapist will have a very difficult time even though what the patient is doing may be judged by others as abnormal or inappropriate. The patient must consent to the rules of therapy and believe some benefit or improvement will follow therefrom. The behavior changes desired must be subject to learning. The patient must be able to talk. It is not clear whether these conditions should be present at the beginning of therapy or whether the early interviews should focus on the development of such responses. We interpret them to mean that the therapist should try explicitly to elicit some of these responses if they are not already present.

Several other response characteristics are mentioned by a few theorists. The patient should have some minimal degree of intellectual ability. He must be able to observe and report in a reasonably accurate fashion. It is better if he is living in a real-life situation, rather than in a hospital, where his reactions occur to "meaningful" surroundings, and where real-life satisfactions are readily available as therapy progresses. It is preferable for him to be relatively free to change his way of life if he wishes to, than to have to defer to the decisions of others, such as parents.

Knowledge Required of the Therapist

There is considerable disagreement among the ten theorists as to what the therapist should know about the patient in order to initiate therapy. Some (Sullivan and Wolpe) insist that the therapist must arrive at a conceptualization of the patient's difficulties before appropriate treatment procedures can be selected. Others seem to believe such a pretherapy evaluation will interfere with rather than facilitate effective therapy (Existentialists, Rogers).

There appear to be two assumptions, both of which must be met, if the therapist can be expected to initiate therapy without some reasonably detailed knowledge of the patient's disorder. If it is assumed that therapy is appropriate for *everyone* and all types of behavior difficulties with no *selection* being required, and if it is assumed that the same general procedures will be used with each patient with no *prescription* being required, then, and only then, would it be appropriate to forego a pretherapeutic evaluation. But neither assumption can be accepted, in the opinion of the writers. Many practicing therapists have encountered cases in which therapy proved to be an unhappy circumstance for particular patients. For instance, depressive episodes are difficult and dangerous situations to manage with characteristic therapy procedures only. The occasional cases in which a behavior disorder was worsened rather than alleviated demonstrates another reason why these two assumptions cannot be maintained. Other cases, rather than being modified by a standard therapeutic procedure, remain relatively untouched. For example, the "psychopathic behaviors," and the behavior patterns characteristically encountered in criminals and alcoholic populations appear to be quite resistant to usual procedures. There are still others in whom changes are effected by a standard therapeutic procedure, but these changes appear uncontrollably and sometimes in undesirable directions. *Effective therapy requires controlled and directional change, not mere change itself! Selection of the steps to be taken to alter a given behavior pattern follows directly from an analysis of the behavior and the conditions under which it occurs.*

Many practicing therapists arrive at a compromise solution, wherein initial evaluation is rarely attempted but diagnosis of a sort occurs. The diagnostic behavior in which they engage is fluid and variable, emerging in the course of therapy itself and often achieving explicit expression only after the therapy series has been terminated. This is characteristic of idiographic positions (Rank, Existentialists) which reject the possibility of general propositions about behavior disorder, and which require a new theory of behavior disorder for each individual. We suspect such theorists have "left the barn door open" in their revolt against theorists who seem to conceptualize all behavior disorder as the same. We think there is ample evidence that there are at least some general propositions concerning behavior disorder, such as the research on fear and its consequences.

Without antecedent analysis, one can do relatively little advanced planning about the therapy. *Ad hoc* diagnoses are of little strategic value, for they can play relatively little part in the choice of therapeutic procedures. Emerging as a consequence of therapy, they perform the function of an overall conceptualization by which the preceding therapy events can all be gathered together and "understood."

The present writers would argue that the first step in the initiation of a therapy sequence is to form some tentative conclusions about the response patterns that are disordered. Naturally as therapy progresses the therapist's hypotheses will become verified or disproved. Certainly as further observations are acquired during the course of therapy, the therapist should expect to modify his hypotheses to some extent, since it is unlikely that he will be completely correct in his original hypothesis. This argument is not directed against the use of observations during the therapy sequence to assist in the planning of therapy, but rather for the careful, initial specification of the behaviors to be changed. This is the only way in which one can avoid initiating unproductive therapy with patients for whom it is not appropriate. We are surprised at how many therapists find it difficult to tell a patient honestly they cannot help him, and how many seem willing to offer therapy to any patient who requests it. In addition, this represents a way to insure that the therapeutic procedures one uses may have direct relevance to the behaviors requiring change.

Behavior Elicitors

There are two aspects to the problem of getting the behavior that must be modified to occur in the therapy interview. One is to elicit the desired responses directly—for example, the inappropriate perceptions—and the other is to introduce changes in those responses that are preventing the desired responses from occurring (resistances). Several proposals appear among these ten systems. Some propose that free association can serve these purposes (Freud, Dollard and Miller, Horney); others suggest that the therapist conduct an inquiry to provoke the responses he wishes to have occur (Adler, Sullivan, Wolpe); still others propose that an effective relationship is the essential requirement (Rank, Rogers).

When one examines the descriptions of how free association, inquiry, or "relationship" are implemented, one finds these concept labels refer to fairly elaborate sets of procedures. Each is not an operation, but a whole set of interrelated events involving verbal instructions as to what responses the patient should and should not make— a variety of questions, comments summarizing what the patient has said, evaluative statements, and nonverbal responses such as bodily position, smiles, voice inflections, and attentiveness. Thus, speaking about technique in such general terms tends to obscure the heterogeneity of procedures actually used and reduces the precision with which therapeutic operations can be communicated to others.

One important controversy dividing this set of theorists is the question of who should take the lead in therapy. In general, "pilot" theorists such as Rank and Rogers emphasize that the patient should be responsible for the initiative in therapy, while theorists who include the "robot" view in their position (Freud, Dollard and Miller, Wolpe) tend to expect the therapist to take the initiative. We suspect both positions have validity for particular purposes, and consider this a topic which deserves extensive investigation.

NONVERBAL RESPONSES. There is agreement among the theorists that certain kinds of nonverbal responses are preferred to some which are undesirable. These include such response characteristics as relaxed positions and gestures, attentiveness to the patient, neutral or friendly facial expressions such as smiles, and voice inflections that are soft, quiet, sympathetic, and friendly. To be avoided are tense, restless, agitated, peculiar, abrupt body movements; attentiveness to events other than the patient; angry, startled, or contorted facial expressions; and harsh, abrupt, threatening, or disapproving voice inflections.

The primary consideration that renders these behaviors advisable or inadvisable seems to be the general classes of response they produce in the patient. Desirable responses seem chosen to elicit positive affect in the patient, as well as thoughts to the effect that the therapist is interested in and cares about the patient. To be avoided are behaviors that elicit negative affect (fear or anger) and lead the patient to think that the therapist disapproves of him, is frightened by him, or does not care about him. The hypothesis is that patients are more likely to discuss themselves in significant fashion if they feel safe with and liked by the therapist, and are likely to resist, defend, mislead, and conceal if they feel frightened of, angry with, or unliked by the therapist.

Sullivan, while subscribing to this as a general pattern, argued that the undesirable responses were sometimes useful for particular purposes. If less obvious procedures failed to interrupt an unwanted stream of verbalizations so that different responses could occur, the therapist might yawn, become inattentive, and look out a window to show his disinterest and thereby terminate the obsessive stream. Freud's procedure of sitting behind the patient would tend to remove the influence of all responses in this category except voice inflections.

There is a difference of opinion as to which of the therapist's observational habits are preferable. On the one hand, Freud proposed the therapist should observe with "evenly divided attention" and Horney argued that the therapist should try to observe everything, suggesting that this would prevent the therapist from overlooking something important. On the other hand, Sullivan proposed that it was impractical and inefficient to try to observe everything. Rather the therapist was more likely to find the crucial factors if he knew what to look for and directed his attention toward such observations, ignoring irrelevant data. Here, again, is an issue which is of considerable theoretical and practical importance, and should be resolved by research rather than debate. We suspect the results of different habits of attending could be most effectively examined first in an experimental rather than a clinical setting.

VERBAL INSTRUCTIONS. Some procedures are elaborated which involve describing to the patient how he is to behave and periodically reminding him when he deviates from the instructions. This is part of the condition of free association. For example, Freud exemplified in his instructions to a patient how he was to observe and report his subjective responses. Dollard and Miller spoke of the need to train the patient in free association. Similarly, in his earlier position, Rogers spoke of "structuring" the therapy situation, that is, discussing with the patient how the therapist and patient should behave. In each of these instances, the instructions were general and intended to guide the patient's behavior over a series of interviews.

Instructions may be used in a more specific way, however. Wolpe would instruct his patients to tell him about all the events which elicited anxiety and to rank them in the order of intensity of the anxiety evoked. Sullivan sometimes instructed his patients to stop talking about one topic and talk about another instead. Adler used instructions to get patients to respond in certain ways outside of therapy. For example, he might suggest they change their job, or join a social group. All probably give at least some instructions about meeting times and places and length of interviews. Rank's end-setting technique seemed to be a different kind of instruction in which the patient and therapist agreed in advance on a termination date as a means of putting some time pressure on the patient, to elicit important responses more rapidly.

The effects intended in the use of such instructions seem to include providing the patient with a definition of the classes of responses that would be desirable, so that he can select his statements to fit the class. For example, a patient instructed to report everything of which he becomes aware may have some angry thoughts about the therapist. His previous social training has taught him not to verbalize such thoughts, but he recalls the therapist's instructions and knows that angry thoughts fall into the category of reportable events. Instructions provide the patient with thoughts by which he can determine what is relevant and what is irrelevant to the therapeutic task. Instructions produce many other effects as well. They can help to reduce the patient's fear of the therapist, by informing him he need not anticipate disapproval if he talks about instances in which he was "bad." They affect the patient's "view" of the therapist by telling him something about the way he evaluates things. Thus, relatively brief instructions by a therapist can produce multiple responses in the patient or carry many "meanings." If one is content to label all of these events in a patient by saying that one is producing a "positive attitude," or "building a relationship," critical features of the exchange come to be overlooked.

EVALUATIVE STATEMENTS. Most of the proposals in this category represent prohibitions for the therapist rather than operations to be performed. There is general agreement that the therapist should avoid making critical or derogatory statements. "Moral judgments" should be avoided. Rather, the therapist should be nonevaluative, neither approving or disapproving. Some propose that occasionally positive evaluation (reassurance) is desirable but agree that its use should be limited. While agreeing with this general position, some (Adler, Sullivan) may use negative evaluative statements with particular kinds of patients to achieve particular results. For example, Adler is reported to have "badgered" a delinquent boy into talking about some deviant behaviors which needed changing. All ten positions agree that the general evaluative attitude toward the patient should be either neutral (Freud) or consistently positive (Rogers).

The purpose of eschewing evaluative statements appears to be to avoid eliciting such responses as fear, or thoughts that the therapist does not like the patient and is not to be trusted. It is assumed that they occasion responses that prevent more primary responses from occurring and becoming modified.

SUMMARIZING STATEMENTS. A number of the theorists emphasize the importance of understanding the patient's behavior and of conveying this understanding to the patient (Rogers, Existentialists). A frequent procedure for accomplishing this appears to be periodic summaries for the patient, reporting the therapist's understanding of what the patient has been saying. In his earlier writings, Rogers emphasized clarification of feeling and restatement of content as the two most important therapist responses. Sullivan typically closed an interview with a summary statement of what had happened. Here again, summary statements undoubtedly have multiple effects. They can be used to keep the patient responding by showing him that useful conclusions have been reached. They may elicit thoughts that the therapist is attentive and trying to help. Because the summary is presented somewhat differently than the patient's actual statement, it may stimulate new thought sequences in the patient. Summaries may also be used to help the patient adopt the therapist's conception of what is happening in his relationships with people, how it makes him feel, and what it leads him to do. Examination of typescripts and recordings of interviews suggests that most therapists use such responses to some extent. It goes without saying that we need a great deal more information about the specific effects of different kinds of summary statements.

QUESTIONS. Some theorists, notably Sullivan, advocate the use of questions to elicit particular responses. This is the complete opposite of instructing the patient to report whatever comes to mind (free association). Questions have as their purpose the arousing of a particular response, usually thoughts and verbal statements, although they may be used to manipulate attending responses and to elicit affective or motoric responses as well. For example, the question "What do you feel like right now?" may draw the patient's attention to some responses he has been ignoring. "Is there really nothing your mother does wrong?" may elicit thoughts and statements about negative parental behaviors the patient has been avoiding thinking about or discussing. Some therapists tend to reject the use of questions, arguing that they place the locus of responsibility in the therapist rather than the patient, and they consider that antithetical to effective therapy (Rogers).

THERAPIST SUBJECTIVE RESPONSES. Although these are not techniques (situational events) in and of themselves, several theorists comment about them as a source of information about what to do with a patient or as a source of interference with effective technique. For example, if the patient provokes anger or fear responses in the therapist of which the therapist remains unaware, these are said to lead automatically to other responses, such as voice inflections or body movements, of which the therapist may also be unaware and which may inhibit rather than induce desired patient responses. On the other hand, by careful attention to the responses the patient is eliciting in him, the therapist may obtain further clues about the patient's interpersonal behavior and thereby select his therapeutic operations more appropriately. Some propose that the therapist cannot prevent his subjective responses from eliciting corresponding overt responses which, in turn, influence the patient (Rogers), while others seem to feel the *sine qua non* of effective therapy is for the therapist to have sufficient control of his behavior so that he can use it in something like the way a surgeon uses a scalpel (Sullivan). We think this question should be a serious topic for research, since it has major implications for the training of therapists.

Typically, discussion of technique by these theorists utilizes higher-order concepts, without clear specification of the therapist behavior involved. Rogers' proposal that the therapist should convey unconditional positive regard to the patient is an example. By this he seems to mean that the therapist should think certain kinds of thoughts, have affectionate feelings toward the patient, and that he should make only some kinds of verbal statements and gestures. This concept covers a great deal of territory. *We think more careful specification on the part of all systems as to the kinds of responses which are included under such abstract concepts would help improve therapy technique and facilitate the verification of the effects of the various kinds of therapeutic procedures.*

Behavior Modifiers

Once the behaviors to be altered become apparent, what can the therapist do to produce the desired change? Here again, all ten systems are very imprecise. We suspect that this arises partly from the lack of adequate propositional statements about how behavior works. The general practice has been to talk about the effects to be achieved rather than the procedures to be used. For example, theorists may speak of reducing anxiety, altering resistances or repressions, teaching discriminations, or developing insight or understanding. *Such statements refer to patient rather than therapist responses, however, and therefore do not designate the responses the therapist can perform to produce such results, that is, techniques.* Without such specification, a verification of the effects of therapeutic procedures is impossible. It is also characteristic of these theorists that they frequently do not separate the problem of modifying behavior from the problem of getting the crucial behaviors to occur in the first place. Undoubtedly these two categories of procedures are related, but the effects toward which they are directed are significantly different and should not be confused. Some procedures are aimed at arranging for one set of responses to occur at a given time rather than another: elicitors. Others are aimed at trying to produce some permanent change in the responses that will occur in particular kinds of situations in the future: modifiers.

The point to be kept clearly in mind is that the therapist can directly modify only the behavior that occurs during the therapy interview. For example, the therapist cannot change the way a patient responds to his mother, since the mother is not present in the therapy interview. However, the therapist may be able to change the way the patient *thinks* about his mother, his *awareness* of the way his mother has affected him in the past as he *recalls* it, the *emotions* aroused when he thinks about his mother, and his *thoughts* planning how he will behave next time he is with her, all of which can occur during the therapy interview. This would not ensure that such changes would be manifest in other situations, however, since behavior is always a function of the situations under which it occurs.[1] Memories of the past, which are always responses experienced in the present, may be as important to change in some instances as the interpersonal habits manifested toward the therapist.

"Successful therapy" is likely to occur when the therapist is explicitly aware of the changes he wants to effect, and skillfully applies specific procedures to effect them. *Each time a therapist responds to his patient, he is implicitly or explicitly making a judgment that his responses may produce certain results at that point in time.* Dozens of such judgments probably go on in every therapy interview. For example, each time a Rogerian conveys his "understanding" to the patient, he is selective in what he says, and this represents an implied judgment that he will try to modify certain responses with certain statements.

[1] The question of how the therapist might ensure that such change will be followed by actual changes in future behavior toward the mother will be discussed later in the section on transfer of change.

Modifiers Change Relationships among Events

Modifiers appear to have two general purposes. Some seem to be directed at extinguishing the relationships among certain responses, or between responses and events. For example, Wolpe might attempt to retrain the patient so that thoughts of social situations do not elicit fear (an *r-r* relationship), or so that fear does not occur in the presence of the patient's boss (an *S-r* relationship). Others seem to be directed at creating new response-response or situation-response relationships. For example, a Freudian might try to alter the defense mechanisms used by a patient to control and discharge his instinctual drives (produce new *r-r-R* interrelationships), while Dollard and Miller might seek to teach new discriminations between the behavior of a man's mother and his wife (changed *S-r* relationships). Generally speaking, the purpose of modifiers appears to be to alter the patterns and sequences of responses that occur in certain situations. What modifiers are used; what changes are they expected to effect; and how are they said to work?

THE RELATIONSHIP. This concept label is currently very popular, and it is purported to represent a set of fundamental therapeutic procedures. It encompasses quite a heterogeneous variety of things a therapist may do to try to modify the patient's behavior. All ten systems speak about this category of events, ranging from Rogers who considers them the single most important ingredient of therapy, to Wolpe who believes they have useful but very limited effects.

What are they? They appear to be patterns of evaluative statements —or, more accurately, nonevaluative statements—and nonverbal responses. The reader may refer to these categories for specification since the same procedures are purported to perform both eliciting and modifying functions. At least some (Rank, Rogers) include summarizing statements and the thoughts and feelings of the therapist about the patient under the rubric of "relationship" procedures. *Obviously, therapy theorists are pointing toward complicated patterns of therapist behaviors when they talk about "the relationship."*

What modifications do they produce? *They seem to be aimed at extinguishing fear responses habitually elicited by the behavior of other people and at developing positive affective responses in the presence of others—specifically the therapist.* It is proposed that this change is necessary before other modifications can proceed. In addition, it is proposed that they may extinguish fear responses aroused by the patient's own thoughts and verbal statements. If the patient thinks and talks about the thoughts and memories that habitually lead to fear in the presence of the "benign" therapist, it is proposed that these thoughts and memories become less likely to elicit fear on future occasions.

How does this process work? Few of the theorists seem to be clear in their proposals about this. In fact, many seem to have ignored the question entirely. Wolpe attempts an answer by proposing that it occurs because the therapist's extended pattern of friendly, understanding behavior elicits some kind of patient responses (r's) which are antagonistic to the fear response and thus prevent its occurrence. When fear is thus prevented on repeated trials, the "connection" is gradually extinguished (reciprocal inhibition). Dollard and Miller suggest it may be a classical conditioning procedure, but do not explain how the therapist behaviors prevent the fear from occurring during the "extinction trials." The rest simply assert that it occurs, without explaining how or why. With such widespread agreement about the importance of such procedures, however, extended research on these issues would appear to be warranted. Much current research is focused on "the relationship" but seems to be concerned with describing it, with process studies, rather than with establishing what effects are achieved and how. *It would seem to us that at least some aspects of this question could be studied experimentally in contrived situations outside the therapy situation itself.* The burgeoning research in "social" psychology may be very helpful in this regard.

Some of the theorists group most, if not all, of their therapy procedures under this category. For example, Rogers argues that if such benign behaviors are consistently directed toward the patient, he will then proceed to alter his own misperceptions, troublesome thoughts, inappropriate value judgments, and ineffective instrumental behaviors. Most of the theorists would appear to disagree with this, however, rejecting it as oversimplified. They propose that extensive use of additional procedures is necessary. We can turn to these next.

VERBAL INTERVENTION. *What the therapist says and when he says it is considered crucial in almost every system.* This group of therapist behaviors is referred to by terms such as interpretation, explanation, labeling, insight, discrimination, and reflection or clarification of feeling and content. In fact, a highly varied set of therapist responses seems to be involved, although these theorists frequently use their concept labels as if they were referring to a particular type of act.

What are the procedures? At the simplest level, the therapist selects from among the things the patient has said, something which seems important, and repeats that back to the patient, usually with some rephrasing (Rogers). The therapist may try to pick out some common element from several things the patient has said and put that in the form of a statement; for example, "You doubt the sincerity of women in general." He may make a simple assertion: "Your voice quavers whenever you talk about your father." He may ask questions: "When your mother shouts at you, how do you feel?" He may point to recurrent relationships between events: "You don't seem to get your headaches except when you get angry with your husband." He may make comparative statements: "Your wife is not the same as your mother"; or "Isn't preparing your favorite food another gesture of her affection?" He may give something a different name: "Most people call those sensations you describe anger." Other examples could be cited, but these should suffice to illustrate the tremendous variety of responses that are typically used.

There is some difference among the theorists as to what should be commented upon. Whereas Rank insisted that the therapist should focus primarily on behavior as it occurred during the interview, Freud was interested in the patient's memories of past events, although memories could occur only in the present. The theorists' view of the nature of behavior pathology also influences the choice of things to be discussed. Rogerians are more likely to respond to the patient's evaluative judgments and the data on which such judgments are based. Adlerians would focus on thoughts about inferiority. Rankians would concentrate on dependent and independent behavior patterns, and so forth.

What modifications do they produce? *This very general category of responses appears to be aimed primarily at modifying habits of attending to events and habits of thinking about those events.* By asking questions, by making comparative statements, by directing the patient to speak about a particular topic, by slight rephrasings of patient statements, or by selectively responding to portions of patient statements, the therapist may get the patient to notice events he habitually ignores. The therapist usually attempts to direct the patient's attention to the kinds of events the therapist thinks are involved importantly in the patient's difficulty. Similarly, the patient's attention may be directed toward important relationships among response and situational events. Thus, the therapist uses words to try to modify habits of attention.

Similarly, therapist statements may provide the patient with different ways to think. If the patient has been responding in an overgeneralized way, he may acquire some thoughts by which he discriminates one situation from another more accurately. If he does not recognize how responses that are effective in one situation might also be effective in another, he may learn some thoughts that help him to generalize about situations and the responses that might be appropriate to them. If he has been basing his evaluative judgments about himself and others on the wrong data, he may learn some thoughts that lead him to identify the correct data. Since most of these theorists seem to believe that it is habits of attending and thinking by which the patient guides his own behavior, such modifications might be expected to influence many other response patterns at a later time and in other situations.

How does this work? Here again, the theorists are quite unclear. One implicit assumption seems to be that if the therapist makes statements to which the patient attends, those statements come to function as thoughts for the patient. A second implicit assumption appears to be that if therapist statements become thoughts for the patient, those thoughts will influence other responses. As every therapist knows, however, thoughts may frequently become modified without exerting any influence on other troublesome behaviors. Therefore, one might ask how thoughts get related to other responses so as to change them. Freud offered a clue when he suggested that a change in thought would not effect other changes unless it was accompanied by the troublesome affect responses involved. The theorists were not able to proceed much beyond this point. *Research devoted to the question of how thoughts become related to other responses so as to effect control over them is something that would be of great value to the field of psychotherapy.*

Procedures for Getting Behavior Change Outside of Therapy

As a group, these theorists devoted almost no systematic discussion to this issue. Most of them seemed to assume that changes accomplished in therapy would automatically generalize to other situations. Such a position would seem to be a logical outgrowth of the assumption that all behavior is controlled by habits of attention and thought;

if one were to change these in therapy, and if the changed habits of attention and thought occurred in other situations as well, they might influence behavior in other situations. Of course, one wonders if the changes in the responses of attention and thought developed within therapy automatically transfer to other situations. We suspect they are far more likely to do so if special techniques are used to facilitate it. Some of the theorists spoke of discussing with the patient his attempts to change outside of therapy, but rarely did they specify any procedures. Wolpe and Adler considered this a very effective procedure, if the consequences could be predicted with reasonable accuracy. This is a most important aspect of therapy, and deserves far more systematic attention than it has received so far.

Sequence of Change

Here again, these theorists have relatively little to say. Where considerable attention has been given to the question (Rogers), it has been in the form of trying to describe the sequence which usually occurs in a consistent form of therapy, rather than in providing a rationale by which the therapist can decide in what order he will attempt to produce changes. One suggestion does appear with considerable frequency, though in several forms; it is that the first step is to "reduce fear," or to alleviate the "avoidance side" of response conflict. There also appears to be some agreement on the gross sequence of (1) reduce fear, (2) alter habits of attention and inattention, (3) modify thoughts, and (4) develop new patterns of instrumental and interpersonal behaviors. Far more specification is necessary, however, for an effective therapy system.

Some rationale about the order in which changes should be attempted is both a conceptual and procedural necessity. Conceptually, the therapist cannot deal with all the patient's difficulties simultaneously. Therefore, he needs some way of deciding what to respond to immediately, what to ignore, and what to defer until later; that is, he must have some notion about the order in which to proceed. Procedurally, it seems likely that there are certain sequences in which change can be accomplished most efficiently. In some instances it seems likely that *b* cannot be changed before *a* is modified—for example, "resistance must first be interpreted away." Much more theoretical and research attention needs to be given to this issue.

Training of Therapists

Since the theorists had such an inadequate and gross specification of principles and procedures for behavior change, it is understandable that they had relatively little to say about the training of psychotherapists. In order to train, one must have some principles about behavior change, procedures for implementing those principles, and some theory about the sequence in which such changes should be accomplished.

Generally, the theorists spoke about the conceptual knowledge the therapist should have, and naturally each theorist tended to assume that the therapist should understand his system. They made comments about the general interpersonal skills desirable in a therapist and generally agreed that the therapist should be relatively free from personal troubles of his own. Beyond that, training involved an apprenticeship and a didactic analysis of his own. At least one theorist (Rank) stated that therapists could not be trained; rather, they had to teach themselves. *Problems of training will be much easier to solve when more of the theoretical and procedural problems we have been discussing have been resolved.*

EVALUATION OF BEHAVIOR CHANGE

Appraisal of Behavior Change

This is a topic about which virtually all the systems had little to say. They all seem to rely almost entirely on the patient's report and on what the therapist can observe in the interview as the basic data for making such judgments. Tests are mentioned occasionally, but no major role has been accorded them. Of course, many of the theorists did their basic work before the psychological testing movement became extensive. However, even those whose writing is more current tend to ignore the use of tests for this purpose. Some do so because they do not consider available tests adequate for their purposes (Dollard and Miller). For others (Rogers), their theory seems to argue against using anything but patient judgment. In some instances, they seem unaware of the limitations and problems associated with interpreting their data (Existentialists).

They are similarly unclear about the criteria by which the judgment is to be made. Wolpe specifies five, emphasizing symptomatic improvement as the most crucial. Most of the others are unclear, or they hand the problem back to the patient, relying on whatever criteria the patient chooses to exercise. We agree that current psychological tests are inadequate for this task. The major problem, however, is a lack of specification of what should be evaluated. *Clear specification of the behaviors to be changed makes easier the development of more effective procedures of appraisal.* One error frequently apparent in the literature should be avoided. *Appraisal should be based only on the behaviors the therapist attempted to change, and these differ from patient to patient.* For example, evaluational studies which assume that all patients will become less dependent are doomed to insignificant results, since not all patients need to change their dependence patterns (Ford, 1959).

Verification of Theory

Here, too, there is very little substance. Rogers stands out from all the others in his extensive attempts to verify his theory using other procedures in addition to the naturalistic observations of the therapist. Wolpe and Dollard and Miller draw on evidence from laboratory experiments primarily with animals as a source of verification. All the rest rely on naturalistic observation by the therapist, although some strongly advocate the use of more rigorous procedures (Sullivan).

This analysis seems to make clear some of the reasons for the paucity of more rigorous attempts at verification. First, many of their concepts are high-order abstractions (organismic experience, life style, ego, existential mode), which cannot be studied in themselves. Unfortunately, the smaller units gathered under such concepts are not clearly delineated and are thus also impossible to study. This lack of specificity makes verification extremely difficult. This fact may also help to account for the shift from "outcome" to "process" research in the therapy literature. Without precise specification of the objectives of therapy and the procedures and propositions by which the specified changes can be achieved, a study of outcomes is not possible. The variable "improvement" reported in so many therapy studies at one time reflects the absence of a rationale for specifying particular changes to be observed. Much of the research that purports to show that therapy is really ineffective suffers from this same type of weakness. It appears likely that the research on "process" and "relationship" may run into similar difficulties because of inadequate specification of the concepts and propositions involved.

The fact that most of their primary concepts represent subjectively observable responses presents another major problem. How can the thoughts, sensations, and emotions of an individual be studied? These theorists rely on the patient's reports as virtually their only source of data. Some (Sullivan) recognize some of the problems in such data and propose a kind of internal consistency criterion to protect the therapist from gross errors. *The fact is that the patient's subjectively observable responses are always a matter of inference for the therapist or researcher. Until rules and procedures are established for making accurate inferences about such responses, verification of the propositions as to how these subjectively observable responses operate and change is not possible.* Establishing a basis for accurate inference making is an extremely difficult task, but one that must be tackled if many theoretical and practical problems about human behavior are to be solved.

It seems clear that evaluations of the behavior changes produced by therapy is possible only when: (1) the changes to be effected with each patient are clearly specified—and these are unlikely to be the same for all patients; (2) the observational data and the criteria upon which the judgment is to be based are clearly specified; and (3) procedures for replication and verification are explicitly identified. *Until the evaluation of behavior change in a particular case is possible, verification of psychotherapy theories in general cannot be done, since the one necessarily depends on the other.*

ONE FINAL WORD

Some readers may feel we have been excessively critical in our analysis and have implied that therapy theories are seriously inadequate. Such value judgments always require a criterion. In the preface we noted that these ten theoretical points of view were being compared to an ideal. To fall short of an ideal does not mean that one has failed.

We complete this task with great respect and admiration for the clinical skill, dedication, and sensitivity reflected in the writings we examined and for the willingness of these theorists to make a serious effort to develop a better theory about human behavior. We think some of their insights are remarkable and some of their contributions among the most important in psychology. Of course, they made some bad theoretical mistakes, too, but even Freud did not expect his grand scheme to be perfect.

Their effort to conceive of human behavior on the large scale is in sharp contrast to the era of "part theories," which now dominates psychology, and to the strident empiricism of the 1930's. We frankly admire all three streams of influence. We hope, however, the current emphasis on "hard-headed" psychology will not deter the brilliant speculators among us from occasional attempts at the challenging task of system building. Questions of fact should not be resolved by debate, but by empirical and experimental study. However, the grand theory (*à la* Hull) may stimulate many people to go out and look for facts as yet ignored and to test ideas as yet untested. It takes courage, and perhaps a little foolhardiness, to try to be a system builder, and we hope there are a few such courageous "fools" on the horizon for psychology and psychotherapy.

Bibliography

Adler, A., 1917. *Study of Organ Inferiority and Its Physical Compensation; A Contribution to Physical Medicine.* New York: Nervous and Mental Diseases Publishing Co.

Adler, A., 1924. *The Practice and Theory of Individual Psychology.* New York: Harcourt, Brace.

Adler, A., 1927. *Understanding Human Nature.* New York: Greenberg Publishers, Inc.

Adler, A., 1929a. *The Science of Living.* New York: Greenberg Publishers, Inc.

Adler, A., 1929b. *Problems of Neurosis.* London: Kegan Paul.

Adler, A., 1930. Individual Psychology. In Murchison, C. (Ed.). *Psychologies of 1930.* Worcester, Mass.: Clark University Press.

Adler, A., 1931. *What Life Should Mean to You.* Boston: Little.

Adler, A., 1935. The Fundamental Views of Individual Psychology. *Int. J. Individ. Psychol.,* 1, 5–8.

Adler, A., 1939. *Social Interest.* New York: Putnam.

Allen, F. H., 1942. *Psychotherapy with Children.* New York: Norton.

Allport, G. W., 1937. *Personality: A Psychological Interpretation.* New York: Henry Holt and Co.

American Psychological Association, 1950. *Conference on Graduate Education in Clinical Psychology.* Training in Clinical Psychology. New York: Prentice-Hall, Inc.

American Psychological Association, 1959. *Graduate Education in Psychology.* Washington, D.C.: American Psychological Association.

American Psychological Association, Seminar of the Education and Training Board, 1959. Education for Research in Psychology. *Amer. Psychologist,* 14, 167–179.

Amsel, A., 1961. Hope Comes to Learning Theory. *Contemp. Psychol.,* 6, 33–36.

Angyal, A., 1941. *Foundations for a Science of Personality.* New York: Commonwealth Fund.

Ansbacher, H., and Ansbacher, Rowena, 1956. *The Individual Psychology of Alfred Adler.* New York: Basic Books, Inc.

Arlow, J. A., 1952. Ego Psychology. In Frosch, J. (Ed.). *The Annual Survey of Psychoanalysis,* Vol. 1. New York: International Universities Press, pp. 109–142.

Binswanger, L., 1956. Existential Analysis and Psychotherapy. In Fromm-Reichmann, Frieda, and Moreno, J. L. (Eds.). *Progress in Psychotherapy.* New York: Grune and Stratton, pp. 144–148.

691

Blauner, J., 1957. Existential Analysis: L. Binswanger's Daseinsanalyse. *Psychoanal. Rev.*, 44, 51–64.

Boss, M., 1958. *The Analysis of Dreams*. New York: Philosophical Library.

Boss, M., 1963. *Daseinsanalyse and Psychoanalysis*. New York: Basic Books, Inc.

Bruner, J. S., 1962. *On Knowing*. Cambridge: Harvard University Press.

Bruner, J. S., Goodnow, J. J., and Austin, G. A., 1956. *A Study of Thinking*. New York: John Wiley and Sons.

Cameron, N., 1947. *The Psychology of Behavior Disorders*. Boston: Houghton Mifflin Co.

Cofer, C. W., 1959. Motivation. *Annual Review of Psychology*, 10, 173–203. Palo Alto: Annual Reviews, Inc.

Deutsch, J. A., and Deutsch, D., 1963. Attention: Some Theoretical Considerations. *Psychol. Rev.*, 70, 80–91.

Dollard, J., and Auld, F., Jr., 1959. *Scoring Human Motives: A Manual*. New Haven: Yale University Press.

Dollard, J., Auld, F., Jr., and White, Alice M., 1953. *Steps in Psychotherapy: Study of a Case of Sex-fear Conflict*. New York: The Macmillan Co.

Dollard, J., and Miller, N. E., 1950. *Personality and Psychotherapy: An Analysis in Terms of Learning, Thinking, and Culture*. New York: McGraw-Hill.

Dollard, J., and Miller, N. E., 1952. Free association. *Pastoral Psychology*, 2, 33–41.

Eisen, N. H., 1962. Some effects of early sensory deprivation on later behavior. *J. abnorm. soc. Psychol.*, 65, 338–342.

Eriksen, C. W., 1951. Perceptual Defense as a Function of Unacceptable Needs. *J. abnorm. soc. Psychol.*, 46, 557–564.

Eriksen, C. W., 1952. Defense Against Ego-threat in Memory and Perception. *J. abnorm. soc. Psychol.*, 47, 230–235.

Erikson, E. H., 1946. Ego Development and Historical Change. *The Psychoanalytic Study of the Child*. Vol. 2. New York: International Universities Press, pp. 359–396.

Erikson, E. H., 1950. *Childhood and Society*. New York: Norton.

Eysenck, H. J., 1957. *The Dynamics of Anxiety and Hysteria*. London: Routledge and Kegan Paul.

Ford, D. H., 1957. Research Approaches to Psychotherapy. *J. counsel. Psychol.*, 6, 55–60.

Frankman, J. P., and Adams, J. A., 1962. Theories of Vigilance. *Psychol. Bull.*, 59, 257–272.

Freud, Anna, 1946. *The Ego and Mechanisms of Defense*. New York: International Universities Press.

Freud, S., 1900. The Interpretation of Dreams. In Brill, A. A. (Ed.). *The Basic Writings of Sigmund Freud*. New York: Random House, 1938.

Freud, S., 1904. The Psychopathology of Everyday Life. In Brill, A. A. (Ed.). *The Basic Writings of Sigmund Freud*. New York: Random House, 1938.

Freud, S., 1905. Three Contributions to the Theory of Sex. In Brill, A. A. (Ed.). *The Basic Writings of Sigmund Freud*. New York: Random House, 1938.

Freud, S., 1910, 1912, 1918. Three Contributions to the Psychology of Love. In Strachey, J. (Ed.). *Standard Edition*, Vol. 11. London: Hogarth Press, 1958.

Freud, S., 1911. Formulations on the Two Principles of Mental Functioning. In Strachey, J. (Ed.). *Standard Edition*. Vol. 12. London: Hogarth Press, 1958.

Freud, S., 1912. A Note on the Unconscious in Psychoanalysis. In Strachey, J. (Ed.). *Standard Edition*. Vol. 12. London: Hogarth Press, 1958.

Freud, S., 1912–15. Papers on Technique. In Strachey, J. (Ed.). *Standard Edition*. Vol. 12. London: Hogarth Press, 1958.

Freud, S., 1914a. The History of the Psychoanalytic Movement. In Brill, A. A. (Ed.). *The Basic Writings of Sigmund Freud*. New York: Random House, 1938.

Freud, S., 1914b. On Narcissism, an Introduction. In Strachey, J. (Ed.). *Standard Edition*. Vol. 14. London: Hogarth Press, 1957.

Freud, S., 1915a. Instincts and their Vicissitudes. In Strachey, J. (Ed.). *Standard Edition*. Vol. 14. London: Hogarth Press, 1957.

Freud, S., 1915b. Repression. In Strachey, J. (Ed.). *Standard Edition*. Vol. 14. London: Hogarth Press, 1957.

Freud, S., 1915c. The Unconscious. In Strachey, J. (Ed.). *Standard Edition*. Vol. 14. London: Hogarth Press, 1957.

Freud, S., 1915d. Mourning and Melancholia. In Strachey, J. (Ed.). *Standard Edition*. Vol. 14. London: Hogarth Press, 1957.

Freud, S., 1915e. *A General Introduction to Psychoanalysis*. Garden City, N.Y.: Garden City Publishing Co., 1943.

Freud, S., 1919. Beyond the Pleasure Principle. In Strachey, J. (Ed.). *Standard Edition*. Vol. 18. London: Hogarth Press, 1955.

Freud, S., 1920. Group Psychology and the Analysis of the Ego. In Strachey, J. (Ed.). *Standard Edition*. Vol. 18. London: Hogarth Press, 1955.

Freud, S., 1922. Psychoanalysis. In Strachey, J. (Ed.). *Standard Edition*. Vol. 20. London: Hogarth Press, 1959.

Freud, S., 1923a. *The Ego and the Id*. London: The International Psycho-analytical Library, 1927.

Freud, S., 1923b. Two Encyclopedia Articles. In Strachey, J. (Ed.). *Standard Edition*. Vol. 18. London: Hogarth Press, 1955.

Freud, S., 1925a. An Autobiographical Study. In Strachey, J. (Ed.). *Standard Edition*. Vol. 20. London: Hogarth Press, 1959.

Freud, S., 1925b. Inhibitions, Symptoms and Anxiety. In Strachey, J. (Ed.). *Standard Edition*. Vol. 20. London: Hogarth Press, 1959.

Freud, S., 1926. The Question of Lay Analysis. In Strachey, J. (Ed.). *Standard Edition*. Vol. 20. London: Hogarth Press, 1959.

Freud, S., 1932. *New Introductory Lectures in Psychoanalysis*. New York: Norton, 1933.

Freud, S., 1937. Analysis Terminable and Interminable. In Riviere, Joan (Trans.). *Collected Papers*. Vol. 5. London: Hogarth Press, 1950.

Freud, S., 1938. *An Outline of Psychoanalysis*. New York: Norton, 1949.

Freud, S., 1955. *The Standard Edition of the Complete Psychological Works of Sigmund Freud*. Strachey, J. (Ed.). London: Hogarth Press.

Freud, S., and Breuer, J., 1895. *Studies in Hysteria*. New York: Basic Books, 1957.

Fromm-Reichmann, Frieda, 1950. *Principles of Intensive Psychotherapy*. Chicago: University of Chicago Press.

Gagné, R. M., 1962. Military Training and Principles of Learning. *Amer. Psychologist*, **17**, 83–90.

Guthrie, E. R., 1935. *The Psychology of Learning*. New York: Harper.

Hall, C. S., and Lindzey, G., 1957. *Theories of Personality*. New York: John Wiley and Sons.

Hall, J. F., 1961. *Psychology of Motivation*. New York: J. B. Lippincott Co.

Harlow, H. F., 1954. Motivational Forces Underlying Learning. In *Learning Theory, Personality Theory, and Clinical Research—The Kentucky Symposium*, New York: John Wiley and Sons, pp. 36–52.

Harlow, H. F., 1958. The Nature of Love. *Amer. Psychologist*, **13**, 673–685.

Hartmann, H., 1939. Psychoanalysis and the Concept of Health. *Int. J. Psychoanal.*, **20**, 308–321.

Hartmann, H., 1947. On Rational and Irrational Action. In Roheim, G. (Ed.). *Psychoanalysis and the Social Sciences*. Vol. 1. New York: International Universities Press, pp. 359–392.

Hartmann, H., 1958. Comments on the Psychoanalytic Theory of Instinctual Drives. *Psychoanal. quart.*, **17**, 368–388.

Hartmann, H., 1950a. Psychoanalysis and Developmental Psychology. In *The Psychoanalytic Study of the Child*. Vol. 5. New York: International Universities Press, pp. 7–17, 53–54, 64–67.

Hartmann, H., 1950b. Comments on the Psychoanalytic Theory of the Ego. In *The Psychoanalytic Study of the Child*. Vol. 5. New York: International Universities Press, pp. 74–96.

Hartmann, H., 1951. Technical Implications of Ego Psychology. *Psychoanal. quart.*, **20**, 31–43.

Hartmann, H., 1952. The Mutual Influences in the Development of Ego and Id. In *The Psychoanalytic Study of the Child*. Vol. 7. New York: International Universities Press, pp. 9–30.

Hartmann, H., 1953. Contribution to the Metapsychology of Schizophrenia. In *The Psychoanalytic Study of the Child*. Vol. 8. New York: International Universities Press, pp. 177–178.

Hartmann, H., 1954. Problems of Infantile Neurosis: A Discussion. Kris, E. (Chairman). In *The Psychoanalytic Study of the Child*. Vol. 9. New York: International Universities Press.

Hartmann, H., 1956. Notes on the Reality Principle. In *The Psychoanalytic Study of the Child*. Vol. 11. New York: International Universities Press, pp. 31–53.

Hartmann, H., 1958. *Ego Psychology and the Problem of Adaptation*. New York: International Universities Press. And in Rapaport, D. (Ed.), 1951. *Organization and Pathology of Thought*. New York: Columbia University Press.

Hartmann, H., and Kris, E., 1945. The Genetic Approach in Psychoanalysis. In *The Psychoanalytic Study of the Child*. Vol. 1. New York: International Universities Press, pp. 11–29.

Hartmann, H., Kris, E., and Loewenstein, R. M., 1946. Comments on the Formation of Psychic Structure. In *The Psychoanalytic Study of the Child*. Vol. 2. New York: International Universities Press, pp. 11–38.

Hartshorne, H., and May, M. A., 1928. *Studies in Deceit*. New York: The Macmillan Co.

Hebb, D. O., 1960. The American Revolution. *Amer. Psychologist*, **15**, 735–745.

Heidegger, M., 1962. *Being and Time*. London: SCM Press.

Hilgard, E. R., 1956. *Theories of Learning*. New York: Appleton-Century-Crofts.

Hilgard, E. R., Kubie, L. S., and Pumpian-Mindlin, E., 1952. *Psychoanalysis as a Science*. New York: Basic Books.

Hollingshead, A. B., and Redlich, F. C., 1958. *Social Class and Mental Illness*. New York: John Wiley and Sons.

Holt, R. K., 1959. A Review of Hartmann's Ego Psychology and the Problem of Adaptation. *Contemp. Psychol.*, 4, 332–333.

Hora, T., 1959. Existential Group Psychotherapy. *Amer. J. Psychother.*, 13, 83–92.

Horney, Karen, 1937. *The Neurotic Personality of Our Time*. New York: Norton.

Horney, Karen, 1939. *New Ways in Psychoanalysis*. New York: Norton.

Horney, Karen, 1942. *Self-Analysis*. New York: Norton.

Horney, Karen, 1945. *Our Inner Conflicts*. New York: Norton.

Horney, Karen, 1950. *Neurosis and Human Growth*. New York: Norton.

Hull, C. L., 1943. *Principles of Behavior*. New York: D. Appleton-Century.

Jackson, D. N., and Messick, S., 1958. Content and Style in Personality Assessment. *Psychol. Bull.*, 55, 243–252.

Jacobson, E., 1938. *Progressive Relaxation*. Chicago: University of Chicago Press.

Jaynes, J., 1958. Imprinting: The Interaction of Learned and Innate Behavior. III. Practice Effects on Performance, Tension and Fear. *J. comp. physiol. Psychol.*, 51, 234–237.

Jones, E., 1953. *The Life and Works of Sigmund Freud*. Vol. 1. New York: Basic Books.

Jones, E., 1955. *The Life and Works of Sigmund Freud*. Vol. 2. New York: Basic Books.

Jones, E., 1957. *The Life and Works of Sigmund Freud*. Vol. 3. New York: Basic Books.

Kahn, E., 1957a. An Appraisal of Existential Analysis. I. *Psychiat. quart.*, 31, 203–227.

Kahn, E., 1957b. An Appraisal of Existential Analysis. II. *Psychiat. quart.*, 31, 417–444.

Karpf, F. B., 1953. *The Psychology and Psychotherapy of Otto Rank*. New York: Philosophical Library.

Kelley, G. A., 1955. *The Psychology of Personal Constructs* (2 vols.). New York: Norton.

Klein, G. S., and Gill, M. M., 1961. The Structuring of Drive and Reality. David Rapaport's Contributions to the Science of Psychology. Unpublished manuscript.

Kris, E., 1951. On Preconscious Mental Processes. In Rapaport, D. (Ed.). *Organization and Pathology of Thought*. New York: Columbia University Press, pp. 474–493.

Lang, P. J., and Lazovik, A. D., 1961. Changes in Phobic Behavior Following Systematic Desensitization Psychotherapy. Unpublished paper.

Lazarus, R. S., and McCleary, R. A., 1951. Autonomic Discrimination without Awareness: A Study of Sub-ception. *Psychol. Rev.*, 58, 113–122.

Lazovik, A. D., and Lang, P. J., 1960. A Laboratory Demonstration of Systematic Desensitization Psychotherapy. *J. Psychol. Stud.*, 11, 238–247.

Lewin, K., 1936. *Principles of Topological Psychology*. New York: McGraw-Hill.

Liddell, H. S., 1944. Conditioned Reflex Method and Experimental Neurosis. In Hunt, J. McV. (Ed.). *Personality and the Behavior Disorders*. New York: The Ronald Press Co., pp. 389–411.

Loewenstein, R. M., 1952. *Psychoanalytic Explorations in Art*. New York: International Universities Press.

Loewenstein, R. M., 1953. *Drives, Affects, and Behaviors*. New York: International Universities Press.

Lorenz, K. Z., 1952. *King Solomon's Ring: A New Light on Animal Ways*. New York: Thomas Y. Crowell Co.

McClelland, D. C., 1951. *Personality*. New York: Sloane.

McClelland, D. C., Atkinson, J. W., Clark, R. A., and Lowell, E. L., 1953. *The Achievement Motive*. New York: Appleton-Century-Crofts.

Marx, M. H. (Ed.), 1951. *Psychological Theory: Contemporary Readings*. New York: The Macmillan Co.

May, R. (Ed.), 1961. *Existential Psychology*. New York: Random House.

May, R., Angel, E., and Ellenberger, H. F. (Eds.), 1958. *Existence: A New Dimension in Psychiatry and Psychology*. New York: Basic Books.

Menninger, K., 1958. *Theory of Psychoanalytic Technique*. New York: Basic Books.

Miller, N. E., 1948. Theory and Experiment Relating Psychoanalytic Displacement to Stimulus-response Generalization. *J. abnorm. soc. Psychol.*, **43**, 155–178.

Miller, N. E., 1951. Learnable Drives and Rewards. In Stevens, S. S. (Ed.). *Handbook of Experimental Psychology*. New York: John Wiley and Sons.

Miller, N. E., 1951. Comments on Theoretical Models. *J. Pers.*, **20**, 82–100.

Miller, N. E., 1952. *Theoretical Models and Personality Theory*. Durham, N.C.: Duke University Press.

Miller, N. E., 1957. Experiments on Motivation: Studies Combining Psychological, Physiological, and Pharmacological Techniques. *Science*, **126**, 1271–1278.

Miller, N. E., 1958. Central Stimulation and Other New Approaches to Motivation and Reward. *Amer. Psychologist*, **13**, 100–107.

Miller, N. E., 1959. Liberalization of Basic S-R Concepts: Extensions to Conflict Behavior, Motivation and Social Learning. In Koch, S. (Ed.). *Psychology: A Study of a Science*. Vol. II. *General Systematic Formulations, Learning, and Special Processes*. New York: McGraw-Hill.

Miller, N. E., and Dollard, J., 1941. *Social Learning and Imitation*. New Haven: Yale University Press.

Mowrer, O. H., 1960. *Learning Theory and the Symbolic Processes*. New York: John Wiley and Sons.

Mullahy, P., 1948. *Oedipus—Myth and Complex*. New York: Hermitage Press.

Munroe, Ruth L., 1955. *Schools of Psychoanalytic Thought*. New York: Dryden.

Murray, H. A., Barrett, W. G., Homburger, E., et al., 1938. *Explorations in Personality*. New York: Oxford University Press.

Muuss, R., 1956. Existentialism and Psychology. *Educ. Theor.*, **6**, 135–153.

Olds, J., 1955. Physiological Mechanisms of Reward. In Jones, M. R. (Ed.). *Nebraska Symposium on Motivation*. Lincoln, Nebraska: University of Nebraska Press, pp. 73–134.

Osgood, C. E., Suci, G. J., and Tannenbaum, P. H., 1957. *The Measurement of Meaning*. Urbana: University of Illinois Press.

Phillips, E. L., 1956. *Psychotherapy: A Modern Theory and Practice*. Englewood Cliffs, N.J.: Prentice-Hall.

Pratt, C. C., 1950. The Role of Past Experience in Visual Perception. *J. Psychol.*, **30**, 85–107.

Prentice, W. C. H., 1958. Perception. In *Annual Review of Psychology*. Vol. 9, Palo Alto: Annual Reviews, Inc., pp. 1–18.

Prokasy, W. F., and Hall, J., 1963. Primary Stimulus Generalization. *Psychol. Rev.*, **70**, 310–323.

Proshansky, H., and Murphy, G., 1942. The Effects of Reward and Punishment on Perception. *J. Psychol.*, **13**, 295–305.

Rank, O., 1929. *The Trauma of Birth*. New York: Harcourt, Brace.

Rank, O., 1932. *Art and Artist*. New York: Alfred Knopf.

Rank, O., 1945. *Will Therapy and Truth and Reality*. New York: Alfred Knopf.

Rapaport, D., 1950a. On the Psychoanalytic Theory of Thinking. *Int. J. Psychoanal.*, 31, 161–170.

Rapaport, D., 1950b. *Emotions and Memory*. New York: International Universities Press, 2nd Ed.

Rapaport, D., 1951a. The Autonomy of the Ego. *Bull. Menninger Clin.*, 15, 113–123.

Rapaport, D., 1951b. Consciousness: A Psychopathological and Psychodynamic View. In Abramson, H. A. (Ed.). *Problems of Consciousness: Transactions of the Second Conference, March 19–20, 1951, New York, N.Y.* New York: Josiah Macy Jr. Foundation.

Rapaport, D., 1951c. *The Organization and Pathology of Thought*. New York: Columbia University Press.

Rapaport, D., 1957. Cognitive Structures. In *Contemporary Approaches to Cognition: A Symposium Held at the University of Colorado*. Cambridge: Harvard University Press.

Rapaport, D., 1958. The Theory of Ego Autonomy: A Generalization. *Bull. Menninger Clin.*, 22, 13–35.

Rapaport, D., 1960. On the Psychoanalytic Theory of Motivation. In *Nebraska Symposium on Motivation*, Jones, N. R. (Ed.). Lincoln: University of Nebraska Press.

Rapaport, D., and Gill, M. M., 1959. The Points of View and Assumptions of Metapsychology. *Int. J. Psychoanal.*, 40, 153–161.

Rapaport, D., Gill, M., and Schafer, R., 1945. *Diagnostic psychological testing*. Chicago: Year Book Publishers.

Ranck, Annette W., 1961. Behavioral Concepts: Frequency of Usage and Relative Modifiability in Experienced and Inexperienced Judges. Unpublished M.S. Thesis, The Pennsylvania State University.

Ray, W. S., 1960. *An Introduction to Experimental Design*. New York: The Macmillan Co.

Rogers, C. R., 1939. *The Clinical Treatment of the Problem Child*. Boston: Houghton Mifflin.

Rogers, C. R., 1942. *Counseling and Psychotherapy*. New York: Houghton Mifflin.

Rogers, C. R., 1951. *Client-Centered Therapy*. Boston: Houghton Mifflin.

Rogers, C. R., 1959. A Theory of Therapy, Personality, and Interpersonal Relationships, as Developed in the Client-Centered Framework. In Koch, S. (Ed.). *Psychology: A Study of a Science*. Vol. II. *General Systematic Formulations, Learning, and Special Processes*. New York: McGraw-Hill.

Rogers, C. R., 1961. *On Becoming a Person: A Therapist's View of Psychotherapy*. Boston: Houghton Mifflin.

Rogers, C. R., and Dymond, R. F. (Eds.), 1954. *Psychotherapy and Personality Change*. Chicago: University of Chicago Press.

Rotter, J. B., 1954. *Social Learning and Clinical Psychology*. New York: Prentice-Hall, Inc.

Rubinstein, E. A., and Parloff, M. B. (Eds.), 1959. *Research in Psychotherapy*. Washington, D.C.: American Psychological Association.

Ruitenbeek, H. M., 1962. *Psychoanalysis and Existential Philosophy*. New York: Dutton.

Salter, A., 1949. *Conditioned Reflex Therapy*. New York: Creative Age Press.

Schafer, R., 1947. *The clinical application of psychological tests*. New York: International University Press, Inc.

Schafer, R., 1954. *Psychoanalytic interpretation in Rorschach testing.* New York: Grune and Stratton.

Simpson, G. G., 1963. Biology and the Nature of Science. *Science,* 139, 81–88.

Skinner, B. F., 1938. *The Behavior of Organisms.* New York: Appleton-Century-Crofts.

Skinner, B. F., 1953. *Science and Human Behavior.* New York: The Macmillan Co.

Skinner, B. F., 1957. *Verbal Behavior.* New York: Appleton-Century-Crofts.

Snygg, D., and Combs, A. W., 1949. *Individual Behavior.* New York: Harper.

Spence, K. W., 1956. *Behavior Theory and Conditioning.* New Haven: Yale University Press.

Spiegelberg, H., 1960. *The Phenomenological Movement: A Historical Introduction.* 2 Vols. The Hague: Nijhoff.

Stevens, S. S. (Ed.), 1951. *Handbook of Experimental Psychology.* New York: John Wiley and Sons.

Sullivan, H. S., 1947. *Conceptions of Modern Psychiatry.* Washington, D.C.: William Alanson White Psychiatric Foundation.

Sullivan, H. S., 1953. *The Interpersonal Theory of Psychiatry.* New York: Norton.

Sullivan, H. S., 1954. *The Psychiatric Interview.* New York: Norton.

Sullivan, H. S., 1956. *Clinical Studies in Psychiatry.* New York: Norton.

Taft, Jessie, 1948. *Family Casework and Counseling: A Functional Approach.* Philadelphia: University of Pennsylvania Press.

Taft, Jessie, 1958. *Otto Rank: A Biographical Study Based on Notebooks, Collected Writings, Therapeutic Achievements, and Personal Associations.* New York: Julian Press.

Thompson, C., 1957. *Psychoanalysis: Evolution and Development.* New York: Grove Press.

Tiebeut, H. M., Jr., 1958. Freud and Existentialism. *J. Nerv. Ment. Dis.,* 126, 341–352.

Titchner, E. B., 1910. *A Textbook of Psychology.* New York: The Macmillan Co.

Underwood, B. J., and Schulz, R. W., 1960. *Meaningfulness and Verbal Training.* Chicago: Lippincott.

Urban, H. B., and Ford, D. H., 1962. Man: Robot or Pilot? In Schneiders, A. A., and Centi, P. J. (Eds.). *Selected Papers from the ACPA Meetings of 1960, 1961.* New York: American Catholic Psychological Association.

Van Dusen, W., 1957. The Theory and Practice of Existential Analysis. *Amer. J. Psychother.,* 11, 310–322.

Willner, Gerda, 1958. Duerckeim's Existential Philosophy: An Evaluation and Critique. *Amer. J. Psychoanal.,* 18, 38–51.

Wolpe, J., 1948. An Approach to the Problem of Neurosis Based on the Conditioned Response. Unpublished M.D. Thesis, University of the Witwatersrand.

Wolpe, J., 1949. An Interpretation of the Effects of Combinations of Stimuli (Patterns) Based on Current Neurophysiology. *Psychol. Rev.,* 56, 277.

Wolpe, J., 1950. Need-reduction, Drive-reduction, and Reinforcement: A Neurophysiological View. *Psychol. Rev.,* 57, 19.

Wolpe, J., 1952a. Experimental Neurosis as Learned Behaviour. *Brit. J. Psychol.,* 43, 243.

Wolpe, J., 1952b. The Formation of Negative Habits: A Neurophysiological View. *Psychol. Rev.,* 59, 290.

Wolpe, J., 1952c. The Neurophysiology of Learning and Delayed Reward Learning. *Psychol. Rev.,* 59, 192.

Wolpe, J., 1952d. Objective Psychotherapy of the Neuroses. *South African Med. J.,* **26,** 825.

Wolpe, J., 1952e. Primary Stimulus Generalization: A Neurophysiological View. *Psychol. Rev.,* **59,** 8.

Wolpe, J., 1953. Learning Theory and "Abnormal Fixations." *Psychol. Rev.,* **60,** 111.

Wolpe, J., 1954. Reciprocal Inhibition as the Main Basis of Psychotherapeutic Effects. *Arch. Neurol. Psychiat.,* **72,** 205.

Wolpe, J., 1956. Learning Versus Lesions as the Basis of Neurotic Behavior. *Amer. J. Psychiat.,* **112,** 923.

Wolpe, J., 1958. *Psychotherapy by Reciprocal Inhibition.* Stanford: Stanford University Press.

Young, P. T., 1955. The Role of Hedonic Processes in Motivation. In Jones, M. R. (Ed.). *Nebraska Symposium on Motivation.* Lincoln, Nebraska: University of Nebraska Press, pp. 193–235.

Young, P. T., 1959. The Role of Affective Processes in Learning and Motivation. *Psychol. Rev.,* **66,** 104–125.

Author Index

Subject Index